Fourth Edition

Choosing Democracy
A Practical Guide to Multicultural Education

Duane E. Campbell
California State University, Sacramento

With contributions by

Peter Baird

Forrest Davis

Edmund W. Lee

John Cowan

Dolores Delgado-Campbell

Francisco Reveles

Allyn & Bacon

Boston   New York   San Francisco
Mexico City   Montreal   Toronto   London   Madrid   Munich   Paris
Hong Kong   Singapore   Tokyo   Cape Town   Sydney

Editor in Chief: Paul Smith
Acquisitions Editor: Kelly Villella Canton
Editorial Assistant: Annalea Manalili
Director of Marketing: Quinn Perkson
Senior Marketing Manager: Darcy Betts Prybella
Marketing Assistant: Robin Holtsberry
Production Manager: Kathy Sleys
Creative Director: Jayne Conte
Cover Designer: Lisbeth Axell
Manager, Rights and Permissions: Zina Arabia
Image Permission Coordinator: Ang'John Ferreri
Cover Art: Getty Images, Inc.
Full-Service Project Management/Composition: Chitra Ganesan/GGS Book Services, PMG
Printer/Binder: Bind-Rite, Robbinsville/Command Web
Cover Printer: Bind-Rite, Robbinsville/Command Web

Photo Credits: AP/Wide World Photos: p. 24; Charles Moore/Black Star: p. 68; National Archives and Records Administration: pp. 104, 204; Barbara Schwartz/Merrill: p. 170; Scott Cunningham/Merrill: p. 191; Anthony Magnacca/Merrill: pp. 266, 290.

Library of Congress Cataloging-in-Publication Data

Campbell, Duane E.
  Choosing democracy : a practical guide to multicultural education / Duane E. Campbell; with contributions by Peter Baird . . . [et al]. — 4th ed.
      p. cm.
Includes bibliographical references and index.
  ISBN-13: 978-0-13-503481-1
  ISBN-10: 0-13-503481-7
 1. Multicultural education—United States.   2. Education—Social aspects—United States.   3. Cultural pluralism—United States.   4. Racism—United States.   5. United States—Race relations.   6. Social classes—United States.   7. Sex differences in education—United States.   I. Baird, Peter.   II. Title.
  LC1099.3.C36 2009
  370.1170973—dc22

                                                                                              2008055914

**Allyn & Bacon
is an imprint of**

www.pearsonhighered.com

10 9 8 7 6 5 4 3 2 1
ISBN 10: 0-13-503481-7
ISBN 13: 978-0-13-503481-1

Foreword

Duane Campbell is an organic intellectual with a deep commitment to a substantive democratic vision. He understands education as a critical activity that unsettles our presuppositions and unstiffens our prejudices such that we can bond with others to alleviate social misery. His acute sense of history enables him to view schooling within a broad multilayered context in which the harsh realities of race, class, and gender as well as the sweet possibilities of freedom, equality, and democracy loom large.

This magisterial treatment of our contemporary crisis in American society, culture, and education takes us step-by-step through the treacherous terrains that impede our efforts to examine critically and expand effectively democracy in our time. His powerful text is the most comprehensive analysis we have of sharpening the practical strategies for multicultural education in America.

Like the exquisite poetry of Walt Whitman and the exhilarating music of Louis Armstrong, Duane Campbell's empowering pedagogy is shot through with profound democratic sentiments. In our frightening moment of class polarization and racial balkanization, his themes of social reconstruction, cultural innovation, and political transformation—themes that link any talk about diversity to the expansion of democracy—are refreshing and uplifting. They also present the principal means by which we can link order to justice, civility to mutual respect, and merit to fairness.

His radical democratic analysis and vision remain a voice of sanity at a time of irrationality—a voice that understands rage yet transforms bitterness into bonding. This bonding is neither naive nor utopian; rather it is rooted in a candid encounter with the sources of our rage and an unleashing of the best in us for serious democratic engagement that goes far beyond our hostilities.

The best of American life has always been embodied and enacted by courageous figures who chose democracy—from Thomas Paine, Harriet Tubman, César Chávez, and Ronald Takaki, to Dolores Huerta. Duane Campbell makes it clear what it means to choose democracy in our classrooms, workplaces, homes, and civic life. In short, like James Baldwin, he frightfully reminds us that we either choose democracy now or ultimately witness the fire this time!

Cornel West
Princeton University

Preface

As teachers, readers of this fourth edition will participate in the construction of the future of our society. In deciding what future is constructed, I anticipate that substantive school reform, including the development of multicultural education, will be necessary for the preservation of our democratic community. *Choosing Democracy: A Practical Guide to Multicultural Education* will help teachers and future teachers to analyze their own cultural frames of reference and to develop a second, multicultural perspective. It seeks to unite teachers' commitments to democratic opportunity and to expand that value position to include cultural democracy in school and equal educational opportunity.

In this new edition of *Choosing Democracy: A Practical Guide to Multicultural Education*, I share the concerns of teachers struggling to develop multicultural curricula and school practices. As a consequence of the dialogues between our students and the several coauthors, and the developmental usage of this text material with hundreds of students over the years, I remain convinced that "a nature of culture" approach, as developed in this text, provides most students with positive alternatives to continuing "business as usual" and allows them to participate in reconceptualizing their own basic assumptions and frames of reference.

Text Organization

Part 1 of this text presents a critical analysis of culture, race, class, gender, and poverty as they apply in school. Chapters 1 through 5 include research evidence and conclusions about societal crises, culture, economics, racism, and gender discrimination to demonstrate how they impact classrooms, teachers, and schools. Prepared with this information, teachers can begin to understand how these matters affect their own classrooms. The work in Chapter 3 & 4 has been revised. Chapter 5 has been revised and updated with the assistance of Dolores Delgado-Campbell.

Part 2 of the text then provides practical strategies for teachers to use in responding to problem areas. In Chapter 6, readers consider the importance of developing quality interpersonal relationships with students and among students—an issue seldom addressed in other texts. It also offers ideas on promoting positive self-esteem and serving as a cultural mediator.

Chapter 7 offers a number of teaching strategies that pursue the goal of empowerment and the philosophy of promoting democracy as well as new material on conflict resolution. In response to reviewers' suggestions, Chapter 8 has been significantly revised to include more descriptions of the interaction between classroom management and democracy. New material has been added on dealing with gangs, with the assistance of Dr. Francisco Reveles of California State University–Sacramento. Chapter 9 has new material on constructivism and defines more precisely the differences between critical thinking and critical theory. It also includes new material on promoting technology literacy, added with the assistance of Dr. John Cowan of California State University–Sacramento.

These chapters present more than five major approaches and hundreds of specific suggestions on how to change the classroom to adapt to our rapidly changing society. These include descriptions of strategies, objectives, and lesson plans on classroom management; guidance and lesson plans to initiate cooperative learning; and information on the theory and practice of bilingual education and second-language acquisition. Chapter 11, which covers the teaching of language-minority populations, has been updated with the assistance of Dr. Edmund Lee.

By Part 3, readers will have developed both a theory and a practice for multicultural education. They will have the background to examine the controversies and enter the dialogue on school reform. Chapter 12 has been significantly revised to become a chapter on curriculum for multicultural schools. It describes the battle of the textbooks in California and New York and the phonics battles in California and analyzes the standards movement of school reform and testing. New to fourth edition is a section on the use of computers and technology to overcome the limitations of published curriculum. Like Chapter 9, Chapter 12 contains new material on technology literacy developed with the assistance of Dr. Cowan.

Chapter 13 has been substantially rewritten to consider the major changes resulting from No Child Left Behind and other efforts at school change. It critiques most reform efforts for devoting inadequate attention to the problems of marginalized students, students of color, and students from poor families and for focusing on blaming teachers rather than seeking solutions. New to Chapter 13 are guidelines for considering reform proposals, a guide for new teachers, and thoughts on education advocacy and change developed with my students in graduate study in Bilingual/Multicultural Education at California State University–Sacramento. It concludes with a vision for pluralistic democracy and a description of some of the successful efforts for school change, including community organizing and school intervention strategies. It includes a new section, "Don't Face School Reform Alone—Organize," with first steps toward teachers working as educational community organizers.

Using This Text

When I use this book with practicing teachers or with students in the pre-service program while they are practice teaching, I often begin with Chapter 10 on cooperative learning and then proceed immediately to Chapter 8 on classroom management. These chapters help readers get started with practical strategies to resolve immediate classroom issues. After experiencing success with these strategies, readers often are more open to considering the alternative perspectives on multicultural education and social justice presented in other chapters.

In working with pre-service teachers, I have found that most of them have little preparation in economics, and what they do have is only of limited usefulness, yet economics is central to arguments about school renewal. This fourth edition has updated economic data throughout the text. I have found the work of Nancy Folbre and the Center for Popular Economics particularly helpful in explaining complex economic issues. You will find their graphs used often in this text. These graphs and others, as well as economic cartoons, are included in an excellent work, *The Ultimate Field Guide to the U.S. Economy* (Heintz, Folbre, & Center for Popular Economics, 2000). I recommend that you get a copy of it so you can photocopy graphs and transfer them to PowerPoint slides or to transparencies for an overhead projector.

Activities and Teaching Strategies

At the ends of most chapters, you will find activities for further study of the subject covered in the chapter. These suggestions are drawn from how we teach this material in our basic Introduction to Multicultural Education class for pre-service teachers. I hope you find these useful.

These activities are followed by teaching strategies, which are written for readers to use as teachers in K–12 classrooms. In Chapters 9, 10, and 11, these strategies include lesson plans designed to introduce readers to issues such as critical thinking and cooperative learning. I encourage you to add to and amend these lessons. Often in dealing with complex issues such as critical thinking, I find that students agree with the concept in general but have only a limited understanding of how to implement the strategies in the classroom. Students better understand the strategies and the need for advance planning for the strategies when they see them applied in lesson plans and lessons.

New to the Fourth Edition

- Major revision of Chapters 1, 7, 12, and 13.
- Up-to-date economic data.
- Improved descriptions of the role and philosophy of democracy.
- A revised Chapter 12 focusing on curriculum change suggested by social justice/multicultural education.

- Significant new material on testing and assessment—and their limits.
- Important analysis of No Child Left Behind and the related policies; consideration of how misuse of accountability has marginalized efforts toward democratic, multicultural education.
- A new section on teachers working as community organizers.

Conclusion

We have the skills, abilities, opportunities, and hopes necessary to renew and sustain one of the greatest social experiments in history: the U.S. democratic republic, where wealth and a high quality of life are shared. It is the hope of the authors that *Choosing Democracy: A Practical Guide to Multicultural Education*, Fourth Edition, will contribute to teachers' opportunities to create a society where all students receive a quality education to prepare them to produce for the world; to compete in the world economy; to trade with the world; and to build a world with diverse, democratic communities.

Acknowledgments

Knowledge is not private property.

Choosing Democracy is a product of years of dialogue with my current and former students. They consistently reteach me and remind me to respect the invaluable contributions that teachers make to the nation and to social justice. I have tried to pass on some of the wisdom that they have taught me.

I want to thank Dolores Delgado-Campbell and Lisa William-White for their coauthorship of Chapter 5 in the third edition. Their perspectives—Dolores, a Chicana and a feminist, and Lisa, an African American—added wisdom and insight to this important chapter on gender issues. Dolores revised the chapter for the fourth edition. I am indebted to Dr. Pia Wong for her excellent work as coauthor of Chapter 13 in the second and third editions, to Dr. Kathryn Singh for her contributions to the first and second editions, and to Dr. Diane Cordero de Noriega for her contributions to the second edition.

Although I graduated from a fine university, I learned more about the commitment to justice and equality by my own participation in several of the social justice movements of the last three decades. These continuing struggles for economic justice and social democracy provided organic intellectuals as tutors, coaches, guides, and teachers. Particularly important to my own education has been working with César Chávez, Bert Corona, Br. Ed Dunn, Dolores Huerta, and Philip Vera Cruz. Movements are more than the individual names. I owe much of my political education and respect for discipline and the working people to service with DSA, the United Farm Workers of America (AFL–CIO), and the U.S. labor movement.

I am grateful to have worked with and learned from Michael Harrington, Cornel West, Barbara Ehrenreich, Rodolfo Acuña, Manning Marable, Jose La Luz, Eric Vega,

Ricardo Torres, Joe Schwartz, Leo Casey, Horace Small, and Hunter Gray, among others. Their insights and critical reflections are found throughout this book.

I am fortunate to have a position within a community of scholars who have worked together for more than a decade and in 1994 comprised the Department of Bilingual Multicultural Education at California State University–Sacramento—a people's university. The collective efforts and integrity of this group sustain me and guide me to resist the individualism and to avoid the narcissism and self-indulgence of many university departments. I am particularly grateful for the many insights that I have gained from my students and that I have sought to record in this text. Our programs have prepared over a thousand new teachers and educational leaders who have gone into classrooms and improved the schools and who have brought their insights back to campus to share with others. In addition to my several contributing authors listed on the title page, I particularly owe a debt of gratitude to Dr. Thomas P. Carter, who served as a mentor until his death in 2000.

The list of other scholars and friends who have helped me, supported me, and encouraged me to refine ideas is too long to enumerate. But particularly helpful have been Bert Corona, Henry T. Trueba (until his passing in 2004), and Hunter Gray. I also wish to acknowledge the contribution of the reviewers, who offered many helpful suggestions: . . .

Dedication

To Dolores Delgado-Campbell, thank you for your more than 30 years of collaboration from a Chicana feminist perspective. You have helped me to cross the borders of culture and to appreciate the dialectics of change.

To Javier Sean Campbell, your sense of conscience and integrity about your issues reteaches me to treat young people with dignity and respect. Hay que pensar en el futuro—y el futuro pertenece a su generacíon. And thank you for the assistance with editing.

Brief Contents

Contents

Part 2
Teaching Strategies to Promote Democracy and Multicultural Education   173

Note: Every effort has been made to provide accurate and current Internet information. However, because the Internet and information posted on it are constantly changing, it is inevitable that some Internet addresses listed in this textbook will change.

Introduction

May the truth of my tale speak for me.
Traditional saying.

This book addresses teachers at a remarkable time in this country's history: the dramatic birth and development of a new, more culturally and linguistically diverse society. In the last two decades, economic turmoil and unprecedented levels of immigration have filled the public schools of the United States with a rich rainbow of faces. In many classrooms, students represent dozens of cultures and use three, four, or even five languages. Few societies have classrooms and schools as diverse as those faced by teachers in the United States each day.

In 1993, the U.S. Congress passed the Goals 2000: Educate America Act. Two of its established goals were "By the year 2000 U.S. students will be first in the world in science and math achievement" and "Every school in America will be free of drugs and violence and will offer a disciplined environment conducive to learning." These goals were not met.

The current basic federal legislation for education is the No Child Left Behind Act (NCLB), passed in 2001. Now, who could be opposed to such a goal? However, in 2003 it was estimated that if the nation makes the same progress on tests that it made during the prior decade of alleged reform, the nation will attain the required level of proficiency in fourth grade math by 2060 and in eighth grade math in 2067 (Bracey, 2003).

If you spend some time in our urban schools and in our low-income rural schools, you will quickly learn that NCLB and state laws have not improved achievement for the nation's low-income schools. By 2014—or before—under current regulations, NCLB will label a majority of all schools in the nation as "failing," even those with high student performances.

1

How could we get to such a place? And how can we get out of this hole and begin to move forward? The lack of significant progress on student achievement requires an explanation, particularly for you as a future teacher.

Schools and teaching reflect society and also participate in constructing a future society. New forms of knowledge and new approaches to teaching have emerged in response to changes in our economy, in our society, and in our schools. Teachers have forged a variety of new strategies to respond to the demands for economic relevancy, democracy, and equal opportunity in response to the schools' remarkable cultural and linguistic diversity.

In this book, I share the insights gained by dozens of teachers working with bilingual and multicultural students as they developed new cross-cultural perspectives, new pedagogies and curricula, and new strategies and programs to respond both to the continuing social crises of schools that are failing and to the continuing need to educate students in these schools. Innovative teachers have found ways to validate students' diverse cultures while preparing them to participate in the social, economic, and political mainstream of U.S. society.

Teachers dedicated to multicultural education hope to build on the cultural diversity of our nation to create a new, dynamic, democratic—and fair—society, one not racked by the problems of poverty, corruption, homelessness, unemployment, community dislocations, and racial division. It is teachers and students in our urban centers who feel the brunt of demographic and economic changes in the United States. It is teachers who are developing the strategies to respond to the poverty and educational crises in our society.

What are these crises?

1. The stress and conflict students bring to school is aggravated by rapidly changing demographics and turbulent economic conditions, particularly in low-income communities.

2. More than one-third of all schools in major cities and rural poverty areas fail to provide a positive educational environment for an increasing number of poor and racial/ethnic minority students.

Teachers now know a great deal more about teaching in a cross-cultural environment than they did in previous years. Effective teaching strategies and programs have been identified, clarified, and developed to take advantage of classroom diversity and to weave stronger, more united communities.

We know that teachers can make a difference. Dedicated teachers from all racial, ethnic, and cultural backgrounds can learn to be effective cross-cultural teachers and brokers of information that provides students with greater access to economic opportunity and social equality. Teachers also know a great deal about teaching. New teachers are fortunate to be able to learn from the experiences of their predecessors.

We know well that schools are not politically neutral. Teachers and schools are situated in specific economic, political environments. Study and reflection on that reality help teachers to select strategies that empower their students and help them succeed. Studies on the nature of culture, race, class, and gender relations in our society provide teachers with a theoretical framework for selecting and evaluating teaching strategies (see Part 1 of this text).

But theoretical analysis of the problems of urban and troubled schools is not enough. Teachers—particularly new teachers—need practical strategies for responding to the dozens of problems they face each day in the classroom—complex problems that have no single solution. In fact, the complexity of teacher decision making often baffles and, at times, overwhelms new teachers. While working through the problems of critical thinking, for example (see Chapter 9), teachers will also need clear, descriptive assistance on issues such as cooperative learning, classroom management, and helping students to learn English (see Part 2 of this text).

On Objectivity

We know that the study of culture, race, class, and gender issues presents some readers with strong conflicts between what they are reading and their own worldviews. This raises the question of objectivity. Objectivity is a very important issue and requires a serious response.

In this book, I avoid the artificial "neutrality" often claimed by those who write using "academic" language. *Choosing Democracy* is written from the perspective that universities and textbooks are not neutral; they in fact present a point of view. Some texts are Eurocentric; some are male centered; some promote the status quo of economic and educational inequality as normal, natural, and inevitable. This work, like all textbooks, has a point of view.

Historian Howard Zinn, in *Declarations of Independence: Cross-examining American Ideology* (1990), deals with the question quite well:

> Writing this book, I do not claim to be neutral, nor do I want to be. There are things I value and things I don't. I am not going to present ideas objectively if that means I don't have strong opinions on which ideas are right and which are wrong. I will try to be fair to opposing ideas by accurately representing them. But the reader should know that what appears here are my own views on the world as it is and as it should be.
>
> I do want to influence the reader. But I would like to do this by the strength of argument and fact, by presenting ideas and ways of looking at issues that are outside of the orthodox. I am hopeful that given more possibilities, people will come up with wiser conclusions. (p. 7)

I do not expect that readers will agree with every statement in this book. Rather, I and my contributing authors encourage you to engage the ideas, to argue with the text, to prepare yourself to debate the conclusions. We say more about dubious academic claims of objectivity in Chapter 7. The concepts of positivism and critical theory and the idea of the maintenance of ideological domination are important aspects of the general idea of academic objectivity. Rather than hiding our point of view, in *Choosing Democracy* we try to make our viewpoint explicit so that you, the reader, can evaluate the point of view and make up your own mind.

As the spiritual says, "May the truth of my tale speak for me." I seek to share a view of our society as I and my colleagues in the schools have come to know it. We recognize both the hope and the problems of our schools.

A Few Words About Words

Language use is constantly changing. Since 1960, the most common term for one group of people has changed from *Negro* to *Black* to *African American*. In the same period, the most common term for another group has changed from *Latin* to *Mexican American* to *Chicano* to *Latino*. These changes reflect substantial redefinition of the problems of race and ethnic conflict occurring in the curriculum, the schools, and U.S. society.

The purpose of language and of books is to communicate. In *Choosing Democracy*, I use terms based on two primary criteria:

1. What terms do the leaders, the intellectuals, and the community itself prefer?
2. What terms most precisely describe the group?

African Americans

I use the term *African American* for the nation's most studied minority group, reflecting the preferred current usage. Ron Daniels, a leading African American political activist, argues that the effort to encourage the use of this term over *Black* goes back to the early 1980s. *Black* is a racial term that attempts to describe a racial group. Sociologists have documented the social importance of race, while biologists encourage us to avoid use of race because the concept is so imprecise (see Chapter 3).

Race and ethnicity are not the same. The racial term *Black* includes significant new immigrant groups of Haitians, Dominicans, and many Puerto Ricans. These groups share "blackness" and are treated as Black by the larger U.S. society. They are, however, distinct ethnic and cultural groups.

Asian Americans

I use the term *Asian American* to describe the common experiences of Asian peoples in the United States. The enormous differences among these peoples in terms of language, culture, and immigration histories will lead more often to my referring to the specific group—for example, Vietnamese or Koreans—rather than using the often-misleading general term. The discussion of population numbers for the Asian/Pacific Islander census subcategory in Chapter 3 illustrates the diversity within this category.

European Americans

In this book, I use the term *European American* to describe persons commonly referred to as *White* and to describe the complex cultural heritage of the majority group and the macroculture in the United States.

Most European Americans come from a mixture of various cultural and national groups, including the German, Italians, Greek, Irish, and English. Members of these groups have been in the United States for generations, and most have little contact with their originating societies. They tend to consider themselves *Americans*. I do not use the designation *American* in this way in this text, as it excludes non-Europeans by implication.

I use the term *European American* in part to encourage members of this group to recognize their own ethnicity and cultural roots. The European American culture is substantially derived from Anglo-Saxon and English culture in the areas of language, common law, and the Protestant denominations. Many immigrant groups, such as Greeks, Poles, Scandinavians, and Irish, have added to the developing common culture, as have those belonging to the Catholic and the Jewish religions. European Americans, often conceptualized as a single group, are in fact a diverse population.

Native Americans

I have chosen to use the term *Native Americans* and *Indians* interchangeably within the text. Both terms are in popular usage, and both have drawbacks. It is most important to recognize the tribal and historical diversity of members of the several native nations. Whenever possible, I refer to a group by its tribal name—for example, the Dineh, Cree, or Lakota nation.

Latinos

I use the term *Latino* to describe those people who are descendants of immigrants from Latin American countries and the Caribbean and those people of mixed Spanish-Indian heritage who were present in the Southwest when the U.S. Army first moved into the area in the 1840s. Until 2003 The U.S. Census Bureau and many people use the term *Hispanic* for this group. At present the census uses the terms Latinos and Hispanics interchangeably. Neither term is perfect, but *Hispanic* seems to overemphasize the influence of Spain and to deemphasize the major contributions of Native American and African cultures. Preference for either term varies by region. In the eastern half of the United States, *Hispanic* is more often used; in the West, *Latino* is more common.

Latinos share some cultural characteristics and yet are widely diverse: 62.3 percent of Latinos are of Mexican ancestry, 12.7 percent are Puerto Ricans, 5.3 percent are descendants of Cubans, and the remaining 19.7 percent are from a variety of other Latin American and Caribbean nations. (See Trueba, 1999.)

The term *Latino* unfortunately connotes the male gender even when used in the plural to describe both males and females. When referring to females only, we use the specific term *Latina* or *Chicana*. While most Latinos are of mixed race, the U.S. Census Bureau attempts to count Hispanics separately by racial categories: Indian, White, and Black. We discuss the variety within Latino culture in more detail in Chapter 2.

People of Color

In referring to the collective experiences of racial groups in the United States, this text will use the term *people of color*. This choice, like all categories, has some limitations. The adoption of the concept of people of color, like other important issues, was a political decision, appropriate for a time but not particularly descriptive. When the concept of people of color is used, the assumption is that the minority groups have similar experiences. This asserts that the experiences of racism are similar for each group, but this assertion needs to be examined for accuracy. Certainly, there are similarities of experience; there are also substantive differences.

The experiences of Vietnamese and Hmong immigrants are distinctly different from the experiences of immigrants such as Mexicans and of forced migrants such as African Americans. There are issues of poverty and fitting into a low-wage part of economy that unite various groups, but there are also significant differences. One of the primary differences is that each group experiences racism differently.

In this text, *people of color* will be used interchangeably with the term *racial and ethnic minority groups*. The *people of color* emphasis highlights the fact that in many urban areas and in some rural regions, such as Texas, Mississippi, and New Mexico, people of color are the majority, not a minority group.

Americans

I deliberately use the term *people of the United States* to refer to U.S. residents and citizens. As noted previously, the common term *American* is a misnomer in this context and seems arrogant to some of the millions of people who live in the Americas. *American* refers to the residents of North, Central, and South America (although it is colloquially used in the U.S., Canada and Europe to refer primarily to residents of the United States). Thus, Brazilians, Peruvians, Costa Ricans, and Canadians are all Americans. The many indigenous groups in these nations are all Native Americans.

In spite of this, citizens of the United States of several racial and ethnic groups commonly refer to themselves as Americans. When other authors have used the term *American* to describe U.S. citizens, I have respected their word choice.

The Poor

The United States has a large poverty class. Official statistics number this group at around 13 percent, while more careful studies show that as much as 20 percent of the U.S. population is poor in any one year. Poverty among children is growing.

When we use the term *poor* in this text, the reference is to people's economic status, not to their lifestyles, morals, values, or family stability. The term *low income* hides the gravity and permanence of poverty in our society. The many euphemisms developed to avoid saying "the poor" significantly obscure the magnitude of poverty in influencing school opportunities. At times, authors are so polite that they refuse to name reality.

The Problem of Categories

The formation of categories of people encourages social scientists to fit everyone into a category. Allegedly racial categories are particularly misleading. Peter Rose (1974) illustrates the issue: "Mexican-Americans are largely the children of Spanish and Indian parentage; Puerto Ricans are the offspring of white and black as well as Indian ancestors; and many people who we call black are very white indeed" (p. 11).

Each person is both an individual and a member of several groups. We may fit into several categories: An individual may be Latino, Catholic, middle class, and a teacher, for example. Each individual's worldview is a complex compilation of diverse influences. Even within a single group such as Guatemalans, there are Indians, Latinos, men, women, children, immigrants, poor, and rich. Categories are necessary for analysis, but they are only transitional starting points for coming to understand the complex varieties of human experience.

PART 1

The Social, Economic, and Cultural Foundations of the Current School Crisis

IN CONGRESS, July 4, 1776.

We hold these truths to be self-evident, that all men are created equal, that they are endowed by their Creator with certain unalienable Rights, that among these are Life, Liberty and the pursuit of Happiness.—That to secure these rights, Governments are instituted among Men, deriving their just powers from the consent of the governed,—That whenever any Form of Government becomes destructive of these ends, it is the Right of the People to alter or to abolish it, and to institute new Government, laying its foundation on such principles and organizing its powers in such form, as to them shall seem most likely to effect their Safety and Happiness.

Declaration of Independence

1

Democracy and the Need for Multicultural Education

Why *Choosing Democracy?*

Our society and our schools are in rapid transition from the old to the new. New global businesses and corporations have propelled our nation into a worldwide market, a place of economic and social instability. Meanwhile, our government structures and schools remain pretty much as they were in the 1950s. The gap between the private, corporate society—growing, dynamic, unstable, and starkly unequal—and the public institutions—underfunded, criticized, and under attack—grows each day. Yet the private sector of society depends on the public sector to provide roads, schools, fire departments, and water and electricity systems (infrastructure); educated workers; and domestic order.

We in the United States have created one of the most free and democratic societies in human history, but at great cost to Native Americans, African slaves, and many immigrant workers. Though far from perfect, our society nonetheless offers our citizens more freedom and self-governance, and a higher standard of living, than are found in most of the world. At the same time, we rank about 37th in the world in health care and life span. Today, we stand in danger of losing our cherished freedom, democracy, and standard of living to chaotic and uncertain global conflicts, terrorism, market competition, and domestic prejudice and intolerance.

As a teacher, you have an important role to play in the decisions about the future of your students and ultimately about the future of our nation. Schools and teachers either promote equality or promote inequality. Schools, whether public or private, can teach and support democratic values, or they reinforce authoritarian, anti-democratic values and increase the hostile divisions in our society. Teachers in most schools have the power to construct classrooms as communities of learners where students learn to develop a democratic life.

We need to learn to live and work together, or to at least tolerate one another, or we may yet tear our society apart. Public schools are the one institution in which we nearly all participate, and the one where we need to teach young people tolerance, cooperation, and the skills of living and working together. Teaching is where we touch the future. In schools, we have an opportunity to teach the coming generations to preserve and extend the United States as an experiment in building a democratic community. The task is far from over, and victory for democracy is far from certain.

The Current State of Public Education

What is the current state of public education in the United States? The answer you get to this question depends a great deal on where you look. For example consider the conditions for teachers in Figure 1.1.

Many of our schools work quite well—students learn to read, to do math, and to write—but in a significant number of schools, children are failing to master such basic skills and are failing to develop the commitments to work, self-sufficiency, and

Figure 1.1   Daily Lives

Scenario:

A first class.

Your class begins today. One of your children, Adam, comes from a home where 11 children, from two families, live. Six of the children are of school age. When Adam has breakfast at school, it will be the first meal since he had lunch at school the day before. At home, chips and soda are the main meal.

Both families are headed by women. No adult men are present. A conflict emerges in the house. Adam's family must move. His family becomes homeless. They arrive at the nearby homeless shelter. The shelter has room, but not for four children.

A second class in the same school is a third grade. Henry, a new student, enrolls on April 16. The child arrives in an oversized T-shirt and clothes that appear to not have been washed for days. The school has a dress code, insisting on a clean white shirt and blue pants. The teacher tries to call the prior school to get some background information about Henry. She finds out that Henry was only in the prior school for two weeks. He has moved eight times this year.

When the cumulative flies arrive, she discovers that Henry has only attended school a total of 90 days since first grade. He is unable to write his own name.

Standardized testing (SAT) begins in one week. Henry is required to take the test. A third class.

Laura is in seventh grade. When asked to read, she stumbles over words such as "justice." The teacher finds that Laura reads at a third-grade level. She can barely read, spelt, multiply, or divide. Laura doesn't like school anymore. "I work as hard as I can, but I feel so left behind," she says. "I am scared of school. I just don't think I can do it."

Laura is known as a remedial student. She is not alone. Fully one-third of the students in this school are at least two years behind in reading and math. Statistics gathered from this school predict that she will drop out of school by ninth grade.

self-government that preserving our democratic society requires. Education researcher David Berliner (2006) describes our current situation as follows:

The United States likes to be first, and when it comes to poor children, we maintain our remarkable status. No other wealthy nation in the world has a greater percentage of children living in poverty, except for Mexico. (And the average per capita income there is a whopping $8,900.) In Denmark, 2.4 percent of kids live in poverty, in Germany, 10 percent. Here, it's nearly 22 percent.

And surely, it's no surprise to hear poor children do worse in school. If the poor were set off as their own country, it would be a largely Black and Latino nation, and compared to other industrialized nations, it would score near the bottom of any academic ranking. Meanwhile, our White and wealthier students, were they a nation, would score up at the top with the likes of Japan and Sweden.

Thousands of studies have linked poverty to academic achievement. The relationship is every bit as strong as the connection between cigarettes and cancer. So why, when we have as much credible research making connections between poverty and school success, do we keep looking for other answers? (For example, it must be the low expectations of teachers!)

Let's look at some data. By 2003, all states were required to participate in tests known as the National Assessment of Educational Progress (NAEP). Fourth graders' reading performance through 2007 (the most recent data available) is shown in Table 1.1.

According to the NAEP, students reading at the Basic level "should demonstrate an understanding of the overall meaning of what they read. When reading text appropriate for fourth graders, they should be able to make relatively obvious connections between the text and their own experiences . . ." (U.S. Department of Education, 2001a, p. 7). Table 1.1 indicates the percentages of students who performed at the Basic level of the reading test. Unfortunately, all states have a significant number of students performing at the Below Basic level. The entities with the most students determined to be Below Basic in 2005 were New Mexico, Mississippi, California, and the District of Columbia. These students would have difficulty with grade-level student work.

Students rated as Proficient (the level above Basic) on the NAEP "should be able to demonstrate an overall understanding of the text, providing inferential as well as literal

Table 1.1   Fourth Graders' Reading Performance as Measured by the NAEP, 1998–2007

	Basic	Below Basic
1998	60%	40%
2000	59%	41%
2002	64%	36%
2003	63%	37%
2005	63%	37%
2007	66%	34%

Sources: *The Nation's Report Card: Fourth-Grade Reading 2005* (NCES 2006-451), by M. Perie, W. Grigg, & P. Donahue, 2006, Washington, DC: U.S. Department of Education, Office of Educational Research and Improvement, National Center for Education Statistics; 2007 data retrieved November 13, 2008, from nces.ed.gov/nationsreportcard/naepdata.

information. When reading text appropriate to fourth grade, they should be able to extend the ideas in the text by making inferences, drawing conclusions, and making connections to their own experiences. The connection between the text and what the student infers should be clear" (U.S. Department of Education, 2001a, p. 7).

Teachers would like to help their students become proficient readers. Figure 1.2 shows the percentages of fourth graders who were at or above Proficient when sorted by race and ethnicity. These results, from the 2005 NAEP, in combination with the reading scores on earlier administrations of the NAEP to the nation's fourth-graders, show a relatively stable pattern in students' average reading scores over the last decade. Reading scores do vary significantly by race and ethnicity.

You can look up your own state's reading scores in Figure 1.3.

Average math scores on the NAEP have improved since 1992. However, as with reading, the wide differences in scores among racial and ethnic subgroups (the achievement gap) have remained (Perie, Grigg, & Dion, 2005).

The NAEP data on reading and math achievement across the states raise two fundamental questions: Why are there differences by racial and ethnic groups (an achievement gap)? And, as a teacher, what can I do about this gap?

Figure 1.2 Percentage of Fourth Graders at or Above Proficient in Reading Achievement Level on the NAEP by Race and Ethnicity

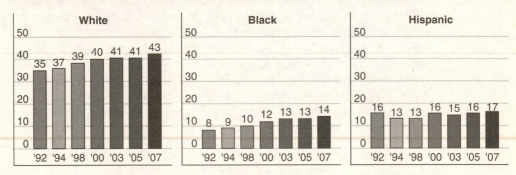

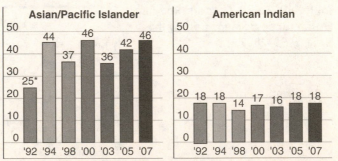

Sources: *The Nation's Report Card: Fourth-Grade Reading 2005* (NCES 2006-451), by M. Perie, W. Grigg, & P. Donahue, 2006, Washington, DC: U.S. Department of Education, Office of Educational Research and Improvement, National Center for Education Statistics; 2007 data retrieved November 13, 2008, from nces.ed.gov/nationsreportcard/naepdata.

Figure 1.3   **Average Reading Scaled Scores and Percentages of Fourth Grade Public School Students Within Each Achievement Level, 2005**

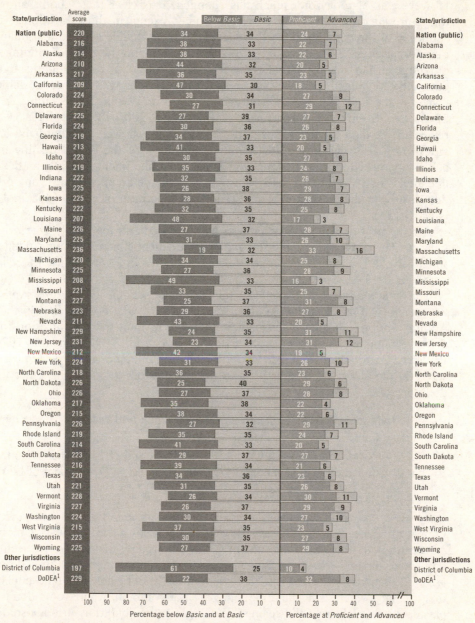

State/jurisdiction	Average score	Below Basic	Basic	Proficient	Advanced
Nation (public)	220	34	34	24	7
Alabama	216	38	33	22	7
Alaska	214	38	33	22	6
Arizona	210	44	32	20	5
Arkansas	217	36	35	23	5
California	209	47	30	18	5
Colorado	224	30	34	27	9
Connecticut	227	27	31	29	12
Delaware	225	27	39	27	7
Florida	224	30	36	26	8
Georgia	219	34	37	23	5
Hawaii	213	41	33	20	5
Idaho	223	30	35	27	8
Illinois	219	35	33	24	8
Indiana	222	32	35	26	8
Iowa	225	26	38	29	7
Kansas	225	28	36	28	8
Kentucky	222	32	35	25	8
Louisiana	207	48	32	17	3
Maine	226	27	37	28	7
Maryland	225	31	33	26	10
Massachusetts	236	19	32	33	16
Michigan	220	34	34	25	8
Minnesota	225	27	36	28	9
Mississippi	208	49	33	16	3
Missouri	221	33	35	25	7
Montana	227	25	37	31	8
Nebraska	223	29	36	27	8
Nevada	211	43	33	20	5
New Hampshire	229	24	35	31	11
New Jersey	231	23	34	31	12
New Mexico	212	42	34	19	5
New York	224	31	33	26	10
North Carolina	218	36	35	23	6
North Dakota	226	25	40	29	6
Ohio	226	27	37	28	8
Oklahoma	217	35	38	22	4
Oregon	215	38	34	22	6
Pennsylvania	226	27	32	29	11
Rhode Island	219	35	35	24	7
South Carolina	214	41	33	20	5
South Dakota	223	29	37	27	7
Tennessee	216	39	34	21	6
Texas	220	34	36	23	6
Utah	221	31	35	26	8
Vermont	228	26	34	30	11
Virginia	227	26	37	29	9
Washington	224	30	34	27	10
West Virginia	215	37	35	23	5
Wisconsin	223	30	35	27	8
Wyoming	225	27	37	29	8
Other jurisdictions					
District of Columbia	197	61	25	10	4
DoDEA[1]	229	22	38	32	8

Percentage below *Basic* and at *Basic*   Percentage at *Proficient* and *Advanced*

[1] Department of Defense Education Activity (overseas and domestic schools).
NOTE: The shaded bars are graphed using unrounded numbers. Detail may not sum to totals because of rounding.
SOURCE: U.S. Department of Education, Institute of Education Sciences, National Center for Education Statistics, National Assessment of Educational Progress (NAEP), 2007 Reading Assessment.

Sources: The Nation's Report Card: Fourth-Grade Reading 2005 (NCES 2006-451), by M. Perie, W. Grigg, & P. Donahue, 2006, Washington, DC: U.S. Department of Education, Office of Educational Research and Improvement, National Center for Education Statistics.

With the publication of *A Nation at Risk* (National Commission on Excellence in Education, 1983), the United States began one of its periodic school reform efforts. However, as of today, not much has changed. It is clear that schools and districts that were successful in 1983 remain so today, except in those locations where the economy of the community itself has changed from middle class to marginalized and poverty stricken. Schools and districts that were failing in 1983, including most of our large urban school districts, continue to fail most of their students today. The data indicate that there have been few substantive changes in student achievement levels in the last 30 years (Darling-Hammond & Wood, 2008; Fuller & Wright, 2007; Lee, 2006; U.S. Department of Education, 2005). Berliner (1995) carefully reviewed the data for the 1990s and concluded as follows: "Standardized tests provide no evidence whatever that supports the myth of the recent decline in school achievement of the average American student. Achievement in mathematics has not declined—nor has that for science, English-language competency, or any other academic subject that we know of. . . . [E]ndless repetition of a myth does not make it true" (p. 34).

Achievement on national reading tests has improved only marginally. It remains essentially similar today, and a significant gap in achievement continues among White, African American, Latino, and low-income students, as shown in Figure 1.2 (Hartocollis, 2002; Kober, 2001; Lee, Grigg, & Donahue, 2007).

The 1980s and 1990s saw an assault on public schools led by conservative policy advocates such as Chester Finn and Dianne Ravitch, who worked first in the Reagan Administration and then with business interests to fault public education for a perceived economic crisis (Emery, 2007; Ravitch & Viteritti, 1997). Then, in 1991–1992, President George Bush and then Governor Bill Clinton, among others, dedicated themselves in the Goals 2000 Initiative to achieving the following, among other things, by the year 2000:

1. Students will be first in the world in science and mathematics achievement, and
2. Every school in America will be free of drugs and violence and will offer a disciplined environment conducive to learning. (U.S. Department of Education, 1991)

These were good intentions and nice promises, but there is little evidence of improved schooling. By the year 2000, the American Civil Liberties Union, Public Advocates and others sued the state of California arguing that what once seemed like a consensus in our society in favor of public education was breaking down. They asserted that we should all agree that children ought to be able to attend public schools that are safe, where gangs and narcotics are not common, where roofs don't leak and plaster doesn't fall from the ceilings. We ought to be able to assure our students that the toilets work and fresh water is available. But, asserted the plaintiffs, we cannot. (Williams v. California, 2000. See also Kozol, 2005.)

In 1954, the U.S. Supreme Court, in *Brown v. Board of Education,* determined that racially separate school systems and schools are inherently unequal. However, the best evidence today indicates that at present schools and the teaching profession are becoming more segregated by race than they were in the 1950s. In *Racial Transformation and the Changing Nature of Segregation* (2006), Gary Orfield and Chungmei Lee argue:

> Past research has documented that for the segregation of black and Latino students the great majority of cases is closely related to concentrated poverty. The important fact is that we are not talking simply about racial segregation but about the whole syndrome of inequalities related to the double or triple segregation these schools typically face. For Latino students, in many cases it also involves linguistic isolation in schools with many native Spanish speakers and few fluent native speakers of academic English, which students must acquire to be successful in high school and college.
>
> Concentrated poverty is shorthand for a constellation of inequalities that shape schooling. These schools have less qualified, less experienced teachers, lower levels of peer group competition, more limited curricula taught at less challenging levels, more serious health problems, much more turnover of enrollment, and many other factors that seriously affect academic achievement. . .
>
> . . . .
>
> This syndrome of inequalities is so profound that there is a very striking relationship between a school's poverty level and its test scores, independent of any other factors. (p. 29)

What is going on here? Do we have a school crisis or a racial crisis? Or is the school crisis a racial crisis?

As you enter the teaching profession, it is important to develop your own position on the central matter of equal educational opportunity. You will soon directly experience one or more aspects of the issue. Will you find your first job in a clean, well-built, modern school with high standards for professional conduct and high expectations for student achievement? Or will you be assigned to a segregated school, or to a segregated program within an integrated school, where students lack the basic conditions of safety and security, where some teachers are demoralized and just marking time while controlling kids? Will your first school have clean windows and modern computers, or will it have broken windows and locked bathrooms?

How did we get to the present situation, where those schools with mostly European American students have decent learning conditions and those with primarily African American and/or Latino students do not?

Schools do not exist in a vacuum. They are not isolated from their neighborhoods and communities. Inequality in schooling usually reflects inequality in society. While schools can be a site for building democracy and equal opportunity, at present many schools are reinforcing inequality. Democratic opportunity can be created only with significant new investment in schools in low-income areas. However, school investment requires a political decision, and each year elected officials decide to continue to underfund specific schools in most local, state, and federal budgets.

The Structural Crisis in Our Society

Schools reflect and re-create our society and its values. To understand the particular failure of schools serving poor children and many students belonging to racial, ethnic, language, and cultural minorities, we must first consider the context and the environment within which these schools exist.

Both our society and our schools are in crisis. In some areas, drugs, crime, and street gangs make travel unsafe at night. While the national crime rate has fallen since 2007, funds for basic government services such as police and fire protection, emergency medical response, public safety, child protective services, youth crime diversion, and schools have remained inadequate. Unemployment has continued at recession levels for decades for young African American males. In 2001, industrial production and high-technology industries entered another recession; by 2007, high technology had recovered, but basic industrial production continued to decline (Mishel, Bernstein, & Allegretto, 2007). While most working people had not yet recovered from the earlier recessions of 1990–1991 and 2001–2003, in 2008 a crisis in the housing market and a resultant crisis in the financial markets, along with a very expensive, protracted war in Iraq, plunged the economy into yet another recession. Teachers were laid off, class sizes were increased, and school budgets were slashed in many states. Some families have been stressed and even destroyed by disasters, poverty, drugs, crime, and violence. Though these economic troubles are found in many regions of the country, they do not affect everyone equally.

Class

Mainstream culture and the media in general typically portray the United States as a classless society (Luhman, 1996). In this work, I present an alternative view—based on actual census data and described in the writings of Rudy Acuña, Barbara Ehrenreich, bell hooks, G. William Domhoff, Michael Harrington, Cornel West, Manning Marable, Michael Yates, and others—that U.S. society in fact has at least three tiers or classes: an upper (affluent), a middle, and a lower (poor). The affluent and well-off have access to fancy cars, the latest technology, exotic foods, and spacious homes. They have large investments and substantial wealth. A few miles away lives a second tier: the middle-class majority. Those in the upper third of the middle class are doing quite well. Those in the middle third are struggling to maintain their standard of living in a rapidly changing economy. And the lower third of the middle class watches as globalization sends industrial production and their jobs overseas, their job security and pensions are lost, their taxes remain high relative to their income, the college tuition for their children increases, and the economic opportunities for their children erode. Most current teachers have come, and most future teachers will come, from the economically stressed lower two-thirds of the middle class.

A third class in our society is that of the working poor, the chronic poor, and those temporarily forced into poverty by the loss of jobs, health crises, or recurring economic recessions. In this tier, we find levels of poverty, crime, and health hazards that are common in underdeveloped nations. Having a job does not always mean that you can provide for your family. The working poor make up more than 20 percent of all poor people. Poverty in our society remains high, much more so than in other developed countries (Mishel et al., 2007, p. 349). As I will detail in Chapter 4, poverty in our society is concentrated particularly among our children.

The extremes of wealth and poverty among our neighborhoods lead directly to extreme differences in the quality of schooling offered to our children. Schools on one side of town serve children of the affluent and the middle class, many of whom can look forward to a bright economic future. In poor neighborhoods, middle-class teachers often face overcrowded classrooms in rundown buildings filled with children from immigrant groups and from the distressed African American and Latino communities where unemployment is high. The quality of instruction and school experience in the schools serving poor and working-class children vary dramatically from those in the middle-class schools (Anyon, 2005; Darling-Hammond, 1995).

In many low-income neighborhoods stressed by the changing economy, there is a much higher incidence of student transience. Families and students are often moving from school to school during the school year. There are higher rates of health crises, incarceration, street violence, and gangs. At the same time, the schools in these neighborhoods are typically underfunded. They have fewer counselors and more security monitors, fewer libraries and books and more gang problems. Schools in stressed neighborhoods have far more new teachers and teachers with limited or no teacher preparation and a higher percentage of teacher turnover. When students have substitutes and new teachers year after year, they fall behind in basic skills such as reading and math. They will arrive in your classroom several years behind, and many will score below the basic level on skills tests. School failure is persistent and endemic in many poor neighborhoods in our major cities.

A related problem, and one of the ironies arising from the growing race–class divisions in our society, is that while the middle class provides most of the teachers, the working class provides most of the students. In addition, most new teaching positions are in districts and schools filled with poor children from a variety of racial, ethnic, cultural, and linguistic backgrounds. The hard truth is that these children come from a separate economy that exists alongside that of the affluent and the middle class in our society. See Table 1.2.

The Economy

In the last 30 years, U.S. government policies have eliminated millions of good-paying jobs, particularly in manufacturing and in the urban core, and have transferred several million more jobs to other nations. The Bush Administration decided to invade Iraq in a war that will cost up to $2 trillion, while officials claim there is not enough money to fix our roads, our bridges, or our schools.

By 2000, the federal tax rates reached their lowest levels since 1983. Then in 2001, the new Bush Administration and Congress passed further massive tax cuts for the very wealthy. *New York Times* reporter David Cay Johnston (2003) describes the current era as follows:

> What surprised me more than anything was the realization that our tax system now levies the poor, the middle class, and even the upper middle class to subsidize the rich. (p. 2)
>   The tax system is becoming a tool to turn the American dream of prosperity and reward for hard work into an impossible goal for tens of millions of Americans and into a nightmare for others. Our tax system is being used to create a nation with fewer stable jobs and less secure retirement income. The tax system is being used by the rich, through their allies in Congress, to shift

risks off themselves and onto everyone else. And perhaps worst of all, our tax system now forces most Americans to subsidize the lifestyles of the very rich, who enjoy the benefits of our democracy without paying their fair share of its price. (p. 21)

Recall that it is the federal, state, and local tax systems that fund our public schools. If the tax systems are manipulated for the very rich (which they are) and the very rich do not send their children to public schools, then the rich and the powerful have every reason to keep taxes low by underfunding the schools, particularly the schools in low-income areas.

The Economics of Business as Usual

The manipulation of the economy to favor the rich was further demonstrated in the scandals exposed by the collapse in 2001 and 2002 of Enron, Global Crossing, and other corporations among the largest and richest in the United States. Enron's political manipulation of the energy markets increased energy bills in California by over 200 percent in 2002, while President Ken Lay made a tidy $127 million personal windfall in just one week. As a result of the Enron corporate bankruptcy, thousands of people lost their jobs and their retirement savings (Blakeslee, 2002; Greider, 2002; Johnston, 2007).

While the rich made billions in the last few years and profits soared, the poor and the working class never recovered from the economic recession of 2001–2003. Employment growth remained a weak 0.9 percent—less than half the rate of earlier "recoveries"—and wages and salaries remained stagnant for millions, while health care and retirement benefits were cut. In particular, workers without a college education suffered economic stress. The economic recovery of 2003 to 2007 was the first in over 40 years to fail to reduce the poverty rate, and more people were without health insurance in 2007 than in 2001 (Johnston, 2007).

Nor were these corporate scandals a one-time event remedied by the legislative reform enacted as the Sarbanes–Oxley Act of 2002. In 2005, just before the Republican Party was swept out of majority control of the Congress in response to a series of corruption scandals, the Congress passed a prescription drug benefit for seniors that protected the drug companies from having to negotiate for lower prescription prices with Medicare (Kroft, 2007). For details of several more such scandals, read *Free Lunch: How the Wealthiest Americans Enrich Themselves at Government Expense (and Stick You with the Bill)* (Johnston, 2007).

In 2008, the underregulated housing market in the United States collapsed under the pressure of subprime loans, creating an $700 billion crisis involving mortgage securities for finance capital on Wall Street and around the world; forcing the closing of a major bank, Bear-Sterns; and pushing the economy into a deep recession. While tens of thousands of working people were laid off, executives departing the stressed and endangered companies received salary packages of over $100 million per year. The resulting recession saw the U.S. dollar decline, gas prices soar to over $4.50 per gallon, and state and local governments suffer severe budget crises, most often leading to deep cuts in school budgets. Economics matters in public education.

While the rich became very rich, the poor continued to be very poor. *The State of America's Children 2005*, by the Children's Defense Fund, describes the state of child poverty:

> After falling for seven consecutive years during the 1990s, child poverty rose for four years in a row to 13 million in 2004; in all, 37 million Americans live below the poverty line. Child poverty has increased by over 1.4 million children since 2000, accounting for more than a quarter of the 5.4 million people overall who have fallen into poverty. More than one out of every six American children were poor in 2004. By race and ethnicity, one in three Black children, almost three out of 10 Latino children, one in 10 Asian children, and more than one in 10 White, non-Latino children were poor. (2005, p. 3)

The U.S. child poverty rate is roughly twice as high as the rates in Canada and Germany and at least six times higher than the rates in France, Belgium, and Austria (Children's Defense Fund, 2001, p. 3). Uncomfortable with homeless beggars and other increasingly visible signs of poverty and suffering and powerless to end the exploitation of the tax system by the rich, middle-class voters have insisted (through local measures and elected representatives) that tax monies be allocated to increase police power and prison space.

As the gap between the lower class and the upper class grows, our secondary schools, particularly in the cities, are allegedly increasingly ineffective in preparing non-college-bound students for entrance into a workforce that requires advanced education and computer skills (National Center on Education and the Economy, 2007). Middle-class children generally have access to higher education, enabling them to prepare for well-paying professional careers. But the majority of children of the working class will end up in the service sector as fast-food employees, service workers, and maintenance personnel (Teller-Elsberg, Heintz, & Folbre, 2006). Unless education gives working-class students access to new careers, knowledge systems, and technology, they will join the working poor.

A Day in the Life

The Children's Defense Fund has earned a national reputation for its advocacy work. In *The State of America's Children 2008*, it describes a day in the life of America's children. See Table 1.2.

In its 2005 report, the Children's Defense Fund reports a poverty rate of 17.8 percent for all persons under age 18, but an African American poverty rate of 33.2 percent, a Hispanic (Latino) poverty rate of 28.9 percent, a non-Hispanic White poverty rate of 10.5 percent, and an Asian/Pacific Islander poverty rate of 9.8 percent. Poverty among the young remains persistently high and results from a variety of causes, including their parents' low-paying jobs, major changes in the welfare system, unstable family life, and neighborhoods dominated by crime, violence, and drug abuse (see Table 1.2). The poor in our society are marginalized in terms of their economic and political participation, and their children usually attend understaffed, poorly financed schools.

Table 1.2 Each Day in America: March 2008

- 2 mothers die from complications of pregnancy or childbirth.
- 4 children are killed by abuse or neglect.
- 5 children or teens commit suicide.
- 8 children or teens are killed by firearms.
- 32 children or teens die from accidents.
- 78 babies die before their first birthday.
- 155 children are arrested for violent crimes.
- 296 children are arrested for drug crimes.
- 1,154 babies are born to teen mothers.
- 1,511 public school children are corporally punished.
- 2,145 babies are born without health insurance.
- 2,467 high school students drop out.
- 2,483 babies are born into poverty.
- 3,477 children are arrested.
- 18,221 public school students are suspended.

Source: The State of America's Children 2008. Copyright 2008. Children's Defense Fund. All Rights Reserved. www.childrensdefense.org. Every Day in America

As described in the Children's Defense Fund's annual reports, the official poverty level is artificially low. Realistically, life is difficult for families living at 200 percent of the poverty level, at about what the U.S. Census Bureau considers the "low budget" line. As jobs move out of the cities and offshore, the poverty and desperation of these families increase. Their lives become increasingly brutal; school dropout and incarceration rates increase. Some young people turn to crime, violence, and acts of rage that make battlegrounds of schools and neighborhoods in some cities (West, 2004).

As a U.S. senator, Barack Obama (2007) described the problems of poor neighborhoods in his adopted home of Chicago as follows:

> What's most overwhelming about urban poverty is that it's so difficult to escape—it's isolating and it's everywhere. If you are an African-American child unlucky enough to be born into one of these neighborhoods, you are most likely to start life hungry or malnourished. You are less likely to start with a father in your household, and if he is there, there's a fifty-fifty chance that he never finished high school and the same chance he doesn't have a job. Your school isn't likely to have the right books or the best teachers. You're more likely to encounter gang-activities than after-school activities. And if you can't find a job because the most successful businessman in your neighborhood is a drug dealer, you're more likely to join that gang yourself. Opportunity is scarce, role models are few, and there is little contact with the normalcy of life outside those streets.

The Emerging Diversity of Students

Ethnic, language, and cultural diversity is increasing in our society and in our schools (Figure 1.4). The U.S. Census Bureau in 2003 estimated that 67.9 percent of the population was White (not Hispanic), 4.1 percent Asian, 13.7 percent Latino, 0.9 percent

Figure 1.4   U.S. Population by Race and Ethnicity, 1985 and 2003

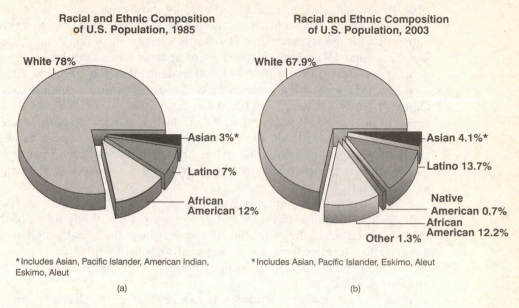

Racial and Ethnic Composition
of U.S. Population, 1985

White 78%

Asian 3%*

Latino 7%

African
American 12%

*Includes Asian, Pacific Islander, American Indian,
Eskimo, Aleut

(a)

Racial and Ethnic Composition
of U.S. Population, 2003

White 67.9%

Asian 4.1%*

Latino 13.7%

Native
American 0.7%
African
American 12.2%
Other 1.3%

*Includes Asian, Pacific Islander, Eskimo, Aleut

(b)

Native American, and 12.2 percent African American. We will consider the diversity among these groups in the next two chapters. Many people can claim more than one ethnic or racial identity, and the Census Bureau now counts these groups. In the 2000 census, less than 2.4 percent claimed multiple ethnic identities.

The U.S. Immigration and Nationality Act Amendments of 1965 created a major change in the number of new immigrants to the United States and in the countries from which they came. The amendments allowed massive new immigration from Latin America and Asia from the 1980s to the present. Wars in Asia and Central America and political upheavals in the former Soviet Union also produced new immigrants. Once these immigrants arrived, family unification provisions of the law allowed them to bring additional family members.

The challenges of teaching an ethnically and linguistically diverse population are being felt throughout the nation. The recent arrival of many students from Latin America, Asia, and the former Soviet Union has created a need for social services and for English as a Second Language and bilingual instruction in schools. Among the new immigrants, Spanish is the most common language (28 million), followed by Chinese (2 million), French (1.6 million), German (1.4 million), and Tagalog (1.2 million) (Shin & Bruno, 2003) Language Use and English-speaking ability: 2000. Census 2000 Brief C2kBR-29). There will be much more on the specifics of language-minority students in Chapter 11.

Since the 1970s, the number of students who struggle to learn English has increased steadily and sharply. The case of California illustrates the impact of immigration on schools. According to the 2006 language census for California public schools (California Department of Education, 2006), language-minority students comprised 24.9 percent of the total school population, up from 15 percent of the student population in 1988. The single largest group of limited-English-proficient students is Spanish speaking (85.4 percent), followed by those who speak Vietnamese (2.2 percent), Hmong (1.4 percent), Cantonese (1.4 percent), and Pilipino or Tagalog (1.3 percent), with the rest speaking 31 other languages, including Khmer, Russian, Punjabi, Farsi, and Mien. Texas has had a similar large increase in language-minority students, growing by 48 percent, to 711,000 students, between 1992 and 2002.

If you take a teaching position in California, New York, Illinois, or Texas or in almost any urban school district, you can expect that out of a class of 28 students, up to 7 will not speak English proficiently. Even if you begin your career in more rural states, such as Iowa, Utah, or Tennessee, you are likely to have a number of immigrant students in your classroom. How are you going to teach them your subject if they do not completely understand English? We will provide you with some strategies in Chapter 11.

Students from these minority language groups are concentrated in specific school districts and in both elementary and secondary grades. While a few of them benefit from high-quality bilingual education programs, the great majority of teachers assigned to these students are unprepared to help them. Most immigrant students receive inadequate English instruction and little academic support in their native language (Gándara, 2007).

In 2001, the Latino population (or in census terms, the Hispanic population) became the largest minority group in the nation (U.S. Bureau of the Census. May, 2001). The Latino (Hispanic) population had increased by over 50 percent in the 1990s, to a total of 35.3 million people. More than 30 percent of Latinos under the age of 18 remain poor (Children's Defense Fund, 2001). High school completion rates for most students have improved but remain lowest for Latinos, who are less likely to attend college than any other group. Latinos and African Americans have substantially higher unemployment rates than other groups (Ramirez & de la Cruz, 2002).

In California, Hawaii, New Mexico, Texas, and Mississippi, the sum of all "minority" students now constitutes a majority of the total student population. Latino and Asian populations are rapidly growing in urban areas throughout the nation. In states such as Maine, Minnesota, Iowa, Indiana, Utah, and Wyoming, the population remains over 80% European American, but large numbers of children from new communities of immigrants have arrived at their schools.

As noted earlier, in the census of 2000, nearly 98 percent of respondents reported they belonged to one race. The largest group reported White alone (the Census Bureau considers Hispanics to be White unless they specify otherwise). The Black or African American alone population represented 12 percent of the total. Some 2.4 percent reported that they were two or more races, an indication of marriages, births, and the blending of different ethnic groups. A total of 12.5 percent of the population reported that they were Hispanic, which is not a racial category in the U.S. census (U.S. Bureau of the Census, 2001, p. 3; see Chapter 3 in this text). Students from all of these ethnic groups, regions, schools, and classes will have to learn to work together and to cooperate in our 21st-century society.

You can get current data and projections for your own state at www.census.gov. When you get there, look for the tables on population estimates.

The Fire This Time

In the absence of quality educational opportunities and supportive social policy, increased racial polarization at times interacts with painful changes in the economy to produce an increase in urban violence. In 1963, James Baldwin published an essay entitled "The Fire Next Time," predicting widespread violence if racial justice was further delayed. In 1965, 1967, and 1968, major U.S. cities were in fact rocked by race riots as economic conditions declined in urban areas. Cornel West claims that there were "329 revolts in 257 cities between 1964 and 1968" (1993a, p. 21). In 1985, 1990, 1992, and 2001, race disturbances returned to plague our cities, the largest insurrection occurring in Los Angeles from April 29 through May 1, 1992 (Table 1.3).

The 1992 Los Angeles riots were costly: 51 dead, 1,032 injured, 3,000 arrested, $1.5 billion in property damage. (See Figure 1.5). The people hurt most by this rebellion and riot were the residents of the neighborhoods where the rioting took place: the people of South Central Los Angeles—a predominantly African American neighborhood—and the people of the Pico Union district—a predominantly Latino immigrant neighborhood (West, 1993a). Racial prejudice had divided neighborhoods—for example, pitting African American families against Korean shop owners. Children watched this racial polarization going on around them and on their television screens at night. It frightened and confused them. In Compton, near one of the riot areas, a group of parents went to the child care center and protected "their school" from arsonists. On Monday, May 4, 1992, following the riots, Los Angeles's 800,000 students returned to school in their devastated communities. In many schools, teachers focused discussion on the recent events. Students wanted to talk, to share their own stories. Some students wrote, some spoke up, some listened.

Table 1.3   Selected Race Riots in U.S. History

Date	Place	Results
1866	Memphis, TN	48 dead
December 1874	Vicksburg, MS	70 dead
July 1917	East St. Louis, IL	49 dead
May 1921	Tulsa, OK	36 dead
June 3–5, 1943	Los Angeles, CA	Thousands of U.S. sailors attack Mexican youth
July 23, 1943	Detroit, MI	43 dead
August 11, 1965	Los Angeles, CA	35 dead
July 23, 1967	Detroit, MI	43 dead
April 4, 1968	Pittsburgh, PA Chicago, IL and other U.S. cities	Riots erupt after the assassination of Martin Luther King, Jr.
August 29, 1969	Los Angeles, CA	3 dead; Chicano anti-war march becomes a three-day battle with police.
May 17, 1980	Miami, FL	15 dead and 743 arrested, mostly African American men.
April 28–May 1, 1992	Los Angeles, CA	51 dead

Figure 1.5a   Los Angeles, 1992
Source: AP/Wide World Photos

Figure 1.5b   Los Angeles, 1992
Source: AP/Word World Photos

The rebellion in Los Angeles and simultaneous disturbances in Seattle, San Francisco, and Atlanta, as well as disturbances in Cincinnati, Ohio, in 2001 and the crisis in New Orleans after Hurricane Katrina, confirm that living conditions for many poor, disenfranchised African Americans and Latinos had deteriorated in the decades of the 1980s and 1990s. The lesson of the riots is that portions of our society once again are moving toward racial and ethnic polarization. Angry, alienated young people—African Americans, Latinos, and members of other ethnic groups—cluster and stagnate in our inner cities. As I will show in Chapters 3 and 4, economic opportunity for the working poor has declined since the conservative political/economic revolution and the changes in government policies of the 1980s. The stagnating economy, particularly in the industrial cities, has not provided the working poor with entry-level jobs, and the schools have not reached many of their children. Some young people adopt an nihilist analysis of urban life as they view their future, abandoned by the economic system and oppressed by entrenched authority, represented on the streets as police power, high rates of incarceration, and the war on drugs (West, 2004).

Unlike the riots of the 1960s, which were followed by a substantial response, the 1992 riots and the 2001 disturbances sparked no national-level investigatory commissions, nor were substantial new programs funded to combat poverty, racial division, and alienation. Outside of Los Angeles and Cincinnati, most of the political leadership went back to business as usual and tried to forget that the riots had occurred, ignoring the economic polarization and other root causes of the violence. They will again be surprised and shocked when the next riot occurs. School leaders and teachers were left to deal with the continuing crises of racial division, crime, and poverty.

By 1995, the U.S. economy had improved for all except the poor and then plunged into another recession in 2001. The racial divisions in the society continued to fester. In 1994, California voters passed Proposition 187, which banned illegal immigrants from receiving prenatal care and other social services and their children from receiving an education in the public schools; it required that teachers and other school personnel report any children they suspected of lacking proper immigration papers. In 1996, a majority of Californians voted to abolish affirmative action. Both of these campaigns later spread to other states and communities. Legislative campaigns against immigrants, against gays and lesbians, and against affirmative action programs became unifying themes that result in conservative political victories around the nation. And in the presidential election of 2000, the critical Florida balloting was seriously marred by tactics that kept over 200,000 African Americans from voting (U.S. Commission on Civil Rights, 2001).

In September 1998, the Advisory Board to the President's Initiative on Race, chaired by distinguished historian John Hope Franklin, wrote the following in *One America in the 21st Century: Forging a New Future*:

> At the dawn of a new century, America is once again at a crossroads on race. The eminent African American scholar W. E. B. DuBois noted decades ago that the main problem of the 20th century would be the color line. Indeed, at the end of the 20th century, the color of one's skin still has a profound impact on the extent to which a person is fully included in American society and provided the equal opportunity and equal protection promised to all Americans in our chartering documents. The color of one's skin continues to affect an individual's opportunities to receive a good education, acquire the skills to get and maintain a good job, have access to adequate health care, and receive equal justice under the law. . . .
>
> The path toward racial progress has had a difficult, sometimes bloody history: Our early treatment of American Indians and Alaska Natives, followed by the enslavement and subsequent segregation of African Americans and then the conquest and legal oppression of Mexican

Americans and other Hispanics, the forced labor of Chinese Americans, the internment of Japanese Americans, and the harassment of religious minorities is a history of which many Americans are not fully aware and no American should be proud. (pp. 35–36)

When the members of the Advisory Board turned to recommendations, they focused in on education, beginning as follows:

Enhance early childhood learning [and s]trengthen teacher preparation and equity. There is a strong consensus that high-quality teachers are our most valuable educational resource, and the need for high-quality teachers is increasing; an estimated 2 million new teachers will be hired in the next decade. . . . If we are serious about ensuring that all children have access to high-quality education and high standards, the Nation must make a national priority the task of increasing the number of high-quality teachers with high expectations for all students. (p. 61)

The U.S. economy recovered from the 2001–2002 recession, and the well-off and the well-educated prospered economically until the recession of 2008. The working poor and industrial workers, however, have not recovered (I will have more to say on this in Chapter 4). Fundamentally, people in the upper income strata are doing well in the new globalized economy. The stock market was up and then declined sharply in 2008. For working people, there has been loss of jobs, wage stagnation, loss of health and retirement benefits, and increased insecurity. The U.S. economy is changing. Significantly, the economy has gone global in production, in finance, and in producing poverty and migration. Immigration and "control of the border" became a major divisive issue in U.S. politics. Over 1 million immigrants and their supporters marched for change in cities all across the nation on May 1, 2006, perhaps among the largest demonstrations in U.S. history. Yet the Congress could not agree on proposals to update our immigration policy. Nations now have less control over their own economies. Preparing students for this new global economy will require improved education and technology skills.

Racial polarization surfaced again in the 2008 presidential election when Barack Obama, born to an African father and a White mother, became a leading Democratic Party candidate. In one case, that of the Reverend Jeremiah Wright, Obama's pastor, his videotaped sermons were copied, edited, and made to seem radical and revolutionary, when if you watched the full 10-minute sermon instead of the 30-second clip, he was making reasonable, rational points. In this case, both the edited video clips on YouTube and the mainstream media distorted the racial context of the message and created an "incident" that polarized millions at a critical point in primary elections. The clips were used again to frighten voters in the general election but with less effect. You can read Senator Obama's response to this racial polarization—which came close to costing him the nomination for President—at www.barackobama.com/2008/03/18/remarks_of_senator_barack_obam_53.php.

As you will read in Chapters 2–5, the contradictions within our society—the positive elements of our great democratic experiment and the troubling legacy of racial, gender, and class conflict—will in many ways shape both the resources available to you as a teacher and your daily decisions of what and how to teach.

The Crisis in Our Schools

Quality public education for all is a cause well worth fighting for. We have inherited our present schools from prior generations who sought to provide all children with the preparation needed for economic opportunity and active citizenship.

Critics of public education repeat and repeat a message of school crisis. And there is a crisis, but some of our schools are working quite well. More and more of our citizens are completing high school and college than ever before. The percentage of high school graduates completing a core academic curriculum—including four years of English and three years each of math, science, and social studies—grew from 14 percent to 57 percent from 1982 to 2000. Many students in high schools are completing advanced math and science courses. The percentage of high school graduates completing advanced math courses climbed from 26 percent in 1982 to 45 percent in 2000. A similar growth has occurred in the sciences (U.S. Department of Education, 2004).

Schools are working reasonably well for the middle class, while many schools serving the poor and ethnic minorities are in crisis (Kozol, 2005). Most urban schools, and some rural schools, as currently organized and funded, are not able to offer an education that will overcome the problems of poverty in our society. Students in low-income areas often have fewer qualified teachers, fewer counselors, and inadequate textbooks and teaching materials. Although teaching conditions vary from state to state and district to district, the dropout rates are high, and the college attendance rates are low for African American and Latino students. With only a few exceptions, these conditions have remained the same for over 30 years.

We have a crisis in some schools—not all—and it is precisely the low-income schools in crisis where there are the most openings for new teachers. Let's look into this crisis. Inadequate funding is a major issue in the school crisis in low-income areas. Governments spent $426.6 billion on K–12 public education in 2005. The problem of inadequate funding is well illustrated in the 2000 lawsuit of *Williams v. California* (Figure 1.6).

In August 2004, the state of California admitted to the facts in the *Williams* case and agreed to provide over $1 billion to remedy the most severe problems. In the settlement, California acknowledged its responsibility for ensuring quality and equal education to all its students. In 2007, a series of over 20 studies commissioned by the state legislature again recognized the ongoing inadequate funding of public education in California (Loeb, Byrk, & Hanushek, 2007). Similar adequacy studies in recent years have found that New York, Ohio, New Jersey, and some 20 other states are underfunding some of their schools (Karp, 2007).

In trying to understand school failure and school funding, it is important to understand how the U.S. economy produces inequality (a topic we explore in more detail in Chapter 4). In our political system, we prize equal votes (as one person–one vote); in our economic system, inequality—even extreme inequality—is normal. We have been growing increasingly unequal in our economy and increasingly unequal in our offering of school opportunities. While the average income of millionaires and billionaires has grown by over 19 percent per year, the average income of 99 percent of households has

Figure 1.6   *Williams v. State of California* (Superior Court, San Francisco County, 2000)

Superior Court, San Francisco 2000. The complaint alleges:

"1. Tens of Thousands of children attending public schools located throughout the State of California are being deprived of basic educational opportunities available to more privileged children attending the majority of the State's public schools. State law requires students to attend school. Yet all too many California school children must go to school without trained teachers, necessary educational supplies, classrooms, or seats in classrooms. Students attempt to learn in school that lack functioning heating or air conditioning systems, that lack sufficient numbers of functional toilets, and that infested with vermin, including rats, mice, and cockroaches. These appalling conditions in California public schools have persisted for years and have worsened over time. The Plaintiffs bring this suit in an effort to ensure that their schools meet basic minimal educational standards.

2. The schools at which these manifestly substandard conditions exist are overwhelmingly populated by low-income and nonwhite students and students who are still learning the English language. In all but three of the schools the Plaintiffs attend, more than half of the student body is eligible for free or reduced-priced meals at school. Nearly all Plaintiffs in this action are black, Latino or Latina, or Asian Pacific American, and in each of the schools the Plaintiff's attend, nonwhite students constitute more than half of the student body. In all but one of the schools, nonwhite students constitute more than 90 percent of the student body." **William v. State of California.**

---

barely grown since 1979. The average income of the bottom 40 percent of households (and over 50 percent of children) has stagnated for over 30 years (Mishel et al., 2007).

We have long known that social class, or socioeconomic status (SES), is directly correlated with school achievement. That is, the rich and the middle class do well, and the poor, by and large, perform poorly on standardized tests and in schools (Berliner, Glass, & Nichols, 2005; Rothstein, 2004).

In the United States, school funding is largely a state and local responsibility, with 47 percent of funding coming from state governments, 43.9 percent from local sources, and only 9.1 percent from the federal government. States spent an average of $9,138 per pupil in 2006, according to the U.S. Census Bureau. New York was the biggest spender, paying $14,884 per student, with New Jersey second at $14,630; California spent $8,486 (below Oregon), while Texas spent $7,561 per pupil. The states with the lowest spending were Utah at $5,437 per pupil, Arizona at $6,472, Idaho at $6,440, Tennessee at $6,883, and Oklahoma at $6,961 (U.S. Bureau of the Census, 2008).

A first requirement for improving schools is adequate funding for all schools, and that requires developing a fair tax system. Adequate funding requires tens of billions of additional dollars over many years, similar to the giant sums of money that have been poured into the military but not into the schools. Few politicians are willing to face this funding reality (Johnson, 2007; Karp, 2007).

A thesis of this book is that schools should serve as a vehicle to provide equal opportunity—not to increase inequality in our society. While inequality is seen by some as normal in our economy, it does not necessarily follow that extreme inequality in terms of basic life needs—housing, health, and food—is appropriate in a democratic society. In particular, we do not need to accept inequality in schooling. If based on democratic theory we assert that each citizen should have an equal vote, the courts, including the U.S. Supreme Court, have decided that all students deserve an equal opportunity for education (14th Amendment; *Brown v. Board of Education*).

Media Myths and School Improvement

As a teacher, you will frequently read media reports and claims that although schools in general are in crisis, some schools have made great progress. Margaret Spellings, while U.S. Secretary of Education, made such a claim on July 14, 2005, which later turned out to be a misuse of the data (Bracy, 2007a; Crawford, 2007; Nichols & Bracey, 2007). School superintendents make, and the press publishes, claims of dramatic turnarounds in urban districts such as Chicago, Philadelphia, and New York City. After a few years, the district's scores no longer look so positive, and the superintendent moves on to another position to start the cycle over again (Nichols & Berliner, 2007).

There are a number of schools, not districts, that have significantly improved student achievement, such as those described in *It's Being Done: Academic Success in Unexpected Schools* (2007) by Karin Chenoweth. Well-functioning low-income schools give us all hope. Other claims of outstanding schools, however, upon further analysis of the data, prove to be far more complex than the claims of the promotional news releases (Bracey, 2003; Rothstein, 2004).

Passing rates on some state and local tests have shown small increases in achievement in 21 states, but there has been little, if any, improvement on national tests such as NAEP (see Figure 1.2 in this text; Bracey, 2007a; Kober, Chudowsky, & Chudowsky, 2008). The gains in achievement we have seen on state tests may be the result of concentrating instruction on narrowly defined reading and math objectives, while cutting science, citizenship, social studies, the arts, and other vital components of the curriculum (Kober et al., 2008; Valenzuela, 2005).

By and large, we have a well-orchestrated process of claims of school improvement, but when you look past the press releases and carefully consider the data, we do not have reformed school systems or districts that demonstrate substantive improvement (Bracey, 2003; Nichols & Berliner, 2007; Rothstein, 2004).

We then need to also ask why, in spite of over 30 years of press and political attention, there has not been systemic improvement in school achievement? One reason is the unfortunate myth that school reform alone can resolve the problems of inequality. The evidence does not support this assumption. A broad and representative group of scholars and school activists, including Julian Bond, James Comer, Ernesto Cortez, Lawrence Mishel, Ted Sizer, and over 40 others, looked at the data and concluded as follows: "A body of research has shown that much of the achievement gap is rooted in what occurs outside of formal schooling. By and large, low-income students learn as rapidly as more-privileged peers during the hours spent in school. Where they lose ground, though, is in their lack of participation in learning activities during after-school hours and summer vacations" (A Broader, Bolder Approach to Education, 2008, p, 3). Much of what is reported as the achievement gap occurs outside of formal schooling.

School reform could offer high-quality education to the populations not presently being served well. However, politicians, advocacy groups, commissions, and news reporters do not teach school—teachers do. It is difficult to improve a complex system like schools without the wisdom of its important participants—in this case, teachers. The organization and implementation of most school reform efforts have avoided and blocked teacher participation—and these efforts have failed. Unless and until we improve the teaching relationship, improve the skills of teachers, build networks of support for teachers, control the violence in some schools, and improve the working conditions of teachers, most schools will not improve. This book is about what you and I can do as teachers to improve schools and make them more democratic.

Schools and Democracy

Ideally, all citizens of the United States consent to a social contract by which we agree to work together to improve our common standard of living, particularly for our children. We all benefit from a society in which children learn to read and write, to be productive in the workforce, to understand the workings of the economy, and to participate in democratic decision making. But only one portion of U.S. society, the middle class, receives quality public education. Most children of the upper class attend private schools, and the children of the poor are too often in low-performing schools. The poor are failed in school, and up to 50 percent leave without graduating. School failure makes most of them ineligible for or uninterested in college preparation. This exclusion, this marginalization, not only damages their future but also endangers the economy and the democratic community.

In this book, I argue that multicultural education is an integral part of the effort to create a more democratic society for us all. One form of democracy is electoral democracy. Dahl (1985) lists the following criteria to describe the democratic process:

1. Equal votes
2. Effective participation
3. Enlightened understanding
4. Final control of the agenda by the people
5. Inclusiveness

Democratic Values

A democratic society encourages maximum citizen participation in political decision making, respects the rule of the majority, and protects the rights of minorities. Fundamental values of our constitutional form of democracy include justice, equality, the protection of individual rights, and the promotion of the common good (Engle & Ochoa, 1988). Since the time of Thomas Jefferson, our nation has recognized that public schools were created in part to promote these democratic values. Others see public schooling as primarily preparation for work. As a new teacher, you will need to consider these two perspectives.

Democracy is about elections, but it is more than elections. Democracy is based on values, one of which is that each person has equal merit and the right to equal treatment before the law. Other values of a democratic society that are expressed in schools include equality of opportunity, equal respect for all, and the encouragement of free choice. Students should learn values in school such as the values of self-determination, economic participation, and self-governance (Engle & Ochoa, 1988; Nai-Lin Chang, Nguyen Louie-Murdock, Pell, & Femenella, 2000). The development of democratic skills, values, and dispositions is seldom discussed in the current school reform efforts.

John Dewey (1859–1952), the preeminent U.S. philosopher of education, described in "The Democratic Conception in Education" his view of the relationship between schools and democracy:

> A society which makes provisions for participation in its good of all its members on equal terms and which secures flexible readjustment of its institutions through interaction of the different forms of associated life is in so far democratic. Such a society must have a type of education which gives individuals a personal interest in social relationships and control, and the habits of mind which secure social changes without introducing disorder. (1966, p. 90)

In a remarkable essay, "Bowling Alone: America's Declining Social Capital," political scientist Robert Putnam says:

> It is not just the voting booth that has been increasingly deserted by Americans. Since 1973 the number of Americans who report that "in the past year" they have attended a public meeting on town or school affairs has fallen by more than a third. By almost every measure, Americans' direct engagement in politics and government has fallen steadily and sharply over the last generation. Every year for the last decade or two, millions more have withdrawn from the affairs of their community. (1995, pp. 67–68)

There are a number of people who were apparently quite satisfied with the decline in political participation—for example, the late Ken Lay, former CEO of Enron, and Bernard Ebbers of WorldCom Inc. (Greider, 2002; Johnston, 2007). When you and I do not participate, it allows such corporate power brokers more power in influencing government decisions. Jim Schultz, in the *Democracy Owners' Manual* (2002), argues that the influence of corporate money in our political process is one of the serious challenges to democracy today:

> At the local level, in the state legislatures, in elections for Congress and the presidency, campaigns are being dominated by the flow of contributions made by wealthy special interest

groups to politicians. These same groups later come calling on those same politicians seeking public favors. The conflict is a clear one. If the money given were in the form of a bribe, stuck in the politician's pocket, the act would be illegal and we would be aghast. Because those funds instead go into the candidates' campaign coffers, the transaction is legal and accepted, but the effect is little different. (p. 16)

Concerned that the U.S. public, and particularly the young, was increasingly disengaged from civic and political institutions and electoral participation, in 2003 a campaign was developed to reassert the long tradition of U.S schools serving to promote democracy. The *Civic Mission of Schools* (www.civicmissionofschools.org), a report prepared by the Carnegie Corporation and published jointly with CIRCLE in 2002, developed a broad ideological framework to promote more understanding of democracy in our schools. Projects in a number of states and school districts have renewed interest in building the democratic agenda of public schools.

In "What Kind of Citizen? The Politics of Educating for a Democracy" (2004), Westheimer and Kahne describe an important debate over what constitutes a good citizen. Conservatives argue that schools should prepare students for citizenship by teaching "good" character, while social justice advocates see preparation for citizenship as engaging students in participatory democratic projects. These are substantive differences. These different conceptions of preparation for citizenship lead to substantially different decisions on teaching strategies and the appropriateness of multicultural education.

Equality

The preservation of prosperity and democracy depends on a system of education that prepares *all* children (majority and minority) equally to be successful at achieving to high standards in the basic skills of reading, writing, and arithmetic and that fully motivates those children to participate in maintaining our democratic community. Democracy requires quality education for all, not just for a favored few (Darling-Hammond & Wood, 2008).

Today, groups that have been historically excluded (African Americans, Latinos, Native Americans, and some immigrant groups) seek opportunity throughout society for jobs, housing, health, and schooling. Their struggle focuses most immediately on U.S. public schools because, although these individuals often cannot undo the hardship and deprivation of their own lives, they can and do insist on equal educational opportunity for their children.

Democracies are characterized by a formal equality of political power for each citizen. In the landmark 1954 court case *Brown v. Board of Education*, the U.S. Supreme Court decided that schools, as public institutions financed by tax dollars, have an obligation to provide equal opportunity for all students. For a democracy to achieve its promise, schools must provide an arena where all students are equally prepared to fully participate in the economic and political life of society. In June of 2007, a sharply divided U.S. Supreme Court decided in cases involving the Seattle and Jefferson County (Kentucky) School Districts to reverse the direction of the *Brown* decision and to limit school districts' attempts to promote racial integration as a tool for achieving equality of opportunity.

Parents in many communities want better schools for their children. The deterioration of order and opportunity in many urban schools and the refusal of legislatures to provide adequate educational funding are a reflection of a more general abandonment of public life in other spheres: feeding the poor, protecting our communities from gangs and crime, and controlling and eliminating drug abuse.

Let us suppose that you coach a basketball team. In your next game, the opposing team has professional players with great talents, it is well funded, and it has massive resources to prepare. On the other hand, your team is made up of well-intentioned teachers. They love basketball, but they know only a few moves, and they have full-time jobs teaching. Clearly, the pro team will win.

A parallel situation often exists today in cases where political leaders are faced with a demand for adequate funding of schools. One side—the corporate side—has professionals, media writers, lobbyists, talented political organizers, and a series of "think tanks," all of which establish the parameters of discussion. They claim that the problem is not money. On the other side are some teachers, their unions, and some very well meaning parents who want to help their children. Can you predict which side will win?

Professor Pedro Noguera (1999) of New York University points to this contradiction:

> The unfortunate fact is that schools produce winners and losers in the economy, and these winners and losers correspond closely with the patterns of race and class. Privileged families usually have high quality schools and teachers, and their children learn well. Children of the poor, African American, Latino, Asian and White, tend to have lower quality schools, fewer resources, less prepared teachers, lower test scores, low rates of attending college, and high school drop out rates. Amazingly, this is seen by many as normal or natural.

Schools can be a site for building toward democracy and equal opportunity. However, this opportunity can be created only by significant new investment in schools in low-income areas. Underfunded schools cannot provide equal opportunity within an unequal society. They cannot prepare workers for employment in the high-tech industries of the future or for full participation in a political or economic democracy. Investment requires a political decision (Darling-Hammond & Wood, 2008). Our elected officials refuse to make this decision each year when approving their local, state, and federal budgets.

Building democracy requires more than frequent elections and two or more political parties. Ultimately, government is about power. Democracy is about the equal distribution of power. To focus on elections as the primary definition of democracy disconnects parents in poor communities from real power and hides the manner in which many communities, abandoned and impoverished by the new economy, are losing their power (West, 2004).

A fundamental purpose of schools is to prepare future citizens to be stakeholders in society. Arnstine (1995) argues that young people should become active participants in building a democratic community. To participate in building a democratic community, young people need curricula and school practices that provide them with the skills and the disposition to advance democratic values. Curricula can change to openly teach democratic values (Westheimer & Kahne, 2004). Chapters 6 and 7 gives examples of how students, parents, and teachers can learn to work together to resolve conflicts and to build democractic classrooms. Public schools are the primary institution designed to produce a public, civic community. Schools distribute knowledge. Unequal schools distribute knowledge unequally. When schools distribute knowledge unequally, they contribute to the decline of democratic opportunity and the continuing oppression of marginalized citizens.

Just as there are pro-democracy forces in our society that seek to distribute power equally, so there are anti-democracy forces that seek to maintain the current imbalance of power based on race and class. The conservative agenda of the last 30 years promoted the idea that governments could not do things well (Frank, 2004). Certainly, an underfunded, poorly managed Federal Emergency Management Agency failed after Hurricane Katrina hit the Gulf Coast in 2005. Many in our society, particularly the working poor, have learned to distrust their government and often to distrust the outcomes of the schools.

Democracy depends upon broad, inclusive participation by citizens. What are we going to do in schools to improve our democracy? To rescue our democracy? What can we do to increase political awareness and participation, including support for pubic schooling, among the largest possible number of people? And what are we going to do to make economic prosperity, a job, or economic security available to all? The increasing divisions among a wealthy class that dominates our political and economic systems, a middle class, and an impoverished lower class with few opportunities divide our communities and endanger our communities and our democracy.

As teachers, what are we going to do to help the entire community—parents, legislators, and others—to understand the importance of public schooling in responding to the challenges of political and economic participation?

A first step is for us, both teachers and future teachers, to understand the scope and the complexity of the racial, cultural, and gender divides in our society and how they impact school achievement. Then, with this understanding, we can design and develop teaching strategies and materials that respond positively to these divisions in order to create what Martin Luther King, Jr., called a "beloved" community.

The Crisis in Our Democracy

Perhaps no event has revealed the incomplete nature of democracy in the United States as much as the presidential election of 2000, when, for the first time since 1888, the person with the majority of the popular votes—in this case, Democrat Al Gore—did not win the election. There were substantive voting problems and irregularities in this Florida election. The balloting ended in a virtual tie, with a difference of only 534 votes between the two major parties. Then, in one of the most partisan decisions in its history, the U.S. Supreme Court intervened to stop the recounting of the Florida ballots and give the Florida electoral votes, and the election, to Republican George W. Bush (Bugliosi, 2001; Latigua, 2001; Palast, 2002).

In the nation, Democrat Al Gore won the popular vote, but Republican George W. Bush won a victory in the electoral college based on highly contested voting irregularities and the partisan decision of the U.S. Supreme Court to stop the counting of ballots (Bugliosi, 2001; Latigua, 2001). There were two additional minor parties on the Florida ballot, each unable to get even 5 percent of the vote.

Journalist John Latigua (2001) described the events this way: "Of the 179,855 votes that were cast but later discarded—either because they contained more than one vote for President or no detectable vote—again it is impossible to know exactly how many were cast by blacks, but statistics make it clear that African-Americans' votes were lost at much higher rates than those of other ethnic groups, involving tens of thousands of votes in total."

The U.S. Commission on Civil Rights (2001) studied Florida's 2000 election as a part of its mandate to protect the civil rights of U.S. citizens. Among its findings was this:

The disenfranchisement of Florida's voters fell most harshly on the shoulders of black voters. The magnitude of the impact can be seen from any of several perspectives:

- Statewide, based upon county-level statistical estimates, black voters were nearly 10 times more likely than non-black voters to have their ballots rejected.

- Estimates indicate than approximately 14.4 percent of Florida's black voters cast ballots that were rejected. This compares with approximately 1.6 percent of non-black Florida voters who did not have their presidential votes recorded. . . .

- Approximately 11 percent of Florida voters were African American; however, African Americans cast about 54 percent of the 180,000 spoiled ballots in Florida during the November 2000 election based on estimates derived from county-level data.

Before 2000, the most controversial election in U.S. history was the 1876 election of Rutherford B. Hayes, who also won on the basis of contested and controversial election results, including contested results from Florida. The 1876 election signified the triumph of anti-Black legislation in the South, known popularly as "Jim Crow" laws.

If African American votes in Florida in 2000 had been permitted, and counted, as were White votes, Al Gore would have become President of the United States. This flawed Florida election process, with its significant racial overtones, combined with one of the most controversial Supreme Court decisions in U.S. history to make George W. Bush President of the United States (Bugliosi, 2001). Such a fundamental violation of democracy might well have produced a sharply divided nation for decades, as it was at the time of the Civil War. However, the attacks on the United States of September 11, 2001, quickly reestablished political unity before such divisions could develop. In 2004, George Bush was reelected in a narrow vote margin that was again marred by electoral irregularities (Palast, 2007).

When democracy does not work well, the public schools suffer. After the flawed election of 2000, George W. Bush became the chief advocate for the No Child Left Behind Act, which has substantially changed education. His administration and the Republican majority in Congress subsequently refused to adequately fund the law.

Unequal opportunity (anti-democracy) is promoted in the schools through unequal government spending. The quality of schooling depends significantly on the funds available for schools, yet the adequacy of funding ranges dramatically from state to state and district to district. State averages of per pupil expenditures provide only a part of the story; there are often great differences between districts within a state. For example, in 2003, school funding in the Chicago area ranged from $17,291 per pupil in the Highland Park and Deerfield area to $8,482 per pupil in Chicago. And in New York State, the Manhasset schools spent $22,311 per student, while the New York City schools could spend only $11,627 per student (Kozol, 2005). Inequality of school funding among districts in a state is a major focus of school reform efforts in Ohio, New Jersey, Tennessee, Texas, Maryland, Michigan, and other states (Weiner & Pristoop, 2006; Karp, 2007).

Political anti-tax efforts have seriously limited school funding in many states. Inadequate school funding, particularly in low-income areas, remains a central issue of school reform, as noted in *Williams v. California* (Figure 1.6). The theory of the *Williams* suit and similar suits around the country is that children attending public schools that lack basic educational necessities are being denied their right to equal protection of the laws because they must learn under conditions that fall fundamentally below prevailing statewide standards. Similar adequacy suits have been filed and won based on state constitutions in New York, New Jersey, and over 20 other states. However, even when the plaintiffs win these constitutional cases, the legislatures and governors have often been unwilling to fund the needed budget changes to equalize funding (Karp, 2007).

School Reform

In the 1970s and 1980s, Ron Edmonds and others located, described, and analyzed so-called effective schools (Edmonds, 1982). They found that approximately 2 percent of schools in low-income areas function well. Planned school interventions involving parents, teachers, and administrators have slowly increased the number of effective schools serving poor and impoverished neighborhoods in the last 30 years. These schools show that effective schools are at least possible in poor areas. Students in these schools learn basic skills and enjoy academic enrichment. The schools work in spite of the economic chaos in the surrounding neighborhoods. Graduates of these schools are as well prepared for college and our new information-based economy as are graduates of suburban schools (Carter & Chatfield, 1986; Grubb & Huerta, 2001).

The fact is that we know how to educate poor and minority children of all kinds—racial, ethnic, and language—to high levels. Some teachers and entire schools do it every day, year in and year out. Karin Chenoweth, of the corporate-funded Achievement Alliance, says the following in describing 16 low-income and minority schools that she studied in *It's Being Done: Academic Success in Unexpected Schools* (2007):

> Make no mistake—every school described in this book has accomplished something admirable. They are taking children who are considered "hard to teach" by many in the educational world, and with thoughtful hard work they are producing academic success. They

could have saved themselves a lot of trouble by falling back on the tired old excuses that many other schools used—that "these kids" can't be expected to do much academically because they are poor, because their parents don't support their education, because their home lives are chaotic, because they don't speak English at home, because they didn't get the proper foundation at an earlier age, because they didn't eat breakfast, because they don't have a culture of academic achievement, or any of a number of other excuses. At none of the schools included in this book did I hear any of this kind of language. The teachers and the administrators know that the children in their school can learn, and they know that it is up to them to figure out how to teach their students. (p. 227)

There are several keys to quality schools and quality teaching. Critical elements include high expectations for all students (establishing high standards, eliminating tracking), protection of academic learning time, well-prepared teachers with time for teaching, a well-organized instructional plan, on-task behavior, and maintenance of a safe and orderly learning environment. Students attending many urban Catholic schools have enjoyed these advantages for years.

Currently, our schools work for some students and do not work for others. As Berliner and Biddle well demonstrated in *The Manufactured Crisis* (1995), schools for middle-class African American, Latino, and European American children fundamentally fulfill their purposes. But the schools for poor African American, Latino, and European American children fail. And while this failure affects all children, it disproportionately impacts the children of African Americans and Latinos. Fully half of all their children are in failing schools. Nationwide, on the 2005 NAEP assessment, over 58 percent of African American and 54 percent of Latino children scored at the Below Basic reading level in fourth grade (U.S. Department of Education, Reading Report Card of the National Center for Educational Statistics, 2005b). Differences in math scores are similarly stark. That is to say, we do not have a general education crisis in the nation; we have a crisis for African American Black, Latino, Asian, and poor White kids. We have an unjust and unequal school system in an unjust and unequal society.

No Child Left Behind

Rather than facing the inequality-of-resources issue, major politically imposed school reform efforts stress standardized testing as the driving force behind such reform at the K–12 level, particularly in low-income districts. Current testing measures the ability to memorize small bits of information. It cannot measure critical thinking skills, the ability to function in a community, or commitment to democratic principles. Testing has not improved schools, improved school funding, or improved teaching. Conservatives such as U.S. Secretary of Education Margaret Spellings argue that opposition to the mandates of the No Child Left Behind Act (NCLB) is opposition to assessment in learning. Nothing could be further from the truth. We need to resist the narrow, reductionist, multiple-choice testing presently being used in place of quality assessment. And we need to resist the misuse of test results by political and ideological advocates of NCLB who do not understand the limits of multiple-choice testing as an assessment tool and as a guide to learning.

This low-quality testing tells us what we already know: Students in low-income schools do poorly (Rothstein, 2004). Studies of 30-year trends in achievement in math and reading as measured by the NAEP show that on average, over this long timeline (including the last 10 years under the testing regime), there has been remarkably little change in achievement by students in our nation's schools (U.S. Department of Education, 2005).

Teachers and schools cannot change the poverty patterns of the national economy. But schools are at the vortex of the struggle for economic opportunity for young people (Anyon, 2005). Poverty creates impoverished schools. For teachers then, the question is, What can we do within an economic system wracked by poverty? There has been only limited improvement in most schools because the interventions used do not deal with the basic causes of low achievement: unequal funding of schools, high teacher turnover, family disruption, and unsafe schools. If the levels of crime, safety, and unemployment have not improved in a neighborhood, then it is far more difficult to improve the local school. What we can do is help some students to achieve and to fight their way out of poverty. And we can teach all students to recognize the need for an expansion of democratic educational opportunity.

We know that good teaching matters. And we know that there are dramatic differences in the preparation and the apparent quality of teachers within states and even between schools within many large urban districts (Darling-Hammond & Wood, 2008).

Schools exist in social and economic contexts that have a powerful effect on how well these schools perform. Many observers argue that our schools are not preparing students sufficiently for the emerging global economy and global competition. Our high school completion rates are too low; our incarceration rates for young African American and Latino males are too high. We are not providing students with the human capital to overcome residential poverty. Our society is asking schools to do more than they can do with their current resources. Schools cannot overcome poverty and racial segregation—at least not as they are currently funded.

The current "crisis" in public education began during the Reagan Administration (1981–1988). The election of Ronald Reagan in 1980 paved the way for the implementation of a conservative political agenda in the United States. A central tenet of this conservative agenda was the reduction of public-sector investment generally, including that in public education. In education literature, *A Nation at Risk* (National Commission on Excellence in Education, 1983) became the manifesto for a conservative ideological assault on the nation's public schools and eventually conservative domination of educational dialogue. Central to components of this effort were demands for nationwide standards, an expansion of testing as both a means and an end, and the introduction of government-supported privatization (tax support for private schools) in the form of vouchers. This conservative domination was consolidated in 2001 under George W. Bush, with the major change being federal mandates placed on schools by Public Law 107-110, popularly known as the No Child Left Behind Act (NCLB). While the states and local communities provide most of the funding for schools (the federal government provides only about 11 percent of education funding), the federal NCLB legislation, supported by the Business Roundtable and other business lobbies, has largely been successful in shaping school policy toward testing and accountability.

NCLB will be specifically analyzed in Chapter 13. For now, let us note that this two-decade effort by conservatives to achieve school reform based on increased testing and accountability has not substantially improved students' scores in reading and math (Lee, 2007; U.S. Department of Education, 2005). However, the testing and accountability effort has transformed teaching and schooling by controlling teachers more, making teaching less interesting, and simultaneously supporting underfunding of schools, a new tracking system, and the privatization of formerly public schools (Nichols & Berliner, 2007).

The domination of the school reform dialogue by conservative political forces and corporate-financed institutes (from 1983 to 2008) produced a shift in the media discussion of school issues away from equal opportunity and toward analysis of the "achievement gap," the gap in scores among ethnic and economic groups (see Figure 1.3). The accountability movement stressed increased testing rather than relying on teachers to make curriculum decisions. It is noticeable in this debate that the children and grandchildren of these conservative policy advocates do not attend the low-income schools where the curriculum and teaching have too often been reduced to drill and test. Their children are in middle-class schools—higher-achieving schools—where the curriculum and teaching strategies remain more open, more child friendly, and more divergent and where educators pursue multiple goals, not just improved test scores.

In political terms, this capture of the media agenda shifted responsibility for children's educational achievement from the unequal funding provided by the government and placed it at the feet of teachers and education professionals, while also demonizing teachers' unions and other education professionals. The accountability and testing movement focused the educational debates away from the discussion of democracy and multicultural education and toward the limited measurement of achievement in reading and math.

These shifts were not accidental nor are they politically neutral. As teachers, we need to understand schools and schooling as contested terrain. We are in a difficult situation; our students' futures and the health of our democracy depend on engaging in the struggle for democratic education. If we want democracy, we must educate for democracy. Democracy depends on the participation of its members in the political, social, cultural, and economic institutions. We educate for democracy through our public schools. The current federal law, NCLB, and most state school reform plans remove teachers, students, and parents from active involvement in decision making about standards, testing, and curriculum and restrict the decision making of elected school boards. That is, the federal NLCB works against democratic participation and decision making. Schools are one of the primary institutions for the nurturing and re-creation of democracy. If, under NCLB, schools become less democratic, then our society itself becomes less democratic.

Teachers Touch the Future

We need education reform to improve the quality of school life for all of our children. Multicultural school reform is directly linked to the pursuit of democratic opportunities. Developing democratic opportunities and dispositions in students is a formidable task in a society divided by inequality and economic insecurity. But democratic practices and economic behaviors are learned, not inherited. Middle-class students—around whose needs the present public school systems are designed—learn to exercise their democratic rights and assume their responsibilities. It should come as no surprise then that the perspectives and agendas of the middle class permeate the schools. Middle-class families provide most of the teachers and administrators for our schools. For democracy to continue, middle-class professionals need to learn to work with the working class and the poor to reform those schools that are currently failing. If our working class and our poor become convinced that they are not expected to participate in the political, social, and economic processes that run our society, then democracy itself becomes at risk. Improving the quality of educational opportunity for the all students is the central task of multicultural education and is essential to the survival of our democratic society (Darling-Hammond & Wood, 2008; West, 2004).

Multicultural Education

Multicultural education assumes that the future of our society is pluralistic. It proposes to restore and fulfill the promise made with the establishment of public schools: to prepare all young people for full participation in the economy and in the democratic community.

Today, teachers in most urban areas face students from a variety of social classes and cultural and language groups. Often, European American children are a minority group. Further, in many rural areas—for example, the Rio Grande Valley of Texas; the central valleys of California; the rural areas of Arizona, New Mexico, Georgia, and Mississippi; and the Appalachian region—the majority of students do not share the middle-class, European American culture common to most college-educated teachers. Teachers find large numbers of English as a Second Language students in their classes from Iowa to Virginia and from Utah to Nevada. Students in our schools will live and work in an increasingly globalized economy. They will need to compete with computer programmers in Ireland and India and with engineers from Pakistan, China, and Germany. Developing an economy with more high-wage, secure, decent jobs—known as the high-wage approach—requires a responsive and well-developed education system, which we presently have for our best students but not for our urban and rural poor. The lower third of our students are in a pretechnology or limited-technology education system. Upon leaving school, they do not receive jobs in high-technology companies, which are instead importing hundreds of thousands of high-skill graduates from other countries to fill their available jobs. This presents a choice: Do we want to fill this growing need for jobs with students from our schools, or do we want to continue to import workers from other societies?

The rapid globalization of the economy also presents a second conflict. Globalization has produced declining rates of economic growth and health improvements in many countries. That is, for many countries globalization enriches the few while making the majority poorer, and thus creating more poverty and more resistance to global corporations (Faux, Scott, Salas, & Campbell, 2001; Stiglitz, 2002b). The terrorist attacks on September 11, 2001, on New York City and Washington, D.C., clearly reveal that some people in some parts of the underdeveloped worldview economic globalization not as a positive force but as an evil force to be resisted. Teachers need to understand the macroeconomic forces, the conflicting forces of globalization, that affect their classrooms in order to assist their students in entering this emerging new economy.

Multicultural educators seek to substantially reform schools so as to give our diverse students an equal chance in school, in the job market, and in the construction of healthy communities. Multicultural educational strategies were developed to assist teachers who are trying to solve the diverse problems imposed on their classrooms by rapidly changing demographics and at times by a crisis-filled society.

James Banks (2008), one of the leaders in the field of multicultural education, describes these dimensions of multicultural education: (1) content integration, (2) the knowledge construction process, (3) prejudice reduction, (4) an equity pedagogy, and (5) an empowering school culture and social structure. In 1995 and 2004, Banks helped document multicultural education as a developing discipline by coediting the *Handbook of Research in Multicultural Education*, in which he notes that "[a] major goal of multicultural education, as stated by specialists in the field, is to reform the school and other educational institutions so that students from diverse racial, ethnic, and social-class groups will experience educational equality" (2004, p. 1).

The ideas for multicultural education in this book come from teachers and from faculty who work directly with teachers. Our viewpoints and strategies are the result of working with these diverse students each day and trying to assist them in achieving success. Teachers, as they work with and motivate the young, must serve as community leaders who observe reality and recognize the gap between the stated ideals of society and its actual living conditions. Democratic citizens respect the rights of their neighbors, including their language and cultural rights. In our role as teachers, we participate in the struggle to extend democracy to students from populations and cultures that were previously excluded. We must not allow the poverty, violence, and anarchy in some of our neighborhoods to overcome our schools and destroy their contribution to the American dream.

In this book, I argue that multicultural education builds on democratic theory to promote the dignity of the individual, the possibility of human progress, and the fundamental equality of all people. Teachers have a responsibility to both teach and reflect these values. We already know how to improve schools. Effective school reform begins with us, the teachers. We need to end tracking; to hold high expectations for all students; to promote success, critical thinking, and self-esteem; and to empower students.

The Process of Multicultural Education

Teachers by and large want to teach well, and they want their students to learn. So why have we created school systems where many students do not learn basic skills and a commitment to our democratic society? Part of the problem is the substantial resistance to change found in most schools. Massive forces keep the schools functioning pretty much as they have in the past. For example, it is clear that the quality of schools and teachers in low-income areas could be improved, but such improvement would cost substantial amounts of money (Karp, 2007; Kozol, 2005). Instead of collecting more taxes and allocating more dollars to bring all schools up to a minimum standard, legislatures have tried endless reforms that do not appear to cost as much money.

During the last two decades, 2 Presidents and over 20 governors have been elected as "educational reformers," yet school performance remains substantially the same. Each of the states has adopted some form of standards- and accountability-based reform (Quality Counts, 1997, 1998, 2008; Swanson, 2006). Elected officials particularly approve of accountability systems for schools prior to, or at times instead of, improving school funding. Accountability means that specific tests are given to measure whether students have met the standards. High standards, accountability, and frequent assessment (testing) are central issues in the school reform package adopted in 2001 as the NCLB Act.

As noted earlier, much of the recent talk of school change has been focused on the achievement gap, a semi-useful measure of learning. The achievement gap measures basic skills—usually reading and math—primarily with multiple-choice tests. As such, it measures what multiple-choice tests can measure—a limited view of education. Advocates of more testing argue that even if lessons are boring and irrelevant to real life, we can increase student learning by increasing the reward for success and the punishment for failure with high-stakes testing, such as high school exit exams. This accountability-driven approach to reform is the opposite of multicultural education and/or democratic education. The accountability-based reforms have driven multicultural education from the schools even while the student population is increasingly diverse. There is little time for providing quality multicultural education or teaching civic responsibility or critical thinking while schools are cramming for multiple-choice tests. And then the test results are usually used to bash teachers rather than to reform instruction and improve teaching.

Multicultural education assumes that teachers want all their students to succeed and that they are looking for positive and effective democratic responses to the economic and demographic challenges taking place in U.S. classrooms. We assume that the future of our society is attending our schools today. We need teachers who are willing to search out the potential of all children. A significant percentage of the U.S. labor force for the next decade will pass through our urban schools. These young people must be prepared to work, investigate, explore, and decide on public policy that will benefit the entire community. If the schools fail, and even if only the urban schools continue to fail, then the U.S. economy will fail.

In our diverse society, multicultural education is an essential component of civic learning. It prepares for the development of unity of purpose in our society and the growth of democracy. Multicultural education—learning to work together with others in our diverse society and encouraging the educational and economic success of all students—is an important part of the democratic mission of schools.

The debates and dialogue in our society over justice, freedom, and equality are a part of our democratic heritage (West, 2004). The very health of our democratic society is at stake. Declining political participation has put our democracy at risk

(Cloward & Piven, 2000; Frank, 2004; Putnam, 2007). We can reverse this trend by educating all young people for a multicultural democracy. Our schools need to teach the fundamental values, ideals, and responsibilities of a pluralistic society—rather than contributing to the conflict in our schools, the continuing divisions in our body politic, and the decline of democracy itself. Multicultural education addresses these democratic goals in ways that testing-based school reform does not. Multicultural education seeks to teach all young people to respect each other and to work together for the common good.

Summary

While the media and the corporations argue that the schools are failing, I think it is more likely that society has failed the schools—in particular, state legislators and local governments have failed the schools. Because good teaching matters, you matter. The following chapters will introduce you to a number of teaching strategies that you can implement in your own school, including multicultural education, cooperative learning, critical thinking, and native language support.

First, we will consider the processes of schooling in the social, political, cultural, and economic contexts that surround the schools and to a significant degree control them. Schools did not create and cannot resolve the racial, class, and gender divisions in our society. But what schools can do is to affect individual students' lives every day. Our multicultural society requires multicultural schooling. Students from all cultural and ethnic groups must succeed and must learn to get along with and to respect each other. As my friend the late Henry Trueba said in the previous edition of this book:

> Education is crucial to the realization of the American dream. The reason is that it is primarily through the acquisition of knowledge and skills associated with formal education that immigrant and low-income students become empowered and a part of mainstream America. It is particularly relevant to speak of multicultural education as the kind of education that will permit Americans to become aware of "democracy at work," realize their full potential, and live in harmony. (p. vii)

Activities

1. Figure 1.3 includes information on NAEP reading scores by state. Look up the reading scores for the students in your state. What effect will the reading scores of your students have on the ways you teach?
2. Figure 1.4 graphs the racial and ethnic diversity in the nation. Look up the statistics on racial and ethnic diversity in your city and in the school district where you are or will be working. Which groups are you most familiar with? Which groups are you least familiar with? What effect will the racial, ethnic, and cultural diversity of your school have on the ways you teach?

3. What is your present viewpoint on No Child Left Behind? What questions do you have about the law's implementation?

4. National statistics will not serve you well as you anticipate what you will encounter in your classroom. You need to have more specific information. For example, what are the major languages spoken by students in your school site? What can you do to prepare to teach these students?

CHAPTER

2

Culture and Schooling

It is difficult for the fish to see the stream.
Traditional Persian saying

Political changes, changing immigration patterns, and the growth of minority student populations have led to renewed interest in multicultural education and bilingualism. In fact, school populations have changed so much that most students in urban classrooms share histories and experiences that differ dramatically from those represented in the curriculum or lived by their teachers. Students in more homogeneous rural areas will also grow up and seek employment in a society and an economy that have been reshaped by demographic changes. As a result, teachers and schools are struggling to find ways to bring success to new and diverse student populations.

When properly understood, the concept of culture explains a great deal about school success and failure for both students and teachers. Unfortunately, many teachers and future teachers have an inadequate understanding of culture. Cultures are often presented as fixed, static, homogeneous; they are not. Nor are cultures sufficiently understood by looking at artifacts, eating ethnic food, or participating in idealized celebrations and dances.

This chapter will help you to recognize, understand, and evaluate the concept of culture—your own and the cultures of your students. The perspective has been developed from the field of anthropology, particularly from the works of Henry Trueba and George and Louise Spindler.

Your active reading and working toward a sophisticated comprehension of culture will provide you with the foundation for developing new teaching strategies and understanding the process of school change.

Source: Roberto Rodriguez, *Uncut and Uncensored* (1997).

The Nature of Culture

A *culture* is a complex web of information that each person learns and that guides this person's actions, experiences, and perceptions of events. We all learn a culture as children. Through it, we learn a broad series of assumptions about people and the world, and then we perceive new incidents and new people through the lens of these assumptions (Hansen, 1979). Culture includes the acquired knowledge that people use to interpret their world and to generate social behavior (Spradley & McCurdy, 1994). As we grow and learn, we reinterpret and modify our assumptions based on our experiences and our perceptions. Culture consists of beliefs and symbols shared within a human group. It is the values, symbols, and interpretations of a people. James Banks, a leading scholar of multicultural education, notes that cultures are dynamic, complex, and changing. Cultures are also systems; they must be viewed as wholes, not as discrete and isolated parts. Cultural groups teach their youth values and behavior styles as well as specific perspectives and worldviews (Banks & Banks, 2001). For further elaboration, see Valentine (1968), Spindler and Spindler (1990), Münch and Smelser (1992), and McDermott and Varenne (1995).

New facts, opinions, and interpretations are presented to us each day. We use the knowledge we have, our culture, to construct meaning from these facts, to define and explain these new events. Some of these events cause us to refine and to reflect on our prior cultural knowledge. King (1995), in developing her own views on multicultural curricula, refers to a people's particular way of interpreting and perceiving reality—their social thought and folk wisdom—as a component of their cultural knowledge.

A culture is the way of life of a group of people. A culture teaches its members how to organize their experiences. To learn a culture is to learn how to perceive, judge, and act in ways that are recognizable, predictable, and understandable to others in the same community.

All human beings learn a culture. All parents teach a culture to their children. A great deal of cultural knowledge is encoded, recorded, and transmitted to the young through language. Culture is also learned and transmitted through the organizations and institutions of a society. That is, cultures are not individuals. Individuals experience and transmit culture uniquely, but culture itself transcends individual experience. Individuals within a culture share an interactive, learned perspective on "appropriate" social conduct. Children bring these cultural values—including language—with them when they enter school, where they may suddenly find themselves in an entirely new community with new values, and perhaps even a new language.

Recognizing cultural practices in ourselves is an important first step in developing a cross-cultural perspective. I frequently encounter students who assert, "I don't have a culture; I'm just an American." In reality, these students are saying that they do not belong to a minority culture. All people, including the majority group, have a culture.

We will call the dominant culture in the United States the European American culture because most of its practices and values, such as speaking English and depending on English common law, come from Europe. If you consider U.S. history, you will recognize that those who colonized North America had relatively weak ties to their homeland (England, Germany, Ireland, and so on). The extended family, important in Europe, was often broken apart, leaving the nuclear family as the main source of community.

Culture shapes what we do, how we act, and what we think. The dominant culture (European American) advocates for democratic forms of government and the rights of the individual. It has been strongly influenced by our economic system, which is a market economy. This market emphasis, along with some important European roots, leads the dominant culture to admire a strong sense of individualism. That is, European Americans expect themselves, and others, to make it on their own. European Americans, as adults, tend to see themselves as separate from nature and often live separate from their extended families.

For more on European American cultural values, see Spindler and Spindler (1991); Bellah, Madren, Sullivan, Swidler, and Tipton (1986); and Putnam (2000). We will look at the development of the European American working-class culture again in Chapter 4.

The School Culture

In U.S. society, the job of training children to participate in the dominant culture of the society has been assigned to the schools. Schools are institutions where we teach all students, including minority students, the cultural rules and norms of the dominant society, such as a future orientation. Many of our school rules and customs come from the European American culture.

Spindler and Spindler (1991) write: "As a teacher, a student, a delinquent, a superlatively good student, or a miserably inept student, we are all caught up in a cultural process" (p. 1). They identify the school system as a "mandated cultural process" and the teacher as a "cultural agent" (p. 1).

The multicultural environment of most urban schools is a culture in its own right; the authority structure of teachers and administrators, the sealed-off quality of the campus, the grade-by-grade hierarchy of the students, and the rich mix of ethnic home cultures create a unique cultural arena. For an immigrant child, entering a public school may be similar to being thrust suddenly into a foreign country. Even if the child knows the native language (and many don't), the habits, rules, customs, and expectations encountered at school can all be dramatically different from those learned at home.

Teachers who have developed a complex comprehension of the role of culture can assist students of diverse cultures as they grapple with the public school experience. They can guide and advocate for these students as they adapt to the school culture and begin to learn the dimensions of the *macroculture* (the surrounding, general, inclusive culture) beyond. From a multicultural perspective, a teacher's task is to respect the cultures students bring from home; to guide students' learning of the basic skills, language, and attitudes of the macroculture; and to nourish each student's self-esteem.

To be guides to culture, teachers must be able to communicate with students. The most appropriate and effective means of guiding children is to build on what they already know. Effective teachers use those concepts and strategies children have acquired at home, their funds of knowledge, to teach new concepts and strategies. The need to build on knowledge acquired at home before a student starts school is most apparent in language acquisition. Languages are central to cultures. When teaching a child a second language, such as English, teachers are most effective when they can provide instruction in the child's home language.

Few issues in education are more controversial than bilingual instruction and English language acquisition by non-English-speaking students. In Chapter 11, we explore in detail bilingual education (including the Ebonics debate) and offer useful teaching strategies for English as a second language instruction.

Students have a need and a right to learn about their own culture as well as the macroculture. For students from minority-status cultures, studying their own culture (including language) can empower them to make important life choices, such as whether to complete high school or college. Studying the culture and historical experience of their people validates minority students' background knowledge and converts it into an accessible base for further learning activities. Incorporating this background information into the official school curriculum gives status to students' parents and communities.

With the security and self-confidence provided by self-knowledge, students can begin to learn about both the school culture and the macroculture, which they must do to gain entry into the political and economic institutions of the larger society. However, if the school system simply imposes the dominant culture's perspectives with little recognition or use of students' home cultures, students may become confused, frustrated, hostile, and resistant—and frequently, education casualties.

Imagine a young boy who enters kindergarten knowing how to read. This student delights in reading, in discovering new stories in books. What would happen to him if the teacher began presenting prereading skills without acknowledging the unique skills the child brings from home? He would feel that his own skills were being devalued, and he would be bored and frustrated with the material.

Many children from Latino, African American, and other minority cultures experience such devaluation of their languages and cultures. Some schools insist that children immediately integrate into the dominant European American culture of the school. But this has proven to be counterproductive. To pull children (or adults) from one culture and place them in another produces anxiety, frustration, and culture shock; it seldom produces learning. In a similar manner, when the dominant culture's language is imposed with little recognition or use of students' home languages to encourage communication, students frequently fail to acquire the basic academic skills of reading and writing (Perry & Delpit, 1997). Children respond in a number of ways to rejection of their home language and culture. Some fail to learn, others withdraw and become passive, and still others engage in open power struggles with and resistance to teachers and the school.

Worldview

All people develop a worldview as a part of learning their culture. A *worldview* is the set of a priori judgments and expectations with which we perceive other people, history, our own culture, other cultures, and daily events. Components of our worldview are taught to us by our parents, family, friends, and, later, teachers.

We also have social experiences and unique individual experiences that shape our worldview. For example, the oldest child in a family will experience some aspects of childhood differently than will the youngest child. The oldest child cannot look to older siblings for guidance, whereas the youngest child will not have younger siblings on whom to practice parenting behavior.

Our worldview is composed of all the things we have learned, all of our experiences. Our culture defines and directs the ways in which we interpret this information and thus how we may react to new experiences. To clarify this point, imagine a family gathering at which a nine-year-old child contradicts the statement of a grandparent. In one culture, this might be interpreted as an expression of self-confidence and independence. The child is learning facts in school that the grandparent does not have. In another culture, however, the same action is seen as being disrespectful, as showing a lack of education (the child has not yet learned respect for the wisdom of elders). The significance of the event differs, depending on the worldview and the culture of those involved.

This process of learning a worldview also applies to students' school experience. Various cultural groups develop their own analysis of schools, which they teach to their young. The development of U.S. schools has been based primarily on the cultural practices of the dominant European American culture. Rules, strategies, curricula, methods of evaluation, and systems of discipline derive primarily from teachers who belong to this culture. Students reared in the dominant culture take these school rules for granted. To them, our school patterns seem natural, normal, and logical. For example, the pressure to compete for grades and attention is often assumed to be a part of universal human experience.

However, if we view schools through the experiences and perceptions of some urban ghetto residents, a different analysis of schools emerges. The real experience of generations of African Americans, particularly those from the lower classes in urban ghettos, is that school is often a place of frustration and failure. More than 50 percent of these students do not complete high school (Orfield & Lee, 2006). Many of those who do graduate have difficulty finding a secure job.

Many African American families have experienced school as a place where their child is measured, tested, and judged to be inadequate. Hard work in school does not always lead to success. In spite of the nation's formal commitment to democracy in schools, the experience of a lower-class African American child is likely to be significantly different from that of her middle-class European American counterpart. School may be a frightening, cold intrusion into the child's life or, conversely, a zone of safety from the street violence in some neighborhoods.

Nigerian American scholar John Ogbu (1978, 1995) argued that some students from subjugated minority groups may believe that teachers and successful students in the school promote "acting White" (see also Fordham, 1988). Such students may perceive that teachers criticize their family members for not monitoring homework or for not attending back-to-school nights. Children who are already defensive about their home culture and who perceive their cultural or ethnic group as under assault may respond to these school messages with withdrawal, distrust, or resistance. Ogbu argued that some students are forced to choose between "acting White," which also means adopting attitudes and behaviors associated with academic success, and building peer-group unity, membership, and support. Such cultural conflict between teachers from the dominant culture and students from the subjugated cultures extends to many places in the nation, including rural Appalachian areas, where European American students often suffer educational neglect similar to that experienced by racial and ethnic minority groups (Eller-Powell, 1994).

The conflict between cultures and worldviews begins when children from a minority culture enter school and may continue throughout their years of schooling. These students learn about the macroculture's values at school but continue to live within, experience, and learn their home culture's worldviews and values.

Keep in mind that culture is complex and multifaceted. Some children within a family may learn to resist the school culture, while other children in the same family may learn to comply based on their experiences in the complex cultural milieu of intercultural conflict at school.

Children's cultural experiences are reconstructed and redefined based on their school experience. For example, parents may teach, "Go to school, get a good education, and get a good job." But the lived experience of many young people may be that school is a boring, alienating, struggle-filled scene of conflict and even degradation. These students learn a different view of school than that intended by parents or teachers. As students mature, they may enter a youth culture with values and views that conflict with both the home culture and the macroculture. This continuing cultural conflict can have a cumulative eroding effect on their confidence and commitment to schooling.

Many young African American and Latino students experience failure and frustration in school. As described in Chapter 1, schools are frequently segregated, underfunded, and poorly equipped. Children in these schools, overwhelmingly from cultural minorities, fall behind in basic study skills. Persistent failure breaks down their self-esteem until some begin to believe that they cannot learn, that school failure is normal and inevitable for children like them. Once a negative attitude is internalized, the pattern of school failure repeats itself. Students who doubt their own capacity to learn will not learn well. They become in-school casualties, or they leave.

The Macroculture and U.S. Schools

The dominant worldview in U.S. society, and therefore in U.S. schools, has been defined by the values, attitudes, beliefs, and folkways of the European American majority.[1] These patterns of communication and life are used as criteria by which to judge right and wrong behavior. In the classroom, this cultural domination is reinforced by the preponderance of middle-class—in elementary schools usually female—European American teachers who unconsciously use their cultural values to judge their students' work and behavior.

A precise term for this European American majority view in U.S. society is *dominant culture*. Although one culture in the United States dominates our social, political, and educational perceptions, in the aggregate United States, society is in fact *multicultural*. Our society includes European Americans, Mexican Americans, African Americans, Asian/Pacific Islanders, Puerto Ricans, and dozens of other cultural groups. It includes Christians, Jews, Muslims, and others. It is in fact made up of all of us—and thus is not composed only of English speakers and only of White people. We will use the term *macroculture* when referring to those aggregate cultural patterns of all peoples living in the United States.

Students from minority cultures and from the working class are generally respected and accepted by school authorities when they imitate the cultural traits of the dominant culture, particularly its middle-class language and customs—that is, when they become assimilated, accepting their socialization with little resistance. They thus learn that the middle-class European American culture represents the preferred way of living, working, and learning.

Using the schools to teach a preferred way of living is called *socialization*. In addition to teaching basic skills, such as English, one of the primary functions of schools has been socialization. Public schools have prepared students to "conform" to the existing social structures of the school and of the society. Socialization is one of several ideological functions of schooling (Arnstine, 1995; Grelle & Metzger, 1996).

Democracy and Cultural Pluralism

One form of democracy is *pluralism*, the belief that multiple viewpoints exist and that each deserves the right to vie for the approval of the majority. *Political pluralism* is the theory that society operates through the interaction of competing interest groups: business, labor,

---

[1]The dominant culture in the modern urban United States is referred to in this text as *European American*. It is composed of the contributions of several ethnic cultural groups (Italian, Irish, German, Greek, and others). At times, the culture is referred to as *Anglo* or *Anglo European* because much of it has been drawn from English language, laws, religion, and customs.

the military, corporations, the finance industry, environmentalists, civil rights advocates, the elderly, and so on. These groups organize and advance their own interests through the political parties and other organizations. The government provides an arena for these competing interests to work out solutions to everyday problems (Carnoy & Levin, 1985).

Political pluralism can provide a model for cultural pluralism. The United States has been pluralist since its founding, composed of several distinct immigrant communities.

It has been recognized throughout U.S. history that European American immigrants may be good citizens even while maintaining their own cultural groupings. Each person had a right to his or her own culture and also had the expectation of participating in a common civic culture. German Americans had their own schools; Finns and Italians had their own neighborhoods and newspapers; the Irish had their own schools, unions, and political organizations. Throughout the 19th century, nativist members of the current dominant culture accused each successive immigrant group of being different, separatist, and at times disloyal. Historian Oscar Handlin described pluralism in 1957:

> In a free society such as the United States the groups which devoted themselves to such nongovernmental functions tended to follow an ethnic pattern. Men with common antecedents and ideas were usually disposed to join together to further their religious, charitable, and social interests through churches and a multitude of other organizations; and through such activities many individuals became conscious of the fact that, while they were all Americans, some were also Swedes or Jews or Dutch or Quakers. (p. 171)

If, as Handlin argued, it has been acceptable to be Swedish, Dutch, or Jewish throughout the nation's history, why then is it controversial today to be Mexican American, Hmong, Puerto Rican, or African American?

Realistically, violence, slavery, terrorism, forced subjugation, annihilation, and attempts at forced assimilation have existed alongside the clearly visible cultural pluralism of our society. The Mormons were driven from their homes in Illinois and Missouri to the Utah desert due to their religious beliefs and practices; Native American children were kidnapped and forced into boarding schools such as the one in Carlisle, Pennsylvania, in an attempt to root out their native cultures; and Japanese Americans in California and Oregon were placed in "relocation camps" during World War II based on their ethnicity even though many Japanese Americans in Hawaii were not incarcerated. Until the 1960s, the goal of "pluralism" was usually reserved for Christian White ethnic groups.

The Civil Rights Movement of 1954–1968 and the elimination of racial quotas from our immigration laws in 1965 extended the rights of political pluralism and cultural pluralism already recognized for European immigrant groups to non-European groups. Those waging the civil rights struggle insisted that race could no longer serve as a factor in determining political and cultural rights. Individuals now must be recognized as having the right to be bicultural (and bilingual); they have the right both to identify with a specific cultural heritage group and to be active citizens of the United States.

The Melting Pot Boils Over Elected officials and public school administrators stressed a *melting pot* point of view or ideology from 1900 until the 1980s. This viewpoint was based on the experiences of European immigrants. It held that distinctions among Swedes, Germans, Irish, Italians, Jews, and others would gradually melt away in the creation of a new "American" culture.

Common observation demonstrates that the melting pot has not worked for many groups, particularly those visibly identifiable "racial" groups. People have not melted into one "model American." In fact, the melting pot viewpoint was often damaging to students from minority-status cultures in schools. Dramatic achievement gaps emerged between students from the dominant group and minority students, as shown in Figure 1.2. Members of certain racially visible minority cultures could not easily assimilate. Their performance in school suffered; to some, this lower achievement was proof of the inferiority of the racial and cultural origins of these students.

Even though racial integration became a national goal and ultimately the law of the land in the 1950s, today's schools are in many ways more isolated, more segregated, and more unequal than those of previous generations (Frey, 2005; Orfield & Lee, 2007). Both schools and society are moving methodically away from integration and equality. Today, schools prepare African Americans, Latinos, Native Americans, and working-class European Americans for unequal, lower-status positions in the economy. Far from melting into one common culture, U.S. society is at times dividing into multiple racial, class, ethnic, and cultural groups that increasingly regard each other with suspicion and hostility, as during the divisive debates on immigration legislation in 2007 (Southern Poverty Law Center, 2007; Wilson, 1999). For individuals to flourish, the community must provide quality education and job training, social services, and meaningful work for all.

Democratic governments protect the dignity of individuals and communities. Positive communities are needed to assist our children to develop supportive, helpful values. For democracy to prosper, we need to consider the schools as community-building institutions. Democratic communities must confront and resist the cynicism and despair so common today in the interaction between young people and elected officials and the government.

Democracy fosters popular participation at every level of decision making. In a democratic community of schools, children learn to work together to solve problems, to share, and to help each other. Public schools should play an important role in building a democratic community.

Cultural Democracy

The Civil Rights Movement (see Chapter 3) and the development of multicultural education have led to advocacy of a new form, an additional form, of democracy: multicultural democracy or cultural pluralism. Participation in the multicultural education project moves us beyond the goals of democracy as developed by John Dewey and earlier philosophers of public education. Multicultural democracy, or cultural pluralism, includes the teaching of civic responsibility, the technical practices of voting (one person–one vote), and critical thinking as well as the development of new, inclusive processes of political participation for all (Banks, 2008). Termed *cultural democracy*, this new approach draws from different perspectives on our nation's history, developments in the social sciences, and a different analysis of the educational process.

Cultural democracy argues that our society consists of several cultures. In this multicultural society, each culture has its own child-rearing practices, languages, learning styles, and emotional support systems. These cultures contribute to and participate in a common culture (the macroculture) by, for example, watching the same television programs, making a commitment to a democratic political system, and attending a public or private school system. Groups may have different views on specific issues, such as secular versus religious schooling or even home schooling, but schooling itself is seldom questioned.

If we adopt the goals of cultural democracy and broad participation in decision making, we will need to create new educational opportunities for all children. Because most parents care about their children and their children's future, developing a broad, participatory multicultural education should begin by creating a community of learners in schools (see Chapter 6).

Democracies are constructed—they are created by human effort. Schools play a role in either advancing cultural democracy or restricting it.

A democratic commitment to a culturally pluralistic life assumes the need for a democratic, responsive, and representative government to ensure a basic level of equality and equity for each citizen, including a democratic school experience. All children deserve a safe school, decent buildings, bathrooms, supplies, a well-prepared teacher, and the opportunity to learn from one another.

For those raised to believe in the melting pot, the change to a culturally democratic viewpoint involves a major conceptual shift. The worldview they learned in their childhood no longer adequately frames society. More precisely, the melting pot view fails to explain the persistent lack of school success by children from dominated ethnic groups and cultures. As the explanatory power of the melting pot view declines and as teachers shift to cultural pluralism, fundamental ideas about schools that were based on the melting pot viewpoint—including curriculum practices, teaching strategies, bilingualism, teacher recruitment, measurement, and motivational assumptions—require reexamination.

In the new multicultural worldview, cultures and cultural values are analyzed relatively. That is, they are investigated by considering the group's own vantage point. This is not, however, cultural relativism. *Cultural relativism* is a perspective adopted by anthropologists to enhance their research abilities. They seek to achieve objective (that is, value-free) research by adopting the view that there are no universal values; rather, researchers should respect and work within the values of each culture in order to understand that culture.

Public school teachers have a different task than do research anthropologists, particularly in the elementary grades. The tasks of public schools include teaching literacy and basic skills, socializing students to the norms of society, and advocating for and promoting democratic values. These goals for schools are not value-free or value-neutral. The multicultural teacher, as opposed to the anthropologist, should not adopt the perspective of cultural relativism. Teachers need to promote democracy, not relativism; to obey the law; and to respect the rights of individuals. These are value-laden obligations.

For example, an immigrant cultural group from Afghanistan may have practiced the forced subordination of women and the early contracting of marriage partners. But when a young girl enters school in U.S. society, she has a right to equal treatment and respect. Practices from other countries such as arranged youthful marriages can violate U.S. laws and democratic values.

Although developing a cross-cultural perspective does not presume ethical relativism, it does require that teachers become precise observers of culture, recognize cultural assumptions, and discard cultural blindness. Rejecting both the past practices of melting pot cultural domination and the laissez-faire, allegedly value-neutral approach, democratic teachers become cultural mediators and present models of ethical behavior that encourage equality and respect among the students.

Teachers and the Concept of Culture

Helping teachers acquire cultural knowledge and understand the nature of culture provides a direct way to help them diminish the effects of prejudice in the classroom. Understanding the complexity of culture helps teachers to work against ethnocentrism and provides a central strategy for reform of schools. Most of us are so immersed in our own cultures that we fail to recognize how much of our behavior derives from cultural patterns. Teachers need to understand how their own cultures affect their lives, their teaching strategies, and the lives of their students. (See Exercise 1 in the "Activities for Further Study of Culture" section at the end of this chapter.)

Each person learns a series of strategies, perceptions, and responses during childhood. Culture, gender, and socioeconomic class overlap within the home to produce behavior patterns, attitudes, and values. For example, some children are reared with a great deal of criticism, others with little criticism but a great deal of modeling, and still others with little or no direction at all. These patterns, learned before the age of four, provide a subconscious framework for much of what children will learn later.

Cultural patterns are not absolute, but they do produce tendencies toward certain behaviors or beliefs within a group. For example, Mexican Americans tend to speak both English and Spanish. Some members of the group speak Spanish almost exclusively, some speak a balance of English and Spanish, and some speak almost no Spanish. A few Mexican Americans also speak German or other languages. A cultural pattern, then, is a possibility—a probability—but not a certainty. Individuals within each group also have their own histories and experiences.

Learning about culture assists teachers in using an intellectually sophisticated view of culture and in recognizing cultural assumptions. For example, the current testing movement and most schools assume that children should compete with one another and that competition produces more learning. This is a cultural assumption of many teachers. There is scant evidence for the view that competition is always beneficial, but it is assumed in the development of many school improvement plans (Nichols & Berliner, 2007).

Efforts to change instruction in the 1960s used a cultural deprivation viewpoint, which assumed that some people had an advanced culture (or modern culture), while others had a lesser culture. While this viewpoint was thoroughly discredited in the early 1970s, it has returned in the instructional strategies of many remedial reading and math programs (see pages 136–137).

While cultures differ, they each have ways of promoting learning. Students have differing perspectives on acquiring knowledge. Some students know well how to achieve in a competitive environment. When students have failed often in school, they may respond to a competitive environment by withdrawing. Some students in the early stages of learning English struggle with their abilities in the language, but in situations where bilingualism is valued, these same students have an expanded ability to communicate.

While it is important for students to learn norms and skills of the majority culture in order to be successful in school, it is also important for teachers to improve their own teaching skills by developing cross-cultural teaching and motivation skills to guide students toward school achievement. Chapters 2–5 offer a number of ideas on developing these skills. The activities at the end of each of these chapters suggest ways to practice learning these new skills.

Teachers should learn to develop culturally proficient leadership skills to be able to design and guide students through learning activities that lead to educational achievement in classrooms with a great deal of cultural, ethnic, and class diversity. Culturally proficient teachers serve as cultural brokers, guiding their students toward improved academic achievement and toward self-confidence and clear identity, both of which assist them in developing a positive self-concept and learning important school knowledge and skills.

Latino, Hispanic, Chicano, or Cultural Diversity?

It is important for teachers to be aware of the variations of experiences within cultural groups and to not assume that all members of a group have similar background experiences. A description of the complexity of the Latino cultural heritage will illustrate this point. (In Chapter 3, we will deal with Asian diversity.)

Latinos comprise all of those people who are descendants of immigrants from Latin American countries and those persons of Spanish-Indian heritage present in the Southwest when the U.S. Army arrived in the 1830s and 1840s. As Figure 2.1 shows,

Figure 2.1   Percent Distribution of the Hispanic Population by Type, 2002

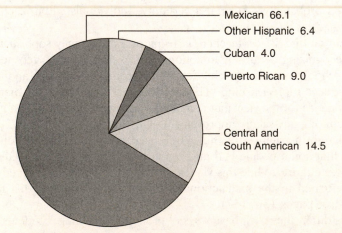

Mexican 66.1
Other Hispanic 6.4
Cuban 4.0
Puerto Rican 9.0
Central and South American 14.5

Source: From *The Hispanic Population of the United States: March 2002*, by R. R. Ramirez and G. P. de la Cruz, 2003, Washington, DC: U.S. Bureau of the Census.

Figure 2.2 Overview of Race and Hispanic Origin, 2002

Reproduction of Questions on Race and
Hispanic Origin From Census 2000

→ **NOTE: Please answer BOTH Questions 5 and 6.**

5. **Is this person Spanish/Hispanic/Latino?** *Mark* ⊠ *the*
   "No" *box if* **not** *Spanish/Hispanic/Latino.*

☐ **No,** not Spanish/Hispanic/Latino   ☐ Yes, Puerto Rican
☐ Yes, Mexican, Mexican Am., Chicano   ☐ Yes, Cuban
☐ Yes, other Spanish/Hispanic/Latino — *Print group.* ↗

6. **What is this person's race?** *Mark* ⊠ *one or more races* to
   indicate what this person considers himself/herself to be.

☐ White
☐ Black, African Am., or Negro
☐ American Indian or Alaska Native — *Print name of enrolled or principal tribe.* ↗

☐ Asian Indian   ☐ Japanese   ☐ Native Hawaiian
☐ Chinese   ☐ Korean   ☐ Guamanian or Chamorro
☐ Filipino   ☐ Vietnamese   ☐ Samoan
☐ Other Asian — *Print race.* ↗   ☐ Other Pacific Islander — *Print race.* ↗

☐ Some other race — *Print race.* ↗

Source: U.S. Census Bureau, Census 2000 questionnaire.

Source: From *The Hispanic Population of the United States: March 2002,* by R. R. Ramirez and G. P. de la Cruz, 2003, Washington, DC: U.S. Bureau of the Census.

there is wide diversity within the Latino (also called Hispanic) culture. Latinos are not a racial group, as measured by the U.S. census (see Figure 2.2).

Understanding Race and Hispanic Origin Data from Census 2000 The federal government considers race and Hispanic origin to be two separate and distinct concepts. For Census 2000, the questions on race and Hispanic origin were asked of every individual living in the United States. The question on Hispanic origin asked respondents if they were Spanish, Hispanic, or Latino. The question on race asked respondents to report the race or races they considered themselves to be. Both questions are based on self-identification. In 2003 the Census Bureau began using the term Latino and Hispanic interchangeably.

The largest component (66.1 percent) of the Latino population in the United States is descended from Mexican parents. In the southwestern United States, descendants of Mexicans predominate, making up more than 80 percent of the Latino population (McCarthey & Vernez, 1997; Shorris, 1992). In northern New Mexico, this population arrived before Mexico was established as an independent nation, and members often

describe themselves as *Hispanos*, a term that retains some sense of historical linkage
with European-Spanish culture.

The Mexican American population in the United States is diverse. Some lived as
Indians on what is now U.S. territory before first Spain and then the United States
arrived to conquer the land. Others immigrated during the major periods of migration:
1911–1924, 1945–1954, and 1965–present. Some of the most recent immigrants are
bringing modern urban Mexican cultural traditions, while others continue the rural
traditions. In recent years, large numbers of Mixtec, Zapotec, and other Indians from
the southern Mexican state of Oaxaca have arrived to perform farm labor.

Puerto Ricans constitute another part (8.6 percent) of the Latino population. Puerto
Rico's native population was decimated by the Spanish invasion and colonization
prior to 1800. They were replaced with African slave laborers who, after abolition,
were integrated into the society. The United States conquered Puerto Rico in 1898 and
gave it commonwealth status in 1952. However, in the early 1950s, new "economic
development" plans drove many Puerto Rican families from their farms. As a result,
millions migrated to the U.S. mainland in search of work, often settling in cities along
the East Coast.

Cuban Americans comprise a third ethnic Latino group in the United States. The
1 million Cuban Americans living in Florida have become a powerful social and political force in that state. They make up about 3.7 percent of the total Latino population in
the country. Their genetic heritage is similar to that of Puerto Ricans, but their history
is quite different. After the War of 1898, Cuba achieved a limited independence. Unlike
Puerto Rico, it was not integrated as a part of the United States. Governed by a series
of U.S.-supported military dictators, Cuba in the 1950s was in a state of economic and
social crisis. Gambling, poverty, prostitution, and underdevelopment were causing
severe problems. In 1959, a nationalist guerrilla group led by Fidel Castro seized
power, turned to the former Soviet Union for support and assistance, and adopted
communism as Cuba's economic and political system.

A large segment of educated middle-class Cubans fled the island at the time of the
1959 revolution. With U.S. government assistance, they established an effective Cuban
American community in Florida that later supported subsequent immigrants fleeing
poverty in Cuba. Whereas Mexican American and Puerto Rican families experienced
decades of economic hardships in the United States, many Cubans were able to move
into successful businesses within a single generation. Eventually, they established
majority status in the economy and government in parts of Florida. Thus, though the
decades of Cuban immigration were difficult, they did not last for generations, and
Cuban Americans did not suffer the cultural disruption experienced by both Mexican
Americans and Puerto Ricans. Assimilation was the major experience for Cuban
Americans, whereas domination by the host culture was the major experience for
Mexican Americans and Puerto Ricans (Crawford, 1992; Llanes, 1982).

In the 1980s and 1990s, large numbers of immigrants arrived from El Salvador,
Nicaragua, Guatemala, and Peru, fleeing deteriorating economies and extended wars
in these areas. In 2002, 40.2 percent of the Latino population in the United States
(about 6 million people) was foreign born. Of these, 50 percent had entered the country

between 1990 and 2002 (Ramirez & de la Cruz, 2003). As they establish families, their children, born in the United States, are U.S. citizens. The 2.2 million recent immigrants from Latin America make up only 14.5 percent of the total Latino population in the United States, but they add even more diversity to that population. Some areas of Latin America (Costa Rica, Uruguay, and Argentina) were so thoroughly shaped by Spanish and European cultures that little of their native cultures or native peoples remains. Other areas (Mexico, Guatemala, El Salvador, and Peru) had such strong Indian cultures and so few Spanish immigrants (and these mostly male) that areas of their societies remain substantially Indian even today.

Recently, hundreds of thousands of Latinos from the Dominican Republic, Haiti, Cuba, and other islands have been landing on the East Coast of the United States, fleeing the political and economic chaos of their countries. They bring yet another distinct cultural heritage.

As these communities live in the United States and adapt to the social and economic conditions they find here, they often metamorphose into another kind of cultural group, one neither native to their country of origin nor imitative of the European American macroculture. Second- and third-generation descendants of Mexicans and Puerto Ricans tend to speak only English (Trueba, 1989). For some, their formative years were spent in communities and schools where being perceived as Latino put them at a social disadvantage. Others lived in barrios and attended de facto segregated schools where, despite being the majority in their own neighborhoods, they were still regarded as a second-class minority by government and school authorities. These groups have developed new cultural experiences based on their lives in the United States. Unlike recent immigrants, who tend to view the school system as a vehicle for assimilation into U.S. life, Chicano students (descendants of Mexican Americans) and Puerto Rican students may see their schools as rundown and shabby, symbols of their oppression and second-class status in U.S. society. These dominated cultural groups have developed new cultural traits, such as bilingualism, and dramatic new poetry and art in the process of creating a culture of resistance to domination.

For many parents from earlier generations, the public schools were the sites of disempowerment. The conflict between home and school at times produced alienation and at other times failure. The culture of the Latino communities is currently in transition. New immigrants arrive each year to reinforce more traditional values, such as respect for home, family, and teacher.

The current Latino culture emerged from people's experiences and the diverse communities' responses. For example, some Latinos have turned to Catholic schools to guard their children from urban violence. Another portion of the community has turned to evangelical religious experiences, while a third group has been overwhelmed by failing schools, gangs, and street violence. These experiences, and others, have continually reconstructed Latino culture.

All of these diverse elements make up the group that the U.S. Bureau of the Census (2002) calls "Hispanics." Similar diversity exists within most cultures, whether Asian, Native American, or African American. The diversity of Asian Americans is indicated

Figure 2.3 Perspectives on Culture for Teachers

What Culture Is
- Dynamic, neither fixed nor static.
- A continuous and cumulative process.
- Learned and shared by a people.
- Behavior and values exhibited by a people.
- Creative and meaningful to our lives.
- Symbolically represented through language and people interacting.
- A guide to people in their thinking, feeling, and acting.

What Culture Is Not
- Artifacts or material used by a people.
- A "laundry list" of traits and facts.
- Biological traits such as race.
- The ideal and romantic heritage of a people as seen through music, dance, holidays, etc.
- Higher class status derived from a knowledge of the arts, manners, literature, etc.
- Something to be bought, sold, or passed out.

Why It Is Important to Know About Culture
- Culture is a means of survival.
- All people are cultural beings and need to be aware of how culture affects people's behavior.
- Culture is at work in every classroom.
- Culture affects how learning is organized, how school rules and curriculum are developed, and how teaching methods and evaluation procedures are implemented.
- Schools can prepare students for effective participation in dealing with the cultures of the world.
- Understanding cultural differences can help solve problems and conflicts in the school and in the community.

Developing a Cross-cultural Perspective: Becoming Aware of Culture in Ourselves
- Involves perception or knowledge gained through our senses and interpreted internally.
- Helps in understanding and avoiding areas of unnecessary conflict and allows us to learn through contrast.
- Calls attention to value positions and value hierarchies of our culture that may be different from the value structures of other cultures.

Becoming Aware of Culture in Others
- Involves a certain degree of ethnocentrism, which is the belief that our own cultural ways are correct and superior to others. Ethnocentrism is natural and occurs in each of us.
- Although ethnocentrism helps to develop pride and a positive self-image, it can also be harmful if carried to the extreme of developing an intolerance for people of other cultures.
- Is, in part, based on the value of cultural relativity, the belief that there are many cultural ways that are correct, each in its own location and context.
- Analyses based on cultural relativity are essential to building respect for cultural differences and appreciation for cultural similarities.

Cultural Democracy
- A teacher's adaptation of the anthropological perspective.
- Recognizes the school role of teaching a common culture.
- When there is a conflict between democratic values and cultural practices, insists that models of democratic values prevail in school (e.g., equal status and opportunity for boys and girls).

Source: From *Perspectives on Culture for Teachers*, by Cross Cultural Resource Center, California State University—Sacramento, 1996, Sacramento, CA: Author. Reprinted with permission.

by the definitions shown in Figure 3.1. Teachers who want to develop a cross-cultural perspective take years to learn the complexities of interaction within this cultural diversity. Often by the time one group is familiar, a new group of students (for example, Filipino, Hmong, Thai, or Russian) will arrive.

Because culture is constantly changing, teachers need to be cautious about all generalizations concerning cultural groups. Do not assume that all Hispanics have a common culture or a common home experience. Most generalizations apply to only one part of a population, and many are overdrawn. While teachers should not generalize, they should observe, listen, and learn. They need to be aware of the differences between ideal and real (lived) culture and foster mutual respect in the classroom. Teachers help students navigate the troublesome terrain between their home culture, with all of its changes and complexities, and the macroculture's traumas, including gangs, school failure, crime, poverty, and social dissolution.

Figure 2.3 summarizes the multiple perspectives on culture useful for teachers working in multicultural education.

Cultural Politics and Cultural Ethics

All cultural groups, including European Americans, continually reevaluate and re-create their culture. Like those in most modern societies, we in the United States have chosen to use schools to introduce students to dominant cultural patterns. Over many years, the idea arose that all students should learn a common civic culture and that schools should teach that culture. Schools are therefore a primary site of cultural transmission. In the process of transmitting cultural patterns—through both formal and informal curricula—the U.S. macroculture is itself redefined (Spindler & Spindler, 1990).

Current European American culture is being forced to change in response to economic transitions, immigration, and urban crises. The melting pot model assumed that over time and with proper instruction people from diverse cultures could be molded into an approximation of an "ideal American." The characteristics and values of that ideal person were assumed to be those of the English-speaking, European American culture. But in California, New York, Illinois, Florida, New Mexico, and Texas, total English dominance can no longer be assumed. In many border and urban areas, the bilingual high school graduate has an advantage in achieving business and educational success.

A Multicultural Worldview

In place of the single idealized "American," the worldview of the multicultural education movement views a society in which members of several different cultures are all equally valued and respected. Most people are not even aware they have a worldview. They assume that all people see reality through a perspective similar to their own. Persians (Iranians) have a saying for this myopia: "It is difficult for the fish to see the stream." In schools, the assumption that "my way is the right way" is revealed when teachers state, "I just want to get beyond this ethnic divisiveness. I treat everyone as an individual. I am tired of having to deal with this ethnic, cultural thing."

Persons making the choice to not recognize diversity fail to recognize that denying the significance of ethnicity and cultural differences is a privilege reserved primarily for members of the dominant group. In our society, the primacy of the individual's rights and needs ("I've got to do what's right for me") derives from cultural patterns rooted in the Protestant tradition of European American culture. In this tradition, individuals—not groups—are the significant elements of a society, and the individual's primary responsibility is to seek personal salvation. Of course, achieving salvation means obeying certain laws and carrying out certain social admonitions such as those found in the Bible's Ten Commandments. But the focus is on the private and personal relationship between an individual and God. Thus, admiration for strong individualism is an attribute of the dominant culture in our society, but it is only a culturally specific choice, not a human universal.

Multicultural educators believe that teachers do not have the right to insist that students from other cultural traditions abandon their less individualistic, more communal values. For example, a young Mexican American child may be taught from an early age to respect the family first, prior to individual advancement. Rural Irish children were taught a roughly similar hierarchy of values based on their shared rural, Catholic culture. African American teenagers may well have learned to stick together to defend their neighborhood friends against the intrusion of drug dealers, police, social workers, landlords, and the political powers of a city.

These students have learned a less individualistic value structure, and the teacher using a culturally democratic approach will recognize and respect these values. Teachers, as cultural mediators who reduce conflict and help children succeed in school, can help students to better comprehend both their own cultures and the demands of the macroculture.

As anthropologist Henry Trueba said in the "Introduction" to the third edition of this book:

> Ethnic resilience and assimilation are the two sides of the immigration coin. Common opinion has it that in order to become a "real" ("assimilated") American, one must forget his/her ethnic identity. Yet, often racial or ethnic identification becomes pivotal in our society to determine a person's relative status and chances for success. Sheer statistical, demographic, and residential information serves to predict educational achievement, income, dropout and suspension rates, size of family, mortality trends, incarceration, tendencies to violence, use of welfare, and other presumed dysfunctional characteristics that configure the U.S. justice system, investment and banking policies and operation, and even the distribution of resources and liabilities (from the location of banks, grocery stores, movie theaters, to that of waste disposal facilities, prisons, and nuclear sites). Additionally, the racial and/or ethnic prejudice in the society at large is reflected not only in the elementary and secondary public schools, but also in higher education institutions. . . .

Identity

Now that we have developed an elaborated view of culture, it is important to be clear about the difference between culture and identity. Culture and identity are closely related but not the same. Culture, as you know, is a learned system of values, beliefs, and practices that guide our everyday lives.

In the last decade, increasing numbers of writers, particularly those focused on the discipline of psychology, have used identity, rather than culture, as an analytical tool. Some see identity as a more dynamic construct than race, culture, class, and gender.

Gee (2001) proposes that there are four major views of identity: nature, institutional, discourse, and affinity group identities. Writers often use these different views of identity, at times confusing their arguments and the readers.

Identity is the way people see themselves. This self-definition may be fluid and changing. It might be ethnic identity, class identity, religious identity, gay/lesbian identity, or a number of other options. Students might have an identity as a good student or a poor student. Some students find their Christian identity or Muslim identity is very important to their lives. Some students may see themselves as Chicano or Latino, although the schools list them as Hispanic.

Ethnic identity is a particular kind of identity. We develop and learn our identities. They are constructed by our interactions with the world, and particularly with those close to us and important to us (Hoffman, 1998). When we learn a culture, we learn a number of possible identities within that culture. For example, Hawaiian identity is learned within a culture.

There are identities related to race and ethnicity, gender, and many more attributes. A person has a racial or ethnic identity when he sees himself, or others see him, as a member of a racial or ethnic group. For example, a student might see herself as an African American, a Mexican, or a White student. These identities, or self-definitions, at times have important consequences for students. We will deal more with these racial and ethnic identities in Chapter 3.

At the same time, the student might see herself as a teenager, a soccer player, or a musician. Clearly, people have multiple identities. There is also class identity, but it is often less obvious. Most students who are successful in the academic track see themselves as middle class, whereas some students practicing resistance may see themselves as working class (see Chapter 4).

Another component of identity is how others see us. Young people may pass through several identities. At times, they seem to be trying on identities. One form of identity is the identity of academic track students in high school. Good students are socialized most of their lives to speak their minds. Their opinions are often taken seriously at school and at home. They are viewed as the future leaders of the nation. Pictures and writings of people who looked like them fill the history books and are placed on walls of the schools. Prior to the 1950s, this was primarily a group of male students; since the women's movement of the 1960s and 1970s, this identity group increasingly has an equal number of young women.

This identity focus of academic track students has many positive components, but consider its opposite. What are the characteristics of groups of students who reject the academic track, who oppose the school culture?

We learn our identities within a culture. Since identities are in part individually selected, they change more often than cultures. Identities are often a confluence or a growing together of social roles. For example, you may be a mother, a student, and a teacher all at the same time. Each of these roles is defined within your own cultural experience.

Students learn new identities and negotiate their identities along the borderlands of cultures. If you live and work totally within one culture, your identity may seem fixed and obvious. However, for students from minority-status groups, school is a place where they learn new identities and, at times, oppose other people. School can be a cultural borderland where new identities are learned, acquired, developed, and at times resisted (Hoffman, 1998).

The teaching and reproduction of identities in schools includes ethnic identities, gender identities, and youth identities (conflicts). In many schools, ethnic identity becomes a political boundary, a distinguishing feature of group membership. During adolescence, identities, including cultural identities, are constantly being negotiated, challenged, and reconstructed. Identities are not fixed. They are chosen and changeable, to some degree. For example, a student can choose to join a gang or to leave a gang (although this is difficult) (Weis, 2004). A student can choose to be a good student—to study hard—or to be a lax or lazy student or to drop out. Some students resist the role of a good student. These choices, made as adolescents, are necessarily immature, yet they contribute to determining each student's life chances, income, and life itself. Teachers can help students to make wise choices. And we need to create a structure within which wise choices are encouraged.

It is important to keep in mind that identities, although seemingly rigid, are often fluid and in transition. For example, a Latino teacher may be a Latina, a teacher, and a female. A White teacher is White, a teacher, and female. In some situations, students (and parents) respond to the teacher based on each identity. You are a teacher; you should be able to control your class and motivate learning. You are a Latina; you should be able to speak to me in Spanish, and you should be willing to stand up for Latino youth. You are female; you should be willing to understand and to motivate young girls in your class.

By examining your own experience, you may be better able to understand the multiple identities of young people. A student in your class may be an African American, a Mexican, and a young woman, all at the same time. Another student could be a Korean American, a young woman, and a good student, all at the same time. Identities have various meanings. For example, consider the identity shift you are making from college student to teacher. To school district personnel, a teacher is a person who follows procedures, conducts classes, and gives grades (among other activities). To your students, your identity as a teacher means you are a person who conducts classes, evaluates their work, and may provide motivation to learn. What does the identity of teacher mean to you?

At times, identities are not fixed; they depend on the setting. A student may be a young man (boy), a gang member, and one who resists schooling and homework. Yet when you visit his home, you may find a respectful, considerate young person. In his home, he may adopt a different identity than he adopts in school or on the street corner. Young girls may adopt gang membership, too.

For most gang members, as they adopt the gang identity, their relationships with their families become strained because they have adopted an identity that is not accepted by the parents. It is not coincidental that gang membership among boys is significantly higher in homes without a male present to teach, and insist on, a positive cultural identity (Fremon, 1995; Schmalleger & Bartollas, 2008).

Multicultural education should assist students as they learn and explore their changing identities. Students can learn safe and positive identities, or they can learn negative and at times dangerous identities. For example, students who use drugs may adopt the identity of a drug user. Soon they are spending their time with a group of students with similar, dangerous lifestyles.

A large number of minority-status students seem to adopt an oppositional identity and oppose the view of the "good students" (Fordham, 1996; Gibson & Ogbu, 1991). Adopting this oppositional identity will affect coursework, courses selected, and the future. Cultural understandings of self and identity may lead to different school performances among Mexican and Mexican American youth (Gándara, O'Hara, & Gutiérrez, 2004). In the middle school years, gender identity and sexuality often become areas of identity conflict (see Chapter 5).

Young girls and boys have identities and roles within cultures. Their preferred identities may be revealed in how they look, how they dress, and how they talk. Young people may try on an identity for awhile and then move on to another identity that they prefer. In the current era, identities have become a commodity to be sold. For example, some young people spend a great deal of money on stylish shoes, clothes, cell phones, and other symbols of their status. In this sense, identity and status are sold. As you approach student teaching, will you wear different clothes to your college classes than you wear to teach? What are you signifying about your teaching by the clothes you choose to wear?

Because determinations of identity are important, teachers need to learn the many skills of discussing identity as well as race, gender, and culture. Applying the prior material on the nature of culture, we should not assume that identities and views of self (self-esteem) are necessarily similar across cultures (Hoffman, 1998).

Teaching About Culture

Students first learn about their culture at home. Lessons about families and roles in the primary grades help students to draw on their home experiences. We know that the very young are often aware of ethnic differences. Students can be empowered by studying the groups and institutions closest to them, including family and school. Studies of concepts such as kinship, education, health, leadership, and community help young children to understand the more general concept of culture.

Children at very young ages can begin to analyze the facets of culture that they have learned from their families. Later, after the age of 10 to 12, when peer groups become more important, students can begin to analyze the differences between the values that their parents taught them and the new values that are encouraged and advocated by society and their peer groups.

Beginning in about fourth grade, children can study themselves in the context of their cultural patterns. They can begin to see that they have *learned* to be who they are. They can study the process of learning and the traits and languages taught at home. It is very important for children to see that they are active participants in the process of acquiring their culture. For example, an African American girl should understand that in her home she is a product of the African American culture. Yet the same child deserves to know that she is also being taught to be a part of the macroculture in school. Some conflict about this is unavoidable, but in a culturally democratic classroom, it can be discussed and analyzed and may become the source of new insight and strategies for survival. If unexamined, cultural conflict creates anxiety that, once internalized, may harden into dysfunctional responses such as a chronic expectation of failure.

For example, U.S.-born children of Mexican descent (Chicanos or Mexican Americans), U.S.-born Puerto Rican children, and African American children frequently do not perform well in English or in reading (Gándara, 1995; Garcia, 2001; Zou & Trueba, 1998). Bilingual education has served immigrant students well but has done little to resolve the cultural conflicts of English-speaking Chicano, Puerto Rican, Hawaiian, African American, and Filipino students. Drill and practice alone will not change the pattern of school failure. Difficulty in mastering English and acquiring reading skills is frequently related to students' conflicts caused by existing in two cultures—one dominant and one subordinate. Some students attempt to overcome this conflict by abandoning their home culture and totally adopting the macroculture. This cultural abandonment strategy has proven to be disastrous for many. It leads to low reading and math scores, withdrawal, passivity, a high rate of school failure, and the tendency to leave school before graduation. Rather than accepting failure, students can study those aspects of their culture that determine their language acquisition patterns and try to understand how those patterns conflict with the job of mastering American English (Trueba, 1989).

Cultural conflict and identity conflict are important subjects of study in the multicultural classroom. For European American students, their cultural values and history are deeply interwoven into the curriculum. Students from other cultures need to be aware that they have learned many cultural patterns from their family and others from their formal education. Students also need to see themselves not only as products of the decisions of others but also as competent individuals who are in charge of the direction of their lives (Reyes, Scribner, & Scribner, 1999). When students learn that they can analyze and overcome educational problems, their self-confidence and self-control increase. By studying the school culture and students' roles, teachers can encourage students to be responsible for and in control of their future (Oakes Rogers & Lipton, 2006).

Schools can offer students the unique opportunity to study themselves and their classmates in the safe context of the classroom. Problems that emerge in the classroom, such as weaknesses in reading and math, can be treated as obstacles for the students to overcome. When students experience failure, the study of cultural conflict may help them to analyze the difficulties and to select ways to overcome educational problems. They will be able to overcome some obstacles by individual effort, such as by acquiring new learning skills; other problems may require group work. The experience of being part of a team that successfully completes a project can help students develop the courage and confidence to overcome educational and psychological barriers.

Cultural Conflicts One type of cultural conflict that frequently arises in classrooms concerns language. Conflict over bilingual education versus English-only language instruction and a 1997 California Ebonics episode reveal the intense cultural and worldview battles over language (Perry & Delpit, 1997). Primary teachers and English teachers have taught formal or Standard English as their primary task almost since the founding of public schools. They are teaching the "standard" communication system of the middle-class members of the dominant culture, and this produces conflicts with other cultures and social classes.

Languages are usually learned at home (not in school), and they are based on culture. Heath (1986) has effectively argued that "all language learning is cultural learning" (p. 145). As children learn a second language, they encounter cultural conflict and require assistance with this conflict. Teaching a second language also introduces teachers to learning a second culture. Strategies for teaching limited-English-speaking students are found in Chapter 11.

Languages also carry cultural assumptions within their expressions. For example, languages influence the manner in which we greet or criticize one another. Languages and cultures differ on how dialogue is initiated (Do elders speak first?) and how it is completed. They also vary considerably in the manner in which they deal with silence and nonverbal expression. Languages permeate and influence most of our social relationships. They both reveal and mark status and education levels. Language and language use within a community and within a school reveal a great deal about power and authority relationships.

Culturally Responsive Teaching: What Can I Do in the Classroom?

Outstanding work has been done in the United States using culturally competent perspectives. King (1995) has developed an extensive and powerful argument that African American studies offer new insights into how to overcome the current crisis in education for African American students. Dr. King served on the California Department of Education committee that drafted the *History–Social Science Framework for California Public Schools* (California Department of Education, 1987; see Chapter 12) and argues that deep biases control the way textbook publishers select what knowledge is important to teach to students.

She proposes that African American cultural knowledge will assist teachers in redesigning education processes for success. Referring back to Carter B. Woodson's important 1933 essay, King (1995) argues that African American young people are miseducated as a result of the current social construction of knowledge and the curriculum: "As Black students move through the educational system, they face 'the school's undermining doubt about their ability.' Their dignity and positive group identity may be further undermined by hegemonic school knowledge and curricula that traumatize and humiliate many Black students" (p. 283).

King focused on intellectual traditions in the African American community. Ladson-Billings (1994a) performed case studies to describe a culturally relevant pedagogy for teachers working with African American students. Based on her studies, Ladson-Billings argues that effective teachers for African American students

- Have high self-esteem and high regard for others.
- "[S]ee themselves as a part of the local community and see their work as contributing, or giving back to the community" (p. 38).
- "[B]elieve that all students can succeed, and organize their lessons based upon this belief" (p. 44).

- "[H]elp students to make connections between their own community and national and global identities" (p. 49).
- See their work as "digging knowledge out of the students" (p. 52) rather than imposing new knowledge on them.
- See their goals as creating a "community of learners" (p. 69) and building positive relationships with students, their families, and their communities.

Eugene Garcia, former director of the Office of Bilingual Education and Minority Languages Affairs in the U.S. Department of Education and dean of education at the University of California at Berkeley, did an extensive literature review in an effort to identify the characteristics of teachers who were working effectively with Mexican-American students. He found that these effective teachers shared many characteristics, including the following:

- Perceived themselves as effective teachers
- Were autonomous decision makers about instructional activities
- Used a communications-based approach to language
- Usually favored thematic curricula and cooperative groupwork
- Had a strong commitment to home–school relationships
- Held high academic expectations for themselves and for their students
- Served as advocates for their students
- "Adopted" their students and were in close, often family-like, relationships with their students' families

This list suggests important for teaching to use their understanding of culture to develop teaching strategies. There are additional suggestions in the section "Teaching Strategies for Use with Your Students" at the end of each chapter.

Keeping Up with Cultural Change

All cultures are dynamic. As students learn about their culture, the culture itself is changing. Some approaches to multicultural education fail to consider this. For example, primary teachers have frequently approached multicultural education by introducing young children to a variety of culturally specific foods. Such an approach teaches that variety exists and little else. Many teaching units on the culture of Mexican children present idealized pictures of people eating tortillas, tamales, and similar traditional foods. Studies of Chinese Americans focus on the use of chopsticks, rice, and fortune cookies. However, if students actually looked at the food most frequently eaten by young Mexican or Chinese American students, they would probably find it is a fast-food hamburger. All cultures are dynamic, including the macroculture.

Many students in a macroculture-based school system are in the process not only of learning how to operate in the dominant culture but also of adapting to continuing change within their own home culture. Acquiring new patterns does not necessarily mean abandoning the home culture; acculturation can be additive. Engaging in and studying this process under the guidance of a teacher skilled in multicultural education helps students to make sense of what is happening to them. Understanding cultural conflict empowers students to make effective choices about how to pursue their education, their careers, and ultimately their lives. When schools do not help students sort out this conflict, street gangs and the criminal justice system may offer more violent alternatives.

Summary

This chapter emphasizes the concept of culture as developed in studies of anthropology and sociology. The intent is to have you as a teacher use the concept of culture to analyze your classroom and your interactions.

As a teacher using the concept of culture, you can examine your students' behaviors and your classroom interactions in an effort to find ways to increase learning. Subsequent chapters will focus on race, class, and gender. These issues blend together in the complex process of school achievement.

Culture is a complex concept central to understanding multicultural education. Culture includes learned behavior and attitudes. A great variety of behaviors and values exists within and among cultures. Understanding cultural patterns and cultural differences assists teachers in understanding student behavior, motivating students, and resolving conflicts in school. Schools and teachers play an important role in preparing students for cultural pluralism.

Culture is a powerful force in the lives of both students and teachers. By developing a cross-cultural perspective, teachers can guide students toward creating a more democratic society. A cross-cultural perspective will also assist teachers in designing and implementing school and curriculum reforms.

Questions over the Chapter

1. Do you think that there is a common "American" culture? How would you describe it?
2. What roles do the school and the television play in teaching a common culture?
3. What are some of the values taught by typical U.S. holidays, such as the Fourth of July, Thanksgiving, and Christmas?
4. Provide at least three examples of how the U.S. macroculture is currently changing (e.g., changes as a result of cell phones and the Internet).
5. Look at the examples of culturally responsive teaching on pages 69–70. Which of these would be most difficult for you?
6. The chapter provided an example of the diversity within the Hispanic culture. What are examples of diversity within the dominant European American culture?
7. Would you prefer to be called European American or American? Explain.

Activities for Further Study of Culture

1. Complete the following chart about yourself and one classmate. Select a classmate from a major cultural group distinctly different from your own. For example, if you are Chinese American, you could interview someone of Polish or Russian descent; if you are Native American, you could interview an African American.

Influences of Family on Learning Cultural Patterns

Family structure (e.g., three children, single parent, extended)		
Major family customs		
Languages spoken at home		
Celebrations		
Religious practices		
Cultural offenses		
Important values		
Memories of grandparents		
Other		
	The person whom you interviewed	Yourself

2. Share the results of your interview with your class.
3. Play BaFá BaFá, a cross-cultural simulation (available from Simulation Training Systems, 1-800-942-2900). http://www.stsintl.com
4. Because you are entering the profession of teaching, consider teachers as a cultural group. What are the norms of teacher culture? How are they enforced? What sanctions are used?

Teaching Strategies for Use with Your Students

1. Recognize that schooling is only one form of education. Plan lessons that incorporate and build on the informal educational systems of home and community.
2. In teaching new concepts, use concepts, strategies, and language students already know.
3. Study the nature of culture and of cultural conflict.
4. Create lessons that excite and engage students.

5. In the elementary grades, focus on reading and language. Materials need to include students from the cultures and traditions found in your classroom. Encourage students to use their home languages and to develop literacy in their home languages as well as in English.

6. In the primary grades, study the concepts of kinship, education, health, leadership, language, beliefs, and community prior to the concept of culture.

7. Build positive relationships with the students. We will have more to say on this in Chapter 6.

8. Do not assume that students accept your management rules. Use direct instruction to teach school-appropriate behavior.

3

Racism and Schools

with Forrest Davis

We have not asked you to give up your religions for ours. We have not asked you to give up your ways of life for ours. We have not asked you to give up your government for ours. We have not asked you to give up your territories. Why can you not accord us with the same respect? For your children learn from watching their elders, and if you want your children to do what is right, then it is up to you to set the example. That is all we have to say at this moment. Oneh.

Chief Oren Lyons [Onondaga], presenting the statement of the Grand Council of the Iroquois to the U.S. Government, 1973

The New Majority

Most of you will encounter in your classroom the growing cultural, racial, religious, and ethnic diversity of our society. Until 2000, the majority of people in the United States were European Americans. In most of our major urban areas, however, a new majority is emerging—one composed of people of color: African Americans, Latinos, Asian/Pacific Islanders, Arab Americans, and many others.

Democracies are based on the rule of the majority. Who is this emerging new majority? It includes (as of 2000) the 34.7 million African Americans, many of them descendants of slaves, who today struggle against segregation, ghettoization, poverty, failing schools, high rates of unemployment, and police brutality (U.S. Bureau of the Census, 2000). African Americans constitute 12.3 percent of the U.S. population. Some 55 percent of all African Americans live in the South (The Black Population of the U.S.A. 2000. U.S. Bureau of the Census, 2001).

This new majority includes the Latino population of 35.3 million, more than double the 1980 U.S. census figure. Nearly two-thirds of the Latino population are Chicano

Civil Rights Activists Cross the Edmund Pettus Bridge with Armed Police officers Watching in Selma, Alabama, in March 1965.

(that is, U.S.-born persons of Mexican heritage). Like African Americans, Latinos experience systematic racial and class oppression. In 2006, 20.6 percent of Hispanics were living in poverty as compared to 8.2 percent of non-Hispanic Whites (U.S. Bureau of the Census, 2006). Latinos and African Americans also suffered double the rates of unemployment and poverty experienced by European Americans (Mishel, Bernstein, & Allegretto, 2007; Teller-Elsberg, Folbre, & Heinz, 2006). Between the 1993–1994 and 2002–2003 school years, the total number of children enrolled in U.S. public schools increased by about 4.7 million; 3 million, or 64 percent of the increase, were Latino children (Frey, 2006).

The new majority includes the Asian/Pacific Islander population, which has doubled in size over the past decade to more than 10.2 million people. Asians are 3.6 percent of the national population. Though portions of this community are economically less disadvantaged than other people of color, some 10.3 percent of Asians and Pacific Islanders were poor as compared to 8.2 percent of non-Hispanic Whites in 2006 (U.S. Bureau of the Census, 2006).

The U.S. Census Bureau describes some of this diversity:

"Asian" refers to those having origins in any of the original peoples of the Far East, Southeast Asia, or the Indian subcontinent including, for example, Cambodia, China, India, Japan, Korea, Malaysia, Pakistan, the Philippine Islands, Thailand, and Vietnam. "Pacific Islander" refers to those having origins in any of the original peoples of Hawaii, Guam, Samoa, or other Pacific Islands. The Asian and Pacific Islander population is not a homogeneous group. Rather, it comprises many Asian and Pacific Islander groups who differ in language, culture, and length of residence in the United States. Some of the Asian groups, such as the Chinese and Japanese, have been in the United States for several generations. Others, such as the Hmong, Vietnamese, Laotians, and Cambodians, are comparatively recent immigrants. (U.S. Bureau of the Census, 2000)

The new majority also includes approximately 1,190,000 Arab Americans, many of whom are subjected to political harassment, racial profiling, media abuse, and ethnic discrimination (Abu El-Haj & Thea, 2002; Al-Qazzaz, 1996; U.S. Bureau of the Census, 2005), and more than 2.4 million Native Americans, who have survived genocide and cultural domination for more than 200 years. The struggle of Native Americans is a political and cultural struggle for national self-determination—and for survival (Mihesuah, 2003). See Figure 3.1.

Included in the total population in 2000 were 28.4 million foreign-born residents (10.4 percent of the total population). Among these 28 million people, 51 percent were born in Latin America, 25.5 percent were born in Asia, 15.3 percent were born in Europe, and the remaining 8.1 percent were born in other regions of the world (U.S. Census, 2000).

The emerging majority is found not only in urban areas; it is also evident in small towns and rural areas of the South and Southwest, where Mexican Americans, African Americans, and Native Americans often constitute a majority population within their communities.

The emerging diversity is even more pronounced among young people and students. In many urban centers, African Americans, Latinos, and Asians each represent a higher percentage of the student population than do the same groups in the total population. In many states and school districts, the increased diversity of the student population has resulted in the districts having no single majority group. *All* cultural groups, including European Americans (or Whites), are minorities. Because there is no majority group, what does the term *minority* mean? In nontechnical writing, such as newspapers, authors usually mean minority-status individuals, or subjugated individuals. As a means of referring to the new reality of the diverse populations in our towns and cities, young people and community activists at times refer to African Americans, Asians, Latinos, and Native Americans collectively as "people of color" rather than as minorities.

The White Minority

Sociologist Joe Feagin (2001) predicts a future time when Whites will be a minority:

Current demographic trends are creating and amplifying societal contradictions that could eventually lead to a major social transformation, including the reduction or destruction of white domination over Americans of color. As we begin a new millennium, Americans of European descent are a decreasing proportion of the U.S. and world populations. Whites constitute less than half of the population of four of the nation's largest cities—New York, Los Angeles, Chicago, and Houston. They are less than half of the population in the state of Hawaii, as well as in southern sections of Florida, Texas, and California. Demographers estimate that if current trends continue whites will be a minority in California and Texas by about 2010. (p. 237)

Clearly, we all need to learn to get along. And historically the public schools are one of the few institutions in our society where this cooperation has been taught.

Race and Racism

Race is the term used to describe a large group of people with a somewhat similar genetic history. Many observers believe that they can describe a racial group based on hair color and texture, skin color, eye color, and body type. In Chapter 2, I noted that we learn culture; in contrast, we inherit race.

Most biologists and physical anthropologists recognize the futility of previous attempts to "scientifically" define race and believe that there are no pure races on earth. In 1997, following the publication of the notorious book *The Bell Curve: Intelligence and Class Structure in American Life* (Herrnstein & Murray, 1994), the American Anthropological Association responded to the confusion on race as follows:

> For several hundred years before this time, both scholars and the public had been conditioned to viewing purported "races" as natural, distinct, and exclusive divisions among human populations based on visible physical differences. However, with the vast expansion of scientific knowledge in this century, it is clear that human populations are not unambiguous, clearly demarcated, biologically distinct groups. As a result, we conclude that the concept of "race" has no validity as a biological category in the human species. Because it homogenizes widely varying individuals into limited categories, it impedes research and understanding of the true nature of human variation. (p. 1)

It is estimated that only 0.012 percent of the differences between individuals can be attributed to racial differences (Cameron & Wycoff, 1998). Although race makes little biological difference in our lives, in the United States it may make a great deal of social difference.

Race is more of a social category than a reliable biological classification. Racial categories have long been used to describe racial groups, cultures, and ethnic groups. These social definitions have changed over time, often based on the relative power of the group in question. The attempt to create racial definitions based on observed physical characteristics became important in the European-dominated part of the world and in the United States between 1490 and 1850.

Ethnic Groups and Ethnicity

Some sociologists seek to deal with the limits of racial theory by describing the role of ethnic groups. Peter Rose (1974) states:

> Groups whose members share a unique social and cultural heritage passed on from one generation to the next are known as ethnic groups. Ethnic groups are frequently identified by

distinctive patterns of family life, language, recreation, religion and other customs that cause them to differentiate from others. . . . Above all else, members of such groups feel a consciousness of kind and an interdependence of fate. (p. 13)

Trueba (1999) further describes an ethnic group as follows: "Their language, culture, religion, art, values, lifestyle, family organization, children's socialization, and worldview are viewed by the members of the group as uniquely linked to their home country and ancestors" (p. 69). In the United States, Mexican Americans, Puerto Ricans, Hmong, Vietnamese, Chinese Americans, and others are considered ethnic groups even though their biological differences are complex.

Although references to ethnic groups are common in sociology, history, and the popular press, Omi and Winant (1986) have written an extensive criticism of the overextension of ethnic group theory, arguing that it tends to blur together European immigrants and racial groups as if treatment of racial differences is not significant.

Figure 3.1   How the Race Categories Used in Census 2000 Are Defined

"White" refers to people having origins in any of the original peoples of Europe, the Middle East, or North Africa. It includes people who indicated their race or races as "White" or wrote in entries such as Irish, German, Italian, Lebanese, Near Easterner, Arab, or Polish.

"Black or African American" refers to people having origins in any of the Black racial groups of Africa. It includes people who indicated their race or races as "Black, African Am., or Negro," or wrote in entries such as African American, Afro American, Nigerian, or Haitian.

"American Indian and Alaska Native" refers to people having origins in any of the original peoples of North and South America (including Central America), and who maintain tribal affiliation or community attachment. It includes people who indicated their race or races by marking this category or writing in their principal or enrolled tribe, such as Rosebud Sioux, Chippewa, or Navajo.

"Asian" refers to people having origins in any of the original peoples of the Far East, Southeast Asia, or the Indian subcontinent. It includes people who indicated their race or races as "Asian Indian," "Chinese," "Filipino," "Korean," "Japanese," "Vietnamese," or "Other Asian," or wrote in entries such as Burmese, Hmong, Pakistani, or Thai.

"Native Hawaiian and Other Pacific Islander" refers to people having origins in any of the original peoples of Hawaii, Guam, Samoa, or other Pacific Islands. It includes people who indicated their race or races as "Native Hawaiian," "Guamanian or Chamorro," "Samoan," or "Other Pacific Islander," or wrote in entries such as Tahitian, Mariana Islander, or Chuukese.

"Some other race" was included in Census 2000 for respondents who were unable to identify with the five Office of Management and Budget race categories. Respondents who provided write-in entries such as Moroccan, South African, Belizean, or a Hispanic origin (for example, Mexican, Puerto Rican, or Cuban) are included in the Some other race category. U.S. Census Bureau

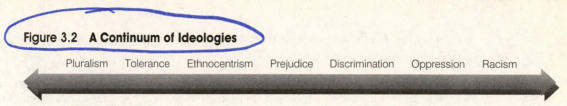

Figure 3.2   A Continuum of Ideologies

Pluralism   Tolerance   Ethnocentrism   Prejudice   Discrimination   Oppression   Racism

They argue for a racial formation position rather than an ethnic group analysis. That is, they argue that the United States's particular preoccupation with race creates racial distinctions among groups, whether those groups are in fact racial, ethnic, or national. Ignatiev (1995) illustrates the creation of a racial group (Whites) out of an ethnic group (Irish immigrants). See Padilla and Lindholm (2004) for more on the problems of definition and measurement in conducting social science research and arriving at social science conclusions on areas of ethnicity.

Pluralism, tolerance, ethnocentrism, prejudice, discrimination, oppression, and racism are ideologies that exist on a continuum (see Figure 3.2). *Pluralism* is a belief in and respect for cultural diversity. *Ethnocentrism* is the belief that one's own cultural ways (ethnic ways) of doing things are the most appropriate and best.

Prejudice is a negative attitude toward a person or group of people. For example, some individuals are prejudiced toward young or old people. In our society, many children learn prejudice against members of racial, cultural, and ethnic groups. Racial prejudice is the prejudgment that members of a racial group are in some way inferior, dangerous, or repugnant to others. Racial *discrimination* refers to one's actual behavior and actions when treating people of a different racial or ethnic group in an inferior manner. *Racism* is the extreme point on the continuum where a dominant group uses its power and often its legal authority to maintain its own privileges and to enforce domination and oppression of others.

Ethnic Identity

Identity was introduced in Chapter 2 in relation to culture. Ethnic identity includes how you see yourself and how you see your group's participation in school and society (Gee, 2001). "Ethnic identity refers to one's sense of belonging to an ethnic group and to the thoughts, feelings and behaviors that are a result of the perceived affiliation. It is composed of factors such as ethnic awareness, ethnic self-identification, ethnic attitudes, and choice of reference group and ethnic behaviors" (Rotheram-Borus, Dopkins, Sabate, & Lightfoot, 1996).

Angela Valenzuela, in an excellent ethnography *Subtractive Schooling: U.S.-Mexican Youth and the Politics of Caring* (1999), describes immigrant students with a dual frame of reference, both U.S. and Mexican. She argues that students in schools such as Seguin High School in Houston, Texas, often learn to devalue their Spanish language, which means they are devaluing their culture and their families (p. 19). This sensitive story gives numerous examples of students negotiating conflicting identities—one the good student and the second the Mexican American student (p. 8).

Curtis Branch (1994) reviewed the literature on ethnic identity and school performance and concludes as follows:

> Ethnic identities assumed by individuals as well as those attributed to them by others, have implications for the learning process because they empower the learner to self define. In the process of creating a definition of one's self with little or no regard for how others see the individual, a sense of determinism and heightened self esteem are likely to follow . . . ethnic identities are important because they are ways by which the learners can exercise some control over their life space. (p. 222)

Your view of your own identity, its significance, and its complexity contributes to shaping your view of the need for multicultural education. Identity has been a source of frequent disputes in ethnic studies and multicultural education. Teachers with clear, or clarified, views of their own identities can assist their students in negotiating new identities rather than having their identities imposed on them from the outside. With supportive teachers, students learn to see school success as an important element in improving life economic opportunities (Valenzuela, 1999).

Individuals construct their identities by defining and interpreting their own experiences and their interactions with others. A person becomes Chicano, or Latino, or White, or Asian American. He or she learns and accepts this identity. Further, this identity is potentially constantly changing (Weis, 2004). The complexity of identity development is well described in *Dreams from My Father: A Story of Race and Inheritance* (1995) by President Barack Obama.

Racism

The danger to our democracy is not ethnic identity or race, but racism, the oppression of a group of people based on their perceived race. Racism is both a belief system and the domination of a people based on these beliefs. Sociologist William Julius Wilson (2001) comments:

> Racism—a term frequently used imprecisely in discussion of the conditions of racial minorities in the United States, especially the conditions of African Americans—should be understood as an ideology of racial domination. This ideology features two things: (1) beliefs that a designated racial group is either biologically or culturally inferior to the dominant group, and (2) the use of such beliefs to rationalize or prescribe the racial group's treatment in society and to explain its social position and accomplishments. (p. 14)

Spain's and Portugal's bloody conquest of Latin America (1492–1811) in search of gold was brutal beyond description. The conquerors sought economic and political, as well as spiritual, goals. The Catholic church made an enormous effort to convert native populations to Christianity. Most of the Indian populations in the territory survived, although their cultures were battered. The conquerors raped and intermarried with Indians on a large scale.

In the English-speaking colonies, intermarriage was not as common for Native Americans and slaves. The English brought African slaves to North America as early as

1619 and Irish peasants as slaves to Barbados and the Caribbean islands by 1648 (O'Callaghan, 2000). In contrast to Catholic law in Latin America, the primarily Protestant European settlers moving west in the territory of the present United States justified their murder of Native Americans (including women and children) and their enslavement of Africans by declaring them to be two separate, not truly human, species.

This expansion and domination of the Americas fostered its own logic of self-justification. Thus, over time the physical characteristics of various non-European peoples (Africans, Native Americans, Mexicans) came to be associated with lower or subordinate status. This subordination was a matter of both ideas (ideologies) and power relationships and had economic and political consequences. For example, in 1849–1850, Mexican and Chinese miners were run out of the new gold mines in California, and Native Americans were forced into slave labor, even though many had been there before European immigrants from France, Scotland, Ireland, and Germany arrived in the gold fields.

Racism has produced a tortuous history in the U.S. intellectual community. Theories of superiority based on an alleged "science" of race that was derived from distorted Darwinism were used not only to find African Americans and Native Americans inferior but also at various times to "prove" the inferiority of women, Irish, Jews, Italians, and Slavs (Feagin, 2001; Omi & Winant, 1986).

For example, between 1840 and 1860 the press and the dominant political groups in the United States actually believed that Irish immigrants were a separate, substandard race. During the early 1900s, the first IQ tests, administered in English and allegedly "scientific," were used to demonstrate that immigrant Jews, Slavs, and people from Eastern Europe were a racial group of inferior intellectual stock. In 1947, a federal court in California ruled that Mexicans could not be assigned to segregated schools because they were legally Caucasians, whereas other courts permitted segregation of Black, Native American, and Asian children on allegedly racial grounds (*Westminster School District v. Méndez*, 1947).

While racial definitions are vague and imprecise, racism continues to divide our society and our schools. Although most scientists agree that humans cannot usefully be distinguished physiologically by race, for a racist nothing could be easier: A race is "them," "those people," the "others"—any group the racist hates and fears. At times, racism is directed at nationality groups (such as Irish, Mexicans, Russians, or Armenians), language groups (such as Spanish, Creole, or Hawaiian), and cultural groups (such as "hillbillies" or "Okies"). *Institutional racism* is the use of the power and authority of a dominant group to enforce prejudice and oppression and to prevent the subjugated group from gaining equal access to employment, quality housing, health care, and education.

Racism and Schools

As shown in Figure 1.2, students of different ethnic groups (Latinos, Asians, Native Americans, African Americans, and European Americans) learn to read at dramatically different rates in our schools.

The ethnic group you belong to makes a substantial difference in school achievement. Mexican Americans leave school at a higher rate than other Hispanics, and Hispanics drop out at a higher rate than do non-Hispanic Whites (Ramirez & de la Cruz, 2003). There has been a dramatic increase in the rate of segregation of Black and Latino students from White students in the nation's public schools (Frey, 2006; Orfield & Lee, 2007). We are becoming a more divided nation. The reason for this is relatively straightforward: Schools for poor children and children of color are inadequately secure, staffed, and funded. Economic choices—for example, to unequally and inadequately fund schools—produce most of the differences in achievement that are used as evidence of racial superiority and inferiority.

In May of 2001, a coalition of civil rights groups filed a class action lawsuit (*Williams v. California*) that documented the deplorable and even unsafe and unsanitary conditions in many of California's schools that serve large numbers of students of color. What causes these unequal conditions? Among the causes is a sustained pattern of underfunding of these schools. These are deliberate decisions to maintain some schools well and other schools in below-humane conditions. The fact that these racial and class disparities exist must be explained.

In 2001, after years of trial, a New York judge, Leland DeGrasse, found that New York State's school funding system denies students in New York City the opportunity for a "sound basic education." Justice DeGrasse ruled that the system violated the state constitution and that the funding system was discriminatory against minority students in violation of the provisions of Title VI of the Civil Rights Act of 1964. Later the decision was overturned by a higher court.

In 2006, the Chicago school district was required to make a list of its failing schools (as now required by new federal law). In Chicago, 365 out of 596 schools, and predominantly African American and Latino schools, were on the list. A 2007 report by the Institute for Democracy, Education, and Access at the University of California at Los Angeles described how California's schools in low-income and heavily Latino and Black areas are significantly more overcrowded, have more substitute teachers, have fewer prepared math teachers, and lack college preparation courses in comparison to similar schools in mostly White areas (Oakes & Rogers, 2007).

If you were a parent of school children in New York, Chicago, or California, would you have confidence that your children were being treated fairly? How do you think such a consistent pattern of underfunding and school failure develops across the nation?

For over 40 years, Jonathan Kozol has been describing the severe inequality of opportunity in many public schools. In 1991, he described school conditions that would never be accepted in adequately funded European American schools:

> The school is 29% black, 70% Hispanic. . . . We sit and talk in the nurse's room. The window is broken. There are two holes in the ceiling. About a quarter of the ceiling has been patched and covered with a plastic garbage bag.
>
> "Will these children ever get what white kids in the suburbs take for granted? I don't think so," says the principal. "If you ask me why, I'd have to speak of race and social class. I don't think that the powers that be in New York City understand, or want to understand, that if they do not give these children a sufficient education to lead healthy, productive lives, we will be their victims later on. We'll pay the price someday—in violence, in economic costs." (p. 89)

Several years later he visited a number of schools for his book *The Shame of the Nation: The Restoration of Apartheid Schooling in America* (2005). He describes some schools in New York:

> I had also made a number of visits to a high school where a stream of water flowed down the main stairwells on a rainy afternoon and where green fungus molds were growing in the office where the students went to counseling. A large blue barrel was positioned to collect the rain-water coming through the ceiling. In one make-shift elementary school housed in a former skating rink next to a funeral parlor in another nearly all-black-and-Hispanic section of the Bronx, class size rose to 34 and more; four kindergarten classes and a sixth grade class were packed into a single room that had no windows. Airlessness was stifling in many rooms; and recess was impossible because there was no outdoor playground and no indoor gym, so the children had no place to play. . . . A friend of mine who was a first year teacher in a Harlem high school told me she had 40 students in her class but only 30 chairs, so some of her students had to sit on windowsills or lean against the walls. (p. 41)

Conditions like those described by Kozol and in the California report can be found in urban and low-income schools across the nation. These are examples of systematic, structural racism. Children in some areas are getting a significantly unequal education—and it has continued for at least the last 40 years.

In 2007, the U.S. government spent over $656 billion for the military, plus over $43 billion for spying and covert operations. How is it that we do not have enough money to fix the broken windows, repair the buildings, and hire teachers for our inner-city schools? And who makes this decision in a democracy?

Our country's history of race relations has been mired in tragedy, including the enslavement of Africans, the murder of Native Americans, and the seizure of one-third of the arable land claimed by Mexico, in addition to all of Puerto Rico and Hawaii, making these people domestic, conquered, subjugated minority groups. We must recognize that, despite decades of resistance and struggle, only limited progress has been made toward ending racial stratification and oppression. Martin Luther King, Jr., a major campaigner for human rights and recipient of the Nobel Peace Prize, commented on the centrality of the struggle against racism in his famous "Beyond Vietnam" speech: "We must rapidly begin the shift from a 'thing-oriented' to a person-oriented society. When machines and computers, profit motives and property rights are considered more important than people, then the giant triplets of racism, materialism, and militarism are incapable of being conquered" (1986, p. 629).

Racism and Privilege

Racism interacts with class, gender, and other variables to construct a complex fabric of intergroup relations. For example, while the African American middle class achieved significant advancement in the last three decades of the 20th century, the African American lower class suffered increased poverty and unemployment (Marable, 2007; Obama, 2007).

Feagin argues that as a part of learning to be White—that is, learning a White identity—children also learn to participate in and to maintain the current social order, including its social injustices (2001, p. 137). We, as teachers, whether European American, African American, Latino, Asian, or other, are either engaged in sustaining the current social order, in significant part by teaching children to fit in, to know their place, or engaged in resisting this social order by teaching children empowerment and responsibility (see Chapter 7).

Some readers may protest their innocence. They will argue that they are just living their lives, not hurting anyone. Most teachers and college students have learned to accept the existing system of racial domination and inequality as normal and natural. This acceptance of racial domination is an example of ideology (Ladson-Billings, 2003).

Feagin (2001) argues that "[f]rom the beginning the system of racial oppression was designed to bring a range of benefits to White Americans. The society, rooted in slavery, provided whites with many undeserved social, economic, political and cultural advantages" (p. 177). He and George Lipsitz go on to describe how these initial advantages have been advanced and maintained down to the present in part through our educational systems (Lipsitz, 2001).

Many authors in the field of multicultural education work from a race-based analysis. In recent times, some have concentrated their focus on White identity and White privilege. An alternative perspective is to focus on race and class (see Chapter 4). From a race/class-based analysis, White supremacy, rather than White privilege, is the major problem. Oppression is the maintenance of political and economic power in the hands of the current controlling elite, most of whom are White. White supremacy is an expression of White/upper-class power in institutions (in schools, curriculum development, and teacher preparation) and in the society. African American feminist author bell hooks has critically noted that White supremacy is supported even by some Blacks, Latinos, and Asians because this maintenance of the status quo, or the current situation, provides benefits of power and wealth to them (2000, pp. 94–96).

Affirmative Action

Racism produces privileges for some and oppression for others. The beneficiaries of racism are taught not to recognize their personal participation in an unjust system. Let us take the example of a European American teacher candidate in California. "Jane" is in a teacher education program at a publicly financed university. Racial privilege provides her with easy admission to the program. Nearly 50 percent of all African American, Latino, and Native American students dropped out of high school. Of those who graduated, another 50 percent decided not to go on to college or were tracked into a nonacademic program in community college. Jane received admission to the teacher preparation program without recognizing the privileges granted to her (and withheld from others) by this academic tracking system.

Jane notices that there are only a few Latinos, African Americans, Native Americans, and Asians in the teacher preparation program, even though more than 50 percent of the students in the schools where she completes her teacher training are from these cultural groups. She relies on folk knowledge to explain this gap. This seems normal to her. She assumes, incorrectly, that African Americans and Mexican Americans must not recognize the importance of education or value the career goal of being a teacher, or perhaps they are unwilling to work as hard as she had to work to get through the university. She has heard that many fail the admissions screening.

Jane does not recognize that her own admission to the program was the result of a quality high school education that others were denied. Instead, she assumes that her admission to the teacher preparation program was the result of a fair and equitable system based on merit. (In California, admission would be based on grade point average in college or a passing score on a standardized teachers' exam.) She also is taught to assume that her college preparation provides her with the appropriate knowledge needed to teach and motivate all children. During student teaching, she will be puzzled and confused when some students from these diverse cultures do not respond enthusiastically to the Eurocentric viewpoint and teaching strategies that she took for granted in her own preparation. Jane, like many others, receives special financial aid from the state because she promises to take a teaching position in a low-income district.

When Jane completes the teacher preparation program, she looks for a job. The first districts she applies to are seeking minority applicants. Jane feels she worked hard to earn her degree and her teaching credential, and she did. She believes in a color-blind society. Programs that focus on recruiting bilingual teachers and those from cultural minorities seem to give those teachers an unfair advantage. Rather than recognizing her own privileges (quality public schools, low-cost public universities, special grants), Jane resents what she sees as special benefits for minorities. Her preferred color-blind philosophy hides the entrenched racial and class inequality that exists in our schools (Guinier & Torres, 2002). These inequalities are not her fault. She believes that good test scores and good grades obtained within the European American–centered university system are proof of superior preparation—a position now challenged by her job search. The truth is that Jane may be well prepared to present the curriculum. Her test scores and English writing skills may be better than those of other applicants, but she may be poorly prepared to teach the majority of children whose cultures and communication styles are different from her own.

In this composite scenario, four applicants seek the teaching position. However, Jane does not get the job; Carmen does. Carmen was born and raised in Arizona. Her home language is Spanish. No bilingual education was available in her school in the 1960s. At age 16, she left school and married. Carmen raised three children. She and her family performed backbreaking labor in the lettuce, grape, and tomato fields for more than 15 years. Finally, because of a death in the family, the family settled in Sacramento, California.

Carmen began to attend community college at age 36. She studied very hard while continuing to raise her children. Learning to read and write English at the college level was difficult; most of her communication for the previous 15 years had been in Spanish. After six years of study, she finally received her bachelor's degree and was admitted to the teacher preparation program. Carmen speaks English and Spanish well, but her college grades are lower than Jane's.

Carmen is an outstanding student teacher. She draws on her skills and competence as a mother, her maturity, and her bilingualism. The school district is under pressure from Mexican American parents to improve the poor quality of education for their children. The teacher selection committee consists of a principal and a bilingual teacher. They select Carmen because for 50 percent of the children in grades 1 through 3 Spanish is their first language.

Three of the four applicants for the teaching position now believe that they were passed over because of preferential hiring. They each assume that they were superior to Carmen. But clearly there was only one job opening. If a European American female (Jane) had received the job, the other three would still be left without a job.

An anti–affirmative action movement, primarily supported by European Americans, became a strong political force, mostly within the Republican Party between 1994 and 2004. In 1996, California voters, following an emotional and divisive electoral campaign, voted 54 percent to 46 percent to end affirmative action programs in their state (Chávez, 1998). Anti–affirmative action efforts emerged in other states, including Texas, Michigan, and Florida, and often focused on admission to universities and law schools. Lawsuits challenging the University of Michigan's use of race in its admission decisions reached the U.S. Supreme Court in 2003. In 2006, Michigan voters voted 58 percent to 42 percent to ban affirmative action in hiring in that state. For teachers, affirmative action was a divisive issue during times of tight economic competition. Now, with a national teacher shortage and plentiful jobs in most states, few people object to extra efforts to recruit, coach, and assist persons in joining the teaching force (for more on this, see www.fairchance.org).

How would you judge Carmen's case? Was the hiring committee acting correctly or practicing "reverse discrimination"? How realistic is this case compared to your own experiences?

Institutional Racism

As the previous example illustrates, racism, poverty, and gender discrimination are interactive, complex, and often misunderstood. Since the 1980s, racial hate groups have increased in number and size, and more incidents of racially motivated violence have been reported than in prior years.

Many teachers find the discussion of race and racism uncomfortable. Well-meaning people have very diverse perceptions of the issue. Some believe that racial discrimination and racism are dated and repugnant doctrines that no longer affect our daily lives.

Racism is much more than acts of violence, expressions of individual prejudice, and the preservation of demeaning stereotypes. Racial domination includes many habits, decisions, and procedures that keep racial and ethnic groups at the bottom of the social and economic order. Racial inequality is primarily a problem not of individuals but of institutions (Guinier & Torres, 2002). For example, examine the racial and ethnic composition of your own teacher preparation program, and compare it with the student population in nearby school districts. In most cases, even in urban areas, the teaching force is more than 80 percent European American and middle class, whereas the student population is much more diverse. How was this largely White teaching population created? It is the product not of individual prejudice but of an entire system of higher education. How was it re-created in your own teacher preparation program?

Racism does its greatest damage in our society when well-meaning people preserve a seldom-examined social structure that benefits some people, while frequently harming others. Current discrimination in wages, schooling, health care, housing, and employment

Figure 3.3   Percentage of U.S. Children Living Below the Poverty Line, 2006

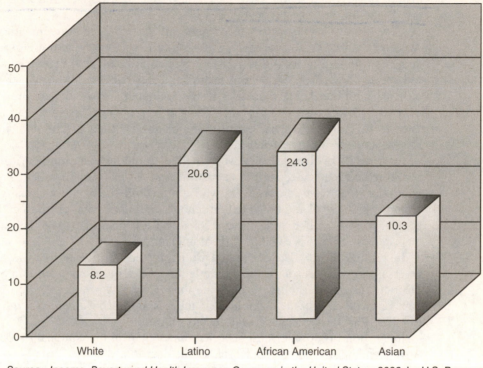

Source: Income, Poverty and Health Insurance Coverage in the United States: 2006, by U.S. Bureau of the Census, 2007, Washington, DC: Author.

opportunities continues the historical pattern of White/upper-class supremacy or White privilege (Lipsitz, 2002). Racism and other forms of oppression, such as classism and sexism, remain because they serve a purpose. Someone benefits from these oppressions. Someone benefits by maintaining inequality. On the other hand, many teachers view themselves as working to oppose this oppression by providing an alternative for their students in spite of the controlling domination of the society.

Scores on national tests like the National Assessment of Educational Progress and on state tests clearly reveal that our educational institutions work well for some students and don't work as well for others. Schools for middle-class European American, Latino, and African American children fundamentally fulfill their purposes. But schools for poor African American, Latino, and European American children often fail. Although this institutional failure harms all poor children, it disproportionately affects the children of racial and ethnic minorities.

The differences in income and poverty levels among racial and ethnic groups are not accidental. They are a result of our economic, social, and educational systems. (See Figure 3.3.) Extreme poverty and even incarceration are a direct result of a lack of employment skills. Educational discrimination and failure in one generation often lead to poverty and school crises in the next. These are cycles that a democratic society should interrupt and remedy.

Low-quality education in prior generations led to a concentration of African American and Latino workers in low-skilled industrial labor fields. As the U.S. economy shifted in the 1980s and 1990s from a reliance on industrial production to a demand for higher-level, more technical skills, millions of jobs in the steel, automotive, and other heavy industries were eliminated. Today, the children of these displaced workers are in school. They must either prepare for new jobs in knowledge-based industries or suffer the poverty of the working poor in low-skilled, low-paying service industries.

As a result of decades of poverty within minority communities, forms of racist behavior became embedded in our institutions. African American and Latino children in urban areas have few teachers who understand their cultural reality. They often attend overcrowded and understaffed schools, and immigrant children are measured by standardized tests biased against persons whose primary language is not English and whose home culture is not that of the dominant culture.

In June 2007, the U.S. Supreme Court decided on the basis of a 4–4–1 vote to reverse prior decisions and to deny the Jefferson County (Kentucky) and Seattle School Districts the use of the law to integrate their schools. In this case, the Court seems to have reversed most of the major ideas in the classic *Brown v. Board of Education* decision of 1954, which insisted on equal access to education.

Julian Bond (2007), civil rights veteran and chair of the National Association for the Advancement of Colored People, said of the decision:

> Today's Court has turned its back on the millions of black and Latino children currently trapped in highly segregated, underperforming schools, leaving them to hang on the ropes of racial and economic disenfranchisement. The Court has paved the way for many more children of color to join them by outlawing the modest means numerous districts have adopted to promote racial diversity and overcome racial isolation. It has denied the very notion that our nation's schools should serve as equalizers. (pp. 18–19.)

In response, a number of school districts, including Jefferson County and San Francisco, have redesigned their school integration plans to consider class as well as race. This new combination has not yet been tested in the courts.

As illustrated, institutional racism seeps into schools through the de facto resegregation of schools in our major cities, through unequal funding, and through a curriculum that focuses primarily on the European American view of history, literature, and language, largely ignoring multicultural views and contributions. It enters schools when teachers and curricula validate and support one group's language and learning styles, while ignoring or even repressing the languages and learning styles of other groups. Institutional racism is embedded in teacher folk knowledge about teaching strategies and inaccurate assumptions about student potential. Its existence is implicit when universities select more than 80 percent of future teachers from European American candidates, excluding people of color and language minorities.

White Supremacy (handwritten annotation)

Racism and African Americans

The African American story is the best known of the many devastating histories of racism in our country. The work of DuBois, Douglass, and others provides a substantial scholarly tradition of African American history. W. E. B. DuBois was a leading scholar–activist in the African American community from 1890 until his death in 1963. He wrote the following:

> We can no longer regard Western Europe and North America as the world for which civilization exists; nor can we look upon European culture as the norm for all peoples. Henceforth the majority of the inhabitants of the earth, who happen for the most part to be colored, must be regarded as having the right and the capacity to share in human progress and to become copartners in that democracy which alone can ensure peace among men, by the abolition of poverty, the education of the masses, protection from disease, and the scientific treatment of crime. [So long as] the majority of men can be regarded mainly as sources of profit for Europe and North America . . . we are planning not peace but war, not democracy but the continued oligarchical control of civilization by the white race. (1975, p. 249)

Accurately including the African American contribution to U.S. history would substantially alter the interpretation of much of the United States' past. Africa, prior to the slave trade, had rich and diverse cultures, major cities, and advanced civilizations.

The domination of life by the slave-owning class in the southern part of the United States created a slave culture. Slave owners developed ideologies of racial superiority, and their apologists defended and extended their brutal system. Together with the European immigrants' genocidal assault on the native populations, the institution of slavery established the racial foundations of present U.S. society (Feagin, 2001).

The Civil War and the end of slavery did not end the terror of racism against African American people. Legal segregation, inadequate schooling, ideologies of racism, lynching, and other forms of open terrorism prevented African Americans from achieving equal opportunity until well into the 1960s (Dray, 2002; see Figure 3.4). The struggle to maintain "White supremacy" in the United States has shaped and distorted the labor movement, the populist movement, our political parties, and our economic system (Feagin, 2001).

Marable (2007) argues that although the United States prides itself on having a two-party system, African Americans faced a one-party system in the South well into the 1960s. The Civil Rights Movement of the 1950s and 1960s grew up outside of the traditional political parties. The movement broke the monopoly of power held by European American Democrats in the South and finally brought a two-party system to the region. When African Americans gained new power in the Democratic Party, large numbers of European Americans in the South became Republicans. By 2000, Republicans won more than half of all congressional seats in the South, allowing Republicans to gain control of the U.S. Congress and the presidency (Feagin, 2001).

The Civil Rights Movement also produced major changes in the relationship between African Americans and the dominant society. Omi and Winant (1986) argue that the Civil Rights Movement changed African American self-perception from an

Figure 3.4   The Life Story of Mr. Charlie Evans as Told by Forrest Davis, November 1997

In November of 1997 I had the opportunity to travel to Birmingham, Alabama, where I grew up from 1943 to 1964. I had visited my home only three times since relocating to California.

I had the impulse to pay a visit to Mr. Charlie Evans, who was a positive role model and who hired me when I was thirteen years old to work on his vegetable truck. During the hot, humid days of the summer I would assist him in delivering produce to areas in Brighton, Westfield and Fairfield. He was surprised but overwhelmed with joy to see me and was even more ecstatic after I told him I was a professor at Sacramento State University. His eyes filled with tears, and he interrupted our conversation and went into his bedroom, then presented me with a manuscript that contained details of his personal life growing up in Alabama.

Mr. Evans's manuscript revealed that he was born in 1914 in Grove Hill, Alabama. His family relocated to Fairfield to work for the Tennessee Iron and Coal Company. Mr. Evans was happy about the move because it presented him with the opportunity to attend Westfield School. This was a company school considered to be the best in the area. A few select black students could attend if their parents were employees of the company. The school was a multigrade classroom from the first through the sixth grade. After completion of these grades, you could not go further because the whites controlled access to the available educational facilities. James Anderson, in *The Education of Blacks in the South, 1860–1935,* documents the influence of the "planter class" and their use of child labor as a major barrier to the education of African Americans. On the other hand, the growth of the coal and iron industry represented a change in the local economy, and competition between these economic forces resulted in an increase in educational facilities. Mr. Evans indicated that his math teacher recognized his potential and offered to pay for his college education because she thought he was one of the smartest students in the class.

Unfortunately the Depression came (1929–1936) and his dream was deferred. Mr. Evans had to work to help support his family. Despite economic hardships, he managed to persevere and save enough money to graduate from Westfield High in 1936. Segregation was predicated on the idea that whites were innately superior. African Americans were denied equal opportunities to compete for employment, housing, and education and denied access to public lodging.

Racism and Schools

This socially sanctioned caste system was enforced by terrorist acts of the Ku Klux Klan.

After World War II, Mr. Evans initiated numerous business ventures, including purchasing a vegetable truck for six hundred dollars. Then he went to a vegetable garden and bought sixteen dollars worth of produce. He said, "I had only two dollars left for gas and two left to make change. On this day I sold twenty-five dollars worth of vegetables from my truck. I built a route that was paying me about three hundred dollars a month. At this time my oldest child was ready for college, so I was able to send her to Alabama State University. Her room, board, and tuition was sixty dollars a month. I would take every half dollar I collected and put it in one pocket. When I got home I would put it in a cigar box. So when it came time for me to pay the tuition I would take the money in half dollars from this box. This is the way I put her through college."

> Later, Mr. Evans supplemented his income by buying and selling houses and then focused his energy on constructing a gas station on Highway 11 between Birmingham and Bessemer, Alabama. He negotiated a joint venture project with a local white businessman who could also see the potential profits. However, the project was immediately aborted after the Ku Klux Klan discovered that the station was going to be owned by a black man. Mr. Evans converted the gas station into a confectionery where he sold Piper Ice Cream, from a company based in Birmingham.
>
> The Evans family had increased to nine girls by 1958, so the business activities were diversified to buying, selling, and renting houses and farming vegetables. He used the income to support his family, and eight out of nine daughters graduated from college.

earlier colonized view to a recognition that their poverty and powerlessness were the products of systems of oppression. This change of viewpoint produced some improvement in race relationships, and the dominant group lost its ideological power to define the boundaries of race relations.

Marable (2007) further argues that the worldview of most African American civil rights leaders, with the exception of the Black Power period of the late 1960s and early 1970s, could be termed *integrationist*. Integrationists called for the elimination of structural barriers that prohibited African Americans from full participation in the mainstream of American life.

Integrationists had a faith in U.S. democracy. The political system could be made to work, they believed, if only people of color and others victimized by discrimination and poverty were brought to the table as full partners. With the passage of the Voting Rights Act of 1965 and other civil rights legislation—the result of a sustained campaign of nonviolent direct action—all members of society supposedly gained equal access to the process of democratic decision making.

Though notably successful in the political and legal arenas, the integrationist strategy lacked a method for advancing democracy against the many means available to those in economic power to dominate and thwart electoral participation.

New forms of racism developed during the 1980s. In the wake of the Civil Rights Movement, it was no longer possible or viable for White elected officials, administrators, and corporate executives to attack African Americans openly. The Ku Klux Klan and other racist vigilante groups still existed but did not represent a mass movement.

Instead, many racists developed a new strategy that attributed racial tensions to the actions of people of color. For example, David Duke, former member of the American Nazi Party and leader of the Ku Klux Klan, received the majority of European American votes in his senatorial race in Louisiana by arguing that "affirmative action" programs discriminated unfairly against innocent European Americans. African American college students were attacked as "racists" for advocating academic programs in African American studies or proposing African American cultural centers. African American workers were accused of racism for supporting affirmative action programs. African American political leaders had to defend themselves against charges of "reverse racism." Conservative academics and think tanks promoted a theory of "reverse discrimination."

As noted earlier, in 1996 the voters of California voted 54 percent to 46 percent to ban affirmative action programs for minorities and for women (Chávez, 1998). The campaign was led by African American Ward Connerly, a regent of the University of California. As a result of the ban, the number of African American and Latino students enrolling in the University of California at Berkeley dropped more than 50 percent by 2001 (Marable, 2007). In contrast, more Asian American students and students who declined to state their ethnicity were admitted (Johnston, 1998). Similar declines in African American and Latino students occurred throughout the University of California campuses (which enroll 230,000 students). The ban on affirmative action had less effect on the California State University system—which enrolls 360,000 students and produces 60 percent of all the state's teachers—and on the California community colleges—while enroll 1.4 million students since these colleges and universities do not usually limit enrollment.

Institutional privilege, discrimination, and prejudice continue to be present within the U.S. economy and U.S. schools. Affirmative action plans and programs have had minimal impact on entrenched patterns of power and privilege.

Although many European Americans in the United States say that they believe that racism and related violence have declined and that great progress has been made, leaders in the African American, Latino, and Native American communities regularly state the opposite. Speakers who testify to the continued violence of institutional racism are often dismissed or marginalized by the media and in educational institutions.

Derrick Bell, a prominent African American professor of law, states in *Faces at the Bottom of the Well* (1992):

> Consider: In this last decade of the 20th Century, color determines the social and economic status of all African-Americans, both those who have been highly successful and their poverty-bound brethren whose lives are grounded in misery and despair. We rise and fall less as a result of our efforts than in response to the needs of a white society that condemns all blacks to quasi-citizenship as surely as it segregated our parents and enslaved their forebears. (p. 3)

Since the 1980s, a profound social crisis—a deep sense of fragmentation and collective doubt—had developed within the African American community. The symptoms of this internal crisis were the widespread drug epidemic, Black-against-Black violence, growth of urban youth gangs, and destruction of Black social institutions. A Black boy born in 2001 has a 1 in 3 chance of going to prison in his lifetime, while a Black girl has a 1 in 17 chance—the same as a White male. A Latino boy born in 2001 has a 1 in 6 chance of going to prison, while a Latino girl has a 1 in 45 chance. By 2004, 2,531 African Americans out of each 100,000 were in prison as compared to 957 Latinos and 393 Whites (Children's Defense Fund, 2007).

Violence inevitably influenced community relationships. People concerned with street violence, robbery, or death were reluctant to attend neighborhood political meetings after dark.

The internal crisis within contemporary African American life was aggravated by corporate and government decisions detailed by sociologist W. J. Wilson in his books *When Work Disappears* (1996) and *Bridge over the Racial Divide* (1999). The refusal of the federal government to initiate economic reconstruction programs opened many neighborhoods to the illegal economies of crack and crime. The level of government abandonment of the poor, and particularly the Black poor, was starkly revealed on national and international television by the lack of an immediate and comprehensive response by the Bush Administration to Hurricane Katrina as it destroyed parts of New Orleans and the Gulf Coast in 2005.

Somewhat paradoxically, at the same time that the economic crisis has grown, the political empowerment of African American leaders also continues to grow. Elected officials now commonly incorporate an African American agenda into political programs. In 1989, Virginia became the first state to have an African American governor. African American mayors lead several major U.S. cities. In 1992, an African American woman from Illinois, Carol Moseley Braun, was elected to the U.S. Senate (although she was subsequently defeated in 1998); and the Black Caucus of the U.S. House of Representatives, including both women and men, reached 38 members in the year 2000.

In *Race, Reform and Rebellion: The Second Reconstruction and Beyond in Black America, 1945–2006* (2007), Manning Marable describes the changes confronting the post–civil rights generation. While recognizing the important contributions of the civil rights generation and civil rights leaders, such as Congressman John Lewis, now the African American community is more diverse, and it faces new problem and possibilities.

The Civil Rights Movement achieved political equality—until 2000, when once again large numbers of African Americans were disenfranchised in a critical election. However, the social and economic policies of the governments of the 1980s and 1990s shifted burdens back onto the working people.

Robert Moses, an activist organizer of the Mississippi struggle in the 1960s and of the Algebra Project for schools in the current era, expresses the conflict this way:

What is central now is economic access; the political process has been opened—there are no formal barriers to voting, for example—but economic access, taking advantage of new technologies and economic opportunities, demands as much effort as the political struggle required in the 1960's (Moses & Cobb, 2001, p. 6)

A division grew in the African American and Latino communities between those who had gained from the civil rights revolutions—a new successful middle class—and those who had lost economic opportunity—the declining industrial working class. In 2005, Hurricane Katrina, one of the costliest and deadliest hurricanes in U.S. history, hit the Gulf Coast and New Orleans. More than 1,863 people lost their lives. The Bush Administration as well as state and local governments failed to provide adequate preparation for evacuation and adequate rebuilding assistance for the people—a majority of whom in the New Orleans area were poor and Black. Thousands were left without food, water, shelter, and health care. The city and the schools have yet to recover. Sustained, oppressive poverty was structured into African American life in many communities, and the promise of the American dream, including quality public schools, was terminated—at least for the time being (Obama, 2006; Marable, 2007; Obama, 2007).

Today, African Americans have far greater access to elected office than in the past. The election of Barack Obama as President is a monumental step forward for the country. His election reveals significant shifts in racial and ethnic relations in the United States. The election does not mean that racism and prejudice are gone, but this significant election certainly marks a change in our history. In the early 1960's voting rights were

U.S. President Barack Obama

brutally suppressed by legal and illegal means throughout the South; in 2008, Barack Obama, the son of an African man and a White woman was elected as President of the United States.

At present the agitational side of the civil rights movement has given way to a generation that looks to elected officials for leadership on questions of social justice and a less confrontational form of identity-based representation. Families in the middle and working classes tried to raise their children in peace and safety by leaving deteriorating urban schools. Some others—including many in the hip hop generation, knowing too little of the struggles of the civil rights era tended to dismiss electoral work and the possibilities of political change through political organizing. A division developed between the Civil Rights generation and some artists in the hip hop generation in politics. The Obama election fused these several parts of the African American community with activists from the Latino and labor communities to create a new coalition dedicated to democracy and justice. Important for the future was the increasing growth of a broad, well prepared, class of African American professionals, doctors, lawyers, teachers, financiers, often educated at the traditionally African American colleges and providing leadership to their communities around the nation.

Racism and Ethnic Conflict in a Nation of Immigrants

Since its founding in 1776, the United States has been a pluralistic society—a society of immigrants. In spite of this diversity, members of the dominant culture have often held somewhat xenophobic attitudes toward foreigners, persons who speak other languages, and native peoples. A brief history of immigration to the United States provides a context for understanding how successive populations entered and transformed a racially stratified society.

The present territory of the United States was first colonized by the Spanish (St. Augustine, Florida, in 1565 and Santa Fe, New Mexico, in 1610); the English (Jamestown, Virginia, in 1607 and Plymouth, Massachusetts, in 1620); the Germans, Swedes, and Dutch (the Middle Colonies from 1624 to 1640); the French (Louisiana in 1800); and the Spanish-Indian Mestizos (the Southwest from 1610 to 1784).

Immigration from Europe

From 1840 to 1920, there was an enormous influx of immigrants from Europe to the "New World." They came in hopes of building a new, more prosperous life. Poor, hungry, adventurous, and at times desperate, they fled European poverty, wars, and oppression. They settled in Canada, the United States, Mexico, and throughout the Americas. Between 1860 and 1920, 28.5 million people arrived in the United States, 74.1 percent of them from Europe (Fix & Passel, 1994). During this same period, the Native American population in the United States was decimated, dropping from more than 4 million to less than 1 million, and Chinese immigration was banned, first by terrorism and then by law (Almaguer, 1994).

From 1840 to 1870, the European migration consisted mainly of English, Scots-Irish, Irish, and, later, German settlers. Immigrants entered primarily through East Coast ports, spoke a variety of languages, and became both the working class for emerging U.S. industry and the farmers in the Midwest. In the 1880s and 1890s, thousands of Swedes, Norwegians, and Finns arrived, most often settling in the upper Midwest.

The first two decades of the 20th century saw the largest immigration wave in U.S. history prior to the present. Between 1860 and 1900, the number of immigrants totaled 14 million, but between 1900 and 1915 alone, another 14.5 million arrived (National Center for Immigrants' Rights, 1979; U.S. Immigration and Naturalization Service, 1997).

These "new immigrants" from Southern and Eastern Europe were Catholic, in desperate economic straits, and often poorly educated. An anti-immigrant, or nativist, movement grew to oppose the influx of immigrants and to maintain the "European American" lifestyle. Power, politics, cultural suppression, and the schools were used to create a myth that all "Americans" were White, Anglo Saxon, and Protestant.

Migration and Immigration from Mexico

Florida and Louisiana were once territories of Spain. Texas was a territory of Mexico prior to 1835, when Anglo-American immigrants rebelled and created the Texas Republic. Parts of the present states of Utah, Colorado, California, New Mexico, and Nevada were seized from Mexico in 1848. The Mestizo peoples in this area did not emigrate from Mexico but were living in the Southwest when the U.S. Army arrived.

The Treaty of Guadalupe Hidalgo (signed in 1848) ended the Mexican American War and ceded more than one-third of Mexico's territory to the United States. Mexican people living in that area were quickly deprived of their land. In spite of resistance, most Mexicans were reduced to cheap and exploitable labor or driven from the country. California, which was a bilingual state by its original constitution, rewrote its constitution in 1879 to make English the only official language .

The border between the United States and Mexico was neither defended nor restricted from 1850 to 1924. Persons of Mexican and Native American ancestry moved freely back and forth. The population of major cities in the Southwest, such as Los Angeles, was often predominantly Mexican in population well into the 1870s (Acuña, 2007; Grisold del Castillo, 1979).

The Mexican Revolution of 1910–1917 became a bloody, extended civil war. Under the leadership of the brothers Enrique and Ricardo Flores-Magón, a significant movement in support of the revolutionaries was organized in the U.S. Southwest. Mexican residents raised funds and protected family members who fled from Mexico into the United States.

Refugees dramatically increased the size of the Mexican population, creating large communities in El Paso, Los Angeles, and southern Texas. European American immigrants had only recently managed to dominate the area, and they perceived the rapidly increasing Mexican population as a threat. In an effort to control these groups, some law enforcement organizations, such as the Texas Rangers, became notorious for eliminating "Indians" and "keeping Mexicans in their place" (Limerick, 1988; Weber, 1973). In the Southwest, many Ku Klux Klan chapters focused on what they termed the "Mexican problem."

Resistance to European American (also called *Anglo* or *Norteamericano*) domination of the area was a constant aspect of Southwest U.S. history prior to 1890. By the 1930s, Mexican/Chicano and native workers actively formed their own unions in mining and agriculture to protect their rights under expanding corporate capitalism. While the population of the cities was largely Mexican, in the rural areas indigenous people (Dineh, Apache, Pueblo) were as often the workers and union organizers.

The companies and the press accused many of these union leaders of being communists as a means to defeat their organizing efforts. In the 1950s, as a result of a program known as "Operation Wetback," hundreds of local Mexican and Mexican American leaders were arrested and deported, the Mexican-American community was terrorized, and many areas were deprived of effective local leaders for more than a decade (M. T. Garcia, 1994).

The deportations set back the political progress of the Mexican and Chicano communities. No single notable national leader emerged. More than six major attempts were made to organize the largely Mexican, Mexican American, and Filipino population of agricultural workers. Finally, in 1964 these efforts unified in the United Farm Workers Union (AFL–CIO) under the leadership of César Chávez, Dolores Huerta, Philip Vera Cruz, and others. The African American civil rights struggle occurring at the same time gave renewed hope to Mexican and Chicano organizers.

In 1968, conditions in schools in Los Angeles and other cities led thousands of Mexican American students to walk out on strike. The current Chicano student movement was born in these walkouts. This movement quickly spread to Crystal City, Texas; Denver, Colorado; and other locations (Acuña, 2007).

The Chicano/Latino civil rights struggles were highly dispersed. Union organizing and educational struggles were major focuses of activity. By 1972, Chicanas/Latinas were asserting their own distinct demands for gender equality within the movement. In the 1980s, Chicano/Latino efforts began to merge with Puerto Rican and other "Hispanic" efforts in the Midwest and East.

The Civil Rights Movement (1954–1968) fundamentally changed the status and participation of Chicano and Mexican American people in the Southwest. These volatile struggles led to a bold assertion of a Chicano identity by many activists.

Young activists, led by Jose Angel Gutierrez and Maria Hernandez, organized politically and took control of Crystal City, Texas. Then they began to challenge the domination of Texas politics by European American officeholders (Acuña, 2007).

Language rights and immigration issues continue to divide voters in the Southwest and in much of the nation today. For example, in 1998 California voters decided to eliminate bilingual education, which served immigrant children in schools.

Chicano-led labor unions and community organizations developed organizing strategies to empower Mexican American communities. The most famous of these efforts was the United Farm Workers Union, mentioned previously. Although there have been many victories in labor organizing, the low-wage economy of the Southwest constantly re-creates conditions of worker oppression. In the 1990s, campaigns to organize strawberry workers in California, apple workers in Washington, tomato workers in Ohio, and garment workers and janitors in major cities helped labor organizing evolve to become a major source of community power among Mexican Americans.

Civil rights struggles changed in the 1980s when a new middle class of Latino professionals and merchants emerged and advocated a less confrontational style of leadership. Many adopted the term *Hispanic* as a description of their identity. A similar layer of middle-class government employees and elected officials, often the beneficiaries of colleges' affirmative action admissions programs, developed within the African American community. In both cases, members of this new middle class politically engaged more cautiously, focusing more on achieving individual advancement and electing candidates to office and evidencing less interest in building community organizations and challenging an unequal political and economic structure.

As the pace of world economic change, directed by the North American Free Trade Agreement (NAFTA) and other economic treaties, has impoverished millions, female workers' organizations such as Fuerze Unida and La Mujer Obrera and unions such as Service Employees International's Justice for Janitors have become important immigrants' rights advocates and important political training grounds for female workers (Yoon Louie, 2001).

In the new century, Chicano and Mexican American students in universities have enjoyed the benefits produced by Chicano participation in the Civil Rights Movement: a great lessening of discrimination (except in the quality of public schools), access to higher education, and access to careers and professions. Meanwhile, the majority of Chicano youth have been left behind in barrios with low-income jobs or no jobs at all. The identities of this new generation have emerged from diverse sources, including Chicano studies courses. The future directions they will take depend in part on the

Figure 3.5   Foreign-Born Population in the United States, 2000

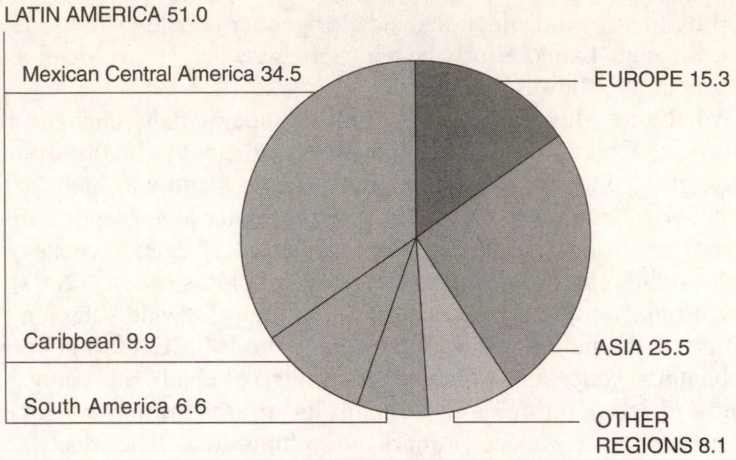

LATIN AMERICA 51.0

Mexican Central America 34.5

EUROPE 15.3

Caribbean 9.9

ASIA 25.5

South America 6.6

OTHER
REGIONS 8.1

Source: U.S. Census Bureau, Current Population Survey, March 2000.

perspectives they will develop through their careers, their participation in community service agencies, and their political struggles such as defense of bilingual education (Yoon Louie, 2001).

In response to globalization and immigration, the Latino population has grown rapidly, reaching 35 million people in 2000. Continued massive immigration into the Mexican and Mexican American communities has produced significant internal diversity (Trueba, 1999). In response to anti-immigrant campaigns, more than 1 million Latinos registered to vote for the first since 1994, fundamentally reshaping elections in several key states, including California, Texas, Florida, and New York. For example, there were 23 members of the Latino Caucus of California out of a total of 80 assembly persons and 40 senators.

The U.S. economy has increasingly come to rely on immigrants as a workforce. On May 1, 2005, over 1 million immigrants and their supporters marched in cities around the country to protest a proposed repressive immigration bill. This was one of the largest political demonstrations in U.S. history.

Although Latinos are exercising new political power and electing Hispanic officials in key states, the Latino high school dropout rate remains the highest in the nation (U.S. Department of Education, 2004). Poorly funded and inadequate schools contribute to the high poverty levels in the Mexican American and Puerto Rican communities. Gangs and youth crime, along with low wages and unemployment, contribute to urban decay.

Most urban schools contribute to inequality in our society by failing to serve Chicano/Mexican American students and African American students, particularly those from families living in poverty. The stark inequality of school opportunity reproduces inequality in our society. One group of students gets well-funded schools with credentialed teachers and textbooks that reflect their reality. African American, Chicano, immigrant, and poor working-class kids in urban areas are consigned to schools that are often starkly unequal (Kozol, 2005; Oakes & Rogers, 2007).

The curriculum is outside of these students' experiences, and often remedial, actually slowing them down in the name of helping them (see Chapter 12). In primary grades, a reductionist curriculum focuses only on reading and math, not providing enrichment, interest, science, and the arts. These schools become boring, a drudgery. One group of students has computers and Internet connections; the other group has few computers and spends too much time on drills and worksheets. Students in run-down schools, with boring, often unprepared teachers or overwhelmingly new, inexperienced teachers, are encouraged to find school irrelevant. They leave school and find jobs at the low end of the economy. And thus the cycle of poverty repeats itself.

Although children are presented with distinctly unequal schools, teachers, and opportunities, states then give them all the same tests and publish the scores in the newspaper. European American students have their culture validated and supported by the currently popular testing movement, whereas students from immigrant cultures are disempowered and prevented from achieving school success.

In 2006, there were 23 Hispanic members of the U.S. House of Representatives and 3 Hispanic members of the U.S. Senate. A major increase in Latino teachers and Hispanic elected officials has impacted immigration policy but has not significantly improved schools, employment, or health conditions for the growing Mexican American and Latino population. In 2006, there were over 1,170 immigration restriction bills introduced in state and local political contests, and citizenship application among Latinos increased by 65 percent. In 2006, a comprehensive reform of immigration law was proposed and failed in Congress.

A recent report from the Pew Research Center summarizes the rapidly changing demographics:

Nearly one in five Americans will be an immigrant by 2050. . . .

The major role of immigration in national growth builds upon the pattern of recent decades, during which immigrants and their U.S. born children and grandchildren accounted for most population increase. . . .

The Latino population, already the nation's largest minority group, will triple in size and will account for most of the nation's population growth from 2005 through 2050. Hispanics will make up 29% of the U.S. population in 2050, compared with 14% in 2005. (Passel & Cohn, U.S. Population Projections, 2005–2050. 2008, p. 1)

You can read the entire report at *www.pewresearch.org*.

Note that Latino children already make up over 29 percent of the students in major states, including California, Texas, New York, and Florida.

Chinese and Asian Immigration

The Chinese—and, later, other Asians—had yet a different and distinct immigration experience. The Chinese began coming to California in the 1840s, while it was still a part of Mexico, primarily because of economic hardships and violence in China. California's vast riches were taken from Mexico and incorporated into the United States after the War of 1848. By 1850, when California became a state, some 25,000 Chinese were working in the gold mines and providing basic laundry and cooking services to the rapidly growing immigrant population rushing to the gold fields of northern California. Exploited with xenophobic cruelty rooted in the racial ideology of the times, Chinese workers quickly learned to live in defensive enclaves, separate from the mining communities.

Anti-Chinese campaigns grew as the gold rush ended. The Chinese, who comprised 10 percent of California's population, became the target of political hate campaigns, terrorism, murder, and violence. These anti-Asian pressures culminated in 1882, when the U.S. Congress passed the first openly racial restriction on immigration, the Chinese Exclusion Act. While immigration from Europe was open and encouraged at this time, immigration from China was made illegal.

Between 1885 and 1894, the Japanese government supported emigration to Hawaii, sending more than 29,000 workers to labor on sugar cane plantations. These Japanese workers were followed by Filipinos. Many of these workers soon moved on to the U.S. mainland. By 1910, there were more than 72,000 (mostly male) Japanese working, often under brutal conditions, in California, Oregon, Washington, and Alaska (Takaki, 1989).

Japanese workers saved money and bought land to begin farming. They imported brides from Japan and established families and family farms. The economic success of the Japanese in the face of severe prejudice and discrimination led to increased hostility from the European American majority population. When the United States and Japan went to war in 1941, anti-Japanese hostility became so intense that all Japanese Americans on the West Coast were arrested and placed in detention camps for the duration of the war (Takaki, 1989). Of all racial and ethnic groups, only Japanese and Native Americans have faced this kind of forced incarceration.

According to the U.S. Bureau of the Census (2000), Filipinos (1,850,314), Koreans (1,076,872), Asian/Pacific Islanders (389,917), Vietnamese (1,122,528), and numerous other groups have moved to the United States in the last 40 years, often in connection with our military installations and operations in the Pacific (see Figure 3.5).

Although some Japanese Americans, Chinese Americans, Koreans, Filipinos, and the first wave of Vietnamese refugees have achieved economic prosperity, Takaki (1989) shows that other Asian/Pacific Islander immigrants and their children continue to face hostility and discrimination. A stereotype of a "model minority" hides the poverty inflicted on many (San Juan, 2002). Anti-Asian attacks, discrimination, and even murders increased as Japan became a major economic competitor with the United States in the 1980s and 1990s. The May 1992 racial rebellion and looting in Los Angeles particularly involved attacks on Korean immigrant store owners by African American youths ("Siege of L.A.," 1992).

As the pace of world economic change has impoverished millions, workers' organizations such as the Asian Immigrant Women's Advocates (AIWA) have become important to Asian immigrants' rights in the United States. More than 100,000 immigrants from Korea, Vietnam, Thailand, China, and elsewhere work in garment industry sweatshops and restaurants enduring illegally low levels of pay and exploitative conditions. Women in these industries have organized worker defense committees to aggressively defend workers' rights and to struggle for immigration rights and reform (Yoon Louie, 2001).

The Asian American communities became an increasing powerful political force in the 1990s, mobilized both to defend immigrants' rights and to protect programs the teach children English in public schools. The welfare and immigration reforms of 1996 impacted these communities particularly severely.

As a consequence of poverty and political repression in some countries, Asian immigration continues to grow rapidly (E. San Juan, Jr., 2002). Recent immigrants have been the backbone of much of the U.S. development of high-technology business, including Jerry Yang of Yahoo and the founders and leaders of technology innovators Intel, Google, and Sun. Immigrants started over 25 percent of all high-technology businesses in the United States.

In addition to permitting permanent immigrants, U.S. immigration law established H-1B professional employment visas, which in 2000 were issued to 195,000 new temporary immigrants, most of whom worked in medicine or the computer industry. Asians from India and Pakistan make up a substantial portion of these migrants (Phillips, 2002). After their temporary status expires, many remain in the United States through marriage and/or a change of their immigration status.

Immigrants from Indochina

The United States was engaged in a war in Vietnam from 1962 to 1975. Since the defeat of the U.S.-backed regime in South Vietnam in 1975, the United States has received a major stream of refugees, averaging more than 70,000 persons per year, leading to a Vietnamese population of 1,122,528 in 2000 (U.S. Bureau of the Census).

Vietnamese refugees came in three groups. Those in the first wave (1975–1978) were primarily from the elite classes or were persons employed by the United States while we were in Vietnam. Those coming in the second wave (1979–1982) were often Hoa (ethnic Chinese) and Catholics from the middle class. The third wave (1983–1996) comprised primarily poorer families from farming and working-class backgrounds. Vietnamese students from the first and second waves of refugees were significantly successful in U.S. schools (Centrie, 2004).

As a result of poverty and underdevelopment in Vietnam and of U.S. immigration policy, which encourages family reunification, immigration from Vietnam continues today. This immigration provides a continual renewal of Vietnamese culture, values, and language within U.S. Vietnamese communities.

The Hmong and Laotian Immigrants The Hmong and the Mien are cultural groups from Laos and the mountains of Vietnam. In 1976, the first of more than 145,000 Hmong refugees came to the United States under the Indochina Migration and Refugee Assistance Act of 1975 (Public Law 94-23). Thousands of Hmong had acted as special guerilla units, mostly in Laos, helping the United States in the war in Vietnam and Laos. The Hmong became particular targets of repression after the Communists won control of Laos and Vietnam.

The first Hmong to arrive were war refugees. Thousands suffered incredible terror and hardship, with entire families being killed, while trying to reach refugee camps in Thailand. Many families had to stay in the camps for up to six years. The extended and brutal terror, along with the long periods spent in refugee camps, divided families and broke up traditional family support systems.

As refugees, the Hmong received several kinds of financial support and assistance denied to other immigrants. By 1990, they were often sponsored by U.S. church groups and charitable organizations. Large concentrations were found in California (more than 65,000), Wisconsin (33,791), and Minnesota (41,800). After their original settlement, many moved a second time to be near other Hmong. In the 2000 Census there were over 169,000 Hmong refugees and their children in the United States. Hmong families tend to have many children. The children born in the United States are U.S. citizens, entitled to all of the rights of citizens but not to the special assistance given to refugees.

One group of Hmong and Laotian students has now been in the United States for a number of years. Years of acculturation and assimilation have produced conflicts within refugee families. Children raised in the United States have faced increased cultural conflict, at times leading them to join gangs. School authorities have been drawn into several disputes between young people adjusting to the U.S. system and families wishing to maintain older systems of respect and family loyalty (Bliatout, Downing, Lewis, & Yang, 1988). In 2004, an additional 15,000 Hmong refugees were admitted to the United States. These new refugees need language services and other special services in schools. The dispersal of Hmong and other refugees to several states is illustrated in the following chart for Minnesota:

Refugee Population in Minnesota as of 1999

Hmong	60,000
Vietnamese	22,000
Somali	15,000
Cambodian	8,500
Laotian	8,500
Former Soviet Republic	6,000

Excellent material for teachers to use to explain immigration can be found at www.mnadvocates.org.

Anti-Immigrant Politics

As each immigrant group grew, so did fear, strong prejudice, and hostility in the majority European American population. Irish, Jewish, Chinese, and Japanese immigrants were each described at one time with stereotypes characterizing them as dirty, uneducated, secretive, and subversive. Racial stereotyping, scapegoating, and violence have continued as a sustained theme in U.S. history, often encouraged by the press and so-called fraternal organizations.

The U.S. economy periodically passes through difficult periods—for example, 1991–1993, 2001–2002, and 2007–2009— and each time anti-immigrant campaigns become popular. In 1994, California passed the highly restrictive Proposition 187, portions of which were later found to be unconstitutional. California Governor Pete Wilson won reelection in 1994 in large part by using a hostile, divisive campaign that blamed the state's economic woes on the Mexican and Mexican American populations (Adams, 1995; Chávez, 1998).

This 1994 California election demonstrated that anti-immigrant campaigns can mobilize angry White voters (Adams, 1995; Chávez, 1998). In contrast, in New York and Texas in 1994 and 1998, both also led by Republican governors, immigrant-bashing never became as popular, and anti-immigrant fervor was marginalized to extremist groups such as the Ku Klux Klan rather than becoming part of the mainstream political debate.

Anti-immigrant politics continues as a popular theme in U.S. political life with the Immigration Reform Act of 1996, the Welfare Reform Act of 1996, and California's 1998 Proposition 227, which banned bilingual education. Some 25 states have passed "Official English" laws, and hundreds of local governments have passed legislation to punish undocumented immigrants in various ways for being in the country—such as denying them driver's licenses. In response, the percentage of Latino voters increased dramatically by the year 2006, particularly in border states.

The production of unemployment, inequality, and poverty around the world continues under the international economic policy known as neo-liberalism. Trade agreements like NAFTA have actually increased poverty for many. NAFTA and free trade have also produced some economic winners. Many corporations moved high-paying jobs to Mexico to cut their labor costs and to increase their profits. In Mexico, several new billionaires were created.

But NAFTA created a loss of at least 879,000 jobs in the United States, and over 1 million jobs disappeared in Mexico. People who lost their jobs moved to the cities in Mexico or to the United States—producing immigration. Since NAFTA was signed, predominantly U.S.-owned transnational corporations have eliminated hundreds of thousands jobs in Mexico and moved them to Vietnam and China, where even more repressive states make labor even cheaper. It is this poverty that drives workers in the developing nations to reluctantly seek better jobs and a better life for their families in the United States and other industrialized nations.

The "push" for mass immigration from the developing nations can best be stemmed by allowing these economies to create productive jobs. The immigrant rights movement in the United States is an important civil rights movement of our generation. Its demand for human rights for all working people challenges the dominant economic ideology, known as "free trade," both in the United States and in the developing world.

Native Americans

Native Americans (indigenous people), of course, were not immigrants, although in their own lands they have often been treated worse than immigrants.

By 1840, the U.S. government had driven Native American tribes, with the exception of the important Iroquois Confederation in Canada and New York, from most of the arable lands east of the Mississippi, but the native peoples of the Southwest and Florida resisted domination well into the 20th century. The growing Spanish and Mexican population of the Southwest intermingled with Native Americans to establish cities and some farming areas, but Native Americans continued to dominate large areas of land. The Navajo (Dineh), the largest remaining tribe, survive in regions of Arizona and New Mexico. The 19 Pueblo tribes have maintained their culture and civilization despite Spanish, Mexican, and European American attempts to defeat them. Most of the Cherokee were forced from their lands in the East and resettled in Oklahoma, beside the Kiowa. The Lakota Sioux maintain established societies and cultures in the Dakotas. A host of other tribes maintain their societies in the intermountain regions. Along the coast in California and Oregon, Native American peoples such as the Chumash and Miwok were virtually eliminated.

One by one, the diverse Native American societies signed treaties and became domestic dependent nations. They signed these treaties to protect the limited land and water rights assigned to them, but few of these rights have been honored by the states or the U.S. government.

Gradually, political control of Native American nations was established and maintained through the Bureau of Indian Affairs. The bureau penetrated the tribes through control of schooling, allocation of "missionary" rights, and deliberate policies aimed at terminating tribes or confining them to reservations on unproductive land.

Today, of the 2.5 million native peoples, approximately 34 percent live on reservations (**U.S. Census Bureau** 2006). With few exceptions, they live in extreme economic poverty. Reservation economies and standards of living often resemble the economies of the most exploited regions of the world (Gray, 2002).

A few tribal nations—the Cherokee, the Navajo, some of the Pueblo, and the Cree—have successfully pursued economic development through education and extended legal struggles to control and profit from the vast natural resources (oil, coal, uranium, etc.) located on their reservations. Recently, other tribes have sought economic opportunity by operating gambling casinos on their land. Nevertheless, for many Native American children, extreme poverty, degradation, disease, and both cultural and physical suicide are the legacy of the conquest of their people.

Public schooling, whether on or off the reservation, often serves a contradictory function in Native American communities. Clearly, schooling provides opportunities to enter the macroculture and to seek economic progress. But even more than other subjugated groups, Native American societies continue to experience cultural repression in the public school system. Many schools and teachers have imposed a colonized perspective on Native American children. Only in the last 20 years have some tribes achieved control over their own schools and colleges, providing needed cross-cultural educational experiences.

One of the most basic struggles of native peoples is to preserve their families, their tribes, their languages, and their tribal cultures (Momaday, 2002).

Some native areas, such as that of the Navajo nation, are rich in the natural resources of oil, gas, and uranium, yet they lack even electrical power for their own people. Native tribes have been in a long-range struggle against corporate development, which often exploits the resources on their land without providing growth and economic opportunities for their own people.

Native people have unique legal rights to their land and resources by the federal treaty and trust relationship based on Article 1, Section 8 of the U.S. Constitution (Gray, 2002).

A shocking example of abuse of the federal trust was revealed in the current lawsuit *Cobell v. Norton*, in which a three-judge federal appeals court found that the Bureau of Indian Affairs failed to account for and/or repay money paid by corporations to the U.S. government for extracting minerals. The corporations had apparently paid the monies to the federal government, but the funds never made it to assist native peoples. The appeals court traced the history of the Indian trust accounts for almost 100 years and concluded: "It would be difficult to find a more historically mismanaged federal program than the individual Indian money trust" (2001).

Similar issues of preservation of sovereignty rights are important among the native Hawaiian population (Au, 2001).

In 2004, the Smithsonian Institution opened the National Museum of the American Indian on the Mall in Washington, DC, bringing together a substantial history of native peoples from all of the Americas and providing material to teachers and classrooms at *www.AmericanIndian.si.edu*. Members of U.S. tribes and indigenous peoples from all of the Americas participated in the September 2007 session of the United Nations General Assembly in Geneva, Switzerland, where the United Nations adopted an important Declaration on the Rights of Indigenous Peoples.

Racial Ideology and Democracy

The specific and diverse historical experiences of each group explain a part of our present racial divisiveness and crisis. Although seldom recorded in public school history books and university courses, popular struggles against racism and toward cultural democracy have also occurred throughout our history. An accurate and comprehensive understanding of history and current race relations will help teachers and this generation of students to build a more appropriate curriculum and more supportive classroom relationships.

Schools teach ideas. Systems of ideas are called *ideologies*. Teachers in their teaching decisions model an ideology of either racism or pluralism, an ideology of either equality or inequality. The dominant ideology in our society supports the present social structure and the resulting stratification of opportunity. Most current school curricula reinforce ideas that legitimize the present distribution of power, money, and privilege. Because U.S. society is currently stratified by race, gender, and class, schools tend to legitimize the racial divisions as normal and natural, even logical and scientific (Feagin, 2001). Power and money—not logic, not science—determine that some students receive a quality education and others a poor education. Multicultural education is a school reform process that challenges the continuing domination of this inherited privilege.

Multicultural education offers an alternative worldview, an alternative ideology. It argues that schools, along with church and family, are potential sources of knowledge and thus sources of power in a democratic society. Schools should promote the growth and extension of democracy rather than sustaining the current inequalities of opportunity. Advocates of multicultural education emphasize the values inherent in and unique to democratic societies: citizenship participation, empowerment, liberty, and equality of opportunity. We recognize that developing a democratic worldview of mutual respect and shared opportunity is difficult in a society divided by race and class. Yet we are hopeful. The school system is one of the few vehicles we presently have that permit us to work toward mutual respect and cooperation as well as political, economic, social, and cultural democracy.

Our once resource-based economy is evolving into a knowledge-based economy that is increasingly dependent on international trade (and therefore rewarding bilingualism). Knowledge of diverse cultures has ever-increasing financial value. As economic changes accelerate, people who have knowledge will gain financial and political power. Children who acquire knowledge and skills and access to computer technology, in school will get ahead. Children who suffer in low-quality schools, have little access to technology, and receive a low-quality education will suffer persistent underemployment and limited economic opportunities.

The European American ideological bias, or *Eurocentrism*, in current public school curricula maintains inappropriate privileges for European American children significantly by avoiding issues of race. Children from all ethnic and cultural backgrounds deserve to see themselves and their families represented in the curriculum in order to see schooling as a path toward a prosperous future. Many young African American and Latino students experience failure and frustration in school; they fall behind in basic study skills. Omission from the curriculum and consistent school failure can lead to an erosion of students' self-esteem. Thus, a cycle of failure begins. The persistent academic failure of African Americans, Latinos, and Native Americans leads some of these students to conclude that schools are negative, intrusive institutions rather than gateways out of poverty and discrimination.

As economic crises in urban areas continue to cause specific neighborhoods to decline and schools to deteriorate, some students turn to resistance. They respond to school failure with open hostility. Some African American, Latino, and alienated White youth have developed cultures and identities of resistance to school authority, rebelling against the school's negative treatment. At times, resistance is necessary and positive, as in the development of a Chicano identity distinct from a Mexican identity. Unfortunately, with little adult support and guidance, many of these young people are choosing destructive forms of identity involving gangs, violence, and drugs. Schools become war zones. Gangs and youth culture make instruction difficult in some urban schools, depriving even dedicated students of their future economic opportunities.

Individuals and families experience school domination or empowerment in their own manner. The ethnic and racial experiences of African Americans are substantially different from those of Latinos and Latinas. The experiences of racial minorities such as African Americans, Chicanos, and Puerto Ricans can be significantly different from the experiences of immigrant minorities from Latin America, such as Mexican, Venezuelan, or Columbian or Asia, such as the Japanese, Chinese, and Vietnamese (Almaguer, 1994; Feagin, 2001.

As a consequence of the increasing hostility, divisiveness, and racial conflict in our society, schools can become cauldrons of individual and intergroup conflict if social justice and nonviolence are not promoted. Figure 3.6 illustrates the complex interrelationships among race, class, gender, culture, and personal histories.

The struggle against racism and for multicultural education calls on teachers and schools to participate in the painful creation of a new, more democratic society. Teachers

Figure 3.6   Interrelationships of Race, Class, Gender, Culture, and Personal History

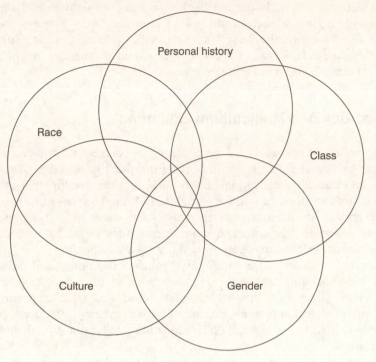

who are democratic seek to claim the promise of the American dream of equal opportunity for all. In part, the struggle calls for a change in worldview. The view of cultural democracy and pluralism presented in this chapter replaces stereotypes of racial ideology and challenges Eurocentric views of history.

The United States is and has been an immigrant and pluralistic society. The current struggle for multicultural education is one more step in the 200-year-old effort to build a more democratic society. Multicultural education poses this challenge: Will teachers and schools recognize that we are a pluralistic, multilingual society in and change our curriculum, testing, ability grouping, and hiring? Will teachers choose to empower children from all communities and races and from both sexes? Or will schools continue to deliver knowledge, power, and privilege primarily to members of the European American majority culture at the expense of students from other cultures?

When students study the ideals of the Declaration of Independence and the U.S. Constitution, they learn a worldview that includes a commitment to democratic opportunity. They are taught an ideology of the "American creed." Multicultural education insists that schools serve as an arena where we achieve the promises of the Declaration of Independence: "We hold these truths to be self evident, That all men are created equal and are endowed by their creator with certain unalienable rights, that among these rights are life, liberty and the pursuit of happiness. . . ."

Throughout the nation's history, citizens have faced conflicts between their ideals and their national reality. Important battles, such as the fight to end slavery and the campaign to recognize women's right to vote, have been won. Some of the battles have been lost, as when several diverse Native American nations failed to survive. But the struggle to create a democratic society continues, and the manner in which we instruct our young people is crucial to that struggle.

The Future of Democracy and Multicultural Education

Achieving political change toward democracy has been a difficult process. Advances were made by the Civil Rights Movement during the 1960s and 1970s, including an emphasis on more equal educational opportunity and the development of multicultural education; however, the end of the civil rights era brought attacks on these advances in the 1980s and 1990s. As conservatives gained local, state, and national political power by electing governors, legislators, and Presidents, they began to advance their social agenda, which includes a particular view of history and schooling.

An ideology of conservative educational "reform" has dominated public discussion since 1982, emphasizing excellence for a few students and pushing aside discussions of equality. Public support for funding education to advance equal opportunity declined. Budgets for vocational and career education were dramatically reduced. School segregation returned to many cities. Public education itself came under attack from the political right.

The victory of George W. Bush in the disputed presidential election of 2000 brought educational conservatives back to power. The powerful reform strategies of standards and accountability included in the Bush Administration's No Child Left Behind Act of 2001, and originally favored by politicians in both political parties, significantly marginalize efforts at multicultural curriculum reform. The election of Barack Obama as President and a Democratic Party majority in Congress may change this direction.

The current efforts to bring about multicultural school reform challenge conservatives' hegemony of ideas and power.

The Way Ahead

The long struggle against racism and cultural oppression continues today. Multicultural education is a part of that struggle. Neo-conservative educational leaders, including Alan Bloom, E. D. Hirsch, Lynne Cheney, Diane Ravitch, Chester Finn, and William Bennett, promote their own careers and resist the change to a more inclusive curriculum. They assert that multicultural education is political and divisive.

One reality of school reform movements is that they come and go—and then often return with different vocabulary. This time, attacks against the idea of equal educational opportunity will fail. As Martin Luther King, Jr., said: "I am convinced that we shall overcome because the moral arc of the universe is long, but it bends toward justice" (1986, p. 207). The demographics of a young, immigrant population assure us that students will be more diverse. These students will speak more languages, not fewer. All of the students in our schools need to study diversity to understand and to participate productively in our emerging global economic dependency.

Multicultural education is an ideological project to move the schools toward cultural democracy. It reasserts the traditional role of the common school to provide economic opportunity for all. This effort necessarily operates within the current contested and disputed worldview of what the appropriate role and functions are for public schools in a democratic society.

Businesses need well-trained workers—not high school dropouts. Unless education improves its ability to prepare many more students, including students from diverse cultures, our economy will continue to suffer a skills shortage. School failure reinforces institutionalized racism and deepens the employment crisis and divisions in our society.

At its best, multicultural education is a process of questioning the dominant school culture, revising the curriculum, and struggling to create greater justice and equity in schools. It is a continuation of the Civil Rights Movement for our children, an effort to create a more democratic, equitable society. Multiracial and antiracist politics and education are central to building a more democratic society. School reform efforts that ignore race and ethnic diversity, and the diversity of experiences students have in school, will fail. Without quality educational opportunities for all, there will be no economic justice. Without economic justice, there will be no social peace. Multicultural education offers a positive alternative to current divisions in our society by preparing all students for dialogue, mutual respect, productive employment, and democratic participation.

What can I do in the classroom?

1. You can learn about, know about, care about, and respect the cultures of your students. Ask them about issues that you do not understand.

2. It is important that you build positive relationships with your students.

3. You can adopt the position that diverse cultures provide opportunities for learning, not problems.

4. As a teacher, you need to support high expectations for all—and plan to provide students with success in achieving these expectations. If you simply hold high expectations and the students fail the lessons, this is not culturally responsive teaching. You need to plan and teach so that the students succeed. If the lesson produces failure, redesign the lesson.

5. You can create lesson plans and lessons that excite, engage, and encourage students.

6. The literature read by your students in the primary grades should include characters from their ethnic and cultural groups. Plan for reading success.

7. You can reorganize your teaching of history and social studies to present a comprehensive, multiethnic view of events. Excellent materials and videos are available from Teaching Tolerance at www.teachingtolerance.org.

8. To be a culturally responsive teacher, seek communication with parents and community members.

9. It is important that you incorporate, use, and encourage students to use their first languages. This will not slow down their English acquisition (see Chapter 11).

There are more ideas in the section on "Teaching Strategies for Use with Your Students" at the end of this chapter.

Summary

The classrooms in U.S. public schools commonly encompass a cultural, linguistic, and ethnic diversity found in few nations. The United States has suffered a long and troubled history of racial conflicts and oppressions. The diverse historical experiences of African Americans, Latinos, Asians, Native Americans, and European Americans explain a part of our present racial divisiveness and our economic and social crises.

A racial ideology emerged in the United States from the cauldron of expansion, settlement, slavery, displacement, migration, and immigration. This racial ideology permeates our history, our view of ourselves, and our society and distorts efforts at school reform. Multicultural education is a part of the 200-year-old struggle to foster democratic opportunity in this society. Multicultural education opposes racial ideology with an ideology of cultural pluralism and equal educational opportunity.

Questions over the Chapter

1. Explain the difference between *race* and *culture*.
2. Define *racism*.
3. Give three examples of racial inequality in schools.
4. How is institutionalized racism different from prejudice?
5. How did racism affect the U.S. tradition of a two-party political system?
6. List four ways that the public school curriculum reflects the macroculture.

Activities for Further Study of Race and Racism

1. Make a list of the advantages or privileges you enjoy because you were born and educated in the United States. Seek out a student in your program who was born and educated in another country. Ask that student to make a similar list, reflecting his or her own background. Compare your answers. (For further information on this topic, see United Nations Children's Fund, *The State of the World's Children*, 2008)
2. Compare the ethnic and gender makeup of your own teacher preparation program with the population of the region where the program is located and with the student population in the local schools. Explain whatever differences you find.

3. In cooperative groups, describe your most vivid memory of racial or ethnic differences. Who was the "other" group? What were the characteristics of this "other"? Who was the source of information about this "other"?

4. In cooperative groups, describe a time when you were separated into racial, ethnic, class, ability, or gender groups. Describe your memory of that event.

5. In a group or individually, assume the points of view of the following different Native American tribes: (a) one of the Plains tribes (Sioux, Crow, etc.), (b) the Pueblo tribe, and (c) the Cherokee tribe. Describe the arrival and settlement of European Americans in the territory of each group.

6. Since 1965, immigration to the United States from Mexico, Central America, South America, Asia, and the Middle East has increased significantly. Immigration reform and control have been major political issues. What is your own view on this increase in immigration? What is good about it? What is bad about it? Should immigration be controlled more?

Teaching Strategies for Use with Your Students

1. Present accurate, truthful information on the separate roles of race and class in determining school and economic opportunity.

2. Study racism and the forces that sustain racial privilege.

3. Use these culturally responsive teaching strategies:
   • Maintain high academic expectations. All students can learn. The task is to plan lessons so that all students will learn.
   • Use instructional materials that include consideration of the students' own realities.
   • Use active teaching strategies for reading, writing, speaking, and listening.

4. Plan strategies to develop the pro-democratic values of equality and the dignity of each individual.

5. At all grade levels, the history/social studies lessons and literature lessons should include the stories and viewpoints of the students' own communities. Students need to see themselves in the stories.

6. Help students to analyze the interactive and complex nature of race, gender, and class oppression.

7. There is interesting material for teachers on immigration at www.mnadvocates.org.

8. Provide all students with instruction in a language they comprehend.

4

With Liberty and Justice for Some: Democracy, Class Relations, and Schools

Nowadays it is fashionable to talk about race or gender;
the uncool subject is class. It's the subject that makes us all tense,
nervous, uncertain about where we stand.
Many citizens of this nation, myself included, have been and are
afraid to think about class. . . .
As a nation we are afraid to have a dialogue about class even though the ever-widening gap
between the rich and poor has already set the stage for a sustained class warfare.

bell hooks, Where We Stand: Class Matters, 2000

Social Class and the Crisis of Poverty

This chapter will examine the economic problems of poverty and social class to further understand the problem of democracy and failing schools.

A basic goal for democratic education is to provide students with equal opportunity. Being African American is not a problem. There are thousands of successful African American businesspeople and professionals and political leaders. Being Mexican American or Puerto Rican or Hispanic is not the fundamental problem. Mexican American and Hispanic businesspeople own and direct major corporations; they are doctors, nurses, professors, congresspersons, senators, and public school teachers. They are represented in all the major professions.

Major progress has been made in racial and ethnic integration, particularly in the southeastern region of the United States, since the 1960s. We now have a distinct African American, Latino, and Asian middle class and even an upper middle class. Now that we have significant racial and ethnic integration in the professions, we can see more clearly the class issues in our economy and in our schools.

Dr. Martin Luther King, Jr., gives his "I Have a Dream" speech during the March on Washington, August 28, 1963.
Photo: National Archives.

Prior to the Civil Rights Movement struggle (1954–1968), writers and social scientists studied poverty, but they saw race. That is, poverty and the cycle of poverty were clearly evident, but most observers described poverty as a racial problem. Researchers looked at poverty and saw ethnicity. Today, particularly since Hurricane Katrina and the economic recession, the poor and the marginalized are more visible. We know that millions of families work more than 40 hours per week and live in poverty. As described by Jonathan Kozol in Chapter 3, poverty and poverty conditions are particularly telling in schools. One group of students gets well-functioning schools, and a second group gets overcrowded, underfunded, poverty-stricken schools. This difference is not about race alone; it is about race and poverty interacting to produce a cycle of poverty—and a cycle of low-performing schools.

Social class, then, is a major barrier to equal opportunity in schools. The issue is school success and school opportunity and access to a college education when the student is African American and poor or Mexican American or White and working class.

To understand economic class, we need to examine the economy. Economist Robert Reich (2007), formerly of the Clinton Administration, describes the major economic trends of an earlier age:

Roughly between 1945 and 1975, America struck a remarkable accommodation between capitalism and democracy. It combined a hugely productive economic system with a broadly responsive and widely admired political system. America (the U.S.) in those years achieved its highest degree of income equality (since measurements have been available). It generated a larger proportion of good-paying jobs than before or since, and more economic security than ever for more of its people. Perhaps not coincidentally, in these years Americans also expressed high confidence in democracy and trust in government, both of which sharply declined in

Figure 4.1   **Family Income Growth by Quintile**

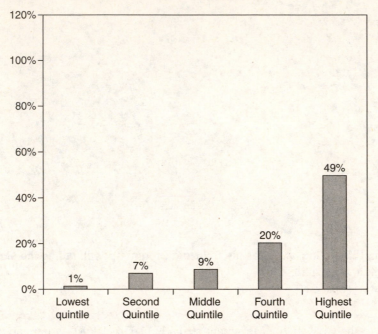

Source: Author's analysis of U.S. Bureau of the Census data. Adapted from *The State of Working America, 2006/2007*, by Lawrence Mishel, Jared Bernstein, and Sylvia Allegretto. Copyright 2007. Cornell University. Used by permission of the publisher, Cornell University Press.

subsequent years. That singular success and that powerful promise extended the moral authority of the American system throughout the world. In contrast to Soviet communism, America became an exemplar of both political freedom and suburban middle-class affluence. (p. 15)

We first need to recognize that our society is increasingly divided along economic lines (Bernstein, McNichol, & Nicholas, 2008; see also Figure 4.1). The wealthy live in luxury housing in affluent neighborhoods, professional workers live in comfortable middle-class suburbs, and working-class and poverty-stricken people make do with deteriorating and substandard housing in the central cities and many rural areas.

Since the late 1970s, and particularly since 1994, our economy has undergone a fundamental change. We are increasingly becoming a part of the global economy. In the United States, poverty has remained high, and inequality has increased, while job security and income security have disappeared for millions. Living standards have eroded for working people, while public services such as public education are underfunded.

It has been the working poor who have been most hurt by the flight of good-paying union jobs to other countries. Clothing, apparel, toy, and manufacturing jobs have been moved out of the United States and now even out of Mexico to other low-wage locations. The Vietnamese workers who produce Nike sneakers get only $.60–$.80 per hour. The shoes cost $70. The Chinese production line workers who make most of our computers get paid about the same. Most of the benefits of economic growth in the age of globalization have gone to a small number of people who own the large corporations.

Global competition regularly drives jobs out of the United States to other countries where unions are almost nonexistent. Those U.S. workers who lose their jobs are understandably resentful of that loss as well as the loss of opportunity for themselves and their families. Political campaigns among the middle and working classes have blamed immigrants and affirmative action for the problems in the economy rather than recognizing the effects of the new global economy on working people.

These economic changes have significant implications for students. In the 1960s and 1970s, most working people in the United States shared prosperity. They got good jobs, particularly when they graduated from high school. They made good products, received a decent wage and health care insurance, and were able to buy a home and raise their families. Since the late 1970s, roughly the time of the Reagan Revolution, this is no longer true. Now students must get a better education, usually from a college or technical school, in order to compete for fewer jobs. Students cannot assume that they will have a safe, stable, secure job in their future. Students who do not do well in school or who leave school are being left behind.

A recent biannual report titled *The State of Working America, 2006/2007* notes that while productivity has increased, living standards for the middle classes and the working poor have declined. Working families continue to work hard to make ends meet, to afford a college education for their children, and to improve their living standards—but the struggle to stay even gets harder and harder (Mishel, Bernstein, & Allegretto, 2007).

Figure 4.1 illustrates the growing inequality in our society. The report *Pulling Apart: A State-by-State Analysis of Income Trends* (Bernstein et al., 2008) describes the last recent economic declines as follows:"Income inequality grew over the last two decades due to both economic trends and government policies. Wages and salaries grew faster for those at the top of the income scale. Various factors explain growing wage inequality including long periods of higher-than-average unemployment, globalization, the shift from manufacturing jobs to low wage service jobs, immigration, the weakening of unions, and the declining value of the minimum wage..." (p. 1). Report coauthor Elizabeth McNichol adds: "Rising inequality raises basic issues of fairness, and harms the nation's economy and political system. It dampens economic prosperity as incomes stagnate for tens of millions of average Americans and it threatens to widen the nation's political cleavages, generating more cynicism about political instutions" (Bernstein, McNichol, & Nicholas, 2008, p. 1).

While their wages have remained stagnant, many working people have lost health benefits and job security in the growing global market economy (Mishel et al., 2007). In the recession of 2001 and again in that of 2007–2009, the U.S. economy slowed, leaving millions without work. A housing crisis caused over $80 billion in losses in equities and the stock market. By 2008, the U.S. economy clearly had entered a recession. There was a real decline in income and the standard of living, particularly for those below the median income. In the crisis, some CEOs of major firms like Merrill Lynch were forced to leave their positions due to equity losses, but they received huge payouts, some as much as $160 million in stock options, and some hedge fund managers made a profit of over $2.5 billion in a single year. Meanwhile, the media and political leaders told us that our standard of living was continuing to improve. But as *The State of Working America, 2006-2007* (Mishel et al., 2007) reveals, the economic problems of the earlier decades continue to produce growing poverty and inequality (see Figure 4.1). In 2005, the *median family income* reached $56,194; however, it was $59,124 for Whites, $35,594 for Blacks, and $37,867 for Latinos (Mishel et al., 2007, p. 51). We have a stagnant national economy and a recession for the vast majority of working people. In this recession, as in prior ones, declining tax revenues hurt our schools, forcing school budget cuts, increases in class size, and teacher layoffs. Most efforts at school improvement that cost money came to an end.

Economists call each 20 percent segment of the population in Figure 4.1 a quintile (one-fifth). The top fifth, of families making over $98,000 per year, are doing quite well. For a detailed description of the U.S. upper class, families making over $170,000 per year in 2003, from opposing perspectives, see Domhoff (2002) and Phillips (2002). In the period covered by the figure, families in the upper quintile increased their income by 49 percent. The middle quintiles, the heart of the middle class, are having a more difficult time. The income of the middle quintile—families making $42,000–$65,000 per year—has grown 9 percent. Income in the fourth quintile—households earning $65,000–$98,000 dollars per year—has grown 20 percent.

The growth of income of the middle quintiles was reversed during the Bush recession of 2001–2003 and the economic crisis evidenced by a falling stock market and the corporate bankruptcies of Enron, WorldCom, and others. The middle quintiles, which include most teachers, nurses, and other professionals, are working harder and harder in an attempt to maintain and protect their current standard of living, health care, and retirement pensions (Pulling Apart, April 2008).

In the 1950s, it was common in most White families to have only one adult working in the paid labor force. One income was enough to buy a home and to raise a family. Today, many in the middle class achieve a higher standard of living by having husband and wife both working for pay outside the home. Stressed families have an important impact on children in school.

The second quintile of the middle class, which would include many teachers who are single-parent heads of households, has gained just 7 percent over the last 24 years. These are people whose household income is between $24,000 and $42,000 per year (in 2003 dollars). This lower part of the middle class is at times referred to as the working class. Working-class individuals in many fields (machinists, assembly line workers, etc.) watch as their jobs are sent overseas, their job security is lost, their taxes remain high, and the economic opportunities for their children erode (Mishel et al., 2007). There will be more on class divisions in the following section.

The growing economic divisions in our society between winners and losers occur because the economy in which we live and work is changing dramatically (Bernstien, McNichols, & Nicholas, 2008; Stiglitz, 2002). For example, most jobs created during the last two decades have been in the low-paid service sector of the economy (teaching assistants, truck drivers, nurses' assistants, janitors). These workers provide services to people and to corporations. The jobs are often part-time or temporary. Even manufacturing jobs in the clothing and computer industries pay poor wages and often do not include job security, health benefits, and retirement plans. These low-wage jobs do not allow working people to provide for their families, to buy homes, or to save for their children to go to college.

The Crisis of Poverty

Many low-wage workers—and their children—are threatened by poverty. The loss of a job or a serious illness in the family could quickly destroy their home and lifestyle. Almost 47 million people in the United States do not have health insurance (U.S. Bureau of the Census, 2007).

In the excellent book *Raise the Floor: Wages and Policies That Work for All of US:* (2001), Holly Sklar, Laryssa Mykyta, and Susan Wefald describe life for members of the working class (see Figure 4.2). And for our purposes, we need to point out that the working poor send their children to school, and you may be their teacher.

The global economic changes of the last decade dramatically affected the work lives of the poor and the educational opportunities for their children. We need to recognize

Figure 4.2 **Raise the Floor**

They work five days a week, often more.

They work full time in the richest nation on earth, yet they can't make ends meet.

They can't make ends meet because their wages are too low.

They are health care aides who can't afford health insurance.

They work in the food industry, but depend upon food banks to help feed their children.

They are child care teachers who don't make enough to save for their own children's education.

They work at vacation resorts, but they have no paid vacation.

They care for the elderly, but they have no pensions.

They work hard.

They work in the backbreaking work of picking lettuce and tomatoes, peaches and strawberries.

They work in the meatpacking plants at jobs so grueling and dangerous they call out for a sequel to *The Jungle.*

They work in fast food places and the finest restaurants where wealthy executives write off lavish meals as business expenses.

They work ringing up purchases at discount stores and luxury boutiques.

They work cleaning the homes and hotel rooms of people who make more in a day than they make in a year.

They work hard and they can't make ends meet in the richest nation on earth.

Most Americans think that's wrong.

Most Americans think work should pay enough to support workers and their families. If you work full time, you should not be poor. It's as simple as that. No one should be working poor.

Source: With Permission, *Raise the Floor: Wages and Policies That Work for Us All* (2001). The Ms. Foundation.

that the economy is working very well for the top 5 percent of the business owners and the corporate elite (Reich, 2007). Conservative writer Kevin Phillips, in *Wealth and Democracy: A Political History of the American Rich* (2002), describes the era: "Between 1979 and 1989 the portion of the nation's wealth held by the top 1 percent doubled from 22 percent to 39 percent. By the mid-nineties, some economists estimated that the top 1 percent had captured 70 percent of all earnings growth since the mid-seventies" (p. xiii). After this came the stock market crash and the fraud revealed in the Enron, Global Crossing, WorldCom, and similar scandals (Black, 2005; Greider, 2002).

Meanwhile, more than one out of six children in the United States lives in poverty—a higher rate than that accepted in other industrialized nations. By race and ethnicity, 33 percent of African American children, 27 percent of Latino children, and 10 percent of White (non-Hispanic) and Asian children lived in poverty in 2006 (Federal Interagency Forum on Child and Family Statistics, 2008). An annual study by the U.S. Department of Agriculture found that child hunger rose by over 50% in 2007 and is expected to get much worse as the recession of 2008–2009 deepens. Some 691,000 children went hungry in the U.S. during 2007 (Sniffen, 2008).

Too many of these children will attend overcrowded, underfunded, inadequate schools in their neighborhoods. Children raised in poverty are less likely to complete high school, less likely to find a decent job, more likely to end up in the penal system, and less likely to have health care.

Yet working families continue to place their faith in education. They have been among the primary supporters of public education since the growth of state-supported schools in the 1840s. Through good times and economic crises, working people have insisted on funding and improving public schools. They expect the schools to teach their children how to participate in a democracy, to prepare them for employment, and to show them how to improve the quality of their lives. They expect equal opportunity for their children.

Four social crises have devastated teachers and schools, particularly in the urban United States, during the last three decades. First, as described above, a global economic system has developed, producing winners and losers. In the United States, the working poor are the losers (Faux et al., 2001).

Second, during the economic crises of the 1980s and 1990s, a new form of market fundamentalism came to dominate political discussion, and social programs were cut back. In pursuit of the ideology of unregulated free markets, public regulation of corporate behavior was repealed, and public financial support for social programs, including schools, was severely cut.

Pulitzer Prize–winning writer David Cay Johnston, in his book *Perfectly Legal: The Covert Campaign to Rig Our Tax System to Benefit the Super Rich—and Cheat Everybody Else* (2003), described the process this way:

> The economic changes remaking our world are affecting all of us from the blue-collar workers whose wages have been falling for the past three decades to the investment bankers whose incomes have soared along with their clients' assets. The response of our elected leaders has been to adjust the tax system to shift tax burdens onto those with good incomes and little political power.

Table 4.1   Some Corporations Pay Lower Taxes than You Do

By 2000, the federal tax rates for corporations had reached their lowest levels since 1983. For example, an average family of four making $30,000 per year had an average tax rate of 17 percent.

But compare Ford Motor Company:

Pretax profits	$18,625,000,000
Federal income tax	$1,050,800,000
Effective tax rate	5.7%

And Microsoft Corporation:

Pretax profits	$21,866,500,000
Federal income tax	$386,000,000
Effective tax rate	1.8%

Source: Bill Moyers; data by Citizens for Tax Justice. Retrieved July 21, 2002, from *www.pbs.org/politics/ taxes* pop/1.html

> The clear trend in America for the past two decades has been to cut taxes on the rich and to raise taxes on those in the middle class and the upper middle class to make up part of the difference. (p. 307)

Johnston describes in detail how the rich and the corporations use their control of the media and the government to shift the tax burden, which is but one of several examples he uses to illustrate how economic power controls our supposedly democratic government. As a consequence, the divisions in our society among the very rich, the middle, and the poor are growing.

During the 1980s and 1990s, in part to gain funds for speculative capital, public funding of most social programs, including schools, was not allowed to grow or was severely cut back; funding for prisons was the exception. Since the 2003 invasion of Iraq, the federal government has been spending over $10 billion per month on war making, leaving very few resources for schooling, health care, or other social services. By 2007, the war had cost over $1,200,000,000.

A third crisis is the societal abandonment of responsibility to care for and guide our children. Families, particularly the families of the poor, are in crisis. The number of teens and unmarried persons having children has soared, as has the number of homes and families with no father present (Children's Defense Fund, 2005). Adults without children pursued their own wealth. Some demanded tax reductions, while increasing their own public benefits.

The rich used their resources and their ownership of the media to help along the careers of politicians and writers who would be useful to them. Reversing a 100-year pattern, voters refused to raise taxes to fund the schools sufficiently. The voting majority of the adult population and their political leaders abandoned the schools, the children, and the future—particularly in the urban areas. The financial and physical condition of urban schools sank into a state of chronic crisis. At the same time, many parents, squeezed by a slow, hidden economic decline of working-class incomes since the 1980s, were working more hours and consequently shifting more of the responsibility for child rearing onto the schools. Poverty has continued to grow, particularly affecting female heads of households and their families, as shown in Table 4.2.

Barbara Ehrenreich gives a series of intriguing first-person accounts of her own efforts to make a living alongside the working poor in *Nickel and Dimed: On (Not) Getting By in America* (2001). You may recognize the situation from jobs you have held.

> So, if low wage workers do not always behave in an economically rational way, that is, as free agents within a capitalist democracy, it is because they dwell in a place that is neither free nor in any way democratic. When you enter the low-wage workplace—and many of the medium-wage workplaces as well—you check your civil liberties at the door, leave America and all it supposedly stands for behind, and learn to zip your lips for the duration of the shift. The consequences of this routine surrender go beyond the issues of wages and poverty. We can hardly pride ourselves on being the world's preeminent democracy, after all, if large numbers of citizens spend half their waking hours in what amounts, in plain terms, to a dictatorship.
>
> Any dictatorship takes a psychological toll on its subjects. If you are treated as an untrustworthy person—a potential slacker, drug addict, or thief—you may begin to feel less trustworthy yourself. (p. 210)

A fourth crisis is the abandonment of the cities by the middle class. With the rapid growth in the ranks of the poor and consequent increases in homelessness, street gangs, drug abuse, and prostitution, many middle-class professionals no longer find the cities a safe environment to raise a family. They may have to work in the city, but increasingly they choose to live in the suburbs. The cities, with their declining tax bases and decaying school systems, are being left to the working poor: White, Black, Asian, and Latino (Orfield & Lee, 2006).

These crises in society have produced crises in the schools. Today's parents are working more hours and earning less money. More than ever, they are looking to the schools to bring up the next generation of children. But schools in many areas have been unable to respond to these momentous changes in the economy and the society. With shrinking budgets, decaying physical facilities, and a deteriorating social environment, the

Table 4.2   Changes in Wages by Gender, 1973–2005

Year	Male	Female	Ratio
1973	$14.08	$8.89	63.1%
1979	$14.39	$9.03	62.7%
1989	$13.07	$9.55	73.1%
2000	$15.81	$12.32	78.0 %
2005	$15.64	$12.82	82.0%

Note: The change in the gap between men's and women's wages is due to both increases in women's wages and decreases in men's wages. For current data, go to www.epi.org.

Source: Adapted from Lawrence Mishel, Jared Bernstein, and Sylvia Allegretto, *The State of Working America, 2006/2007.* Copyright 2007. Cornell University. Used by permission of the publisher, Cornell University Press.

schools in many cities are falling behind. The burden of this failure weighs most heavily on the children of the working class and people of color because their parents can escape neither the public school system nor the cities where the problem is most acute (Kozol, 2005).

Social Class as an Analytical Concept

The racial and cultural analyses of school achievement described in prior chapters use the concept of identity and reveal only part of the story. Social class and gender interact with culture, race, and identity to influence each individual child's school achievement.

Social class is a *concept*, an intellectual construct, a tool that helps us to categorize, store, and retrieve information. In Chapter 2, we used the concept of culture to organize a wide variety of information about how groups of people live. We may not remember all of the particulars of a group of people, but we recognize the general concepts of culture and identity. Having learned these concepts, we can approach learning about new groups of people using the same organizing ideas.

Class is a multidimensional concept. G. William Domhoff (2002) has written one of the classic studies of the U.S. class system. He argues as follows:

> First and foremost, the term [class] refers to an intertwined economic and power relationship between two or more groups of people who have specific roles in the economic system. Owners of businesses and the employees of those businesses are the most obvious example of this dimension in the nation-states of the Western world, but not all societies have economies that feature owners and employees. Second, class is a category that refers to the social institutions, social relationships, and lifestyle within the various economic groups: common neighborhoods, common clubs, and recreational activities, and a strong tendency to interact primarily with people from one's own economic class. (p. 4)

An important attribute of concepts (such as culture and class) is that they shape the thinking of their users. Thomas Kuhn, in his landmark work *The Structure of Scientific Revolutions* (1970), described how the selection of basic concepts for research strongly influences researchers' methodologies and results. For example, a researcher who sought explanations for school failure by examining the concept of social class (usually a sociologist or an economist) would pay attention to different evidence than a researcher who looked at failure through the concept of psychology (identity) or the neo-conservative philosophies of the recent school reform movement.

As a result of the personal histories and the worldviews and cultures of most professional educators and many U.S. sociologists and psychologists, the literature in education pays only limited attention to class issues or avoids discussing class.[1] Instead, researchers refer to *socioeconomic status* (SES). The social status approach, one of

---

[1]The complexity of definitions of social class in the United States and the rapid changes in professional jobs in the middle class lead some researchers to avoid class issues. But the difficulty of arriving at a clear definition of *class* is not an adequate reason to avoid using it as an analytical concept (Ehrenreich & Ehrenreich, 1979; Parker, 1972; Yates, 2007).

two approaches commonly taught in university sociology courses, follows the tradition of W. Lloyd Warner (1898–1970). The concept of SES blends the economic issues of jobs and income (or lack of work) with the status issues of role relationships, consumption patterns, and implied values to determine a prescribed socioeconomic status. Education research usually follows the Warner tradition and uses the concept of SES rather than the concept of social class to describe differences among families, neighborhoods, and schools. While SES studies explain some issues, the concept, as Kuhn (1970) noted, also shapes the perceptions and the conclusions of social scientists and teachers.

The use of SES as an analytical tool emphasizes the role of the individual in determining success or failure. Status can be improved, for example, by getting more education or earning a big promotion at one's workplace. Researchers using SES as an organizational concept usually assume that people improve their position in society primarily by individual effort and that schools serve as vehicles for economic and social advancement. The SES approach rarely challenges the inequality of the system. The use of the concept of status leads educators to seeking incremental improvements in the schools to benefit those students who appear to be willing to try harder.

The assumptions behind status research reinforce the position that it is the individuals who need to change, not the schools. Decades of education research and policy development from this perspective have described the deterioration of education opportunities for students placed at risk by declining economic opportunities in many regions, but the research has not led to the development of democratic alternatives for teachers and students (Anyon, 2005; Weis, McCarthy, & Dimitriadis, 2006).

Research organized around the concept of social class works from substantially different assumptions. For purposes of clarity, let us define the major economic classes in the United States. For this purpose, I am closely following the writings of Michael Yates in *More Unequal* (2007). He says:

> The working class are those people with relatively little power at work—white collar banktellers, call-center workers, and cashiers, blue-collar machinists, construction workers, and assemblyline workers; pink-collar secretaries, nurses, and home health-care workers—skilled and unskilled, men and women of all races, nationalities, and sexual preferences. The working class are those with little personal control over the pace or content of their work and without supervisory control over the work lives of others. There are nearly 90 million working-class people in the U.S. labor force today. The U.S. has a substantial working-class majority. . . . (p. 174)

The usual talk of a mass middle class in the United States, with some rich and some poor on the fringes, is fundamentally misleading. It confuses analysis.

The middle class are professionals, small business owners, and managerial and supervisory employees. They are best understood not as the middle of an income distribution but as living in the middle of two polar classes in capitalist society. Their experiences have some aspects shared with the working class and some associated with the corporate elite.

Small business owners, for example, share with the capitalists an interest in private property in business assets, defeating unions, and weak labor regulations. But they share with workers the work itself, great vulnerability to the market place, and government power, and difficulty securing adequate health insurance and retirement security. (Yates, 2007, p. 175)

When we look at the experiences over the last 30 years of professionals in the middle classes, we see a division. The economic and social standing of those professionals who work with and for the working families—for example, public school teachers, community college teachers, and lawyers in public defender positions—has by and large stagnated along with the declining prosperity of the working class. However, if we look at the lives of those professionals working with and linked to the corporate elite, often called the professional managerial class—such as corporate lawyers, stock brokers, and high-status doctors and large business managers—they have prospered significantly, as illustrated in the upper quintiles of income on the Chart 4.1 (Yates, 2007).

Bowles and Gintis (1976), Carnoy and Levin (1985), Domhoff (2002), Anyon (2005), Apple (2001), and others whose research is based on a social-class perspective argue that our economic system produces social classes and that these classes are group phenomena, not individual choices. Social class is more than a position on a scale; it is always a relationship to others. That is, the working class, the middle class, and other classes exist in relationship to one another. The huge, even obscene, profits garnered by CEOs and owners of high-tech companies in the 1990s and by elites in the corporate meltdowns in 2001–2002 and again in 2007–2008 were an issue not because these people were rich but because their profits were so disproportionate in comparison to the salaries of the workers in their companies and because their actions resulted in the loss of jobs, pension and health benefits for the broad sector of working people (Phillips, 2002).

The Working Poor

Barbara Ehrenreich, in *Nickel and Dimed: On (Not) Getting By in America* (2001), gives detailed personal testimony of the lives of waitresses, housecleaners, salesclerks at Wal-Mart, and the vast array of the working poor. These workers, many of them White, spend more than 40 to 60 hours per week as nurse's aides, gardeners, day laborers, janitors, and meat packers, and they do not earn enough wages to afford health care or an adequate diet for their families. *Hardships in America: The Real Story of Working Families* (Boushey, Brocht, Gunderson, & Bernstein, 2001 provides a detailed analysis of wages and living costs around the nation to demonstrate that 29 percent of all families with one to two adults and one to three children under 12 have incomes below adequate family budget levels. These families go without food, have utilities turned off for lack of payment, face medical crises, and at times are thrown into homelessness (Boushey et al., 2001). These serious and persistent crises dramatically affect the children's stay in school.

The working poor live in inadequate and often unsafe housing; they rely on emergency rooms to obtain health care and on church food closets and clothes closets to feed and clothe their children. Each day in their lives is a struggle to just hang on and to survive until the next paycheck. And these are people who all live above the poverty line!

A clear majority of the working poor is European American or Latino, but this class is distinctly multiracial. The lives and difficulties of White, Asian, Latino, and African American workers in hotels, restaurants, construction, gardening, and day-labor markets were described in Figure 4.2. The service economies of most of our major cities, and the entire South and Southwest, would not function without these low-wage workers.

Changes in class composition occur as a result of changes in the economic system. The structural changes presently occurring in our economy are having this effect. Good-paying union jobs in the auto, steel, electronics, and other industries are being transferred to other countries and are being replaced by low-paying service jobs. These are class changes—not individual changes—and they impact the role of schools in preparing students for economic participation.

Attention to social class, rather than SES, yields additional insights into the functions of schooling in our race- and class-polarized society. Scholars, teachers, and researchers interested in promoting equality in schooling use the concept of social class to explain how the gaps in school achievement among students from the upper, middle, working, and poor classes reproduce and maintain inequality in society. According to Bowles and Gintis (1976), only when we grasp the role of class in our educational system can we begin to counteract its effects:

> Understanding the dynamics of class relationships is essential to an adequate appreciation of the connection between economics, racism and education. For the institutions of economic life (including schools) do not work mechanistically and mindlessly to produce social outcomes, but rather change and develop through the types of class relationships to which they give rise. The educational system is involved in reproducing and changing these class relationships and cannot be understood by simply "adding up" the effects of schooling on each individual to arrive at a total social impact. (p. 67)

When class is not considered, or when ethnicity or SES is substituted for class, the analyses fail to recognize how hard many people work to survive in this economy. Workers struggle 12 to 14 hours per day, six and seven days per week, in sweatshop, clothing manufacturing plants, in hotels and restaurants, and elsewhere in order to have a home and to put food on the table for their families.

Parents working in these grueling jobs, often women and single parents, have a difficult time helping their children in school. Few of the children have dental care or health care. School policies such as required homework where the parents are expected to monitor and to check the homework fail. And in difficult times when companies move their work and their factories to other countries, the families of these most exposed workers are often destroyed (Yoon Louie, 2001). These workers are struggling to survive, to take part in the American dream, and to keep their children in school.

Education researchers such as Michael Apple, William Julius Wilson, Richard Rothstein (2008), and Jean Anyon (2005), who pay attention to class issues, view the way in which education is presently dispensed as a part of the system of maintaining class relationships. Tracking, ability grouping, teacher expectations, counseling services, and inequitable school expenditures reinforce already existing social class differences (Anyon, 2005; Emery, 2007; Weis, 2004). Researchers who approach these problems from the perspective of social class usually have different goals for schools than those using a status-based approach. They argue that democratic schools should produce more equality rather than advancing a few individuals within the present unequal system. This viewpoint regards schools as a product of public policy and as institutions that are subject to change based on the democratic demands of the majority.

Formation of the European American Working Class

To have an accurate understanding of our society, it is important to know not only that the majority of the population is White but also that most White people belong to a working class. Each part of the macroculture has its own history and identity. As an example, we will consider the Irish in the United States.

The Irish Americans are descendants of immigrants. They trace their roots to Ireland. Ireland had always produced a surplus of food. Between 1641 and 1652, one-fourth of the population of Ireland was killed in an invasion by the English general Oliver Cromwell, and English masters sold more than 100,000 Irish children to serve as slaves and prostitutes on plantations in places such as Barbados (O'Callaghan, 2000).

The forced imposition of the English ownership of the land after 1640 changed agricultural production in Ireland and forced the remaining peasantry into extreme poverty. In 1846 and 1847, the Irish potato crop failed, and more than 1 million people faced starvation. During this time, Ireland produced sufficient food for all its people, but the control of the food production was in the hands of English nobility.

When the potato famine hit, starvation was so severe that the bodies piled up by the side of the roads. There were not enough healthy people to bury the dead. More than 50 percent of the male population either fled or died. Some moved to England to earn a few dollars and then fled to Australia, Latin America, and the United States. Families survived by sending their young men, and later young women, to the United States looking for work. Irish workers were recruited in England, in Ireland, and in the cities of New York and Boston to build railroads, work in the coal mines, and dig canals. By 1850, a majority of people in many of the major cities in the United States were immigrants, predominantly the Irish.

Not all immigrants reached the U.S. cities alive. Workers and families crossed the ocean as cargo. They had to bring their own food and water on the ship. They were packed below deck on the large ships. Diseases and epidemics killed tens of thousands of immigrants on their way to the United States.

Irish immigrants enjoyed a few advantages: They spoke English, they had a history of political organizing, and they brought several community organizations with them, notably the Catholic church. Irish immigrants used these skills in the United States to create labor unions and political organizations to defend themselves from factory owners. The Irish had long developed resistance societies in Ireland, and political organizations soon arose in the United States. The Irish developed their own schools and universities, known today as Catholic schools.

In the United States, the new Irish immigrants faced racism and prejudice, as did the Italians, Finns, and others who followed them. Irish workers and their unions were attacked as subversive. Fortunately for them, the Irish entered an economy with an expanding frontier and a rapidly growing job market. The factories, mines, and railroads and the U.S. Army needed workers. Immigrants could enter the job market without an education.

The children of the immigrants went to school, and some even went to college. The better-paying jobs—the public service jobs such as police and fire and the jobs that required training—were opened to the Irish through kinship networks, political patronage, and Catholic schools.

Factories and mines grew in the North after the Civil War. More unskilled and menial workers were needed to do the dangerous and exhausting work. Unions began to form in the mines and on the railroads and to spread to more industries. Factory owners responded by recruiting new immigrant workers in Europe. They sent recruiters to Poland, Germany, Lithuania, and Italy in search of more workers.

When Irish and U.S. workers went on strike, Polish, Italian, or Finnish workers were imported to do the work. These workers were brought here by labor contractors and did not speak English. Like the Irish before them, they were fleeing the poverty of peasant life in Europe. They came to earn money and to feed their families. They could be used to break the strikes of the Irish and the German immigrant workers.

These migrants hoped to find farmland in the West, but many got no farther than Cleveland, or Detroit, or Milwaukee, wherever the most jobs could be found. Some of the immigrants were legal; many were not. Men, women, and children worked 12 to 14 hours per day for barely enough to eat. Living conditions in the urban immigrant communities (ghettos) were almost subhuman. Housing was unbearable. Workers in factories often could rent only a bed, which they shared with workers on other shifts. Women and children 12 and 14 years of age worked. If they couldn't find a position in a mill, they would be forced to work as servants; losing those jobs, many were forced into prostitution. After 10 years of hard labor, many immigrants were too diseased or mutilated to continue to work, so they were thrown out on the street. Criminal behavior and drunkenness were common in immigrant quarters.

Slowly, painfully, each community was able to get its children into the newly established public schools. It took more than 80 years of struggle to create unions, in part because each immigrant group could be used against the other. After one or two generations, with union wages and working conditions, stable families began to develop.

Throughout the East and Midwest, ethnic communities developed around industries: the Irish in Boston and in the coal fields of Pennsylvania; the Poles, Italians, and Irish in Pittsburgh; the Slovaks and Italians in Cleveland and Buffalo; the Germans in Milwaukee and Chicago; the Finns in the iron mines of Minnesota; and the Irish and the German and Russian Jews in New York.

People in these immigrant communities worked hard. They sent their children to public or to Catholic schools. Schooling offered the families a hope for a better life. The schools were vehicles to "Americanize" the children, to teach them English. After decades, a new, fiercely "American" culture developed among the working-class descendants of these immigrants.

After World War II, many in these communities began to redefine themselves as "Americans" rather than Irish or Polish, and working people began to move out of the central cities to the new places called *suburbs*. Federal home loans (subsidies) helped veterans purchase homes, and the GI Bill (financial aid) allowed many of them to attend college. During and after both wars, large numbers of African Americans migrated from the South to the North, often coming into conflict and economic competition with the working-class descendants of European immigrants.

In their own communities' view of history, these descendants of immigrants believed that they worked hard, built their unions, played by the rules, educated their children, and became "good Americans." This European American working-class culture, like other cultures, passed on a perspective, a worldview, of the melting pot to its children. And they saw this worldview as accurate history.

Each new immigrant group became economic competition for those already here, and they were often faced with hatred. Immigrant groups were easily turned against one another. In the 1830s, "native" working people rioted when the Irish began to arrive in large numbers. Political parties were created to keep the Irish out. In 1846, Irish immigrants became the soldiers for the U.S. invasion of Mexico. In the 1860s, Irish workers in New York rioted rather than be drafted to fight in the Civil War. In the 1870s, the new Republican Party campaigned against the Irish with opposition to "Rum, Romanism [Catholicism] and Rebellion" (Ignatiev, 1995).

Although they had been treated as "outsiders" themselves, by the 1850s Irish workers and other "natives" used both the courts and terrorism to demand that Mexican workers be driven out of the gold fields of California and their land seized. In the 1880s, Irish political leaders led the Workingman's Party and demanded that the Chinese workers be kept out of California (Almaguer, 1994). The Irish, Czechs, Poles, Italians, Russians, and Jews were each, in turn, considered aliens, foreigners, a threat to the "American Way" of life by nativist forces. By the 1920s, immigration laws were passed to control the influx of the newer groups of European immigrants.

In the 1920s and again in the 1940s, unions, political forces, and terrorism were used to keep African Americans from gaining political power as they migrated from the South to take jobs in factories in the North. Unity between Protestant and Catholic European immigrants could often be achieved within the working class by pitting them against African Americans—or more recently, Mexican and Latino immigrants—who seemed to pose a threat of economic competition.

These European immigrant groups, along with others, built the railroads, dug the coal, produced the steel, and made the autos. As they achieved economic stability, they created schools and universities and enrolled their children. The formerly separate Irish, Italian, Polish, and other subgroups have widely intermarried; as a result, their children have a substantially mixed, and new, cultural heritage. Having benefited from education, the children, particularly the women, of these European American working-class families have sought a secure job in the lower-level professions, such as teaching and nursing.

At present, many European American working-class families, like others in the working class, are under severe financial pressure to keep a secure job with good pay and benefits. The international economic restructuring has replaced many of the good-paying, unionized, industrial jobs. Young people in the working class could at one time rely on getting a reasonably well paying union job in industrial production. Manual labor jobs have declined from 36 percent of the economy to only 23 percent, while (nonunion) clerical and sales jobs have increased dramatically from 17 to 26 percent. Those with a college education have managed the transition; those who left high school early have been left behind in this new economy, at times creating bitterness as expressed in the election campaingn of 2008 (Teixeira & Abramowitz, 2008). Most members of the European American working class see themselves not as a class but as "Americans" or sometimes as Whites (Guinier & Torres, 2002). This lack of class consciousness, in part taught in schools, hides and distorts significant job loss and class inequality.

Since the 1990s, right-wing political candidates such as Patrick Buchanan, talk show hosts, and conservative opinion shapers in the media and on college campuses have blamed minority advancements and the women's movement for the economic stagnation of working people in our society, a view accepted as valid by some (Domhoff, 2002). Since 2001, much of the focus of hostility and blame has shifted to immigrants, particularly immigrants and their children from Latin America, Asia, and the Caribbean nations of Haiti and the Dominican Republic. A populist anti-immigration movement and supporting ideology were developed by author Samuel Huntington, news anchor Lou Dobbs on CNN, former Congressman Tom Tancredo of Colorado, and Sarah Palin when she ran to become the Vice-President of the United States in 2008.

An American Dilemma: Poor Children in Poor Schools

There often exists a direct relationship between poverty and school failure. Under our present structure of schooling, poor kids fail more often than kids from middle-income families. The number of poor people in our society is growing. We can therefore predict that a growing number of children will fail in school. *Why* they are failing is a more complex question.

To understand the crisis of poor children in urban and rural schools, we need more information about the growth of poverty in our society and how poverty, schools, race, ethnicity, and economic class interact to produce school failure.

As described earlier, substantial economic transformations are causing rapid changes in our society and our schools. Figure 4.3 shows the historical pattern of poverty in the United States. Trends described in *The Field Guide to the Global Economy* (Anderson, Cavanagh, & Lee, 2000) indicate that both the absolute and the relative sizes of the poverty class will grow. As poverty increases, school problems increase.

During the 1960s, as a result of economic growth and government programs known as the War on Poverty, there was an overall decline in poverty in the United States. As the economy entered the current period of structural change, poverty levels increased in recessions and remained high during recoveries. Clearly, some segments of society do not benefit significantly from current economic recoveries.

The official poverty rate in 2006 was 12.3 percent, or 36.5 million people. This rate has remained constant for the last three years. A person living in poverty is a person living in a household with an annual income of $19,178 or less. This is the lowest

Figure 4.3   **Number of Poor and Poverty Rate, 1959 to 2006**

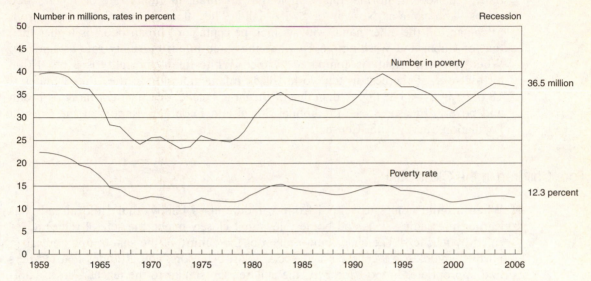

Note: The data points represent the midpoints of the respective years. A recession began in July 1990 and ended in March 1991. Another recession began in 2001.

Source: From *Income, Poverty, and Health Insurance Coverage in the United States: 2006*, by U.S. Bureau of the Census, 2007, Washington, DC: Author.

quintile in Figure 4.1. The poverty rate was 23.9 percent for African Americans, 20.6 percent for Hispanics, 10.3 percent for Asians, and 8.2 percent for non-Hispanic Whites. The poverty rate for children under age six was 20 percent (U.S. Bureau of the Census, 2007). It is generally recognized in the research community that the U.S. official estimate of poverty is an understatement of real poverty (Mishel et al., 2007).

The Children's Defense Fund (CDF) is a respected source of information on income levels for families with children. The CDF says that more than one out of six children in the United States lives in poverty—a higher rate than accepted in other industrialized nations (Mishel et al., 2006/2007; OECD, 2006). By race and ethnicity, 1 in 3 African American children, almost 3 out of 10 Latino children, and more than 1 in 10 Asian and White children live in poverty (Children's Defense Fund, 2005, p. 3).

Federal tax changes and budget cuts enacted by the Reagan and Bush Administrations (1980–1992) significantly increased the presence of poverty. Since the 1980s, structural changes in the economy and the removal of government social-support programs have produced a growing semipermanent class of poor families with children.

In 1996, the Republican Congress passed and President Clinton (a Democrat) signed a welfare reform law that again substantially reduced federal spending for the poor and significantly changed the 60-year-old program for assistance to poor families. Without an antipoverty policy, we pay the enormous social and human costs of creating a poverty class.

One of the very real human costs is that poverty affects whether children live or die. San Francisco, California, for example, has an infant mortality rate of 7 per 1,000 births—the same as Norway or Switzerland. The infant mortality rate in Detroit, Michigan, on the other hand, with its high percentage of urban poor, is higher than that of Cuba, and Washington, DC, has the same infant mortality rate as Jamaica. When infant mortality is compared by race, White infant mortality is 8 per 1,000 births—one of the best in the world. Black infant mortality in the United States is 18 per 1,000—a rate higher than that of Bulgaria, Poland, or Cuba. For more on health and poverty measures, see the annual Social and Economic Report of the Current Population Survey (U.S. Census).

Poor Children in the Classroom

When a child comes to school from a middle-class family, that child already has learned prereading skills and home values that closely match the school values advocated by teachers. The child knows much of the culture of the school upon entering. Further, middle-class children have social skills, behaviors, and attitudes that teachers find appropriate. In most respects, the children are similar to the teachers' own families. Because the middle-class child's culture is similar to the teacher's culture, most teachers react positively to their middle-class students, and supportive bonds develop between them. In elementary school, more than 90 percent of the teachers are female, producing particularly supportive bonds for girls.

A child from a poor, marginalized family is more likely to enter school less prepared with prereading skills (Anyon, 2005; Coley, 2002; Lareau, 2003; Rothstein, 2008). While the school expects children to know the themes of mainstream children's literature—Cinderella and other European folktales—some children come from homes where few people read. Other children's language skills may be extensive in Spanish or Vietnamese but limited in English. Yet the school culture expects knowledge of concepts and performance in English. Some kids come from homes where computers and the Internet are often used, while others come from homes dominated by television. The punishment and reward systems used by schools are often confusing and different from those familiar to the child.

Some children arrive at school from homes where poverty or divorce has disrupted stable living arrangements, although disruption and disorganization of home life are not unique or universal to families living in poverty. Middle-class families also frequently experience disruption and are made dysfunctional by divorce, alcoholism, drug abuse, and physical or psychological abuse.

Poor but stable families usually prepare their children well for school success. The safety and security of a stable home environment enhance the child's ability to view the new environment of school without undue fear. Getting a good start in school in a safe, protected environment helps children learn the culture of school and the new ways of doing things. Children who fail to learn the new behaviors and values required for school success may encounter conflict at school.

Children in poor neighborhoods move from school to school at a high rate, which degrades the quality of their school experience. Poor people often lose their jobs and their apartments. Poverty, as well as health and economic crises, requires them to move. Some even become homeless. For children, frequent moving produces a pattern of health problems and school disruption with a constant array of new teachers, new classmates, and new curricula.

The truly poor have severe financial problems simply getting through the month. A doctor's visit can require two days of waiting for service at a public health clinic. For recipients of Temporary Assistance to Needy Families (TANF), contacts with government institutions are intrusive, overwhelming, and full of dangers. In poor neighborhoods, a simple school request for family information may cause fear and alarm at home. Parents may fear that yet another social worker is going show up to reduce their already inadequate benefits.

In spite of the very real problems of poverty, most poor parents still look to school as the best hope for their children's future economic opportunity. They believe in the ideals of our school system. They recognize schooling as the best available route to ending their own cycle of poverty. These parents sacrifice for their children. Other parents, too often destroyed by the drug trade and violence, may not support the schools.

When poor children come to school, too often they encounter frustration and failure. Large urban school districts with bureaucratic, authoritarian structures and intrusive cultural demands seldom ensure success for poor children. Not one of the major cities provides a quality education to all of its students. Real dropout rates of up to 50 percent are common (Bridgeland, DiIulio, & Morison, 2006). More than 30 percent of the schools in these urban areas fail to educate their students even to basic levels of literacy (Children's Defense Fund, 2005). The children fail to learn the rules of the school and find it difficult to meet the school's expectations. Middle-class psychologists and educators may label the students "bad" or "unmotivated."

Even in "difficult" neighborhoods, most of the parents are struggling to achieve an education for their children. These efforts are sometimes counteracted by overworked and burned-out school staff whose main focus is to maintain control of the school campus. Tired school faculty too often hold low expectations for the children; routinely practice tracking; and ultimately blame the children, their parents, and their communities for the problems. The parents blame the schools, and the schools blame the parents. Neither approach helps the children. Rather than continuing this fruitless cycle, teachers need to accept their responsibility to work with parents, to educate children, and to make their classrooms locations of respect and success for all.

In the face of impoverished school conditions, families can lose hope and confidence in themselves and in the schools. Other families, who recognize the violence happening to their children and see their own dreams of opportunity fade, become defensive or hostile toward the schools. They are convinced to vote for tax limitation plans and "choice" or voucher plans that reduce school funding. Some parents make enormous financial sacrifices to place their children in tuition-based private schools, such as the Catholic school network. Some frustrated parents avoid their children's school. Others, angry at a society that seems to have abandoned their children, encourage students to engage in open conflict with school authorities.

Society's Obligations to Our Children

The interaction between poverty and schooling is complex and changing. Teachers have always needed to control and redirect a few children in each class who fail in their schoolwork or who refuse to adjust to reasonable standards for school social behavior. In many impoverished neighborhoods today, however, matters are much worse than in prior years. Whereas a teacher in the 1950s might have faced 2 disruptive children per class, today's teacher may face 6 or, in some classes, up to 10.

Two worldviews of society's obligations to its children are contending for support. Voters and taxpayers have long insisted that our democratic society promote the common good. Our federal Constitution and most state constitutions assign the government the task of promoting the "general welfare." One view holds that a society needs to arrange itself so that children are cared for, their health protected, and their education provided (Labaree, 2000; Parker, 2003; Schwartz, 2008). This view has been the mainstream opinion since at least the 1850s and provides the justification for establishing schools as a public responsibility.

A theory of "the common good recognizes that if a society stops caring for its children, all parts of society suffer" (Schwartz, 2008). Even a family that is responsible, protective, and nurturing can lose children to the war zones found in some urban neighborhoods. Society as a whole loses when a child is shot in random gang violence, killed as a bystander at school, or kidnapped by a person who ought to be receiving mental health care and perhaps be hospitalized. Parents in marginalized neighborhoods recognize the danger to their families, and they resent the refusal of political leaders to respond to their children's most basic needs of both security and educational opportunity.

Unfortunately for children, since the 1980s the ideology of the conservative political activists has promoted an alternative view of society. Radical conservatives or fundamentalist conservatives convinced a majority of voters that by saving money and not paying taxes, they would be promoting the common good. This was a reversal of traditional conservative thinking. As Robert Reich described in *The Work of Nations* (1991b), the wealthy seceded from the cities, bought beautiful homes in suburbs, walled off their neighborhoods, hired private security forces, and richly funded their children's schools. They promoted their individual consumption of wealth rather than the public good. They tried to blame the deterioration of life in poverty areas on welfare recipients, immigrants, and minorities. Their flight from poverty into walled enclosures replaced concern for the common good.

Yet no part of society remains healthy when the other parts are sick. Violence and drug abuse in one part of the community endanger us all. Even in the suburbs, teenage runaway and suicide rates have reached epidemic proportions. The conservative strategy of withdrawing into the suburbs and funding more prisons worked only until gangs, violence, and drug abuse appeared there, too.

In the bottom tier of our society—the semipermanent poverty areas—the decline in good-paying jobs has substantially damaged family life. Families are divided and some are destroyed by crime, drugs, health crises, divorce, abandonment, and permanent underemployment.

These are crises that most people choose not to acknowledge. Wilson, in *When Work Disappears* (1996), describes how unemployment, economic decay, and the deindustrialization of society rob the lower tier of workers of hope and economic opportunity (see also Schwartz, 2008, on Wilson's contributions). Neither the schools nor the police are adequately funded or prepared to handle this growing crisis.

In *Where We Stand: Class Matters* (2000), hooks comments: "Given the huge gap between those who have a lot, those who have a little, and those who have nothing, it is difficult to understand how citizens of this nation can imagine that ours is still a classless society" (p. 158). But political leaders and education writers can pretend that we have a classless society. They are able to sell this ideological position because we are constantly taught in school that we live in a classless society and benefit from a classless school system. Nothing could be further from the truth.

Children bring their crises to school each day (Kozol, 2005). Poor and middle-class children mix in some schools. The deterioration of life opportunities among the poor adds to a deterioration of schools. Some students bring to school the same disorder, crime, and gang violence they see in their neighborhoods. Dealing with these problems inevitably takes away from safety and instructional time. Tax cuts and the demand to spend extra funds on school security, plus the need for remediation of basic skills, stress many urban school budgets.

Only major increases in public spending will improve the schools and promote the common good. But the rich and most corporations paid a higher percentage of taxes in the 1960s than they do today. As a result of the tax cuts for corporations and the wealthy over the last 20 years, the tax burden has been transferred from corporations to the middle class and has produced a middle-class tax revolt (Domhoff, 2002). The rich, the middle class, and the elderly are defensive voters and as a group have fewer children in public schools than do the poor and the working class.

The crisis for working people also produced a crisis in our democracy. Robert Reich (2007) describes it as follows:

> Meanwhile the democratic aspects of capitalism have declined. The institutions that undertook formal and informal negotiations to spread the wealth, stabilize jobs and communities, and establish equitable rules of the game—giant oligopolies, large labor unions, regulatory agencies, and legislatures responsive to local Main Streets and communities—have been eclipsed. Corporate statesmen have vanished. In this way the triumph of capitalism and the decline of democracy have been connected. Democratic Capitalism has been replaced by supercapitalism. (p. 50)

> The economically privileged tend to vote to limit taxes and to limit school spending. Taxation wars and tax rebellions over school funding have rocked state after state, including New Jersey, Massachusetts, California, Michigan, and Ohio. Elected officials have responded to the demands of mobilized voters. The poor too seldom vote, and the children cannot vote. Consequently, the needs of poor children have been given less priority by many elected officials who have given little weight to arguments for promoting the public good when voters are demanding tax relief.

Interaction of Culture, Race, Class, and Poverty

Research on race, class, and poverty in the United States and their cumulative effect on schools is notoriously inadequate. Media descriptions of poverty with their emphasis on gangs, drugs, and violence produce distorted images of inner-city youth. The isolation of teachers (many of whom live in the suburbs) from the communities surrounding their schools combines with a frequent lack of parental participation to produce misunderstandings and the perpetuation of harmful stereotypes.

The subjects of stereotyping are not limited to racial and ethnic groups. There is class stereotyping as well. Michael Harrington (1928–1990) spent much of his life studying the class divisions in our society and wrote dozens of books and articles on the subject. In 1962, he wrote *The Other America*, a landmark work on poverty in the United States. His research led directly to the War on Poverty of the 1960s and influences the perspectives of this chapter. Harrington reviewed decades of research on poverty and pointed out that the average poor family is White and headed by a person working full-time at a low-paying job.

One particularly large portion of the poor studied by Harrington was the people of Appalachia and other rural areas. Rural poverty is often not taken into account when considering social class. Yet, according to the U.S. Census Bureau, the states with the highest numbers of people living in areas of concentrated poverty in 1999 were usually rural: Louisiana (41.7 percent), Mississippi (41.7 percent), New Mexico (37.1 percent), West Virginia (33.8 percent), Arizona (24.4 percent), and Arkansas (23.7 percent). These states have poverty levels similar to those in our major urban areas, such as the District of Columbia, with 41.9 percent (U.S. Bureau of the Census, 2005; Areas with Concentrated Poverty, 1999).

Most Appalachian children are White. They are descendants of the Scots/Anglo immigrants who came to our country in the 1700s (Webb, 2004). Their distinct culture at times clashes with school expectations (Sullivan & Miller, 1990).

Now, some 40 years after the War on Poverty, areas of the Appalachian region remain economically impoverished. In spite of decades of popular struggles by local organizations, wealth still flows out of Appalachia, while poverty, and often political domination, intensifies (Couto & Guthrie, 1999). Nearby areas, such as the Piedmont region of the South, have developed a modern industrial society and achieved significant economic prosperity.

Race and Class

Misunderstandings about the causal factors of school achievement occur because in our society there is a strong congruence between race and class. Educational failure by students from the lower class is often reported as a racial issue. But school failure is in fact a race–class problem. We collect clear data on race and confusing, indirect data on class. Each year the Economic Policy Institute, in *The State of Working America*, provides data on the interaction between poverty and race. Scholars working from the standpoint of a race-based analysis have described and focused on the injuries of race and the privileges of being White. But not all White people are privileged. Nobel Prize winner Martin Luther King, Jr., described this issue as follows in 1968:

> You [poor white people]ought to be marching with us. You're just as poor as the Negro. . . . You are put in the position of supporting your oppressor. Because through prejudice and blindness, you fail to see that the same forces that oppress Negroes in American society oppress poor white people. . . . Now that's a fact. That the poor white has been put into this position—where through blindness and prejudice, he is forced to support his oppressors, and

the only thing he has going for him is the false feeling that he is superior because his skin is white. (King, in Washington, ed. 1986, p. 264)

Several academic feminists in the 1990s further developed the concept of White privilege to describe what they saw as the inherent benefits of their own experience of being White in the United States. As we saw in Chapter 3, there are certainly benefits to being White in a society structured by racial privilege and White supremacy in institutions (Lipsitz, 2001). For example, White people are less likely to be stopped by the police in most states and less likely to be ignored by salespersons in upscale stores.

But from a race–class perspective, we need to consider White-class privilege rather than White privilege because most of the gains and benefits asserted as privileges of the European Americans, the White privilege, are substantially gains for people who identify as middle-class professionals (like college professors) and upper-class women (Gimenez, 2007). As demonstrated well by Ehrenreich in *Nickel and Dimed: On (Not) Getting By in America* (2001), poor and working-class White women, particularly the working poor and recipients of TANF (Temporary Assistance to Needy Families), have only a few privileges based on their race. For example, they remain less likely to be suspected of illicit drug abuse and prostitution than many women of color—however, their children attend the same low-quality, often disruptive, schools.

Author and activist bell hooks (2000) is particularly critical of middle- and upper-class African Americans for abandoning the African American poor. She claims,

[I]t is evident that the vast majority of privileged class black folks feel they have nothing in common with the black poor. Whenever well-to-do black persons justly complain about the ways racism operates to keep them from reaching the highest pinnacle of career success or the way everyday racism makes it hard for them to get a taxi or does not exempt them from being treated unjustly by the police (white privilege) if these complaints are not linked to an acknowledgment of how their class power mediates racial injustice in a way that it does not for the poor and underprivileged, they collude in the nation's refusal to acknowledge the solace and protection class privilege affords them. (Hooks, 2000, p. 94)

The deadly combination of poverty and racism that oppresses some families in the United States was demonstrated vividly on television for the whole world to see after Hurricane Katrina struck New Orleans in September of 2005. Over 1,800 died, and thousands of homes and families were destroyed; U.S. citizens were threatened and controlled at gunpoint. You can see this event for yourself in the Spike Lee–HBO movie *When the Levees Broke*. With funding from the Rockefeller Foundation, the Teachers College at Columbia University has produced a teachers' manual that will be useful if you decide to show this film in your classroom.

On the other hand, middle-class African American, Chicano, and Filipino students succeed significantly like their middle-class European American (White) peers when they attend schools in middle-class neighborhoods. Meanwhile, poor and working-class European American students in poverty schools fail remarkably like their poor African American and Chicano peers (Finn, 1999; MacLeod, 1987; Mehan, 1992; Orfield & Lee, 2006; Weis, 2004). Princeton University philosophy scholar Cornel West commented on this dilemma when he was asked what he thought of public schooling for African American youth: "I think it's magnificent for [the] black middle

The Hurricane Katrina disaster (2005) and the failed government response revealed many of the race–class divides in the United States.

Photos: Cypress Image Gallery.

class and above, but it's a national disgrace for the black working poor and the very poor. There is a class difference that we have to acknowledge" (quoted in Kilsen, 2007). *As reported in Black Commentator, Dec. 20, 2007, Dr. Martin Kilsen (2007)*

Cultural and Linguistic Deficit Explanations of School Failure: The Attempt to Avoid Class

Early writings on "disadvantaged" young people in the 1960s focused on their alleged cultural and educational "deprivation" or deficits. Middle-class education writers and policy advocates created harmful myths of cultural and linguistic deprivation to explain the school failure of some children (Labov, 1970). The cultural- and linguistic-deprivation theses were then incorporated into teacher folk knowledge and curriculum plans (Gorski, 2008; Payne, 2001).

Compensatory education services based on the culture of poverty thesis continue as an important element in the school curriculum through the federal program known as Chapter 1. But three decades of this program have resulted in only marginal improvements in the achievement gap between middle-class students and students living in poverty. The program has never been adequately funded, but an additional problem is conceptual. Compensatory education programs and the culture of poverty thesis—as interpreted by a generation of mainly European American, mainly middle-class education researchers—often worked from the unexamined assumption that there must be something wrong with poor people or they wouldn't be poor.

In the view of William Julius Wilson, the Civil Rights Movement of the 1960s and the government policies that followed resulted mainly in the strengthening of the Black middle class. Wilson's emphasis on the importance of economics in race relations followed the lead of Dr. Martin Luther King, Jr. Early on, King recognized the need for a broad, inclusive movement to promote economic justice as well as racial equality. The Southern Christian Leadership Conference (SCLC), along with others, promoted a multiracial struggle for economic justice with the Poor People's Campaign of 1967–1968 (Dyson, 2000). According to King: "We're going to take this movement and … reach out to poor people in all directions in this country … into the Southwest after the Indians, into the West after the Chicanos, into Appalachia after the poor whites, and into the ghettos after the Negroes and the Puerto Ricans. And we are going to bring them together into something bigger than just a civil rights movement for Negroes" (quoted in Guinier & Torres, 2002).

King united the struggle for civil rights with union struggles and other efforts to end class oppression. Unfortunately, King was assassinated on April 4, 1968, before the Poor People's Campaign could organize a sustainable movement for economic justice.

Since the 1980s, the economic problems of the poor have increased significantly. Major corporations closed their plants in the industrialized and unionized northeastern United States, depriving hundreds of thousands of working-class African Americans and Latinos of good jobs and steady income. Plants moved to nonunion areas of the South and the Southwest and to Third World nations, devastating the economic base of the African American and Latino communities and the lives of many in the working class. In 1977, General Motors Corporation had 77,000 jobs for hourly workers in Flint, Michigan. By 1998, it only had 33,000. Working-class union families lost their jobs or were pushed into marginal employment in low-paying service industries. The economic crisis in urban industrial areas has devastated many African American families since the 1980s. Sociologist Wilson describes the consequences of this economic shift in urban areas in *When Work Disappears: The World of the New Urban Poor* (1996) and *The Bridge over the Racial Divide: Rising Inequality and Coalition Politics* (1999). Jean Anyon, in *Radical Possibilities: Public Policy, Urban Education, and a New Social Movement* (2005), describes how race, class, and the lack of a government policy on economic growth continue to work together to reinforce school failure. Both authors recommend government policies to promote economic growth and change for the entire lower class. In this view, general programs for the poor, such as jobs, housing, and health, are needed to go along with school reform.

Reading about the schools and the very poor in areas like Chicago, New York, Boston, Philadelphia, and Los Angeles does not tell teachers much about the life experiences of children in midsize cities like Sacramento, Portland, Seattle, and Denver. Nor does the concept of an urban underclass adequately describe their experiences in Atlanta, Birmingham, New Orleans, and the other large cities of the South.

Even in large northern urban ghettos where the economic crisis is most severe and social institutions have often failed and where some communities are dominated by gangs and the drug culture, not all of the families have lost the battle for their children. Most parents love their children and want the best for them. They work long, hard hours, often at demeaning jobs, to feed and clothe their children. It is important that teachers avoid stereotypes about poor and working-class students.

Some ultra-conservative foundations, such as the Ollin Foundation, have generously funded a branch of advocacy writing that purports to demonstrate genetic differences by class and by race. *The Bell Curve: Intelligence and Class Structure in American Life* (1994), by Richard Herrnstein and Charles Murray, is an example of these works. The authors have sought to revalidate the discredited theories of genetic and cultural deprivation from the 1960s. Charles Murray's previous book, *Losing Ground* (1984), helped to set the agenda for the current attacks on the welfare system. A wide range of social scientists have demonstrated the flaws in argument and psychological measurement found in *The Bell Curve*. In spite of the numerous errors, a series of policy organizations continue to promote the ideas of genetic and cultural deprivation.

More recently, the culture of poverty arguments from the 1960s have reemerged in the popularly written teachers' manuals and workshops of Ruby Payne (2001).

Figure 4.4   Talking About Class: Making it Personal

This issue is so central to the thesis of this book that I will change out of textbook style writing and use a personal example to illustrate. I, the author, was raised among the working class. I experienced the way the working people see and experience the world, how they relate to food, money, relationships, education, conflict, and other aspects of life. Both of my parents worked in factories for most of their lives. My cousins, uncles, and grandparents, all worked in the factories. My mother finished high school, but my father did not. I worked in factories for five years myself while going to college.

Today, I have a doctorate and a position as a college professor. In my view, none of the descriptors of generational poverty found in Payne's writings fits the experiences in my family or the families that I grew up with. And now I have read the research on social class as reviewed in the prior pages of this chapter. Neither my own experience nor the research supports the poverty ideas suggested by Ruby Payne.

And more. My wife (coauthor of Chapter 5) was raised in a Mexican American and Tigua Indian family along the U.S. border. Her father and mother both worked hard all their lives. They had extended families of aunts and cousins. A generation later most of the family has made it distinctly into the middle class; all are English dominant. None of the descriptions of poverty found in Payne's writings fits the experiences of this family.

Although her writings have encouraged teachers think about issues of poverty and family disruption, the reintroduction of the cultural deficit framework has all of the problems of earlier deficit thinking.

Payne has described some of the interactive manners in which poverty and family disruption contribute to school problems. Indeed, the middle class, to which author Payne claims to belong, has many examples of family disruption, lack of order, and living in the moment—maladies that Payne describes as representative of poverty.

Certainly, the school killings in Jonesboro, Arkansas (on March 24, 1998); Littleton, Colorado (on April 20, 1999); Santee, California (on March 5, 2001); and Blacksburg, Virginia (on April 16, 2007, when 32 were killed at Virginia Tech)—as well as the ongoing crisis of domestic violence and incidents of extreme violence in middle-class schools—indicate that dysfunctional lives and lack of preparation of children also occur within the middle class.

Payne, in her writings and her workshops, describes a stereotype of people in poverty. Do these people exist? Certainly. Are they representative of the poor or the working class? No evidence is provided in her writing. Instead, the social science research evidence contradicts the stereotypes and has consistently indicated that a culture of poverty does not exist (Gorski, 2008; Weis, 2004; Wilson, 1996). Poor people do not have one way of thinking or one way of relating to others. These traits all vary across cultures, ethnic groups, and living experiences. It is almost as if you were to say, "All Americans are arrogant." There are some Americans who are arrogant and others who are not.

Payne's anecdotes are well received in workshops in part because they support and reinforce stereotypes that many middle class teachers have of the poor as well as stereotypes commonly repeated in the media. They also provide an explanation—albeit a faulty one—of the observable connection between poverty and school failure. Unfortunately, the explanation faults the individual child and the family, while avoiding analysis of how the U.S. economy reproduces poverty and economic inequality. Author Paul Gorski (2006) describes the issue well: "Then I read *A Framework*. And I was horrified. Instead of a commitment to equity and justice I found a framework for understanding poverty that frames poverty as a deficit among students and parents and draws upon racist and classist stereotypes" (Gorski, 2006).

As an author and a presenter, Ruby Payne describes the important work of Rueven Feuerstein in a manner that projects his ideas far beyond the original research samples (Payne, 2001). Using concepts from mental disability research to describe class differences is an overextension and thus inappropriate. If there is evidence to support the application of mental disability research to poverty, it has not been presented in Payne's book.

Some middle-class teachers find the interventions suggested by Payne useful, while some scholars (Bomer, Dworin, May, & Semingston, 2008; Gorski, 2008) find them insulting. The teaching strategies may work, but they would also be useful with middle-class kids. There is not much evidence of a distinct poverty culture or lifestyle. There is significant evidence that the problems experienced by the unemployed can overwhelm poor families. And when a school has a large number of children from impoverished families, these problems come to school. Payne's writing and presentations unfortunately add to the students' problems. Now, in addition to all the problems of poverty, students face a teacher with a stereotype—a faulty explanation—of school behavior.

Payne's *A Framework for Understanding Poverty* (2001) is easily written, based upon anecdotes rather than reasoned evidence and accessible without serious consideration of the role of class or the role of racial stereotypes in our society. She reports that it has sold over 1 million copies. While extreme poverty and family disruption due to a severe illness or the incarceration of a parent may explain the lagging achievement of individual students, they do not explain why an entire class of students—the poor—has fewer experienced teachers and fewer resources in their schools. Lack of prepared teachers and lack of resources are the result of political decisions made by taxing authorities and state legislatures.

The conceptual framework used in *A Framework for Understanding Poverty* opens the doors again to the deficit hypothesis about culture, which has historically proven to be a destructive analysis (Bomer et al., 2008). The presentations and workbooks fit well into a conservative ideology about poverty in which racism and oppression are not significant issues; it is all about individual behavior. Focusing on individual behavior rather than social structural change is the opposite of using a social-class perspective. Clearly, success in our society is dependent on both individual behavior and the social structural opportunities provided to children (Rothstein, 2008). It is precisely these kinds of oversimplifications and stereotypes that Payne offers, wrapped up and presented as if they were research, that contribute to the creation of the compensatory educational policies of drill and more drill encouraged by No Child Left Behind. These conservative ideologues do not understand poverty (and race), so their solutions miss the mark.

School Responses to Poverty

While avoiding stereotypes, we need to recognize that class (or poverty) may explain some of the problems of school failure (Sampson, Sharkey, & Raudenbush, 2008). Patrick J. Finn (1999), in one of the few books that deal positively with working-class children and schools, argues as follows:

> When it comes to schooling, the working class suffers because of the dynamics of class and language in two ways. First, their habitual use of implicit, context-dependent language, and their relative lack of comfort in using explicit language (in school settings) puts them at a tremendous disadvantage in terms of acquiring higher levels of literacy that rely on highly explicit language. Second, their style of authority and their attitude of powerlessness in dealing with institutions and agencies explain why they wind up in classrooms like Anyon's working-class classrooms. . . .
>
> The language of the school, especially the language of school books, is explicit. The explicit language that more affluent children learn at home prepares them for the ever so much more explicit language of the school, particularly the language of books. The implicit language that working-class children become accustomed to at home doesn't.

Finn also points out that reading scores on standardized tests confirm this viewpoint:

> By fifth grade the correlations between reading scores and the status of their parents' occupations are considerable. Not that all working-class children do poorly or that all rich children

do well, but it is a safe bet that the average reading score for one hundred randomly selected affluent kids would be considerably higher than the average reading score for one hundred randomly selected working-class students. . . .

As working-class children progress through school, their reading scores fall farther and farther below their actual grade level. (Finn, 1999, p. 90)

Finn (1999) argues that teachers, even well-meaning teachers, treat working-class children and children from affluent families very differently. He describes reading lessons where one group is given a collaborative lesson, and the lower group is given a very traditional directive lesson:. "The resulting inequality—empowering education for some and domesticating education for others—is about as savage as any I can think of . . ." (Finn, 1999). And while the most recent scores from the Program for International Student Assessment (PISA) show that U.S. students continue to lag behind students from other nations, these results also reveal that social class has more of a negative impact on math and science achievement in the United States than in other modern nations (Organization for Economic Cooperation and Development, 2006).

Because race and class interact, improving schools for the working and the poverty classes would improve schools for the majority of African American, Latino, Asian, Native American, and European American students.

We have not tried in any significant manner to improve schools by overcoming poverty, by providing high-quality health care and high-quality child care, so that children arrive at school healthy, well-fed, and on time (Berliner, 2005; Children's Defense Fund, 2006). And in the age of testing and accountability, we have few examples of the implementation of bilingual and/or multicultural education in an organized, high-quality curriculum with appropriate teacher support. There will be more on improving schools in Chapters 12 and 13.

Those who respect democratic values insist that all students deserve schools and teachers of equal quality. Most states do not provide a semblance of equity (Kozol, 2005). Lawsuits in California, for example, point out the extremes of dilapidated, rat-infested, falling-down schools for the poor (e.g., *Williams v. California,* 2000), and the Education Trust (2006) has published a well-documented report, *Funding Gaps 2006,* that details inequitable funding patterns in other states.

So What Can I Do in the Classroom?

It is harmful and stereotypical to assume that children in poverty-stricken neighborhoods or from poor families have "characteristic" problems in school. Children have different language patterns, but all of these can lead to literacy (Finn, 1999). Living in a poor neighborhood does not always produce low reading and math scores, although living in a violent and disruptive family or attending a violent and disruptive school might. A wide variety of people and families lives in poverty. Some are homeless; some are chronically unemployed, low-skilled, and even criminals. Most are not. Teachers' attitudes and decisions about teaching strategies may produce substantial differences in reading (Finn, 1999; Gee, 2001; Taylor, 1998).

As teachers, it is important for us to focus on what we can do rather than spending our time blaming families for their economic hardships. Classrooms need fewer disruptions. Teachers need more time to work with children. Special compensatory education programs must not interrupt the normal flow of classroom instruction. Children need a safe and orderly environment in order to learn basic skills.

As Jonathan Kozol has pointed out in his many books, schools could serve to promote democracy instead of recycling a society divided into the rich, the middle, and the poor. They could serve as a response to poverty. If we made this political choice, marginalized neighborhoods and cities would have safe, clean, well-constructed schools, with counselors, nurses, security, and high-quality instruction. To date, political leaders have not decided to provide such schools. Teachers working in the difficult environments of the current school systems deserve support from political leaders and the media.

Schools and teachers can improve opportunity by recognizing the often conflict-centered role of oppositional culture. Teachers need to assist students to work out their culture conflicts and their identity conflicts; they cannot leave these vital matters primarily to gangs and peer group influence. School would be a more positive location for working-class kids if the theater, music, arts, sports, and leadership development programs were returned to the curricula, particularly if the arts, media production, and music studied were from working-class culture. And, importantly, not only middle-class kids but also working-class kids need to be involved in the schools' leadership development programs. We need to build on the students' strengths and offer young people positive reasons to go to school.

Much of the current curricula fails the working-class students, both those who are European American and those who are from ethnic and linguistic minority groups. Students need to see their real lives in the curriculum and textbooks. By high school, history/social studies and economics classes should study the economic classes, not pretend that these classes do not exist. We need to tell students the truth about economics and power. When alienation and withdrawal have occurred in middle schools and secondary schools, some states have developed quality school-to-career development programs. By the junior or senior year, many disaffected students should be working part-time in quality jobs (not fast-food restaurants or other sales jobs) where math, science, computer use, and writing skills are required. Carnegie-Mellon University in Pittsburgh, Pennsylvania, demonstrated that significant opportunities for school-to-career development are available by arranging for working-class high school students to partner with university-based programs that provide jobs and job preparation. Certainly, working on college campuses, in paid positions as student assistants, encourages high school students to consider higher education opportunities.

High schools have been particularly weak in finding ways to build a mutually beneficial relationship between the family and the school. While many adolescents work hard to keep the family away from school, teachers need to work even harder to overcome these separations. Divisions between home and school strengthen youth culture and often undermine school and home values. Teachers from working-class families can learn to serve as cultural mediators to improve the communications systems between school and home. Middle- and upper-class homes have developed new, online methods of tracking assignments, attendance, and homework. New systems that reach out to the working poor need development. The working poor want the same educational opportunities for their children. And because working people are so overwhelmed by work schedules, they are less able to provide the needed supervision of home life. This leads students to rely on peers for advice and support, a process often in opposition to school culture and school success. There are more ideas in the "Teaching Strategies for Use with Your Students" section at the end of this chapter.

Summary

A growing crisis of poverty, particularly among children, contributes to many of the failures in our school system. Multicultural education employs the concept of social class along with race, ethnicity, culture, and gender in describing, designing, and improving schools.

While poverty and family disruption may explain the performance of individual students, they do not explain why an entire class of students receives fewer resources. Schools serving poor communities usually are underfunded, are staffed with less-experienced teachers, and frequently practice tracking and accept low standards of achievement. These school practices, not the individual characteristics of children, provide unequal educational opportunity and produce failure. Federally funded and directed compensatory education programs have not remedied the problems of our failing schools in urban areas. Attention to social class helps to explain the persistent failure of students in poverty-stricken schools.

Questions over the Chapter

1. List factors that contributed to the significant increase in the number of children living in poverty.
2. List three recommendations for school improvement from each conceptual scheme: (a) socioeconomic status and (b) social class.
3. From 1967 to 1968, Dr. Martin Luther King, Jr., and the Southern Christian Leadership Conference expanded their emphasis from civil rights to include economic justice.

a. What were the important elements of an economic justice agenda in the 1960s?
b. Describe the elements of an economic justice agenda today.
4. What are the differences in policy recommendations that result from a racial analysis and from a race–class analysis of school achievement?
5. What can schools and teachers do to respond to the rise in poverty among children?

Activities for Further Study of Class Relationships in Schools

1. Observe and document the broad spectrum of diversity found in a classroom, such as culture, ethnicity, gender, social class, and gifted and talented. What are the different groups in the class? How many members are there in each? Does the

teacher devote more time to students from certain groups? Do certain students receive more criticism and punishment?

2. Take a walking tour of the immediate neighborhood of the school in which you are working. Record your impressions and share them with your classmates.

3. Several members of your class may be among the working poor. Ask them to describe their monthly budget for a family.

Teaching Strategies for Use with Your Students

1. Find literature, music, and videos that begin in the students' own experiences and reach to universal themes and skills.

2. Validate the students' own languages and cultures.

3. Integrate reading and oral and written language instruction and skills into several subject-matter areas.

4. Include hands-on learning activities whenever possible.

5. Plan and teach specific study skills as a part of the curriculum. Begin at the students' actual skill levels. Teach the use of texts, paragraph writing, and other necessary skills.

6. Maintain the goal of reading and writing at the skill levels of the middle-class suburban schools (or of the state standards). Do not lower your expectations for achievement.

7. Teach standard, appropriate, academic English as a valuable system of communication in addition to the students' vernacular expressions.

8. Build a classroom climate of safety, trust, and community building.

9. Study and encourage pro-school values.

10. Maintain high expectations. Support students as they develop their language and literacy. Insist that they develop academic language and literacy.

11. By high school, teach about economic classes and the economic consequences of school leaving. The video and curriculum *When the Levees Broke* will assist with discussions of class. The book *Field Guide to the U.S. Economy* (Teller-Elsberg, Heintz, & Folbre, 2006) has excellent graphs and cartoons that can be reproduced for classroom use.

12. Seek positive relationships with families.

13. Use active teaching strategies: reading, writing, speaking, and listening.

5

How Society and Schools Shortchange Girls and Boys

with Dolores Delgado-Campbell

> All I ask our brethren is that they take their feet from
> off our necks and permit us to stand upright on the ground
> which God destined for us to occupy.
> *Sarah Grimke, 1837*

> No person in the United States shall, on the basis of sex,
> be excluded from participation in, be denied the benefits of,
> or be subjected to discrimination under any education program
> or activity receiving Federal financial assistance. . . .
> *Title IX of the Education Amendments of 1972, U.S. Congress*

Gender Roles and Schools

There are strong similarities between sexism and racism. Both teach role relationships that leave one group in a subordinate position. Both are primarily expressed through institutional arrangements of privilege for some and oppression for others. Both are forms of violence: individual and collective, psychological and physical. Previous chapters described how African Americans, Latinos, and Native Americans, among others, are harmed by low expectations; being female also leads to subtle forms of tracking—even by female teachers (Ginorio & Huston, 2001).

Amott and Matthaei (1991) argue that gender, like race, is as much a social as a biological category:

Gender differences in the social lives of men and women are based on, but not the same thing as, biological differences between the sexes. Gender is rooted in societies' beliefs that the sexes are naturally distinct and opposed social beings. These beliefs are turned into self-fulfilling prophecies through sex-role socialization; the biological sexes are assigned distinct and often unequal work and political positions, and turned into distinct genders. (p. 13)

The school site is a stage on which gender roles are developed in our society, and thus schools contribute to the assignment of unequal status and work opportunity in our rapidly changing economy. Schools serve as "gatekeepers," providing opportunity to some but not to all.

In 1992, the American Association of University Women (AAUW) issued an important report, *How Schools Shortchange Girls*. In part, it said:

> The absence of attention to girls in the current educational debate suggests that girls and boys have identical educational experiences in schools. Nothing could be further from the truth. Whether one looks at achievement scores, curriculum design, self-esteem levels, or staffing patterns, it is clear that sex and gender make a difference in the nation's public elementary and secondary schools. There is clear evidence that the educational system is not meeting girls' needs. Girls and boys enter school roughly equal in measured ability. In some measures of school readiness, such as fine motor control, girls are ahead of boys. Twelve years later, girls have fallen behind their male classmates in key areas such as higher-level mathematics and measures of self-esteem. (p. 2)

The AAUW issued important follow-up reports in 1998 and 2008, keeping track of progress and limits in school reform. There has been a near revolution for majority group (European American) girls since the 1992 publication of *How Schools Shortchange Girls*.

Although problems continue in areas such as Advanced Placement course enrollments, in general girls are achieving better than boys in almost all grades (Corbett, Hill, & St. Rose, 2008). The crisis in public schools, particularly the crisis in low-income and predominantly minority schools, impacts the girls in these schools as well as the boys. The AAUW's 1998 follow-up report Gender Gaps: Where Schools Still Fail Our Children and *¡Si, Se Puede! Yes, We Can: Latinas in Schools* (Ginorio & Huston, 2001 make it clear that many Latinas are not achieving primarily because they are in low-achieving (poverty) schools, not because they are girls.

Tracking Female Students

For girls, especially middle-class European American girls, attending school in the United States can mean getting a head start in the early grades only to be tracked and subsequently held back or diverted into less challenging fields in the higher grades. *Tracking* is a system wherein individuals are identified according to specified physiological, cultural, socioeconomic, or academic criteria and placed in academic course sequences (tracks) designed to fulfill select educational prerequisites, develop a specific skill set, or prepare them for specific careers. Oakes (1985) amplifies this definition:

> Tracking is the process whereby students are divided into categories so that they can be assigned in groups to various kinds of classes. Sometimes students are classified as fast, average, or slow learners and placed into fast, average, or slow classes on the basis of their scores on achievement or ability tests. Often teachers' estimates of what students have already learned or their potential for learning more determine how students are identified and placed. Sometimes students are classified according to what seems most appropriate to their future

lives. Sometimes, but rarely in any genuine sense, students themselves choose to be in "vocational," "general," or "academic" programs. (p. 3)

Tracking of women occurs in our schools despite the fact that the schools are predominantly female turf. For example, women now constitute a majority of all college students and 79 percent of all teachers, concentrated particularly at the elementary school level (National Education Association, 2003).

The women in charge of these classrooms and schools are usually European American. In most elementary schools, girls are not systematically disparaged and criticized by teachers for being girls, although they may be disparaged for being lower-class Latinas, African Americans, or Asians. The emotions and turmoil of middle-class European American girls are sympathetically understood by elementary school authorities, both teachers and principals. The female-dominated institution produces success for European American girls during the critical early years when each one is defining her own identity and her relationship to learning and schooling (Sadker, Sadker, & Long, 1989).

Self-Esteem

Although racism and sexism both have damaging effects on the oppressed and on the oppressor, their manifestations in the early years of school are often quite different from their adult forms. While the excellent AAUW report argues that positive cross-sex relationships may be more difficult than cross-race relationships, in elementary schools the problem is more complex. This is because families and schools generally are much better at giving young children positive cross-gender experiences than they are at giving them positive cross-racial experiences. Several examples can be seen in the typical home.

Children develop a view of self in their very early years, usually in the intimate and nurturing surroundings of the home. Evidence indicates that children learn both about themselves and about others by at least age four. Most learning of "appropriate" role relationships takes place under the guidance of females, either in the home or in child care.

When children or adults work in an intimate relationship with another person in a positive environment, they learn to like and respect that person. This equal-status interaction teaches mutual respect (Buteyn, 1989; National Education Association, 1990; Sadker et al., 1989). Most little boys have an intimate, trust-building relationship or an equal-status relationship with at least one female—usually their mother. In the early formative years, most boys learn to respect and love their mother or some other female caregiver, such as a grandmother or an aunt. Few young boys learn to dominate their mothers. This early relationship should provide a basis for future learning of mutual respect and cooperation in relationships with women.

Of course, this picture does not match the experience of all children. In a home with an abusive or dominating parent, children may learn abusive and dominating patterns. In homes with a single female head of household, boys may still learn respectful relationships. In some such homes, however, boys may fail to experience positive relationships with males. They then may get guidance from television and the streets—both inadequate substitutes for a caring family. However, generally speaking, prior to age six, most young boys and girls learn to interact with their peers without male dominance.

Their early experience of respect and cooperation provides a basis for learning future equality-based relationships.

While families provide opportunities for cross-gender respect, they seldom provide opportunities for cross-racial respect. Most U.S. neighborhoods, cities, and families are segregated by race and culture. Most of our cities were more racially segregated in 2000 than they were in 1960 (Orfield & Lee, 2006). Too many of our young children do not develop an intimate, loving, caring relationship with persons of other races.

The teaching profession remains female dominated and racially segregated (National Education Association, 2003). As a result, too few young students have a positive relationship with a teacher from a minority racial or ethnic group. The lack of this intimate, perception-shaping experience makes learning mutual respect and cooperation in cross-cultural relationships more difficult. Some children learn to fear the "other," the outsider. This fear establishes a basis for future learning of prejudice.

The lack of cultural diversity in the upbringing and schooling of young children hits the children of minority cultures hardest. When African American, Vietnamese, or Latina girls enter school, they enter a new culture, often one where they are regarded as "other," "different," and "inferior." The shock may be profound. Some of these children may suddenly feel uncertain about themselves and become withdrawn or defensive. Their ability to learn may also suffer. Too often failure and frustration in school attack a student's self-image and distort her view of her home culture (Au & Kawakami, 1994; Foster, 1994; Ginorio & Huston, 2001). Young girls (and boys) of color usually first experience an inferior, castelike status in their neighborhood school.

Entering school is a major, traumatic event in the lives of many girls (and boys) from these cultures. The average African American or Latina student enters school a few months behind her middle-class counterparts in skill development and remains behind for the next 12 years (Ginorio & Huston, 2001). Although school may not be the primary source of this society's oppressions, it is often the institution where tracking, labeling, and failing first occur.

Oakes (1988) documents the negative results of tracking African American and Latina youths away from college-bound classes and into general, homemaking, and business courses. Evidence indicates that Catholic schools track Latinas less than do public schools (Oakes, 2005) and that tracking remains a problem for Latinas in public schools (Ginorio & Huston, 2001).

Research on European American Girls

School failure and intrusion are substantially different for European American girls than for members of racial and linguistic minorities. Studies by Sadker et al. (1989) and others (which focus mainly on European American girls) show that gender-based bias in school is significant and powerful. Some schools still track girls to mothering roles and boys to college. In the 1980s and 1990s, girls scored lower than boys on some math and science measures, but by 2000, these differences had been virtually erased (U.S. Department of Education, 2007).

In the primary grades, the school's failure of girls takes different forms. The average girl enters school academically ahead of boys her age and remains ahead (as measured by grades and test scores) through the elementary grades (AAUW, 1992). For these girls, the major problems with school achievement occur after they leave the predominantly female turf of elementary schools.

A multiracial perspective on gender and student achievement leads to distinctly different conclusions for students of color. Unlike students of color, young European American girls normally do not come to school and encounter a new environment run by "others." These girls go from a usually female-centered home culture to a female-centered school culture. Schools and teachers have positive expectations for them. Young, middle-class European American girls do not encounter the substantially destructive attacks on their gender that young minority children (male or female) encounter in their culture. When students share class, race, and gender with the teacher or the counselor, they are usually encouraged to "become the best they can be." Female students from several minority cultures encounter the oppression of race and class in school.

Fortunately, gender-role stereotyping in schools is decreasing, but it remains a problem (National Coalition for Women and Girls in Education, 2002). The efforts to reduce gender stereotyping among teachers create new questions about school achievement across cultural groups.

It is often boys, particularly African American, Latino, and Asian boys, who lack role models for the first six years of schooling. Whereas European American girls benefit from their female-centered primary school experience, children of color—particularly boys—fail. It is boys who encounter the most conflicts, receive the most punishments, and most often get placed in special education and remedial programs (Flood, 2000).

The positive school experiences of girls begin to change in adolescence. The teenage years in our society are a time of redefining self and roles. Young girls and boys who were once self-confident now search for new identities. Earlier self-definitions shift. For many teenagers, belonging to a group becomes a major goal. Young people look to their peers for guidance through these difficult and troubling years.

Schoolgirls, at least those European American girls studied, suffer significant declines in self-esteem as they move from childhood to adolescence. A nationwide study commissioned by the AAUW in 1990 found that on average 69 percent of elementary school boys and 60 percent of elementary school girls reported being "happy the way I am"; among high school students, the percentages were 46 percent for boys and only 29 percent for girls.

The AAUW survey revealed sharp differences in self-esteem among girls from different racial and ethnic groups. Among elementary school girls, 55 percent of white girls, 65 percent of black girls, and 68 percent of Hispanic girls reported being "happy the way I am." But in high school, agreement statements came from only 22 percent of white girls and 30 percent of Hispanic girls, compared to 58 percent of black girls. However, these black girls did not have high levels of self-esteem in areas related to school success. Obviously, self-esteem is a complex construct, and further study of the various strengths and perspectives of girls from many different backgrounds is needed in order to design educational programs that benefit all girls. (American Association of University Women, 1992, pp. 12–13)

Young girls who excelled in elementary school may begin to falter as they enter the middle grades (6 through 8). Particular concern has been expressed by teachers over the falling grades of girls in science and math (National Coalition for Women and Girls in Education, 2008). Gilligan, in her groundbreaking work *In a Different Voice* (1982), hypothesizes that many girls acquire feminine ways of learning and relating to others that are distinctly different from the behavior described as universal to boys and girls by psychologists. In critiquing prominent theories of moral behavior, she states, "While the truths of psychological theory have blinded psychologists to the truth of women's experience, that experience illuminates a world psychologists have found hard to trace" (p. 62). Another researcher, Tannen (1990), describes differences in communication styles learned by boys and girls. It is important to keep in mind that these roles, like all roles within cultures, are constantly changing.

The writing and research of feminist authors also provide important insights into classroom differences. Tavris (1992) systematically examines the research on differences between males and females and finds that many assumptions and assertions have been overgeneralized beyond the available evidence. Her book, *The Mismeasure of Woman*, provides an excellent analysis of overinterpretation from limited data, criticizing work in learning styles and brain activity as well as Gilligan's assumptions about value orientations and relationships. We must assume, until proven otherwise, that gender differences do not explain or cause differences in school achievement; these differences can be attributed to how teachers and schools treat children (Tannen, 1990; Tavris, 1992).

Early research by Dweck and her associates suggested that girls may learn "helplessness" in math based in part on teacher expectations and on how teachers respond to and evaluate student work. Teachers of either gender could unknowingly concentrate their responses to girls in a way that discourages intellectual effort, particularly in math (Dweck, 1977). Various researchers have chronicled the several ways that females and males do not receive the same support from teachers. Carinci (2007) notes that this teacher behavior has a cumulative destructive effect on female students. The most recent data we have are from the National Assessment of Educational Progress (NAEP) for 2007. In reading, girls consistently outperform boys at the fourth-grade level, and in math, girls score within two points of boys (U.S. Department of Education, 2007). On the SAT test, often used by the most selective colleges to determine admission, boys continue to significantly outperform girls in math (Corbett, Hill, & St. Rose, 2008). On the other hand, as a consequence of their overall achievement, girls are admitted to college at a higher rate than are boys.

Years of effort and emphasis on closing the achievement gap for girls, encouraged by Title IX, may have produced significant change since the early research by Dweck. Concerns continue about girls' success in math. If you ask what percentages of boys and girls are at or above "proficient" in math for their grade level, you get the data shown in Table 5.1.

Table 5.1 reveals a 4 percent to 7 percent advantage for boys in math proficiency as measured by this test. When the same data are sorted by ethnicity, as in Table 5.2, the differences between boys and girls are small, while the differences between ethnic groups (both boys and girls) are large. Corbett, Hill, and St. Rose (2008) say it well: "Large discrepancies have long existed in the American educational system and continue today.

Table 5.1   At or Above "Proficient" in Math for Their Grade Level in 2007

	Girls	Boys
Grade 4	36%	43%
Grade 8	29%	33%

Source: *The Nation's Report Card: Mathematics 2007*, by J. Lee, W. Grigg, and G. Dion, 2007, Washington, DC: U.S. Department of Education, Institute of Education Sciences, National Center for Education Statistics.

Table 5.2   8th Grade

Average Score	White	Black	Latino	Asian/Pacific
Females	289	260	264	296
Males	292	258	265	297
At or Above Proficient				
Grade 8 Both genders	41%	11%	15%	49%

Source: *The Nation's Report Card: Mathematics 2007*, by J. Lee, W. Grigg, and G. Dion, 2007, Washington, DC: U.S. Department of Education, Institute of Education Sciences, National Center for Education Statistics.

These long standing inequalities could be considered a 'crisis' in the sense that action is urgently needed. But the crisis is not specific to boys; rather, it is a crisis for Hispanic, African American, and low-income children—both boys and girls" (p. 68).

It is in middle school, as adolescents, that many girls crash into cultural expectations, an emphasis on looks, and a perceived lack of power. Although most girls make it through adolescence and redefine themselves and their gender roles in healthy ways, too many end up with severe emotional problems.

As young people reach adolescence, they become much more interested in their peer relationships and more distant from their families. In early adolescence, young people often struggle with family, wanting to be with their peers more. Their caregivers, parents, and teachers serve as models for how to interact with peers. Adolescents learn "appropriate" behavior from both their parents and their peer group.

In the last 30 years, we have witnessed a strong penetration of the home and school by popular culture, frequently observed in music and videos. Popular culture, such as music videos, also teaches and models another proposal of "appropriate" dress and behavior, a model that has been dramatically sexualized since the 1980s. Now, people as young as 9, 10, and 11 are presented with open and confrontive sexuality, drugs, and violence as a normal and natural process. Children develop their identities with both the popular culture choices and the family cultural choices presented to them, and market forces are very strong (Kilbourne, 2000; Leadbeater & Way, 1996).

In middle school and high school, when young women's concern with appearance peaks, some experience harassment for their looks, and others are harassed because they avoid sexuality. Peer pressure can lead to using drugs, having early sexual relations, and leaving school. School can be a harsh and difficult world to negotiate. Depression and eating disorders are frequent introductions to crises. Young women need coaches and support during this time (Pipher, 1994). We discuss this further in Chapter 6.

Feminist researchers have developed the concept of "silenced voices" among students. Fine (1993), in her study of a major New York City high school, found that systematic "silencing" of girls' voices (by not respecting their opinions) helped teachers to preserve an ideology of equal opportunity, when in fact the schooling practices reinforced inequality. Fine's research offers dramatic examples of the conflict between what some teachers want to pursue as democratic goals and the reality of public school experiences.

At the high school level, teachers' discomfort with discussing sexual issues prevented the school from serving as a source of valid and valuable information, so girls turned elsewhere, to the streets, for information. The work *Urban Girls: Resisting Stereotypes, Creating Identities* (Leadbeater & Way, 1996) deals with the multiple struggles of girls from diverse racial/ethnic and cultural groups. When schools refuse to deal with the urgent issues of young women—contraception, sexuality, and so on—some women choose to leave school (Fine, 1993).

By high school, girls begin to make career choices. Influenced in part by the ideology of movies, television, teen magazines, and popular culture, some—not all—young women learn to prefer nonacademic, unchallenging classes. They come to regard intellectually rigorous classes as "unfeminine." Faludi (1991, 2006) describes this as an "undeclared war" on women and feminism, arguing that some current counseling practices continue to track girls to become nurses rather than doctors, legal secretaries rather than lawyers, and elementary school teachers rather than college professors. The American Association of University Women (1992) reports that between 40 percent and 50 percent of female dropouts leave school because they are pregnant. Their child care responsibilities sharply limit their future economic opportunities. Later, deprived of a quality education, they will find themselves laboring long hours doing unfulfilling work for low pay in a gender-stratified workforce (National Coalition for Women and Girls in Education, 2002).

The Lure of the Beauty Myth

Many girls become preoccupied with their personal image and their relationships with others. Later, by high school, this becomes the "beauty and romance" myth. Television and other popular media teach that a girl can achieve success, defined as marriage and wealth, by becoming beautiful and shrewdly using her sexual powers.

Wolf (2002) discusses the destructive effects of the beauty industry and its ideology. As she describes in *The Beauty Myth: How Images of Beauty Are Used Against Women*, the myth is that girls do not need to prepare for a career; they can just be beautiful and become a model, a star, or at least a mother. (The male equivalent of this myth is to plan to become a major league sports figure and make millions of dollars.)

Girls who are heavily represented in Advanced Placement and higher track classes usually have a number of ways to express and to represent themselves and are less likely to buy the "beauty hype." For example, these girls may participate in band, dance, sports, clubs, and/or student government. On the other hand, African American girls and Latinas are underrepresented in these classes and usually have fewer school-based support systems to help them withstand the corporate beauty barrage. African American girls and Latinas are, at the same time, less represented in the ads and promotions of the beauty culture.

The Sexualization of Girlhood

The popular culture gives girls contradictory messages about womanhood and sexuality and masks the violence that is perpetrated against them. The media disseminate a vast number of messages about identity and acceptable forms of self-expression, gender, sexuality, and lifestyle (American Psychological Association, 2007; Gauntlett, 2002), while the adolescent culture often also yields inaccurate and uninformed expectations about sexuality. Further complicating the realities of gender messages are societal conditions that girls are raised in: growing divorce rates, chemical addictions, casual sex, and violence against women—all have had a profound impact on the development of women's roles.

Dr. Mary Pipher's study of adolescent girls, *Reviving Ophelia* (1994), examines the challenges for young women growing up in a looks-obsessed, media-saturated, "girl-poisoning" culture. Increasingly, girls have been sexualized and objectified in every facet of the popular culture—advertising, movies, music videos, and video games—leaving few protected spaces where they can claim a true and wholesome identity.

Wolf (2002) argues that some girls' self-esteem may be predicated on being admired by boys, usually for their physical beauty or sexual availability. Adolescents become increasingly influenced by their peer culture as they begin to form a new identity. And vulnerability to peer groups generally peaks in early adolescence and remains important as individuals move through high school into young adulthood. Lack of knowledge and awareness of one's sexual identity makes one more susceptible to peer pressure (Levy, 2005). This realization peaks in adolescence during a time when middle school girls sense their lack of power in society but generally are unable to articulate what they sense.

According to Pipher (1994), "bright and sensitive girls" are most likely to understand the implications of the media around them and be alarmed, yet they lack the cognitive, emotional, and social skills to handle this information. "They struggle to resolve the unresolvable and to make sense of the absurd" (p. 43). Less perceptive girls miss the meaning in sexist ads, music, and shows entirely, thereby aiding their subordination in a consumer-based society that capitalizes on their experiences.

How do young girls cope? Pipher (1994) identifies four general coping styles that girls display: conformity, withdrawal, depression, and anger. Ariel Levy, in *Female Chauvinist Pigs: Women and the Rise of Raunch Culture* (2005), argues that another way that some girls deal with this is to become sexually provocative. Each of these strategies can be debilitating without adequate intervention from people who can help these girls to analyze the culture pressures and to reclaim a sense of self-worth. Pressure to fit in with the peer group expectations and norms has a cost. For example, a recent study conducted by the Alan Guttmacher Institute, a nonprofit organization that focuses on sexual and reproductive health research, policy analysis, and public education, found that the younger the women are when they have intercourse, the more likely they are to have had unwanted or involuntary sex (Guttmacher, 1999). Many young women try too hard to fit the mold—to be slender, feminine, and perfect; to fit a false male-imposed expectation (American Psychological Association, 2007). They have been trained to be what the culture wants of its women.

More recently in the United States, feminists have examined the oversexualization of womanhood and ultimately girlhood. The Dove campaign for real beauty (*www. dove.us*) attempts to send a positive message to young women: Accept yourself, your face, your body, your size. Acceptance of our physical self is vital, and women continue to be valued primarily as sex objects in the media.

Hollywood presents an alternative scenario. Notice all the attention given to the escapades of the once popular singer Britney Spears. She had a 24-hour marriage, a quicky annulment or divorce, and car crashes; she was seen drinking, driving under the influence, driving with no underwear, shaving her head, and driving around town with no proper safety seats for her sons. Now divorced, she has lost custody of her sons.

Consider Lindsay Lohan, Amy Winehouse, Paris Hilton, and Nicole Ritchie. These young women are promoted as role models—as persons that young people should admire and try to look like. Drugs, alcohol, and questionable sexual behavior are promoted as positive. Our daughters and our sons are constantly reminded of just how important—and rich—these people are. The media record their every move. Extreme behavior, regardless of how bizarre, is written, text messaged, and blogged about and placed on Facebook. News headlines and television specials thrive on this behavior.

How does this affect young girls? A student of mine and her daughter were visiting me in my office. As I greeted them, the young single mother whispered in my ear, "Help me with Sydney. She is driving me crazy wanting me to buy her clothes like Britney Spears wears." Sydney is 5½ years old.

Before our sons and daughters get to school, they are bombarded with television ads, billboards, and magazine ads. Among the heavily promoted items are the Bratz Dolls. They are a more cutting-edge Barbie—dressed in mini skirts, tops with plunging necklines, and belly-showing clothing, with multicolored hair and gaudy jewelry—for 5- to 10-year-olds. The copyright battle between the Bratz and Barbie has gone to court.

In recent years, television has attempted to regain the youth market through "reality" shows such as *Survivor*, *Roommates*, *The Bachelor*, *The Bachelorette*, and *Girls Gone Wild*. *Girls Gone Wild* is a program emphasizing, encouraging, promoting, and publicizing raunch female culture. Most often the camera follows girls and guys on spring break at beaches in Mexico, Florida, and Hawaii. College life is portrayed as sun, fun, drinking, dancing, and hooking up. Little is left to the imagination. The bikinis are skimpy, and girls flash their bodies—their breasts, butts, and genitals—for the camera. Hooting and yelling are the primary script. For this exhibition, girls get a hat, a T-shirt, and 1–2 minutes live on television.

Joe Francis, the creator of *Girls Gone Wild*, likens the flashing girls he captures to feminists burning their bras in the seventies (a media distortion). He argues that his productions are sexy for men and liberating for women—good for the goose and good for the gander. Francis estimates that *Girls Gone Wild* is worth $100 million (Levy, 2005).

What do young people learn by watching such programs?

Recently, the television hit *Sex in the City* was made into a movie. In its prime years, it was targeted to appeal to young professional women living and loving in New York City. As more women go to graduate school and move into the professions, this show claims to portray their lives. Some new television series such as *Saving Grace*, about a female detective in Oklahoma, and *The Closer*, about a female deputy chief investigator in Los Angeles, attempt to portray strong, complex women in professional roles.

Jeane Kilbourne is a major writer who has recorded the effects of sex-role stereotyping in the media. She argues that television viewing makes an independent contribution to adolescents' sex-role attitudes over time, given that the average American is exposed to more than 3,000 advertisements a day and watches three years' worth of television ads over the course of a lifetime. Kilbourne suggests that this barrage of advertising drastically affects young people, especially girls, by offering a distorted reality regarding women's lives and portrayals in popular culture.

In addition, she argues that there is a reciprocal relationship between the amount of television viewing and the degree of congruence between sex-role attitudes and behavior. Consequently, the amount of television viewing, coupled with what adolescents learn from their families about media sexuality, is the strongest determinant of how young people's behavior is affected by popular cultural images (Childers & Brown, 1989; Kilbourne, 1999). Newcomer and Brown's (1984) study found a strong and significant relationship between the amount of sexually oriented television programs watched (as a proportion of all television viewed) and the probability of an adolescent's having had intercourse.

Given the power of the media's negative messages about women, young girls must be educated to recognize and reject this socialization. This begins with teaching young people to understand how the media and our culture impact our thinking, in order to gain self-knowledge and to develop their total capabilities. Only when this occurs can we help young women to make conscious choices about who they are and what they want rather than subconsciously conforming to society's expectations (Fitzell, 1997).

Young women need models in their lives that display assertiveness, strength, self-pride, and social responsibility. They need to see women in their lives who value their self-worth and their self-image and men who respect and validate self-confident women. As a result of the feminist movement of the 1960s and 1970s, today women are writers, producers, anchors, editors, and publishers of important newspapers, magazines, and television and online news sources. They are on each of the national television networks and on local television and radio. In a consumer world captivated with fashion advertising, media hype, the music and video pop culture, and gender stereotypes, girls need these tangible female models who base their self-worth on who they are and not what society says they should be.

Television, film, the print media, and the culture of consumerism often shape teenage girls' worldviews more than does their school experience. For many, the shopping mall is the campus of choice.

Positive television viewing could help to counterbalance negative images. For example, cable networks such as the Disney Channel, UPN, PBS Kids, Nickelodeon, and Fox Family each provide positive programming that is appropriate for young viewers and teens.

Media Literacy

Issues such as violence against women and girls, eating disorders, coping with grief and loss, date rape, the rising rate of HIV/AIDS in teen populations, and the impact of teen pregnancy on girls' mobility should be integrated into classroom discussions and into school-based educational programs at an appropriate level of maturity. Teachers can have young people write letters to magazine editors and advertisers to let them know that they are offended by an ad. Young people can be encouraged to boycott products whose advertising is offensive. Teachers can also integrate meaningful and relevant biographical and nonfiction reading about women and girls into classroom content.

The number of school-based health centers has significantly increased. They provide an important source of counseling and medical care for low-income and uninsured young people. Although conservatives have attacked such clinics as interfering in the parents' role, the authors of the present chapter believe that it is better to not have 11- to 14-year-old girls getting pregnant and encountering sexually transmitted diseases. We prefer that young women grow beyond 16 before having children. To make it through adolescence without birthing children requires that young women and men clarify their own views on sex and sexuality and that they be taught adult decision-making skills.

Many online resources provide rich and age-appropriate information to use for classroom discussions on gender issues. *Ms.* magazine is one source that is at the forefront of exposing media stereotypes and helping young people learn about issues that affect women everywhere. Girlzone at *www.girlzone.com* is a lively resource where teachers can access girl-centered information on topics such as college, careers, health-related issues, sports participation, and summer reading lists. In addition, girls can read about how the world views and defines women and girls. This site provides a bulletin board where questions are posted and young people are able to express their views on issues. The site also provides opportunities for teens to post messages on topics that are important to them, and the staff has committed to respond to all girls' inquiries and questions. Teachers can construct classroom bulletin boards encouraging students to anonymously post their ideas about issues. This sharing can then be used as a springboard for weekly discussions on contemporary topics.

Adolescence is a time of high risk. Peer pressure to participate in sexual relationships at a young age has grown significantly in the last 20 years. Young women need self-confidence and support from others to protect themselves from the peer pressure and the sexual harassment they encounter in school (Rotheram-Borus, Dopkins, Sabate, & Lightfoot, 1996).

When questioned, young women report that the peer pressure to engage in sex by both boys and girls, and their own desire to love someone and to be loved, leads to sexual behavior and pregnancy (Hechinger, 1992; Pipher, 1994). Early pregnancy and childbirth lead many to leave school and face subsequent lifelong poverty. For some, early pregnancy is an introduction to a life of abuse and behavioral problems that are then passed on to their children (Children's Defense Fund, 2001).

Not all young people become interested in sex at age 11, or 12, or 14, or even 16. Interest in sex is a result of a complex series of social, psychological, biological, and cultural events. In our society, television, magazines, and movies regularly define being female as to "grow up" fast, to have breasts, to have a boyfriend, and to become sexually active. Many young people are pressured to be sexual—and to be sexually active—while they would still prefer the safety of early adolescence (Kilbourne, 1999; Pipher, 1994). Girls and boys, particularly in middle schools, deserve the support of empathetic teachers, counselors, and parents in their times of changing identities (Children's Defense Fund, 2001; Valenzuela, 1999).

Sexual behavior, particularly by the very young, has severe consequences (Pipher, 1994). Sexually transmitted diseases are on the rise. AIDS due to unprotected sex and drug abuse presents a serious crisis. Sexual education could be included in several areas of the curriculum, including literature, science, health education, and social studies. English literature classes, for example, could use stories or poems dealing with teenage sexuality. Role-playing peer pressure and writing journal entries can further explore these themes.

Assisting Young Women

Women teachers, with their own role identity clear, can assist young women by serving as mentors and encouragers and by providing a sounding board for young women's role and gender questions. Teachers, counselors, coaches, librarians, and nurses have opportunities to establish trusting and helping relations with these young women. If a teacher acts in a trusting and friendly way and respects students' confidences, she will attract students who are looking for support, a smile, and a person with whom they can talk. Often, a teacher's small gestures of encouragement and expressions of interest and support can change a student's direction (Figure 5.1; see also the discussion on coaching in Chapter 7).

Teachers can be the first to notice such crisis signs as bulimia or anorexia and to ask for the assistance of the school nurse or counselor. Teachers can bring out into open discussion the commercial overemphasis on looks, dress, and being thin that endangers some young women's lives. They can also be aware of signs of abuse: bruises, cuts, or broken bones. The pressure that some girls feel to "have a boyfriend" may include staying with a person who is possessive and abusive. In this situation, girls need to talk with a teacher, and the teacher can refer them to a local women's center. You can initiate these discussions by placing a domestic violence poster in your room or by handing out the business cards of a responsible center or by discussing material from *www.girlzone.com*. To keep current on these issues, we recommend *Ms.* magazine.

Many adolescent girls respond to their natural body growth with an unwarranted fear of weight gain. Young girls are dieting and skipping meals far too often for good

Figure 5.1 **A Teacher Inspires a Student**

> Maria's family moved, so she was forced to change schools in sixth grade. She was shy and insecure about her abilities. Her new teacher, Miss Vernon, taught both English and Spanish classes. She was gentle and encouraged Maria's comments, even though Maria spoke softly and avoided attention. Miss Vernon smiled and encouraged her with comments, a touch on the shoulder, and support.
>
> One day Miss Vernon stood next to Maria's desk and handed her an English paper with a large gold seal on it. She smiled and said, "Maria, you are a smart girl." Maria felt warm, glowing, and proud. This small event continues to inspire Maria to this day. She went on to college and is now a teacher herself. Whenever she faces a difficult problem, a confusing assignment, she remembers the encouragement and the faith that Miss Vernon had in her.

health. Schools cannot change the commercial media's emphasis on the "perfect" image, but they can promote a healthy balance of personality development, social skills development, good health, and physical fitness. Friendly teachers can advise young women on dress and makeup, countering the sometimes bizarre messages of magazines and television and thus helping students to develop healthy self-confidence.

The feminist movement of the 1970s and 1980s affected many teachers' views of themselves and of their roles as advocates for young girls. Weiler (1988) argues that feminist sociologists constructed a new way of looking at school success and girls' several forms of resistance to the arbitrary limitations on their futures Her work offers a detailed analysis of how several female teachers experienced gender issues. These teachers were committed to working with their students to challenge traditional gender roles. They each had a strong sense of social justice and drew from their commitment in selecting teaching strategies. Many believed that they, themselves, had suffered professionally as a result of the prior generation's rigid gender roles. In this study, each teacher's own sense of self, her view of her own relationship to feminist goals, was an important factor in her selection of instructional strategies. Teachers can find excellent materials on this subject at the Gender, Diversities and Technology Institute website, *www2.edc.org/gdi*.

Sexual Orientation

Friend (1993) argues that our schools and society have "a systematic set of institutional and cultural arrangements that reward and privilege people for being or appearing to be heterosexual, and establish potential punishments or lack of privilege for being or appearing to be homosexual" (p. 211).

Adolescents face many crises of identity. Some young people, about 10 percent, face a conflict between their emerging sexual orientation and the socially approved norm (Friend, 1993). Deciding on or accepting a sexual orientation other than the socially approved one involves a number of social, psychological, and personality conflicts. Recognizing homosexual orientation can provoke crises in students' lives. Students who acknowledge and exhibit homosexual behaviors are often subject to assault, harassment, and violence in school (Gipson, 2002). Violence toward homosexual students is a major problem for some students, and it deserves to be dealt with in the same manner as other hate crimes (Friend, 1993).

When students face such difficult decisions as whether to acknowledge or hide their sexual orientation, they need to talk with adults, with teachers, and with counselors. When the curriculum silences any student voices and omits coverage of sexual orientation issues, the vulnerable students are left on their own. When school administrators are unwilling to stop sexual violence, failing or leaving school and even considering suicide are among the consequences for these students. In addition to protection, students need opportunities to think and rethink their emotions, feelings, and decisions (Reveles, 2000). Human relations lessons on name-calling and homophobia provide opportunities for students to explore identity conflicts. Gay, lesbian, bisexual, and transgender (GLBT) issues are best taught in ways that are both age appropriate and situation appropriate. We do not teach young children about sexuality, but it is appropriate to discuss bias, discrimination, and identity at the appropriate maturity level. Harassment of students must be opposed and stopped. Under Title IX decisions, school districts that fail to stop harassment have been subject to significant awards for damages.

The school environment can be made more accepting. Some middle schools have social justice clubs with sponsored activities. Sexual orientation is a sensitive issue because students are often unsure of themselves and may not have come out to friends and family. This is more volatile in adolescence when identity and acceptance are such important issues (Leadbeater & Way, 1996; Reveles, 2000). Students who do acknowledge an orientation other than heterosexual are too often harassed and intimidated by classmates (Gipson, 2002). It is helpful if there are community agencies or support groups that can help these students and their families think through these issues and that can provide counseling, social activities, and support groups.

Limited Choices for Non-College-Bound Women

Until recently, the typical U.S. high school had little to offer non-college-bound female students in the way of technical and professional preparation. Business courses, for example, offered little more than secretarial training. Yet the business office of today requires advanced computer, graphics, and technology skills.

The conservative school reform movement (1982–2007) sought to reestablish a common academic curriculum for all students in high school. Schools concentrated their time, energy, and funds on improving academic programs. Opportunities for college-bound students improved. But in their emphasis on academic excellence, these reformers neglected vocational preparation—a critical omission at a time when job opportunities and the skills needed to take advantage of them were rapidly changing. Thus, the post–high school opportunities of non-college-bound students became more restricted than ever (Weis, 1988, 1990).

In 1994, the U.S. Congress passed, and President Clinton signed, the School to Work Opportunities Act (Public Law 103-239) to encourage states and local school districts to develop new high-technology programs to help students move from school to employment. The law was supplemented in 1998 by the Carl Perkins Vocational and Technical Education Act. Most states now have developed and implemented their own school-to-work programs. While states vary widely in their commitment to improving school-to-work opportunities, in general this segment of education has been desperately underfunded since the 1980s. Working-class students who are not going on to college often do not receive equal opportunities in secondary schools.

School-to-work programs offer preparation for the new knowledge-based economy to students as part of their high school and community college preparation. Well-developed programs motivate students to remain in school by providing them with workplace experience and introducing them to the adult world of work (see Figure 5.2). School-to-work counselors assist students in exploring new, emerging industries for their career choices. Equity efforts in school-to-work programs should include preparing girls for high-technology-based positions (National Coalition for Women and Girls in Education, 2002).

Teachers can assist students in taking advantage of school and work opportunities by sharing their own life histories and by encouraging young women to get a good education. Young women 16 to 18 years old often look mature and dress in an adult manner. Many even engage in adult sexual behavior. Yet their consciousness of the reality of the working world remains underdeveloped.

Feminist scholarship argues that girls benefit in school from assistance in developing self-confidence rather than relying on beauty images (Carinci, 2007; Erkut, Fields, Sing, & Marx, 1996). Girls should receive praise for their intellectual work, not for their conformity and obedience to marketed images of women. All young women need to be encouraged to pursue a well-rounded, rigorous education. Female teachers sharing experiences from their own lives validate the experiences of younger women.

Figure 5.2   A School-to-Work Success Story

Noemi was a troubled teenager. She daily considered leaving school. She was sexually involved and feared that she was pregnant. Her group of friends was into drugs, gang activity, and frequent petty crime. Her grade point average was 1.5, and she missed more than 20 days of school each semester.

Then a school-to-work counselor got her a position working in food preparation and catering. The work schedule forced her to be on time and to improve her cleanliness habits. Entering the world of work gave Noemi a feeling of maturity, an exit from her adolescent troubles. Her circle of friends changed as she worked daily and met new people, many of them more mature and with a sense of purpose.

She says, "I feel that I am more prepared for work than the college-bound students. I work in a real hospital, with real patients, employees, and customers. Every day I am learning something new.

"For me, getting an education now means more than just going to school. This [school-to-work] program (school-to-work) has really helped me to focus. Now I want to finish high school and go on to college."

Often neither the working class students nor their families understand the entry points for professions. Working as a nurse's aide or a teacher's aide places career alternatives in front of the students while they earn money. And the career world places them in daily contact with a number of adults and encourages adultlike behavior, such as preparing for the future.

Students appear to understand the system but do not. Few, for example, know that it takes five years to be a teacher or that most doctoral study is financed. We regularly encounter teenagers who do not know that tuition at state schools is very different from that at private colleges. Some teenagers pay thousands of dollars for training in a career or technical institute when the same preparation is available at the local community college for one-tenth of the cost. Most young people do not know the economics of jobs and careers. Teachers can ally with the students by helping with these immediate issues. If students do not know these basic issues, then they certainly do not know more subtle issues.

The number of high school (and college) students who work has tripled since the 1970s. Work hours and school assignments are often in conflict, with work winning out. Students, of course, are affected by the consumer culture and the beauty myth, as advanced on television, radio, the internet and other media. Young girls and boys know that self-esteem is often measured by the things you own, the clothes you wear, the car you drive, and even the cell phone you use.

One consequence of this extreme materialism is the desire to leave school for work. Many young people work not to contribute to the support of their family but to compete in this material world. Results include less homework turned in, lower grades, less participation in extracurricular events, and less commitment to schooling itself.

The new high-skills economy demands that students acquire both academic knowledge and workplace skills. School-to-work placements and multiple pathways approaches help students to earn money and to see the immediate application of their school courses. Work sites provide interesting, relevant, and paid experiences to encourage young women toward further training, two-year colleges, and quality entry-level jobs. Often work placement is a major motivation for students, and effective programs provide a guided transition from adolescence to adulthood.

Gender, Race, and Class

The importance of gender issues can change from one generation to the next and is culture specific. It is often difficult or impossible to separate race, class, and gender discrimination because the oppressions interact with each other. Research on the school behavior of girls and young women of color was notably absent until recently. Most researchers have assumed that young girls have similar experiences across cultures (Leadbeater & Way, 1996).

Women of color have gained university positions and political leadership in recent decades and have turned their research skills to documenting the conflicts faced by African American, Latina, and working-class girls in schools. Weis and Fine (1993) have documented some of the ways young women face and react to sex education in high schools, collecting powerful essays that begin to move beyond the more restricted early research boundary of European American women.

Boys Have Problems in School, Too

Recently, there has been recognition that boys, particularly African American and Latino boys, have increased problems in schools. In elementary school, boys are more likely to be diagnosed with learning disabilities and assigned to special education, are more likely to be suspended for behavior problems, and regularly score lower on standardized tests (Gurian & Stevens, 2005). In high school, boys drop out more and are more likely to be involved in serious disciplinary cases. Over 80 percent of violence in schools is initiated by boys (Flood, 2000). The excellent work of the Children's Defense Fund (2007) on the "cradle to prison pipeline" notes the increased incarceration of young men.

One reality is that with the dramatic changes in family structure, more and more single-parent families are headed by women and young boys in these families have fewer males to teach them appropriate, mature male behavior (U.S. Bureau of the Census, 2006). Increasing numbers of young boys bring disruptive and potentially violent behaviors to school. Schools, with few male teachers in the elementary grades, have difficulty dealing with this behavior (King & Gurian, 2006).

A special task force in the state of Maryland examined the particular crisis in school behavior and success of African American boys and recommended, among other ideas, single-gender classrooms in some schools (Task Force on the Education of Maryland's African-America Males, 2006).

We know from studies of incarceration and studies of working-class life that young women are being far more successful in avoiding incarceration and developing a professional life than are young men (Schmalleger & Bartollas, 2008). In a rapidly changing and globalizing economy, young women are being more successful than are young men (Weis, 2004).

A particular concern has been voiced about the destructive impact on African American children, particularly boys, of common public school practices such as negating children's home cultures and using biased assessment methods, usually carried out in elementary schools by female European American teachers. Researchers King, Foster, Ladson-Billings, and others have documented several basic issues facing African American girls and boys in classrooms in *Teaching Diverse Populations: Formulating a Knowledge Base* (Hollins, King, & Hayman, 1994b). They have suggested characteristics and tendencies in the African American culture that teachers can use as background information to reduce the cultural conflicts in the classroom and to improve student achievement. The excellent work *Urban Girls: Resisting Stereotypes, Creating Identities* (Leadbeater & Way, 1996) offers a needed balance to the earlier limited research.

The predominantly European American teaching profession needs such research to begin to understand the diverse classroom roles of girls and boys within specific cultures. For example, young Latinas who succeed often have supportive parents, particularly mothers (Gándara, 1995). These insights support the importance of schools offering programs to develop parental support for pursuing education and for attending college (Gándara, 1995; Ginorio & Huston, 2001). One persistent social myth is that women do most of the work in the home and men do most of the work outside the home. Amott and Matthaei (1991) provide a multicultural history of how farm and working-class women have labored for wages in increasing numbers since the beginning of the Industrial Revolution in the Unites States in the 1840s. The great historical and social events of the 20th century—the Great Depression (1929–1939), the shift from a rural to an urban society, the worker shortages caused by World War II—brought even more women into the paid labor force. More recently, the economic stagnation that began in the 1970s has produced a dramatic increase in the number of middle-class women entering the paid workforce (see Figure 5.3). Although more than 50 percent of all women of color have been in the paid labor force since the 1950s, since the 1970s more than 50 percent of *all* women over age 16 have worked for wages (Amott & Matthaei, 1991). According to the AFL–CIO (2002):

> More women are working than ever before. And they're looking for solutions to the problems of juggling work and family, making ends meet and finding respect and opportunity on the job. . . . Over the past century, women workers have grown steadily in number and as a proportion of the workforce.

- The number of working women has grown from 5.3 million in 1900 to 18.4 million in 1950 and to 70 million in 2006.

- Women made up 18.3 percent of the labor force in 1900, 29.6 percent in 1950 and 46.6 percent in 2006.

Figure 5.3   Women's Share of the Labor Force, 1870–2000

Source: Facts About Working Women. AFL–CI0. Available at *www.AFL-CI0.org/women.* Used with permission.

In the United States, many women of color must assume extra responsibilities to protect and advance their community's interests. African American women, for example, are often looked to as the center of strength and the source of leadership within their communities. Perhaps because they are regarded by the macroculture as less threatening than African American men, African American women may be less impeded and more accepted as they assume positions of responsibility in their communities or seek career advancement in the professional world. West (1993b) describes the fear of black men and the acceptance of African American women as in part a result of "psychosexual racist logic." Yet many African American women are well prepared for their role as economic provider. Many African societies had strong female leadership. Slavery forced a matrifocal family structure on the African American community. The women of many African American families have drawn strength from this long tradition of female leadership.

Latinas share many of the racially based economic burdens of African American women, including the responsibility of caring for the elderly and for extended families. Strong female leadership was also common in many Mesoamerican societies prior to the Spanish conquest. Currently, matrifocal family structures have developed in Mexico in response to the migration of millions of male farm workers to labor in U.S. agricultural fields. Most Mexican American and Latino families in the United States remain patriarchal, similar to those in the dominant European American society (for more on this complex issue, see Gándara, 1995; Garcia, 2001; Ramirez & Castañeda, 1974; Váldes, 1996). Girls and young women have paid a price for this continued patriarchy, lagging behind African American women in entrance into college and professional schools until the 1990s (Ginorio & Huston, 2001).

The oppression of African American, Latina, and some rural European American women has taught them to work in cooperative communities. Families take care of the elderly, care for children troubled by divorce and abandonment, and take extended family members (cousins, aunts, etc.) into their homes. In these communities, women serve on school–parent advisory councils and keep churches functioning. Women are the primary social service providers in these communities.

School curricula should acknowledge and recognize the extensive contributions of women to the community's health. The female-centered home and community provide a rich and extensive breadth of background knowledge on which to build an educational curriculum. Moll, Vélez-Ibañez, and Greenberg (1992) assert that children gain when classrooms draw on this community knowledge and use it to advance literacy instruction. Multicultural education is important in this context because curriculum and literacy efforts should give more emphasis to women's contributions in order to provide role models for female students and to counterbalance the devaluation of women by the media and by the patriarchal traditions of the macroculture.

Although European American women have attended colleges since the 1840s and African American women have had access to the traditionally Black colleges that rose up in the South after Reconstruction, substantial numbers of other women of color did not gain access to higher education until the 1970s. The development of both ethnic studies and women's studies on campuses has opened new doors of scholarship and expression. In *Teaching to Transgress: Education as the Practice of Freedom*, Hooks

(1994) offers several powerful essays on how race, class, and gender interact in the classroom.

An outpouring of African American, Latina, Native American, and Asian women writers has redefined women's sphere in the United States to include women of color. Amy Tan, Gloria Anzaldúa, Maya Angelou, Bell Hooks, Olivia Castellano, Paula Gunn Allen, Wilma Mankiller, Marian Wright Edelman, and others provide insights into the diverse voices and insights of the many peoples of our nation.

Title IX and Affirmative Action

Title IX of the Education Amendments of 1972 describes the federal commitment to equal gender treatment where the federal government provides financial assistance:

> No person in the United States shall, on the basis of sex, be excluded from participation in, be denied the benefits of, or be subjected to discrimination under any education program or activity receiving Federal financial assistance. . . .

Title IX was authored by U.S. Representatives Edith Green (Oregon) and Patsy Mink (Hawaii). As a result of the passage of Title IX in 1972, the role of women and girls in education has changed substantially. Title IX prohibits sex discrimination and sexual harassment in educational institutions receiving federal funds. The act prohibits discrimination in recruitment, educational programs, activities, financial aid, counseling, athletics, employment assistance, and other school functions.

The reforms instituted by Title IX have restructured our society, bringing significant changes to women's participation in the workforce and in athletics.

Affirmative action programs and Title IX enforcement have been effective in promoting women in careers and in breaking down traditional rigid gender roles in many universities. Currently, college-bound students benefit from changing work opportunities and the victories of the feminist movement. There are now more women doctors, lawyers, elected officials, and college professors than ever before. In 2006, women received 50 percent of medical degrees compared with 9 percent in 1972, 49 percent of law degrees compared with 7 percent in 1972, and almost 50 percent of all doctoral degrees compared with 25 percent in 1977. Women now make up the majority of the students in U.S. colleges and universities and the majority of recipients of master's degrees (Musil, 2007). In the 110th Congress (2007–2008), women held 16 percent of the 100 seats in the U.S. Senate and 17 percent of the 435 seats in the U.S. House of Representatives.

Women's studies, apprenticeship programs, and mentoring have opened important new opportunities. Special programs provide additional counseling and encouragement for Latinas and African American women to attend college (Ginorio & Huston, 2001). Well-educated young women are choosing careers as doctors, attorneys, and politicians. As yet, however, the benefits and advantages of the feminist revolution of the 1970s are less apparent in the school lives and career opportunities of the 50 percent of female high school graduates who do not go on to college.

In spite of Title IX, tracking remains an issue. We still see female students over-tracked to classes in cosmetology, whereas boys take advanced computer and information technology programs (Gaines, 2002; Oakes & Saunders, 2007).

Many school districts now provide continuing education through alternative schools for the increasing number of pregnant middle school and high school students. It is particularly important that these students receive the quality academic and technology preparation necessary to give them an equal chance at success in the world of work (National Coalition for Women and Girls in Education, 2002).

Women's History in Textbooks

Although feminist scholarship has made strides in the university, this progress is only beginning to have a significant impact on public school textbooks. Tetreault (1989) and Moraga and Anzaldúa (1981) have written about the invisibility and fragmentation of women's history, particularly that of women of color, in literature and text illustrations.

Some progress is being made. Publishers have started to delete linguistic bias and to use gender-neutral terms. States are requiring that texts move beyond depicting women in stereotypical roles. The National Women's History Project has developed excellent new materials to overcome this invisibility.

Students seem to develop self-esteem and a sense of being socially centered when they see their role models in books and other educational materials. Women's literature, history, and sociology assist female students in evaluating their own experiences and traumas. Readings in these areas can help young women gain perspective on the pressures to surrender self and goals for temporary status and temporary relationships. Social history and popular histories record the extensive participation of women in building our communities, public schools, and social institutions. Readings from the era in which the "cult of true womanhood" was promoted (1800–1860) help students to reflect on how public images and role models can promote profit seeking rather than developing human potential. Readings from the Progressive Era (1890–1920) help students to see how immigrant women organized unions and (European American) women made significant advances in attending colleges and entering the professions.

The curriculum should be authentic, realistic, and inspirational. Reform requires more than adding a few new heroines to existing textbooks. The writings and speeches of Dolores Huerta, Fannie Lou Hamer, Shirley Chisholm, Rosa Parks, Marian Wright Edelman, Hillary Clinton, and others are important additions to the curriculum.

Women students can keep journals to reflect on their own lives. Recording a journal helps young girls through times of doubt and insecurity, as does developing friendships. Teenage girls can learn to accept themselves as they are and build a positive future instead of dreaming of cosmetic makeovers.

Young women also gain from learning about the leadership and activism of women in their communities. Working-class women and women of color have raised families and survived. They have created a positive life for their children. Presenting guest speakers from the community teaches that average, normal people run unions, institutions, and essential community organizations. Guest speakers bridge the gap between the school and adult reality. The curriculum empowers and motivates students when it presents hope and optimism without a superwoman model of accomplishment.

Wilbur (1992) states that a gender-fair curriculum has six attributes:

1. *Variable,* accommodating similarities and differences among and within groups of people
2. *Inclusive,* allowing both females and males to find and identify positively with messages about themselves
3. *Accurate,* presenting information that is data-based, verifiable, and able to withstand critical analysis
4. *Affirmative,* acknowledging and valuing the worth of individuals and groups
5. *Representative,* balancing multiple perspectives
6. *Integrated,* weaving together the experiences, needs, and interests of both males and females

Wilbur and the 1992 AAUW report argued that so far no major curriculum reform efforts have explicitly used gender-fair approaches. The AAUW report offers a list of more than 40 action items for change. Individual teachers may pursue the following 12 items from the list (American Association of University Women, 1992):

1. Teachers must help girls develop positive views of themselves and their futures, as well as an understanding of the obstacles women must overcome in a society where their options and opportunities are still limited by gender stereotypes and assumptions.

2. The formal school curriculum must include the experiences of women and men from all walks of life. Girls and boys must see women and girls reflected and valued in the materials they study.

3. School curricula should deal directly with issues of power, gender politics, and violence against women. Better-informed girls are better equipped to make decisions about their futures. Girls and young women who have a strong sense of themselves are better able to confront violence and abuse in their lives.

4. Curricula for young children must not perpetuate gender stereotypes and should reflect sensitivity to different learning styles.

5. Girls must be educated and encouraged to understand that mathematics and the sciences are important and relevant to their lives. Girls must be actively supported in pursuing education and employment in these areas.

6. Existing equity guidelines should be effectively implemented in all programs supported by the local, state, and federal governments.

7. Local schools and communities must encourage and support girls studying science and mathematics by showcasing women role models in scientific and technological fields, disseminating career information, and offering "hands-on" experiences and work groups in science and math classes.

8. Continued attention to gender equity in vocational education programs must be a high priority at every level of educational governance and administration. Have students discuss how gender roles are changing in their own generation.

9. Testing and assessment must serve as stepping-stones, not stop signs. New tests and testing techniques must accurately reflect the abilities of both girls and boys.

10. Girls and women must play a central role in educational reform. The experiences, strengths, and needs of girls from every race and social class must be considered in order to provide excellence and equity for all our nation's students.

11. A critical goal of education reform must be to enable students to deal effectively with the realities of their lives, particularly in areas such as sexuality and health.

12. Child care for the children of teen mothers must be an integral part of all programs designed to encourage young women to pursue or complete educational programs. (pp. 84–87)

Kay A. Chick reviewed studies of textbooks and asserts that history, social science, and literature books have made "some progress" toward gender balance. In *Teaching Women's History Through Literature: Standards Based Lesson Plans for Grades K–12* (2008), she proposes a number of ways to integrate the teaching of these subjects and to encourage gender balance. This valuable publication of the National Council for the Social Studies unfortunately limits its focus almost exclusively to Black and White women, leaving invisible the role of Latinas, Native American women, and Asian American women in the development of the nation (there is one example of a Latina). The book and the lesson plans, while a step in a positive direction, fail to achieve Wilbur's goals of being inclusive, accurate, and representative.

Despite the efforts of feminist scholars, educators, and some textbook publishers, self-image and role-stereotyping problems for girls continue (National Coalition for Women and Girls in Education, 2002). Clearly, schools and textbooks are less powerful in their influence than is the commercial marketplace. They are no match for television programs and multimedia advertising campaigns portraying the popular youth culture. We are unlikely to make much progress on this front until large companies and the advertising agencies they hire cease to exploit sex and gender stereotyping for profit.

Teaching for Equity

Teachers may use several strategies to improve the success of girls in school. Cooperative and collaborative learning approaches work well (see Chapter 10). Teachers can place students in small groups of six to eight to listen and work together for part of the curriculum.

Girls and young women can be assigned the status of experts on a given topic and make presentations to the class. Students can learn to critique and improve the work of their group. As Carinci (2002) notes, cooperative learning advances equity only when there is clear planning for equal status interaction. Girls should have equal opportunity to be in charge or to assume responsibility in the classroom. This generation has many young women who are experts on computers, microscopes, and other forms of technology. Effective teachers place young women in high-status positions as appropriate.

Many teachers have found success by emphasizing young women's verbal and written communication strengths. Girls often do well on assignments involving journal writing. Keeping journal records of their observations in science, history, and biology may produce more success for girls. Establishing a positive, trusting relationship with your students is the first step. This is the subject of Chapter 6.

Teachers can encourage girls to keep journals and to read literature about their many adolescent conflicts. They can make close and consistent contact with the home. Although home contact is frequent in elementary school, it usually declines in middle and high school. This decline in contact hurts students. Many adolescent girls and boys prefer to build a wall separating the home and the school. The break in communication allows them a space of liberty. However, the communication gap separates young women and men from the consistency of support they need from the adult world. Teachers can extend themselves to get to know families. As a teacher, you can refuse to be a party to young people's attempts to build the wall between school and home.

You can find other excellent materials and teaching ideas at the website of the National Women's History Project (*www.nwhp.org*).

The Counterattack

In 1994, Congress passed revisions to the Elementary and Secondary Education Act (ESEA), which governs the basic federal programs for the schools. The decades of feminist scholarship—particularly the work of the AAUW—led to efforts to strengthen the gender-equity provisions of the ESEA by allocating some $3 million in new money for gender-equity activities. A counterattack was launched by Diane Ravitch, former undersecretary of education during the Reagan and Bush administrations, and other critics of feminist and gender-based research. Ravitch claimed that the proposed allocation "takes as findings of Congress that all these flawed research claims were true" (quoted in Schmidt, 1994, p. 1). Senator Nancy Kassebaum also argued against the legislation, saying that gender-inequity claims were "supported only by a small body of research which has questionable findings" (quoted in Schmidt, 1994, p. 16). Finally, Professor Joseph Adelson of the University of Michigan called the AAUW studies "a propaganda machine that does not seem to respond to any contrary evidence" (quoted in Schmidt, 1994, p. 16).

In 1996, California voters passed Proposition 209, which banned equal opportunity programs in the state. In 2006, Michigan passed a similar law. Conservatives claimed that affirmative action programs amounted to reverse discrimination. Conservative activists were able to cut the funding for major Title IX enforcement efforts (National Coalition for Women and Girls in Education, 2002).

Like the attacks on multicultural education (see Chapter 12), critics accuse advocates of gender equity of promoting an ideology. (In the following two chapters, we discuss the role of ideology in shaping research perspectives and educational philosophies.)

As shown in Tables 5.1 and 5.2, girls, particularly White girls, have made significant achievement gains in the last two decades. And women are filling the colleges. At the same time, conservative forces have fought back against these feminist gains, using their power in federal, state, and local governments to rescind gains in access to birth control. Plan B is emergency contraception, the "morning after pill." In 2003, nearly all of the medical advisors to the Food and Drug Administration urged the agency to make the pill available without a prescription. The agency delayed the decision until 2006, and then it ruled that Plan B could be sold without a prescription only to women over 18 years of age. Pharmacies in several states have refused to make this pill available in their stores even to adults.

In 2000, Christina Hoff Sommers wrote a major article in *Atlantic Monthly* on the "War Against Boys" and published a book, *The War Against Boys: How Misguided Feminism Is Harming Our Young Men*, arguing that the gains made by girls in schools also produced crisis and failure for boys. The data for these arguments have since been analyzed and refuted by the AAUW reports, including *Where the Girls Are* (Corbett, Hill, & St. Rose, 2008).

In 2007, the U.S. Supreme Court in a 5-to-4 decision ruled in the case of *Ledbetter v. Goodyear* that Ms. Ledbetter could not sue for pay discrimination based on gender after 30 years of employment. The Court ruled that under Title VII of the Civil Rights Act of 1964, which prohibits gender discrimination in employment, she had to sue within 180 days of the alleged act of discrimination. The U.S. Senate failed to gain the 60 votes needed for a supermajority to pass the Ledbetter Fair Pay Act, which would have corrected the Court's decision.

This chapter concludes Part 1, exploring the social–political foundations underlying multicultural education. The emphasis in Part 2 shifts to concrete teaching strategies to help empower all cultural groups to seek cultural democracy.

Summary

Schools, particularly elementary schools, are primarily female institutions. Young girls do well in elementary school. Recent evidence from the National Assessment of Educational Progress indicates that girls are doing as well as or better than boys in reading in grades 4, 8, and 12 and almost equal to boys in math in grades 4 and 8.

Gender issues interact with race, culture, and class to influence the development of young girls and boys. Gender stereotyping and sexual identity become volatile issues in middle and high school. Girls need supportive teachers to deal with dangerous cultural practices, including sexual behavior and dieting. Students need adult assistance and guidance in these difficult years. Feminist research has been valuable in identifying problems and developing responses for teachers to use in making their classrooms more supportive.

Questions over the Chapter

1. Girls tend to be more successful than boys in school in kindergarten through grade 6, but many begin to encounter difficulties at grade 7 and above. What factors contribute to this change?

2. List some ways schools may track girls. Why is this practice damaging? Were you tracked in high school? Explain.

3. What is the "beauty myth"? How does it negatively impact girls?

4. List at least four attributes of a gender-fair curriculum. Provide examples of gender-fair curricula that you have seen.

5. List ways that Title IX has impacted your school life and career choices.

6. What factors contribute to a "crisis of self-esteem" in middle and high school?
7. How has sexual responsibility changed in the last decade? What evidence do you have for your statements? How have the new patterns of sexuality and child rearing impacted schools?
8. What behaviors are prohibited by Title IX?

Activities for Further Study of Gender Relationships

1. In small groups, discuss and summarize the effect of gender relationships on schooling. Each team should report to the class.
2. Invite a Chicana or African American feminist to speak on the relationship between ethnic and feminist struggles.
3. In small groups, describe recent experiences in which you were treated unfairly based on your gender or race. Then share your stories with the entire class.
4. Complete a life history interview with a female over age 40. Share your interview with the class.
5. Compare *racism* and *sexism*. How are they similar? How are they different? How does socioeconomic class affect each?
6. In a class discussion, predict five major changes in gender-role relationships that will take place in the next decade. Discuss how these changes may affect schools.
7. Bring to class four advertisements from women's magazines that promote "the beauty myth." What messages are the ads sending to readers?
8. Ask students in your class who are mothers or fathers to describe the financial difficulties of graduating from college.
9. Describe to the class the reasons for your choice to become a teacher. How did the female domination of the profession affect your schooling and your career choices?

Teaching Strategies for Use with Your Students

1. Include the study of power and gender equity in the curriculum.
2. Teach students to recognize and oppose gender stereotyping.
3. Study stereotyping presented in commercial media. Identify what values are being advocated, and develop ways to present alternative values to students.
4. Use self-esteem–building lessons for girls and boys to combat the stereotyping messages of commercial media.
5. Use role-playing and role-reversal strategies to resist stereotyping.
6. Use a nonracial definition of women's achievements. Include the contributions of women of color.
7. Make the curriculum inclusive, including examples of women in nontraditional careers.
8. Write for and use the excellent materials of the National Women's History Project.
9. Praise and encourage girls for their academic excellence and skills, in addition to areas such as neatness and compliance.
10. Use strategies and lessons found in Schniedewind and Davidson's *Open Minds to Equality* (1998).

PART 2

Teaching Strategies to Promote Democracy and Multicultural Education

CHAPTER

6

Human Relations and Multicultural Education

It takes an entire village to raise a child.
Traditional African proverb

Teachers Touch the Future

Good teachers make a difference. Each year schools, districts, individual states, the Disney Corporation, and the President recognize a few of the many excellent teachers working in schools all around the country. Excellent teachers illustrate the truism that the quality of interaction between teachers and students is the single most important element in learning. Quality teaching may occur even in underfunded, racially segregated, or isolated schools. Quality teaching depends on creating trusting and supportive relationships between students and their teachers.

Perhaps the most important ingredient in quality schools is a quality teacher. Good teaching matters. To improve the quality of education in poor and marginalized communities, we need to improve the quality of teaching. Other important ingredients are experienced teachers to guide, assist, and mentor new teachers and time for teachers to plan, assess, and work with students (Haycock, 2001).

To be successful, teachers must engage the students in high-quality, caring, supportive relationships. It is unlikely that you, as a teacher, will build a quality, caring, supportive relationship with students if you do not respect their families and their cultures (Gay, 2003; Valenzuela, 1999). Teachers who are intolerant of diversity, who are not interested in cultural varieties, will be unlikely to establish caring, nurturing relationships. Such teachers should not be working in schools with a diverse student population.

175

Promoting positive human relations.

This chapter will introduce five major teaching issues in promoting positive teacher–student relations:

1. Serving as a cultural mediator
2. Building a community of learners
3. Teaching social skills
4. Building positive relationships
5. Resolving conflicts

Underlying Assumptions of Human Relations

We teachers and our students are, of course, all human. As humans, we are much more alike than we are different, and many teachers begin their approaches to multicultural education by affirming our common humanity. Lessons thus focused are called *human relations* lessons. Discussions, particularly of race, make many new teachers uncomfortable. They would rather affirm our common humanity, putting aside the histories of race, class, and gender oppression described in prior chapters. Certainly, many students in your teacher preparation program hold this view. It is important for new teachers to understand this position, to analyze it, and to develop their own philosophy concerning human relations and the other approaches to multicultural education.

The human relations approach to multicultural education emphasizes our common humanity—the enormous similarities in physical, psychological, and social patterns among humans—and builds lessons to emphasize human similarity. For example, we can see differences in skin color, but well over 98 percent of all human biology is identical—we all have hearts, kidneys, toes, eyes, and so on (Cameron & Wycoff, 1998). Recent DNA evidence indicates that we are more similar than different and that groups of people have been mixed and intermarrying for centuries.

This human relations approach traces many of its intellectual roots to efforts after World War II to understand the terror and brutality of the Holocaust (Sleeter & Grant, 2007). Scholars and activists sought to develop lessons that schools could use to promote an end to the prejudice and discrimination observed in U.S. society. They feared that intolerance and prejudice could damage our society as it did the German and other European societies.

As a new teacher, you enter the profession believing in the positive possibilities of children and looking for strategies to build on children's humanness. Applications of human relations research are currently commonplace in public schools, with human relations being accepted and the dominant form of multicultural education in grades K through 4. Such approaches remain an important aspect of multicultural education throughout high school and college.

Human relations theory suggests strategies for new teachers to begin pursuing democracy and equal opportunity in the curriculum. The human relations approach is the least controversial of several approaches to multicultural education and the one that requires the least change of worldview on the part of teachers. However, teaching even human relations can become controversial. Teaching students about the contributions of their own people is a common human relations strategy. In 2008, groups of mostly Mexican American students in several cities in California walked out of their high schools to protest the lack of coverage of César Chávez in the curriculum and by their teachers, even though there is a state holiday to mark his birthday and state legislation specifically calling for instruction about his contributions to history (Carreon, 2008).

The Work of Abraham Maslow

Psychologist Abraham Maslow described a hierarchy of needs that he argued provides a model for understanding the need for human relations in the classroom (see Figure 6.1). Needs lower on the pyramid, such as physical and safety needs, must be met before an individual will consider higher-level needs.

This hierarchy explains important components of behavior, including school behavior. Teachers often assume that the physical security and safety needs of their students are ensured, but in many schools, they are not. Increasing numbers of homes and schools are unable to provide simple safety. When physical security and safety, including sleep, are challenged, students will use most of their time, energy, and creativity simply trying to survive. This struggle interferes with learning.

Belonging needs are often strong in school. Children need to know they are a welcome part of the class. The teacher cannot allow derogatory name-calling and other

Figure 6.1   Maslow's Hierarchy of Needs

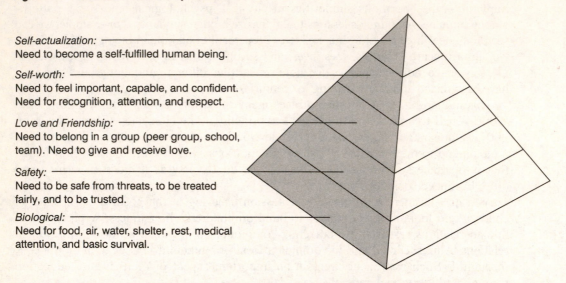

Self-actualization:
Need to become a self-fulfilled human being.

Self-worth:
Need to feel important, capable, and confident.
Need for recognition, attention, and respect.

Love and Friendship:
Need to belong in a group (peer group, school,
team). Need to give and receive love.

Safety:
Need to be safe from threats, to be treated
fairly, and to be trusted.

Biological:
Need for food, air, water, shelter, rest, medical
attention, and basic survival.

Source: From *Motivation and Personality* (3rd ed.) by Abraham H. Maslow. © 1954, 1987 by Harper &
Row Publishers, Inc. © 1970 by Abraham H. Maslow. Reprinted by permission of Addison Wesley
Educational Publishers, Inc.

forms of bullying and exclusion to dominate the classroom. These peer group relations substantially influence school success. It is difficult to learn in hostile, conflict-filled classrooms and schools. Classroom planning and curriculum decisions, such as the decisions to teach cooperative learning (see Chapter 10) and peer group mediation (discussed later in this chapter), can help to convert the classroom environment to one of support and belonging.

Maslow did not consider this hierarchy a rigid one. Students will partially fulfill some needs and thus become prepared to consider higher-level needs. The highest level, self-actualization, is a theoretical position Maslow described as a goal, usually for adults. *Self-actualization* is, at most, a goal advocated by practitioners of Gestalt therapy—anthropologists would not necessarily recognize it as a cross-cultural, universal human experience (Pastor, McCormick, & Fine, 1996).

Teachers can help students learn to meet their own safety and friendship needs and to recognize their own self-worth by building a positive classroom environment. These basic needs must be met before education can take place in school.

Human relations theory, including the work of Maslow, provides the psychological and sociological basis for the democratic claim that schools should promote equal opportunity. Once accepted, the concept of equal opportunity suggests a need for fundamental changes in school financing and in curriculum and teaching strategies.

Human relations theory assists teachers in promoting a safe and supportive environment at school. However, the Children's Defense Fund (2001) points out that our society also must change in order to promote a safe and supportive environment for children, considering both psychological and physical needs. In many schools, roofs and windows need repair, buildings need reconstruction, failure needs to be reduced, violence needs to be controlled, and the children need sufficient food and safe homes.

Current conditions in our streets in many communities make the learning of positive self-worth difficult. In human relations lessons, all students are treated as individuals, often ignoring that the student is also a member of a group (gender, cultural, ethnic). Because each person is regarded only as an individual, human relations theory suggests there are few reasons to change or to adapt lessons to account for cultural, gender, or class variables. The same human relations teaching strategies are suggested for diverse racial, ethnic, cultural, language, class, and gender groups, denying the important contributions of culture to student learning and the importance of culturally proficient teaching strategies.

Human relations theory also assumes Maslow's universal human hierarchy of needs and values that emphasizes individual differences and individual independence. Other cultures emphasize more group solidarity and interdependence with others in the community. In the dominant U.S. culture, children are encouraged to learn self-esteem and self-worth for themselves. This works for members of the European American community and for most teachers. But human relations lessons may fail to recognize that self-esteem and self-worth are significantly influenced by culture (Ladson-Billings, 1994b; Valenzuela, 1999).

The central insight of the human relations approach is that creating positive and nurturing human relationships between teachers and students and among students is one of the most important issues of school improvement. Young people do not learn math, reading, or English well if they are intimidated, defensive, and fearful.

Violence and the Urban Crisis

As described in prior chapters, some children live in decaying parts of communities stressed by racism, class and gender prejudice, job loss, crime, and poverty. Changes in the economy described in Chapter 4 left the poor and the poorly educated increasingly marginalized and unemployed. In 1996, Congress and the President passed new welfare legislation (the Temporary Assistance to Needy Families Act) that ended the 60-year-old guarantee of food and housing for the poorest families. These social conditions create conflict and violence in communities and in schools. When children are abandoned by the society, some children learn violent responses to the violence they encounter. And they bring the violence with them to school.

During the last 20 years, teachers working in inner city schools have witnessed a disturbing decline in student behavior, including classroom behavior, that parallels the rise of violence and crime in our society. There has been an increase in bullying, assaults, gang involvement, and drug abuse as well as sexual activity. The report *Indicators of School Crime and Safety: 2007,* published jointly by the U.S. Department of Education and the U.S. Department of Justice, indicates that violence, theft, drugs, and weapons are serious problems in many schools for both students and teachers (Dinkes, Cataldi, & Lin-Kelly, 2007). The violence makes it difficult to learn in many schools.

Most often the schools respond by turning to the police and creating campus security forces. These make up only one part of an appropriate overall response. In addition, we need to teach students values that respect life and schooling. The streets are teaching violence; we need to teach nonviolent alternatives—and we do so in the way we manage our day-to-day classroom interactions. In addition, schools need counselors, community service programs, and gang intervention. These interventions will be considered in Chapter 8. Later in this chapter, we begin with some things teachers can do to modify the day-to-day environment of the classroom and school.

Teachers, social workers, and police cannot by themselves stop the violence in society. But schools have an obligation to provide safety and security to children while they are in school. Schools must become islands of safety in an often conflict-filled urban landscape. The teacher's difficult task is to build positive relationships, to organize the curriculum, and to respond to the students in a positive, nurturing, and constructive manner that encourages them to learn respect and nonviolence. In order for teachers to teach and to nurture, political leaders—Presidents, governors, legislators, mayors—have the responsibility to make certain that the schools are adequately funded, and school administrators—from school board to principal—have the responsibility to keep school grounds safe and clean and to keep drugs, gangs, and violence off campus. They often fail.

To reform schools in the direction of multicultural democracy, we must build communities of learners (see p. 190). Teachers must improve the quality of respect and interchange in the classroom. Teachers create positive environments by their decisions, choices, expectations, and interactions with students.

How Research Limits Our Views of Students and Schools

Unfortunately, present practices in psychology and the social sciences provide only limited insight into the growing crisis of urban decay and into teacher–student relationships and interactions. The dominant approaches in psychology, the social sciences, and educational studies generally accept the present impersonal and control-oriented structures of schools as natural, as the result of progress and "scientific planning." As you have read in prior chapters, multicultural education challenges these basic assumptions, asserting that present school practices are often unequal and discriminatory with respect to racial, gender, and class issues.

Positivism

To understand the problem of accepting an impersonal and, at times, unjust and violent school structure as natural, we must look at the philosophy of positivism, which provides the basis for most education and social science research. *Positivism* derives from the belief that human behavior, including thought, can be adequately understood by isolating variables for study. It includes the assumptions of hypothesis-testing research and a belief that natural laws of human behavior may be understood and manipulated in terms of "universal" facts, generalizations, and regularities through use of the "scientific method." Most scholars and teachers in the United States have been educated within the positivist viewpoint.

This philosophy developed during the Age of Enlightenment (1600–1860). Early scientists, such as Sir Isaac Newton and René Descartes, developed a scientific method based on a philosophy of realism and sought to isolate variables for study. Other scientists, such as Galileo, created experimental processes to look for natural causes for events. The landmark research of Louis Pasteur and Charles Darwin, based on experimentation and observation, was admired and copied by others.

The social sciences emerged in the late 1800s, following the earlier dramatic developments in the natural sciences. Early social scientists hoped to discover natural laws about human society similar to those laws discovered in the natural sciences by Pasteur, Gregor Mendel, Newton, and others. They searched for universal law–like statements and predictive explanations. These scientists hoped to move beyond the moral philosophy of their time by applying a "modern," scientific approach to human behavior. Currently, this "modern" scientific approach dominates education research and writing. Work based on positivist assumptions is referred to in contemporary social science and education literature as *behaviorism, empiricism*, or *reductionism*.

The Overreliance of the Social Sciences on Positivism Efforts to develop scientific methods in human matters were frustrated by the complexity of human experience. Human institutions—economic systems, school systems, cultures—are so complex that it is often impossible to create quality experimental designs and to isolate variables. In response to frustration, social scientists continually refined their "scientific methods," their proof processes, and their statistical processes. Social scientists who depended on the philosophy of positivism adopted a faith that improved methodology would lead to truth, as it seemed to have done in the natural sciences. This faith in science can be termed *objectivism* or *scientism*.

In pursuit of objectivity, psychologists and other social scientists developed increasingly precise methods of controlling variables. Unfortunately, psychologists usually dealt with these variables under isolated laboratory conditions, and sociologists used statistical manipulation instead of directly studying real life. In this manner, they were able to describe correlations and to imply causation. Psychologists and education researchers limited and restricted what they considered appropriate topics for study.

Over time, social scientists developed the separate disciplines of geography, economics, political science, psychology, and sociology. Each of these disciplines had positivist, objectivist origins. Most practitioners in these disciplines sought objectivity and believed that the scientific method and processes offered methodological neutrality. Researchers working within the assumptions of positivism presumed that if they continued to refine their research methods, they would eventually achieve their goal of developing universal laws and predictive explanations. In part in response to their claims of being based on "scientific research," conclusions from psychology and psychological perspectives came to dominate education research and teacher preparation.

The philosophical limitations of positivism have been examined by Giroux (1979). He argues that the culture of positivism seeks to put aside the normative, value-laden issues—the issues of supreme importance to the teacher. These value-laden issues are central to an effort to reconstruct schools in a democratic manner that would empower minority students. For an excellent analysis of these trends, see Bernstein (1983) and Torres and

Mitchell (1998), and specifically Popkewitz's (1998) chapter within. Posivitism is not, of course, wrong. It is merely limited. But when researchers are unaware of its limits, the errors they make may be called *scientism* or *objectivism* (Bernstein, 1983).

Behaviorism

Social scientific research based on positivist assumptions emphasizes work that is quantifiable, measurable, and verifiable. By the 1960s, the so-called behaviorist school of social sciences had developed. *Behaviorism*, based on the work of Edward Thorndike and B. F. Skinner, emphasizes control of behavior and is predicated on the belief that one may correctly identify and diagnose inner physical and mental states by studying outward behavior. The researchers in this tradition seek to monitor behavior that is observed and measurable. They tend to ignore or cast aside idealism, consciousness, ethics, and faith because they cannot be measured. Behaviorism became the dominant trend in education psychology and sociology in the 1970s. Applications of behaviorism in education include behavioral objectives, many remedial approaches to reading (including phonics), the Madeline Hunter model of direct teaching, and the current testing and accountability emphasis in school reform (Dorn, 2007).[1]

Behaviorism and cognitive psychology both provide hypotheses about how students learn basic skills. Some students do learn basic skills when teachers use these behaviorist strategies, as in the politically imposed Open Court Reading Program. Behaviorist research and behavioral psychology serve reasonably well in the laboratory to describe how a rat or a pigeon learns (Weinberg & Reidford, 1972). However, you probably have never met a rat or a pigeon that could speak a language or do mathematics. Behaviorism also describes strategies to socialize mostly middle-class students to a culturally congruent classroom. Although behaviorism can assist some English-speaking students to learn to read, it has done little to teach students to succeed in the chaotic, decaying social structure of inner-city schools and neighborhoods.

Behaviorism usually does not serve democracy well because a preference for democracy is not reducible to practicing isolated skills (Kohn, 1993). Behaviorism offers few insights for the oppressed. Behaviorism, for example, teaches students from the lower classes to conform to the existing social system, but it does not teach them to use their education to struggle for better schools, educational opportunities, and a more just distribution of wealth and income.

Reductionism

Clearly, applying scientific methods to the natural sciences has led to great advancements in modern society. The use of scientific methods in the social and behavior sciences has led to similar major advancements, but these methods also have significant limitations.

[1]For more on behaviorism and education, see Bernstein (1983), Bowers and Flanders (1990), Hartoonian (1991), Kohn (1993), Popkewitz (1998), Torres and Mitchell (1998), and Wexler (1989).

One version of the scientific method developed a tendency termed *objectivism*, *empiricism*, or *reductionism*.

Reductionism occurs when a complex problem is "reduced" to an issue that can be measured, even though the entire problem is quite complex. For example, learning to read is a complex problem. Children learn many skills of reading. An emphasis on phonemic awareness measures only one of those skills. But if researchers reduce and restrict their attention only to phonemic awareness, they will fail to understand the complex problems of learning to read.

Reductionism distorts complex and comprehensive observation and limits both the analytical and the explanatory powers of much school research. The conceptual frameworks or research paradigms of objectivists and behaviorists led them to isolate variables and to study learning behavior out of the real context of schools.

In the pursuit of objectivity, behaviorist and reductionist research has ignored vast amounts of important information on the purposes and intents of learning as well as on the importance of quality relationships between students and teachers (Kohn, 1993). The effort to be objective, to be empirical rather than normative, directed these research designs away from important issues of power. The pursuit of objectivity and methodological precision distorted and limited research in education and the social sciences. As a consequence, the present unequal distribution of wealth, power, and opportunity in our society and in our schools—in other words, racism and class bias—was usually not considered an appropriate subject of study by researchers committed to procedural objectivity and neutrality.

Objectivist and reductionist psychologies, restricted by positivist assumptions, avoid questions of oppression and domination as research topics in explaining school failure of students of color. Giroux (1979) describes the problem as follows: "Wrapped in the logic of fragmentation and specialization, positivist rationality divorces fact from its social context and ends up glorifying scientific methodology at the expense of more rational modes of thinking . . . more important, it leaves unquestioned those economic and social structures that shape our daily lives" (p. 271).

In particular, these research efforts leave unquestioned cultural domination and race and gender bias in teaching, learning, and curricula. Objectivists' and behaviorists' thought processes dominated most research in education well into the 1980s and reemerged as the dominant viewpoint in the popular testing and accountability movements of today. The behaviorists' view of learning produced reductionist forms of teaching and curricula, particularly in compensatory programs for children from poverty-stricken neighborhoods. The conservative school reform effort and its faith in allegedly objective testing and a test-driven curriculum are direct results of this narrow and restricted view of research (Berlak, 2000; Dorn, 2007; Valdés & Figueroa, 1994).

The errors or distortions of positivism have led to some very specific school intervention strategies. For example, in the controversy in reading education between phonics and whole language, many phonics proponents base their stance largely on a limited, behaviorist view of linguistics. These advocates regularly assert that theirs is the only reading system based on research. The National Reading Panel, which established much of the background research for the Bush Administration approach to school reform, provides an excellent example of the language and ideology of positivism in the following:

> Third, there should be an exhaustive and objective analysis of correlational, descriptive, and qualitative studies relevant to reading development and reading instruction that is carried out with methodological rigor following pre-established criteria. Fourth, experimental research should be initiated to test those hypotheses derived from existing correlational, descriptive, and qualitative research meeting high methodological standards. (National Reading Panel, 2000)

The linguistics used to support the phonics approach to reading results from looking only at very limited, controlled data (reductionism). Phonemic awareness research reveals some reading problems, and phonics is a useful approach on some issues. The behaviorist and reductionist research approach has helped teachers to recognize the important role of phonemic awareness. Behaviorism adds important knowledge but also ignores critical information, tending to negate both the importance of students' own constructions of meaning and the value of a student speaking a second or third language.

The best summaries of reading research at the present time argue for a balanced approach that includes both phonics and an emphasis on encouraging reading in a complex context (Eldredge, 1995; "Every Child Reading," 1998). Note also that no one strategy for the teaching of reading works for all students and that students who speak a second language or a divergent dialect of English need strategies for reading that build on the language they already know. We discuss this issue further in Chapter 11.

Taylor (1993) describes this limitation on reductionist research processes that has led to an overemphasis on phonics and phonetics in reading education. For more on this issue, see Taylor's writings, particularly *From the Child's Point of View* (1993).

In a similar manner, the faith in objectivism and scientism has led directly to the current overemphasis on testing, and particularly to testing with inadequate measurement instruments and to the control of teacher decision making by testing (Berlak, 2000). By 2001, all 50 states used some form of multiple-choice testing to measure their schools, whereas only 7 states used essay exams in areas other than English ("A Better Balance," 2001, p. 87). The current emphasis in school reform efforts on testing and test scores provides an example of how reductionism can shape policy. Legislators and conservative policy advocates argue that you can measure the quality of education in a school by looking at a few test scores on limited multiple-choice exams. This approach is limited and insufficient (Bracey, 2006; Nichols & Berliner, 2007).

Alternatives to Reductionism

A countervailing tradition of reporting and analysis has developed in four arenas: clinical psychology and counseling, the sociology of knowledge, the politically informed movements of empowerment, and the research process of ethnography.

Gestalt therapy, humanistic psychology, and Rogerian counseling have contributed to the understanding of interpersonal relations and communication styles. Practitioners have developed alternative ways of understanding human psychology, emotions, and behavior that do not draw all of their conceptual framework from positivism (Weinberg & Reidford, 1972). In *The Culture of Education* (1996), Jerome Bruner, one of the pre-eminent psychologists in the United States, describes how culture informs and directs psychological processes. These important concepts provide a conceptual framework for human relations teaching strategies.

Over the last several decades, education anthropologists and linguists have developed ethnographic approaches to describe in detail the sociocultural and linguistic context of classroom teaching and learning. In contrast to positivist psychologists, who usually sought to isolate variables for study by following traditional scientific research formats, ethnologists discovered new insights by focusing on the dynamic, complex, and often subtle nuances found in diverse classrooms (Heath, 1995; Ladson-Billings, 1994a; Trueba, 1989).

Rather than looking for improvement in student achievement as a result of a single intervention, such as the use of a new phonics curriculum or testing strategy, education ethnographers incorporate anthropological research tools to examine the day-to-day phenomena unfolding in schools and classrooms. Foremost among these tools is the use of extended participant observation (often over several years) and informant interviews (usually teachers, administrators, staff, parents, and, at times, even students).

Valenzuela, for example, in *Subtractive Schooling: U.S.-Mexican Youth and the Politics of Caring* (1999), provides a fascinating, rich description of the personal and social relationships among teachers and among students in a Houston, Texas, high school. Her in-depth ethnographic research and interviews reveal several important insights into the school, including the multiple roles of identity formation and rejection, youth culture, and student alienation and the politics of caring in schools.

In *The Dreamkeepers: Successful Teachers of African American Children* (1994a), Ladson-Billings describes the context and the cultural perspectives of eight teachers, both European American and African American, who regularly encouraged excellence from their mostly African American students.

The work of Trueba, Rodriguez, Zou, and Cintrón (1993), Ladson-Billings (1994a, 1994b), and Valenzuela (1999) reveals that a broader ethnographic framework provides a more complex, detailed, and interactive description of school realities than does the limited reductionist approach common in prior education research.

Developments in the sociology of knowledge first brought into question the domination of positivism within education research and its role in fragmenting and segregating knowledge. Torres and Mitchell (1998) and Popkewitz (1998), among others, have critiqued popular understandings of the role of research and pointed out the improbability of scientific neutrality. Through careful reasoning, workers in the sociology of knowledge have demonstrated the intertwined nature of empirical data collection and value judgments. This important theoretical development recognizes that, within the social sciences, ideology and science are inextricably interconnected.

In Brazil in the 1960s, Paulo Freire and his coworkers taught peasants to read in about 30 hours using cultural circles. They developed a theory to explain their action. The theory required praxis, an interaction of consciousness, and social action on the side of the poor (Freire, 1972). Freire was not neutral, nor was he "objective." He and teams of cultural workers engaged peasants in dialogue to develop literacy and to democratize knowledge, culture, and power in their societies.

The works of Freire and his teams have had a profound effect on education practices worldwide, including in bilingual and multicultural education in the United States. Some teachers emphasize Freire's plans for reading, others emphasize his use of dialogue, and still others emphasize the close relationship between education and a political commitment to struggle for justice.

From my own experience in working with students, I find that Freire's writings and practice assist in describing developments and relationships of oppression and the struggle for justice and in explaining that we, as teachers, can engage in these struggles for justice in order to understand our reality and the options we face. Thus, working with the United Farm Workers union or other group teaches me a great deal about education, ethics, and the practice of freedom. It is this participation in social justice struggles that educates profoundly.

In one of his last books, *Pedagogy of Freedom: Ethics, Democracy, and Civic Courage* (1998a), Freire makes clear again the important connections between values (such as ethics and democracy) and education processes.

In the United States, developments in psychology, ethnography, and the sociology of knowledge translated Freire's insights into the language of the U.S. academy. *Consciousness*, a central concept in Freire's work, is an awareness of one's own existence and of the environment. Both philosophy and experience demonstrate that consciousness exists. Gestalt psychology argues that consciousness is centrally important to understanding human behavior. Studies of the struggles of the feminist movement and the Civil Rights Movement testify to the importance of consciousness raising. However, behaviorist and reductionist education researchers are unable to measure the role of consciousness. Because they cannot measure it, they fail to use this important concept in developing education programs. But failures of measurement do not deny the importance of awareness of self, consciousness, and self-knowledge.

On the contrary, the strategies best designed for empowering students depend on an understanding of consciousness. The teacher's choice to promote either equality or inequality in the classroom is a product of the teacher's awareness and consciousness. Freire's work is further discussed in Chapter 7.

Human relations theory beyond behaviorism also provides important insight into the process whereby teachers either motivate students or alienate and discourage them. Teachers promote either equality or inequality through their interaction with students. Some teachers are supportive, motivating, and demanding, whereas others are tentative, distant, disengaged, and, at times, oppressive. These different interaction styles significantly influence student motivation and achievement (Valenzuela, 1999).

Differences among interaction styles are substantially a result of the human qualities and the cross-cultural competence of the teacher. Interaction styles are subject to study and improvement. Ethnographic studies add significant power to education research by focusing on the interaction, context, characteristics, and consciousness of both teacher and students (Ladson-Billings, 1994a; Mehan, Lintz, Okamotoa, & Wills, 1995; Trueba, 1989; Valenzuela, 1999).

Figure 6.2   Models of Classroom Interaction Research Paradigms

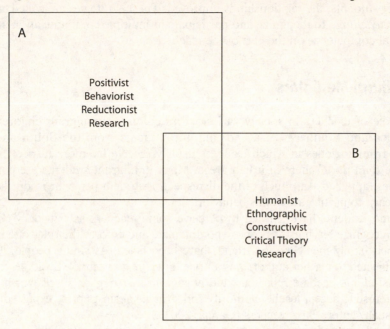

A

Positivist
Behaviorist
Reductionist
Research

B

Humanist
Ethnographic
Constructivist
Critical Theory
Research

Interaction styles and communication among teachers and students consist of far more than words and sentences. Communication improves when teachers and students respect each other, when they know each other's realities, when they are aware of the assumptions they hold, and when they can "read" each other's body language and tones. Communication styles differ among cultures and between genders (Bruner, 1996).

Students' classroom experiences improve when teachers design their instruction and interaction using insights from both of the models, or paradigms, shown in Figure 6.2. Exclusive use of the information in paradigm A may result in improvements in instructional strategies, but it will not inform or significantly assist in student human relations empowerment.

In the humanist, constructivist paradigm B, teachers are concerned with the quality of their interactions with students. Both teachers and students enter the classroom with motivational styles that are, in part, culturally influenced (Ramirez & Castañeda, 1974). For example, research summarized by Garcia (2001) asserts that, although many children achieve well in our increasingly formalized, depersonalized classrooms, young Latino children learn more when the teacher provides a positive, supportive human interaction. Research summarized by Bennett (1986) asserts that African American children tend to learn better in an oral-interactive environment than they do in situations in which they individually read a text and write answers on a worksheet. King (1995) and Ladson-Billings (1994a) have researched the attributes of teachers who are successful with African American children as listed in Chapter 2. Native American children may learn more in cooperative settings and where observation and listening are respected. When teachers use communication and motivation styles that respect students, the relationship is improved. These strategies are called *culturally proficient teaching*. To recognize and participate in multiple communication styles requires cultural competence on the part of the teacher.

Teachers as Cultural Mediators

The role of teachers in society varies across cultures. Immigrant children from Latin America and Southeast Asia and migrant students from the South and Southwest come from societies in which teachers usually receive far more respect from working people than do teachers in urban areas. Many immigrant students are confused—and at times, appalled—at much of the disrespectful student behavior in our schools. Then they learn to participate in this behavior.

Some students have learned to perceive some teachers as outsiders (Ogbu, 1995). They recognize teachers as people who dominate and enforce the rules of a school system in which family members and friends have been failed. As young people, these students are subjected to teacher authority as a price for staying in school. By adolescence, some of these students become rebellious and engage in a struggle for self-worth and identity. They refuse to accept teacher authority and struggle against norms expected by the school and usually enforced by teachers (Garcia, 2001).

Schools reward compliance with a promise of future success. Neither our consumer culture nor students' life experiences prepare them to work for long-term educational goals (West, 1993b). When the teacher chooses domination as the framework for the teacher–student relationship, older students (grades 6 through 12) will respond by struggling for their own arenas of power, such as gangs, sports teams, bathrooms, and play areas (Garcia, 2001). Other students adopt domination as an appropriate strategy and use this strategy to bully other students.

Quality interpersonal relations between teachers and students are particularly problematic in marginalized neighborhoods. Too few teachers live in the neighborhood of the school and participate in the cultures of the students. The teaching profession and teacher preparation programs remain predominantly centered on the European American experience. A cultural and communication gap is growing between many teachers and students from the several diverse cultural communities.

When communities suffer economic distress, students' stress levels are such that these students require even more supportive teacher–student relationships. Quality schools in marginalized neighborhoods must provide a positive alternative to the decaying urban social order. In the primary grades, teachers establish positive relationships with their students by directly teaching appropriate role behavior and communication systems. The social skills needed to be a productive student are taught rather than assumed. Effective teachers repeatedly encourage rather than demand cooperation among the student, the home, and the school.

James P. Comer and the School Development Program, based in New Haven, Connecticut, and at Yale University, developed an extensive system of schools working closely with communities to produce a positive, child-friendly school environment. The program teaches children and teachers positive social and emotional skills. This approach of concentrating on the safety and environment of the school for all of its participants— students, staff, teachers, parents, and so on—produced remarkably positive results in about one-third of the schools. The Comer School Development Program concentrates on developing positive and nurturing adult–student relationships (O'Neil, 1997). I discuss the program and other similar approaches in more detail in Chapters 8 and 13.

Improving the quality of teacher–student relationships and reducing depersonalization are essential to school reform, particularly in middle and high schools. Teachers facilitate a democratic relationship by respecting students' rights and by encouraging them to display responsible behavior. At the same time, teachers need to discourage and prevent bullying and similar abusive and disrespectful behavior. (See Chapter 8.)

Identity

The issues of identity and identity development are vitally important, particularly in the adolescent years. This is when young people try on differing identities, and the choices they make can influence a lifetime. Some young people, particularly the most marginalized, develop a crisis of confidence, of purpose—a crisis that develops rapidly in grades 6 through 9 (Valenzuela, 1999). Their crisis becomes a school crisis. It is at the school, as an institution, where students are most imposed on and most often criticized and disrespected. Students respond to this disrespect by resistance to schooling. Gang involvement is but one manifestation of adolescent youth trying to adopt a new identity. Others students may express their problems and insecurities by engaging in substance abuse, becoming pregnant, dropping out of school, or completely withdrawing into a lonely world where they suffer in silence and fear.

As we described in Chapters 2 and 3, identities develop over time in both the communities and the schools. In middle and high schools, as in the primary grades, young people need adults who know their names and respond to their ideas. Schools need a number of faculty members with these skills. The quality of relationships between students and faculty, the quality of caring expressed, is one of the most important variables in schooling (Valenzuela, 1999).

European American students are in schools where the majority of the teachers are of their same culture, and they receive a variety of supports. The struggles of students against schooling, and against conforming to school norms, are often identity struggles. The most alienated students are the most attracted to gangs and/or drugs (Garcia, 2001, p. 159). To respond, we need programs and faculty in the schools to offer positive alternatives.

Schools in low-income areas are brimming with students in crisis. Successful teachers serve as cultural mediators or even cultural therapists for these students (Spindler & Spindler, 1991). These teachers assist students in their often-painful transition from secure members of their home culture to individuals with a bicultural identity who can effectively participate in the society. New faculty members may well be so overwhelmed by the processes of becoming teachers that they are not yet prepared to be coaches during the many conflicts over identity.

The economic, social and school crises in our society make students more and more isolated and alienated. They blame themselves, other ethnic groups, and politicians for their loss of equal opportunity. At the same time, schools and the knowledge and credentials they control are ever more important to students from the working classes. Alienation from school is ever more damaging to their economic future. Teachers committed to democracy must help students to fashion a way out of this conflict.

Building a Community of Learners

As explained in Chapters 1 and 2, schools both transmit the dominant culture and socialize students to that culture. Schools are transitional institutions where society insists that students adjust to the social stratification of the emerging global economy (Thurow, 1996).

When curriculum by omission or commission attacks a student's culture or gender, it attacks the student's self. In particular, invisibility, intimidation, and failure in the school attack the student's "enduring self" (Spindler & Spindler, 1991). The teacher as a mediator must help students identify and work toward more positive alternatives.

Students need to learn effective resistance to economic and racial oppression. Students are more successful when they understand the changing economy and how to pursue individual and community progress. They are also more successful when they understand their own culture and the forces of assimilation and when they know how to choose new strategies and when to adapt past practices to new situations. Effective teachers help, coach, and guide students through this turmoil.

We can prepare students for a democratic life by building communities of learners in the classroom (Sapon-Shevin, 1999). Students learn democratic preferences from the lives they live, including school lives. Students need to learn to affirm each other's cultural and linguistic identities and to respect one another in day-to-day classroom experiences. Classrooms need to be places where each individual is valued. We do that, in part, by creating a positive, supportive classroom environment. This includes controlling and directing the comments and behaviors of the students. In the primary grades, communities of learners can achieve positive results by including the families of the children (McCaleb, 1994).

When the school and the families work together, the students achieve more. In the upper grades, involving the families becomes increasingly difficult but remains an important facet of improving schools. For Mexican/Latino/Hispanic kids, creating communities of learners that include the families has been demonstrated to be particularly important to school success (Paredes, p. 12; Reyes, Scribner, & Scribner, 1999).

By middle school, many students from marginalized groups act out resistance to school rules in a form of expressing "I don't care." Valenzuela (1999) describes how effective teachers demonstrate caring in large urban high schools. This concern for the student, expressed as a part of a school community, is vital to keeping students engaged with school and with learning. One advantage of having some new teachers in a building is that most new teachers have not yet learned as much cynicism. The alienation of some in the youth culture, and of marginalized cultural groups, is made worse when students believe that the school and teachers do not care about them (Valenzuela, 1999, p. 109).

By middle school, the curriculum should study issues of youth identity, alienation, and cultural and racial conflict. A number of minority-status students seem to adopt an oppositional identity and oppose the view of the "good students" (Fordham, 1996; Ogbu, 1995). Adopting this oppositional identity will affect their schoolwork and their future opportunities. In the middle school years, gender identity and sexuality often become areas of identity conflict (see Chapter 5).

Young girls and boys have identities and roles within cultures, and yet they seldom understand their role choices (Hoffman, 1998). Their preferred identities may be revealed in how they look, how they dress, and how they talk. Given the temporary nature of some identity formulations, teachers need to help students to make positive identity choices that prepare them for a prosperous future. Hanging out with friends may seem like an important event to adolescents, but more mature choices such as completing their studies and preparing for college are also important.

Because determinations of identity are important, teachers need to create an environment where they can discuss identity, as well as race, gender, and culture.

Students, including the alienated and the gang wannabes, seek identity in their resistance to schooling. Identity is a complex phenomenon. The students' identities are in transition. Decisions on clothing and appearance (tattoos, earrings, nose rings) place the student in a group. The group, the peer group, provides validation and support, whereas some classrooms produce frustration and alienation.

It may be that the stronger the conflict is between school and home, the more the student is looking for a new, in-between identity. This is a draw of gangs. They provide an identity for the insecure and the frightened—although usually a negative identity. (See more on gangs in Chapter 8.)

Well-off students go through a similar process by purchasing the latest clothes, buying late-model cars, or being on a sports team; these are symbols of membership in the in-group. Kids from working-class and working-poor families cannot acquire these symbols of group membership, so they invent others. Baggy pants, shoelaces untied, a refusal to care about their appearance—any number of strategies can be used to create group membership symbols. Unfortunately, teachers, counselors, principals, and the police often misinterpret these styles and assertions of identity as "gang" related (Valenzuela, 1999).

It is very important that adults express caring and remain in dialogue with the students. Adolescents need adult guidance. Without it, they turn to their peers, at times with negative results (Garcia, 2001; Schmalleger & Bartollas, 2008).

For example, at Lee Middle School in Woodland, California, Enrique Sepulveda conducted a special class one day a week for students alienated from school and prone to joining gangs (personal communication, February, 1998). They dealt with real issues, such as personal responsibility for becoming pregnant and for staying in school and peer group pressures to act out in school. Separate classes were held for boys and girls, with a female counselor facilitating the girls' classes. Alienated young people need to know that some adults care, that some listen, and that school is a place where they can learn to work through their very real problems of adolescence. Young people need counselors and social workers in the schools. Studying the conflicts they face helps students to comprehend and validate their own identity and to fashion productive responses (Valenzuela, 1999). Teachers as mediators encourage students to find alternatives. Cultural mediation helps students to draw on their own cultures and experiences as resources, as sources of knowledge for developing strategies to overcome the barriers of an often hostile society.

Teachers who are emotionally well adjusted and comfortable with themselves are able to establish a healthy classroom environment that promotes quality relationships among students and quality teaching (Trueba, 1989). Being well adjusted in an urban school includes being comfortable with one's ethnicity and the complexity of one's culture. Well-adjusted teachers are not overstressed by fear of others or by guilt. Teachers are not personally responsible for the decline in order and economic opportunity in many urban neighborhoods or for the inadequate funding of most urban schools. Teachers *are* responsible for creating a positive classroom climate and for promoting high achievement and educational opportunities for the students in their classes.

Teachers help most by encouraging students and demonstrating caring (Valenzuela, 1999). Positive human relations are helpful for teachers as well as for students.

Maria Delgado—A Teacher Serving as a Cultural Mediator

The case of Maria Delgado, a Mexican American (Chicana) high school teacher in Texas, illustrates the importance of positive social relationships between teachers and students. Because her presence at the school establishes the idea that Chicanas can go to college and become teachers, Maria serves as a positive role model to young Chicanas. She can be particularly helpful and sensitive to other immigrant students.

Maria makes close personal contact with some of her students. She looks for opportunities to talk privately and supportively with her students. She uses a little Spanish, the endearment *mija*, and some friendly advice to establish rapport with her female students. Expressions of empathy and understanding, as well as active listening skills, serve her well. Students often need to talk and explore ideas and emotions with adults other than their parents. When a safe, supportive environment is established, many students approach the teacher for advice.

Maria's female students perceive her as a woman who "understands" that their daily turmoil and conflicts—dress, looks, boyfriends, parents, rules—all are critical issues. Most of these conflicts are personal rather than academic. Maria's own training as a counselor taught her to use active listening skills to establish empathy. With more than 160 students per day, each week 3 or 4 students need help. She can put her arms around a young girl and give her a hug and reassurance. She can provide them with important information on crisis intervention, dating, birth control clinics, and counseling support for family crises.

It helps that Maria is a Chicana, but teachers do not have to be Chicano to encourage Chicano students or African American to encourage African American students (Ladson-Billings, 1994a; Valenzuela, 1999). Two of Maria's mentors were European Americans.

Support behavior, both verbal and nonverbal, is often culturally specific and precise. Family supervision styles often vary across cultures and are changing. A female

European American may lose contact with some of her Mexican American students if she fails to comprehend or respect traditional Mexican American values of close family supervision or Catholic values on birth control. An insider to the culture is more likely to know of the complex diversity within Mexican and Mexican American cultures. A European American female teacher could provide most of the support that Maria provides. Indeed, it was a European American teacher—not a Mexican American teacher—who first encouraged Maria to go to college.

Some teachers from other cultures learn about Chicano culture, work closely with the Mexican American community for years, and become a part of the community. They are seen in the neighborhoods and get invited to family rituals such as baptisms, first communions, and weddings. They become a friendly and supportive aunt or uncle, *padrino* or *madrina*—a significant and accepted member of the community. These teachers and many teacher assistants provide desperately needed guidance for students and important communication between home and school (E. Garcia, 1994).

Being Chicana is not a guarantee of empathy with Chicana students, nor is being African American a guarantee of support for African American students. Some Mexican American and some African American teachers choose to remain apart, uninvolved in their students' lives. They do not recognize that they have a special responsibility to serve as a mediator. All individuals, including teachers, respond uniquely to their life circumstances. The teachers' personal goals and the major differences within the culture—generational differences as well as differences in language usage and the degree of assimilation—divide some students and teachers.

The lack of male role models in elementary school produces a particular problem for young boys of several cultures. By the middle school years, coaches and a few male teachers provide an additional support system and guidance for boys. Female teachers and principals may extend themselves to assist boys, but the gender difference creates barriers that only more self-assured or more desperate male students will cross.

The increased incidence of harassment charges and actual sexual molestation makes it more difficult today for teachers to use hugs and physical comforting with students of the opposite sex. Racism, racial fears about sexuality, and homophobia frighten many teachers. Lawsuits, abuse charges, and many district policies prevent teachers from using even small amounts of physical force to direct a child (such as holding onto a child's arm while scolding him or physically breaking up a fight). What seems a simple, obvious, and supportive touch to you as the teacher may cause concern among a small number of parents. Some children, and unfortunately some teachers, are immature and prone to exaggerate. Children often have little comprehension of or concern for the consequences of their accusations. As a new teacher, particularly if you are a male teacher in elementary or middle school, you should exercise care and learn the professional and safety guidelines for touch in your particular school district.

In our society, where many children need more attention, more comforting, and even more encouraging touches, we have yet to develop useful professional guidelines and reasonable procedures.

By high school, a strong emphasis develops in some families on working to raise money for the family. School-to-career programs are particularly needed when families do not have experience at professional levels. Without helpful advice, students often settle for a job in retail sales, fast food, or other service industries because they provide immediate income. But with guidance, career professionals can assist the students to understand how to mix school and work and to develop a profession.

Several valuable intervention systems have been developed in schools to decrease the dropout/push-out rate of teenagers. Particularly noteworthy have been Puente and AVID, two successful programs that combine academic and career preparation (Garcia, 2001).

Teaching Social Skills

Children and adolescents need to be taught to work together cooperatively and to respect one another. These goals are not attained unless they are taught and promoted by specific teaching strategies. For kindergarten and first grade, teaching social skills such as cooperation is a normal part of the social studies curriculum.

Teaching role behavior and respectful, positive communication styles, as well as other social skills, is an important component of cooperative learning. Such instruction should begin by at least second grade and continue thereafter. In classes with a mix of cultures and in schools serving economically marginalized neighborhoods, the study of social skills, human relations, and conflict resolution strategies is essential for teachers to achieve a positive classroom environment and improve school social climate.

Skills and attitudes promoting positive communication and positive human relationships must be taught. Some older students do not use respectful communication because their life and school experiences have not taught them to value respect and the use of positive communications in school. An increasing number of young people have not learned to interact positively with schools and teachers—particularly when they are stressed by failure. Meanwhile, their peer group experiences on the streets reinforce aggression, competition, and disdain and disrespect for many school norms[2] (Garcia, 2001; Schmalleger & Bartollas, 2008).

These same students are clearly able to learn under certain conditions. Gangs are, in themselves, schools that teach role relationships and communication styles, albeit negative ones. If the school and family do not offer positive alternatives or if the school and family are in conflict, the street culture in many cities offers incentives and communication—and motivation styles that are opposed to school success. The economic result that affects all of us—student alienation from school—has already reached crisis proportions. The crime results are staggering.

Teachers use human relations lessons to help students to work together and to assist one another in the classroom. Social skill lessons teach respect, cooperative social behavior, and problem-solving techniques. Teachers can use assigned roles in cooperative learning groups to help all students to belong to positive social groups in the classroom (see Chapter 10). Additional human relations lessons may deal with stereotyping, bullying, and scapegoating—long identified as problems that contribute to interethnic conflict.

---

[2]It is important to not overgeneralize. Many students have learned appropriate role behavior at home, and they also may have learned aggressiveness and rebellion at school. This conflict is not unique to disenfranchised students or students of color.

Teachers present a model of positive human relations when they treat students with dignity and respect, when they show that they care for students, and when they insist that students treat each other with dignity and respect.

Building Positive Relationships

Safety and Security

Most students need a strong sense of comfort and safety from both physical and emotional abuse and criticism in their classrooms. Teachers need to have enough order that students do not intimidate, bully, insult, or overly criticize each other. You achieve this sense of positive order by teaching and developing positive social skills. Students do well when they believe that they can depend on the teacher and their classmates. This comfort is achieved by rules and regulations in the classroom that are sensible and consistently enforced. Teachers build a trusting relationship by helping and encouraging students and by stopping inappropriate behavior, such as racial and gender harassment.

At all ages, students are very sensitive to what they perceive as unequal treatment. When students believe that their teacher favors some students over others, conflict grows in the classroom, and their trust in the teacher declines.

In secondary schools, teachers have more students and therefore often know them less well. Secondary teachers place more emphasis on teaching subject matter, and some tend to place less emphasis on serving as coach, mentor, counselor, or cultural mediator. The lack of opportunity to develop personal relationships and the variety of teacher and student personalities create alienation. Students want to be listened to and respected as human beings with wants, desires, fears, and emotions (Valenzuela, 1999).

Over the years, students need to develop a strong sense of security, and they should have the opportunity to develop a trusting personal relationship with some teachers and students. For some students, the school's teams, clubs, and student government projects contribute to this important sense of belonging. Each student should encounter at least one teacher or counselor who is interesting and motivating each day. If this does not occur, the school will lose the student. Without positive personal relationships, schools become warehouses for students rather than learning centers.

Teachers and students without a sense of security develop symptoms of stress, anxiety, and alienation. They resist change to a multicultural paradigm. When schools are full of interethnic conflict, bullying, or sexual harassment, the violent environment prevents many students from learning. Human relations lessons and strategies, such as those found in the curriculum *The Wonderful World of Difference* (B'nai B'rith Antidefamation League, 1996), help to build classrooms where students feel safe and comfortable.

Self-Worth

When schools serve students well, students develop a sense of self-worth and competence and come to expect to succeed at classroom and social projects. The curriculum should be planned and presented so that all students succeed each day.

In the primary years, students should learn to read. If they are not successful readers, additional support in the form of increased teacher time, tutors, and special instruction along with a rich variety of reading strategies must be provided so that students learn to love reading and so that they do not fall behind (Slavin, 1998). Learning successful reading skills and acquiring joy and interest in reading contribute to a positive sense of self-worth in school.

A strong relationship exists between poverty (social class) and reading scores (Finn, 1999). Teachers of grades 4 through 8 need to help students to improve their reading. Lessons in history, science, and literature should systematically include high-interest literature, allow students choice, and emphasize skill development.

Upper elementary school students (grades 4–6) and middle school students (grades 6–8) also improve their sense of self-worth by learning to set immediate, accomplishable goals and establishing clear criteria for achieving them. With clear goals and lessons, students can recognize and improve their study and interpersonal skills. Quality literature and guest speakers can regularly present positive lifestyle choices to students.

Students who believe themselves competent become more willing to take risks. They generally feel successful at important tasks and school subjects. Such students are willing to share their ideas and opinions and to recognize the accomplishments of other students. Too often teachers use theories of motivation based on the competitive tendencies in the macroculture and poorly informed teacher folk knowledge about testing, measurement, and grading (Nichols & Berliner, 2007).

Students in supportive environments develop a positive sense of self. Violence, drug use, and alienation among teenagers indicate a struggle for a clear identity. Students bridging two or more cultures and identities may suffer increased stress and conflict as they develop their own identities (Foley, 2001). Literature and lessons about teen conflicts, challenges, and successes offer opportunities for support. Students need to find themselves and recognize their conflicts in the curriculum, and the literature used must include teens from the cultures represented in the classroom. As a consequence of political power, state content standards often are ethnocentric and impede inclusion of diverse literature and authors.

A process of supporting students through asset development has been devised developed by the Search Institute and others (Scales & Leffert, 1999). This approach focuses on building on the students' strengths, such as energy and creativity. Focusing on strengths can help students develop resiliency to deal with serious problems, such as teen pregnancy, violence, and dropping out of school.

Sense of Belonging

Students at all ages have a strong need to belong to groups. The desire to fit in provides a major source of motivation and—at times—challenges to school rules. Students may feel conflicting desires to belong to an ethnic or cultural group, girls' or boys' athletic teams, or any one of a number of other groups. Learning to work positively within a social group is important to maturity.

Promoting self-esteem.

Students strengthen their sense of self-worth when they receive recognition, approval, appreciation, and respect from their peers. Lessons should promote inclusion and acceptance of all students. You can promote these important feelings in the classroom by using cooperative and collaborative learning and classroom projects. Lessons should draw on the diversity of languages and skills students bring to school. Make every attempt to recognize leaders, authors, scientists, filmmakers, and teachers from all cultural groups.

Deliberately developing peer support groups and recognizing the diversity of talents—for language, music, math, social leadership, and so on—help students to develop a sense of belonging to one or more of the groups in school.

By adolescence, group affiliation can at times challenge school rules and norms. Teen culture, like African American, Latino, or teacher culture, must be respected. If schools set themselves against teen culture, the conflict will destroy many students. Only negative aspects of teen culture, such as drugs, violence, and theft, should be opposed (Garcia, 2001; Reveles, 2000). In the many classrooms and schools that seek to impose a Euro-centered culture and to defeat teen culture, student conflict and opposition can reach destructive levels. Defeated students withdraw from school and peers; they become isolated, alienated, lonely, and, at times, dangerous to themselves and to others.

Principals have turned to peer conflict resolution and gang and narcotics units of police departments to augment inadequate resources for gang intervention. Students need to be recruited and encouraged to support the positive aspects of school through clubs, team building, conflict resolution, and leadership development programs. The school must become a student-friendly, safe environment.

Self-Esteem

The theories of promotion of positive self-esteem derive primarily from a humanistic psychology that has taken too-limited notice of cultural differences. Behavior that would illustrate a positive self-concept in one culture, such as assertiveness, might be interpreted as a sign of poor education in another (Bruner, 1996). Separate from this debate, teachers have developed a series of classroom strategies to encourage students to conduct themselves appropriately.

A Sense of Direction Although young students often accept the direction of their parents and the school, by adolescence many students are redefining their roles and their choices. Some students need repeated lessons on setting goals and establishing their own sense of responsibility and direction. Students can learn to make decisions and identify consequences. Experiential education programs and outdoor programs help students with goal setting and motivation. Through coaching and counseling, teachers can help students make preliminary career and college choices. Teachers serving as advisors to clubs—such as MECHA, MAYA, African American clubs, ski clubs, teams, and journalism clubs—often play important roles in helping students to define and to select their future.

A Sense of Purpose Students succeed more when they have a sense of purpose to their school life. Essentially, success at school is their job. School needs to prove its worth to them. Students benefit from lessons on and experiences with decision making and cooperative problem solving.

Teachers encourage positive self-esteem when they recognize, validate, and respect students' own cultures. Cooperative learning and other human relations strategies teach students how to achieve positive interdependence and how to create and maintain a cooperative working environment . Students learn the rewards of shared responsibility and cooperation.

Teachers make decisions to structure their classrooms in ways that encourage learning and cooperation or in ways that produce anxiety, frustration, competition, failure, and disruption. In particular, a highly competitive classroom environment discourages trust and cooperation. Some students always lose, and these students legitimately feel alienated and angry. Students must come to trust that the teacher has their own best interests at heart, even in difficult times. Teachers achieve this goal by demonstrating their respect for the fundamental dignity and worth of each student (Valenzuela, 1999).

Stopping Demeaning Comments Too often, particularly in grades 4 through 10, classrooms are the scene of bullying, intolerance, and demeaning comments among students. All students deserve a safe environment in which to learn. Teachers should prohibit demeaning and derogatory comments, particularly those that invite racial and gender conflict (see Chapter 8). Teachers need to work against this intolerance by presenting lessons and activities that promote tolerance and respect and lessons that oppose scapegoating.

You improve your classroom climate by modeling positive, supportive communications skills and by teaching these skills to students. The great majority of interactions in classrooms are among students. You can influence and encourage respect in these interactions by teaching positive skills. Lessons in listening actively, using "I" messages, and negotiating conflicts show students how to treat each other with respect. Teaching democratic participation and decision making encourages positive self-esteem.

Resolving Conflicts

Students and teachers encounter stress, anger, and fear in their lives. Life in many neighborhoods makes one angry or fearful. Intergroup conflict is frequent. Physical danger is a reality on some streets and often in schools. This conflict, anger, and fear must be dealt with, not silenced or ignored. Teachers who make irrational or impossible demands on students also contribute to classroom tension. Suppressing or not talking about these problems may create an even more dangerous setting.

Many schools have successfully taught groups of students and parents to serve as conflict mediators, allowing teachers to invest more time in teaching. Developments in the area of peace studies and conflict resolution have become increasingly valuable for teachers. Classroom management systems work when the general atmosphere of the school, the neighborhood, and family life is positive, helpful, and supportive. (See Chapter 8.) But management alone, even skillfully applied management, will not resolve conflicts that are deeply rooted in poverty, racism, and schools that rely on authoritarianism to respond to adolescent growth and change.

Teaching Conflict Resolution and the Social Studies

Many elementary school teachers have responded to administrative demands to improve reading and math skills by reducing the time spent on social studies. This is an unwise choice. Social skill development provides students with an opportunity to be proud of who they are and healthy in who they are becoming. Quality social studies encourages students to develop the social skills necessary to cooperate with others and to resolve problems. Social studies lessons should encourage students to analyze their own environment and their society and to plan and prepare to take charge of their own future. In schools in impoverished areas, where government services are inadequate and voter turnout usually low, students need additional assistance to learn to believe in, to value, and to advocate for a democratic society and to develop civic competence and courage (Acuña, 1996; Carnegie Corporation, 2002). Young people can learn these things by studying the history of African Americans', Latinos', women's, and working people's struggles for justice, dignity, and democracy.

Teachers and students gain from preparation in conflict resolution. The conflict students experience may reach dangerous and unhealthy levels. Teachers alone cannot "control" the violence that comes into the schools from outside. They need to enlist students in a cooperative effort to reduce violence, at least in school. Lessons on Martin Luther King, Jr., Rosa Parks, César Chávez, and others can introduce the important values and strategies of nonviolence. One way to lessen the impact of these stresses is for students to learn clear communication skills. Students can learn alternative, nonviolent strategies for reducing conflict. They can learn mediation skills. Most important, they can learn that even major social problems such as conflict can be faced and dealt with within a cooperative community.

Teachers' choices of what to teach in social studies and in literature can contribute to reducing stereotyping, misunderstanding, and unnecessary conflict. They should introduce discussions of race, ethnic, class, and gender relations. Students live in a world of intersecting demands. Studying these demands, and multiple perspectives on these conflicts, assists students in making deliberate and wise choices. In community action projects, they can learn to advocate skillfully for their own interests. It strengthens community to learn to resolve conflicts in a democratic and cooperative manner.

Many classes require a time of trust building and attention to issues of group dynamics. Continued attention to trust building is called for in our increasingly polarized society. Schools should be places where children learn to work and play together. They should be places where children learn to judge others on their merit and on their actions rather than on stereotypes, fear, and mistrust. A long period of working together on sports teams, in classrooms, and in student leadership programs can significantly reduce intergroup hostilities (Sapon-Shevin, 1999).

By converting the violence of adolescent lives into something to study, to analyze, teachers move from coercive power to adult authority. Father Greg Boyle in Los Angeles argues that many adolescents need additional amounts of adult authority in their lives. Students need guidance. They need help making fateful choices. Students are full of fear about joining gangs, using drugs, bringing weapons, establishing sexual identity, and similar explosive matters. If the school is silent or ignores these issues, issues that are consuming children, then the school becomes an accomplice in the violence in parts of our society (Fremon, 1995).

Schools must be about developing positive and respectful relationships. Classrooms, forums, and clubs should discuss values central to democratic living, such as respect for the opinions of your opponents, fairness, honesty, and willingness to listen to others. The curriculum and the school culture can be shaped to give students practice in democratic, open decision-making.

In communities where parents do not usually participate in the school, outreach workers should be employed to recruit and foster parent participation. Lacking funding, teachers oriented to community participation can create parental participation systems. Local universities' social work departments and teacher preparation programs should assist. Many parents in immigrant communities literally do not know how to participate. Schools can sponsor workshops by community leaders, religious leaders, and migrant education specialists to teach the fundamental skills of parent participation as well as holding English as a second language classes (Olsen & Dowell, 1997).

There are several emerging strategies for resolving conflict. One, classroom meetings, is described in Chapter 8. Johnson and Johnson (1992) describe successful efforts in Edina, Minnesota, to develop a peer mediation program in the schools. Similar programs are emerging in schools across the country.

Communication skills taught to students include the following:

1. Checking for understanding of the opposing viewpoint
2. Clearly stating one's own position
3. Sharing one's needs, feelings, and interests in the conflict

Mediators can assist by doing the following:

1. Recognizing negotiable and less negotiable conflicts
2. Helping to restate conflicts in negotiable forms
3. Reframing the issues (talking about the issues in a new, nonpolarized manner)
4. Seeking rather than suppressing solutions to conflict

School administrations must state clear rules for conflict management in schools.

The report *Reducing School Violence: Schools Teaching Peace* (1993), by the Tennessee Education Association and the Appalachian Educational Laboratory, concludes by stating the following: "Training and practice in conflict resolution can give students the skills to explore peacefully the differences among them. Tolerance and empathy can be taught, and, at a time when incidents of violence and hate are at an all-time high, the need has never been greater" (p. 9).

Curricula have been developed to assist classroom teachers and mediators with training. For more information on conflict resolution, see the excellent resource *Connected and Respected*, available from

Educators for Social Responsibility

23 Garden Street, Cambridge, MA 02138

www.esrnational.org

Teachers using the work of Spencer Kagan (1985) to help students improve their communications skills have posted charts displaying a list of alternative behaviors available to students under stress. Students practice and role-play these alternatives. Then, when conflicts arise, they have a choice of responses. Kagan and others working in the field of conflict resolution suggest using and posting on the classroom wall the methods for resolving conflicts shown in Figure 6.3.

The coaching practices described in Chapters 7 and 8 are useful strategies for helping the increasing number of students with extremely high stress and conflict levels.

Figure 6.3   Kagan's Methods for Resolving Conflicts

Share
Take turns
Compromise
Change
Seek outside help
Postpone
Avoid
Use humor

Human Relations and Values in Democratic Schools

Multicultural education as we have defined it is a project to extend democracy in our society. As such, it has continually been under political assault by persons and forces who want to continue their domination through the present distribution of political and economic power. At the current time, as a consequence of the drive for content standards and increased testing, multicultural education is losing ground.

Recognizing that this is a struggle for access to power and economic opportunity, it is important to be clear about the role of democracy and values in our work. The literature in political theory clearly indicates that values and valuing are central processes in our society (Appiah & Gutmann, 1996; Arnstine, 1995; Banks, 2001; Batstone & Mendieta, 1999; Carnoy & Levin, 1985; Freire, 1998; Green, 1998; West, 2004; Westheimer & Kahne, 2003). James Banks, a leader in multicultural education, incorporates the theories of schooling for democratic citizenship into his work by calling for strategies of values analysis as a part of the curriculum (Banks, 2008). The following chapters will demonstrate that values and dispositions are central to both the theories we use in teaching and the ways we organize our classrooms.

Currently, one form of values education is referred to professionally as *character education*. A good source for the study of character education is *www.character.org/principles/index.cgi*.

Teacher Self-Confidence Many teachers, particularly during their first year, too often experience the frustration of failure. These feelings cause many new teachers to transfer schools or to leave teaching altogether.

Several aspects of teachers' work environment—disruptive students, undermotivated students, feelings of failing as a teacher, and demeaning professional work conditions—may combine to attack a teacher's self-confidence. Both teachers and students respond to attacks on their self-concepts in a defensive and at times hostile manner. Parents may expect that teachers can teach responsibility in a society characterized by violence, self-indulgence, the need for immediate rewards, and consumerism. This expectation is unrealistic and represents an overreliance on schools. As the now well-known traditional African proverb contends, "It takes an entire village to raise a child."

The clash between teacher and student can be quite a power struggle and often produces an unfortunate, nonproductive, and conflictive environment for both parties in the classroom. Adolescent conflicts are particularly severe in at-risk schools where both the number of students suffering in their home lives and the number of new, inexperienced teachers increase.

Multicultural education offers an alternative form of resistance. Students can be incorporated into a cooperative, positive school culture engaged in the study of their real-life issues (Rogers & Oakes, 2006). They can learn to respect communities and cultures. Successful students contribute to their community's health and safety rather than leaving school to join a gang (Ayers, Hunt, & Quinn, 1998; O'Neil, 1997).

In schools all across the country, hundreds of involved, positive teachers of all cultural groups engage and motivate students. Unfortunately, many students also encounter rigid, alienated, resentful teachers who produce troubled, conflict-filled classrooms. In positive classrooms, both the teachers and the students gain; in negative classrooms, both the teachers and the students lose.

Cultural Competence

Understanding their position as cultural mediators helps teachers work with students to establish positive interpersonal relationships. When teachers are comfortable with their own cultural perspectives, they can accept cultural conflicts as normal. Students need instruction in the culture of schools. Some students need to learn to negotiate cultural conflicts and to seek positive, respectful resolutions. Winning, losing, and revenge injure the positive interpersonal relationships needed in the classroom. Culturally competent teachers are able to help to resolve student conflicts. They do not waste their energy in endless struggles for power and control.

A teacher's real power to manage a classroom productively comes from cultural competence, experience, and maturity—not from using punishment and physical force. Teachers committed to empowerment for students of color help students to analyze and resolve their own cultural conflicts.

Teachers are a unique cultural group. Like other cultural groups, teachers tend to communicate well with and accept students who share their culture and agree with the norms and values of the school.

Many students learn in school. There are hundreds of success stories as a result of schooling poor and minority students (see Ayers, Hunt, & Quinn, 1998; Meier, 1995; Olsen, 1997; Olsen et al., 1994). Students learn best when teachers believe in them. But for teachers to have confidence in students, teachers must first have confidence in themselves. Teachers must model and teach the value of education and of social service. Encouragement and guidance help students win the difficult struggle to develop a positive, productive life.

Most middle and high schools are larger than elementary schools and use more hierarchical, impersonal, and formal control mechanisms. The formality of the schools and the rigidity of their controls produce more conflict and win–lose situations. Teachers establish personalized and supportive relationships in their classes in order to work against the problems of size and rigidity. Students and teachers under great stress at times need an accepting, even therapeutic relationship. Young people need the opportunity to belong, to

Figure 6.4   A Summary of Human Relations Approaches in the Multicultural Classroom

Societal goal	Promote respect for others, unity and tolerance, and cultural democracy.
The problem	Racial, gender, and identity problems and conflicts exist primarily because of prejudice. Prejudice is seen as an individual problem.
The theories	Abraham Maslow's proposed hierarchy of human needs. Changing individuals' attitudes, knowledge base, and behaviors will lead to a reduction or elimination of prejudice. Equal status interaction.
School goals	Promote positive working relationships among students. Help one another. Promote positive self-concepts and positive identity.
Students	K–12: All students need anti-bias education. Children from groups that are targets of bias need support and protection. All students need to learn anti-bias behavior in a positive, integrated class environment.
Curriculum	Teach lessons about stereotyping, name-calling, self-worth, individual differences, positive role models for all students. Lesson plans are available from A World of Difference (Anti-bias curriculum), Teaching Tolerance, and others. Include a contributions approach to topics. Teach positive social skills, e.g., cooperation. Key concepts: identity, community, relationships, self-worth, sense of belonging, self-esteem.
Key concepts, vocabulary	Self-worth, self-esteem, community of learners.
Classroom instruction	Use of cooperative learning, role-playing, and simulation games. Create a community of learners in the classroom. This theory seeks to change attitudes and values; you need to use values and attitudes teaching strategies in addition to accurate cognitive information. Teach conflict resolution skills.
Teacher skills	Cultural competence. Cultural mediator. Self-awareness. Provide support. Student advocate.
Assessment	Assessment of attitudes and affective objectives is complex; it takes time. Frequently, assessment is based on teacher observation over a time period.

*As defined by Sleeter and Grant (1996) and Gibson (1976).

be successful in school life even while they make errors. They are, after all, children or adolescents.

Teachers assist students by developing supportive relationships—particularly with those students who are resisting the depersonalization and hierarchical structure of the school.

Summary

Improving the quality of the human relationships between teachers and students is central to multicultural education (see Figure 6.4). The dominant trend of positivism in education and the behavioral sciences has not been helpful in developing cross-cultural, positive teacher–student relationships. Multicultural education and ethnographic research offer new strategies for developing positive relationships.

The diverse cultures of teachers and students affect their interactions and the classroom climate. Multicultural education encourages teachers to become culturally competent. Dedicated teachers can learn about cultural conflict and improve their skills as cultural mediators.

Questions over the Chapter

1. What are four important goals of the human relations approach?
2. Describe why children from the working class need a human relations teaching approach in the primary grades.
3. How can a teacher influence the quality of the student–teacher relationship?
4. Define *cultural mediator* and *cultural competence.*
5. Which cultures do you feel competent within?

Activities for Further Study of Human Relations

1. Interview a student about the teachers who most influenced him or her. What are the characteristics of the influential teacher? Ask the student to compare this teacher with another who was less influential. What are the characteristics of the less influential teacher?
2. Conduct library research on the causes, symptoms, and consequences of teacher stress. Prepare a written summary of your findings.

Teaching Strategies for Use with Your Students

Teaching strategies for human relations vary somewhat according to students' age level and maturity.

At the Primary Level

1. Select a student of the week. Have students bring in pictures of themselves and their families. Feature one student each week.
2. Consistently use positive statements. Try to make a positive statement to each child each day. Start each day with a positive statement.

In Intermediate Grades

1. Designate one of the bulletin boards in the class for student work. Groups of students can take turns, and responsibility for, placing materials on the board.
2. Have students write their autobiographies. Use Writer's Workshop or other strategies to edit and improve these autobiographies. Take pictures of the students and post the writings with the pictures.
3. Deliberately create a positive classroom spirit. Use a banner, a mural, or a class newspaper to create a positive view of the classroom.
4. Involve parents and other community members in your class. Invite parents to come in and to make presentations. Inform parents of what is happening in the class. Perhaps produce a classroom newspaper to facilitate this effort.
5. Identify, recognize, and build on students' strengths. Emphasize the skills they have learned.

In Middle and High School

1. Invite a guest speaker to address the issue of gangs. Encourage the speaker to discuss these questions: Why are young people attracted to gangs? Why do young people join groups? What are the advantages and disadvantages of joining a group?
2. Make a list of classroom activities that promote and respect diversity. Perhaps have students make murals or posters of these behaviors and then display the posters prominently.

At All Grade Levels

1. Ask students to list their favorite three movies or television shows. View these programs for insights into student interests.
2. Record a current music video. Transcribe the words to the song. Play the song in class and read the words. Analyze the themes of the song. Ask students their views of the themes in a popular song.
3. Select a student in your class who is not actively involved in class discussions. Make an effort to talk to this student informally before or after class at least three times per week. If the student finds the experience uncomfortable, change to another student.

7

Teaching to Empower Students

with Peter Baird

Cuando somos realmente honestos con nosotros mismos debemos
admitir que nuestras vidas son todo lo que verdaderamente nos
pertenecen. Por lo tanto, es cómo usamos nuestras vidas lo
que determina qué clase de hombres somos. Es mi creencia más
profunda que solamente con dar de nuestra vida encontramos la
vida. Estoy convencido de que el acto más verdadero de valor
. . . es el de sacrificarnos por los demas en una lucha
totalmente no violenta para la justicia.

When we are really honest with ourselves, we must admit that
our lives are all that really belongs to us. So it is how we
use our lives that determines what kind of people we are.
It is my deepest belief that only by giving our lives do we find
life. I am convinced that the truest act of courage . . . is to
sacrifice ourselves for others in a totally nonviolent
struggle for justice.[1]

César Chávez (1927–1993)

Five Approaches to Multicultural Education

At least five major approaches to multicultural education are commonly used in U.S.
public schools. Each approach has both strengths and weaknesses. Some approaches
concentrate on improving intergroup relations, others on making the curriculum more

---

[1]Statement made at the termination of a 25-day fast for nonviolence, March 10, 1968, in Delano, California. From César
Chávez Foundation, *Education of the Heart, Cesar E. Chavez in His Own Words* (accessed Dec 3, 2008). Reprinted by
permission.

César Chávez (1927–1993).
Photo: National Archives.

inclusive, and still others on raising academic achievement. Often the discussion of multicultural education becomes confused by mixing references to the different approaches as if they were aspects of one program. They are not.

Human Relations Approach

In Chapter 2, I described an approach termed *the nature of culture*, which incorporates the best of a recent anthropological perspective to overcome the limits of an earlier and very limited educational approach frequently called *teaching the exceptional and the culturally different*.

Sleeter and Grant (2007) have developed a typology of approaches to multicultural education, as has Gibson (1987). (See Table 7.1.) Both these typologies recognize a human relations approach. Human relations approaches (such as those described in Chapter 6) have been popular among teachers since the 1960s. These approaches include valuable materials and techniques for breaking down habits of thought that lead to prejudice, stereotyping, and discrimination. Human relations and intergroup relations strategies are an important part of a good curriculum, particularly for the elementary grades and for students from the macroculture. However, as demonstrated in Chapter 3, the worst damages of racism, class bias, and sexism are structural or institutional. Human relations strategies for teaching students to eliminate their individual prejudices, though an essential part of an enlightened curriculum, are by themselves inadequate for teaching middle and high school students and for meeting the crisis of our increasingly divided society.

Table 7.1 A Typology of Approaches to Multicultural Education

Paradigm	In This Book	Source of Goals	Curriculum
Teaching the Exceptional and the Culturally Different	See linguistic deprivation. Chapters 2 & 4.	Popular in the 1960s. Remains popular in special education. Treats cultural differences as a problem to be fixed.	Based on reductionist psychology.
		Includes cultural and linguistic deprivation theory. Includes the gifted.	Uses remedial education and scripted phonics lessons in reading.
Human Relations	Chapters 5 & 6.	Maslow, human relations theory. Inclusive of gay and lesbian issues.	A world of difference. Teaching tolerance.
Single-Group Studies	Chapters 3 & 5.	Ethnic studies/women's studies. Includes bilingual education.	Usually found in colleges.
Transformative Multicultural Education	Advocates cultural pluralism. Chapters 3, 4, 5, 7, & 11.	Based on ethnic studies and the nature of culture. Curriculum must be meaningful to students.	Teaching tolerance. Infuses new material into the curriculum.
Multicultural Education That Is Social Justice Oriented	Advocates democracy and antiracism. Chapters 7 & 12. Critical theory. Critical pedagogy.	Based on the Civil Rights Movement. Empowerment as goal.	Includes social action. Students learn to shape their own futures.

Single-Group Studies Approach

An approach called *single-group studies* or *ethnic studies/women's studies* has led to major debates in the popular media over appropriate curricula or "canons" of study in colleges since the 1980s. The descriptions in Chapter 3 detailing the diversity of U.S. ethnic and cultural experience are a strong argument for the usefulness of single-group studies. Students need and deserve to know their own histories, and many are empowered by this information. But ethnic studies and women's studies have primarily served only the target groups; they have added new specializations but have not recast the macroculture's basic conceptual framework of history, literature, and the social sciences. The great majority of students in the United States are still learning the dominant culture's worldview. The single-group studies approach has challenged, but not revised, the canons of the academic disciplines.

Choosing Democracy argues that each of the latter four approaches in Table 7.1 is appropriate for specific age levels and situations. In addition to human relations as described in Chapter 6, *Choosing Democracy* argues for multicultural education in a "strong sense," as a process that engages students in building a more democratic society. *Strong-sense multicultural education* includes the humanist approaches described in Chapter 6, but it also emphasizes social responsibility. As Sleeter and Grant (2007) point out, multicultural education that is social justice oriented incorporates ideas and strategies from each of the prior traditions and adds the philosophy of *social reconstruction*, the idea that schools should participate in efforts to create a more just and a more democratic society. The social justice position can also be termed *antiracism education*. In the remainder of this chapter, we will argue for multicultural education positions that include a commitment to social justice, as this offers the best hope for achieving educational equality and cultural democracy.

The federal education law, the No Child Left Behind Act of 2001 (NCLB), states some goals that are useful to consider as we begin to examine alternatives:

Sec. 1001. Statement of Purpose.

The purpose of this title is to ensure that all children have a fair, equal, and significant opportunity to obtain a high-quality education and reach, at a minimum, proficiency on challenging State academic achievement standards and state academic assessments. This purpose can be accomplished by—

1. ensuring that high-quality academic assessments, accountability systems, teacher preparation and training, curriculum, and instructional materials are aligned with challenging State academic standards so that students, teachers, parents, and administrators can measure progress against common expectations for student academic achievement;

2. meeting the educational needs of low-achieving children in our Nation's highest-poverty schools, limited English proficient children, migratory children, children with disabilities, Indian children, neglected or delinquent children, and young children in need of reading assistance;

3. closing the achievement gap between high- and low-performing children, especially the achievement gaps between minority and nonminority students, and between disadvantaged children and their more advantaged peers. . . . (Public Law 107-110)

[Note: The No Child Left Behind Law is due for re-authorization in 2008/2009. These goals are not likely to change.]

Changing—or restructuring—schools in pursuit of these goals requires us to end tracking and rigid ability grouping. Violence is done to democratic opportunity when students in some schools receive funding at over $14,000 per child, while other schools spend less than $6,000 dollars per child. Violence is done to democratic opportunity when students in "honors" classes and magnet schools receive quality instruction using technology and critical thinking, while students in low-income schools receive remedial drills and practice sheets. Students from all cultural groups deserve the opportunity to learn democratic principles as well as reading and math skills. Our commitment to democratic opportunity requires that we reform many schools—particularly those where students are presently failing in substantial numbers.

Goals for Democratic Schools In addition to the goals set out by NCLB, as argued in Chapter 1, schools should develop democratic participation in our society. We should teach all students to have a commitment to civic values, including the dignity of the individual, free speech, and a democratic form of governance.

The Campaign for the Civic Mission of Schools argues that we need an urgent reform of schools to teach students to participate in their communities, to act politically, and to develop positive moral and civic virtues. Its recent report states that "an essential goal of civic education is to provide skills, knowledge and encouragement for all students, including those who might otherwise be excluded from civic and political life" (Carnegie Corporation, 2002).

Our schools at present are not meeting these democratic goals. In addition, in our diverse and divided society, multicultural curriculum reform is required to achieve substantive democracy. James Banks is a lifetime leader in the multicultural education movement. He argues that among the goals of the curriculum should be

1. Empower the students, especially the victimized and marginalized.
2. Develop the knowledge and skills necessary to critically examine the current political and economic structure.
3. Teach critical thinking skills and decision making skills including the analysis of the way in which knowledge is constructed. (Banks, 2008a, pp. 41–49)

The following explains how multicultural education encourages these democratic and participatory goals for schools.

Democratic Schools and Values This work is about a value position called *pluralism*. Prior chapters have argued that students should learn to respect the cultural diversity in our society and in our schools. This value of pluralism is promoted or limited by what teachers choose to teach, how they teach it (critical thinking), how they assess what they have taught, and how they choose to implement classroom management.

I argue that whereas many values are relative and changing, such as attachment to your home language, other values are absolute. For example, in Chapter 1, I argued that democracy represents a series of values that we choose and will not compromise. Classrooms should promote democracy, and therefore, we insist that children should be treated with respect and should learn to treat each other with mutual respect. At the same time, there are major disagreements in our society over issues such as bilingualism and an inclusive curriculum. We cannot impose a value position on students in these areas of major, substantive values.

In Chapter 2, I focused on the concept of culture and argued that values and value clarity are important parts of learning about culture in others and learning about culture in ourselves. Values lead to our behavior. The behaviorist (reductionist) approach to values is to use behavior to shape values and includes the direct teaching of values. Behavior does shape our values. And value clarity is essential in dealing with cultural conflict, identity conflict, and the problems of drugs and violence (see Chapter 8).

Let's assume that you wish to teach students the value of engaging in electoral decision making. How would you go about teaching trust and confidence in government? If you were a resident of New Orleans or the Gulf Coast after Hurricane Katrina struck in 2005, how would you engage students? Or how do you encourage civic participation when the students can easily see that their schools are underfunded? Is it reasonable to teach democracy in an environment that is obviously unequal?

Our schools need to actively teach the fundamental values, ideals, and responsibilities of a pluralistic society, or they contribute to the conflict in our schools, the continuing divisions in our body politic, and the decline of democracy itself. Although behaviorist strategies and direct teaching work for management issues and in the early primary grades, as children mature, they develop values and attitudes through more complex processes. The work of Lawrence Kohlberg and his students has traced a possible continuum of valuing processes (Gibbs, 1977). As students mature, certainly by about fourth grade, an additional series of strategies, called *values analysis and clarification*, becomes useful for teachers, particularly for those teachers interested in promoting democratic processes (Kirschenbaum, 1992). The strategies of values clarification help students to choose and to clarify their values (Raths, Harmin, & Simon, 1966). Engle and Ochoa (1988) provide an additional approach of values analysis and investigation, as does James Banks (2008). Character traits or dispositions—such as honesty, trustworthiness, empathy, and caring—are closely related to values. Some people refer to the development of these as character education. The character education movement grew exponentially in the 1990s, with over 23 states adopting lists of virtues and character traits that schools should impart (Glanzer & Milson, 2006; Johnson, 2008). Central multicultural issues of prejudice, discrimination, and domination are as much about learning and exploring values as they are about learning new content. Values and dispositions are an important part of civic education and are central to multicultural education (Parker, 2009).

How the Present Curriculum Fails Students The present curriculum is too often divorced from students' actual lives and experiences. Lessons in history and the social studies should provide a natural starting place for students to engage in multicultural education. However, since the 1990s the pressure to raise scores on standardized tests (particularly in math and reading) has intensified. In response, social studies lessons on the development of self-concept, cultural identity, and empowerment have been practically eliminated in the primary grades. Instead of lessons about the self and the society, priority has been given to additional time for reading, language, and math instruction.

In the elementary grades, schools focus on teaching to the math and reading standards and too often rely on haphazard and fragmentary approaches to culture. The intermittent units that do exist too often touch on cultural holidays, heroes, "foods of other lands," and similar activities; while they may be fun, they do not lead to cultural clarity and empowerment. In most states, the standards promote only the majority culture's view of society and schooling. Instead of providing an intellectually defensible view of a multicultural society, many middle and high school courses are even further distanced from students' reality. The curricula generally follow the canons of establishment history and culture taught in universities and imposed by the standards and the textbook publishers. Most curricula avoid a rigorous analysis of race, culture, class, and gender, even though many students' daily lives are immersed in these conflict areas.

Students need multicultural education content and strategies to understand the society as it really exists. These strategies should include goal clarification and establishment of clear measures of progress. For example, immigrant students want to become proficient in English, but many give up and accept low levels of language learning. Their failure is not from a lack of goals or of practice. Failure develops from alienating school experiences that do not provide measurable progress toward language mastery. Language acquisition programs fail when they approach lessons as if language is only a skill. Attitudes toward language, toward culture, and toward self all influence language acquisition (Freire & Macedo, 1987). Positive experiences with language use and reflective thinking about cultural conflict and assimilation encourage students to learn English, to stay in school, and to continue toward graduation.

The conservative school reform movement of the 1980s and 1990s—led in part by Diane Ravitch, Paul Gagnon, and Chester Finn, among others—along with the promotion of the California Framework for History and Social Sciences, successfully convinced many state and district textbook buyers and publishers to focus on history and geography—avoiding the more open-ended social sciences of economics and sociology as well as social and controversial issues. In the upper elementary grades and in middle and high schools, inadequate and unrealistic texts predominate. Instead of engaging students' interest, most history texts offer a sterile, inaccurate, and incomplete view of our society in boring prose. Teachers resort to grades, tests, and worksheets in futile attempts to motivate students from diverse cultural and language communities to pay attention. Some teachers have become wardens, forcing rote memorization on reluctant students, thereby adding to the students' growing impression that school, particularly history, is oppressive and irrelevant to life.

Transformative Multicultural Education

Multicultural education helps students to develop the self-confidence and competence needed to stay in school and to prepare for their own future. Henry Trueba described the process as follows:

> A strong personal cultural or ethnic identity is providing the individual with legitimacy and recognition for his or her enduring self. The psychological justification for retaining a personal framework for self-understanding and for self-acceptance, the setting to which we feel attached as children—the quintessence of what we are in our own eyes, our enduring self—remains justified and unchanged regardless of other adjustments. This is the basis for deeper

emotional peace and stability. In contrast, being forced to abandon this inner frame of enduring self, especially when the home language is lost, isolates a child from the world of his dreams, the world of his affection. How can a child deal with two different worlds and transfer information from one to the other, if the bridge between the two worlds (the language) is broken? How can a child retain a measure of psychological integrity if he is not allowed to reconcile conflicting values from home and school? How can a child enrich his home learning environment if going home is seen as degrading? How can a child seek emotional and cognitive support from parents who are seen as unworthy and despicable? Sooner or later, a child will comprehend that the rejection of one's own language and culture is ultimately the rejection of one's own self. (Trueba, Rodriguez, Zou, & Cintrón, 1993, pp. 147–148)

The multicultural curriculum is designed to help students to analyze their own cultures, to learn about the cultures of others, and to use this knowledge to make decisions about their own futures. Rather than excluding the study of culture, race, class, and gender, multicultural classes provide students with frequent opportunities to examine these issues and constraints. Schools need to meet the students halfway and provide them with a curriculum, teaching faculty, and strategies that assist them in analyzing the society as it really exists. Figure 7.1 provides an overview of this transformative multicultural education approach.

Our society cannot afford the continuing assault on its youth. When we fail to teach children from diverse cultures about their own heritage, we reap a harvest of low self-esteem, greater alienation from school, and higher dropout rates. We must offer students the opportunity to learn the beauty and refinement of their own cultural heritage as well as to acquire essential knowledge and skills for employment and democratic citizenship.

The multicultural curriculum must include academic skill development. To succeed in school or to get a better job, students need to improve their reading and writing skills. It is better for students to develop reading and math skills in fourth or even eighth grade than to struggle with remedial classes in high school or college. Practice in reading and writing helps students to experience more school success and to develop a positive attitude toward school. The reading and writing lessons need to be about the diverse mosaic of the kids in U.S. schools. Lesson plans and curricula should include developing improved study skills among the attainable, measurable goals appropriate to young people and directly related to economic success and opportunity.

Following the lead of Thomas Jefferson and John Dewey, our schools should prepare all students to become active, participatory citizens in the society. Engaging in multicultural education, learning to work together with others in our diverse society, and encouraging the educational and economic success of all students comprise a process to advance democracy. With the new demographic reality—the increasing diversity of students in our schools—all students must be prepared for civic participation.

We can reverse the trend of declining political participation by educating all young people for democracy (Frank, 2004; Putnam, 2000). Multicultural education responds to these democratic goals. It seeks to teach all young people to respect each other and to work together for the common good. Young people who have a positive self-concept and a positive personal identity and who see members of their own communities participating in government are more likely to acquire democratic values and dispositions.

Figure 7.1   Transformative Multicultural Education

Societal goal	Promote respect for others, cultural pluralism, and democracy.
The problem	While intolerance and prejudice may be individual acts, they are more often replicated in societal structures—including public schooling.
The theories	Cognitive theory.
	Builds on human relations theory.
	Adds cognitive theories, constructivism, and sociology of power.
	Eliminating racism requires restructuring power relationships in economic and educational institutions (such as schools).
Source of goals	Democratic theory, ethnic studies, women's studies, gender studies, bilingual education, the Civil Rights Movement.
Students	Appropriate for all students. Usually found in grades 6–12.
	Has a particular relevance for minority students from groups that are targets of oppression.
Curriculum	Uses all lessons from human relations.
	Recasts the curriculum from a multiethnic point of view.
	Includes critical thinking, constructing a confident self-identity, funds of knowledge. Requires revisions of standards.
Key concepts, vocabulary	Ethnicity, culture, gender, identity, cultural mediator, values. cultural democracy, pluralism, civic values.
Classroom instruction	Cooperative learning.
	Role-playing.
	Teaching conflict skills and conflict resolution.
	Teaching to empower.
	Social participation.
	Directly teaching critical thinking skills, media literacy, and decision making.
	Concern with the achievement gap.
	Teaching academic skills for success.
Teacher skills	Cultural competence.
	Cultural mediator.
	Informed on diverse histories and struggles.
	Teach critical thinking and cross-cultural awareness.
	Project-based learning.
	Bilingual and English as a second language instruction.
	Teach reading and writing skills.
Assessment	Traditional assessment processes measure a portion of the curriculum.
	Need for authentic assessment of new topics and themes.
	Rubric assessments.
	Portfolios.

Multicultural education is a vital component of civic learning and is essential for the development of unity of purpose in our divided society and for the growth of our democracy.

Multicultural Education with a Social Justice Focus

Beginning in the 1970s, a new approach to schooling for student empowerment developed in the United States. This alternative intellectual tradition, known as *critical theory and critical pedagogy*, had four major historical contributors in the United States: the work and influence of Paulo Freire; the work and influence of scholars who followed the lead of Althusser and Gramsci (Aronowitz & Giroux, 1985); feminist scholars who were searching for alternative understandings of gender relationships; and the political movements of empowerment, from the Mississippi Freedom Schools of the Civil Rights Movement to current struggles to rebuild the schools for democratic citizenship.

Critical Theory Educators using critical theory assume that men and women have a moral imperative toward developing their own humanity and freedom. This assumption differs from the "scientific" positivist or empiricist scholarly tradition, in which researchers assume the need for neutrality and objectivity of investigation (see Chapter 6). Critical theorists further assume that the current problems of any society are subject to investigation and change. They assume that individuals and groups can and should work together to build a more democratic education system and a more democratic society.

Education writers urging the use of critical theory in the United States include Paulo Freire, Henry Giroux, Peter McLaren, Lois Weis, Alma Flor Ada, Jim Cummins, Kathleen Weiler, Carlos Torres, Joan Wink, Antonia Darder, Stanley Aronowitz, and several of the coauthors of this book.[2]

The following concepts are central to critical theory and are useful in trying to comprehend and analyze your own teaching experience:

- **Consciousness:** Awareness of yourself and your environment. Consciousness includes self-awareness. For example, *multicultural consciousness* refers to a recognition of the ethnic, racial, and social divisions in our society.

- **Culture:** The collective knowledge of a group of people (described extensively in Chapter 2). Please note that European American critical theorists have tended to rely on European authors for descriptions of culture—authors who tend to emphasize class differences and to pay less attention to differences among cultures and ethnic groups.

- **Domination:** The act of controlling an individual or group of people.

- **Empowerment:** Education processes that lead to political courage and political efficacy. Empowerment strategies teach students to analyze and to act on their analyses. Empowerment strategies also help students gain social, political, and economic power, including the power to make their own decisions.

---

[2]See, in particular, Aronowitz and Giroux (1985), Freire (1997), Freire and Macedo (1987), Giroux (1988), McLaren (1989), and Weiler (1988).

- **Ethics:** Normative preferences and recognition that decisions are often based on values rather than exclusively on objective research.

- **Hegemony:** The overwhelming domination of ideologies or economic systems by a single group or source of power. Often ideological hegemony leaves learners unaware of alternative viewpoints. For example, most schools and teachers have an unexamined commitment to competitive grading.

- **Hidden curriculum:** The variety of values and ideas taught informally in schools. These values, attitudes, and assumptions permeate school but rarely reveal themselves in lesson plans or tests. For example, U.S. schools commonly teach individualism, competitiveness, and a European American perspective on our nation's history.

- **Ideology:** A series of interrelated ideas, such as racism or cultural pluralism. A dominant ideology is often taught in schools as if it was the only truth. For example, we are taught that the United States has a democratic government. Our system is then presented as the definition of democracy: two competing parties, regular elections, a free press, and limited government intervention in the economy. There are other models of democracy, but our particular system is taught as an ideology. In similar fashion, we are taught an ideology that our schools are politically neutral, even though they are clearly committed to the maintenance of the present economic/power system.

- **Ideological domination:** Controlling the ideas presented to students by, for example, writing standards and selecting the content of tests and textbooks.

- **Social class:** A group identified by its economic position in the society—for example, the working class, the poor, the wealthy, owners of corporations. There are several contending descriptions of classes in the United States (see Chapter 4).

- **Social construction of knowledge:** The observation that most knowledge is created by persons. What we regard as knowledge was created for a purpose. The concept of the social construction of knowledge treats knowledge as being purposeful and as serving particular interests rather than as being neutral and merely discovered. For example, IQ tests were generated for a particular purpose: to predict school success. They do not define intelligence; instead, they measure a specific kind of mental aptitude in relation to a specific purpose. As an alternative, Gardner (1983) proposes that the concept of multiple intelligences provides a different, more useful description of thinking processes.

Critical Pedagogy At the turn of the last century, John Dewey (1859–1952) argued that a central purpose of schooling was to prepare students to build a democratic society. He thought that critical analysis and learning by doing were essential for the preparation of citizens in a democracy (Dewey, 1916/1966). Influenced by the massive European immigration from 1890 to 1920, Dewey was not an advocate of multicultural education as we presently know it. Like Jefferson before him, Dewey favored having schools lead the nation in developing a new, idealized, democratic American. Today, in a parallel period of massive immigration, Dewey's works provide important insights for the role that schools can play in the cause of creating a democratic society.

In the 1970s, Brazilian educator Paulo Freire contributed to a new interest in and extension of Dewey's ideas about the field of education as a means of advancing a pluralistic democracy. Freire's work revolved around a socially responsible humanism. Like Dewey, he believed that education has a central role in building a democratic society. But Freire's writings offered a new and fresh view of education's role as a participant in the political struggle to liberate oppressed people. He argued that ending oppression and the "culture of silence" in Brazil was essential to the process of building a democratic, participatory community.

Freire first gained attention for the methodology he and his colleagues developed to teach literacy to the impoverished people of the Recife area of northeast Brazil. His first major book, *A Pedagogy of the Oppressed* (1972), described a revolutionary educational and social change process for the poor in Latin America. Freire believed that education workers could help empower adults by engaging in dialogue with them instead of falling into traditional teacher–student roles. The Brazilian military government's official response to his work was to arrest him in 1964 to stop the mobilization of the poor. After his imprisonment and eventual deportation, he worked for the World Council of Churches in Geneva, Switzerland. *A Pedagogy of the Oppressed* was soon being read and discussed throughout Latin America and among small circles of intellectuals in the United States and Europe (Freire, n.d., 1985; McFadden, 1975; McLaren, 2000). In it, Freire described the oppressive and colonizing functions served by traditional teacher-dominated schooling. Freire's ideas have important ramifications for understanding the education of oppressed cultural and class groups in U.S. schools.

Prior to Freire's work, most published education research and university work in social science education in the United States had suggested only technical improvements to the existing school curriculum. The "scientific study" of schools, common even today, used positivist, reductionist research methods (see Chapter 6). This research generally strengthened the school's role in the domination of oppressed communities. Freire's writings suggested new analytical concepts to describe the experiences of students. His work offered new hope and insight for teachers working with alienated and oppressed students in our own society. Teachers and activists searched his works and found alternative strategies for work with immigrant and working-class students. Freire's work suggested solutions to the structural failure of poor children in U.S. schools, whereas the narrow research paradigms of positivism hid the critical questions of race and class domination and provided few real alternatives.

Freire openly acknowledged that his views included a political pedagogy (Freire, 1998). His writings revealed the political and class dimensions underlying any education system. Education and schools could reinforce the domination of the existing structure, or they could introduce students to citizenship and freedom. Education could help young people to lead free and self-empowering lives. Following Freire's lead, education teams in Brazil, Chile, Venezuela, and Nicaragua taught the poor to read by helping community members analyze their life situations. Poor peasants engaged in community organizing to effect social change. Freire used the term *praxis* to describe the process of critical analysis leading to action. The experience of praxis empowers people to participate in democratic struggles. It gives students and teachers hope. Multicultural education applies the principles of cultural action and praxis to U.S. public schools, particularly schools serving students of oppressed classes and cultures.

Conservative scholars accuse advocates of multicultural education of politicizing the curriculum. This charge has intimidated some multicultural education advocates and placed them on the defensive. Yet clearly the writings of John Dewey were profoundly political. Critics attack the political dimension of both Freire's work and multicultural educational theory, while refusing to acknowledge that Dewey's major works provide the intellectual foundations of social justice teaching. Dewey argued that the schools should promote immigrant assimilation and build a democratic society. These are political goals. Freire's work, like Dewey's, recognizes the essentially political nature of education.

Both the present Eurocentric curriculum and its multicultural alternatives are highly political. The current standards-based, test-driven curriculum is a political project imposed by legislatures and the President. Realistically, a teacher's choice is not between being political and being neutral. Claiming political neutrality for schools actually supports the continuation of the current tracked, starkly unequal system—a profoundly political position.

The teaching strategies and attitudes described by Freire and adapted for social justice multicultural education in the United States begin by respecting the prior cultural knowledge that all students bring to the classroom. Freire, like Dewey, argued for rooting the education experience in students' real experiences. Freire believed that speech, language, and literacy can be understood only in a social context and that students learn language and literacy best in the context of their social experience. He worked with a number of adult literacy campaigns that have applied this principle and that have had enormous impact in societies seeking transition to democracy. Cultural action in literacy contributed to social change in Brazil, Chile, Guinea-Bissau, and Nicaragua (Freire, 1997). In his writings, Freire also applauded successful efforts in the United States—notably the Highlander Folk School in Tennessee.

Both ethnographic research and Freire's work in Latin America considered culture as a field of struggle, not as a fixed or static object. In this view, developing an understanding of their culture helps students to respect themselves, to learn from the past, and to participate in the active creation of a democratic future. The literacy programs designed by Freire and his colleagues used an ethnographic perspective to assist peasants in learning about their culture as a means of empowering them (Freire & Macedo, 1987). While many teachers at bilingual and multicultural sites were drawn to the work of Paul Freire and his collaborators by its emphasis on culture and the power of the struggle for social justice, other teachers and authors, primarily African American, were engaged in developing a parallel U.S. approach known as *culturally relevant pedagogy*, as described in Chapter 2.

Critical Race Theory   Following developments in legal studies and the work of Derrick Bell, activists, scholars, and teachers in the 1990s focused again on examining race and racism as they have played out in the United States and in our schools—a movement known as *critical race theory*. Advocates of critical race theory argued that race theory complemented critical theory in the struggle for social justice, since race and racism had not been sufficiently recognized and analyzed in developing most bilingual and multicultural programs.

Empowerment as a Goal When students recognize their own cultural context, they can learn to think critically about it and make meaningful decisions about their life opportunities. Critical pedagogy, or problem-posing education, seeks to help students to understand the world they live in and to critically analyze their real-life situations. Critical analysis, practical skills, value clarity, and self-confidence lead to empowerment. Participation in community development helps students to develop the political courage to work toward the resolution of their real problems. Community action teams working with preliterate peasants in Latin America helped them to learn to read and perhaps to create a labor union or farmer cooperative. For students from oppressed or marginalized groups in the United States, the goals might be gaining admission to college, receiving a good-quality high school preparation for work, or counteracting crime in their communities.

The strong, democratic social justice perspective in multicultural education, including critical race theory, has adopted the goal of empowerment as central to education reform. By urging that schools help students build a more democratic society, multicultural education moves away from positivism's stress on being an objective observer of events. Education projects designed for empowerment help students to take a stand. They provide opportunities for students to intervene in their own families and communities—to analyze situations, decide, and act and then to analyze their actions anew. Empowerment is taught to overcome disempowerment.

Teachers can teach about social justice at all levels, including the primary grades. Even the youngest children are interested in the value of fairness. The question is one of emphasis. There is more reason to stress a multicultural social justice approach in high schools, where the students are adolescents and approaching maturity.

High school students are ready and interested in studying their own realities and how to operate within the limits of our political/economic system. It is more urgent in high school that the students learn to take control of their own lives and to overcome low achievement and tracking. The economic consequences, including incarceration, are more severe if students get left behind during their high school years.

Multicultural education that is social justice oriented deals directly and forcefully with social and structural inequities in our society, including racism, sexism, and class prejudice. It prepares students from oppressed groups to succeed in spite of existing inequalities. This approach argues for a bold commitment to democracy in schooling based on a belief in the learning potential of students from all races and classes and from both genders. Figure 7.2 describes the approach of multicultural education that is social justice oriented.

Selecting Themes for Empowerment and Hope

Prior to 1998, teachers made the most fundamental decisions on what themes and concepts to teach and to emphasize in their classrooms. Since then, the dominant standards movement assumes that teachers should follow a curriculum controlled

Figure 7.2   Multicultural Education That Is Social Justice Oriented (Also known as Strong Sense Democratic Multicultural Education)

Societal goal	Build a more inclusive, democratic society, create a more equal social structure, and ensure social justice in the school and the society.
The problem	Both individuals and institutions in the society benefit from and wish to continue the present distribution of power and resources; only a few want to change.
	The political and economic systems often block democratic change.
The theories	Critical pedagogy, critical theory.
	Social reconstruction viewpoint.
	Conflict theory.
Source of goals	Commitment to democracy, justice, and individual dignity; the Civil Rights Movement.
Students	Particularly for students from oppressed cultural, ethnic, class, and gender groups.
	It is a pedagogy of the oppressed.
	Most often developed with high school students and adults.
Curriculum	Uses strategies from prior perspectives plus service learning, social participation, and social action.
	Coaching.
	Often considered a curriculum that is "politicized" around current social issues.
	Project-based curriculum: projects in the community/city.
Key concepts, vocabulary	Consciousness, empowerment, hegemony, ideologies, ideological domination, social class, social justice, social construction of knowledge, culture, values clarity.
Classroom instruction	Project-based curriculum.
	Critical thinking.
	Inquiry.
	Working with others.
	Analysis of their own realities.
	Modeling activism and political participation.
	Cooperative learning.
	Democratic decision making.
	Empowerment (see page 235).
	Dialogue.
	Praxis.
	Teach social action skills.
Teacher skills	Community organizing, organizing support.
	Dialogue.
	Critical thinking.
	Cultural, ethnographic analysis.
	Cultural broker.
	Advocate.
	Political courage.
Assessment	Rubrics.
	Participant observation.
	Authentic assessment of process and products.
Other	This is a distinct minority position.
	There are a few published concrete examples in elementary grades.
	Most often, this is fundamentally an approach for secondary schools and adults.

and provided by the state or the district (see Chapter 12). In the area of reading and phonics, this often includes scripted lessons that tell the teacher precisely what to say (derived from remedial perspectives and the teaching-the-exceptional-and-the-culturally-different viewpoint). In this manner, the standards committee, or the district, or often the textbook publishers have decided precisely what the teachers should teach.

Both critical theory and a strong sense of multicultural education suggest an alternative approach: that teaching and learning should begin in the interests and lives of the students. This multicultural approach, often in conflict with the standards movement, encourages teachers to make important choices with the students on appropriate and important topics, themes, and concepts for study.

Because it is difficult for teachers, particularly new teachers, to resist the imposed curriculum of standards, you may want to pursue a compromise—a combination of standards-based imposed topics and facts some of the time and student-centered teaching at other times. Selecting student-centered themes and concepts in literature and social studies is often difficult because new teachers do not know where to begin to find themes rooted in students' lives. Language and literacy teachers will refer to themes and social science teachers will refer to concepts for these closely associated ideas. A theme can be a topic or subject that recurs frequently in the life of a child. The process of studying themes from their own experiences validates students' cultures and helps them to recognize the importance of school. To help students understand that school and lessons are valuable, school lessons should help to explain real life.

Selecting Themes for Kindergarten Through Grade 6

Many good teachers begin the process of discovering their students' interests by observing and listening. What do they do? What do they talk about? You can also ask parents what the most important things are for their children. In particular, you should ask the parents of a child who is mildly off-task or disruptive to share some of the activities and interests the child responds to at home.

Teachers' bookstores and conferences, as well as conversations with interesting experienced teachers, provide resources for new teachers. States and districts often have lists of supplementary and extension children's literature that suggest themes. Many of the conversations now occur online in teacher chat rooms. You can look for these through professional organizations such as the International Reading Association and the National Council for the Social Studies. You will find that others have done some of the work for you and have located high-quality children's books about children's themes. In larger cities, there are bookstores that specialize in the literature of our diverse cultures. Many of these resource lists are online and can be found with popular Internet search engines. Online teacher chat rooms are particularly valuable because you may find suggested lessons and assessments already prepared for you to use with the literature books.

Student teachers should begin to collect supplementary materials, bulletin board ideas, charts, and other supplies during their practice teaching.

Singing for Social Justice with Children One way to approach important social justice concepts and themes is through music.

A study, *Children's Song-Makers as Messengers of Hope* (Baird, 2001), has brought together some of the most influential and beloved children's songmakers in the United States to discuss the issue of introducing social justice ideas for children and what they think educators, parents, children, and other musicians can do about it—including suggestions for songs and how teachers can use them.

> Chief among the participants is Pete Seeger, who started sharing his folk and original songs with school children in 1938 at the age of 19 and has never stopped, even when he was blacklisted for singing for labor, civil rights, and peace and other organizations. Some of the songs he has written or popularized with children and adults that still are sung today by the generation of teachers and musicians who were raised on his music are songs against racism ("We Shall Overcome"), to protest war ("Where Have All the Flowers Gone," "Waist Deep in the Big Muddy"), songs to urge us to clean up the environment ("Ballad of the Sloop Clearwater," "Rainbow Race") and proclaim the power of love ("Kisses Sweeter Than Wine"), to work for international understanding ("Guantanamera," "De Colores") and strive for a better world for our children ("Abiyoyo," "Visions of Children"). No one song can sum up a lifetime of songmaking for social justice, but "If I Had a Hammer," by Lee Hays (words) and Pete Seeger (music), comes pretty close. . . . (pp. 112–113)

Even young children can understand the essence of complex social issues when they are tied to child-friendly concepts such as fairness, sharing, and nonviolence. Song leader Jacki Breger tells preschool and primary-age children in the Los Angeles area, "Social justice means that you don't do things that are not fair, or that hurt other people." Then she tells them positive stories from the Civil Rights Movement and shares the songs that the actual people sang to raise their spirits and spread the message of their cause: the story of Rosa Parks and the Montgomery bus boycott ("If You Miss Me at the Back of the Bus"), student sit-ins ("We Shall Not Be Moved"), freedom marches ("Ain't Gonna Let Nobody Turn Me 'Round"), determination and inspiration ("Woke Up This Morning," "This Little Light"), and the anthem of the Civil Rights Movement ("We Shall Overcome").

All the songmakers urge teachers and parents to start singing early and keep singing often with children—to connect their natural love of music and singing with their capacity to help make a better world. Early childhood musician and legend Ella Jenkins tells teachers to begin with what they know ("Twinkle, Twinkle Little Star"), to not worry about having a trained voice, and above all to be respectful of children. Argentine-born Suni Paz reminds teachers to sing Spanish and other native language songs such as "De Colores" and "Corrido de Dolores Huerta" and to include such strategies as using recorded music, inviting parents to participate, and bringing in visiting musicians. To find the best music resources, songmakers advise looking on the Internet for (1) the Children's Music Network, which many of them belong to, and (2) the Smithsonian Folkways Recordings, a wonderful collection of socially conscious children's music by Woody Guthrie, Pete Seeger, Ella Jenkins, and Suni Paz, recently reissued on CDs.

Selecting Themes for Intermediate Grades 6 Through 8

At this level, you can start with inventories of student interests. One example, created by Sidney Simon and his colleagues (Simon, Howe, & Kirschenbaum, 1972), is the values clarification exercise shown in Figure 7.3. In the original exercise, the lists were kept private. The teacher then guided students through the process of analyzing values and calculating factors of risk, cost, and parental influence for each item on their lists (Simon et al., 1972). Changing the exercise to have you collect the lists provides you with an excellent source of themes in students' lives.

A similar exercise has students list their favorite television shows. You or the students compile the lists, which you then analyze. Analysis of television viewing can provide important curriculum themes. Also, you can watch programs such as *Reading Rainbow* or look at websites such as *www.discoveryschool.com* for ideas.

You also may discover student themes by attending student events, talking to experienced teachers, and reading teaching periodicals and online resources, such as *Teaching Tolerance* and *Rethinking Schools*. In doing so, you are not abandoning the standards-based curriculum in search of students' interests. Instead, you are searching for themes in students' lives that make the officially approved curriculum valuable, useful, and motivational.

Selecting Themes for Grades 8 Through 12

The examples of student inventories, literature, and values clarification lessons described for grades 6 through 8 also apply to grades 8 through 12. However, the students in these grades are older and will need to further investigate their own experiences and cultures. Because adolescents often feel as if they are under attack, they benefit from talking about their frustrations, conflicts, and anxieties. Teachers should listen to the problems of adolescents in a rapidly changing and often dangerous society. Students' own problems constitute important themes for study.

Your choices of what to teach in social studies and in literature can contribute to empowering students (Apple & Beane, 1995; Banks, 2008a). Concepts of race, ethnicity, class, and gender relations should be addressed. Your students live in a world of intersecting and at times conflicting demands. Studying multiple perspectives on these demands assists students in making deliberate and wise choices. Students will not necessarily make positive choices by themselves, so they need the sensitive guidance of a teacher.

Figure 7.3   Values Clarification Exercise

The students prepare a paper by listing the numbers 1 through 20 down one side. The exercise calls for students to make a rapid list of their favorite activities. The teacher explains in advance that she will collect the paper. Students should not write intimate items on this paper. Names are not needed on the paper.

When the teacher gives the signal, the students make a rapid list of the items they would most like to do. The items are not listed in any priority.

Example:

Things I Would Most Like to Do

1.
2.
3.
4.
5.
6.
7.
8.
9.
10.
11.
12.
13.
14.
15.
16.
17.
18.
19.
20.

Source: Adapted from *Values Clarification* (p. 30), by S. B. Simon, L. W. Howe, and H. Kirschenbaum, 1972, New York: Hart.

As a teacher, you may select your content from the standards, from a textbook, or from a district curriculum guide. I also encourage you to choose to take the time and effort to teach units in social studies on the cultures represented by students in your school, the cultural conflicts common in your school, and the personal development skills your students will need in an increasingly divisive society (Banks, 2008a). Like gang behavior and drugs, it is best to bring these topics into the open in order to study and discuss them.

Open discussion of race, gender, and class conflicts may reduce the physical conflict in your school but may also increase the level of disagreement in your classroom. Some teachers are uncomfortable even discussing these topics with students. Your own self-confidence and recognition of your role as a cultural mediator permit you to openly discuss volatile issues.

Analyzing advertising aimed at young people reveals additional themes. For instance, many clothing advertisements encourage teenagers to believe that a certain look will win them access to a desired social group. Some advertisements for clothing encourage conformity, and some encourage aggressive sexuality, while others encourage eccentricity. These themes are ever-present in students' lives. Initially, students may deny advertising's effectiveness, but more thoughtful examination usually reveals its function in defining "the good life" (see Chapter 5).

Teenagers particularly respond to stereotypes about teenagers. Often, the stereotypes are revealed in name-calling and group forming. Gangs for the poor and exploited and cliques and fraternities for the middle class are expressions of young people's need to belong to a group. Social studies classes should study the roles and functions of gangs and cliques. There is further discussion of content selection in Chapter 12.

Reality: Its Place in the Classroom

In spite of the national ideal of promoting pluralism, racism, sexism, and discrimination remain realities of our society. Whereas human relations approaches may be sufficient for kindergarten through grade 6 and for majority group students, students of color need more powerful strategies to prepare them to overcome the institutionalized inequality in our schools and our society. An inaccurate, conflict-free view of our society and our government invalidates students' own life experiences as sources of knowledge. An empowerment curriculum should offer the opportunity for students to study racism, sexism, and pluralism, among other themes, and encourage them to search for new democratic alternatives.

The violence of racism, sexism, and class oppression provide important subjects for study and analysis. By studying oppression in historical settings and analyzing its constituent parts, students develop a perspective that stops placing the blame on the victim. In empowerment classes, this sort of critical analysis leads to planning for social change. By middle school (grades 6 through 8), students should be encouraged to consider empowerment strategies that include seeking their own individual advancement through education and collective advancement through elections, social change projects and political struggle.

Current opportunities for schooling are unequal, but educational opportunities are more equal than are economic or housing opportunities. Since at least 1900, schooling has been considered a preparation for life and an opportunity to achieve a better standard of living. Advocacy groups fought long and hard for educational opportunity, culminating in *Brown v. Board of Education* (1954), *Lau v. Nichols* (1971), and the Civil Rights Movement of the 1950s and 1960s. An empowerment curriculum seeks to bring the orientation and the results of these struggles for equality into the classroom. On the other hand, present school tracking by "ability groups" promotes the ideology of meritocracy and strengthens discrimination (Oakes, Rogers, & Lipton, 2006). Students in the upper, college-bound tracks have an inherent advantage. Low-income students in the middle and lower tracks need to understand the school system they are subject to and become more mature and more goal-oriented in order to gain equal educational opportunity (Oakes & Rogers, 2006). The study of racism, sexism, and class oppression in schools helps students to comprehend their place in this unequal system and to make personal decisions to take advantage of their school experience to prepare for the future.

Television and the youth culture present a competing, less mature, more immediate, self-indulgent life philosophy. The abundance of wealth in our society bestows on middle-class students the luxury of extended adolescence. They can get serious about growing up later, in college or even after college. But working-class students may sacrifice their future educational opportunities when they substitute the values and sexuality of the commercial youth culture for hard work in school. These young people especially need adults to present a commonsense, real-world perspective on opportunity.

Social Participation in Schools

Anthropologists and sociologists refer to two aspects of school curriculum—the formal and the informal. The *formal curriculum* consists of the goals, course outlines, strategies, and materials used to teach and evaluate lessons and skills. The *informal curriculum* includes the messages conveyed by a combination of rules, regulations, procedures, and practices, including the attitudes of teachers, staff, and administrators. The formal and the informal curricula sometimes conflict. The formal curriculum may encourage students to take a position and to defend that position with argument, but students are seldom coached and supported for taking action on controversial issues in schools, such as tracking, alienation, and violence.

Schools have long recognized the value of participation in student councils and student governments, but these structures typically serve a small, select few. It is not an accident that middle-class schools have numerous opportunities for participation and decision making, whereas inner-city schools tend to emphasize control of the student population. These differences reveal attitudes that are potentially harmful to many students: A small portion of the middle class is taught to lead, while the poor are contained and controlled. The informal curriculum of many schools serving working-class students discourages these students from getting involved in self-governance. The cultural democratic alternative argues that because all students need preparation for democracy, all students should be engaged in decision making (Banks, 2008).

Since the time of Dewey, we have recognized that humans learn best by doing. Yet schools often seek to teach citizenship to students from dominated cultural groups through passive methods, such as readings, discussions, films, and worksheets.

To prepare students to participate in our democracy, we must make room in the curriculum for more active strategies that teach democratic participation (Engle & Ochoa, 1988).

Students need to develop their own relationship with society—a responsible relationship (Parker, 2003; Westheimer & Kahne, 2003). Society imposes a curriculum and school practices on students. Strategies and lessons need to be developed to help students to form an active, purposeful relationship with society—not just to be the subject of adult authority. Students come to prefer democracy when they participate and experience success in their efforts. These experiences of success can be developed through project-based learning and service learning projects.

Active strategies expose students to meaningful social and political choices and give them opportunities to act as responsible citizens. For example, in 1996 and in 1998, California students participated in election campaigns in support of affirmative action and in defense of bilingual education. In 2002, students in Massachusetts organized demonstrations to oppose the state school exams. In 2006, Los Angeles students working with the UCLA's Teaching to Change LA institute carried out research projects on how schools and school budgets were shortchanging students in minority-dominant schools. School administrations, counselors, and advisors know how to reach the "good" students who are already committed to schooling. We need new strategies to reach the isolated, alienated students who are potential dropouts. Programs for college preparation such as AVID and Puente provide an important positive direction for these students. Reluctant and passive students are in great need of the participatory strategies presently offered primarily to the academically successful.

Schools encourage democratic behavior when students engage in substantial decision making. Some teachers achieve this by having students participate in management decisions and discipline systems in classroom meetings. Many elementary, middle, and high schools have engaged student teams in conflict resolution and violence reduction strategies. The strategy of teaching democratic behavior, attitudes, and analysis through encouraging students to participate in social controversy and social movements is called *social participation*. Introducing social participation into the curricula in the upper grades produces a positive, pro-democratic effect on both formal and informal curricula (Wade, 2000; Westheimer & Kahne, 2003).

Teachers promote social participation and service learning by encouraging projects at a level of safety and controversy appropriate to each school community. Social participation projects offer excellent ways to complete thematic units that integrate two or more subjects. For example, fourth-grade students might design a campaign to rid the school of litter. Sixth-grade and older students can participate in conflict resolution training to reduce bullying and violence on the school grounds. Tenth-grade students might want to lobby for auto insurance reform or school financing of intramural athletics. Urban students can work to make their school grounds or neighborhood a drug- and violence-free zone. Philadelphia students have worked with the Algebra Project, and Los Angeles students have engaged in political processes insisting on adequate funding of their schools (Oakes & Rogers, 2006). Students learn academic skills and increase their sense of efficacy and self-worth when they study issues, make decisions, and then take actions that help to eliminate problems they have identified. In the

Anti-Bias Study Guide of the Antidefamation League, one lesson has students developing an individual action guide for community action (p. 275). Another asks students to reflect on their own perspectives on taking a stand in the case of Rosa Parks.

Through skillful training in decision-making and problem-solving processes, students can learn to accurately predict the possibility of achieving specific changes. Teachers guide students in conducting research on topics and appropriately selecting targets for their efforts. Later students analyze their results to measure the accuracy of their predictions and the effectiveness of their chosen strategies.

Multicultural curriculum reform often includes civic and community participation projects. Increasingly, this process is being called *service learning*. Students develop social and work skills along with pro-democratic values through active, guided participation with community service agencies. By working with a range of groups, such as antipoverty agencies, local community-based organizations, political parties, and labor organizations, 11th- and 12th-grade students can gain a realistic and diverse view of their community and of the political process. In 2000, the California State Legislature encouraged service learning in the state's schools by including service as a part of the César Chávez holiday curriculum. Social participation develops both the skills and the sense of political courage needed to overcome the present alienation between many students of color and the schools (Banks, 2008; Oakes & Rogers, 2006; Wade, 2000; Westheimer & Kahne, 2003).

Too many working-class students have been trained for defeat. Sitting in classes completing endless worksheets confirms a cynical belief that schooling and education make little real difference in life. On the other hand, social participation—and school-to-work opportunities—empowers students and provides a means to break out of these defeatist patterns. Work in community agencies gives students a realistic view of the processes of change. Adult community activists serve as mentors to students and encourage them to complete their education. Students begin their transition to the world of work and return to school more mature and focused on improving their own education.

Interaction with life, work, racism, and poverty will convince many students of the value of education. Students gain a sense of social responsibility when they participate in projects that actually contribute to the health of their own communities. It is important to select social participation activities that provide both safety and success. Some schools have fifth-grade students become "buddies" who are responsible for helping first graders adjust to school. In other schools, tenth-grade students staff tutoring centers to help seventh- and eighth-grade students complete their homework. Students, the school, and the community gain by these efforts. Students learn to work to achieve goals. Social participation teaches that we can accept responsibility and control our own lives, an important step toward believing in the value of education.

In earlier decades, some of the finest traditions of the social studies were built on a conception of curriculum that stressed service and social participation. Dewey (1916/1966) stressed the need to create a new society by democratic participation in the construction of such a society. Westheimer and Kahne (2003) describe efforts to get students involved in productive community service projects as integral parts of their classroom experiences. Shaver (1977) and others advocate further development of the ideas of participation. Sheldon Berman, founder of Educators for Social Responsibility, updates this earlier work and describes successful efforts to engage students in projects and learning (Berman, 1999; see also Westheimer & Kahne, 2003).

A standards-driven curriculum is often the opposite of service learning. Conservative forces favor the presentation of an "approved" curriculum, often sterile and irrelevant academic lessons that continue the current ideological hegemony. Conservative academics, not teachers, dominated the standards-writing processes, particularly in history and the social sciences. These lessons teach many students that school does not matter; thus, they teach apathy and alienation from school and from society. Conservatives blame the home and the neighborhood for school failure, ignoring the irrelevance of much of the imposed curriculum. They often consider social service and the political participation strategies of multicultural education to be radical attempts to "politicize" the schools (Campbell, 1980; Ravitch, 1990).

Social justice teaching, or antiracism education, like other education philosophies, is political. Multicultural education that is social justice oriented encourages participation as a strategy to develop a critical consciousness about the roles of race, class, and gender in structuring our society and controlling our schools. Students from working-class communities should engage in advancing democracy and advancing their own education. Future citizens from *all* cultures and classes deserve to learn the skills and acquire the political courage needed to make government work for their interests.

Empowerment Strategies

Empowering students is central to the social justice approach to multicultural curriculum (Figure 7.2). Many schools empower middle-class students. And even though problems of drugs, suicide, and violence clearly indicate that not all middle-class students are empowered in school, most are taught the skills, attitudes, and behavior patterns needed to succeed in our society.

Schools presently empower students from dominant classes and too often disempower working-class students and selected cultural and gender groups. As Henry Trueba explained, empowerment contests with disempowerment. Schools systematically disempower cultural minority groups by silencing students, denying the validity of their culture, or rendering their culture and language useless in school (Trueba et al., 1993).

Trueba describes the process of empowerment as follows:

> In this context of cultural contacts between mainstream persons and those from different linguistic and cultural backgrounds (such as between teachers and students), the least conflictive position is taken by those persons who adopt multicultural responses. Yet, cultural therapy, as a means to compare and contrast cultural values and understandings, can enhance communication and resolve conflicts arising from misunderstandings in inter-ethnic and intercultural exchanges. There are at least two main ways in which cultural therapy can help. First, it can help develop a strong personal identity based on a better known and better understood cultural background. Second, cultural therapy can also increase the ability to identify areas of value conflict, differences in interpretations of messages and expectations, range of acceptable etiquette, preferential protocol, and other expected behavioral responses. (p. 147)

For our democracy to survive and prosper, schools serving students of color need a fundamental shift in emphasis. Democratic teachers should design teaching strategies to empower all students. Schools should teach all students to read and provide them with the skills needed to find employment as well as to gain access to both higher education and the knowledge industries of the future. Students from all social classes and ethnic groups deserve to learn the skills of analysis and organization as well as to develop the self-confidence needed to engage in struggles for political equality (Anyon, 2005; Freire & Macedo, 1987; Oakes & Rogers, 2006).

Students from minority cultures and linguistic groups who have been excluded from democratic participation particularly deserve education designed for empowerment (Cummins, 1986), as described in Figure 7.2. We can summarize the main teaching strategies for empowerment as follows:

1. Study the nature of culture.
2. Study the nature of cultural conflicts and value conflicts.
3. Study the powerful analytic concepts that reveal students' real culture and current status. (See Chapter 2.)
4. Use students' home, school, and community experiences as source material for curricula and as a basis for analysis.
5. Compare racism and pluralism as options for the individual and the society.
6. Plan lessons to use success as a strategy. All students deserve the opportunity to succeed.
7. Teach critical thinking (reflective thinking). (See Chapter 9.)
8. Use problem-posing education. (See Chapter 9.)
9. Critically examine students' own social realities and help them plan for change.
10. Develop critical literacy.
11. Use coaching. (See the following section, "The Teacher as Coach.")
12. Use cooperative learning strategies. (See Chapter 10.)
13. Respect children's home languages. (See Chapter 11.)
14. Promote dialogue. (See Figure 7.5.)
15. Encourage social participation and praxis as part of the curriculum.

Subsequent chapters in this book provide you with practical advice for these empowerment strategies.

The Teacher as Coach

We need not restrict our view of teaching and learning to large-group instruction. Often, educational encounters that empower occur between a teacher and one or two students. A question, a comment, or a few words of encouragement from the teacher sometimes help students to continue their struggle for an education.

Figure 7.4   A Coaching Process for Teachers

1. Identify the issue or individual of concern.

2. Set time aside for coaching. Meet with the student individually.

3. Establish clear goals for the coaching. Your role as coach is to assist the student in achieving the student's goal. Coaching is inappropriate for punishment (see Chapter 8).

4. Cooperatively analyze specific steps that the student can take to achieve his or her goal232.

5. Break the task down into manageable steps.

6. Support and encourage the student in taking each step.

7. Meet regularly. Encourage continued effort.

8. Establish a means or criteria for evaluation.

9. Check back with the student on progress.

Students who experience regular success in school receive affirmation and support from their daily school experiences. Unfortunately, many students simply pass through school. They seldom reflect on their experiences or consider taking charge of their educational and economic future.

When a teacher coaches a student, a simple comment or a student conference can lead the student to reconsider his skills or behavior and to plan for improvement. Good teachers use coaching to conduct conferences on motivation and skill development and to build on student strengths. A pedagogy for empowerment should make coaching a deliberate, planned series of experiences for all students.

Coaching is begun by teachers noticing the performance of their students. Students who are performing well should be encouraged to continue. Students who are performing poorly should be coached to change their study strategies. Students who are in the middle seldom get noticed. A carefully thought-out strategy of coaching will encourage the success of *all* students (see Figure 7.4).

Set a goal of getting to know one student per week by talking with the student and listening to the student's perception of reality. A suggestion, a prompt, or a little praise can encourage students to consider themselves important and to make changes in their study habits. Teachers make time for coaching by planning lessons that provide the opportunities for one-on-one interaction (see Chapter 10).

Working in Teams

Students and adults in many communities are divided and isolated. They quarrel with each other and are frequently alienated from government and society. But when residents of low-income communities work together on projects ranging from crime control to school improvement, both the communities and their members gain power (Anyon, 2005; Moses & Cobb, 2001).

In Chapter 10, we explain how structured activities in group work, decision making, consensus seeking, and group evaluation can prepare students for community leadership development. Some social action projects should require students to work together in teams. Working in groups helps students learn interpersonal skills and increases their chances of experiencing success. Working in groups helps students learn to practice behavior that supports the values of cooperation, noncompetitiveness, sharing of resources, and peer respect.

Cohen (1986) argues that there is an urgent need to structure groups purposefully so that cooperation and caring emerge because American youngsters are so heavily influenced by forces leading to individualism and competitiveness. Students in the middle school years (grades 6 through 8) want to belong to groups to overcome the alienation and fear of rejection common in their lives. Group membership, both positive and negative, is also a strong motivation in high school. Schools that build on group values make important and vital connections with students' concerns and offer an alternative to gang values (see Chapter 8). A curriculum of social participation and empowerment can support group values, while redirecting students away from gang membership and crime.

Teams of students can work together to combine analysis and action on the following projects:

1. Changing the classroom environment (such as bulletin boards or seating arrangements)
2. Helping to solve neighborhood problems (such as preventing teenage pregnancy, providing tutoring, or eliminating litter)
3. Visiting the aged and helping in food lockers and kitchens for the homeless
4. Volunteering at day care centers and breakfast programs
5. Participating in political party efforts
6. Joining with student groups to support neighborhood organizations, unions, and civil rights organizations

In Chapter 10, we discuss in detail developing teams and processing their work.

Dialogue

The empowerment strategy of teacher–student and student–student dialogue is a powerful approach that assists students in improving their thinking, language, and communication skills. Working in teams and coaching are improved by teachers engaging the empowerment strategy of dialogue.

Patrick J. Finn (1999) describes dialogue in Figure 7.5. Dialogue strategies are important both for working with students and for working with other teachers to promote a social justice curriculum.

Figure 7.5   Dialogue

Dialogue:
    I search for basic agreements.
    I search for strengths in your position.
    I reflect on my position.
    I consider the possibility of finding a better solution than mine or yours.
    I assume that many people have a piece of the answer.
    I want to find common ground.
    I submit my best thinking hoping your reflection will improve it.
    I remain open to talk about the subject later on.

Anti-dialogue:
    I search for glaring differences.
    I search for weaknesses in your position.
    I attack your position.
    I defend my solution and exclude yours.
    I am invested wholeheartedly in my beliefs.
    I assume there is one right answer, and that I have it.
    I want to win.
    I submit my best thinking and defend it to show it is right.
    I expect to settle this here and now. (Finn, 1999. p. 169)

Summary

It is important for students to learn that attendance, study, and analysis in school can help them make life decisions and learn skills that will help them succeed in their adult lives. Positive school experiences make a difference in students' lives and lead them to conclude that further schooling can provide an entrance into the dynamic sectors of our economy. Multicultural education with a social justice emphasis uses empowerment strategies as important vehicles for the growth of our democracy and our economy. Teaching analysis, social participation, service learning, and social action skills provides confidence and political courage. When students see that the process of critical analysis can lead to positive action (praxis), they learn that they can take real steps to improve their lives. Multicultural education that is social justice oriented encourages students to participate in the valuable, long, and difficult effort to build a more democratic society.

Questions over the Chapter

1. List two of Paulo Freire's pedagogical ideas that are similar to those of U.S. philosopher John Dewey.
2. What are at least two examples of Freire's statement that all education is political? What are the political dimensions of your current teacher preparation program?
3. Describe the power relationships in your current school or current program. Who has power? Who does not? What is the nature of power in your school?

4. List four ways that your curriculum may not be politically neutral.
5. What are the goals of empowerment?
6. What would be important empowerment goals for a group of immigrant students?

7. List four examples of social participation projects appropriate to the specific grade level you intend to teach.

Activities for Further Study of Empowerment

1. List social participation opportunities that you can relate to some element of your curriculum. Work out a strategy with your students for one of these, and guide them in implementing it. Evaluate the results.
2. Role-play a coaching session in your university class. Encourage a student to work to improve his or her study skills.
3. Choose two objectives from each group, and write specific lesson plans for them.

Grades 1–3: Students will do the following:

a. Volunteer to assist a limited-English-speaking student with her lessons.
b. Participate in class meetings about student behavior.

Grades 4–8: Students will do the following:

a. Work as a volunteer tutor with younger students.
b. Learn negotiation strategies for conflict resolution.
c. Serve as a conflict resolution monitor in school.
d. Make an education plan to improve their own reading and writing skills.
e. Assist the teacher with classroom tasks.

Grades 8–12: Students will do the following:

a. Work as a volunteer feeding the hungry.
b. Make an education plan leading toward higher education or a career.
c. Follow through on the first steps of the education plan.
d. Identify and analyze their own specific academic skills.
e. Plan and practice to overcome a specific skill weakness (for example, writing a paragraph).
f. Conduct research comparing learning conditions in an affluent suburban school and a school serving low-income students.
g. Work on a team within a community service organization. Analyze and improve the team's work.
h. Interview a community activist about what forces prevent community agencies from achieving increased success.
i. Complete a study of conflict resolution strategies. Establish a student-run system of conflict resolution in the school.

4. Provide students with a list of local community agencies accepting volunteers. Help students identify an area they may like to experience, help them identify the appropriate agency, and encourage them to participate in its activities.

Teaching Strategies for Use with Your Students

1. See the empowerment strategies on page 230.
2. Plan community participation and social participation as part of your curriculum.
3. Investigate the present reading and writing levels of your students. Generate plans to advance them at least 1.5 years in 1 year. (Your goal will be to get low-achieving students up to their actual grade level in 2 years.)
4. Integrate reading, writing, and language development into all aspects of your curriculum.
5. Plan lessons on the importance of staying in school, clarifying values, and developing skills to achieve success in school.
6. Implement dialogue strategies in your classroom.

8

Democracy and Classroom Management

with Francisco Reveles

> Of all the civil rights for which the world has struggled and fought for
> 5,000 years, the right to learn is undoubtedly the most fundamental. . . .
> The freedom to learn . . . has been bought by bitter sacrifice. And whatever
> we may think of the curtailment of other civil rights, we should fight to the
> last ditch to keep open the right to learn, the right to have examined in our
> schools not only what we believe, but what we do not believe; not only what
> our leaders say, but what the leaders of other groups and nations, and the
> leaders of other centuries have said. We must insist upon this to give our
> children the fairness of a start which will equip them with such an array
> of facts and such an attitude toward truth that they can have a real chance to
> judge what the world is and what its greater minds have thought it might be.
>
> *W. E. B. DuBois, "The Freedom to Learn"*

Personal Safety

For many students, schools are not safe. Without a safe environment, it is difficult for teachers to teach and more difficult for students to learn. According to a report by the National Center for Education Statistics, students 12–18 years of age were the victims of about 1.5 million nonfatal crimes, including thefts, simple assaults, and 628,200 serious violent crimes (rape, aggravated assault, robbery, and sexual assault) in 2005. Students in this age group are more likely to be victims of theft at school than away from school. Ten percent of teachers in central city schools reported that they were threatened with injury by students as compared to 6 percent in suburban schools. More than 2 percent of public schools reported daily or weekly occurrences of racial tension and conflicts between students (Dinkes, Cataldi, & Lin-Kelly, 2007). Such statistics illustrate in part a clear response to the loss of economic prosperity and political opportunity in parts of U.S. society. Acts of violence and disruption have increased among working- and middle-class citizens. The economic stagnation and decline of the last 30 years for working people and the decline of effectiveness of schools in preparing cultural minority and working-class young people for economic success have substantially eroded teacher and school authority.

The United States has the highest homicide rate of any modern industrialized country and the highest number of its youths placed in prisons. Life in our society is teaching some young people and adults that violence and force are useful and practical instruments.

In the 1980s and 1990s, order declined in our society, particularly in urban areas. Middle and high school students increasingly challenged the legitimacy of schools and the roles of teachers. Youth gangs became a major problem for schools, and gang members had more and more powerful weapons. Gangs are also a problem for their members; as many as 6 percent report carrying weapons in school in the last month, usually, in their view, to protect themselves from the violence of others (Dinkes et al., 2007). Students were victims of 1.4 million crimes while they were at school, and these crimes were roughly evenly divided between males and females (Dinkes et al., 2007). An increasingly disorderly environment in many schools demoralized even the most dedicated students and teachers.

Increased racial and class divisions between teachers and the communities they serve isolate and divide teachers so they are unable to exert effective family and neighborhood influence. Young people need schools and families working together to reduce violence. The increase in street crime parallels increased disruptions in school. Both are produced by the growth of poverty, marginal employment, and unemployment; and neither street crime nor chaos in the schools can be cured by school practices alone (Schmalleger & Bartollas, 2008).

During the 1990s, some school districts and communities began to create programs to reverse the violence and to allow schools to return to their educational mission. An important part of regaining control is for schools to create caring and supportive relationships among students. A California report (Dear, 1995) states, "Severe acts of violence such as shootings, rape and assault are best handled by law enforcement and the criminal justice system. The school's focus should be on basic academic development and, to a lesser extent, personal and social enhancement" (p. 2).

Developing Democracy in Schools

James Banks (1997), a leader in the field of multicultural education, argues as follows:

A fundamental premise of a democratic society is that citizens will participate in the governing of the nation and that the nation-state will reflect the hopes, dreams, and possibilities of its people. People are not born democrats. Consequently, an important goal of the schools in a democratic society is to help students acquire the knowledge, values, and skills needed to participate effectively in public communities. Educating students to be democrats is a challenge in any kind of society. It is a serious challenge in a society characterized by cultural, ethnic, racial, and language diversity, especially when these variables are used to privilege some individuals from some groups and to deny others equal opportunities to participate. (p. 1)

In Chapters 1 and 7, I argued that the promotion of democracy should be a central goal of schooling. Teachers should promote and cultivate democratic values. One way we promote democracy is to teach about civic responsibility, the electoral process, and the U.S. Constitution. A second way is to teach about the use of social participation and service learning strategies (see Chapter 7). A third way to promote democracy in the classroom is to develop in students a preference for fairness, justice, and mutual respect; these are issues of classroom management.

In Chapter 7, we defined *empowerment* as a goal for students and stressed the empowerment of students currently marginalized in our society. Empowerment is often encouraged by creating a classroom environment of civility and is nurtured by the quality of relationships among students and teachers as well as by the themes, concepts, and strategies of the curriculum.

Democratic values are usually studied in the formal curriculum of history and the social studies. Our commitment to developing democracy derives from an ideology espoused by Thomas Jefferson, John Stuart Mill, John Dewey, and many others. We believe that democracy is good. Rule of law is superior to arbitrary power or rule by an elite. Teaching students to have a commitment to a common set of democratic values is a major goal of multicultural education and provides one of the main cohesive forces in our society. Developing democratic values and skills in young people is, along with teaching reading, writing, and arithmetic, a primary reason we build public schools.

Youth Culture

Schools need to respond to youth culture to help young people develop life-supporting community values. Documents such as the Carnegie Council on Adolescent Development's *Great Transitions: Preparing Adolescents for the 21st Century* (1995) offer a thoughtful perspective on contemporary youth culture.

Aspects of youth culture and popular culture in our society produce a crisis of meaning, purpose, and direction for many teens. The alienation of youth culture, and of marginalized cultural groups, is aggravated when students believe that the school and teachers do not care about them (Valenzuela, 1999; West, 2004).

The development of this youth culture has a significant impact on school attendance, classroom management, and discipline for younger students. Some young people see little reason to attend school. When at school, they often miss class or ignore instruction in the classes they do attend. Some students miss up to 20 classes per semester, making it difficult for their teachers to teach them and establish relationships with them.

In some urban high school classrooms, it has become "normal" for students to talk out, bring cell phones, and "stand up" to the teacher. While this is a management issue, it is also a time-on-task issue. If the disruption in a class is significant, if the teacher has to spend half his or her time managing, then little learning gets done. The negative side of youth culture contributes significantly to the achievement gap. When students think that it is "normal" to not do their work, when they waste class time, all the students fall further and further behind. In these cases, a major intervention is needed for the teacher to get back in control of the class and to have time to teach.

Youth culture has a positive side as well as a disruptive side. When young people are engaged in projects like media production and events, you can locate and recognize students with particular talents and skills—such as computer and media production. Recognizing these students provides an important opportunity to build on the students' strengths.

Schools need to teach students a culture of student success. Learning this culture is not automatic. In particular, in schools with a great deal of disruption, this culture is difficult to encourage.

Promoting Democratic Values

Teachers learn to promote democratic values, or promote obedience, or promote anarchy, nihilism, and destruction in their classrooms. Order is necessary; you cannot teach math or chemistry if you cannot get students to sit in their seats and allow you to present information. But a reliance on force and obedience and compliance, particularly in urban schools that are failing, has led to a refusal to learn and disruption on the part of many students. Schools are microcommunities where students learn how real-world communities both do work and should work. Think of the schools you have visited. Do they present positive, goal-oriented introductions to the emerging economy and society or dreary, policed, control-oriented negative views of the students' own future? Teachers need to develop strategies and use management techniques to teach democracy, to encourage a culture of school success, tolerance, respect, and human dignity.

Students and teachers promote a democratic community when they develop an inclusive classroom and school environment, one where all students can participate with fairness and justice. We promote democracy when students learn to work together, to respect one another, and to resolve conflicts and achieve community goals. These vital lessons are taught in the day-to-day management of each classroom as well as on sports fields and in student government. Where these lessons are not learned, schools become dreary warehouses, and teachers spend most of their time managing and controlling young people rather than teaching them.

Classroom management is necessary for schools to function. By redirecting management toward democracy and empowerment, strong-sense multicultural education promotes a very clear set of values, a culture of school success, and fairness and justice for all.

Instead of using force and threats of force, we need to develop school societies where democracy is nourished (Kohn, 2005; O'Neil, 1997). Such positive school societies nurture the democratic ethos of community building. Students in safe schools learn to prefer democratic values of justice and fairness because they live with these values in school. For example, the curriculum in such schools offers students opportunities to reflect on their values and behavior and teaches them to think critically (see Chapter 9).

To better serve alienated and marginalized students, schools must formally teach democracy and fairness as a part of the curriculum. Schools should be places where children experience safety, trust, and respect. When gangs, bullying, and violence dominate and when the police serve as a virtual occupation force, young people seldom learn to respect the law or to respect each other. Life is teaching them violence and revenge, while schools are preaching about respect. In our current society, many schools must contend with both academic failure and the increased violence, alienation, and disruption of street culture.

Too often, schools in marginalized and oppressed areas have too many new teachers and too many teachers on "emergency" credentials who are just learning classroom management. New teachers tend to respond to discipline crises either by withdrawing or by resorting to force and control. More than 80 percent of new teachers are European Americans, encounter ethnic conflict in the school, and have not learned democratic management skills, and many, not having studied multicultural education, harbor unfortunate misunderstandings and stereotypes about student behavior. Some of these teachers even fear their own students. Too much cultural and class conflict produces school failure.

The use of coercive power may serve to control a class for a few hours, but it will not teach democratic values (Etzioni, 2008). Coercive power will allow teachers to survive day to day but leads directly to overlarge numbers of new teachers quitting the profession within the first three years .

Some school districts assist new teachers by having mentor teachers and local school experts show them how to manage classrooms. But teachers need both to develop a management system and to promote students' democratic empowerment, particularly for students of cultural and linguistic minority groups. They need to develop consistent, respectful relationships with students in order to help them learn.

Democratic values are not promoted only by presenting social studies lessons about democracy. We must also construct the school environment to teach the important values of mutual respect and tolerance for differences. It is difficult for a single teacher to create a democratic community in a school. Teachers must work together.

In this chapter, we will explore classroom management styles that permit schools to function and teachers to teach. Teachers, even new teachers, have the power of adult expertise and must learn to manage their classrooms so that students are safe and are willing and able to learn.

A Safe and Orderly Environment

Children learn best in a safe and orderly environment. Research on "effective schools," common sense, and teacher experience indicate the need for a reasonable and supportive classroom environment. Both teachers and students need order in the classroom (Etzioni, 2008; Goodlad, 1984). Teachers want order to encourage learning. Excessive disciplining and lack of classroom order cause extensive waste of teaching time and learning time. Violence and intergroup conflict, combined with academic failure and the many problems of young people, deny many students a classroom environment that supports learning (Children's Defense Fund, 2005).

When teachers are unable to create a positive atmosphere, when they fail in their attempts to productively manage their classroom, students lose instructional time. Most off-task student behavior is not dangerous, confrontational, or violent, but it is a frustrating waste of academic learning time. Students who are off-task tend to become disruptive. The disruptions are cumulative, in that talking and other inappropriate behavior spread from student to student. Students who are off-task learn less and fail more. In many neighborhood schools with high levels of disruption, a cycle develops of off-task behavior leading to failure, failure leading to discouragement, and discouragement providing a further incentive to get off-task.

Constant discipline and management problems frustrate and discourage teachers. Teachers prefer to teach, but classroom conditions require them to manage disruptive behavior. They pay a price in lower self-esteem and less professional satisfaction. For many teachers in difficult schools, the price soon becomes intolerable: Some transfer, some quit, and some give in to student pressure, demanding little and expecting even less.

Acquiring the skills of effective classroom management takes first priority for most new teachers. These skills are best acquired in a public school classroom during student teaching with supportive supervision; they are difficult to learn in a college classroom. When cultural differences and class differences divide teacher and students or when cultural and ethnic conflict is common among students, conflict resolution and management skills become even more valuable.

When new teachers fail, it is more often in their attempts to produce classroom control and motivation than in their efforts to provide instruction. The remainder of this chapter will provide you with detailed and specific ideas for establishing and maintaining positive, democratic classroom management. The principles and goals of democratic classroom management have long been accepted, but classroom practice suffers from frequent conflict and failure. Too many teachers, particularly new teachers, struggle and are frustrated in their futile attempts to control students, particularly in schools in marginalized neighborhoods. Disruptive and rebellious students demand so much of the teacher's time and energy that little remains for teaching. Teachers can reduce discipline problems and design their classrooms for better democratic control by (a) creating a positive classroom environment, (b) promoting student choice, (c) promoting on-task behavior, (d) promoting positive teacher–student communications, and (e) promoting a positive school culture. We discuss these concepts in the following sections.

Reducing Discipline Problems

You probably chose to enter teaching to make positive contributions to students' lives—not to control unruly kids. But when teachers fail to achieve classroom control—and new teachers often fail at this—a common response is to seek more power, more control. A major problem in this struggle is that teachers—and future teachers—have a great deal of experience with authoritarian practices and very little with democratic alternatives. They soon discover that their efforts to gain more control through power strategies fail. Endless power struggles exhaust them and remove much of their motivation for teaching. Teachers and students alike pay an enormous price in lost instructional time and damaged self-esteem.

To reverse this unwelcome state of affairs, democratic teachers learn strategies that promote learning and deal effectively with disruptive students. One way to begin effective classroom management and reduce discipline problems is by creating a positive classroom environment in which students feel safe and secure.

Beyond Rewards and Punishment

The behavior management systems of Fred Jones and Lee Canter—using points and taking away student time, among other strategies—may serve a useful purpose by allowing teachers to get control of an unruly class. At times, teachers may need to use these techniques (see "A Guide for New Teachers" later in this chapter). However, once control and reasonable rules have been established, teachers should move on to systems that teach students democracy and how to accept responsibility for their own conduct (Kohn, 1993, 2005).

Teachers should decide on their own orientation toward class management by reflecting on their core values. Throughout this book, I argue that a central value of schools should be to promote democratic behavior and responsibility. Democracy is not anarchy. Nor is it a laissez-faire approach. Democracy includes the development of a series of fair rules and a respect for the rights of all members of the classroom and the school community. In a democracy, citizens (the students) participate in setting up the rules within the limits established by a social contract or a constitution (school policy). Then students are made responsible for keeping their own rules and for complying with reasonable class norms. Teachers and students need to work together to establish norms for acceptable behavior, to promote a positive learning environment, to encourage respect for all, and to develop sanctions for those who do not cooperate.

Creating a Positive Classroom Environment

Choose Instructional Strategies That Encourage Success One thing successful teachers do to create a positive environment is to choose instructional strategies that help students to succeed and to feel confident. Students need to believe that they are acquiring important information and skills. Success builds confidence, whereas failure produces anxiety, hopelessness, and resistance. The environment, the teaching strategies, and the curriculum should produce success.

You can ensure the success of instructional strategies by selecting quality curriculum materials and demonstrating to students the value and usefulness of the subjects they are studying. An interesting, culturally relevant curriculum assists with class management, whereas a boring curriculum invites students to respond with boredom, indifference, and disruption.

Communicate a Belief in Students' Ability to Succeed Students, particularly those in low-performing schools, need to be convinced that they can succeed. You can plan and teach this vital lesson. Students who have poorly developed study skills frequently encounter a failure-filled, tense, anxious environment. Unfortunately, experience has taught many teachers to have *low expectations*, to *accept* the failure of poor and minority children as normal. But failure seldom helps young people to achieve instructional objectives. Failure produces tension and anxiety and interferes with learning. Success works. You need to plan each lesson to produce success.

Give Positive Feedback to Students When classrooms are chaotic, full of tension and conflict, and students are fearful that teachers will respond to them with insults, the classroom is not a safe environment. Young people who fear sarcasm and demeaning comments from teachers or bullying from other students respond with anxiety and frustration. Arbitrary enforcement or settlements imposed by power and bullying do not promote democracy. Such classrooms produce failure for both students and teachers.

Communicating positive feedback to students, however, helps both you and your students. You, as the teacher, need to maintain a positive attitude. The school may be underfunded and the school administration less than helpful, but that is not the students' fault. You need to ally yourself with the students. They need confirmation that you are there to help them succeed and to provide them feedback on *how* to succeed. They need to learn the rules and norms of school success. When their needs for success are being met, they are less likely to be abusive and critical of other students. When a positive environment is created, you have fewer discipline problems and can spend more time on actual instruction.

Your task then is to learn to create a positive, productive environment that enhances the lives of both you and your students. Democratic teachers set up structures and systems that guide students toward positive interpersonal behavior and toward appropriate school behavior. You need to recruit students and encourage them to cooperate in creating a positive classroom environment.

Promoting Student Choice

Free and responsible choice is at the heart of democratic behavior. Students learn to make responsible choices, or they learn to comply, or they learn to resist. The emphasis in your classroom is significantly up to you. Some mistakenly believe that they enter teaching only to instruct students in math or biology, but such a limited view of the teacher's role seldom leads to success. Teachers must also help students learn democratic behavior by assisting them in making responsible choices.

Not all issues in school are subject to choice. For example, students may not choose to disrupt your class without consequence. But they may choose to either work cooperatively in class or leave. And you, the teacher, may choose to help them learn constructive behavior or to subject them to the school disciplinary system.

Problems and conflicts occur daily in school. Problems provide teachers with opportunities to instruct students in responsibility. They provide opportunities to teach pro-democratic behaviors. Whenever possible, convert the problem into a choice situation instead of suppressing or trying to control the conflict or allowing a power struggle to develop.

For example, student A hits student B. Student B must choose whether to respond, to walk away, or to move on to conflict resolution. Through role-playing and discussion, students can learn to evaluate a conflict or violent situation and to make their own choices, including choosing safety for themselves and others. Students should learn decision-making and leadership skills in order to direct conflicts toward nonviolent resolutions. There are a number of available curriculum packages for teaching nonviolent conflict resolution (see the section on conflict resolution in Chapter 6).

Teachers assist students by making their choices conscious. Students need to be aware of the choices they are making. Discussion of conflict and choice should be a part of your curriculum. Such study can actually save class time for academic subjects. You can create and examine scenarios and practice alternative responses. Such practice can help students to deal with violence in the school or neighborhood. Students are empowered when they have thought through in advance potentially violent situations.

Students can engage in planning and creating a safe school or a safe classroom environment. You can encourage your students to take leadership roles in decision making by advocating school policies that lead to mutual respect and democracy.

Lessons and discussions are appropriate on self-control, boundary setting, and impulse or anger management. Lessons are helpful on self-determination and the recognition of those realms in which students have decision-making responsibilities. For example, if a student initiates a conflict, you can take her aside and explain, "You have a choice. You may choose to cooperate in this class, or you may choose to disrupt it. If you insist on obstructing class, I will ask you to leave." Responding to conflict by providing choices opens opportunities for coaching (discussed later in this chapter).

Particularly after the primary grades, students need to learn to take ownership of their own behavior. Self-evaluation and self-regulation are far superior to teacher control. Counseling theory provides you with a powerful instrument in the understanding that you usually cannot change a student or force him to change. You may force compliance, but this is usually temporary and requires a great deal of your effort to maintain. Forced compliance, at times necessary for the safety of others, seldom leads to learning responsible, democratic behavior.

You can, however, provide powerful assistance to help students to change when they want to change. You can encourage change through coaching; maintaining a safe, democratic environment; and helping students to make responsible choices. You gain additional influence by making contact with students' homes. Teachers and parents need to work together to guide young people. Unless home and school can learn to work together, the urban education crisis will continue (Children's Defense Fund, 2007; Meier, 1995). Your curriculum should include opportunities for students to actively work toward making their own community and school safe and productive places. This may include initiating parental and/or community engagement projects and volunteering with community service agencies (see Chapter 7).

Promoting On-Task Behavior

Positive use of classroom time is an important issue. Students waste a great deal of time. Researchers have reported that they are off-task, not studying, and not learning a great deal of the time (Aronson, Zimmerman, & Carlos, 1998; Charles, 2008). Students in schools impacted by poverty are off-task far more often than are students in middle-class schools. Older students are often off-task because they believe that what they are being asked to study is boring or irrelevant to their lives. Teachers promote on-task behavior by providing success and by demonstrating the relevance of lessons to students.

Demonstrate the Relevance of Lessons to Students Effective teachers use a variety of instructional strategies that engage students in active learning. One way you can show students how schoolwork relates to their lives is by allowing some student choice and choosing student-centered projects. You can find excellent ideas for student-centered educational projects in *It's Our World, Too! Stories of Young People Who Are Making a Difference* (Hoose, 1993) and in *Open Minds to Equality: A Sourcebook of Learning Activities to Affirm Diversity and Promote Equity* (Schniedewind & Davidson, 1998). At other times, you will need to teach the approved curriculum and teach to state or district standards (see Chapter 12). A well-informed teacher who is a cultural mediator will use a variety of strategies and emphasize those elements of the standard curriculum that have practical or current relevance to students.

Use Positive, Managed Intervention Strategies Teachers need to learn skills to help students to stay on task and to pursue goals. Effective teachers plan for and manage potential conflicts and discipline problems before they even arise. Positive classroom management keeps students working on interesting, useful, and rewarding tasks.

In the elementary grades, when students are off-task, effective teachers intervene early and frequently to call on students to return to the learning task. In grades 4 through 8, early interventions produce success and can be employed with low levels of power, thus avoiding failure and confrontation.

Some teachers respond to off-task behavior by becoming more authoritarian and more aggressive toward students. Their efforts may achieve control, but authoritarian action interferes with efforts to provide the safe and supportive environment students need for success. Often, aggressive teacher behavior is self-defeating because it produces more control problems, exhausts teachers, and interferes with productive learning—a cycle of frustration, failure, and repression. For many students during adolescence, constant power struggles between student and teacher disrupt the learning environment and encourage more off-task behavior, even for those students interested in learning.

Frequent, low-level, managed intervention provides an alternative. Teachers learn to use eye contact, body language, physical proximity, facial expressions, and gestures to structure and manage the class and keep everyone on-task. This strategy combines commonsense teaching practices with rewards. Reward students for increased on-task learning time by giving them planned leisure and recreation time. Interventions can be effective and nondisruptive, encouraging students to return to the task at hand. Once classroom order is established, and at least by sixth grade, democratic management systems should be used.

Try Task Analysis Your first management task is to establish a working system in the classroom for students and groups of students to learn. Rules, procedures, and routines are each important. Task analysis permits teachers to select rules and procedures and to design a positive environment to help students to succeed. For example, numerous studies have demonstrated that cooperative learning is a helpful strategy, particularly for African American, Latino, and

Native American children (Garcia, 1995; Ladson-Billings, 1994b). Both children and adults need instruction in how to work cooperatively. As teachers begin to use cooperative learning, they must teach the skills necessary for cooperative work (see Chapter 10).

Task analysis separates the skills of cooperative work into several teachable, learnable sets. For example, essential skills for a fourth- to eighth-grade class might include moving chairs, selecting persons for roles (e.g., monitor, checker, encourager), staying on the subject, listening to one another, taking turns, and supporting the authority of a student leader. Each of these skills is isolated, taught, practiced, and evaluated to improve the quality of cooperative work and classroom relationships.

Direct Instruction Madeline Hunter of UCLA developed a process known as *direct instruction* that is useful and effective in teaching students new behaviors (Hunter, 1982). The format works well both for addressing behavior issues and for introducing new concepts in lessons. Direct instruction is most appropriate when teaching clear, identifiable behavior or a specific concept and is far more effective than criticizing and punishing students for inappropriate behavior.

To use direct instruction, you first identify the specific behavior you want to change. For example, you might want all students to be in their seats when class begins or to raise their hands before talking. You then plan lessons on the behavior. Dr. Hunter has developed a sequential series of steps for direct instruction. Figure 8.1 illustrates the use of Dr. Hunter's steps to teach students to raise their hands before talking.

Figure 8.1   Direct Instruction

1. *Anticipatory set.* Get students' attention to the subject. Start with an example from their own lives or an example of the problem that just occurred.
2. *Explanation.* Explain the lesson objective clearly. Tell students what they are going to learn and why it is important.
3. *Input.* Give students more information on the task. Explain why it is important for everyone to raise their hands before speaking. Explain the consequences of not establishing rules for polite discourse.
4. *Modeling.* Demonstrate, or have students demonstrate, the actual behavior you are trying to teach. It is essential that students see the actual behavior, not just talk about it.
5. *Check for understanding.* Ask students to explain the reasons for establishing the behavior. Perhaps have two or three students explain or model the behavior.
6. *Guided practice.* Have students actually practice the behavior. For example, several students could simultaneously attempt to answer a question you pose. You may want to repeat this practice two or three times.
7. *Independent practice.* Monitor and comment on the behavior for the next several days. If there are any problems, return to step 4 and repeat the process.
8. *Closure.* Summarize the lesson. Review its importance. Thank students for their participation.

Promoting Positive Teacher–Student Communications

Teacher behavior either contributes to or detracts from the building of a positive class-room environment. Studies indicate that the average teacher uses negative comments and commands much more often than positive comments. Positive communications strategies are important at all levels. They become increasingly important during ado-lescence. Violence and domination teach violence and domination, whereas respect teaches respect. Good teachers contribute to a positive environment by practicing posi-tive comments that guide and structure student behavior (see Figure 8.2).

Learn to Describe Positive Behavior Successful teachers learn to describe positive behav-ior. Consistent repetition of positive directions guides most students to respond with-out increasing defensiveness. Such repetition directs student behavior and lowers the anxiety and frustration levels in the classroom. Teachers often produce success through encouragement and cooperation.

Redirect Students' Disruptive Behavior Effective teachers practice the skill of redirecting students from nonhelpful to helpful behavior by clearly describing precisely *how* to perform a task. Primary teachers often model the task rather than relying on oral instructions. In grades 4 through 8, role-playing and physical practice of a task reduce the need for criticism. A clear explanation of how to perform a task provides students with a positive alternative to criticism. Teachers who overrely on criticism and correction attack students' self-esteem and make them feel hostile, defeated, alienated, or self-doubting. When possible, it is best to avoid strategies built on negative responses.

Give Clear Directions Teachers frequently need to give instructions and commands on how to perform tasks. Giving clear, brief instructions provides a structure within which students can succeed. When a few students do not carry out the instruction, repeating the command is often more effective than criticizing them (e.g., say simply, "Open your books now. Please open your books to page 45.").

Giving clear, appropriate instructions is essential to managing your class. But when instructions are demeaning or issued in an attacking manner, they become criticism, and students receive them defensively. Of course, in real classrooms, you occasionally

Figure 8.2 Alternatives to Negative Comments

Instead Of	Alternative
"Stop talking and get busy."	"Open your book now."
"You haven't started yet?"	"How did you answer question 1?"
"Why aren't you working?"	"Can I help you with the first problem?"

will need to criticize. It often helps to explain your reasoning when critiquing a student's response. Effective teachers try to call students' attention to the purpose behind the instructions. When it is evident that you give your instructions out of concern for the welfare of the class, even criticism can be heard in safety and can lead to positive student behavior. For example, saying, "Please stop talking, I want to go on with the lesson," works better than saying only, "Please stop talking."

Use a Supportive, Encouraging Speaking Style Democratic teachers seek to give instructions, even commands, without using an aggressive or dominating style. They seek to replace divisive and demeaning communication with communication that encourages students to cooperate and support one another. Positive communication contributes to the positive social climate in the classroom necessary to promote personal and social growth.

For students beyond grade 6, *feedback*—or constructive direction—is a useful instructional strategy. The following guidelines promote positive, nurturing communication:

1. Concentrate on criticizing the act or the idea—not the person. Personalizing criticism is worse than useless because it interferes with the possibility of future positive communication.

2. Practice giving feedback and correction when the action occurs and then move on. Repeatedly reminding students of past offenses (nagging) frustrates both teachers and students. No one can change the past. Students cannot undo past mistakes. Concentrate on the present and the future.

3. Feedback and correction should be as specific and concrete as possible. Telling students to be respectful or to behave does not provide the information they need to change their behavior. The best feedback tells students precisely what they can begin doing correctly rather than offering negative evaluations of what they have done.

4. Labeling students and using sarcasm are not helpful. They seldom contribute to behavioral change or instruction.

5. Encouragement always works better than criticism because it helps students to build self-esteem.

Classroom management systems enable teachers to design student success. Unfortunately, not all students will respond to a positive environment. Prior school and home experiences may have taught some students to disrupt and to resist learning.

For students from low-status cultural groups who are experiencing cultural conflict in schools, the intensity of criticism can reinforce a desire to withdraw from participation and to flee school. Others resist even reasonable school norms. Teenagers frequently experience conflict, self-doubt, and lack of confidence. The overuse of negative messages by teachers (and other students) alienates and divorces some students from schooling.

Respect Students Young people can be cruel to and critical of each other. It is a mistake for the adults in a school to enter into the teenage culture of putdowns and sarcasm

(Kagan, 1986). Even when a specific student appears arrogant or overconfident, public sarcasm is damaging because it intimidates and injures other students. Although students may have developed apparent defenses against sarcasm from other students, too much criticism from teachers can be devastating. The consistent application of positive communication helps students develop a positive attitude. Respecting students encourages them to internalize new values supportive of civility and of classroom instruction.

Schools were established to instruct youth in information, values, and skills. The teacher has a right and a responsibility to establish a positive classroom atmosphere. Students do not have a right to be disruptive or disrespectful. The school and the classroom need clear, reasonable parameters of appropriate behavior, and effective teachers enforce the rules. Democratic behavior can best be encouraged within a safe environment. When teachers and the school administration fail to consistently enforce a positive, appropriate, fair structure of discipline, peer group pressures will disrupt the school. Young people deserve and need adults in charge who will establish and maintain reasonable standards of school-appropriate behavior (National Economic and Social Rights Initiative, 2007).

Simple and clear rules help everyone to succeed. Figure 8.3 provides guidelines for developing school rules.

Figure 8.3   Simple and Clear Rules Help to Establish a Safe and Productive Classroom Climate

1. Everyone affected should have a voice in determining school rules. Language barriers to full participation should be removed.

2. Rules should be clearly stated in behavioral terms.

3. Rules should be reasonable.

4. Rules should be enforceable.

5. Rules should be easily understood.

6. Rules should be taught as part of the curriculum.

7. Rules should be communicated to parents in the language spoken in the home.

8. Rules should be consistently enforced by teachers.

9. Rules should be perceived by students as being fair.

10. Rules that disproportionately impact any one group of students should be changed.

Source: Based on suggestions made in *The Good Common School: Making the Vision Work for All Children: A Comprehensive Guide to Elementary School Restructuring*, by National Coalition of Advocates for Students, 1991, Boston: Author.

Isolate Disruptive School Groups and Provide Appropriate Intervention Classes tend to have several student-centered groups: some supportive of instruction and a positive school climate, others disruptive. By the middle grades (grades 6 through 8), most students will want to belong to a group. Peer group influences become increasingly important. If peer group behavior is positive and supports instruction, most new students will accommodate to the group. A major teaching task is to establish a positive, productive atmosphere and then to encourage and recruit the majority of the students to cooperate.

By the teenage years, peer group and gang pressures can dominate a class. Teachers who encounter difficulties with gang members in classes should seek support and additional resources from the school administration and from parent groups (see pages 261–264).

Reteach Appropriate School Behaviors If Necessary Young students often need to be taught appropriate behavior. Even adolescents at times need to be retaught basic interpersonal skills, such as talking to others without making "putdowns." You identify and teach the skills of positive behavior just as you would teach the skill of writing a sentence. If you want students to move from a large group into smaller groups, giving clear directions and rehearsing will help students learn the skills involved. In the primary and intermediate grades, practicing class-appropriate behavior helps students to belong within a positive group and to participate in creating a positive environment. In middle and high school classrooms, you need clear instruction and practice time early in each semester to establish the appropriate behavior for your class.

Provide time for teaching, practicing, and evaluating social skills. It helps to make teaching school-appropriate behavior a part of your curriculum. It will save you time for instruction. You and your students will experience success from teaching and practicing appropriate behavior. Instruction and practice lead to change. Management and punishment lead to control that is usually temporary (Kohn, 2005; Charles, 2008).

Major, lasting changes in student behavior occur slowly. Disruptive behavior in class may be the result of years of experience in school and at home. Producing major changes in classroom behavior for some difficult students often requires months and supplementary counseling resources.

Extending the Teacher's Influence Through Coaching

Our society has become increasingly depersonalized in the modern era. Many children have less positive supervision by parents. Some disruptive children literally need more parenting. In our troubled society, many students need guides, coaches, and counselors.

Coaching and conferencing extend teachers' influence in managing the classroom. Successful democratic teachers use conferencing and coaching with those students who continue disruptive and off-task behaviors. Coaching strategies provide monitoring, advising, and instruction, which are particularly important to students in the middle grades (grades 6 through 8) as well as in high school. Students need positive, adult interaction and interventions in school. Setting up coaching and advising sessions helps teachers to guide classroom behavior and build important connections between students and the school (Comer, 1988).

Teachers plan and implement coaching processes with students when weeks of instruction and reinforcement in cooperative behavior have not worked. Just as planning improves instructional delivery in math, science, and the social studies, systematic planning of coaching will improve most students' behaviors, and eventually their attitudes. One valuable form of coaching is the restorative justice conference (McGarrell, 2001).

Effective teachers need an intervention system to redirect disruptive students toward prosocial and constructive classroom behavior. A counseling and coaching strategy provides such a system. The system of individual psychology, as developed by Alfred Adler, Rudolph Dreikurs, and subsequent researchers, provides an effective democratic approach for helping students to move away from disturbing and destructive school behavior.

A Theory of Antisocial Student Behavior

The Dreikurs system (Dreikurs, Grunwald, & Pepper, 1998; Dreikurs & Stoltz, 1964) proposes a theory of how students learn their worldviews and role behavior and assists in developing an intervention system.

Martinez (1978) describes the theory of Adlerian psychology and of Dreikurs intervention systems as follows:

> From infancy, the individual begins to formulate a cognitive representation, a picture of himself/herself, the world, and the individual's place in that world. This view is like a multi-dimensional puzzle with many sides and levels. The child perceives pieces of data and like a puzzle, he/she puts the pieces into some kind of picture (world view). This picture becomes a map which gives direction and purpose to the child's life. Children observe the environment, evaluate it, and arrive at conclusions about themselves, their worth, their potency, and their place in the environment. They decide on a view of what the world demands of them and how they can acquire a sense of belonging to or a sense of being part of that world. The family is the first social group the child encounters. (p. 59)

Martinez quotes Mosak and Dreikurs (1973) to say that through the child's interaction with the family,

> [each child] stakes out for himself a piece of territory which includes the attributes of abilities that he hopes will give him a feeling of belonging, a feeling of having a place. If, through his evaluation of his own potency (abilities, courage and confidence), he is convinced that he can achieve this place through useful endeavors, he will pursue the useful side of life. Should he feel that he cannot attain the goal of having a place in this fashion, he will become a discouraged child and engage in disturbed or disturbing behavior in his effort to find a place. For the Adlerian, the "maladjusted" child is not a "sick" child, he is a "discouraged" child. Dreikurs classifies the goals of the discouraged child into four groups: attention-getting, power-seeking, revenge-taking, and declaring deficiency or defeat. It should be emphasized that Dreikurs is speaking of immediate, rather than long-range goals. These are the goals of children's "misbehavior," not of all child behavior. (Quoted in Martinez, 1978, p. 117)

Life, like culture, is dynamic rather than static. The world around children is continually changing, and they are changing. Children are continually confronted with new information. Some new data agree with their existing worldviews. Other new information conflicts.

Conflicting information presents the recipient with two alternatives. She can incorporate it in her worldview in place of old information and thus alter her view of the role she is playing in the classroom. Or she can reject or distort the new information so that it appears consistent with her existing self-image.

Worldviews and views of self serve as cognitive maps, guiding students in their actions. Immaturity, perceptual biases, distortions, and incomplete data make students' worldviews incomplete, but they appear adequate to their holders.

Students behave based on their worldviews and their perceptions of reality. A student's cognitive map and worldview guide her in comprehending new information. These perceptions are culturally influenced and largely subconscious. Students are aware of their behavior but usually unaware of its underlying worldview, cultural frame of reference, perceptual set, and motivation.

Dreikurs et al. (1998) argue that when teachers share the above assumptions, they respond to disruptive students as if the students are discouraged. Children's prior life in and out of school may not have provided them with either the strategies for successful classroom behavior or the motivation to succeed. Prior experience has taught them to pursue short-term self-interest, such as attention getting through disruption or fighting. Children need to learn to pursue their own long-term self-interest by contributing to a positive social environment where they can experience support and success.

Class Meetings

Teachers using the democratic recommendations of Alfred Adler (1870–1937) and of Dreikurs and Stoltz (1964) have developed classroom meetings as an important aspect of problem solving to improve behavior. Democratic teachers provide leadership and structure to assist students in taking responsibility for resolving some class problems.

Students as young as first graders are taught to clearly identify the problem-causing disruption. In many classrooms, from grades 1 through 8, students set an agenda for the next classroom meeting by listing a problem behavior on an agenda sheet. At a specified time of the day or week, a classroom meeting is called. Classroom meetings work best when students have been taught cooperative learning skills (discussed in Chapter 10). The teacher and students together examine the problem behavior, and the students work together to suggest potential solutions. The teacher provides a structure for the meeting by insisting that all solutions be reasonable, related, and respectful. Suggesting solutions does not resolve problems; students need to agree on the nature of the problem, and they need to agree on the solution.

Class meetings are useful at all grade levels, although rules for conducting them should change based on students' maturity. Typical rules for grades 1 through 4 include giving compliments as meeting starters, using the agenda to keep focused on the problems, and identifying logical consequences for misbehavior rather than punishment (see Figure 8.4). The Tribes Curriculum provides a useful guide to class meetings (Gibbs, 2001).

Perhaps as a consequence of John Dewey's strong influence on educational theory, most teachers want to assist students in practicing democratic behavior even though

Figure 8.4   Sample Problem-Solving Scenario

The students in Mrs. G's fourth-grade class have practiced classroom meetings. They know the rules and the skills they need to facilitate conflict resolution. Mary places Heather's name on the agenda for the next meeting. At meeting time, the students sit in a circle. Mrs. G serves as a facilitator. She asks Mary to explain the issue. Mary says that Heather constantly calls her a "dirty Mexican." She wants the name-calling stopped.

Several classmates confirm that they have heard this name-calling. The children discuss name-calling and stereotypes. They decide that children often repeat what they hear from adults. But at school, all children deserve respect. The teacher guides the children in role-playing some name-calling events to clarify the issues.

After a time, the subject changes to consequences.

they frequently do not know how to advocate for these positions. In classroom meetings, strategies for empowerment and for cooperative learning combine to provide teachers with powerful strategies for encouraging democratic behavior.

Coaching Using Dreikurs's Ideas

Classroom meetings use the powerful motivations of group cohesion and group belonging to encourage students to learn cooperation, but some students will resist. Many individual students have strong desires to disrupt or to seek control of the classroom agenda. These powerful drives at times are too complex to simply turn the problem over to a problem-solving group; coaching and conferencing are additional strategies for you as a democratic teacher.

Even though students frequently bring enormous conflicts from their home and peer lives into school, your first task is to redirect their behavior to help them succeed and to function effectively in the classroom. Set up a coaching/counseling session to redirect the behavior of consistently disruptive students. The coaching/counseling relationship will encourage them to learn the motivation and strategies necessary to operate positively within your classroom environment.

As a harried student teacher, you may protest that you do not have the time or the skills to arrange for counseling and coaching. Only a few urban schools have adequate counseling and support resources. In some states such as California, schools stressed by repeated budget cutbacks have eliminated most of their school counselors. These budget cutbacks leave the teacher to deal with the significant issue of some very disruptive students. Several leading educators advocate that teachers deserve substantial additional support and assistance to deal with the several children per class who are potentially disruptive, particularly in communities suffering a high degree of economic and social stress (Comer, 1997; O'Neil, 1997).

But in the face of few resources, teachers have little choice. They must respond. The continued use of power and force for discipline does not resolve conflicts. Power only temporarily suppresses students' disruptive behavior. The conflicts will emerge or explode at other times when teachers will be unprepared to manage the problems. If teachers do not develop effective response systems, such as coaching, students will continue to disrupt their classrooms.

As a teacher–coach, you first schedule a meeting with a disruptive student to analyze the problem and to plan for behavioral change. Initiate a positive, therapeutic relationship so that your coaching process can move forward. Typically, you and the student can agree on some fundamentals. You are in charge of the class. Disruptive behavior is not acceptable. You want to set up a system in which the student is not disruptive. After clearly explaining these fundamentals, analyze together the specific behavioral problem displayed in class and attempt to identify the problem's relationship to the student's own goals.

When you have established a safe relationship and a clear goal for coaching, the student can openly examine his behavior and select alternatives that will help him belong positively to the class. Work together with the student to give up the disruptive behavior and practice appropriate behavior (see Figure 7.4). Successful coaching often requires a number of sessions to help a student gain more positive and productive control over his classroom behavior. Detailed analysis and practice of each step help you direct most students toward constructive behavior (see Figure 8.5).

In our violence-prone society, teachers will encounter a few students who, as a result of a dysfunctional family life, drug abuse, or similar trauma, refuse to permit the classroom to function. The school administrator must provide alternative resource classrooms or other resources for such students. Teachers seldom have the time or skills for therapy, but they can advocate for and demand additional staff with appropriate skills.

When children in elementary school are taught self-direction and social cooperation skills, they improve in terms of school achievement and develop strong self-esteem. By 10 to 12 years of age, disruptive behavior may become a way of school life for some students, and ever more sophisticated and powerful intervention systems are needed—including counselors and trained therapists. Fortunately, older students can conceptualize, discuss, and relearn school-appropriate behavior.

Figure 8.5 When a Disruption Occurs

1. Talk to the student privately.

2. Remove the student from the scene.

3. Establish a coaching relationship.

4. Teach the appropriate behavior rather than punishing inappropriate behavior.

5. Have the student practice the behavior.

6. Contact the parents. Ask for their assistance.

The Work of James P. Comer

James P. Comer (2001) has developed a psychotherapeutic perspective to assist educators in creating nourishing and safe environments for schools and communities. Such a community-building approach, while beneficial for any school, is particularly important for schools in disenfranchised and marginalized communities.

When schools fail to attend to safety problems and to teach positive social behavior, the cost is quite high, leading eventually to students leaving school and often entering the far more expensive criminal justice system.

Comer (2001) argues:

> Given the purpose of education—to prepare students to become successful workers, family members, and citizens in a democratic society—even many "good" traditional schools, as measured by high test scores, are not doing their job adequately. But test scores alone are too narrow a measure. A good education should help students to solve problems encountered at work and in personal relationships, to take on the responsibility of caring for themselves and their families, to get along well in a variety of life settings, and to be motivated, contributing members of a democratic society. Such learning requires conditions that promote positive child-and-youth development.
>
> Children begin to develop and learn through their first interactions with their consistent caretakers. And the eventual learning of basic academic skills—reading, writing, mathematics—and development are inextricably linked. Indeed, learning is an aspect of development and simultaneously facilitates it. Basic academic skills grow out of the fertile soil of overall development; they provide the platform for higher-order learning.

Working with the Rockefeller Foundation, Comer schools have demonstrated the value of schools and families working together, even in some of the most depressed neighborhoods.

> People at school can then influence children's development in ways similar to competent parents. To be successful, schools must create the conditions that make good development and learning possible: positive and powerful social and academic interactions between students and staff. When this happens, students gain social and academic competence, confidence, and comfort. Also, when parents and their social networks value school success and school experiences are positive and powerful, students are likely to acquire an internal desire to be successful in school and in life, and to gain and express the skills and behavior necessary to do so. (Comer, 2001)

Comer and his associates have developed school reform systems in a number of communities that stress the importance of teachers themselves being both healthy and culturally competent in order to deal with the stresses of urban education. Creating positive, nurturing relationships for children requires a positive, supportive environment for adults as well as a close working relationship between home and school.

The Rockefeller Foundation has supported extensive development and evaluation of school reform based on these Comer principles. The schools achieve very positive academic success by focusing on the quality of the social and supportive climate in the school (Cook, 2001).

No one psychotherapeutic theory has proven adequate and useful to teachers in all situations. Nor have adequate quantifiable data validated any one theory's explanation of student behavior. Meanwhile, teachers need a strategy to work with on a daily basis.

The Adler–Dreikurs theories presented are the theories most connected to the practice and extension of democracy. The promotion of democracy in the classroom is difficult and substantially underdeveloped (Banks, 2008; Cagan, 1978; Parker, 2009).

A Guide for New Teachers

Schools in minority neighborhoods have a high proportion of new teachers. Many experienced teachers transfer out of such schools to places where they can spend more time teaching and less time managing the classroom. Initially, new teachers experience a difficult time of trial and error. Their teaching skills are learned through practice while on the job (see Figure 8.6).

New teachers in difficult schools face a number of hardships, and students inevitably suffer from having less experienced teachers. In turn, new teachers often suffer from having to learn to teach with some of the most difficult students.

As a new teacher, you will work with children from diverse cultures and can benefit from getting to know the school community. Prior to the first day of school, you should travel around the community, visiting its churches, its youth clubs, and its neighborhoods. It helps to visit your school early to acquaint yourself with the principal, the secretary, and the resources you will need.

The school is not an island apart from the community. Teachers who arrive at school, spend their time teaching, and leave just after school will misunderstand their students. In the past, prior to the current concern for multicultural education, some teachers displayed an offensive colonial attitude in their relationship to school. They entered the community to teach. They received pay from the community, but they did not respect the community. They appeared like missionaries bringing outside culture to the natives. This colonial attitude led to misunderstanding, hostility, and resentment. Most parents know that education and schooling are important to economic success, but a colonial relationship prevents mutual support and respect between teachers and parents. When a gap exists between parents and schools, younger children suffer. Older students and gangs exploit the communication gap to resist school. To avoid

Figure 8.6   New Teachers Can Learn the Skills of Classroom Management

Effective teachers

- communicate clearly and positively with students.

- demonstrate concern for students' many conflicts, including gender and cultural issues, peer pressure, and academic success.

- are respected and trusted by students for their fairness and equity.

- set clear, consistent limits.

- defuse or divert many potential disruptive situations with coaching or with conflict resolution.

such strained relationships, teachers should think of themselves as employees of the community and make it their responsibility to learn about the community so they can use community resources and culture to support the education program (Olsen & Dowell, 1997).

Instruction isolated from a community context too often fails. Quality teaching requires you to understand children's reality rather than holding a series of stereotypes. Knowing students' reality allows you to select experiences in their lives to build on.

One of the fundamental differences between successful middle-class schools and failing schools is that middle-class teachers in middle-class schools share the cultural perspectives of their students. They draw from a common source of experiences for reading, writing, and skill development. When teachers draw from students' own experiences, it validates and empowers the students. In contrast, teachers with a colonial attitude seek to impose curriculum content on students. This imposition of culture invalidates and negates students' own experiences and culture. Students are made to feel inadequate. They do not learn confidence in themselves, their families, or their cultural competencies.

For students to succeed, your classroom must be reasonably orderly. Teachers and students have varying tolerances for disorder. Teaching should start on time, and the classroom needs to provide a safe and orderly environment, an environment that encourages learning. You need to provide students with successful learning experiences, particularly in the first few days of instruction. You should start with a well-organized, firm, and fair process of management and discipline. Management strategies must be practical and understood by the students (through modeling). And they must be applied consistently over time. When you are able to minimize disruptive behavior, you gain time on task, learning time (see Figure 8.7). When you have established order and have learned more about students' individual characteristics and personalities, you can move toward a more democratic environment.

Most teachers benefit from personalizing their teaching. Personal influence, personal knowledge, and personal contact provide you with your best instruments of instruction as well as your best instruments of classroom control. When you know students and communicate with them in ways that acknowledge their selfhood, as when you learn a few words of their home language, your classroom environment improves dramatically.

You can be more helpful when you know your students well. Elementary school teachers master this problem with ease, whereas middle and high school teachers facing 150+ students per day have difficulty. Instructors who do not learn about individual students are reduced to giving commands and instructions. This command relationship, in turn, produces student resistance. Such depersonalized relationships produce a significant portion of the discipline and conflict management problems of upper-grade teachers.

Small steps, such as calling students by name and asking them about their interests, personalize your interchanges. You can use transitions between activities and time provided by cooperative learning to talk with students about their lives and interests. Students from cultures that value reinforcing interpersonal relations before engaging in business and task exchanges (such as Latinos, Asians, Arabs, and Native Americans) will particularly benefit from your efforts to personalize your teaching.

Figure 8.7   Minimizing Disruptive Behavior

1. Teach positive rules. Reinforce positive rules.
2. Teach positive roles.
3. Respond to small disruptions.
4. Teach responsibility.
5. Share responsibility with students through cooperative strategies.
6. Try to avoid power struggles. Provide students with a cooling-off period.
7. Maintain your adult composure and decision-making skills.

Teachers acquire a powerful set of connections when they get to know students individually. You will soon get to know the "good" students. To improve classroom control, make an effort to get to know the potentially disruptive student, the clown, the resister. Talk to them. Telephone their parents or guardians. This individual contact will give you information that will help you direct them toward cooperative rather than disruptive behavior.

Your efforts to personalize your interactions with students will help make your classroom a safe environment. Students respond more positively, more respectfully, to teachers who treat them with respect.

It is easier for you, a new teacher, to establish a positive environment in the first few days than it is to dominate the class. A tense environment where commands are common and cooperation is minimal produces resistance and disruptions. Beyond grade 6, trying to win consent exclusively through the use of power is seldom effective with students, particularly when some students are skilled in resistance.

This is not to argue for a hands-off, laissez-faire approach. Most students, except for those in kindergarten and first grade, already have experience with school and teachers. Students evaluate new teachers during the first few days to decide what kind of classroom to expect and to determine what they can get away with. It helps to make your goals clear: a safe and orderly classroom, clear and reasonable rules, a high degree of academic engaged learning time, and a personalized classroom where students and teacher all respect one another.

During the first few days of school, establish a few basic rules and post them where all students can read them. Rules commonly used by primary teachers include the following:

1. Only one student out of seat at a time.
2. Raise your hand to speak.
3. Keep your hands and feet to yourself.

Rules common to middle school include the following (note the overlap with the primary school list):

1. Only one student out of seat at a time.
2. Raise your hand to speak.
3. No putdowns or negative personal comments.

Establishing a positive, productive classroom climate is particularly difficult in schools with large numbers of students who are at risk. By adolescence, the cultural gaps between teacher and students are more clearly recognized, producing miscommunication and conflicting expectations. Establishing a positive, personal, supportive environment can turn an ineffective classroom into an effective one.

You have both a right and a responsibility to provide an organized, calm classroom. Once you have established rules, enforce them. Students require more than just reading and discussing rules. Demonstrate, model, and practice appropriate behavior. If lack of respect for a particular rule becomes a generalized problem, reteach the rule and practice the behavior again. You will save yourself important time and energy by teaching and reteaching rules instead of trying to manage and control each individual child.

Try to identify management problems within the first few days of class. Task analysis works well to design positive management alternatives. Some teachers have difficulty because six students need to sharpen their pencils just before an assignment, or four students come to them for assistance at the same time, or the noise level becomes intolerable when asking students to move into groups.

When problems appear, isolate and analyze the problem. Try to identify the precise behavior that is causing disruption, and then develop a process for teaching the appropriate skill and practicing the appropriate behavior. Learning to behave appropriately in school is like learning to play soccer; it takes practice. Practice improves student performance far more than do criticizing and making demands.

As a new teacher, you can gain valuable insight by recruiting an experienced teacher as a mentor, someone who can answer the hundreds of simple questions you will have. You also benefit from recruiting an ally, someone with whom you can share frustrations and anxieties. If there are no other new teachers in the school, consider taking a course at a nearby university where you can discuss your concerns with other teachers.

There are a number of good guides for new teachers, including *The Teacher's Guide to Success* (2008) by Ellen L. Kronowitz. Interested readers can find excellent guides to classroom management in C. M. Charles's *Today's Best Classroom Management Strategies: Paths to Positive Discipline* (2008) and Vern and Louise Jones's *Comprehensive Classroom Management: Creating Communities of Support and Solving Problems* (2007).

Drug Interventions

Students in their adolescent years are often trying out new identities. For some it is a dangerous world, and gang affiliation and crime may appear to be attractive options. Schools need to offer alternative, positive affiliations through sports, clubs, service groups, and clinics. These supplemental services require the support of parents, church groups, and civic groups. If these positive alternatives are not available, encouraged, and made attractive, students seeking more connections may become alienated or drift into gang membership and drug use.

Crime statistics reveal that schools are among the most dangerous locales in many communities. An alert visitor to many campuses can quickly identify areas of a school where discontented students "hang out." Smoking and drug sales may be common there. These areas place many students' lives at risk (Hechinger, 1992). Teachers, principals, and security personnel know these areas and in most cases can identify those students who are placing themselves and others in danger.

School personnel must be willing to intervene and to stop illegal drug sales and pre-gang activity on school grounds rather than trying only to control the behavior. As a first step, the school should not permit drug use and weapons under any conditions. Administrators who allow such developments must be replaced by education leaders willing to work hard to create positive environments for students. School personnel unwilling to help implement plans to ban drugs and weapons should be removed from the school. Employee unions and parents alike should support such actions to protect the safety of students, faculty, and staff. Schools cannot allow young people to make life-threatening decisions. It may be true that in some areas government authorities have failed in the war on drugs and have not provided sufficient police, probation, and clinical recovery support. In these cases, education leaders need to recruit parents and civic groups to stop these self-destructive behaviors on school grounds.

In addition to strategies for controlling behavior problems, a principal, a vice principal, or a respected teacher should set up a class, with attendance mandatory, for all students in this alienated group. The class can study the drug abuse, physical abuse, and violence that the students experience. Local antidrug and antigang community groups, such as Narcotics Anonymous and Alcoholics Anonymous, and the local probation department may also become involved. The teacher may choose to hold separate classes for boys and girls to facilitate free discussion of issues such as media influence, physical abuse, sexual practices, and other sensitive topics. By converting the violence of adolescents' lives into something for them to study and analyze, the teacher moves from coercive power to adult authority.

Many adolescents go through a period of exploring a drug- or gang-related identity. During this time, they are alienated from their families. With appropriate support, most will mature to become productive citizens. However, ongoing crises in some families require that schools provide persons in assertive leadership roles, substitute parent roles, for some young people. We cannot simply state that this is not the school's job, that the school is to teach only subject matter, not life skills. Many adolescents need additional adult authority in their lives. Students need guidance. They need help making fateful choices. They are full of fear about gangs, drugs, weapons, sexual identity, and similar explosive matters. Unless these students are helped, they will disrupt school and endanger their own lives (Children's Defense Fund, 2007; Dinkes et al., 2007; Fremon, 1995; Media Literacy Summit, 2001). We know that coaching and mentoring work. If schools are silent or ignore these issues, issues that are consuming students, then they become accomplices to the violence and terror of that part of society.

Gang Interventions

Gangs have increasingly become a part of the urban school environment, often making the school violent and unsafe and thus contributing to the degradation of learning environments (Schmalleger & Bartollas, 2008). Gangs are constantly recruiting new members, some as young as 10 or 11, and students may well be physically assaulted and threatened if they refuse to join. Conflicts between gangs at school events are an increasing problem, forcing some schools to cancel sports, dances, and other events.

For the past few years, a law enforcement paradigm has driven the quality of information educators receive with regard to gang-associated youth. As a consequence, simplistic definitions and approaches to youth gangs have come to shape the limited preparation that teachers, counselors, and administrators receive. While law enforcement does provide many valuable security services to schools, its influence and impact on gang awareness training for educators need to be critically reexamined (Deprived of Dignity, National Economic & Social Rights Initiative, 2007).

Why Do Youth Join Gangs?

Young people join gangs because many of them come from disrupted homes, perhaps with one parent in jail or out of the picture, and they have felt the pain and anger of failed or frustrated dreams, racist educational practices, violence, and an educational system unwilling or unable to respond (Henry, 2000). Gang involvement can best be understood when viewed as a response to extreme frustration and failure, as an act of resistance. Gang involvement is but one manifestation of adolescent youth trying to make sense of or cope with grinding circumstances. Others may express their disillusionment by engaging in substance abuse, becoming pregnant, or leaving school.

In some neighborhoods, joining a gang is strictly an issue of personal safety as students daily navigate a gauntlet of the competing dangers of violence and predators in the school halls and on the streets. It's a sad fact that many students tend to associate with gangs simply because they have no other choice. Gang membership reveals a loss of faith by students in teachers, school administrators, and police to protect and keep them safe (Henry, 2000).

What is a Youth Gang?

A gang is usually defined as a loose-knit organization of individuals generally between the ages of 12 and 24, although some tend to be much younger and others can carry gang affiliations and loyalties well into adulthood and membership may be generational in nature (Howell, 1998). Usually, the group has a name derived from geographical identifiers such as streets, neighborhoods, or public housing units. Others tend to identify themselves along ethnic or cultural lines, and all exercise a degree of control or influence over a specific territory, school, or playground. A distinguishing characteristic of gangs in contrast to general youth associations is the degree of their involvement in criminal activity against other youth gangs or the general population. While the existence of gangs in a school or neighborhood may be obvious, identification of individual students as gang members is much less precise.

Misidentification and over identification of gang membership can wrongly foster a blanket zero-tolerance approach in schools to anything that could even remotely be considered gang related. Youthful expression is confused with gang behavior and squelched. Religious icons and cultural symbols become suspect; low-rider car shows, pep rallies, and benign styles of dress are banned; and physical altercations between students are construed as gang related. At times, a mentality of a school under siege takes hold, and an educational institution begins to resemble more a correctional facility than a school (Deprived of Dignity, 2007). When the gangs are perceived to be much more prominent and much more of a threat than they really are, the school is giving power to the gangs rather than taking it away from them.

High Expectations in the Classroom

Teachers need to maintain high expectations and provide lessons that encourage high levels of achievement (not failure). Teachers who may be intimidated by gang-affiliated youth in their classrooms may unwittingly enter into an unspoken contract with these youths whereby they lower their academic expectations in exchange for some sort of classroom peace or calm. This type of academic blackmail has a price and is extremely corrosive to attempts to maintain order in the classroom. As Huff (1989) writes:

> Contrary to much "common wisdom", teachers who demonstrate that they care about a youth and then are firm but fair in their expectations are rarely, if ever, the victim of assault by gang members. Rather, it is those teachers who "back down" and are easily intimidated who are more likely to be the victims of assault. During two years of interviews, not one gang member ever said that a teacher who insisted on academic performance was assaulted. Such teachers are respected far more than those perceived as "weak", and "weakness" generally represents a quality to be exploited by gang members in an almost Darwinian fashion, much as they select targets on the street. (p. 534)

Clearly, teaching well and maintaining high academic and behavioral expectations are the best way to convey respect to students as well as to reduce the likelihood of violence in the classroom.

Teaching Gang-Associated Youth

Many successful teachers have their own unique and personal ways of motivating and building relationships with gang-associated youth. Their various approaches tend to rely on the consistent application of specific educational principles, which are really the hallmark of good teaching for all students. These include the following:

- Maintaining consistent and fair classroom routines, structures, and expectations. Youth involved in gangs can be acutely aware of instances involving disrespect or differential treatment of students by teachers. The emphasis should be on interacting with all students equitably and making attempts at offering academic assistance to all—even to students who have previously failed—in very explicit ways.

- Allocating time to understanding and being sensitive to the cultures and histories of students. As described in prior chapters, teachers and administrators must reach out and connect with the families and better understand the home culture and family life of the students. Building positive relationships is especially important if the student comes from a home where gang involvement is generational. Attempting to draw a student away from the gang lifestyle by demeaning or belittling his or her gang involvement may serve only to insult the student and his or her family.

- Maintaining a set of graduated sanctions in the classroom that are logical and reasonable. Teachers or staff who consistently depend on and regularly call on administrators or the police to help maintain order in the classroom will see a gradual erosion of their authority in the classroom. This disempowering effect is insidious and will only subject the teacher to more frequent and intense challenges by gang youth. These youth may sense weakness, and they will exploit it.

- Emphasizing positive opportunities is just as important as having a clear set of consequences for negative behavior. Negative consequences may stop disruptive behavior, but positive interventions changes it. Rewards, recognition activities, and positive communications to the home serve to demonstrate to young people and their families that they have an existence beyond the gangs and can be productive students.

- Incorporating cooperative and hands-on learning experiences that address different learning modalities. Enlist gang-involved students to work with other students on class projects and in extracurricular activities. In doing so, it is equally important for teachers to have an awareness of current gang tensions, rivalries, and dress in order to avoid student groupings by default that enhance gang affiliation and intimidation in the classroom.

- Requesting that school administrators offer gang awareness workshops that involve more than simply having the local police come in and share gang intelligence and related paraphernalia. Insist instead that a panel format be utilized that includes community leaders and elders, parents, and peer educators with a successful record of working with gangs (Deprived of Dignity, 2007).

Building Hope

Youth who are involved in gangs tend to receive contradictory or mixed messages about adulthood, rites of passage, respect, power, and success. Simply being in a gang means having fewer friends, more enemies, and fewer places one can go and feel safe. Schools are in a pivotal position to offer these youth real alternatives away from this skewed existence.

Perhaps one of the most important things that educators can do with gang-associated youth is to impart a sense of hope and optimism to these students. Ultimately, success in school means creating situations in the classroom where students can practice new behaviors, take risks without fear of reprisal or ridicule, and plan in a way that fosters real hope.

Summary

Public schools offer one of their best chances for equal opportunity for low income students. Teachers need to use classroom management skills with a commitment to cultural and social democracy. Without this commitment, management skills lead to control, not to student responsibility and self-direction. Neither teacher domination nor chaos and anarchy prepare young people to live responsible, democratic lives. Teachers can develop management skills that promote academic achievement and a democratic, trusting, caring environment in the classroom.

Questions over the Chapter

1. List three classroom rules that would reduce interpersonal conflict.
2. What three student behaviors in your classroom produce the most off-task time for students? What steps could you take to prevent these behaviors in the future?
3. How can a teacher get enough time for coaching?
4. Give two examples of personalizing the interaction between students and teachers.
5. List areas of authority where teachers should assert their adult–teacher responsibilities.
6. What are major in-school causes of class management problems?

Activities for Further Study of Classroom Management and Power

1. If you are having difficulty with class control, enroll in a workshop for assertive class management. See the supplementary texts mentioned on page 260.
2. Consider new forms of student assessment (see Jones & Jones, 2007).
3. Attend a teen Narcotics Anonymous or similar self-help group meeting. Find out if there is such a group in your school. Listen to teens discuss their own experiences and dependency on drugs.
4. Observe an experienced teacher conducting a classroom meeting at your grade level.
5. Contact your local probation department. Investigate what programs they have for schools and for drug or gang intervention.
6. Role-play a coaching session with a student.
7. Observe and participate in training for conflict mediators in a school district. Learn these skills.

Teaching Strategies for Use with Your Students

1. Decide on your three most important classroom rules. Post them. Teach them. Consistently enforce them.
2. After completing strategy 1, add no more than one new rule per week. Clearly describe and practice appropriate behavior.
3. Isolate off-task behavior and reteach the rule and appropriate behavior to those who are off-task.
4. Step out of power struggles. Refer to strategies 1 through 3.
5. Use positive communications whenever possible. (See the suggestions given in this chapter.)
6. Teach and practice appropriate social skills.
7. Plan and implement a coaching strategy.
8. Teach the skills of conflict resolution to students.
9. Refer again to Figures 8.5, 8.6, and 8.7. Identify and practice ways to integrate these concepts into your relationships with students.

CHAPTER

9

Promoting Democracy and Critical Thinking

> The educator with a democratic vision or posture cannot
> avoid in his teaching praxis insisting on the critical
> capacity, curiosity and autonomy of the learner.
>
> Paulo Freire, *Pedagogy of Freedom:*
> *Ethics, Democracy, and Civic Courage*

This work is about choosing democracy. Teachers either choose democracy or choose inequality when they select their curriculum, their teaching strategies, and their management strategies.

The classroom teacher makes the most important decisions concerning teaching processes. Teachers choose daily whether to stress equality or inequality, content coverage or understanding, skill development or critical thinking. And teachers choose based on their own view of students and their learning potential and on their own view of society. In our knowledge-driven economy, fact-based approaches to education are inadequate to the task.

Teachers dedicated to building a democratic classroom recognize that teaching decision making and critical thinking plays a central role in moving away from inequality and toward cultural pluralism. Based on their own values and philosophy of democracy in education, teachers can make the important decision to emphasize critical-thinking strategies.

The educational literature is full of terms such as *constructivism, reflective thinking, inquiry, decision making, critical thinking, higher-level cognitive skills*, and *evaluation*. Researchers use these terms to describe multiple aspects of complex thought processes. Most educators agree that students gain from instruction in critical thinking (Costa,

2008). This instruction teaches students to carefully consider ideas and to examine the assumptions on which ideas are based. This instruction also teaches students to process evidence, to draw precise conclusions, and to limit their conclusions. A variety of instructional strategies exists to teach students processes for gathering evidence, determining patterns of data, and stating the results of their analyses.

This chapter provides an overview of critical thinking, of critical-thinking skills, and of how, in many schools, low expectations for students and an overreliance on drill-and-practice activities have hindered the development of such critical thinking. Finally, this chapter describes several strategies for teaching decision-making and critical-thinking skills.

The Processes of Learning

Descriptions of the processes of thinking were developed in the modern era by William James (1842–1910) and converted into educational theory by John Dewey (1859–1952). They based their theories on the developing field of psychology and on philosophical works dating back to Plato. Philosophers, beginning with Plato, have argued that quality education should move beyond the memorization of facts to teach the processes of learning. An inquiring mind and spirit are admired and promoted. Modern philosophers of education have advanced the idea that the development of rational thinking should be a primary goal of schools (Arnstine, 1995; Gardner, 1999).

Cognitive psychologists, notably Jerome Bruner and Jean Piaget, used observation as a primary research technique to further advance the theory that cognitive processes develop based on experience. Vygotsky (1978) amplified and clarified the important relationships among experience, social relationships, and learning.

The Constructivist Perspective

In the 1960s through the 1980s, advocates of critical thinking would term their psychological perspective *cognitive psychology*. Today, they are more likely to term it *constructivism*. Constructivism presumes that teachers cannot give knowledge to students. Instead, students use received information to construct knowledge and give it meaning in their own minds. Teachers facilitate this process by using strategies that make information meaningful and relevant, by teaching students to use critical-thinking or metacognitive skills, and by encouraging discovery learning. The essential insight is that we cannot transfer knowledge from one person to another; rather, we can only assist students in constructing their own.

We will use this text as an example. In Chapter 2, we discussed the nature of culture; in Chapter 3, race; in Chapter 4, class; and in Chapter 5, gender. These presentations— and your teacher's accompanying lectures, videos, and activities—did not give you a comprehension of culture, race, class, and gender. You did not accept completely what the text or your instructor said. Instead, you received examples and concepts and then developed your own definitions based on how your prior experience blended with the information received. Each student in your class defined these key issues differently. A constructivist psychologist would say that each of you constructed your own knowledge about culture, race, class, and gender.

Bruner (1996) describes the constructivist tenet as follows:

> The reality that we impute to the "worlds" we inhabit is a constructed one. To paraphrase Nelson Goodman, "reality is made, not found." Reality construction is the product of meaning making shaped by traditions and by a culture's toolkit of ways of thought. In this sense, education must be conceived as aiding young humans in learning to use the tools of meaning making and reality construction, to better adapt to the world in which they find themselves and to help in the process of changing it as required. (p. 20)

A constructivist perspective encourages teachers to consider learning as an active process. Students should not only read, listen, and do exercises but also debate, hypothesize, investigate, and defend a point of view. This constructivist perspective stresses that knowledge is learned in a social manner—that is, we learn by dialogue and interaction with others. This part of the constructivist paradigm will be extended in Chapter 11, which considers language. And constructivism emphasizes that students often benefit from creating and re-creating knowledge for themselves, as you have hopefully done in struggling with concepts such as class, race, ethnicity, gender, and authority in reading this book (Perkins, 1999).

Constructivism uses a different viewpoint than does behaviorism (termed *reductionism* in Chapter 6). Howard Gardner and others argue that in the constructivist class, students try out ideas, experiment, and explore to develop their own conclusions. Our job as teachers is to help them to be clear, systematic, and rigorous about learning (Mansilla & Gardner, 2008).

Critical Thinking Defined

Most teachers would agree that schools should teach students to solve problems, to make decisions, and to arrive at conclusions based on evidence and reasoning. The formal written goals of state standards, most schools, and many curriculum guides include providing students with experiences in developing critical-thinking skills. A central task of multicultural education is to extend the teaching of critical thinking to all students.

Critical thinking is a process encouraged within the constructivist perspective. We can begin to define *critical thinking* with Beyer's (1988) definition: "Our graduates should be able to make well-reasoned decisions, solve problems skillfully, and make carefully thought-out judgments about the worth, accuracy, and value of information, ideas, claims, and propositions" (p. 1).

Paul (1988) clarifies further:

> A passionate drive for clarity, accuracy, and fair-mindedness, a fervor for getting to the bottom of things, to the deepest root issues, for listening sympathetically to opposite points of view, a compelling drive to seek out evidence, and intense aversion to contradiction, sloppy

thinking, inconsistent application of standards, a devotion to truth as against self-interest—these are the essential components of a rational person. (p. 2)

A group associated with Paul's work, the National Council for Excellence in Critical Thinking (2008), defines critical thinking as follows:

Critical thinking is that mode of thinking—about any subject, content, or problem—in which the thinker improves the quality of his or her thinking by skillfully analyzing, assessing, and reconstructing it. Critical thinking is self-directed, self-disciplined, self-monitored, and self-corrective thinking. It presupposes assent to rigorous standards of excellence and mindful command of their use. It entails effective communication and problem-solving abilities, as well as a commitment to overcome our native egocentrism and sociocentrism.

On the other hand, conservative scholar E. D. Hirsch (1996), a professor of English, dismisses much of the emphasis on critical-thinking skills as romantic and unscientific nonsense.

Critical Thinking for All

Recently, research on critical thinking has focused on comparisons of how "experts" and "nonexperts" reason and make decisions. When monitored, experts in a field use a variety of testing strategies and intuitive leaps, demonstrating more skillful intellectual performances than do amateurs.

Reflective thought resembles the process scholars admire, write about, and prefer to believe they engage in. This romanticized, egocentric view, coupled with the lack of precise analysis, leads to a common folk culture of schooling from middle school through the university. If the teacher presents the material and students learn, then the students are considered capable and intelligent. If the teacher presents the material and students fail to learn, then the students are considered limited or not bright. Many teachers and entire school systems respond to students they consider "not bright" by selecting for them a behaviorist model of drill, practice, and testing strategies rather than encouraging the construction of knowledge and critical thinking (Renzulli, 2002).

This inaccurate and nonreflective view of learning ignores numerous intervening factors, including poverty, inadequate school resources, and the important subjective interaction between the instructor's communication and motivation styles and the corresponding communication and motivation styles of students (Bruner, 1996). Because these styles are learned in cultures, conflict between teacher and learner styles frequently produces school failure in learning (Anderson, 1988; Garcia, 2001; Ramirez & Castañeda, 1974). As a consequence of the power relationships between teacher and learner, failure to master the material is blamed on the student and too often attributed to limited intellectual capabilities—an often inaccurate analysis.

Nonacademic Sources of Rational Intelligence

Most authors and teachers assume, without much evidence, that a critical, rational life develops primarily in school. Italian intellectual Antonio Gramsci supplemented school-based definitions by describing the role of "organic intellectuals," those in the working class who demonstrate intellect based on their life experience, usually without being subservient to school or university norms. Gramsci described persons without formal training who often develop the reflective ideal and assist others in reconceptualizing world–work relationships (Aronowitz & Giroux, 1985; Giroux, 1988). Some parent activists and community organizers fit Gramsci's description of organic intellectuals.

People are experts in a variety of fields. The rice farmer in Africa is an expert in measuring and planting rice. His approach to problem solving offers solutions not available to a novice planter, even if she is college educated. The pursuit of intellectual excellence is not an exclusive domain of schools and formal schooling.

If we are cautious to not confuse the lifestyle and culture of professional academics with intellect, we can still agree that it is useful to pursue a deep understanding of concepts, rational analysis, and critical awareness. It remains a normative assumption that schools should promote intellectual life and intellectual integrity.

Although philosophers since Plato, and U.S. schools since Dewey, have been advocating critical thinking and rational processes, researchers do not yet know enough about human brain activity to describe the processes adequately. We operate from a series of hunches. One important body of work argues that instead of the recent focus on one fixed definition of intelligence, derived from reductionist views of psychology, teachers should adopt the theory of "multiple intelligences" to explain the variety of student thinking patterns (Gardner, 1999, 2006). Developments in so-called brain-based research are beginning to suggest that teachers can select teaching and language strategies that are more compatible with the human mind and that enhance learning (Gardner, 1999; Pool, 1997).

Overcoming Low Expectations

Schools in poverty areas commonly use more drill and practice and place less emphasis on teaching intellectual processes than do middle-class schools. Drill-and-practice exercises keep children quiet, and the children complete their work. Because many poor and minority children score low on standardized exams, a myth has emerged that these children are less capable of advanced thinking. A series of rationalizations, each based on biased or incompetent research or applications, developed to demonstrate the alleged limited abilities of poor children (Banks, 1997). Even some well-meaning research on cognitive styles has been abused to reach conclusions not based on sufficient evidence. There is no reason to assume that children from diverse subcultures have any less need for training in knowledge construction and critical thinking (DeAvila, 1987; Garcia, 2001; Miller-Jones, 1991).

Too often, teachers in multicultural settings are forced to choose between compensatory education strategies of drill and remediation, or what Renzulli calls the "ram–remember–regurgitate" model, and more open-ended, constructed, critical-thinking strategies (Renzulli, 2002). This choice is one of the most fundamental decisions in choosing democracy. The power to choose lies in the hands of each teacher. In this important arena of students' lives, teachers have more power than the legislature, school board members, principals, or unions. The choice for critical thinking is an expression of teacher power and a rejection of biased research, and it reaffirms basic democratic values and your reasons for becoming a teacher.

The pattern of stressing drill and practice over critical thinking in de facto segregated schools has major social consequences. Under slavery, Africans brought to this country were prohibited from learning to read as a form of social control. In our present schools, social control is further advanced when students living in poverty areas, particularly students of color, are directed away from classes that encourage critical thinking, decision making, and creative use of technology and into classes that emphasize drill and practice and remediation. Promoting the development and practice of critical thinking must be a major concern in school reform (Boyer, 1983; Garcia, 2001; Goodlad & Keating, 1990; Renzulli, 2002).

Critical thinking, or reflective decision making, should be central to the agenda school reform (Darling-Hammond & Wood, 2008). Whereas many schools have not stressed thinking skills and processes enough, students of color and working-class students receive the least training in these areas. Many urban schools have an honors track or a magnet program in which thinking skills and processes are taught and a basic track in which students are incorrectly assumed to be incapable of abstract thought. Poor and minority students are regularly assigned to the basic track (Gardner, 1999; Kozol, 2005; Oakes, 2005; Renzulli, 2002).

The process at C. Wright Mills High School (situated in a large urban district) illustrates how students of color are scheduled away from critical-thinking classes.[1] Mills is an integrated school: 23 percent Asian, 22 percent African American, 20 percent European American, and 35 percent Latino. Mills has a magnet program emphasizing the humanities and fine arts. Students in the program receive an excellent education stressing critical thinking and college preparation. Visitors to the magnet program are surprised to find that 90 percent of the students are European American and Asian in an otherwise integrated school. Visits to the military science (ROTC) and vocational programs reveal more than 80 percent Latino and African American students. In this manner, a legally integrated school has tracks based on race, and students of color are tracked away from classes likely to stress critical thinking. Internal school tracking practices are common throughout the nation (Oakes, 2005).

We know that effective schools should emphasize higher-level cognitive processes (critical thinking) (Elder & Paul, 2008, Education Trust, 2006). Yet, particularly since the development of standards-based and assessment-based instruction, in schools with students from poverty-stricken areas, critical thinking has been driven from the curriculum, while drill-and-practice exercises abound. Teachers respond to student failure on tests by turning to behaviorism and reductionism and away from critical thinking. Worksheets and control have replaced efforts to motivate and encourage divergent thinking (Kozol, 2005).

Teachers with low expectations of students design their classes in ways that produce students with low achievement (Oakes & Rogers, 2006). Such low expectations mean that teachers do not expect students to excel in reading and writing and do not engage

---

[1]The name "C. Wright Mills" is a pseudonym for an actual school I have often visited.

them in tasks that require higher-order thinking. Low expectations are a primary factor in school failure. They are displayed in low cognitive-level instruction, such as that demonstrated by an overreliance on worksheets and drill and practice. Combined with other school barriers to success, teachers' low expectations communicate to students not to expect much of themselves or their future. In this, cognitive science has failed to inform and to shape the instructional practices of teachers. Instead of using what we know, many teachers rely on a "folk wisdom" of low expectations.

No significant evidence demonstrates that children from minority cultures have less ability to perform high-demand cognitive tasks (critical thinking). Yet students from minority cultures are regularly underrepresented in programs for gifted children (Ford & Harris, 1999). Children from all cultures benefit from instruction in critical thinking and the related higher-order thinking areas. Schools and curricula need to develop learning experiences in which the children's repertoire of knowledge (including language) is used to stimulate their intellectual processes (DeAvila, 1987; Garcia, 2001).

Teachers focused on democracy will try to develop strategies to teach using a constructivist perspective and critical-thinking processes. Teachers will work to get equal access to gifted and high-track programs for all children. Failure in the areas of abstract thinking is most often a result of inappropriate or insufficient clarity in the presentation and practice of skills necessary for the process.

Teachers may ask questions from the textbook or teacher's manual and silence follows. Communication barriers may be caused by lack of attention to cross-cultural learning and motivational styles. Rather than assuming the students are unable to learn the material, you need to examine the structure and pattern of your questions. When questions seek data from students' own experiences and are clearly organized on a retrieval chart, students from all racial, cultural, and class groups readily perform higher cognitive functions, such as predicting and evaluating (see Figure 9.1).

The Need for Teaching Strategies to Develop Critical Thinking

The "back to basics" movement of the 1990s and the test-driven standards movement of the last 10 years have often led poor and minority schools to emphasize skill remediation and rote practice rather than problem solving. In spite of the importance of critical thinking, schools often pay little attention to it and seldom evaluate the development of critical-thinking skills (Renzulli, 2002).

There are many reasons for schools' failure to focus on teaching for deep understanding and critical thinking (Costa, 2008; Willingham, 2007). The most obvious is that most schools have seldom tried. Teachers are hired and given a job to cover a specific body of content. University professors seldom model constructivism and critical thinking in their content courses. Few university students are trained to teach critical-thinking skills. Further, college courses are usually divided into content areas, and exams largely emphasize content. This problem is made even more difficult when districts hire "intern" teachers who have neither teacher preparation nor a major in the field in which they are teaching. Untrained teachers, overwhelmed by the task of learning to teach, tend to teach without reflection. And significant evidence exists that these

Figure 9.1 Critical Thinking; Intellectual Processes

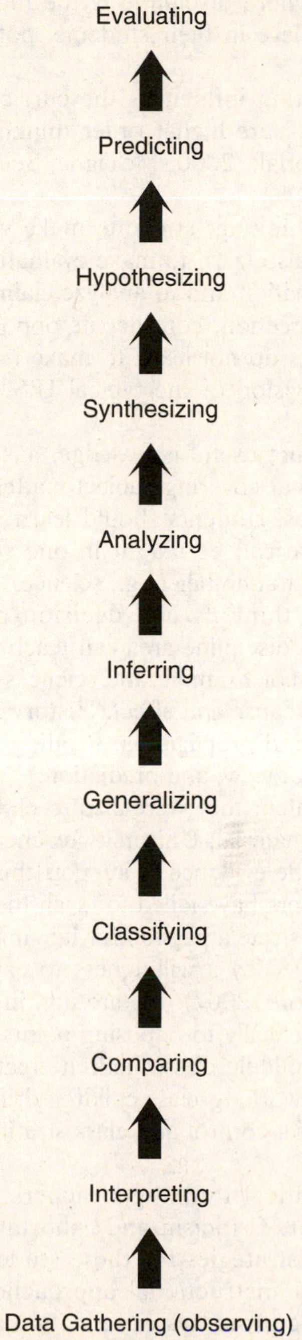

Evaluating

Predicting

Hypothesizing

Synthesizing

Analyzing

Inferring

Generalizing

Classifying

Comparing

Interpreting

Data Gathering (observing)

Based on Hannah and Michaelis, 1977.

intern teachers are overrepresented in schools serving low-income students (Haycock & Crawford, 2008; Kozol, 2005). In schools where discipline is the major problem, there is seldom motivation for teachers to believe in their students' potential and to emphasize critical thinking.

The current emphasis on standardized testing influences the curriculum toward content memorization. Few tests exist that measure higher-order thinking skills, and those tests that do are expensive to employ (Berlak, 2000; McTighe, Seif, & Wiggins, 2004; Nichols & Berliner, 2007; Popham, 1999).

When schools successfully teach critical thinking, students make well-reasoned judgments and solve problems skillfully. They also learn to make evaluative judgments about the worth, accuracy, and value of information and to analyze claims, ideas, and ideologies. To clarify the importance of this direction, consider its opposite. Create a vision in your mind of a school where students do not learn to make reasoned judgments and solve problems. Now you have a vision of the typical U.S. high school. Would you like to spend four years there?

Clearly, learning to think actively, to construct useful knowledge, has not been the incidental outcome of classroom study directed at covering subject matter such as history, math, or literature. In the primary grades, students should learn skills such as sequencing, grouping, and categorizing. These can be taught in one subject matter (e.g., reading or social studies) and generalized to another (e.g., science).

By about the fourth grade, some critical-thinking and decision-making skills become more specialized by subject field. Each discipline area can teach the appropriate skills with attention to their transferability. For example, the sciences can focus on observation, the use of data, and recognition of cause and effect. History and the social studies can focus on the identification of bias and propaganda. Reading and literature can focus on similarities and differences, point of view, and prediction.

Teachers once assumed that by teaching content they were also teaching the operations and skills needed to learn or process the material. University teachers often operate from this perspective. There is, however, little evidence to support this assumption. From elementary school to the university, teachers have failed to teach the processes of learning. In elections our citizens do not demonstrate a passion for fair-mindedness and accuracy. Our political processes are not typified by a willingness to explore difficult issues or a propensity for open-mindedness (Gore, 2007). We are not, in general, willing to suspend judgment and to listen sympathetically to opposing points of view. Particularly troubling is the fact that, if we teach middle-class children creative processes and higher cognitive processes, while we teach working-class children drill and remediation, we are using the schools to promote social control and class stratification rather than democracy.

Instead of encouraging reflection and critical thinking, teachers often simply exhort working-class students to work harder. Criticism and exhortation have not served as effective critical-thinking teaching strategies for these students. Instead, teachers deserve assistance in planning their instructional approaches to include strategies that encourage students to learn the processes of reflection and the skills of thinking. Emphasis on content, on questions, and on worksheets does not, by itself, help students improve their thinking. Questions may encourage thinking and, at times, may even provoke thinking, but they do not teach the skills of reflective inquiry.

Direct Instruction in Critical Thinking

One step in the process of learning critical thinking is to learn a series of specific skills, such as defining and clarifying problems, gathering evidence, and distinguishing between statements of facts and opinions. Students should receive direct instruction in developing thinking skills. Separating the many facets of critical thinking into clearly identifiable skills allows teachers to focus on, teach, practice, and evaluate each skill (see Figure 9.1). In Chapter 8, you were introduced to the strategy of direct instruction to teach a new behavior. Direct instruction also works well with the initial steps of teaching critical thinking. To use direct instruction to introduce a critical-thinking skill, follow this strategy:

1. Select the skill.
2. Give clear and precise instructions.
3. Model the skill for students.
4. Have students practice systematically.
5. Provide students opportunities for practice under your guidance.
6. Assess students' abilities with the skill.
7. Have students practice independently.

Direct instruction is a useful strategy for initial critical thinking, cooperative learning, classroom management, and other lessons. Used in conjunction with other strategies, it provides an opportunity for initial skill instruction. When students have acquired the necessary skills, you can vary your strategies. For example, you may use direct instruction to teach a student to compare. The student may then use comparison as a skill within more extended problem-solving tasks. Direct instruction can teach appropriate group roles for cooperative learning, after which the group can explore divergent and imaginative social participation projects. In the midst of an active project of experiential learning, you may want to reteach some basic skill, such as writing a paragraph, using direct instruction.

Dewey argues, and I think he is correct, that reflective teaching requires more than the isolated practice of skills. It requires that these skills be used in real problems (Dewey, 1916/1966, p. 152). Figure 9.2 provides examples of critical thinking skills that students should learn.

Sample Critical-Thinking Lessons

Kindergarten Through Grade 2 In kindergarten through grade 2, we should teach students lessons on grouping and categorizing. You can use students themselves as participants by categorizing them into groups, such as those with brown hair or red shoes or girls and boys. (Some teachers use ethnic groups as one of several categories for grouping, but it causes much confusion!)

Figure 9.2 **Essential Critical-Thinking Skills**

Cause/effect

Evidence

Point of view; perspective

Forming a conclusion based on evidence

Differences between fact and opinion

Differences between statements of facts and value judgments

Analyze

Identifying the elements of an argument

Identifying the strengths of an argument

Classifying

Comparing/contrasting

Evaluating a source

Decision making

Determining relevance

Lessons on sequencing can also be taught. For example, students should recognize the opening, body, and ending of stories. Teachers can direct discussions about the concepts of cause and effect with students in literature, science, and other subjects.

The following lesson is from a split kindergarten/first-grade bilingual class in Woodland, California. The teacher, Lisette Estrella-Henderson, describes the events:

> The leg of the reading table which we had been using since the beginning of the year fell off one day without any warning. All of our materials went flying, and by the time we had finished cleaning up the mess, there was no time left to do the activity which the students had been looking forward to. Needless to say, my students were upset and frustrated—not to mention how angry I was, since I had asked the secretary to tell the maintenance department about the problem two weeks before!

> I finally realized that the only way I was going to get any action was by illustrating to the administrators how their apathy directly affected my students. I engaged my students in a discussion about what they thought we could do about the problem. (They knew that I had already asked for the leg to be fixed once before.) It was wonderful and enlightening for me to see how their ideas developed and evolved as a result of thinking out loud and putting their ideas together.

> The final consensus was to write a class letter explaining our problem and sending it not only to the principal but to the maintenance department and the superintendent as well. The students also drew pictures illustrating the situation and took them home to show their parents as they explained the situation to them. I had the parents and maintenance department at my door the very next day to fix the table, not to mention the visit from the principal and the call from the superintendent. I asked the parents and the maintenance department to let us borrow their tools, and the children fixed the table leg themselves! I could not have come up with a better problem-solving lesson that promoted higher-level thinking skills if I had planned it.

The students really learned that by combining their brains, physical power, and the skills of working cooperatively, they really could make a difference.[2]

Grades 3 Through 6 To teach critical thinking in grades 3 through 6, teachers integrate lessons on evidence, cause and effect, stereotypes, and similar skills into the curriculum. For example, you could show a portion of the film *Amistad* and then have one group of students write a description from the point of view of the African captives. Have a second group write a description of slavery from the point of view presented in their textbooks. Each group should support its point of view with evidence.

As another example, after you give direct instruction on the concepts of sequence and character, students can read a work of literature and describe a sequence of events from the perspective of various characters. The tales *The Eagles Who Thought They Were Chickens* (Winn, 2002) and *The Streets Are Free* (Kurusa, 1995) provide interesting opportunities for reflection.

Grades 6 Through 8 Students can build a retrieval chart to compare the experiences of European immigrants with those of Native Americans, Mexican Americans, and African Americans in previous centuries and in the present (see Figure 9.3).

By this age, you can teach a decision-making process like the following:

1. Identify a problem and clarify the issues.
   - Is the conflict definitional?
   - Is the conflict empirical?
   - Is the conflict value-based?
2. Suggest alternative solutions.
   a. Plan a system of criteria to use to evaluate each aternative.
      - State probable outcomes.
   b. Have teams evaluate each proposed solution.
3. Implement the preferred alternative.
4. Evaluate the outcomes.
5. Have students give an oral or written report on the process of problem solving.

At these grade levels, students might also develop a plan to assist immigrant students in their classroom or in the school. Then they can implement and evaluate it.

Grades 9 Through 12 Divide students into teams. Provide them with the titles of ethnic group and women's history texts available in your school or community library. Have each team select a period of U.S. history and compare the histories of Native Americans, Latinos, Asians, African Americans, and women as given in their textbooks with the information in the library books. Students should consider omissions, assumptions, and the effect of learning a particular point of view in history. See also the excellent work on problem-based learning at *glef.org*.

---

[2]From L. Estrella-Henderson, Woodland, California. Used with permission.

Figure 9.3   Sample Retrieval Chart

	American Indian	Mexican	African American	European American Northern/ Southern
Reason for coming?	Already here.	Already in Southwest when Europeans arrived.	Slavery, brought in chains by force.	Economic opportunity and religious persecution.
To what degree is the group a victim of racism and discrimination?	Faced genocide. Still face some discrimination.	Forced off of their land. Still face some discrimination.	Enslaved until the 19th century. Still face discrimination. Terrorism used to oppress.	Incidents of discrimination have decreased after one generation.
Present status?	High suicide rate. Many continue to live on reservations. 50 percent urban.	High school dropout rate is high. Current attempts being made to limit additional immigration.	High unemployment in urban areas. Some political power.	Assimilated into mainstream.

Critical Theory and Critical Thinking

Critical theory, as described in Chapter 7, incorporates critical-thinking strategies and extends them beyond their positivist roots to include the empowerment of students and oppressed peoples. Critical theory raises important issues regarding ideology and the social control of knowledge. When teachers raise the issue of the ideological loading of education and the curriculum, the political right often counterattacks with vehemence and vigor, accusing them of "politicizing" the curriculum.

The conservative school reform movement of the last two decades displaced liberal concerns of human relations and civil rights with an emphasis on "core knowledge" and standards in discussions of schooling and the curriculum. When critical theorists discuss the political and ideological content of current curricula and when they emphasize critical thinking and the values of democracy and pluralism, this offends or frightens the conservative forces in education (Hirsch, 1996). Many of the most divisive battles over textbooks and curricula were provoked by the challenge of multicultural education advocates, revealing the ideological control of the present curriculum (Apple, 2001; Cornbleth & Waugh, 1995; Gay, 2003; Leming, Ellington, & Porter, 2003).

Critical theory encourages learners to always look at facts and theories in their context. Our education systems, including universities, public schools, and teacher preparation programs, teach not only facts but also norms, values, and acceptance of the existing relationship between schools and the economy (Bruner, 1996).

Critical theory denies that social systems such as schools are neutral but assumes that, as systems designed by people, schools contain within themselves the values of the designers. The same is true of textbooks and of teacher education programs. Think about it for a moment. Is your teacher preparation program neutral, or is it based on a specific worldview and a specific set of values and assumptions? Critical theory seeks to uncover and to reveal these perspectives, these worldviews, and to reveal the hidden curriculum of schools (Carnoy & Levin, 1985; Darder, 1991; Gordon, 1995). For examples, see Loewen (1995) and Zinn (1990).

Critical theory contributes two additional concepts to the discussion of how we know things: student voice and praxis.

Student Voice

Both critical theory and feminist pedagogy have added important ideas about the role of student voice in the constructivist classroom. In order to learn powerful knowledge, students need opportunities to enter into dialogue with other students, with teachers, and with other members of the community. Encouraging students' expression of opinion, of concern, is fundamental to developing their democratic interests. For example, having students write narratives and then analyze them in class provides students excellent opportunities to develop habits of critical and reflective thinking (Darder, 1991; Freire & Macedo, 1987).

Many language arts curriculum efforts have focused on developing and encouraging student voice. For immigrant students, this development is often in their native language; for African American students, voice may be expressed in Black English (Ebonics) (see Chapter 11). Language instruction has recently been substantially reconstructed based on the recognition of the power inherent in students sharing their own ideas. The importance of voice, of adolescent voice, extends beyond language instruction to all areas of the academic and arts curriculum. Progressive teachers encourage expanding student dialogue and reflecting on student ideas (Finn, 1999; Wink, 1997).

We think through language; we cannot think or express thoughts we have no words for. Students with limited mastery of English express their most powerful and most intimate ideas in their home language. Teachers who use only English will prohibit the expression of student voice on many issues.

Freire's work in Brazil and elsewhere—along with the powerful messages of Martin Luther King, Jr., César Chávez, Ernesto Cardenal, and others—illustrates that when people find their own voices, when they can name their own realities, they begin an empowering process of problem-posing education. Students from silenced cultures begin a revolutionized form of reflective education through finding their own voice (Freire, 1997, 1998; Freire & Macedo, 1987).

Debbie Meier (1995) describes the important development of "habits of the mind," when schools encourage mutual respect between students and teachers as well as diversity of and disagreement on intellectual issues. She describes her students as they learn to focus on ideas and themes across the curriculum. They do not find that critical thinking or reflective thinking is a product of a single subject matter area. Teachers work to integrate the school curriculum so that students can understand the unity of experience and knowledge.

Lawrence-Lightfoot (1994) provides dialogues and narratives about six prominent African American citizens. By reading their stories and hearing their narratives, students and teachers learn about perspectives and about those persons who have been left out of history and literature.

Praxis

The concept of praxis is a second powerful critical-thinking tool that developed from critical theory. *Praxis* is the process of learning by doing and then reflecting on the activity (see Chapter 7).

As a learning process, praxis introduces students to critical theory. You learn to read by reading, to write by writing, to teach by teaching. But action alone, work and experience as a teacher alone, will not necessarily improve your teaching. Praxis is learning by doing and then reflecting on (analyzing) and improving your efforts. Figure 9.4 diagrams the process.

Figure 9.4   Praxis

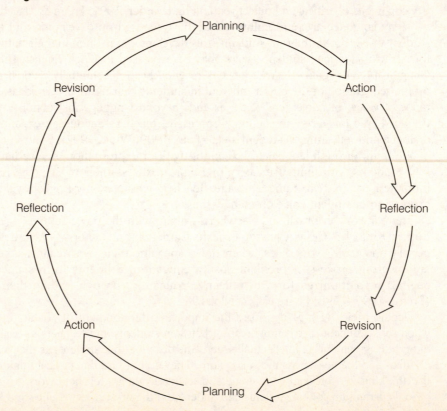

Problem-Posing Education and Social Inquiry Teachers encourage praxis though a process known as problem-posing education. Problem-posing education engages students in analysis and action on a problem (Freire, 1972). Dewey argued that students could construct the curriculum out of real problems they face (Dewey, 1916/1966). The problem might be anything from racial or gender stereotypes among students to an apparently irrelevant curriculum. Students set up a project to investigate the problem. Then, based on their investigation, they take a selected action.

For example, your students might believe that their math class is not relevant to the jobs available in their community. They could investigate the local job market and compare math requirements there to the curriculum. Then they may draft ideas about how the math curriculum could be made more relevant. Or they might choose to examine the current theory that Algebra 1 should be an entrance point for college preparation. The investigation process will necessarily teach them more about math. Students engage in social inquiry along with political participation by conducting research projects into their own circumstances. Their own experiences, such as tracking, school failure, violence, gangs, and suicide, are arenas where students can learn to use the tools of critical inquiry—such as evidence—through engaged and active investigation.

In Los Angeles, one group of high school students investigated access to Advanced Placement classes; others documented dilapidated school facilities, leading to lawsuits against the school district and the state. In these projects, students come to understand the social and economic context of a problem, putting decisions on school budgets and the unequal distribution of resources into a more complex context (Oakes & Rogers, 2006). And so the process continues, with the teacher serving throughout as coach, guide, and fellow investigator.

Multicultural education should go beyond teaching isolated critical-thinking skills to encompass decision making and social inquiry. Praxis and problem-posing education are powerful forms of intellectual development that involve more than acquiring a series of isolated skills. Problem-posing education encourages acquiring both skills and attitudes that support a deep understanding of concepts, inquiry, discovery, and decision making. Social inquiry assumes the radical, democratic stance that all students and adults can resolve their own problems and make their own decisions. Democratic multicultural education, building on the insights of critical theory, seeks to reveal the ideological domination that keeps political and cultural power in the hands of a small segment of society.

Media Literacy

Achieving Computer Literacy Today for Good Jobs Tomorrow The changes that turned the U.S. economy into an information-based economy require fundamental changes in our schools. All schools, not only the affluent ones, need modern technological equipment and teachers prepared to assist students with access to higher education and careers in computers and information technology fields. A constructivist viewpoint should include instruction in technology (Rosen & Salomon, 2007). More than 40 percent of the new jobs in our society will not require a college education. Students should be offered specific work skill preparation, such as computer and information technology offerings, while in high school (Partnership for 21st Century Skills, 2008). These new facilities—and if necessary, new institutions—should be constructed in communities with high rates of school leaving and unemployment. To advance equal opportunity, schools need both technology and teachers who are well prepared to use the new tools for learning, including, remarkably, cell phones and iPods.

Media Literacy: Using the Internet The development of the Internet could have led to the creation of new opportunities to close the achievement gap; instead, it has often led to a digital divide, in which the privileged move ahead in a high-technology world, and the less privileged once again get left behind. Teachers can make a difference. The critical steps are for you, the teacher, to become proficient with technology and to use it in your teaching. You can save a great deal of time, and prepare more interesting lessons, by using the technology currently available. When textbooks and standards leave multicultural themes out of the curriculum, you can access lessons and material on the Iinternet.

Important ideas from technology-enhanced learning include "just in time" learning. Students need to learn to use the Internet and other media technologies as tools in their work. Even if you only have one computer in your classroom, it should be put to work. Resourceful teachers can usually get several computers donated. One good source is *www.computers.fed.gov/school/user.asp*.

For you to assist students, you need to be comfortable with both using the technology and allowing students to lead you in the use of new technologies. In this constructivist environment, teachers are no longer the sole purveyors of knowledge; instead, we are guides and coaches that assist students in their pursuits. The Internet can be a useful source of data and evidence for students to use to arrive at their own conclusions. They need guidance and assistance in gathering data, evaluating it, arriving at conclusions, and limiting their conclusions to the data available. Excellent lesson plans and programs exist to guide teachers. Use a search engine (such as Google) and look for Media Literacy + Lessons.

> Not since Gutenberg invented the modern printing press more than 500 years ago, making books and scientific tomes affordable and widely available to the masses, has any new invention empowered individuals or transformed access to information as profoundly as Google.
>
> David Vise (2006)

Searching for Information—How to Use Google Effectively The most popular search engine today is Google. It is a very effective and easy-to-use search engine that does a very good job of producing relevant results. In February 2008, a Google search for the term *multicultural education* produced 2,530,000 "hits." This is far too many pages to look through one by one. The challenge of today and tomorrow, in terms of the technology skill set needed, is not only how to find information but also how to find the specific, current, and accurate information we need at a given time and place.

There are two main elements in this information-seeking skill set. The first element is that teachers need to be able to access information. Many teachers and students have already acquired this skill—most people know how to access Google and type words to initiate a search. But the second, and perhaps the more critical, aspect of the information-seeking process is that users need to know how to use advanced features of Google to narrow down their topic to the specific, current, and accurate information being sought.

Here are some strategies for narrowing search criteria in a Google search.

As of February 2008, Google included 28 specialized searching features that allow users to specify their media of choice. Users of Google can refine and/or limit their searches to

1. *Media:* Using the blue underlined terms at the top of the Google window, users can search for media by types, such as images, music, and maps. In February 2008, entering an image search for *Cesar Chavez* returned 166,000 images of the late founder of the United Farm Workers Union.

2. *Definitions of Terms:* Typing *Define:* in front of a term or phrase will return a variety of definitions for that term or phrase. Entering *Define: Multiculturalism* resulted in a listing of 12 definitions for the term, plus links to the sites providing the definitions.

3. *Full Text of Books:* Whenever you search for a term or phrase that is the title of a book that is available online, Google will list the book at the top of the search results. A February 2008 search for "The Tell-Tale Heart" by Edgar Allan Poe produced not only several full-text listings of the story but also, at the end of this list, a 1953 black-and-white video of the story. Searches for books that are not available freely online, such as Sandra Cisneros's *The House on Mango Street*, return results showing where the book can be seen online for purchase or purchased online.

The complete listing of the 28 searching features of the Google search engine can be found at *www.google.com/intl/en/help/features.html*.

Technology and the Internet are changing the way we gather, select, and use information and the way we teach. For more ideas, see *Teaching and Learning with Technology* (2008) by Judy Lever-Duffy and Jean B. McDonald.

A classroom that has been reorganized to engage and use technology is much more than a place for the teacher to make more visually appealing presentations. The classroom should be redesigned to foster divergent learning and to engage students in active learning about topics they care about (Rosen & Salomon, 2007). Technology has the potential for skipping over obstacles. For example, South Dakota has recognized that technology can bring the best of instruction to even remote schools. It can also provide virtual field trips to students in the most isolated classrooms. Students can be introduced to a virtual world on the Internet, enabling them to learn about going to college and about a wide variety of careers. One of the most accessible careers made possible by the technological revolution is a career in information technology.

Some career-oriented teachers in high schools have taught students to assemble and repair computers, and then the students construct their own computers and take them home. There are numerous sites for free Internet access, and the students will quickly find them. Students who were preparing to leave school can be provided with instruction leading to Cisco and other certifications for computer repair, making them eligible for jobs paying $30 per hour or more. In one case, students on the career or work track were given positions as student interns on a college campus. They became the computer tutors for the faculty and earned good money while still in high school in a school-to-work program. And working on a campus is a great recruitment process. They found they were interested in college, which gave them more motivation to complete their work in high school and get on to a more adult world.

Through bold and creative changes in the classroom, students' interests can be tapped, their minds engaged, and introductions made to the world of the information sciences.

Summary

It is vitally important that teachers in multicultural settings choose to emphasize critical thinking, a constructivist perspective, and problem posing instead of relying on compensatory education strategies. In too many schools, low expectations and overreliance on drill-and-practice activities have prevented students from developing critical-thinking skills, reflective attitudes, and a value commitment to education. Teachers committed to establishing democratic classrooms can use the sample critical-thinking strategies described in this chapter to help their students develop the skills necessary for processing evidence, drawing accurate conclusions, solving problems skillfully, and believing in their own decision-making abilities.

Questions over the Chapter

1. What is the relationship between having low expectations for students and teaching critical thinking?
2. List four critical-thinking skills appropriate to your grade level.
3. Researchers have noted that teachers in schools serving low-income areas and people of color frequently rely more on drill and practice and less on teaching critical thinking. How would teachers you know justify this decision? What are some consequences of this decision?
4. Which value positions or value orientations support teaching critical thinking in schools?
5. Why would the objectives and strategies of critical-thinking lessons in grades 1 and 2 be different from those in grades 10 through 12?

Activities for Further Study of Critical Thinking

1. Write objectives that call for the use of critical-thinking skills in studying topics in multicultural education. (See the examples in the following section, "Teaching Strategies for Use with Your Students.")
2. Write lesson plans or unit plans that include the teaching of at least one specific critical-thinking skill.

3. Plan the evaluation of critical-thinking skills.
4. Prepare lessons in which students analyze their own K–12 textbooks. Students can compare how the books portray African Americans, Latinos, Asian Americans, or women in literature or history. Have students write a comprehensive, multicultural, inclusive history of a week or a month in their classroom. Students will need to deal with significance, evidence, point of view, and similar problems.

Teaching Strategies for Use with Your Students

Critical-Thinking Lesson Plans

The following list of objectives will help you begin to plan critical-thinking lessons. Students will be able to

1. Cite evidence to support a stereotype.
2. Cite evidence to contradict a stereotype.
3. Form a conclusion about stereotypes.
4. Analyze school inequality from two points of view.

You may use a variety of lesson plans based on the theories of instruction that you favor. There is no one correct form or format. An actual lesson would include additional objectives and strategies to achieve human relations or multicultural goals in addition to critical thinking.

The following lesson plans are provided to help you as a new teacher get started in planning critical thinking. Your instructor may want to include additional components. For example, many teachers include a component on evaluation.

Sample Lesson Plan for Grades 2 Through 4

Students will be able to

1. Categorize data as learned or inherited.
2. Group data based on the categories provided.
3. Recognize that students learn both at home and at school.
4. Recognize that culture is learned behavior.
5. Read words on the board.

First, list the following categories on butcher paper or the chalkboard:

Things I Learned	Things I Inherited
language	hair color
food preferences	skin color

Then provide students with some clear examples of each category. In a class discussion, have students categorize skills and characteristics as either learned or inherited.

After students have made the first categorization, list the following categories on butcher paper or the chalkboard:

Things I Learned at Home	Things I Learned at School
language	reading

Then have teams of students meet to create lists using this second group of headings. A reporter from each team should share the ideas from that group. You then record the students' ideas on butcher paper or the chalkboard.

As you summarize the information students generate, provide the conclusion that students learn both at home and at school. This conclusion is important to their understanding of lessons on culture. See Chapter 2.

Sample Lesson Plan for Grades 8 Through 12
Students will be able to

1. State a thesis and support it with evidence.
2. Arrive at a conclusion based on evidence.

First, introduce the subject of inequality and review the process of using evidence to support a position. Provide students with a model by stating a conclusion, supporting it with evidence, and then formulating a thesis. For example, you might use this thesis: Students suffer from unequal funding of schools.

Through class discussion, have students offer evidence to support this thesis.

After this class discussion, have students draft a series of thesis statements on inequality. Record the theses on butcher paper.

Assign teams of students to collect evidence to support each thesis. Allow each team 30 minutes to 3 days to collect evidence to support its position, depending on the subtlety of the inequality in question.

Have each team prepare an outline of a report on its research responses to the thesis about inequality. Each report should begin with a thesis statement, followed by the evidence the team has gathered to support it. Finally, each team reports its conclusions and supporting evidence to the class. Provide time in class for feedback.

Have each team write a short essay (two to six paragraphs) using its thesis as its main idea and presenting its supporting evidence. Allow each team to edit and improve its essay prior to submission.

Finally, offer a summary of the importance of using evidence to support a conclusion.

CHAPTER

10

Cooperative Learning, Democracy, and Multicultural Education

All of us together know more than any one of us alone.
Source Unknown

Cooperative Learning

Teachers generally have chosen to structure classrooms in a win-or-lose manner, where competition and individual effort are rewarded or punished. As shown in prior chapters, the working-class students and students of color systematically lose in this system. As a part of the response to the challenge of teaching in the multicultural classroom, some teachers have developed strategies whereby pairs and small groups of students work together, learn from each other, and master the material, while building respect, solidarity, and a sense of community. These strategies collectively are called *cooperative* or *collaborative learning*.

A conservative view of democratic education has students learning political concepts, skills, what is in the Constitution and the Bill of Rights, and students' rights. Often conservatives use this approach to urge values inculcation and character education. No significant evidence supports the conclusion that this approach works.

A more active approach is to consider that democratic education requires social education in the arts of democratic living. Classrooms are sites where students practice and learn skills of cooperation and working together. Cooperative learning is an important part of this approach to democratic education (Parker, 2009).

Cooperative learning strategies engage students from diverse cultures who may be alienated from the macroculture. Cooperative strategies are particularly valuable for language-minority students and students below grade level in language skills. This high-energy approach also has shown success with students across social classes whose interest in learning may have been dulled by rapid changes in society and an increasing

287

dependence on television. Teachers can no longer assume that the home has nurtured in the student positive attitudes toward school and toward working with others. Using the cooperative learning approach, we can teach students how to build positive relationships with other students and with adults.

A variety of teaching strategies exists to encourage social interaction and collaborative learning, including learning buddies, jigsaw study, literature response groups, reciprocal teaching, and cooperative group work. Practice and success in these activities develop what Gardner has termed *intrapersonal intelligence*, a highly useful perspective for students' social, political, and economic future (Gardner, 1993). Development of intrapersonal intelligence and collaborative skills empowers students, parents, and communities.

Collaborative learning strategies take advantage of the complex relationship dynamics that exist in all classrooms—teachers instructing students and students interacting with each other. Students learn more when they talk about a subject, explain an idea to other students, and even argue about an idea than when they hear a lecture or read a book. Instead of trying to suppress student-to-student interaction in the interest of "classroom order," teachers who use collaborative learning regard such interaction as an important learning resource, and they present strategies to capture this energy to support and strengthen learning. The total amount of teacher talk is reduced, and the amount of teacher-directed student-to-student interaction, and thus student learning, increases.

Teachers integrating computers and the Internet into their classrooms should particularly develop the cooperative skills of their students. Students learn better in the technology world when they work together. And, importantly, new leadership skills will emerge within these groups.

Cooperative learning provides both elementary and secondary teachers with strategies to teach positive social skills, such as listening, sharing, and working together. These lessons are particularly needed in depressed neighborhoods, where economic and social stresses combine to thwart student achievement. The process of improving group interaction is enormously interesting to young people, and they soon become engaged in creating a positive supporting classroom environment. They learn from one another.

Groupwork conducted within multicultural classes encourages students to exchange viewpoints, check their validity, and gradually engage in dialogue. It teaches students to work together and reduces prejudice in the classroom (Slavin, 1995). Groupwork can move the class away from seatwork and worksheets to cognitively demanding instruction. Well-planned collaborative learning also encourages students to take responsibility for their own education (Berman, 1999).

Ladson-Billings (1994a) argues that collaborative structures and team building are important elements used by effective teachers of African American students. She states the issue like this: "Culturally relevant teaching encourages students to learn collaboratively and expects them to teach each other and take responsibility for each other" (p. 70).

The teachers in her study found significant improvement in their students' conduct when they taught collaborative skills. Garcia (2001) similarly asserts that consistently effective teachers of Mexican American children organized so as to ensure small, collaborative academic activities requiring a high degree of heterogeneously grouped student-to-student social (and particularly linguistic) interaction.

Skilled teachers use cooperative groups to break down the effects of ability grouping and to establish high expectations for all. Cooperative strategies counter traditional tracking and ability-grouping strategies, which undercut student perceptions about equality of opportunity and democratic principles. Kagan (1986) cites evidence to suggest that cooperative learning can equalize achievement among students in subjects such as math and science, providing a needed step toward equal educational opportunity.

The use of cooperative learning results in improved academic achievement for many underachieving students. While cooperative strategies are valuable in all schools, they are particularly important in a multicultural environment because they produce high achievement levels for all, promote equal-status interaction among students, and teach students to work together to resolve problems (Johnson & Johnson, 1999; Slavin, 2001). Cooperative learning is a direct way to teach language and positive intergroup relations. Research indicates that when students are taught how to cooperate and are placed in teams, student friendship and respect across racial lines increase (Kagan, 1986).

The Tracking Debate

A sharp debate has developed around the nation over ability grouping and tracking. Recall that in Chapter 1 we defined *tracking* as a system wherein individuals are identified according to specified physiological, cultural, socioeconomic, or academic criteria and placed in academic course schedules (tracks) designed to fulfill selected educational prerequisites, develop a specific skill set, or prepare them for specific careers. See also "Tracking Female Students" in Chapter 5. Most multicultural education advocates oppose tracking. They see classes for the gifted and for low-track students as contributing to the problems of unequal access to the curriculum. Significant evidence supports this view (Oakes, 2005). Advocates of programs for the gifted and talented argue that heterogeneous classes prohibit "bright" students from seeking educational excellence. They, too, have substantial research to support their position (Darling-Hammond, 1995).

Although excellent work is being done by a minority of teachers to oppose tracking, most take ability grouping for granted. High school teachers accept that some students are college bound and others are not. Teachers often avoid low-track classes, and principals assign these classes to the newest faculty. Teachers in low-track classes find it difficult to establish positive, productive learning environments because many of the students recognize their low status and conform to the school's low expectations. Students exhibit defeatism, alienation, and resistance to academic work. Soon both teachers and students develop low expectations of these classes. There is more authoritarian teacher behavior and more student-to-student violence in these classes. In racially integrated schools, low-track classes have an overrepresentation of African American, Latino, and Native American students (Darling-Hammond, 1995).

Not only are students tracked, but schools and teachers—particularly new teachers—are tracked as well. Schools in low-income areas of cities often have fewer resources and fewer fully credentialed teachers than do schools in more affluent areas. Schools in low-income areas have more teachers instructing in a field other than their major (e.g., physical education majors teaching social studies). Meanwhile, affluent schools have only math majors instructing math classes and only science majors instructing science classes. Tracking occurs when schools considered difficult have eight classes of general English or math and only one class of honors or advanced English or math. Even bright, motivated students in such schools will not have access to a demanding curriculum. When these students graduate, they compete for access to universities with students from schools where most students took Advanced Placement history, math, and English (Darling-Hammond, 2001; Oakes & Saunders, 2007).

You must consider several important issues when developing a professional view on tracking and ability grouping. Substantial evidence indicates that students are frequently identified and placed into ability groups based on poor measures and inadequate placement decisions (Oakes, 2005). Oakes and others have demonstrated that race and social class strongly influence the placement of individuals. High-track programs are available in middle-class schools, whereas urban schools have a preponderance of low-track, remedial, and terminal programs. The placement process itself is unequal and unfair (Oakes & Rogers, 2006).

A major problem is that placement in low-track classes or low-ability groups is unnecessarily and inappropriately rigid. Students change and mature. Schools help students to learn. But rigid placement systems punish students for poorly informed or biased decisions made by students and faculty in prior years. The rigidity of ability grouping reduces the value of hard work (Sapon-Shevin, 1999). A fixed conception of ability and intelligence has long been abandoned by most serious researchers (Gardner, 1999).

Being placed in a low track contributes to the several attacks on self-esteem that devastate many students—particularly adolescents, girls, and students of color. Ability grouping, as presently practiced, frequently contributes to racial, ethnic, and class isolation. Lawsuits in Boston, San Francisco, and other cities have challenged school integration plans that guarantee access for African Americans and Latinos to prestigious high schools by limiting access for European American and Asian students (Guthrie & Brazil, 1999; Walsh, 1999).

If these criticisms of tracking are true, then what about the arguments of advocates for gifted and talented programs (Ford & Harris, 1999). Aren't bright students bored and held back in "regular" classes? Haven't magnet schools and programs for the "gifted" kept European American students in urban public schools when they would have otherwise fled? These arguments also have merit. Changing to heterogeneous classes will not, by itself, overcome the failure to motivate and interest students common in too many classrooms. Without other significant improvements in the quality of education, ending ability grouping might simply bore all students equally.

In real-world classrooms, the two positions on ability grouping should not be treated as only polar opposites. Concern for equal opportunity leads to the conclusion that students should be primarily taught in heterogeneous classes. Teachers can change their teaching strategies to encourage all students to learn. Cooperative learning strategies are some of the fundamental strategies for teaching in heterogeneous classes (Cohen & Lotan, 1997).

In a few subjects that are highly sequential, such as math, students can be grouped based on their demonstrated abilities. That is, some students can study math, while others study calculus. Some students can study Spanish 1, while others study Spanish 5. But these groupings are less harmful if they are not rigid. That is, while the students may be placed in a "gifted" class for math, they should be in heterogeneous classes for social studies, physical education, and other less sequential courses. Schools should offer advanced classes in art, music, and other subjects where students might also be "gifted." In addition, students with special needs sometimes require special services to gain access to the mainstream curriculum. For example, limited-English-proficient students might be separated for part of the day to give them increased opportunities to learn and practice English at their appropriate level. At other times, these students might be in a class that studies literature or some other appropriate subject in Spanish.

A change to a less-tracked curriculum requires teachers to adjust their strategies. Most important, teachers need to consider multiple definitions of intelligence (Gardner, 1999) and abandon current fixed and static views.

Language–Minority Students

Collaborative strategies are particularly helpful in a classroom where some students have limited English skills. Placing students in teams provides second-language learners with a significantly improved learning environment by dramatically increasing the number of student-to-student exchanges. Those learning a second language usually understand these exchanges better than they comprehend teacher-to-student talk. Dialogue among students provides context cues and opportunities for comprehension checking that are missing from most formal teacher presentations (Cummins, 1996). In Chapter 11, we present additional strategies for oral language development through collaborative learning.

Not only does groupwork stimulate the development of language skills, but also increases learning across all subject matters. A teacher's professional vocabulary and interests often create a gap between presented material and students' prior knowledge. This gap interferes with learning. The student-to-student exchanges common in cooperative learning help to close the gap by allowing students to discuss presented material using terms and contextual clues that are meaningful to them (Vygotsky, 1978).

As you know, traditional strategies of competition do encourage some students to work. Collaborative learning does not replace the competitive approach, but it does provide additional strategies to encourage the participation of students who may not flourish under individual, competitive practices. There is no evidence to show that time spent on cooperative interaction slows down academically talented students. These students actually learn more—not less—as they interact with the material in group discussions and explain difficult sections to others.

When students have practiced cooperative learning and have learned a few basic rules and roles, groupwork resolves many classroom management problems. For example, students can learn to work independently on clearly defined tasks. One student per team serves as a task monitor to assist the teacher in keeping students involved in their team project. The teacher serves as monitor, helper, and coach.

Teachers in the middle grades (grades 6 through 8) particularly benefit because they can spend less time trying to control the class and more time working with individuals. Well-run cooperative groups allow teachers the time and freedom to build the positive human relationships required for effective teaching.

Preparing a Class for Cooperative Learning

You should take four initial steps to prepare a class for cooperative learning:

1. Design the environment.
2. Select appropriate tasks.
3. Teach appropriate roles.
4. Encourage positive interdependence.

Designing the Environment

Students need to be *taught* to work together. Learning how to work in groups requires instruction and practice. To prepare for teamwork, teachers design practice sessions so students can learn new roles (such as checker and praiser) and new social skills. Long-range projects covering a week or two are appropriate only after students have developed skills of cooperation and processing.

For very young students and for students new to cooperation, instruction often begins with extended practice working in pairs. In these early stages of cooperative learning, select tasks students can complete within 5 to 10 minutes. Later combine pairs to create teams of four to six students, groups small enough so each student can participate. Assign one student per team as team recorder and have all teams document their activities.

Teachers design the classroom environment to encourage cooperation and learning. Chairs are moved, computer stations designed, partitions and tables selected, and materials placed so as to encourage student responsibility and cooperation.

Reorganize and rotate team membership every two to four weeks. In elementary school, form separate teams for different subjects so students do not think that the teams are ability groups. When language-minority students are in the class, place a bilingual student and an English language learner in a group together. The English language learner will gain English practice and comprehension. The bilingual student will gain academic status as well as practice in his/her home language.

Require frequent oral progress reports from each team. These reports encourage high expectations. Any member of the team can use the recorder's notes and report for the team. You may say, for example, "The person to the left of the recorder will make the report." Distributing the reporting function helps to keep the entire team responsible for quality work. Encourage and monitor student participation by regularly collecting and reviewing team notes.

Teaching students how to engage in cooperative learning takes time, and there are no shortcuts. A lecture on role behavior is no substitute for practice. You must define the roles, help students practice those roles, evaluate the practice, and then help students improve their role behavior. (See the information on direct instruction on page 247.) Some teachers may be reluctant to devote valuable class time to this training for groupwork, but time so used will result in time saved over the school year. Having students who have learned on-task behavior and know how to work in teams to pursue independent study projects will more than make up for the time spent in learning these skills.

Teachers have developed a variety of team-building exercises to begin instruction in cooperative learning. Guides to these exercises can be found in Kagan (1993) and in the "Teaching Strategies for Use with Your Students" section at the end of this chapter.

Selecting Appropriate Tasks

Collaborative assignments work best when they provide intrinsic and immediate rewards based on successful completion of appropriately challenging tasks. These tasks should require multiple skills and encourage students to take diverse viewpoints. Whenever possible, draw on students' personal experiences as subjects for study.

In the first month of cooperative learning, begin with small, quick, easy-to-evaluate tasks and projects that have clear ending points. Effective tasks for cooperative learning should involve conceptual thinking rather than a group search for a single right answer (see Figure 10.1). Tasks where students can share their own experiences and engage in creative problem solving also work well.

Figure 10.1 **Suggested Cooperative Tasks**

Primary Grades (Kindergarten Through Grade 2)

Sharing of feelings

Language practice

Upper Elementary Grades (Grades 3 Through 5)

Math problems

Language practice

Science projects

Reciprocal teaching

Middle Grades (Grades 6 Through 8)

Process writing

Language practice

Secondary Grades (Grades 9 Through 12)

Discussion of controversial issues

Process writing

Student governance

Social participation projects

Not all tasks are appropriate for group investigation. Groupwork lends itself to problem solving rather than to rote memorization of predetermined material. While you can use a group structure for memorizing the definitions of adverbs and nouns, it is more useful in helping students to edit their own writing. Groupwork is of marginal value in memorizing historical or geographical facts but very useful for teaching critical thinking in the course of a history or social science investigation. Groupwork is particularly valuable for process approaches to writing and to Internet work.

Teaching Appropriate Roles

You begin cooperative learning by teaching appropriate cooperative role behavior. The roles suggested in Figure 10.2 have proven useful in many classrooms.

The several tasks of group maintenance are too complex to assign to a single individual. Assigning multiple roles allows all students to learn and practice leadership skills. It works best to rotate role assignments within the group to ensure that each student acquires the skills necessary for each role.

Often, after a week or two of work on a project, the teacher needs to review and reestablish the roles. This is an ongoing process. When cooperative learning is not

Figure 10.2 **Suggested Roles for Cooperative Learning**

> **Checker:** This student checks for agreement in the group and makes certain all students understand the answers.
>
> **Praiser:** This student praises the students' efforts, ideas, and role behavior.
>
> **Recorder:** This student records ideas and decisions and shares the final product with the class.
>
> **Task Monitor:** This student keeps the group on the assigned task and monitors time.
>
> **Gatekeeper:** This student encourages all students to participate and keeps any one person from dominating.

working, it is usually because the roles or the goals are not clear. When you see groups not functioning well, it is time for some evaluation and practice of role behavior.

Science and math projects often involve handling materials and objects, and it is helpful to assign some additional roles to group members. The Finding Out/Descubrimiento Project uses a "gofer," a safety monitor, and a cleanup director (Cohen, 1986). The gofer has the task of getting all materials to the work area. Assigning this role discourages dozens of students from getting out of their seats to get materials. The safety monitor remains alert for sharp objects, spills, and other safety concerns. The cleanup director supervises and monitors the cleanup activities for all team members. Once established, such roles assist the teacher and reduce stress. Even within groups, assigning language buddies can assist the English language learner.

Encouraging Positive Interdependence

When you use cooperative learning, you seek to establish positive interdependence among students. Arrange tasks and evaluation so the group does better when it cooperates. The task of broken circles is a good example.

Students in a group are supplied with a series of parts to circles. Each group has all the parts necessary for all members to make complete circles. Group members are expected to assist their teammates in completing their circles. However, if a few students seek only their own success and ignore the needs of others, they will complete their circles using parts that their teammates need to complete theirs, thus preventing the group as a whole from completing the task.

Projects for which the entire group receives a common grade engender positive interdependence. Encourage teams to look for ways in which they can use to their advantage the artistic or mechanical aptitude or computer skills of apparent underachievers. Kagan (1993) describes ways teachers encourage positive interdependence by establishing a grading system in which bonus points go to the team that has the fewest members with low scores. He notes that having students help a teammate to review basic multiplication and division improves the teammate's score, the team score, and all students' math competence.

Traditionally, the grading systems and curricula of most schools have emphasized competition and the resultant sorting of students into winners and losers. Cooperative learning, and particularly group grading, counteracts these school folkways (Johnson & Johnson, 1999). Figure 10.3 lists some of the differences between cooperative and traditional learning groups.

Reciprocal teaching is a strategy that will help students to work in teams for reading, writing, and math. Teams regularly use collaborative strategies to improve members' reading and research skills. Each team member has the task of helping the others become more proficient. Students engage in dialogue and serve as monitors for each other's work (Carter, 1997).

Teamwork serves particularly well for social action projects in middle and high schools. The ideas and diversity of a two- to four-member student team bring originality, intellect, and creativity to bear on resolving real-life problems of classrooms, agencies, service organizations, and community groups. Going on to six-person teams requires even more skill. I would wait until the students have practiced teamwork for two to three months before proceeding with six-person teams. Teamwork skills developed in social action projects, like the development of critical thinking, prepare students for employment in the growing world of knowledge-based industries. Projects provide a bridge from the passive-receptive behavior common to students in teacher-centered classrooms to the active and responsible behavior required in the adult world of work.

The proliferation of computers and Internet access in classrooms offers opportunities to enhance collaborative work. Students usually perform better research by working together in teams on computers and can assist one another with technology problems. A collaborative team approach to Internet investigations encourages students to verbalize their thought processes. Student teams plan the research; some investigate on the Internet; some prepare documents with student-friendly software, look for photos, edit, proofread, design, and print.

Figure 10.3   Differences Between Traditional Groups and Cooperative Groups

Cooperative Learning Groups	Traditional Learning Groups
Positive interdependence	Little interdependence
Group accountability	Individual accountability
Heterogeneous	Homogeneous
Shared leadership	One appointed leader
Shared responsibility for each other	Responsibility only for self
Groups process their effectiveness	Little or no focus on group processes

Source: Adapted From *Circles of Learning* (p. 10), by D. W. Johnson, R. T. Johnson, E. J. Holubec, and P. Roy, 1984, Alexandria, VA: Association for Supervision and Curriculum Development.

Figure 10.4   Evaluation of Small-Group Work (I)

In addition to the task assigned, you should be learning to improve the processes of your groupwork. Please complete the questions below and then discuss your responses with your team.

How well is the group working toward completing the task?	Very Well	Not Well
Defining the task?		
Gathering information?		
Sharing information?		
Making a decision?		

What issues were discussed? _____

Was agreement reached on any issues? _____

Well-designed student projects can be improved and repeated year after year. Projects are worthwhile when all the students, not just a few, have a positive experience. Your role is to encourage and help the less assertive to participate and to learn.

Cooperative learning works best when the students engage in both reflection and evaluation. Student teams need time built into the process for thinking about their thinking. The teacher can guide this through stopping and asking questions of the team, such as "How well is this work going? What would make it better?" Another important process question is "What could we do to involve all the students on the team?"

Periodic evaluation of teamwork is critical. Teams should regularly monitor their processes and work on improving team skills. Figures 10.4 and 10.5 show sample evaluation sheets. After completing the evaluations, the quality of the groupwork becomes the subject of analysis and discussion.

A Classroom Example

Miguel Hernandez teaches eighth-grade social studies in Merced, California, a medium-sized city in California's Central Valley. He wants his students to think about

Figure 10.5   Evaluation of Small-Group Work (II)

How well are the members contributing to the group effort?	Very Well	Not Well
Helping each other?		
Sharing?		
Expressing different points of view?		
Seeking solutions to group problems?		
Encouraging each other?		

the world of work and their own future job prospects, to recognize the advantages of staying in school, and to improve their writing skills.

Miguel initiates the project by first discussing these issues and sharing a short auto-biographical paper he wrote on schooling and his own job. He encourages students to comment on the paper and to critically evaluate its ideas.

Miguel directs students to move into their prearranged small groups. Each group spends about eight minutes reacting to Miguel's paper and recording suggestions for improvement. Then Miguel refocuses the discussion. He tells each group to brainstorm ideas and issues the members could use in writing their own papers. Each group delegates a recorder to write down all of the ideas. This brainstorming might last 10 to 15 minutes. Each team member makes a copy of the ideas from the recorder.

After brainstorming, group members write a draft of an outline for their individual papers. Each student must record three to five ideas. Students are allowed to share and discuss their ideas during this time. If students have difficulty, the team helps them to draft their initial ideas. Miguel monitors progress during this time, visiting each group and offering his assistance, if needed.

Once rough outlines are done, each student writes an opening paragraph based on the outline. Paragraphs are then revised to improve spelling and sentence structure.

Back in their groups, team members read their opening paragraphs aloud. This is called a *read-around*. The other team members comment and make helpful suggestions. They are encouraged to offer ideas on content, clarity, and style. Team members may also make "me, too" comments to affirm a writer's themes. Team members suggest additional ideas that might illustrate or support the themes. The writer takes notes and considers the teammates' ideas.

After all opening paragraphs have been discussed in the teams, each writer prepares an initial draft of the paper. Usually, the drafts are short—one to two pages. Writers prepare their draft for further discussion by correcting spelling and sentences. If a photocopier is available, each author makes four copies of the paper.

The team now takes the time to read each paper and to make marginal notes. Members discuss each paper while the author takes notes, focusing on its main ideas, clarity of expression, and communication. At times, Miguel assigns tasks such as having one student provide feedback on sentences or paragraphs, while another provides feedback on clarity.

At this point, Miguel groups the writers into pairs to rewrite, proofread, and edit a final copy of each paper. Once that is done, the papers are "published" on a computer (you could use a copying machine). Finally, Miguel reads the papers, grades them, and confers with each student on how he or she is developing as a writer. Miguel's strategy for conducting a cooperative learning writing project is shown in Figure 10.6 in outline form.

After students complete the project, Miguel further guides them in processing the experience and in selecting cooperative learning skills for future development.

Confronting Racism and Sexism Through Equal-Status Interaction

Cooperative learning helps teachers to deal with the societal problems of racism and sexism. It provides excellent strategies for directly working against different forms of prejudice.

Figure 10.6 Outline for Cooperative Learning Writing Project in Miguel Hernandez's Class

1. Brainstorm on themes	(Small group, 2–4 students)
2. Build an outline	(Cooperative)
3. Write first draft	(Individual)
4. Read-around	(Small group, 2–4 students)
5. Critique draft	(Small group, 2–4 students)
6. Redraft	(Individual)
7. Edit	(Pairs—writer and team member)
8. Rewrite	(Individual)
9. Second read-around	(Cooperative)
10. Edit or rewrite	(Individual)
11. Publish/print	(Cooperative)
12. Distribute	(Cooperative)

Children Learn Prejudice

In a society such as ours, where racial, sexual, and homophobic ideologies contend with more liberal and humanistic philosophies, prejudice is easy to learn. Children learn prejudice, often at an early age, from their parents and peers.

For students from stressed and disrupted families, where safety and security are often missing, misinformation and prejudice are often projected onto groups that serve as convenient targets to blame for problems in the family, the neighborhood, or the economy. In other families, the burden of learned racism is passed down from generation to generation.

Teaching students positive human relations helps to reduce prejudice by providing the support and self-esteem they need. Teachers must themselves provide a consistent model of behavior that respects the diverse cultures and abilities in the classroom. Your modeling will contend against other examples in society. You can bring up these issues by presenting accurate information, rather than stereotypes, about all cultural groups. The empowerment strategies described in Chapter 7 reduce prejudice by moving the potential victim out of the position of low status or subjugation. When students achieve equality, when they work in equal-status groups, it is very difficult for oppressors to maintain their prejudices except by the most distorted logic.

Cooperation, interdependence, and mutual respect are central goals of the multicultural curriculum. You should plan for and work toward these goals instead of only hoping that they will emerge in your classroom. Gordon Allport, in his classic work *The Nature of Prejudice* (1979), says, "Prejudice (unless deeply rooted in the character structure of the individual) may be reduced by equal status contact between majority and minority group members in pursuit of common goals" (p. 281).

Cooperative learning that includes equal-status interaction strategies works against prejudice by providing students with regular experiences of mutual support, dependence, and caring. You consciously plan the control of status in your class. To achieve equal-status interaction, carefully teach the roles of group behavior (see the preceding section). Select group members and integrate each group to the degree possible by race, ethnicity, gender, observed talents, languages, and perceived ability. Once learned, rotate role positions so that all students have an important function in helping the group achieve its common goals.

A substantial body of research shows that cooperative learning reduces prejudiced behavior in the classroom when teachers use planned interventions to control for social status. The effects of these cooperative efforts are strong and long lasting (Slavin, 2001). Few, if any, other strategies have as strong a claim to prejudice reduction, although combinations of strategies can promote school reform (Levine & Lezotte, 2001).

Students who initially do not perform well or who lack academic or cooperation skills are given extra instruction and assistance rather than criticism and avoidance. Teachers consciously plan to place students who might be low status in high-status positions for group projects and assist them in performing there. Try to design cooperative groups in ways that ensure the distribution of high status to all, particularly to those who might otherwise be left out.

One way to achieve this status improvement is to place most of the dominant talkers in one group. Quickly, you will find that leadership emerges in the other groups. Encourage and support these new leaders. Further, evaluate and consistently improve groupwork. Expect students to function well. This activity requires caring for and supporting all group members (Cohen, Lotan, & Whitcomb, 1992).

All of Us Together Know More than Any One of Us Alone Consistent planning of role-playing, use of simulation games, and rotation of roles within cooperative learning, along with planning of status interventions, will significantly reduce the stereotyping, prejudice, and social distance among students in your class.

Students with strong acquired prejudices may resist working cooperatively in groups, but you should exercise leadership and insist on positive, democratic behavior in your classroom and in the school. Do not permit prejudices brought from outside to structure your classroom interaction. If some students resist even more, you may want to use coaching (see Chapter 8) to encourage them to behave cooperatively and respectfully. The successful activities of cooperative groups in the classroom teach democratic behavior and attitudes.

Certain cooperative learning programs have developed a sophisticated approach to equal-status interaction among ethnic groups and between genders. Through careful planning and monitoring, students participate in equal-status role relationships rather than hierarchical or oppressive relationships. Prejudices tend to be reduced when students working cooperatively succeed at a mutual task (Cohen, 1986).

One of these cooperative learning programs was developed by Elizabeth Cohen, Ed DeAvila, and their associates at Stanford University. Called Finding Out/ Descubrimiento, this bilingual math/science curriculum project combines curricula, teaching strategies, and evaluations to effectively establish equal-status interaction. It provides numerous insights into critical thinking, classroom management, and group processes (DeAvila, 1987).

By rotating students through roles, all students practice and develop the skills of leading and assisting others. Students learn to participate with and depend on students from diverse language, ethnic, and cultural backgrounds. The teacher designs tasks so students must turn to all of their peers, not just the ones they may feel most comfortable with.

Well-planned cooperative learning encourages students to use the multiple talents in the group. Some cooperative learning tasks may require a good artist, some a person with advanced computer skills, some a good negotiator, and others a bilingual advocate. Cooperative projects demonstrate the slogan "All of us together know more than any one of us apart."

If you are teaching in a class with two to six (or more) children with limited English skills, design role relationships that place bilingual children in roles as experts. For example, bilingual children could serve as translators for their group, translating from English to the target languages and from those languages to English, allowing all students to learn. Bilingual children gain status by using two languages to communicate, while students learning English in the group are assisted in comprehending and participating in group tasks. Using bilingual translators in cooperative groups creates a win–win situation for students and allows you to continue teaching.

Most countries other than the United States use the metric system, and many immigrant children can excel in tasks related to metric measurement. You can enlist the assistance of immigrant children as experts when teaching this system. English-dominant students on a team reciprocate by helping these students with their English.

During the Civil Rights Movement (1954–1968), young people working together to solve problems of segregation and injustice learned to believe in their own worth and to make demands on the government for redress of grievances (Cass, 2002). Today, students from low-income areas and students of color seldom encounter opportunities to work together successfully for positive, constructive purposes. Teamwork in schools that focuses on social service and participation tasks provides the instruction in morals and values necessary to extend our democracy to include students from low-income families and ethnic minorities in public participation rather than excluding them. Teamwork also involves students in social issues vital to their own future by helping them to learn to respect diversity of skills, talents, and perspectives and the values essential to community building.

Cooperative learning empowers both teachers and students. Students learn problem-solving strategies and reflection. Student teams identify problems, draft solutions, consider the possible outcomes of each proposed solution, choose and implement a solution, and then work to overcome barriers. Teachers are empowered by having 6 or more task masters or students guiding teams to stay on task. Teams working toward problem resolution provide excellent preparation for participation in a democratic society and development of a civic culture.

Classroom Management

Teaching cooperative learning in an increasingly self-centered, individualistic, and competitive society shaped by the popular culture is difficult. Many children are not prepared to cooperate. You must teach the skills of cooperation and the attitudes supporting cooperation. You will need to use the classroom management strategies described in Chapter 8 to teach and promote cooperation.

Two groups of students are particularly resistant to adopting collaborative learning strategies: those who consistently win in the competitive classroom and those who have mastered the art of avoiding teacher attention and scrutiny. You must use a balance of cooperative and individualized learning to provide both competitive and cooperative students with an environment where they can succeed.

When a small number of students fail at cooperation, carefully reteach the skills and roles of cooperative learning. Teaching and insisting on role behavior sometimes need to be done assertively, especially in the early stages of learning cooperation. Later, once the groups are functioning well, new students can receive orientation and skill training from other students in the group (Johnson & Johnson, 1999).

You, the teacher, should address major problems of management, alienation, or non-participation by a few students, not assign them to the group. When one student refuses to work, it frustrates other group members. The task of correcting student behavior is potentially very divisive to the group, particularly when students have little or no experience in conflict resolution. They may resort to nagging, sarcasm, and other brutal and severe strategies. After several weeks of cooperative learning, these problems will decrease as groupwork becomes rewarding and students learn to prefer working together.

Heterogeneous grouping works best for most collaborative learning. After practicing roles, structure the teams to maximize integration of ethnic, gender, class, and perceived ability levels. When cooperative work is initiated prior to second grade, interethnic tensions are quickly reduced. Interethnic cooperation may take time with older children. For lessons on these issues, see *www.teachingtolerance.org*.

In communities where racial conflict is significant, weeks of student preparation and extended social skill practice will enhance the success of cooperative groups. When tensions are high, students need clear goals and rules of conduct for working together. These goals should be established and maintained throughout the school. Students need to practice social skills as a part of preparation for collaborative work. Team-building activities can contribute to the creation of an equal-status, integrated environment. Systematic development of cooperative learning in the classroom will reduce ethnic conflict and divisions in class and contribute to reducing violence in the school.

Cooperative learning produces a change in classroom management. The noise level often increases in classrooms using groupwork. Teachers and administrators learn to distinguish between productive, on-task noise and idle chatter. As students develop increasing skills in cooperation, your role changes from one of struggling for control to one of giving direction and guidance. You will become more involved in initiating, coaching, and encouraging, plus insisting on reflection and processing, and less involved in delivering information. You will spend more time establishing the cooperative environment and designing tasks for it and less time criticizing students for their behavior. Initially, designing appropriate tasks takes a great deal of time and ingenuity. Fortunately, once designed, the tasks are useful year after year. You will gain time, ideas, and support by working with other teachers—cooperating—in project design.

Summary

Schools and teachers need additional strategies to respond to the growing diversity of U.S. society and the growing alienation of some students. The recent development of collaborative and cooperative teaching strategies provides a direct and interesting approach to democratic, multicultural education. Cooperative learning empowers students and teaches self-confidence as well as a sense of responsibility for the welfare of others. It also teaches students to listen, to share, and to advocate for their own interests. Cooperative learning strategies change the relationship between teacher and student to promote dialogue and a sharing community in the classroom.

Questions over the Chapter

1. What are some skills for kindergarten through grade 3 that are taught through collaborative learning?
2. Define *tracking*. Are there examples of tracking in your school?
3. What are the results of tracking?
4. Give examples of groupings that are not tracked.
5. Why do many teachers assume that tracking is beneficial?
6. How can cooperative learning provide an alternative to tracking?

Activities for Further Study of Cooperative Learning

1. Teach the cooperative skills lessons presented in this chapter to your students. Develop lesson plans for your class using cooperative strategies.
2. After teaching cooperative skills to your students, periodically assess their use of cooperation (see Figures 10.4 and 10.5) and identify skills you need to reteach.
3. Use coaching sessions to teach the skills of cooperation to a group of students in your class who will serve as assistants and tutors for language-minority students.
4. Investigate and use the strategies for assigning status within cooperative learning described by Cohen and Lotan (1997).

Teaching Strategies for Use with Your Students

Sample Objectives for Cooperative Learning Lessons

Students will

1. Work cooperatively in a group.
2. Share materials with others.
3. Stay on the subject while working in the group.
4. Listen to other members of the group.
5. Gather information by listening to others.
6. Contribute ideas to others in the group.

7. Accurately report on the group's progress.
8. Assist other members of the group.
9. Serve in a specific role (for example, checker, task monitor).
10. Contribute to improving the process of the group.
11. Select a skill for the group to work on next.
12. Evaluate the effectiveness of the group.
13. Plan and practice group improvement.

Sample Lesson Plans for Cooperative Learning

Lessons in cooperative learning teach values, skills, content, and critical thinking, while using cooperative strategies. The following lessons focus only on the cooperative strategies. You should add content, values, and skills to these preliminary lessons.

Sample Lesson Plan for Grades 1 Through 3
Students will

1. Listen to others.
2. Work in a group (or pairs).
3. Get to know other students in the class.

Have students line up based on height (from shortest to tallest). Other variables for lineups might include number of brothers and sisters and birth dates. Once lined up, the person at one end steps forward and walks to the opposite end. The persons second from the end will follow in a line.

Each student is now facing a partner. Designate which line of students should share their ideas first. Select some easy-to-answer question, such as "What is your favorite ice cream/food/television show/sport/game?" or "What do you like to do after school?"

Students in the first line share their responses to your question. Then students in the second line share their responses to the same question. Have students return to their seats and pose to them sample discussion questions such as these: "What is one thing you learned about your classmate?" and "What did you do to show you were a good listener?" Praise students who exhibit specific examples of positive social and academic skills during the activity.

Sample Lesson Plan for Grades 4 Through 8
Students will

1. Work cooperatively in a group.
2. Stay on the subject while working in a group.
3. Practice specific role behavior (for example, checker, task monitor).
4. Contribute to improving the group's functioning.

Present the specific roles shown in Figure 10.2. Describe and discuss each role.

Provide the task. Each group will discuss cooperation. Each group should make a list of the advantages and disadvantages of cooperation. The assigned persons will practice their roles within each group.

After an eight-minute work session, each group reports on their list. Each member of the group gives one evaluative remark to the checker. The group plans to improve the practice of working as a team. Rotate the roles one person to the right, so that each group member has a new role to practice.

The group discusses improved group functioning, with each student practicing the new role. Provide an assessment system in advance. Have the students evaluate how well the group members are sharing opinions and how well they are respecting the points of view of others.

Evaluate the discussion. Then summarize the skills practiced this day. Use these skills with discussions again the next day.

Sample Lesson Plan for Grades 9 Through 12
Students will

1. Work cooperatively in a group.
2. Define the task prior to beginning work.
3. Consider the viewpoints of others.
4. Give feedback to each other.
5. Decide to reduce the name-calling in class.

Divide the class into small groups and assign appropriate roles. Instruct students on the importance of clearly defining the task prior to initiating group discussion.

Provide the task. Each group is to decide on three suggestions for reducing the use of derogatory names in class. In a small-group discussion, each group member should suggest ideas.

Each person should practice his or her assigned role. Have the reporter from each group report on the group's ideas. Record the ideas on the chalkboard. Later students can make charts of these ideas for posting in the class.

Select the three to five most common or most interesting suggestions. Assign two groups this task: Describe the positive and negative consequences of these suggestions.

Assign two other groups this task: List the influences that will help students follow or prevent them from following these suggestions.

Have the recorder in each group report for the group.

Have the groups evaluate their work, using a form like those shown in Figures 10.4 and 10.5.

As the teacher, you should comment on positive and helpful behavior observed while the groups were working. Remind students of the importance of having a clear definition of the task prior to beginning work.

11 Teaching Language-Minority Populations

with Edmund W. Lee

There is no equality of treatment merely by providing students with the same
facilities, textbooks, teachers, and curriculum; for students who do not
understand English are effectively foreclosed from any meaningful education.

Lau v. Nichols, 1974

As the student population in the United States becomes increasingly diverse, more and
more teachers find themselves teaching students who speak a language other than
English.

In the 2003–2004 school year, English language learner (ELL) services were
provided to 3.8 million students (11 percent of all students). California and Texas had
the largest reported number of students receiving ELL services. In California, there
were 1.6 million students (26 percent of all students) who received ELL services; and
in Texas, there were 0.7 million students (16 percent of all students) who received ELL
services (NCES, 2006). What should you as a teacher do when you have students in
your class who do not speak English as their first language?

This chapter will provide background information for teachers working with language-
minority students.

Language-Minority Students in the Schools

In periodic waves in the 1980s and 1990s, immigration and immigrants became a
focus of concern in the nation and in our schools. Worldwide economic restructuring, increased ease of transportation, and changes in U.S. immigration law produced

major increases in immigration to the United States. Whereas in the 1970s the United States received some 400,000 immigrants per year, by 1997 that figure had increased to more than 900,000 per year. Even though the number of immigrants has increased significantly, current immigration is proportionally less than European immigration of the late 19th century. In 1910, immigrants made up 15 percent of the national population, whereas today they make up only 11.7 percent (U.S. Bureau of the Census, 2004).

Schools and employment are the entrance points into our society for many new immigrants. Some immigrants bring families with them. Children born here of immigrant parents are immediately citizens of the United States and are eligible for all school services. Recent immigrant populations, particularly Latino and Asian, are young people and usually have a higher number of children entering school than do U.S.-born European Americans (Fix & Passel, 1994). Each year thousands of new immigrant children enter school speaking a home language other than English.

During the 2003–2004 school year, close to 4 million limited-English-proficient (LEP) students were enrolled in the public schools of this nation, a number that doubled in the last decade. California and Texas had the largest reported numbers of students receiving English language instruction. In California, there were 1.6 million students (26 percent of all students) who received English language instruction; in Texas, there were 0.7 million students (16 percent of all students) who received such instruction (Sable & Hill, 2006).

Language representation of students was as follows: 54.4 percent Spanish, 8.8 percent French, 7.3 percent Chinese, 6.5 percent Vietnamese, 2.5 percent Native American languages, 1.7 percent Cambodian, 1.6 percent Pilipino/Tagalog, 1.5 percent Hmong, 1.3 percent Korean, and 14.5 percent other (Pérez, 1998).

For almost 100 years, schools served as the primary vehicle to "Americanize" immigrants. They taught the children of immigrants to speak English. From the 1870s until the 1940s, many—even most—immigrants failed in school and left school prior to eighth grade (Rothstein, 1998). As in any industrializing economy, there were jobs for unskilled labor. Today, the rapid change toward a technology-based economy has eliminated many of these jobs and lowered the wage scale for unskilled labor. School dropouts no longer have access to well-paying industrial jobs and economic opportunity. Schools must now prepare all students, including those who are learning English as a second language, for entrance into the new, high-technology economy.

Immigrant and other students whose first language is not English are classified as language-minority students as compared to students whose native language is English. Language-minority students include not only those students born in non-English-speaking countries but also the first-generation, and possibly second-generation, children born in the United States to immigrant parents.

Within the language-minority population, two distinct subpopulations can be identified on the basis of English proficiency. The fluent-English-proficient (FEP) student population is represented by students who, when assessed, demonstrate the oral and literacy skills in English necessary to succeed in school without specialized instructional programs such as bilingual instruction or English language development. Students who cannot demonstrate adequate oral and literacy skills in English are identified as limited

English proficient (LEP). These students clearly need specialized and differentiated instruction to promote acquisition of English and mastery of subject-matter content. More recently, the terms *English learner (EL)* and *English language learner (ELL)* have been applied to students with limited English proficiency.

All language-minority students have unique educational needs that, when met, result in their successful integration into the rapidly changing economy. These students learn the structure and rules of the dominant culture—particularly the English language—primarily in school. Schools in major cities and certain states (New York, Florida, Illinois, Massachusetts, California, and Texas) are heavily affected by the rapid growth of the English language learner student population. The arrival of large numbers of English language learners has required the addition of English language development (ELD) programs and the preparation of ELD teachers in school districts throughout the nation (Goldenberg, 2008).

Language-minority students bring extensive language and cultural skills to our classrooms. They arrive at school with the knowledge and wisdom of many cultures. They and their families have learned to survive in many lands. Classrooms with language-minority students are filled with knowledge about societies, customs, and languages that English-speaking students need to study. Bilingualism, particularly literate bilingualism, provides these students with a distinct advantage in the emerging global marketplace.

Linguistic research indicates that bilingual instruction and sheltered English programs (modified instruction that is comprehensible to English learners) offer the best ways to encourage students toward academic success and employment (Collier, 1995; Krashen & McField, 2005; Ramirez, Yuen, & Ramey, 1991). However, none of the states with large concentrations of English learners has an adequate number of bilingual teachers to serve the rapidly growing student populations. And several states and districts have followed the lead of California in banning or severely limiting bilingual education.

Each immigrant group, each language group, has its own culture and experiences. Language, experiences, traditions, and cultures all vary dramatically. Even within a cultural group, children who have spent most of their lives in the United States have experiences substantially different from those of recent immigrant students (see Figure 11.1).

We have learned through the experiences of numerous students and educators that a submersion program (which uses a sink-or-swim approach) can be a very painful and unsuccessful process for learning English and for acquiring academic material (Crawford, 1999). Those who were submersed in the pool of English often failed later in school.

Adaljiza Sosa Riddle, a retired professor of political science at the University of California at Davis, tells what the sink-or-swim programs were like for her as a young child:

> I speak as a child of immigrants who attended a public school system in southern California in the 1940s–1950s prior to the development of bilingual programs. I, along with 25–30 other poor children of Mexican immigrants, entered kindergarten speaking only Spanish. We did not know how to read or write anything. We learned a second language by coercion, fear, intimidation, punishment, shame, and the need to survive. There was no pleasure in anything

Figure 11.1 Success Stories

Miguel Perez

After fleeing with his mother from the war in El Salvador, Miguel Perez entered the United States illegally. He struggled for years to learn English and to stay in this country. Soon after he came to the United States, his mother died. Once he was even ordered deported by the Immigration and Naturalization Service (INS). However, in 1992, he graduated as valedictorian of his class from California State University—Dominguez Hills. He won his case with the INS and received permanent resident status. When eligible, he wants to become a U.S. citizen.

Moa Vang

At age nine, Moa and his family walked three weeks to flee the invasion of their village in Laos. Half of his family died en route to the refugee camps in Thailand. After four years in the camps, Moa and one brother were allowed to come to the United States. A sponsor took him in and helped him to succeed in school. As a refugee, he did not have the fear of deportation experienced by Miguel. Now 34, Moa has spent more than a decade getting permission for other family members to immigrate. The war, the refugee camps, and the difficulty of immigration and adjustment have devastated his family and much of his community. After working for three years as a teacher assistant, Moa began the long, difficult task of becoming a teacher.

Ann Ngo Tran

As a young girl, Ann remembers life in Vietnam. Then she and her family had to flee. Because her father was in the military, they were able to fly out of Saigon. Many members of her family were left behind. When she arrived in Portland, Oregon, Ann spoke only a few words of English, but she was able to attend school and struggled to learn English. The stresses of migration and learning to live in this country have produced great divisions in her family. One brother is a gang member. But Ann is a respectful daughter. She has watched her generation achieve and has watched her parents' generation struggle with their loss. She has now graduated from college and has become a bilingual teacher, hoping to assist other immigrant students with their difficult transitions.

Note: The descriptions of Moa and Ann are composites, drawn from the experiences of several students in the bilingual program at California State University—Sacramento.

we did in school. Even making valentines was a dreaded activity. It seemed to us as if teachers stayed up late to devise new means to torture us. It was no wonder that only half of my classmates finished high school and none went to college, even when they were clearly capable.

Our acquisition of English was uneven within each class, and even within each family. Our ability to learn Spanish beyond the level of a 5-year-old was completely thwarted. I was lucky because my parents and my oldest sister had taught themselves to read and write Spanish and they in turn taught me as best they could. This was very difficult in a family of nine children and extreme poverty. The loss of talent was indeed great, unhealthy, and destructive. I don't praise myself for surviving that. Instead, I am brought to tears remembering all those years. (Personal communication, May 18, 1998)

History of Bilingualism in the United States

Bilingualism has a long history in our nation of immigrants. Forms of bilingual education were in common use in the early years of the nation. The framers of the Constitution considered guaranteeing German language rights. Spanish language rights were implied in the Treaty of Guadalupe Hidalgo (signed in 1848), by which the United States acquired what is now the Southwest from Mexico, and were explicit in California's and New Mexico's first state constitutions (Crawford, 1999).

From 1880 to 1910, the United States experienced massive migration from Europe and Mexico. In response, fraternal and social organizations were formed to limit immigration and to insist on the dominance of English. During World War I, government-sponsored anti-German pressures led to the cancellation of German language schools, and several states passed laws restricting schools to using English only. Public schools were charged with promoting the rapid assimilation of immigrants and encouraging the use of the "American" language (Crawford, 1999).

Policies to eliminate ethnic enclaves and use of foreign languages were advocated as good for students. Crude and inaccurate racial theories developed, based on early Darwinism, to argue for the superiority of Anglo Saxon culture against those of the Greeks, Slavs, Italians, Mexicans, and other immigrants (Crawford, 1999; Omi & Winant, 1986). A legend began circulating that U.S. schools served as the vehicle for immigrant opportunity, in spite of significant evidence to the contrary (Aronowitz, 1973; Boyer & Morais, 1955; Colin, 1975; Davis, 1986). In this period, leaving school early was not viewed as a crisis; a young person could get a job in industry with little formal schooling or preparation.

In a diverse, fragmented, and, at times, divisive society, conservative business groups advocated for language uniformity. Crawford (1999) notes that Henry Ford made attendance at Americanization classes mandatory for foreign-born workers. If immigrants used Polish, Yiddish, or Finnish to organize radical unions, conservatives used their control of government to promote "Americanism" and the enforcement of language uniformity. Insistence on speaking English was an important mechanism for weakening ethnic group loyalty and group support for labor unions. Speaking English became the approved way for immigrants to "Americanize" their families. Bilingual schools (most often in German) were eliminated (Crawford, 1999; Davis, 1986).

From the 1880s until the 1950s, the Bureau of Indian Affairs operated boarding schools and applied harsh measures to promote English over tribal languages (Crawford, 1999).

English language domination became closely connected with "Americanism" in popular culture. Only the competition with the Soviets in the 1950s during the Cold War finally called into question these English-only and English-first policies. In 1959, a rebel army led by Fidel Castro wrested control of Cuba from the U.S.-backed Batista government. The new Castro government turned to the Soviet Union for support and adopted a Soviet-style authoritarian government. More than 100,000 Cubans fled to the United States. The U.S. government rushed to cover the substantial resettlement costs of these anticommunist Cuban refugees and their families and made provision for temporary bilingual schools in Florida (Crawford, 1999).

In the same era as the Cuban exodus, the Civil Rights Movement (1954–1968) in the United States emphasized education reform as a strategy to gain equal economic opportunity for minorities. A Mexican American political movement and an emerging Chicano student movement in the Southwest (1958–1980) demanded bilingual education programs to overcome the education failures of Spanish-speaking children (U.S. Commission on Civil Rights, 1975; see also Chapter 3). Legislators were convinced to include provisions prohibiting the denial of state services and voting rights on the basis of national origin in the 1964 Civil Rights Act. On January 2, 1968, President Lyndon Johnson—a former teacher of Mexican American children in Texas—signed the Bilingual Education Act which was the first federal commitment to assisting language minority students (Crawford, 2004).

In 1974, the U.S. Supreme Court ruled in *Lau v. Nichols* that the San Francisco School District had violated the 1964 Civil Rights Act. The Court upheld guidelines established by the Office for Civil Rights in the U.S. Department of Health, Education, and Welfare, which stipulated the following: "Where inability to speak and understand the English language excludes national origin-minority group children from effective participation in the educational program offered by a school district, the district must take affirmative steps to rectify the language deficiency in order to open its instructional program to these students" (35 Fed. Reg. 11595 (1970)).

The *Lau* decision thus established the principle that children have a right to instruction that they can understand in the public schools and that school districts must proactively develop remedies to overcome existing inequalities of opportunity. It did not require school districts to implement any specific remedy, such as bilingual education. Instead, bilingual education was cited as one of several available legal options.

Two other federal court decisions, *Castañeda v. Pickard* (1981) and *Keyes v. School District #1* (1983), are significant because they formulated a three-part test to determine a school district's compliance with the Civil Rights Act of 1964 and the Equal Educational Opportunities Act of 1974. The three test components include theory, practice, and results:

- **Test #1:** Is the school district providing an instructional program for English learners that is based on sound educational theory?
- **Test #2:** Is the school actually implementing its program for English learners with the instructional practices, resources, and personnel necessary to make the theory work?
- **Test #3:** Has the school collected and analyzed program data in order to eliminate those programs that have failed to yield positive results? (Crawford, 2004)

The protections given to English learners through federal law helped to establish bilingual education laws and programs in states with high concentrations of students who did not speak English. Bilingual education programs were designed to use the child's native language in order to learn English and to promote mastery of basic subjects. However, those opposed to bilingual education see the use of a student's home language as a threat to English and have organized campaigns to ban bilingual education in public schools. California's experience provides an example of the ongoing controversy over bilingual education.

English Learners in California

Individual states responded to the *Lau* decision by enacting laws to guide school districts in providing special programs for LEP students. By 1976, California had one of the strongest bilingual education laws in the nation.

The 1976 bilingual education law required schools to establish bilingual programs taught by licensed bilingual teachers whenever 10 or more LEP students of the same language group enrolled in a grade. However, the law included a 10-year authorization, and in 1986, it expired. Although a bill to reauthorize the law passed both houses of the legislature, it was vetoed by the Republican governor. Subsequent revisions to the bill were passed through the legislature four times, only to be vetoed each time by a governor.

The immigration waves of the 1970s through 1990's resulting in part from wars and civil unrest in Indochina, Central America, and Eastern Europe, significantly increased the diversity of the state's student population. California schools enrolled 6.2 million K–12 students during the 2006–2007 school year. Of this population, 2.7 million students (40 percent) were identified as language-minority students, representing more than 90 language groups. Some 1.1 million students were identified as FEP, and over 1.5 million (25 percent of the total school population) were identified as English learners. Although Spanish speaking–background students constitute the largest language group in the state, significant numbers of students speaking Vietnamese, Pilipino, Cantonese, Hmong, Korean, Mandarin, Punjabi, Arabic, and Armenian are also represented (California Department of Education, 2008).

Attacks on Bilingual Education

Even though bilingual education has provided a positive and supportive environment for the academic and social growth of many language-minority students, politically motivated opposition to bilingual education has prevailed in most states. Conservative forces mobilized throughout the nation in the 1980s and 1990s to attack taxes, schools, and bilingual education. Since the 1990s, these same groups have frequently attacked multicultural education as divisive to national unity. Some English speakers are offended that immigrant children are taught in their native tongue for part of the day. Political leaders argue that bilingualism handicaps children.

For example, Porter (1998) argues, "Bilingual education is a classic example of an experiment that was begun with the best of humanitarian intentions, but has turned out to be terribly wrongheaded. . . . The accumulated research of the past thirty years reveals almost no justification for teaching children in their native languages to help them learn either English or other subjects (pp. 28–29).

As in the debates on affirmative action, conservatives have created the deception that minorities are gaining an advantage, that bilingual education is discrimination against

Table 11.1   California Voting Patterns on Proposition 227 by Ethnicity, 1998

	Yes	No
European American	67%	33%
Latino	37%	63%
Asian[1]	57%	43%
African American	48%	52%

[1]The Asian vote, less than 4 percent of the total, is widely diverse, ranging from Chinese Americans to Vietnamese Americans. Useful conclusions on voting cannot be drawn from this limited sample. *Los Angeles Times*. June 5, 1998.

European Americans (Guinier, 2002; Krashen, 2002b). The attacks on bilingualism continue, with voters in several states voting for anti–bilingual education measures.

After a volatile political campaign, California's electorate (then 69 percent European) responded to crises in the state's educational system by adopting Proposition 227, the so-called English for the Children initiative, drafted by English only advocate Ron Unz. Latinos made up 29.4 percent of the state's population and more than 36 percent of its school-age children but only 12 percent of its voters. Table 11.1 shows the voting results for Proposition 227 by ethnic group, drawn from exit polls conducted at the time by the *Los Angeles Times*.

The resulting new law dramatically altered the way in which English is taught in California schools. Proposition 227 effectively abolished bilingual education for immigrant children (whose parents are often not citizens and cannot vote) by making the use of other languages for instruction illegal except under special circumstances. It mandated intensive 10-month "sheltered English immersion" programs as the instructional strategy, except in very limited circumstances where a waiver of the bilingual education ban might be granted. As a result, in 2000 less than 10 percent of the English language learners in California were receiving bilingual education (Gandara et al., 2004). Since 1998, similar initiatives have passed in Arizona and Massachusetts but have been defeated in Colorado.

The public debate on bilingual education often deals with a false dichotomy, that of choosing either English or the home language. All immigrant parents want their children to learn English. Both languages are valuable. Bilingual advocates argue that the nation gains from the language resources of its immigrant communities, while antibilingual advocates stress the need for national cohesion through one language.

In January 2002, Title VII of the Elementary and Secondary Education Act, also known as the Bilingual Education Act, was allowed to expire. It was eliminated as a part larger "school reform" effort President Bush's No Child Left Behind Act (Public Law 107–110) that abolishes most efforts at bilingual education and substitutes increased funding for English language acquisition efforts. The 34-year federal effort to investigate and experiment with bilingual education at the federal level has ended. Anti–bilingual education forces have won. Even the U.S. Department of Education's Office of Bilingual Education and Minority Languages Affairs has been renamed the Office of English Language Acquisition, Language Enhancement, and Academic Achievement for Limited English Proficient Students. English learning has always been the primary function of this office, but now even the limited efforts to learn in a home language are discouraged and not funded (Crawford, 2002).

As anti-immigrant activism continues to grow, including attempting to influence the 2008 presidential campaign, antibilingual efforts have also increased, with California and Arizona, among other states, preventing even limited use of native language materials to assist children while they are learning English.

The several court decisions requiring special services for language-minority students so they can learn English and gain access to the core curriculum (*Lau*, *Castañeda*, and *Keyes*) remain in effect. In spite of the conservative political mobilization against bilingualism, the rapidly growing language-minority populations require schools to respond to the language needs of their children.

Effective Bilingual Programs

High-quality, effective bilingual programs have been created in a number of school districts, such as El Paso and Ysleta in Texas and Calexico, National City, Los Angeles, and Montebello in California, where residents recognize bilingualism as an important economic asset in the face of an emerging global economy (Cummins, 1996; Gold, 2006; Hakuta, 2001; Krashen, 1996). A number of upper-income private schools in and near major cities have adopted programs of dual immersion, another form of bilingual education. (See, for example, the Atlanta International School at *www.Aischools.org*.) Bilingual education by itself, however, cannot overcome the student achievement crisis for English language learners within failing public school districts (such as Oakland, Los Angeles, Sacramento, Chicago, Philadelphia, and New York).

As a consequence of political controversies, bilingual education faces unusual and rigorous demands for evidence to support its claims. Substantial and adequate research has been collected in the last two decades to support bilingual strategies. The study by Hakuta (2001) is one of a long series of supportive research reports. Studies clearly show that bilingual programs help students increase their scores on standardized tests measured in English. Research by Krashen and McField (2005) also indicated the positive impact of bilingual programs, as does that of Genesee, Lindholm-Leary, Saunders, and Christian (2005). For more on this topic, see the review of the research by Goldenberg (2008). Resistance to bilingualism is usually at its core a political campaign, not a debate about the usefulness of the approach.

Goals of Programs for English Learners

All instructional programs for English learners have three common goals: to teach students to (1) speak, read, and write proficiently in English; (2) achieve in school; and (3) develop positive sociocultural skills. In short, effective programs for English learners result in students who are English proficient and academically successful. The 2001 reauthorization of the Elementary and Secondary Education Act, also called the No Child Left Behind Act, reaffirms these goals, stating that federal education programs are "to help ensure that children who are limited English proficient, including immigrant children and youth, attain English proficiency, develop high levels of academic attainment in English, and meet the same challenging State academic content and student academic achievement standards as all children are expected to meet . . ." (Public Law 107-110, Title III, § 3102(1)).

Most English learners and their parents recognize the need to immediately learn English. Children want to learn English, learn in school, and fit into their new society (Olsen, 1997). Substantial evidence indicates that students who were educated in their homeland and acquired school skills there readily transfer their academic skills to English in U.S. schools (National Research Council, 1997). Similarly, those students without a solid educational foundation and their teachers face greater challenges in meeting the aforementioned goals.

Teachers need to understand the language acquisition process, not simply turn to their own English–language arts preparation for guidance on teaching and learning strategies. Learning English as a second language is not the same process that a native speaker uses in learning to read. Heath (1986) argues as follows:

> Language learning is cultural learning: Children do not learn merely the building blocks of their mother tongue—its sounds, words, and order; they learn also how to use language to get what they want, protect themselves, express their wonderings and worries, and ask questions about the world. The learning of language takes place within the political, economic, social, ideological, religious, and aesthetic web of relationships of each community whose members see themselves as belonging to a particular culture. (pp. 145–146)

Knowing English and having effective English-language teaching techniques in general are not enough. Teachers need to examine their attitudes toward language-minority students, help students learn a second language, and reorganize their classroom, if necessary, to meet the needs of this large segment of the U.S. school population.

National English Language Development Standards

In 1997, in response to the recent standards-based education reform movement, Teachers of English to Speakers of Other Languages (TESOL), a national association, published a set of English as a second language (ESL) goals and corresponding standards for the effective education of English learners from pre-K through grade 12. The TESOL vision emphasizes that all education personnel are expected to take responsibility for the education of English learners through the provision of quality and accessible programs (TESOL, 1998).

Eight key principles generated from research and theory pertaining to language learning and language teaching guided the development of the TESOL standards. These principles provide a good introduction to language theory and are summarized here:

1. *Language is functional.* Oral and written language are means of communication that involve more than simply learning the elements of grammar and vocabulary. English learners need to be able to use their English in a variety of settings as they move toward English proficiency.

2. *Language varies.* Language is not monolithic, and its variation depends on numerous factors, such as person, topic, purpose, and situation. Regional, social class, and ethnic differences may also impact language varieties.

3. *Language learning is cultural learning.* Each language reflects the norms, behaviors, and beliefs of a unique culture. Consequently, the learning of a new language also involves the learning of new norms, behaviors, and beliefs.

4. *Language acquisition is a long-term process.* Each individual moves through specific developmental stages toward English proficiency. Whereas conversational skills may be learned relatively quickly, acquiring the academic language skills to be successful in school may take five to seven years.

5. *Language acquisition occurs through meaningful use and interaction.* English learners must have numerous opportunities to use English in different social settings and for different purposes.

6. *Language processes develop interdependently.* Language learning does not always follow a linear progression. The skills of listening, speaking, reading, and writing can develop simultaneously and interdependently.

7. *Native language proficiency contributes to second-language acquisition.* English learners use proficiency in the native language to help in the acquisition of English. Students who have native language literacy already have the basis for developing English literacy.

8. *Bilingualism is an individual and societal asset.* Having proficiency in more than one language can lead one to greater educational and economic opportunities as well as social mobility.

TESOL proposed the following goals for English language learners: "to use English to communicate in social settings, to use English to achieve academically in all content areas, and to use English in socially and culturally appropriate ways." TESOL developed standards for multiple grade levels to achieve these goals. You can access the standards at *http://www.tesol.org/s_tesol/seccss.asp?CID=1186&DID=5348*

The goals and standards developed by TESOL, considered along with state and local standards, provide teachers with direction and guidance for developing and delivering strong ELD programs and improving student achievement.

Factors Affecting the Acquisition of English

The Language Acquisition Process

Professor Stephen Krashen of the University of Southern California has been a major contributor to language acquisition theory and literature. In 1981, Krashen argued that language needs to be acquired rather than learned. In acquiring a language, students follow many of the same patterns and strategies used in learning a first language (California Department of Education, Bilingual Education Office, 1986; Crawford, 1999; Krashen & Terrell, 1983). Terrell (Krashen & Terrell, 1983) termed this process of fostering second-language acquisition the *natural approach* because it seeks to follow seemingly natural language acquisition patterns of children. Students acquire language when they understand the language. The focus in language acquisition must be on communication, not on drilling rules of grammar.

Krashen (Krashen & Terrell, 1983) also suggested an "input" hypothesis. He argued that only comprehensible input, or comprehensible language, will help students acquire a second language. This hypothesis suggested that students' language proficiency emerges over time as a result of communication. Further, it emerges under conditions of comprehensible input and low anxiety. Teachers promote a low-anxiety environment by avoiding overcorrection of language errors. Constant correction impedes and frustrates communication in the classroom. Soon many students are reluctant to volunteer and to speak. Overcorrection actually slows down language acquisition. Students learning English or any second language, like children learning a first language, will hear and correct many of their own errors as they seek improved communication.

Comprehension precedes production. Receptive language is usually stronger than expressive language; second-language learners will usually understand more than they can produce themselves. It is usually easier to listen or read than to speak or write.

Language Acquisition Stages Following the work of Krashen and Terrell, most researchers recognize that children learn a second language in a manner similar to that by which; children learn their first language. Most students progress through these stages:

- During *preproduction*, also known as the *silent period*, students are observing and trying to "make sense" of the new language. They can understand a limited amount but are not yet ready to speak. At this stage, students need to be involved with activities that allow them to listen and to respond nonverbally. They are building vocabulary and starting to learn basic grammatical structures. Reading and writing should be limited to one to two words at a time.

- *Early production* involves utterances of one to two words with many errors. Receptive language is still much stronger than expressive. Students at this stage can answer simple questions or make statements with one- to two-word answers. Structures need to be kept very simple, preferably in the present tense and in active, not passive, form. Reading and writing can include basic sentences.

- In the *speech emergence* stage, students are able to produce longer sentences with fewer errors, although still noticeably nonfluent in nature. At this point, students can answer with complete sentences, ask questions, and make more complex statements. Reading and writing can reach a higher level, with students being able to write paragraphs and even simple essays.

- With *intermediate fluency*, statements are longer and are often grammatically correct. There may be some subtle errors, such as misunderstanding idioms or incorrectly choosing a word. Intermediate fluency students can be introduced to reading and writing at their grade level with some assistance. You should not expect these students to function at the same level as native speakers, although they may appear to be fairly proficient in English.

- Students who have achieved *fluency* have begun using language at a level that approximates that of a native speaker. Not all learners reach this level. At this level, students can read and write at the same level as native speakers. Occasionally, some words or structures will continue to pose difficulties.

A classroom focus on communication helps students to learn more English. When students negotiate meaning in a relevant setting that focuses on getting the message across rather than on grammar or syntax, they tend to acquire the language more easily and retain it longer.

The Contributions of Jim Cummins Jim Cummins is a Canadian researcher who has contributed significantly to our understanding of language acquisition. He focuses on how language use is related to the empowerment of students and their families and looks at how different types of language are developed. He emphasizes the role of the first language and culture in the process of learning a second language (Cummins, 1996).

- **Types of language:** Cummins writes about two types of language: social and academic. *Social* language is used by second-language speakers to perform day-to-day tasks, such as greeting, taking leave, initiating conversation, apologizing, making excuses, explaining what one did over the weekend, and so on. *Academic* language is a higher level of language needed in order to function in content classes such as math or science. Academic language takes approximately five to seven years to acquire.

- **Context and cognitive demand:** Tasks can be examined in terms of how embedded they are in context and how cognitively demanding they are. Teachers must provide greater context when working with students who are LEP. An example of this would be involving students in a demonstration where they actually see one form of matter change into another (such as making ice cream) rather than just talking about solids, liquids, and gases and their ability to change form. Limitations in English do not indicate limitations in cognitive ability.

- **Transfer:** Once someone learns something in his first language, he can transfer the knowledge and skills to his second language. An example would be learning how to find the main idea in a paragraph. Once you learn how to do that, you don't need to learn the skill again in another language—you just need to learn the language.

- **Personal factors:** Age, motivation, aptitude, self-esteem, degree of risk taking, and personality also affect language acquisition. When students want to learn a new language, they will work hard at it. When second-language acquisition brings prestige and new opportunities, students put in intense hours of work. On the other hand, when learning a second language is mixed with criticism, ridicule, cultural conflict, and self-doubt, language acquisition is slowed (Cummins, 1996; Olsen, 1997).

- **English itself:** This presents a number of issues: dealing with a new sound system, tackling a possibly different syntax or word order, figuring out rules for putting words together, and discovering subtle meanings connected to verbal and nonverbal messages. It will be easier to learn English when the primary language is a European language similar to English.

Children trying to learn a new language often encounter cultural conflict. The following excerpts from *Immigrant Students and the California Public Schools: Crossing the Schoolhouse Border* (California Tomorrow, 1988) illustrate several of the conflicts encountered.

> I just sat in my classes and didn't understand anything. Sometimes I would try to look like I knew what was going on; sometimes I would just try to think about a happy time when I didn't feel stupid. My teachers never called on me or talked to me. I think they either forgot I was there or else wished I wasn't. I waited and waited, thinking that someday I will know English. (Ninth-grade Mexican girl who immigrated at age 13, p. 62)
>
> You don't know anything. You don't even know what to eat when you go to the lunch room. The day I started school, all the kids stared at me like I was from a different planet. I wanted to go home with my Dad, but he said I had to stay. I was very shy and scared. I didn't know where to sit or eat or where the bathroom was or how to eat the food. . . . I felt so out of place that I felt sick. Now I know more, but I still sit and watch and try to understand. I want to know what is this place and how must I act? (Eighth-grade Vietnamese girl who immigrated at age 9, p. 71)

Learning English for school success requires learning the dominant (English-speaking) culture. Acquiring English requires that the student learn an additional frame of reference and a new worldview. Learning a new language produces cultural conflicts about the status of English learners' families and parents in this society. Intense cultural conflicts can slow English learning. To succeed, the student needs to learn the academic language and also the cultural norms and sanctions of the school. Students who are skilled in negotiating cultural conflict can direct and influence their own language acquisition. When students come to our schools with a strong education background and literacy in their native language, they learn English much more rapidly. These students know who they are, and they have a clear view of their identity. For them, learning a new language (English) is not as wrapped up with identity and cultural conflicts.

Teachers assist language learning by serving as cultural mediators—or cultural brokers—and helping students to work their way through cultural conflicts. Strategies for assisting with cultural conflict are described in Chapters 2, 6, and 7.

Language lessons assist with cultural conflict by including value examinations such as these:

- Why do I want to learn this language?
- What is the value of learning the language?

- How will other people who are important to me perceive me if I study, practice, and learn this language?
- How do I feel when I fail to use English properly?
- What steps can I take to acquire English without giving up my language, culture, family, and friends?

Support and Empowerment

Cummins (1989) has combined the insights of critical theory in the sociology of education with current theories of second-language acquisition. He lists the major components of a language acquisition and empowerment strategy:

1. A genuine dialogue between student and teacher in both oral and written modalities,
2. Guidance and facilitation rather than control of student learning by the teacher,
3. Encouragement of student–student talk in a collaborative learning context,
4. Encouragement of meaningful language use by students rather than correctness of surface forms,
5. Conscious integration of language use and development with all curricular content rather than teaching language and other content as isolated subjects,
6. A focus on developing higher level cognitive skills rather than factual recall, and
7. Task presentation that generates intrinsic rather than extrinsic motivation. (p. 64)

Educators play an important role in helping or encouraging students and their families to become empowered. *Empowerment* means that an individual has control over her destiny and is able to make changes (see Chapter 7). Cummins (1996) expresses the concern that we often see students' native language and culture as being inferior, not worthy of being used as tools in the school setting. In fact, when we do not allow students to build on their existing language, we and they lose a great deal of richness and value, and we perpetuate the myth that non-English languages are not school languages.

Instructional Program Design for English Learners

How can teachers best develop students who are proficient in English and academically successful? How can you meet the desired goals for teaching English learners? This section explains three main components common to effective instructional programs for English learners: English language development (ELD), specially designed academic instruction in English (SDAIE) or sheltered instruction, and primary-language instruction (bilingual education).

Know Your Language-Minority Students

Knowing the backgrounds and experiences of your students is an important first step in building your instructional plan. Language-minority students arrive at your classroom door with experiences that may or may not be similar to those of their native-English-speaking classmates. It is important that you provide a comfortable environment that supports all students and that you find out as soon as possible about the experiences that students do bring. Building shared experiences into instructional activities serves as a strong base for English lessons. Please keep the following in mind:

- Not all English learners are alike. Each comes from a unique background and has her own abilities, needs, interests, and goals.

- Instructional strategies and materials must be modified to ensure that language-minority students can comprehend and make connections with material. Without modifications, students are faced with lessons they cannot learn.

- Language-minority students need social and emotional support. They find themselves in a setting that may not be aligned with their experiences. They may face cultural conflict, discrimination, and exclusion due to their language, race, or ethnicity. (Olsen, 1997)

The English Language Development Component

As illustrated in the TESOL standards, one of the primary goals of any instructional program for English learners is the development of English language proficiency. Each English learner must receive ELD instruction appropriate to her level of proficiency in order to develop appropriate listening, speaking, reading, and writing skills in English. Teachers must know each student's initial level of proficiency and the corresponding ELD content standards in order to select the proper lessons to teach.

Most states require the assessment of English language skills for language-minority students upon school enrollment. New teachers should check with their school district to find out which tests are used and how to interpret the scores. Since 2001, California, for example, has required all school districts to use only the state-developed California English Language Development Test.

From these assessments, English learners can be grouped into one of the following stages of language proficiency: preproduction, early production, speech emergence, intermediate fluency, and fluency (see the "Language Acquisition Stages" section earlier in this chapter). As the teacher, you should select teaching strategies that are most effective for each stage of proficiency. For example, students at the preproduction level will need more teacher guidance and language modeling. As students become more proficient, less guidance and modeling will be needed, and more dialogue and language integration will be possible.

Ideally, students with similar levels of English proficiency can be grouped together for ELD instruction. The first priority is to teach students to communicate in English so they can survive in school as well as to provide the basic language needed for understanding academic instruction. To be successful in subject-matter lessons, students must have specific vocabulary and be aware of certain language structures (such as the expression "How much?" in mathematics). The teacher helps students to achieve comprehension by carefully developing the context of language through interactive, experiential lessons. Several ESL instructional programs provide a well-developed sequence of lessons that allows students to develop vocabulary and grammatical structures in a meaningful context. English can be taught through direct language lessons (which focus on vocabulary or grammar) and through content-based experiences, such as planting seeds, collecting items of various shapes, and interviewing a family member about moving to the United States.

Typical strategies used for ELD lessons may include role-playing, poetry, readers' theater, chants, songs, total physical response (responding by movement to commands given by a teacher or other students and gradually building grammatical structures and vocabulary), art projects, games, predictable literature, interviews, the matching of words with pictures, dialogue journals, and computer games. As much as possible, teaching strategies should encourage dialogue between students rather than lecture and presentation by the teacher. Particularly useful are lessons that connect to the students' own lives, including how to be successful in school.

Teachers who have the responsibility of teaching a small number of English learners in their classroom will need to plan their curriculum to provide specialized instruction in ELD, at an appropriate level, to those students who need it.

Middle and high school teachers may find themselves in situations similar to those of their elementary colleagues when only a handful of English learners populates each class period. These situations call for the regrouping of students through teaming or schedule changes for specific ELD instruction. In addition, language and literacy instruction should be developed in all classes across the curriculum, including math, social studies, and the arts. Teachers must find the time and resources to provide the appropriate ELD lessons to their students while they are in integrated classes. Failure to do so will put English learners in a sink-or-swim position and violate basic civil rights law.

Literacy and the Language Experience Approach

English literacy development for second-language learners continues to provoke considerable controversy ("Every Child Reading," 1998). Educators question whether it is more appropriate to develop reading skills in children's home languages or in English (Hakuta, 2001; Ramírez, 2000). New Mexico continues to permit bilingual instruction, while California and Arizona prohibit it in most circumstances. Texas permits a particular form of dual-language instruction. Even in states where bilingual instruction is permitted, many school districts have decided that primary-language literacy development is not feasible due to the multiplicity of languages present in their classrooms. These districts often promote English-language literacy even when students are not yet proficient in English.

Most of our strategies for learning to read in English are developed from theories of emergent literacy in English-speaking children. These theories can mislead the teacher planning an ESL program. A strong oral language development program provides much of the foundation needed to learn to read. A young English-speaking child in school has had five to six years of oral language development in English prior to learning to read.

For ESL students, as they hear and speak their first English words, they are learning the sounds of the new language. Next, they need to learn the symbols (or written language). Packaged programs and phonics readers concentrate on learning letter/sound correspondence and decoding printed words. These skills are helpful but lack the critical element of comprehension. Recall that, for ESL students, comprehension is everything. ESL students need extensive and active oral language development in addition to the popular phonics-type programs in order to succeed. They need interesting lessons that build language background knowledge and vocabulary as well as the many strategies of a whole-language approach. To foster success, teachers with ESL students need specific instructional strategies and materials designed for the second-language learner as well as the specific skills necessary to integrate language acquisition into the curriculum.

A major concern is deciding when it is appropriate to introduce reading in English to students who are already reading in their primary language. Teachers find that even students who are literate in their first language and who speak English adequately may have an advantage learning to read in English. Comprehension is always a problem. Second-language learners seldom have all the sight vocabulary of typical English speakers. Researchers claim extensive evidence of the value of phonemic awareness for reading, but in your teaching, you will quickly learn that there are numerous exceptions to this claim of phonemic regularity (Adams, Foorman, Lundberg, & Beeler, 1998). For example, students who are literate in Spanish are accustomed to its regular sound/symbol relationship. Learning to read English, with its extensive irregular use of vowels, may be difficult and confusing for such children.

The language experience approach to reading was introduced in the United States in the 1920s. Unused for decades, it was rediscovered by Roach Van Allen, who observed the method being used in Texas with bilingual Spanish-speaking children. The basic premise, as explained by Van Allen and Allen (Van Allen & Allen, 1976), is simple: What I think about, I can say. What I say, I can write. I can read what I have written. I can read what others have written for me to read. Research on the language experience approach to reading reveals positive results (Hall, 1981). It offers several useful steps to assist English language learners.

While students acquire the English language, they learn to read (Green, 1998). In the language experience approach, readers "write" their own story. They use their own words to write about their own experience. This real-life experience becomes their context for reading, and they comprehend all of what they read.

For students struggling to learn to decode in English, language experience lessons provide an opportunity to move into reading English with comprehension supported by experience. In these lessons, error correction must be kept to a minimum.

Language experience lessons allow the teacher to be very creative. The process motivates students. Children love to read stories about themselves, but these are not just stories about themselves—they are stories the children themselves have written. With computers and programs such as *Bilingual Writing Center,* you and your class can print high-quality and visually appealing stories to share with students' families. Thus, developing more language experiences leads directly to a literature-based approach to reading. The Optimal Learning Environment (OLÉ) Project provides teachers with excellent ideas, strategies, and materials for developing reading and writing skills (Ruiz, Garcia, & Figueroa, 1996).

Teachers may also expand on the traditional language approach to include teaching phonemic awareness, grammar, and other skills necessary to enable English language learners to be successful readers.

Teaching Phonemic Awareness Phonemic awareness lessons, whether included in language- or phonics-based reading programs, require teachers to be aware of the phonemic structures of other languages. For example, children who read Spanish are accustomed to its regular series of vowels, whereas English constructs a diverse series of phonemes from its vowels. Children who speak Asian languages are accustomed to several distinct phonemes that may interfere with their recognition of English phonemes.

English language learners may have difficulty hearing and recognizing English sounds and phonemes because equivalent sounds may not exist in their language. Spanish speakers, for example, may have difficulty recognizing English sounds such as /sh/ as in *shirt* and the initial /s/ as in *skirt*. Simply adding more drills will not resolve the problem. The teacher must stop and articulate the sound, explain the language differences and help students hear the phonemes.

When using a balanced approach to reading for English language learners, the teacher needs to attend to both the skills of teaching English as a second language—listening, speaking, reading, and writing—and the reading skills of vocabulary development, word attack, and comprehension.

Teaching English Grammar Older or more advanced students may be ready to refine their language by paying attention to points of grammar with their written stories. They can look for verbs and then edit for correct tense and person. They can look for adjectives in their stories and add descriptive words or change those already there. They may develop new vocabulary in this fashion. Some students may find English's irregular plurals difficult to master. A good exercise for them is to find all the nouns in their stories, write them down, and list their singular and plural forms. Prepositions are also difficult and are developed late in the sequence of English language acquisition. Students can look for prepositional phrases and edit them for correctness.

The Sheltered English Component (or Sheltered Instruction)

Learning subject-matter content, particularly in this era of standards-based instruction, is the second vital component of the EL instructional program. *Specially designed academic instruction in English (SDAIE)*, also known as *sheltered English*, involves teaching in modified English so that English language learners can comprehend and participate successfully in the classroom. Having a program designed to get students to meet appropriate standards, or levels of subject-matter comprehension, is required by federal court decisions. A list of frequently used Sheltered Strategies is provided in Figure 11.2.

Figure 11.2 Sheltered English Strategies

Sheltered English strategies are appropriate after students have reached an intermediate level of English. These strategies include the following:

- Extracting the important points of a lesson or unit and focusing on them rather than on numerous details

- Modifying text

- Simplifying teacher talk (e.g., shorter and less complex sentences, more consistent word choice, face-to-face communication, use of active rather than passive voice)

- Involving students more actively in hands-on activities

- Providing comprehension supports, such as buddies or cooperative groups

- Promoting comprehension by providing a great deal of context through gestures, visuals, and other graphic tools

- Accessing and using students' background knowledge

- Finding multiple ways to check for understanding and to assess lesson objectives

Instruction with sheltered English strategies should begin in context-rich subjects such as art, physical education, and music and eventually move on to math and science, where demonstrations, modeling, and experiential learning are common. The final stages of implementation would include social studies and language arts, both "word-intensive" subjects whose texts at times have few illustrations or graphic depictions. Classrooms can use their connections to the Internet to provide both context and primary-language support for important concepts.

Sheltered English has as its goals achievement in the subject field and improved use of English. Teaching in a sheltered English mode requires thoughtful selection of objectives, incorporation of active student participation, delivery in a very concrete and inclusive way, and assessment techniques that allow students with limited English ability to show what they have understood. Sheltered English calls for rich and contextualized lessons at the appropriate level of delivery (this is why sheltered instruction is inappropriate at the early production stages). In effective classrooms, sheltered lessons are not simplified lessons but extended and enhanced lessons about the subject matter.

Bilingual Education Programs

Bilingual education is a series of instructional strategies for teaching students school subjects, in part in their home language, and for teaching them English. In bilingual classes, the instruction might be in Spanish or another language for part of the day and English for another part. In this manner, the student learns math, reading, and other subjects while acquiring English. The immigrant student does not fall behind the other students. Bilingual education uses ELD strategies to help students acquire

English. Quality bilingual education encourages the development of bilingual and biliteracy skills in both languages—valuable assets in our increasingly international economy.

It is difficult for children to learn when the instruction is in a language they barely understand. Bilingual education teaches other academic subjects as it teaches English. While children are learning English, they are also taught the difficult tasks of reading, math, and science in the language they best understand. After two or more years (and preferably after five to seven years) of instruction and practice in English, instruction in most subject areas gradually changes to all English (DeAvila, 1997).

Most states have been unable to obtain a sufficient number of bilingual teachers to provide native language instruction for students who need it. Voters in California, Massachusetts, and Arizona have chosen to limit or prohibit bilingual instructional programs. In areas of a high concentration of a specific language group (such as Cantonese, Navajo, or Spanish), school districts can organize classrooms to provide bilingual instruction. All students need education in a language they can comprehend. They deserve an environment that encourages their enthusiasm, an environment that makes them independent and autonomous learners. The U.S. Department of Education estimated in 1992 that only 11 percent of students who have a legal right to English language support actually receive bilingual services (McKeon, 1994). By 2006, as a consequence of the antibilingual Proposition 227, only 7.5 percent of California's rapidly growing language minority population was still receiving bilingual education (California Department of Education, 2007).

California education leaders violated the federal laws protecting the rights of language-minority students until they were forced to change their practices by direct court orders. In 1985, 1996, and 2001, the courts found that the state superintendent of public instruction was not enforcing the existing laws (*Comité de Padres v. Superintendent of Public Instruction*). In 2002, when the state school board began to take the court orders more seriously, several of the major school districts in the state were found out of compliance with both state and federal laws (California Board of Education, Minutes, January 10, 2002).

Congress passed the Bush Administration's No Child Left Behind Act of 2001 and allowed the Bilingual Education Act to expire in 2002. The new education legislation does not reference bilingualism, and federal funds are now provided only for ELD programs, not for bilingual programs. The limited continuation of bilingual education programs is now dependent on the efforts of local schools and school districts; there is no federal support and only limited state support for such efforts. There are still significant federal court requirements regarding the provision of extra and supplementary services to LEP students.

Both bilingual instruction and ELD programs respond to students' needs to learn English. By law and by practice, well over 80 percent of all bilingual programs are transitional; that is, they use the home language for only a few years while the student learns English. A few bilingual programs also maintain and develop academic skill in the home language as well as English. Rarely do primary-language skills get preserved and developed in sheltered English programs, thus ignoring and negating the significant language skills these students bring to school. In an increasingly international economy, our society needs to preserve and develop language skills in primary languages.

Bilingual education and extended use of sheltered English allow students time to transition to all-English instruction. A common underlying language proficiency and common learning skills facilitate rapid progress once English has been acquired. Students may have learned important concepts in school in their home country. For example, children need to learn to read or learn math only once. Most reading and math skills learned in another language readily transfer to English (Krashen, 2003).

Native-language instruction is helpful for young children and adolescents. Children learn better when their native language is used to develop English and school competency (Gold, 2006; Thomas & Collier, 2002). Children receive their primary instruction about respect, motivation, values, and life from their families. They need extended and consistent guidance. At times, school personnel who are poorly informed about language acquisition have urged families to stop talking to their children in their home language. This has usually proven to be a disastrous recommendation. Children respond best to positive communication. Lack of communication, even in the home language, impedes children's learning of concepts and skills.

The misguided advice to stop speaking Spanish, Cantonese, or Hmong results in reduced talk and communication between parents and children. School pressure may divide children from their home, and they lose their major source of instruction in cooperation, fairness, personal responsibility, and attitudes toward work. They may become alienated from both home and school (Wong-Filmore, 1991).

Teachers and language specialists have developed several approaches to bilingual education. Programs differ based on (1) how much the primary language is used and (2) how long the primary language is used for academic instruction (Gold, 2006; Thomas & Collier, 2002).

Elementary school teachers typically have responsibility for teaching the entire curriculum to a group of children every school day. In some cases, you may have only a few English learners in your class. In others, the majority of your class may consist of English learners. Compounding either situation may be the fact that your students vary widely in their English proficiency and ability levels. Each situation requires you to thoughtfully organize your students and your instructional day in order to maximize the learning opportunities for your students.

Considerations for Teachers

Elementary School Teachers

The following suggestions may assist elementary teachers in the organization of their class:

- To the extent possible, group English learners by their English proficiency level when teaching ELD and subject matter.
- Provide small-group reinforcement (follow-up) for your English learners to ensure subject comprehension.
- Use additional resources such as bilingual parents or instructional assistants to support your teaching.

- Use bilingual students to support classmates who are English learners (cooperative learning).
- Team with another teacher to regroup students by English proficiency levels.
- Above all, maintain high expectations and standards for all your English learners.

Middle and High School Teachers

Middle and high school teachers are normally responsible for teaching a single subject area. Depending on the school's student population, secondary teachers may find themselves in situations similar to those of their elementary colleagues when either only a handful of English learners populates each class period or the class consists of a majority of English learners. In either circumstance, secondary teachers feel particular pressure to deliver the content of their subject and typically focus their teaching on subject matter rather than on English language instruction.

Ideally, secondary teachers can teach their subject matter while developing the language skills of their English learners. Secondary teachers must find the time and resources to provide the appropriate ELD and sheltered content lessons to their students who are learning English. Failure to do so will put English learners in a sink-or-swim position. The following thoughts are offered to assist secondary teachers of English learners:

- Know who your English learners are and their specific English proficiency levels as well as their history of schooling. Some immigrant students are highly literate in their native language and come to the United States with a solid educational background.

- Analyze your school's curriculum to determine whether students can be scheduled into a specific sheltered subject course. If not, ask yourself how you can effectively shelter your teaching for the English learners in your class.

- Work in conjunction with the ELD teacher to determine ways in which ELD lessons can support specific subjects, such as history, mathematics, and science.

- Use bilingual resources such as volunteers, instructional assistants, or students to support your teaching.

- Above all, maintain high expectations and standards for all your English learners.

Putting the Pieces into Practice

Effective classroom practices translate theory into action. The following ideas can assist teachers, regardless of grade level or subject, in providing solid learning for English learners.

Classroom Environment

A classroom that is bright, colorful, full of student work, print-rich, personalized, and comfortable will support students as they learn English. Seating students in groups rather than rows allows them to interact and to support each other academically. Making materials accessible to students means that the classroom is student centered.

The way in which you and your students interact with each other also has an effect on the environment. In positive environments, teachers talk less and allow students to talk more. The strategies of student-to-student dialogue are encouraged and respected.

Comprehensible content delivery is extremely important. Students spend most of their day studying subject-matter material. The use of active learning strategies and sheltered instruction techniques makes instruction more comprehensible.

Development of the primary language should be a component of instruction for all language-minority students (Krashen & McField, 2005; Thomas & Collier, 2002). The teacher should help students develop their primary language because (1) it is their dominant form of communication both at school and at home, (2) they can use it as a tool for acquiring content knowledge and skills, (3) it can act as a base for them as they move into English instruction, and (4) it is an unnecessary tragedy for anyone to lose their language. We do not help students by making them less well educated. Teachers who do not speak the primary language of their students can still validate and support their students' first languages. Native-language support builds a cooperative relationship among students, their parents, and the school. We need a closer home–school relationship to reduce crime, the school dropout rate, and the growing social decay in many cities.

English is necessary for both social and academic transactions. For the ESL student, most lessons are English language lessons. As students see word banks, read language experience stories, look at labeled classroom objects, work with classmates in cooperative groups, participate in circle sharing time, and take part in science and social studies field trips, they are learning English. If the English is comprehensible, then they will acquire it. When the teacher gives students opportunities to use English in a supportive, negotiable way, their knowledge and their English improve.

Getting Started

What are some things that you, as a teacher, can do to provide a positive and productive experience for language-minority students and their families?

- *Find out as much you can about your students and their families.* Talk with your students and their parents, try to visit their homes, attend community events, read, see films or documentaries, and talk with other teachers about their experiences.

- *Provide a positive physical, social, and academic classroom environment.* Students should feel wonderful from the minute they walk in the door to the minute they go home. As the primary adult throughout the major part of their day, your attitude and actions make a difference. You are also responsible for making sure that all students are included, respected, and validated.

- *Use your classroom and its routines to teach English.* Label, post word banks, build patterns into your routines (such as circle time, calendar), and post procedures for doing things (such as writing process, heads together, share with a partner).

- *Provide ELD time daily to your English language learners.* Do not assume that students will pick up English through language arts or through classroom routines alone. Language learners need a block of time with you, or occasionally with an instructional assistant or volunteer, during which they can be exposed to and can practice vocabulary and language structures. Make sure you teach both social and academic language. Respect the stages of language development, tailoring your ELD lessons to the students and what they are comfortable doing. Use fun, engaging activities that focus on meaning rather than form. Try to get students listening, speaking, reading, and writing in a natural setting. Be kind with error correction.

- *Scaffold! Scaffold! Scaffold!* Many teachers have adopted the strategies of scaffolding as a process to help students learn English. Scaffolding is a metaphor. Think of repairing a major building. First, workers build a scaffold so that they can reach and work on the building. A significant amount of language work has been influenced by Vygotsky (1836–1934) and his view of the "proximal zone of development" (Vygotsky, 1978). Scaffolding is used in a classroom when the teacher helps students to understand a concept by using gestures, objects, questions, and responses. The teacher helps them to use English to describe an event or an opinion. She may ask questions that require students to reflect on their experiences and use English words to describe them. The teacher accepts students' tentative use of English and then elaborates on or extends the descriptions by supplying more descriptive and useful words.

- *Find ways in which to involve your students in decision making, encouraging them to take responsibility for their own learning and for the classroom in general.* (See Chapters 7 and 8.)

- *Involve parents in meaningful ways.* Find out how to get parents to school if they are not already coming to the site. Provide translation.

- *Work closely with anyone at the school providing assistance to language-minority students.* This might include language specialists or ELD teachers, instructional assistants, volunteers, peer tutors, and those working with Title I programs and after-school tutoring programs.

- *Provide support in the form of peer or cross-age buddies.* They can help language-minority students to find their way around campus as well as assisting them with school work.

- *Promote understanding and cooperation by taking the time to talk and listen to new students.* In the first few weeks, it is important to check in with new students each day. Chat before school, during recess, or at lunch. You gain insight into students' viewpoints and culture by listening to their views on how well they are adjusting to the new language and the new school.

Summary

Teaching language-minority populations is an exciting and perspective-widening challenge. Schools have developed a variety of strategies in response to the needs of language-minority students, including English language development (ELD), sheltered English (also called SDAIE), and bilingual education. All bilingual programs are designed to teach students English. Few programs encourage the development of the language resources of immigrant populations. Most U.S. schools have yet to recognize the advantages of bilingualism.

Language acquisition and a multicultural curriculum should provide students with meaningful, comprehensible, challenging, and substantive school opportunities. Bilingual education and sheltered English instruction teach students from cultural and linguistic minorities the macrocultural values and language necessary for survival in the public schools.

Electronic Resources for Teachers

California Department of Education, *www.cde.ca.gov/sp/el*
California Tomorrow, *www.californiatomorrow.org*
Center for Research on Equity, Diversity, and Excellence, *www.crede.berkeley.edu*
National Association for Bilingual Education, *www.nabe.org*
National Clearinghouse for English Language Acquisition, *www.ncbe.gwu.edu*
Teachers of English to Speakers of Other Languages, *www.tesol.org/index.html*
U.S. Department of Education, Office of English Language Acquisition,
    www.ed.gov/offices/oela
University of California Language Minority Research Institute, *www.lmri.ucsb.edu*
WestEd, *www.wested.org*

Questions over the Chapter

1. Schools often "Americanize" immigrants. In what ways is this Americanization appropriate? Give examples of inappropriate Americanization.
2. In what ways is learning a second language like learning a first language? In what ways is it different?
3. Which strategies help teachers stress communication rather than formal language rules?
4. What are some advantages to teachers of becoming bilingual?
5. The *Lau v. Nichols* (1974) decision requires that all students be provided with access to the mainstream curriculum. Which teaching strategies help provide immigrant students with access to the curriculum?

Activities for Further Study of Language Acquisition

1. Make a list of the advantages to becoming bilingual.
2. If you have studied a second language, describe to a classmate your experiences in trying to learn it. How did you respond to your teacher's correction of language errors? Based on your own language experiences, what strategies would you employ as a teacher to help your students learn a second language?
3. Talk with bilingual adults about their experiences in learning English and about the support they felt, or didn't feel, for their first language and culture. Were they enrolled in a bilingual program? Was their education experience positive?
4. Find out about the types of ELD and bilingual programs offered in your area. Do the schools provide transitional, maintenance, or immersion programs? Which languages are served?
5. Observe a sheltered classroom. What types of strategies does the teacher use to make sure that students are included and able to participate?
6. Investigate your district to find out what efforts are made to include parents in the education of their language-minority children. What types of committees are in place? How are parents encouraged to take part in school functions, both special and ongoing?
7. Take a look at some programs commonly used for teaching English as a second language. How are they structured? What do they include? What types of activities are used? Are they meaningful, focusing on communication rather than on grammatical correctness? Is language developed in a natural way?
8. Visit a bilingual classroom. How are the two languages used? How are students encouraged to develop both languages? Are parents involved? What are the goals of this particular program?

Teaching Strategies for Use with Your Students

1. Create and maintain a low-anxiety environment.
2. Focus on communication rather than on correct language form.
3. Be tolerant of errors, and minimize correcting them.
4. Simplify information whenever possible to make it comprehensible. Use pictures, movement, simple language (see strategy 5c), and other strategies.
5. Use sheltered instructional strategies, such as the following:
   a. Extract the important points of a lesson or unit, and focus on them rather than on numerous details.
   b. Modify text.
   c. Simplify teacher talk (use shorter and less complex sentences, use words consistently, communicate face to face, and use active rather than passive voice).
   d. Involve students more actively in hands-on activities.
   e. Provide supports such as buddies or cooperative groups.

     f. Provide a great deal of context through gestures, visuals, and other graphic tools.

     g. Tap into and build on students' background knowledge.

     h. Find alternative ways to check for understanding and measure final outcomes of lessons.

6. Focus on concepts. Evaluate, reuse, and expand concept lessons.
7. Provide students with visible context for ideas and concepts: pictures, videos, field trips, role-playing.
8. Scaffold students' communication and your own.

PART 3

The Dialogue Between Democracy and Multicultural Education

Chapter 12: Democracy, Curriculum, and Multicultural Education

Chapter 13: Democratic School Reform: How Do We Get from Here to There?

12

Democracy, Curriculum, and Multicultural Education

with John Cowan

> Once social change begins, it cannot be reversed. You cannot un-educate the
> person who has learned to read. You cannot humiliate the person who feels pride.
> You cannot oppress the people who are not afraid anymore.
>
> *César Chávez, November 9, 1984*

Civil Rights and Education are Human Rights

Quality schools are an issue of civil rights. Our public schools should provide all students with a high-quality education. At present, they often do not (Kozol, 2005; Moses & Cobb, 2001). Receiving a quality education is necessary for economic opportunity, economic survival, and the development of a democratic community.

Multicultural education is part of a movement of school reform whose aim is to provide quality education for all and to make schools more democratic. Its intellectual roots lie in the civil rights struggles of the 1960s, the ethnic studies movements of the 1970s, and the struggles for bilingual education (Banks, 2008).

The Curriculum

The curriculum of a school or district is the plans and materials for guiding instruction, the lesson plans, and the plans for assessment of objectives. These are typically written down and available to teachers as guides. The curriculum in a school includes the program of study for all students as well as the specific plans for courses of study, such as math, English, and history.

Curriculum study and development have become an area for social control. The educational philosopher most often associated with developing curriculum based on the interests of the students and the development of a democratic society is John Dewey (1859–1952). In his writing, Dewey strongly emphasized his view that schools should access student interests in developing curriculum. He recognized that all knowledge has a social origin. Since the existing knowledge had a social origin and carried with it the perspectives of the dominant groups, Dewey argued that to prepare students for democratic decision making, students should practice critical thinking and decision making about important issues of their day. He thought students should learn democratic practices by practicing democracy in schools.

In 1949, Ralph Tyler wrote a small book, *Basic Principles of Curriculum and Instruction*, which framed much of the debate of the next 50 years. He argued that the curriculum should meet the needs and interests of the students and the needs and interests of the society and incorporate the choices of experts in the academic fields. The study of curriculum development has produced a relatively stable series of viewpoints and publications that are at times referred to as the dominant canon. The developed curriculum products usually sought to provide a common core of experience for students in the United States. The curriculum products (the canon) were widely accepted by professionals as sufficiently comprehensive to accurately describe the histories, cultures and experiences of U.S. society which should be studied in schools. Decisions about what is important to study were made by committees and working groups representing an academic elite that typically had little current experience in public school classrooms (Apple, 1979; Apple and Smith eds., 1991).

Someone makes the decisions necessary to plan the curriculum. A committee selects goals, objectives, materials, learning strategies, and processes for student evaluation. Then the teacher in the classroom makes decisions on how the curriculum is delivered.

A curriculum is developed based on the writers' values and views of the appropriate goals for society. Its adoption usually rests with state or district decision makers. It is taught based on the values and views of the teachers and relevant learning theories. Even today, in the period of standards and testing, the teacher in the classroom makes significant curriculum decisions each day.

The curriculum has often been the battleground for U.S. education. Advocacy groups, business groups, religious reformers, teachers and their unions, and elected officials have sought to use the curriculum to define and to direct schooling. Multicultural education enters into the conflict over the curriculum because a multicultural social justice perspective most often reveals a conflict between the promises of education for a democracy and the view of the society taught as accurate and complete in the existing courses offered in the schools.

Curriculum change or improvement can be pursued as a means of trying to move a school from one level of achievement to another. Curriculum change involves choices. A major emphasis of the 1980s and 1990s was to upgrade the high school curriculum for college preparation. A result of this emphasis was the sharp reduction—almost elimination—of vocational education programs in some states, such as California. Yet fully 80 percent of all high school students will not graduate from college. It was an ideological choice to decide that we should design the high school curriculum as if all students were going to college.

The development of multicultural education calls for a reanalysis of curriculum basics and a revision of the textbooks and curriculum experiences where appropriate. We need to recognize that many curriculum decisions are based on ideological choices. From a critical theory point of view, knowledge is not neutral. Knowledge is power. Those who control the access to knowledge, including publishers, bureaucracies, teachers, and the curriculum, control a source of power in our society.

Michael Apple (2001) refers to *ideological domination* in the following:

> Reality, then, doesn't stalk around with a label. What something is, what it does, one's evaluation of it—all this is not naturally preordained. It is socially constructed. This is the case even when we talk about the institutions that organize a good deal of our lives. Take schools, for example. For some groups of people, schooling is seen as a vast engine of democracy: opening horizons, ensuring mobility, and so on. For others, the reality of schooling is strikingly different. It is seen as a form of social control, or, perhaps as the embodiment of cultural dangers, institutions whose curricula and teaching practices threaten the moral universe of the students who attend them. (p. 46)

A goal of the multicultural education effort is to rewrite curricula and textbooks so that all students—members of the United States's diverse communities—recognize their own role in building our society and economy. Multicultural advocates choose to rewrite the curricula so that all students experience a school that serves as an engine of democracy and opportunity.

Curriculum content, usually expressed in textbooks, is very important. These materials often direct and shape what students read and often outline the teaching strategies to be employed. Among other things, curriculum decisions determine *whose knowledge is of most worth*.

Curriculum Goals

The complete curriculum for a K–12 school district has many goals and tasks to fulfill, including preparing students with skills needed for everyday life and work (English language, reading, writing, and math); introducing students to the history and norms of our society and our several cultures; preparing students for life in a rapidly changing global economy; assisting students with life adjustments (work habits, identity, and conflicts); and preparing students to actively participate in the political system and to create a more democratic political and ecoomic system.

As described in Chapter 7, James Banks (2008a), a lifetime leader in the multicultural education movement and a former president of both the National Council for the Social Studies and the American Educational Research Association, described the multicultural curriculum efforts as a transformative curriculum of empowerment (see Figure 7.2). He argued that in addition to the traditional curriculum goals (the canon) a curriculum should among other things:

1. Empower the students, especially the victimized and marginalized.
2. Develop the knowledge and skills necessary to critically examine the current political and economic structure.

3. Teach critical thinking skills and decision making skills including the analysis of the way in which knowledge is constructed. (p. x)

Further, as described in Chapter 8, a recognition of the life difficulties of many of our students, particularly in distressed areas of our country, suggests that schools and teachers should also help students to make improved choices on issues such as joining gangs and staying in school and that we will need to help students to deal with some of the harsh realities in their lives, including homelessness, drugs, and incarceration.

Curriculum Balance

Public schools have multiple goals, as listed above, and these goals require a balanced curriculum. A balanced curriculum is concerned with the academic subjects such as English, reading, math, and the social sciences, and it also teaches critical thinking, social skills, bilingualism, social adjustment, and civic responsibility. A well-constructed curriculum is concerned with both what is taught and how it is taught. Unfortunately, many of the recent efforts to use prepackaged curricula and to promote drill-based instruction, particularly in the low-income schools, have failed both to teach important skills and to provide the students with a balanced curriculum that deals with some of their immediate needs.

The Role of Democracy in the Curriculum

Advocates of democracy in schooling, led by John Dewey, argued that public education was needed to educate the children of working people. Universal voting, along with universal education, would make our society more democratic. An educated electorate would understand politics and the economy and make wise decisions. Later, by the 1960s, public education advocates argued that educating working people to a higher level (as through the G.I. Bill) would complete our transition to a deliberative or participatory democracy. This position is well developed by political philosopher Benjamin R. Barber in *Strong Democracy: Participatory Politics for a New Age*, first published in 1984 and republished in 2003.

An alternative view of democracy is presented by Richard A. Posner, a federal appellate judge, in *Law, Pragmatism, and Democracy* (2003). Posner argues that the U.S. political system is not so much self-rule (democracy) as it is "rule by officials who are chosen by the people and who if they don't perform are fired by the people" (p. 144).

The multicultural education view, following in the tradition of Thomas Jefferson, John Dewey, Martin Luther King, Jr., Fannie Lou Hamer, and others, is that schools should include substantive developments to prepare all students for deliberative democracy. The report *Democracy at Risk* (Darling-Hammond & Wood, 2008) says it well:

The welfare of our nation rests heavily upon our system of public education. We strive to provide all of our children with equal access to a high-quality, free education because we know that without it, our democratic way of life will be at peril. As Thomas Jefferson once said, "If Americans desire to be both ignorant and free, they want what never has been and will never be." Indeed, it is our democratic system of governing, based upon the twin pillars of equal rights and responsibilities, which requires we have a system of public education. (p. i)

Multicultural education must foster the development of citizenship. And good citizenship, in turn, fosters multicultural education. That is, citizenship must be broad, inclusive, and pluralistic to be democratic. So multicultural education and good citizenship are intimately linked.

Multicultural education is for everyone: the middle class, the poor, European Americans, and communities of color. If you live in this nation and plan to participate in building this community, then you need multicultural education in order to enter into the civic dialogue with your fellow citizens and future citizens.

Further, multicultural education should include preparation for an active, participatory citizenship. Our critics accuse us of promoting particularism, when in fact our goal should be building a new, inclusive, democratic society. Frank Parker (2003), after examining the contributions of Martin Luther King, Jr., to our society, concludes: "Cultural pluralism and racial equity are best served by nurturing the kind of public life that, in turn, protects and nurtures cultural pluralism and racial equity. On this view, multicultural education and citizenship education are one thing, not two" (p. 13). Parker argues that the curriculum is not sufficient unless it prepares all students for democracy. Current projects in civics education are not sufficient because they do not include the substantive necessity of bringing all of our young people to the table of democracy (Parker, 2003).

James Banks describes the balancing forces in *An Introduction to Multicultural Education* (2008):

> Citizenship education must be transformed in the 21st century because of the deepening racial, ethnic, cultural, language and religious diversity in nation-states around the world. Citizens in a diverse democratic society should be able to maintain attachments to their cultural communities as well as participate effectively in the shared national culture. *Unity without diversity results in cultural repression and hegemony. Diversity without unity leads to Balkanization and the fracturing of the nation-state* (emphasis in the original). Diversity and unity should coexist in a delicate balance in democratic multicultural nation-states. (p. 20)

Planning curriculum for multicultural democracy involves making some value choices. We need to move beyond the idea that the schools are neutral. They were established and funded to promote democracy and citizenship. A pro-democracy position is not neutral; teachers should help schools promote democracy. The myth of school neutrality comes from a poor understanding of the philosophy of positivism. Rather than neutrality, schools should plan and teach cooperation, mutual respect, the dignity of individuals, and related democratic values.

Schools, particularly integrated schools, provide a rich site where students can meet one another, learn to work together, and be deliberative about decision making. In addition to democratic values, teaching deliberative strategies and decision making provides core procedures for multicultural education.

The Achievement Gap

During the 1970s and the 1980s, before the standards and testing movement, school achievement rose dramatically among poor and minority students, and the achievement gap was cut by half. In this period, just before the state tax revolts slashed school budgets, income inequality was declining, and multicultural education and English language assistance became a part of the curriculum. In recent years, some states and some school districts have continued to excel despite financial challenges. Latino, African American, Asian, and poor White students excel in some schools and in some states (Chenoweth, 2007; Haycock, Jerald, & Huang, 2001).

The United States has recently experienced over 30 years of national focus on and debate about schools and school reform. Presidents, governors, and legislators have been elected promising new, more robust school systems. However, as described in numerous studies, since the 1990s the achievement scores in most schools have not significantly improved. Middle-class schools have generally continued to offer quality education, and schools serving poor and minority students have generally continued to fail (Bracey, 2003; Rothstein, 2004).

The persistent difference in achievement scores between White students and African American and Latino students and between middle-class schools and schools in poverty areas is called the achievement gap. The large achievement gap between White students and African American and Latino students is generally presented by legislators and the media as a failure of our public schools. Writers and paid policy advocates claim that this gap results from ineffective teaching, low expectations, unqualified teachers, poorly designed curricula, and a host of similar school problems. They refuse to recognize that low scores can be produced by children living in poverty conditions and attending schools in poverty (Rothstein, 2008).

In 2008, a diverse bipartisan group cochaired by Helen F. Ladd, Pedro Noguera, and Tom Payzant and including many of the scholars cited in references throughout this book signed a statement entitled *A Broader, Bolder Approach to Education*. It said, in part, the following:

> Evidence demonstrates... that achievement gaps based on socioeconomic status are present before children even begin formal schooling. Despite the impressive academic gains registered by some schools serving disadvantaged students, there is no evidence that school improvement strategies by themselves can close these gaps in a substantial, consistent, and sustainable manner....
>
> The potential effectiveness of [No Child Left Behind (NCLB)] has been seriously undermined, however, by its acceptance of the popular assumptions that bad schools are the major reason for low achievement, and that an academic program revolving around standards, testing, teacher training, and accountability can, in and of itself, offset the full impact of low socioeconomic status on achievement. The effectiveness of NCLB has also been weakened by its unintended side effects, such as a narrowing of the curriculum, and by the incentives that NCLB generates for schools to focus instruction on students who are just below the passing point, at the expense of both lower-performing and higher-performing students. (p. 1)

As described, the achievement gap is real and persistent. Unfortunately, the gap has also been used to frame the issue in a politically conservative—keep my taxes low—manner. Writer Jim Crawford argues, "The No Child Left Behind Act—though a policy failure in many ways—has nevertheless been a rhetorical victory for conservative policy advocates...." The emphasis on overcoming racial "achievement gaps" has served as a moral high ground, to oppose those professionals who have worked for years to improve schooling for the poor by insisting on equal resources and equal funding for students. (Crawford, 2008). Framing the Debate over No Child Left Behind (Jim Crawford).

When advocates asked for funds, teacher preparation and assistance for English Language Learners they were accused of "the soft bigotry of low expectations." When teachers working in the schools pointed out that many of the ideas being proposed by outside foundations were unrealistic in schools as they were presently funded, they were accused of "making excuses for failing schools" (Crawford, 2008, p. 1).

Cognitive linguist George Lakoff explains that "frames are mental structures that shape the way we see the world." In this case, Crawford is arguing that language frames—such as "achievement gap" and "No Child Left Behind"—shape our discussion of reality, much as Chapter 4 argued that concepts shape our perceptions of school reality (Crawford, 2008, p. 1).

As explained by conservative think tanks and advanced by conservative politicians such as George Bush, the concept of an achievement gap was used to ignore poverty, crime, and unemployment in neighborhoods and to blame teachers. The arguments deployed around the achievement gap and NCLB did not look at the inequities offered to the students in school in terms of, for example, class sizes, teacher preparation, and resources.

Recent analyses of the data by the Education Trust and others indicate that some specific schools have overcome the school obstacles of poverty and racism. Low-income and minority schools, such as the KIPP Academies and others around the nation, have organized themselves so that their students score near the top in state tests of all kinds (Education Trust, 2006b. Also see, "Don't Trust Ed Trust," Krashen, 2002a). In some cases, improved test scores are achieved by encouraging and inviting low-performing students to leave the academies and to go to other public schools. In general, however, two decades of research and practice show that schools can improve for children—if we choose to do so.

The Standards Movement

Given the increasing diversity of our students (see Chapter 3), it is clear that the nation cannot achieve economically or politically unless we learn to educate all of our students (The New Commission on the Skills of the American Workforce, Tucker et al., 2007). Our task then is to create new policies and practices to foster high academic achievement and to develop pro-democratic preferences, including mutual respect among students in our diverse schools.

To change our current failing schools and to create more equal school systems will require new, substantial investments and will require that those investments be targeted where they will do the most good—in the classrooms of low-achieving schools.

The most popular approach to school change since 1992 has been to rely on standards and assessments (Cuban, L. & Shipps, ed., 2000; Swanson, 2006). Politicians and the business community declared that there was a crisis of mediocrity and low performance in public schools (Emery, 2007). Elected officials did not know how to improve instruction and were unwilling to invest new money, so they called for standards as a substitute for more funds for failing schools. A school reform "industry," usually funded by corporations, developed to advocate, lobby, and give advice to elected officials (Education Trust, the Thomas B. Fordham Institute, Brookings Institution, etc.). The business community and elected officials called for "clear" standards, and school districts and professional organizations responded. Advocates in state departments of education, professional organizations, and most local school districts embraced the new standards movement with a passion. Writing standards became a growth industry for policy advocates and staff and for leaders of educational advocacy organizations.

There are now standards in math, geography, history, English, English as a second language, the sciences, career technical education, and most core curriculum areas, and all demand more, often much more, of students than was previously required. While high standards may help middle-class districts, ironically most impoverished districts were already not meeting the previous low, poorly defined standards. Even during economic recessions when school budgets were cut, removing programs such as counselors, summer school, and reading tutors, the standards are not changed.

To understand standards, let's take an example. A district decides that fourth-grade students should be able to read and do math at a fourth-grade level. (There are, of course, problems with how to define this level.) This district defines a fourth-grade level as the 50th percentile on a nationally normed test, which is the average for fourth graders nationwide.

Then a group of professors, advocates, and teachers gets together and tries to define what student work appropriately demonstrates mastery at this level. This definition becomes the *standard*. Using this standard, committees of advocates and professionals define what reading and math to include in the fourth-grade curriculum.

In Massachusetts, Texas, California, and other states, proposed standards sparked intense battles over whole-language versus phonics approaches to reading, hands-on math versus drill-oriented math, and whose history was going to be taught (see Taylor, 1998). Standards became a new battleground in the curriculum wars.

Once standards were established, the next step was to develop assessment instruments to measure student work. In most cases, states and districts purchased commercial tests. (The test production industry in the United States is a highly profitable enterprise.) As a result, a shift occurred in many states. Test scores became as important as, or even more important than, teachers' grades. As a result, the curriculum shifted to respond to the demands of the tests.

In 1996, at the National Education Summit, governors and business leaders concluded that "efforts to set clear, common . . . academic standards for students in a given school district or state are necessary to improve academic performance" ("Quality Counts," 1997, p. 320). By 1998, virtually all states and most school districts had adopted some form of standards as central to their efforts to improve student achievement (Swanson, 2006). By 2008, 22 of the 50 states had decided that students must pass state tests to graduate from high school (U.S. Department of Education, 2007).

Conservative advocates often merge the terms *standards* and *accountability* into one idea when in fact they are two distinct ideas. Standards have been described above as a level of achievement. Accountability is a decision about who is responsible for achievement or lack of achievement. When schools in poor areas have low test scores, politicians and editorial writers tend to blame and shame the teachers, even though the teachers have not been provided with the resources, quality school facilities, experienced teachers as mentors and coaches, and health and nutrition support needed to overcome academic failure in these areas. The school has standards, but the students are not meeting the standards. Who should be accountable?

In some cases, standards and testing may work together to drive good teachers out of teaching or out of low-income schools. For example, teacher Rachel Bravo worked in a low-performing school in the Sacramento region. Over half of her students were limited-English-proficient. She was an excellent teacher and spent long hours helping her students. But as in most poverty-area schools, her students' test scores and the school's tests scores remained in the low percentiles. Each year the district and the principal complained and criticized, stating that the test scores needed to improve.

So Rachel abandoned her creative, rich, and interactive teaching. Her principal insisted on a very skill-oriented teaching approach, emphasizing only reading and math. Teaching this way took the joy and the pleasure from teaching and from the children. Frustrated with drill and remedial approaches, Rachel found another job in a middle-income school in a nearby district. Now, she can return to her creative, rich, and rewarding teaching methods and her important professional decision making. Her new middle-class students score in the 70th–80th percentile. According to the data, she has gone from being a "poor" teacher to being an "excellent" teacher merely by changing schools. She did not change—her students changed. And now the students in the low-income school have lost their excellent teacher.

Standards serve a positive function in that they help a teacher to decide what to teach and they indicate what is probably on the test. This information is particularly helpful for new teachers (Glidden, 2008). The standards movement to date has had a substantially negative impact on multicultural education. Most states and national groups have developed "content" standards. These content standards stress facts and skills, such as reading, writing, and math. By their nature, content standards usually ignore the important issues of developing a positive and democratic sense of self—that is, they ignore vital multicultural education goals. At its most basic level, multicultural education is about developing a positive sense of self, respect for others, and a well-informed, comprehensive, balanced, and critical analysis of our society. Further, multicultural education is about promoting democracy. The standards movement works against each of these goals.

Schools with a high percentage of English language learners have been particularly impacted by standards. The test scores in these schools tend to be low, in part because the tests are in English. As a consequence, these schools particularly focus on reading, writing, and English learning. In such schools, each and every spare minute must be spent on language drill (Gándara, 2000; Gutiérrez, Baquedano-Lopez, & Asato, 2000; McNeil & Valenzuela, 2001). Yet, as described in Chapter 11, language learning is intimately connected with studies of culture and self-esteem, topics that once were studied in social studies classes. Teachers report that they often go an entire year without teaching either science or social studies. The intervention systems of the controlled curricula used often leave the teacher no time for teaching about important issues of culture and identity. In this manner, standards reduce the curriculum.

Standards usually include long lists of content items, selected from a Euro-centered view of history and positivist-dominated social sciences. In some states, these have been supplemented with a few isolated pieces of multicultural history. But it is this fragmented and isolated approach to facts that itself works against developing both a multicultural perspective and critical thinking. For example, the California eighth-grade history standards include the following:

California. History–Social Science, Grade 8.

Students analyze the divergent paths of the American people in the West from 1800 to the mid-1800s and the challenges they faced.

4. Examine the importance of the great rivers and the struggle over water rights.

5. Discuss Mexican settlements and their locations, cultural traditions, attitudes toward slavery, land-grant system, and economies.

6. Describe the Texas War for Independence and the Mexican-American War, including territorial settlements, the aftermath of the wars, and the effects the wars had on the lives of Americans, including Mexican Americans today.

New York educators developed the following standard:

Intermediate Students:

4. The skills of historical analysis include the ability to investigate differing and competing interpretations of the theories of history, hypothesize about why interpretations change over time, explain the importance of historical evidence, and understand the concepts of change and continuity over time.

The New York Standards are here: *www.emsc.nysed.gov/ciai/socst/pub/ssframe.pdf*
Here is K–8 Curriculum, *www.emsc.nysed.gov/ciai/socst/pub/sscore1.pdf*
Here is 9–11 Curriculum, two years of Global History and one year of US History and Government. *www.emsc.nysed.gov/ciai/socst/pub/sscore2.pdf*

The California and New York standards, like many others, provide enough latitude for the creative teacher to include democratic multicultural education in the classroom. California followed the direction of long, endless lists of historical facts and positions. New York avoided this direction and cited James Banks, saying, "Implementation of the standards should go beyond the addition of long lists of ethnic groups, heroes, and contributions to the infusion of various perspectives, frames of reference, and content from various groups. As a result, students better understand the nature, complexity, and development of United States society as well as societies in other nations throughout the world" (New York Department of Education, Curriculum Instruction and Assessment for the Social Studies, New York, 1995) located here: http://www.emsc.nysed.gov/ciai/socst/pub/ssframe.pdf

The detailed lists in standards seldom get to the important idea of students applying this content in their own lives. Bill Bigelow, in *Rethinking Schools* (2002), suggests that additional standards such as the following would be appropriate such as:

Evaluate the role that racism has played—and continues to play—in shaping the experiences of social groups, especially with respect to economic and political power.

Appreciate the impact social movements have had in addressing injustice of all kinds, and evaluate the effectiveness of these efforts. (p. 9)

These two examples from Bill Bigelow would be rejected by test makers as difficult to measure with multiple-choice tests. In this manner, the standards in many states shape the curriculum toward learning isolated facts and away from studying such complex issues as racism.

Assessment and testing must be aligned with the curriculum in order to improve student achievement (Popham, 1999, 2003). For example, if the state adopts a standard that fifth graders should know a specific skill, then teachers should teach that skill, and tests should measure it. Tests not aligned with curricula will measure student performance on skills they have never been taught. A great deal of the measured failure of schools can be explained by the mismatch between what is taught and what is tested. Keep in mind that the content of the tests has been developed far from the classroom.

Teachers and Accountability

In the last decade, the federal and state emphasis on standards and testing has established a new system of teacher accountability. Prior to the standards movement, teachers could teach poorly and have virtually no measure of their success or failure except their ability to control a classroom. Standards, tests, and accountability programs have begun to change this situation. Some teachers in low-performing schools simply are not successful with these students. They will not raise their standards, and they will not do the extra preparation required to assist all students to learn. With standards and accountability, these teachers can be identified, coached, and provided with opportunities to improve their teaching—or to leave the school.

The movement toward having national standards has been successful in gaining the political support of most elected officials. Advocates (Chenoweth, 2007; Wilkins, 2006) assert that high-poverty schools have improved by focusing on standards and accountability. The evidence supporting these claims is far from conclusive.

Rather than working on improving school conditions in order to assist teachers, the conservative school reform movement has successfully tied arguments for accountability and testing to the demands for standards. And, too often, the standards/accountability mantra has been used to limit teachers' professional decision making and to prevent their modification of lessons and strategies to respond to the needs of the students.

The problem is not that accountability is bad or that it is a conservative (business interests) reform. It is that our current processes of testing and accountability are crude and inaccurate measures that deliver power into the hands of state school boards and test writers who have shown limited knowledge of the reality of classroom life and no particular commitment to the democratic role of schools and multicultural education. The flaws in most test processes have produced a condition where testing has been practically useless in improving curriculum or teacher delivery of instruction. In most districts in low-income areas, standards and test-based accountability have not improved school achievement—they have only placed someone else (an administrator, a state department) in charge of measuring achievement rather than the teachers (Kober, 2001; Nichols & Berliner, 2007).

There should be accountability. The next step is for teachers to participate, often through their unions, in shaping this accountability by participating in the legislative battles over NCLB and in the district-level decision making about testing and accountability measures. There is nothing inherently wrong with a national test that measures the basic skills of reading, writing, and math and that can be used for comparisons. We should also measure other items, such as graduating from high school, voting, graduating from college, and getting a decent job. Collecting this information would not be more expensive than the current test production and administration costs. States and school districts already collect some of this information.

The crisis in urban education is not just a school issue; public policy decisions on school funding, housing, jobs, transit, crime, and rehabilitation have accelerated the urban school crisis. The current corporate-imposed process of accountability based on test scores has failed. The problem with the current accountability systems is that they are too narrow, focusing primarily on reading and math scores and ignoring other valuable skills such as bilingualism.

Testing and Standards

Assessment (including testing) is closely tied to the standards movement. The argument is that if a district cannot assess performance, then teachers do not know whether the student has met the standard. District leaders also do not know the areas where the school or the district needs to improve. There is little doubt that quality assessment practices, including testing, are important to school improvement.

Texas Assessment Texas is a high-poverty state. It provides the major example of using testing to drive school reform. The Texas Assessment of Academic Skills (TAAS) was begun in 1990, and when George W. Bush became governor in 1994, he inherited that system of testing. Tests and sanctions then became a centerpiece of his campaign for presidency and his stated first priorities as the "education president."

Several school districts in Texas, with concentrations of students from high-poverty areas, claimed to have made dramatic improvements in student achievement in between 1992 and 2000, as evidenced by the TAAS. In the Ysleta Independent School District near El Paso and elsewhere, entire schools made significant gains in student achievement. In several cases, previously low-performing schools improved. The Ysleta district focused on high standards for all students; accountability with strong alignment to the written, taught, and state-tested curricula; and bilingual education, when appropriate, to assist language-minority students (Hart, 2006).

Over a period of more than 10 years, TAAS scores improved for many schools in Texas. Houston Superintendent of Schools Rod Paige later became U.S. Secretary of Education under George Bush. He was a strong advocate of testing and the TAAS system of frequent testing, remediation, and sanctions. As President, George Bush adopted the slogan of the Children's Defense Fund, "leave no child behind," as the title for his proposed legislation, which included frequent and regular testing. Often referred to as NCLB, this legislation became law in January 2002 (PL 107-116).

In *The Harmful Impact of the TAAS System in Texas* (2000), Linda McNeil and Angela Valenzuela offered extensive research evidence to show that behind the improved TAAS scores is a major shift in the curriculum toward test preparation. The test became the curriculum. Test preparation activities, rather than quality teaching, became a norm, particularly in low-performing schools. It appears that students may have answered more test questions correctly, but they did not necessarily learn to read better (McNeil & Valenzuela, 2000). High-performing schools were allowed to continue with an emphasis on creativity, art, development of self-worth, and self-governance, while low-performing schools were forced to change their curriculum to emphasize more drill-and-practice activities in an effort to raise their test scores.

Evidence indicates that the curriculum in low-performing schools was restricted and reduced. The curriculum was changed to a more remedial education model based on cultural and linguistic deficit theories. The study of topics such as science and social studies (preparation for democratic life) that are not on the test was significantly reduced (McNeil & Valenzuela, 2000). In response to criticism, extensive cheating, and apparent manipulation of the data, by 2003 Texas had adopted a new series of tests, the Texas Assessment of Knowledge and Skills. The Texas approach of relying on testing remains popular with elected officials focused on fixing an endangered school system.

Teachers need to understand the limits of our current testing systems. What you count, what you measure, and what you don't count bring ideological preferences to bear. The current testing pressure has moved many schools away from seeking multiple goals, including democracy, and toward responding to what is tested (Rothstein, 2007). The standards and the tests have come to drive the curriculum. Usually, standards and testing have reinforced a consensus point of view rather than an oppositional or nuanced point of view about issues such as race and racism.

Tests, particularly multiple-choice tests, measure limited fact-based items. Thus, the standards and testing movement, or accountability, has shifted the curriculum significantly toward coverage of facts and away from multicultural education, critical thinking, and civic values. The focus on testing is a reflection of the corporate ideology that has grown throughout our society with little acknowledged analysis (Emery, 2007; Nichols & Berliner, 2007). While testing has become a dominant form of school control, most people using the tests do not understand testing well or recognize its significant limits (Lee, 2007; Nichols & Berliner, 2007; Popham, 2003).

Education is cumulative; learning to read and to do math accumulates from year to year. A single year of testing does not appropriately evaluate instruction. Further, testing what students learn of reading, citizenship, or other skills not only evaluates the teacher but also assesses the entire school, the family, and the community (Rothstein, 2004).

A tragedy of current programs is that low-performing schools are using more and more time for drilling in math and reading rather than teaching science or social studies or the arts or focusing on hiring teachers with reading and math preparation. The test preparation focuses on easily tested basic math and reading skills rather than attempting to measure deeper comprehension of math concepts and written language. The high stakes attached to the current testing have led schools to limit curriculum and school experiences to those that focus on test preparation, robbing low-income children of motivation and opportunities to engage in school (Wood, Darling-Hammond, Neill, & Roscheweki, 2007; Perlstein, 2007).

President George Bush and Secretary of Education Margaret Spellings use a sales or promotion approach to claim that No Child Left Behind reforms have resulted in significant improvements in student achievement in both reading and math and that they have reduced the achievement gap for African Americans and Hispanics. They cite as evidence the National Assessment of Educational Progress (NAEP). Less ideologically committed researchers have pointed out that there has been no change in average reading scores in the nation on the NAEP between 2002 and 2006 and only a small gain in math scores (Fuller, Wright, Gesicki, & Kang, 2007). A lively debate continues over what the test scores actually mean (Kober, Chudowsky, & Chudowsky, 2008; Nichols & Berliner, 2007; Perlstein, 2007).

Perhaps the Focus on Testing Has Not Produced Improved Achievement

In the report *Assessment, High Stakes, and Alternative Visions: Appropriate Use of the Right Tools to Leverage Improvement* (2006), Professor Laitsch writes:

> [T]he current high-takes system assumes that it is self-evident that all schools should pursue increased test scores as their dominant goal and that those scores offer the most reliable evidence of how well a school is performing. . . . The federal No Child Left Behind act has helped promote the high-stakes model of assessment, in which test scores are used to make decisions affecting both individual students and the schools they attend—up to and including whether those schools will remain open.

Negative consequences, Laitsch writes, include "[n]arrowed curriculum and instructional strategies," resulting in "an impoverished academic experience" for students. In their excellent book *Collateral Damage: How High-Stakes Testing Corrupts America's Schools* (2007), Sharon Nichols and David C. Berliner provide powerful examples of how the focus on testing has produced a significant pattern of cheating by students, by school officials, and by politicians (p. 81). In Chapter 4, they describe how states use statistical manipulation to claim improved test scores. There are disturbing data indicating that high-stakes testing has increased schools' dropout and push-out rates (McNeil, Coppola, Radigan, & Heilig, 2008). In 2008, the *New York Times* revealed that the New York City Schools had begun to use student scores to measure the alleged quality of individual teachers—increasing the stakes for testing without having improved the quality of test instruments (Medina, 2008).

While the NAEP and state tests typically hold schools accountable and may cast blame on teachers, another form of testing—exit exams—seeks to hold individual students accountable. By 2006, some 22 states required students to pass an exit exam to receive a high school diploma. These tests are always in English, creating a major barrier to graduation for immigrant students who enter our schools at the high school level. There is no evidence yet that the students in states using exit exams learn more than the students in states without exit exams.

Among the several problems in testing described by Nichols and Berliner are that few who make policy decisions understand the processes of test development and the limitations of current test instruments and that even fewer understand the processes of determining test scores and cut scores. Policy recommendations are made based upon a simplistic and often misinfromed view of the validity and the reliability of test scores. The determination of cut scores, which are used to define such categories as pass/fail, proficient, and basic, is a political decision; it is not done using an objective or a scientific process. Yet schools are closed and superintendents promoted based on weak and inappropriate use of the data.

Many states claim improvements in reading and math scores and cite student scores on some state and local tests. But there has been little, if any, improvement in scores on well-established national tests such as the NAEP (Lee, 2006). In 2007, measurable gains nationally were finally made in math. The small gains we've seen may be the result of concentrated instruction on narrowly defined objectives in reading and math. Achievement in math on national tests has improved in grades 4 and 8 and has declined in grade 12, while achievement in reading had increased from 1992 to 2001 and has leveled off since then (Fuller et al., 2007). The most recent research finds that achievement as measured by state and national tests is moving marginally in a positive direction. The definitions used to distinguish the categories and the differences between basic and proficient on state tests are often dramatically different than the definitions of proficiency used in the NAEP. As a consequence, the percentages of students considered proficient in some states are distinctly different depending on whether one looks at the state or the federal tests (Kober et al., 2008). The testing and accountability efforts have transformed teaching and schooling, often for the worse, by controlling teachers more, making teaching less interesting, and at the same time supporting underfunding of schools, a new tracking system, and the privatization of formerly public schools (Nichols & Berliner, 2007).

Curriculum Alignment

Curriculum alignment has been one of the most frequently used forms of curriculum development since the start of the standards movement. Essentially, curriculum alignment adjusts the curriculum so that it covers the same information as the standards and the tests. Since most standards focus only on content, this gives priority to content coverage over other approaches to learning such as critical thinking and the development of democratic values. Curriculum alignment is particularly useful in skill-based courses such as reading and math. Here, providing a consistent series of skills and knowledge as well as practice in these skills improves achievement.

Discussions of curriculum alignment among teachers provide opportunities for them to work together to share and to solve problems. These discussions are particularly helpful for new teachers, who have so much to learn about actual teaching. At other times, alignment discussions have become oppressive, particularly when they are connected to irrational demands by administrators. For example, there is some evidence that 20–30 minutes of direct phonics instruction helps many children, and particularly those with dyslexia, to learn to read (U.S. Department of Health and Human Services, 2000). It does not follow that 60–90 minutes of direct instruction in phonics is twice or three times as good. This is faulty reasoning and irrational.

Several moderately successful programs such as Success for All have insisted on a 90-minute reading/language arts period. Then, when poorly informed or desperate administrators see that students are still not learning to read at grade level, they extend the scripted lessons to 2½ hours. There are no data to support such decisions. This is the equivalent of learning that drinking 8 glasses a milk per day is good for you and then drinking 24 glasses per day since that must be better. When imposed without professional competence, more curriculum alignment and more curriculum control have not been shown to improve achievement.

The Debate Over Textbooks

Textbooks have long been a major source of control of the curriculum. Challenges to Euro-centric textbook coverage have increased as our schools have become more diverse. Today, several communities refuse to be rendered invisible in textbooks, as if they had not contributed to the development of the United States.

Lacking sufficient preparation time and support services, teachers usually do not have the time to write their own materials. Additionally, many teachers feel they do not have the expertise to design a math or science curriculum, so they rely on state or district standards, textbooks, and curriculum guides to organize their lessons. Throughout our school systems, most teachers accept many of the curriculum and teaching decisions made by textbook writers and publishers.

The struggles over the content of public school curricula are of great significance. Groups arguing for multicultural education must contend against the established and preferential political power of the standards committees, publishers, and many educators. Teachers' overreliance on textbooks makes the content and structure of these textbooks very important. In some school districts, teachers enjoy a great deal of latitude in selecting and using materials. In these districts, principals and other administrators consider the teachers professionals and do not usually impose decisions made outside the classroom.

In other schools and districts, administrators closely monitor the curriculum. Schools and districts where test scores are low often insist that there be a uniform curriculum, that all teachers follow a set of commercially prepared lesson plans, and that a blanket set of rules governing homework and tests be implemented as a strategy to improve achievement. The strategy taught to many administrators is to control teachers' use of time and curriculum delivery in an attempt to improve test scores. One way to improve test scores is to force teachers to teach to the test. Unfortunately, this approach assumes that the tests reflect a viable and valuable curriculum; they do not. In addition, in most cases the textbooks are written by content experts and editors, not by teachers or by writers familiar with the lives of children and young adults. Teaching is less personally rewarding in such harsh school environments, so creative and experienced teachers may flee to other school sites. Another method administrators use to improve test scores is to encourage low-scoring students such as immigrants to leave school— or at least to leave their school. The strategy of more administrative control as opposed to teacher empowerment seldom improves learning.

The failure of schools to achieve the equal educational opportunity that enables all students to prepare for entrance into the economic and political life of the nation and the increased diversity of our society require multicultural curriculum reform. Textbooks and curricula should be changed to do the following:

1. Eliminate bias and stereotypes in instructional material.

2. Reduce overreliance on worksheets and other materials of questionable educational merit.

3. Reduce reliance on materials and strategies that focus primarily on direct teacher instruction.

4. Include higher-order thinking skills (critical thinking) in the curriculum for all students.

5. Provide time for teachers to prepare enriching instructional material.

6. Revise texts and materials for all students to provide a comprehensive, complete, and inclusive view of society and its history.

7. Encourage cooperative learning, sharing, and helping one another.

8. Base materials on students' life experiences.

9. Emphasize the development of language and communication skills.

10. Develop materials that explore cultural and national differences and that teach students to analyze diverse viewpoints.

11. Provide all students with introductions to the rich contributions of many cultures.

12. Build on and extend students' experiences.

13. Build on and extend students' languages.

14. Promote dialogue between teachers and students.

15. Help students analyze and comprehend their real-life situations—that is, peer groups, gangs, drugs, violence, romance, youth culture, and music.

Most existing textbooks do not respond to these minimum qualitative criteria.

Multicultural school wars are far from new. Battles over the place of ethnic groups and immigrant groups and culture date back at least to 1840 (Glazer, 1997). Textbook battles frequently occur over religion, sexual orientation, and women's issues as well as multiethnic education. Recently, when a father sued to eliminate the phrase "under God" from the Pledge of Allegiance, Congress and the media exploded in a storm of criticism, even though this phrase was added only in 1954 to a pledge originally written by a socialist minister.

Efforts to rewrite texts to achieve comprehensive representation of diverse cultures often produce rancorous conflicts and frequently are opposed by textbook writers (often college professors) and commercial publishers (Ansary, 2005). These conflicts reveal the underlying struggle for power in education. When long-hidden issues are unmasked, persons who have enjoyed the undeserved and unwarranted privileges of defining "history" and literature react with alarm. Presently, standards-writing committees, state curriculum committees, and textbook publishers control the selection of common knowledge. The control of knowledge determines who controls the future. Changing who controls the selection of knowledge is central to school reform (King, 1995).

Apple (2001) and Carnoy and Levin (1985) discuss the importance of control of knowledge. Apple contends that control of knowledge has been a primary factor in controlling women and devaluing women's work in the field of education. Critical theorists have paid particular attention to ideological control and domination within education, arguing that the historical record has been persistently slanted to support ideological control and institutional racism (Apple, 2001). When scholars use a multicultural perspective to reveal historical biases, when they criticize narrow definitions and perspectives of history, they frequently encounter hostile responses and a vigorous defense of a European American–centered viewpoint as the only truth (Ansary, 2005; Gitlin, 1995; Glazer, 1997; Leming, Ellington, & Porter, 2003; Schlesinger, 1992). Teachers come under attack also. In 2008, a powerful Republican senator introduced Senate Bill 1108 in the Arizona Senate. Among other provisions, it would have defined Mexican American and La Raza studies as anti-American and bar their teaching in public schools.

Textbook struggles in California and New York reveal the opposing viewpoints. The view that won out in California was crafted by neo-conservative historian Diane Ravitch and supported by Paul Gagnon and former California State Superintendent of Public Instruction Bill Honig, among others (Cornbleth & Waugh, 1995). Their view argues that textbooks and a common history should provide the glue that unites our society. Historical themes and interpretations are selected in books to create unity in a diverse and divided society. This viewpoint assigns to schools the task of creating a common culture. In reality, television and military service may do more to create a common culture than do schools and books.

Conservatives assign the task of cultural assimilation to schools, with particular emphasis on the history, social studies, and literature curricula. Historians advocating consensus write textbooks that downplay the roles of slavery, class, racism, genocide, and imperialism in our history. They focus on ethnicity and assimilation rather than race—on the successful achievement of political reform, representative government, and economic opportunity for European American workers and immigrants. They decline to notice the high poverty rate of U.S. children, the crisis of urban schooling, and the continuation of racial divisions in housing and the labor force.

In arguing for this unity, the authors consistently take primarily one viewpoint in their recounting of historical events. They select heroes who champion unity and events that support their theses, while ignoring heroes who champion diversity or class struggle (see Figure 12.1). Loewen (1995) and Weatherford (1988) illustrate the narrow misrepresentations of history favored by this group (see also the discussion in Chapter 3).

This *consensus conservative viewpoint* of history, as opposed to multicultural perspectives, dominates textbook publishing, but these partial and incomplete histories do

Figure 12.1 **Common History Textbook Heroes**

Unity Heroes	Diversity Heroes
Alexander Hamilton	Daniel Shay Patrick Henry
Andrew Jackson	Chief Pontiac Chief Tecumseh
Stephen F. Austin	Gregorio Cortez
Abraham Lincoln	John Brown
General George Custer	Sojourner Truth Sitting Bull
Samuel Gompers	Eugene Debs
Teddy Roosevelt	Big Bill Haywood Emma Goldman
George Washington Carver	W. E. B. DuBois Elizabeth Cady Stanton Jane Addams Alice Paul Lucia Gonzales Parsons
Martin Luther King, Jr.	Malcolm X Martin Luther King, Jr., 1967–1968

not empower students from our diverse cultural communities. By recounting primarily a consensual, European American view, history and literature extend and reconstruct current White supremacy, sexism, and class biases in our society. When texts or teachers tell only part of the story, schools foster ideological domination (Cornbleth & Waugh, 1995).

In 1991, the New York State Social Studies Review and Development Committee argued against continued ideological domination and for diversity in the curriculum: "If the United States is to continue to prosper in the 21st century, then all of its citizens, whatever their race or ethnicity, must believe that they and their ancestors have shared in the building of the country and have a stake in its success" (p. 1).

The differences between the consensus viewpoint and the multicultural viewpoint are profound. They differ both on what happened and on whose knowledge gets validated. Young people have their own background knowledge. They have a worldview based on their daily experiences in their homes, among their friends, and on the streets. If the curriculum reaches out to build on and extend this knowledge, they feel validated as part of the larger society. Students need to see themselves and their lives as part of history and as part of our society. A curriculum of diversity and inclusion treats them as members of the community: Inclusion encourages all students to partici-pate in building a more tolerant, more just, and more democratic community.

Students of several diverse cultural groups encountering the traditional consensus view in textbooks find their own history discounted or ignored. When their background knowledge is ignored, they are invalidated (Gay, 2000). They are made invisible. The discounting of working-class history, significantly a history of people of color, com-bined with economic subjugation and poor job prospects, leads to the alienation from school and the pain and rage that periodically explode in crime, in violence on school grounds, and occasionally in urban riots.

The struggle between the two viewpoints is a struggle over worldviews, as explained in Chapter 2. The new multicultural worldview contends against the currently domi-nant Euro-centric view. Both sides can marshal evidence, and both sides have compe-tent historians. Both sides have advocates who refuse to give a fair rendition or just consideration to the viewpoints and evidence of their opponents (Ansary, 2005; Gagnon, 1995; Gay, 2003; Gitlin, 1995; Leming et al., 2003).

Instead of just choosing sides or using only a consensus text, the journal *Rethinking Schools* gives numerous examples of critical teachers recognizing that the interpretation and analysis of history and the social sciences are a continuous project in which students can participate. In *Rethinking Columbus* (Bigelow & Patterson, 1998); *The Line Between Us* (2007), on immigration; *Whose Wars?* (2006), on the Iraq War; and other publica-tions, the journal demonstrates that there is often not a historical agreement on any single viewpoint. To present only the conclusions of the unity advocates in textbooks encourages poor scholarship and limits students' freedom of thought and public responsibility.

Each worldview selects specific concepts to present and specific content to cover. Power relationships, along with research paradigms, are expressed in defining and selecting the categories (Apple, 2001; King, 1995; Popkewitz, 1987). Teachers need to know about the various viewpoints and their nuances in order to present materials that provide academic balance and supplement commercial textbooks.

Multicultural education works to transform textbooks to achieve democratic goals and to present an inclusive curriculum. For example, most U.S. and state histories use the concept of the *frontier* in telling the story of the conquering of the Midwest and the West. Textbooks portray European settlers as bringing civilization to a previously uncivilized land and people.

Any reasonable analysis of the lifestyle of gold miners, cattlemen, and others in com-parison to that of Native Americans reveals that the settlers were not "more civilized" and the Native Americans "less civilized," even though textbooks frequently perpetuate these views. The Europeans were not less violent; more family-oriented; or more respectful of life, social mores, and other community values. They were better armed and more numerous; the native nations were divided against each other—and the Europeans won. Most public school texts present a romanticized, Euro-centric view of the frontier and civilization (Foner & Werner, 1991).

A similar misapplication of the concepts of frontier and civilization occurred in recording the Europeans conquering Africa and initiating the transatlantic slave trade and the terror of White supremacy in the South. Textbooks too often portray the expansion of European culture as a historical inevitability, as natural. The resultant destruction of peaceful societies and the deaths of millions are dismissed as historically insignificant.

When teachers, parents, and others seek to balance textbooks to offer a less Euro-centric view of territorial expansion, they can expect to be attacked by intellectual elites and neo-conservatives in education, government, and private foundations. Although neo-conservatives do not totally control the public discussion, their network of professors, institutes, and foundations is effective in garnering media attention (Apple & Christian Smith, 1991; Asante, 1991; Cornbleth & Waugh, 1995; Glazer, 1997; Leming et al., 2003; Ravitch, 2003).

Writing the California Framework for History and Social Sciences

California has the largest population of any state, with more than 6,286,000 students in school in 2006. California students make up more than 11 percent of the U.S. total. California, along with Texas and some 15 other states, adopts textbooks for the entire state instead of district by district. This makes the California adoption the largest single textbook sale in the nation. Succeeding in this market is an important goal for textbook publishers. Many publishers write and edit their books in a targeted attempt to win control of the large and lucrative California and Texas markets. Publishers promote and try to sell books developed for California and Texas throughout the nation in an effort to increase their profits.

The election of 1982 began 16 years of conservative Republican control of the California governorship, and governors appoint the members of the California State Board of Education. The conservative control changed the history–social science, language, and reading curricula and textbooks for the state and influenced textbook decisions throughout the United States. The California Department of Education's 1987 draft of the *History–Social Science Framework for California Public Schools* (a guide for teachers and textbook selection still in use today) excluded an accurate history of Latino and Native American settlement of the Southwest and did not cover the substantial Asian history in the West (see Almaguer, 1994). By electing to concentrate on a melting pot, consensus point of view, the *Framework* assumed that telling the history of European immigrants adequately explained the experiences of Mexicans, Native Americans, and Asians.

The *Framework* does not describe the displacement and destruction of Native American, Mexican, and Mexican American communities from 1850 to 1930 throughout the Southwest, including in Los Angeles and San Diego. The authors—among them, educational historian Diane Ravitch—failed to note that the present mosaic of Southwest culture was created by the subjugation and domination of previously existing groups, both Native American and Mexican American. This California document won the praise of conservative school advocates around the nation. Honig and Ravitch and numerous funded advocacy organizations such as the Brookings Institution cited it in their writings and speeches as a positive example of the kind of multiculturalism they supported.

In California, committees and the state board of education select textbooks for all K–8 students in public schools. The U.S. history books submitted for the California adoptions in 1990, 1998, and 2005 were required to be based on the *Framework*. The 2005 *Framework* expanded the coverage of African American, Native American, and women's history but was totally inadequate in its coverage of Latinos and Asians—both significant population groups in the development of the West. Now, Latinos make up 48.1 percent of California's student population and Asians make up 8.1 percent. The only significant change between the *Framework* adopted in 1987 and that adopted in 2005 was the addition of a new cover, a cover letter, and a photo of César Chávez. The treatment in seventh- and eighth-grade texts of the history and cultures of Africa and the U.S. slave system was promptly challenged by members of the African American community (King, 1992). The history of African Americans was presented as if it was not central to understanding U.S. history. (For a detailed analysis of this curriculum conflict, see Cornbleth & Waugh, 1995. For an opposing view, see Gitlin, 1995.) The conservatively defined *Framework* became the controlling conceptual framework for the California History–Social Science Standards of 2000 and the basis for the selection of textbooks until the present day.

In 1998, California adopted new reading–language arts guidelines that focus intensely on phonics instruction for kindergarten through grade 3. The reading (and math) scores of California's children had dropped perilously from 1982 to 1994, as the state struggled with an economic crisis and critically underfunded its schools. Class sizes mushroomed to more than 33 students per teacher. Conservatives blamed falling reading scores not on the largest class sizes in the nation but on the whole-language approach to reading education and on inadequately prepared teachers. Most of the press and other media accepted and repeated this viewpoint as the truth in spite of substantial evidence to the contrary (Krashen, 2002a).

The state board of education and the legislature held hearings at which only phonics advocates were allowed to present their ideas. Almost none of the research on phonics has been completed with language-minority children, who constitute 1.5 million, or nearly 25 percent, of the total student population. Taylor (1998) describes how reading research was distorted and ignored, while academic careers were created, in the successful right-wing campaign to change reading instruction. The legislature, ill-informed on reading and language instruction, passed laws requiring phonics lessons in new textbooks, smaller class sizes in the primary grades, and phonics training for all new teachers (see also Arlington & Woodside-Jiron, 1999). Now, with almost 10 years of emphasis on phonics, there is no substantive evidence on national tests of improved reading scores beyond grade 4 (Fuller et al., 2007: Gutiérrrez et al., 2000; U.S. Department of Education, 2005). In 2008, leaders in the Bush Administration were found complicit in imposing nationwide phonics approach to reading known as Reading First. After six years of implementation, there was no evidence that the imposed curriculum approach, which emphasized phonics and used a scripted curriculum, improved reading scores (Boulay et al., 2008).

The New York Curriculum of Inclusion

California is not alone. Similar textbook and curriculum struggles have occurred elsewhere in the United States. After an earlier dispute, in 1991, the New York Commissioner of Education's office drew together a curriculum review committee, whose members included several eminent scholars, to recommend a curriculum for teachers in the state. This committee wrote *One Nation, Many Peoples: A Declaration of Cultural Interdependence* (New York State Social Studies Review and Development Committee, 1991). In July 1991, the New York Board of Regents adopted the "Understanding Diversity" policy recommendations based largely on that report (http://www.emsc. nysed.gov/ciai/socst/pub/ssframework.pdf). The committee report offered extensive guides and suggestions to teachers to supplement the inadequate textbooks available. The report was attacked as too multicultural. Arthur Schlesinger, Jr., resigned from the committee in protest, while historian Oscar Handlin and others defended the report. The California State Board of Education had adopted a "consensus" view, and the New York Board of Regents had adopted an "inclusion" view (Cornbleth & Waugh, 1995).

Texas

Texas, with 4.1 million students, buys textbooks for the entire state; thus, like California, it creates a large, lucrative market (more than $344.7 million per year). Texas law mandates that approved books promote democracy, patriotism, and the free enterprise system. In July 2002, the process of social studies textbook selection began again in Texas. Members of conservative groups objected to some proposed books as anti-American and anti-Christian. They claimed that the books had errors because they failed to say that Indian tribes were as much to blame as fur traders and tourists for wiping out the great buffalo herds of the Plains by shooting the animals for sport (Mabin, 2002). The textbook battles in Texas continue to the present (Ansary, 2005; Dallas News, Jan 16, 2008–March 28, 2008).

Political Control of Standards and Textbooks

The standards movement that began in the 1990s has changed the textbook debates substantially. Now texts are written to cover standards. In many states, the ideological battles of the consensus versus the multicultural perspective have shifted from writing frameworks and resource guides to writing standards.

Even though sociologist Nathan Glazer can claim *We Are All Multiculturalists Now* (1997), the implementation of standards-based programs, particularly where enforced by testing, has significantly reduced multicultural education in the curriculum and shifted instruction back toward a Euro-centric traditionalist viewpoint. The gap between current historical, sociological, and economic scholarship and available textbooks contributes significantly to students' alienation from history and social science courses (Gay, 2003). The problems of textbooks and the problems revealed in the battles over them are not errors or accidental. Political forces use their control of governments to advance their worldview, as in the elimination of bilingual education from the reauthorization of the Elementary and Secondary Education Act in 2002. These struggles are the product of choices by people in power to use the teaching of history, the social sciences, and literature to promote a specific worldview. This worldview is being challenged from the right by evangelical Christians and from the left by those who support the multicultural education movement. The views that pass for a consensus history, at times called the *canon*, have been developed in universities' history departments and reveal the current distribution of political and ideological power in these departments.

Cornbleth and Waugh (1995) describe the process of opinion shaping and media control in curriculum battles as follows:

> Also noteworthy is the organizational location of individual members (of the conservative network) which lent status and authority to their pronouncements. One speaks not for oneself but for a committee, commission, council or center or a university or federal government agency. Network members supported one another and their reform cause by praising each other's work in public statements and journal articles, appointing one another to advisory boards, hiring one another as consultants for their various projects, and helping to fund these projects. (p. 18)

These institutions and conservative networks resist emerging multicultural perspectives because the emerging multicultural society challenges the traditional distribution of power (Apple, 2001).

The multicultural curriculum should help students understand society and their place in it, and it should prepare them for a positive, productive future. To achieve these goals, a democratic multicultural perspective argues that students' histories should not be left out of the curriculum. All students need to learn that they belong and that they are participants in the democratic project. The curriculum should help students to learn that they are important. They need to learn the skills, information, and attitudes that will protect and extend democracy and allow them to participate in the 21st-century economy.

Clearly, U.S. society is more democratic today than it was in 1776. It became more democratic as a result of popular struggles to expand democracy—most recently, the Civil Rights Movement (1954–1968). Textbooks and curricula should tell the stories of struggles for democracy—for women's right to vote; against slavery; and for labor unions, civil rights, and economic justice—and teachers should get to these parts of history. The curriculum can help empower students by teaching them that past struggles have made our society more democratic. In studying these events, students learn that conflict is a normal and natural way to make change and that progress is the result of hard work.

Beyond the Text: Technology

Just as it can be argued that a student's access to a higher quality of life is enhanced or hindered based on their ability to read and understand print (a literacy divide), so, too, a student's access to the economy and a higher quality of life is enhanced or hindered based on whether or not he or she has the skills to access and utilize computer technology and the Internet (a digital divide). It was this belief that drove the United States to invest heavily in the 1990s to place computers into schools and to connect those schools to the Internet.

There was a belief by some in the early years of the 21st century that placing computer technology into schools and connecting schools to the Internet would somehow bring equal opportunity to the classroom, that it would level the technological playing field. This view ignored a critical tenet of truth regarding public education—all schools do not begin with equal resources.

In 1980, Jean Anyon wrote in *Social Class and the Hidden Curriculum of Work* that in working-class neighborhoods, school knowledge was rigidly defined and learning occurred in a rote fashion, with little choice or discussion. Knowledge was construed and delivered as individual chunks with little connection made between the various pieces of knowledge presented. Knowledge in the working-class school meant learning the basics, primarily through repetitive practice. In wealthy neighborhoods, schooling was quite different. In these schools, knowledge was seen as fluid. Learning involved interaction between teacher and student. Students were often asked to express what they thought and were supported in thinking critically about connections between various portions of the curriculum (Anyon, 1980). Today, unfortunately, technology can be used in either manner. Most middle-class schools are preparing their students for technology literacy—and most poor schools are not.

Technology is shaping the world, from the Internet to iPhones, from cell phones, to social networking sites such as facebook and myspace and it is shaping the business and trade world. Those who are well prepared will prosper; those who are not well prepared will fall behind. The future economic prosperity of our nation depends on decisions we are making now. Either our students will gain access to technology and learn to learn with technology, or the computers in their classrooms will be used primarily for low-level tasks such as performing drills, keeping grade books, and recording attendance.

The problems of using technology to move beyond the limited textbooks help to form a new awareness that the use of computers and the Internet needs to be combined with support for faculty to develop technological skills and quality educational practices ("Quality Counts at 10," 2008).

Every student, every school, should have access to the skills to use technology and to access the vast media world around us, from libraries, to databases, including YouTube and others. Henry Jenkins et al. of the Massachusetts Institute of Technology, in an important paper written in 2006 for the MacArthur Foundation, says:

> Educators must work together to ensure that every American young person has access to the skills and experiences need to become a full participant, can articulate their understanding of how media shapes perceptions, and has been socialized into the emerging ethical standards that should shape their practices as media makers and participants in online communities. . . .
>
> Fostering such social skills and cultural competencies requires a more systemic approach to media education in the United States. Everyone involved in preparing young people to go out into the world has contributions to make in helping students to acquire the skills they need to become full participants in our society. (pp. 3–4)

Moving in this direction requires a revolution in how teachers use their time and resources. The wide use of technology and the Internet will interest some students and will even motivate some students to remain in school. The information on the World Wide Web (Web) that comes from museums, libraries, and special collections such as the Martin Luther King collection at Stanford University can provide students with excellent, interesting material that is urgent and relevant to their lives.

Technology is already changing our world and our schools. Our challenge is to be certain that all our students join in this development rather than being left behind by a new form of tracking where the middle class and the elite students have technology and the students of color and language minority students have electronic worksheets and test preparation drills.

Teachers working together and accessing the Internet can find and create useful materials for their classrooms. Access to the Internet and the Web has revolutionized our ability to find exciting, interesting, and accurate information and to move dramatically beyond the limits of current textbooks. Look on the Web for the Hmong home page (*www.hmongnet.org*), for example, and you will find links to a variety of information sources. Native American, Latino, and Asian resources on the Web are seemingly limitless. Each group has its own news services, which can be found using a search engine. There are Web pages and resource guides for all. (The Web changes rapidly, and pages listed here may become out of date. You need to use a search engine to look for materials.) There are more than 100,000 lesson plans on the Web. Good places to start are *www.rethinkingschools.org* and *www.nea.org*. The problem is not the lack of material but the need to develop the skill of selecting good material.

Students need to learn the skills of locating relevant information and evaluating information in order to use the Web as a data source. Teachers should select a search engine such as Google and teach their students to use it well. As an initial step, teachers can provide prescreened useful sites. It is difficult and disheartening for students to simply look up a topic. They may get thousands of hits and little guidance as to which sites are valuable as opposed to weak or worthless. You can start with some megasites, such as Paul Gorski's Multicultural Pavilion and the Discovery Channel and PBS sites as well as websites listed in professional journals. Web quests provide a particularly engaging process, and now there are over 1,000 Web quests (*www.webquest.org*). They even have a Web quest on evaluating Web sources. By engaging in project based learning (see glef.org), students develop technological literacy while producing their own materials.

You can use cooperative learning strategies to assist students whether you have a one-computer classroom or a classroom that has a bank of computers. It is helpful to identify which of your students can assist you as computer experts. Give these students the responsibility for caring for the computer and teaching others to use it well.

After weeks and months on the Web, students can begin to record and to create their own stories music and videos. The video of students producing their own stories at *www.edutopia.org/san-fernando-education-technology-team* provides excellent examples of this work. In fact, the Edutopia megasite is a great place to find additional lessons and learning modules on technology use and integration. Students can record their own stories and pass them along to the next class. A group of students in Los Angeles designed and implemented a research project on tracking in their high school. Once created and presented as a multimedia project, such research can become the basis for the next semester's or the next year's research. Students can learn from, build on, and extend each other's work—each year improving on research and presentation skills.

When students create multimedia projects such as those discussed above and make interesting presentations of their own work, they are learning skills valuable in their preparation for both college and the workforce. Students living in poverty are less likely to have Internet access at home or to have only dial-up access. School use of the technology and the Internet is even more important if these students are to learn important communication and presentation skills.

Teachers benefit from using technology as a resource in preparing and improving lessons. There are thousands of lesson plans and resources on the Web. Useful starting points include university sites, Kathy Schrock's guide, the Multicultural Pavilion and So.Just.net sites (*www.edchange.org/multicultural*), and textbook Web supplements.

Teachers working to promote positive relationships with students and teachers working to promote multicultural education need a positive, supportive work environment. Critical is having an environment of support and feedback for teachers. The Internet can assist with this by enabling the discussion boards and blogs that allow teachers with similar interests to create networks. We can discuss and learn from each other—as well as from our students. This will make us better teachers and more satisfied, more creative, and more imaginative people.

Using the extensive resources of photos, virtual field trips, and lessons available on the Web, teachers can develop their own materials and share them with others. After brief presentations on the issues of copyright, students can assist in developing lessons, digital media and web resources. You can teach the students some of the basics and they will take it from there into advanced video and digital production. Learning these skills is excellent career preparation for well-paying jobs.

There is a even possibility of open licensing for some textbooks and other educational materials so that schools and teachers will be able to freely use quality materials now on the Web. There are already interesting opportunities to use such material through Google Books.

The Multicultural Curriculum Alternatives

Whereas all groups accept the education goals of mastering the English language and acquiring work skills, advocates of multicultural education reject the thesis that it is also a school's function to force cultural assimilation on students.

The multicultural worldview insists on preparing students for participation in a democratic society and requires that students develop a more comprehensive and inclusive view of history, the social sciences, literature, and the humanities than has been presented in curricula thus far. The domination of the language and literacy curriculum by researchers familiar only with the macroculture has led to teaching strategies that fail many students (Taylor, 1998). The majority of strategies and materials used for language arts instruction were developed based on assumptions of working with English-dominant students even though large numbers of these prereaders are English language learners (Au, 1993; Garcia, Kleifgen, & Falchi, 2008). Knowledge is required for self-identity (Banks, 2008; Gay, 2000; King, 1995; Ladson-Billings, 2003).

Figure 12.2   Banks' Approaches to Multicultural Curriculum Reform

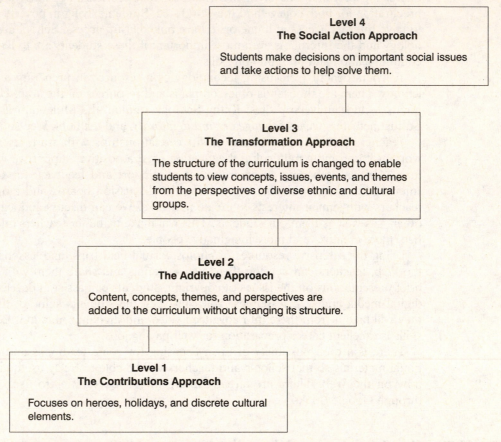

Level 4
The Social Action Approach

Students make decisions on important social issues and take actions to help solve them.

Level 3
The Transformation Approach

The structure of the curriculum is changed to enable students to view concepts, issues, events, and themes from the perspectives of diverse ethnic and cultural groups.

Level 2
The Additive Approach

Content, concepts, themes, and perspectives are added to the curriculum without changing its structure.

Level 1
The Contributions Approach

Focuses on heroes, holidays, and discrete cultural elements.

Source: "Banks Approaches to Multicultural Curriculum Reform," in James A. Banks, 2008, *An Introduction to Multicultural Education*, 4th edition. Boston: Allyn and Bacon, p. 48. Reprinted with permission.

The existing curriculum rests on the ideological position that experiences of the European American male adequately represent all of our history and culture.

James Banks (2008) proposes a perspective on how to integrate ethnic studies content into the elementary and high school curriculum. See Figure 12.2.

Contributions Approach

A few textbooks and a few lists of standards have taken the first step—a contributions approach. Publishers and teachers using the *contributions approach* add a few women and ethnic heroes and subjects to the present curriculum. The primary grades use biographies, literature, and holidays to "integrate" the curriculum.

With the contributions approach, typically a school selects a few important dates, such as El Cinco de Mayo and Martin Luther King, Jr.'s birthday. Students participate in lessons, pageants, and celebrations of the events. The contributions approach, along with human relations strategies such as those described in Chapter 6, is the most common approach to multicultural education. In particular, multicultural curriculum reform in the sciences and math has focused primarily on a contributions approach.

The contributions approach, however, has several limitations. It leaves the existing curriculum unchanged and unchallenged. Children are first taught the main story, history, and literature of society primarily from a mainstream European American point of view. Then a few interesting stories are added. The contributions approach does little to validate students' own diverse cultures and background knowledge. Most students still find their own histories left out of the story—and thus many do not recognize their own place and their own responsibility in the society. Because students do not look at society from several perspectives, they fail to learn the concept of *multiple perspectives*. The contributions approach does not recognize that the mainstream curriculum carries a fundamental ideological slanting.

The heroes and holidays of the contributions approach tend to isolate the story of the several diverse communities from inclusion in the development of our society. The Houghton Mifflin elementary history texts authored by Gary Nash, for example, adopted first for use in California and subsequently for schools around the nation, are particularly limited by the contributions approach. For students in middle and high school, the history of African American, Latino, Asian, and indigenous cultures would more accurately be presented in the context of the struggle against racism and the struggle for decent jobs in society instead of through a heroes and holidays approach.

Ethnic Additive Approach

Several textbooks, school districts, and curriculum guides now offer units and materials on specific ethnic groups—this is the ethnic additive approach. While moving one step beyond the contributions approach, this approach continues to isolate ethnic history and society from the mainstream curriculum. Teachers using this approach add ethnic content and units without restructuring the curriculum.

The *ethnic additive approach* assumes that the present conceptual framework and viewpoints of society are accurate but incomplete. Teachers and curriculum guides add some African American, Chicano, or Asian history or literature. Like the contributions approach, the ethnic additive approach views the history and culture of the United States from the mainstream perspective. Writers select heroes and contributions to supplement and support mainstream views. For example, students will study the Civil Rights Movement and Martin Luther King, Jr., but they will seldom study the separatist challenge of Malcolm X or the deepening radicalization of King's own ideas from civil rights to economic justice in the latter years of his life.

With Internet access, however, students can pursue much more lively and participatory history. For example, several websites are devoted to Martin Luther King, Jr. Students can read and download texts and photos, hear his actual speeches, and read contemporary press accounts of this movement. A similar collection is being assembled about César Chávez at *www.farmworkermovement.org/news/index.php*. These news stories are more local, detailed, and interesting; include more conflict; and contain more evidence than the rather sterile generalizations and descriptions of King and Chávez that make it into published textbooks. Using the Web, students with computer access can overcome the limits of most published textbooks and standards-based lessons.

Native American nations and African slaves certainly had different views of history than the view presented in most textbooks. For example, Native Americans were not considered citizens of the United States until 1924. They were residents of domestic, occupied, defeated nations. From Jamestown to Hawaii, native peoples and cultures were displaced and destroyed by the advancing "Christian civilization." The Native American viewpoint of the expansion of European America cannot be adequately presented in a single chapter or reference.

In the ethnic additive approach, minority groups and minority languages are too often presented as a problem, usually an unexamined opposition to majority "progress."

Transformative Approach

Just as political power established the Euro-centered curriculum, the political shift to democratic empowerment of all peoples in this multiethnic nation requires a similar shift to a multicultural curriculum. The *transformative approach* to multicultural curricula recognizes that present textbooks and most state standards are a product of past power, not a reflection of "truth" or of a neutral or an "objective" analysis. Transformation of the curriculum involves revising standards and reconsidering basic themes, units, and courses.

The transformative approach, as informed by critical theory, is appropriate and may even be necessary to reduce the dropout rate and the achievement crisis of many working-class students and marginalized students of color. Studies in history, the social sciences, language, and the humanities should particularly break with current content coverage to assist students in defining themselves and their own worldview.

Popkewitz (1987) describes the issue well:

> The social sciences are social productions, being neither neutral, disinterested, nor unrelated to their political context.... The methods and procedures of science are produced often in response to particular social agendas. The modern testing and measurement industry has its origins in a political movement of eugenics to improve the quality of racial stock.... The values underlying our science help us to understand that there is no one notion of science but multiple traditions for understanding and interpreting. Our social sciences contain paradigms or different constellations of value, commitment, methods and procedures. (pp. 338–339)

In a transformative curriculum, students study the relationship of knowledge to power. They learn that there is a strong relationship between whose knowledge gets validated and whose power is respected. Apple (2001) describes this important issue of textbook content: "[I]t is naïve to think of school curriculum as neutral knowledge. Rather, what counts as legitimate knowledge is the result of complex power relationships and struggles among identifiable class, race, gender and religious groups" (p. 44).

The transformative curriculum involves students in considering the social, cultural, and political interests of those who select "school" knowledge and define success.

Teachers require a great deal of assistance in transforming the curriculum. Their university coursework prepares them for admission to the field of teaching but, because of its Euro-centric domination, seldom provides them with an adequate background for curriculum revision. New standards, new books, and new course outlines are needed. Teachers who have taken a number of ethnic studies courses and become cross-culturally competent in their disciplines will be better able to transform the curriculum. Teachers who have not had classes in ethnic and women's studies can access the Internet for much of this information, as described in the following section. Problem-based learning as exemplified by the interesting video, discussed above, about students in the San Fernando Valley (*www.edutopia.org/students-find-their-voices-through-multimedia*) and by Web quests promotes a transformative approach. *Rethinking Columbus* (Bigelow & Peterson, 1998) provides excellent and interesting models of transformative education on the experience of European colonization of the Americas.

Social Action Approach

The *social action approach* applies the ideas of social participation and uses the empowerment strategies described in Chapters 7 and 11. Only a few teachers, programs, and schools have attempted social action approaches to reconstruct the curriculum. An early example was the Foxfire curriculum development projects for Appalachian students. (For information, contact the Foxfire Fund, P.O. Box 541, Mountain City, GA 30562.) Many English as a second language (ESL) classes for immigrant students have used whole-language lessons and a social action approach to record students' own histories of immigration. The writers' workshops and computer programs teach students to write, edit, and publish their own stories. Some high school technology projects teach students to build and to rebuild computers for themselves and for residents of low income neighborhoods. These materials add social action elements to the curriculum.

The social action approach often arises out of local curriculum development efforts, such as the current work of the Ojibwa in Northern Wisconsin and the Student Nonviolent Coordinating Committee's Freedom Schools of 1965, not from standards and textbooks. The social action approach goes farther than the other approaches to include important critical-thinking and decision-making processes essential to multicultural curriculum reform.

Social action curriculum reform happens when teachers move outside of textbooks. The economics of textbook publishing dictates that commercial texts will be slow to respond to social change. Emerging computer technology already permits high-quality, low-cost printing and publication of student-created materials. Students learn from well-organized class discussions of current and vital issues in their communities. Particularly by middle school (grades 6 to 8), students need places to discuss their concerns about race, violence, fear, sex, power, and drugs. The participatory social inquiry projects of students in Los Angeles described in *Learning Power: Organizing for Education and Justice* (Oakes & Rogers, 2006) provide interesting and valuable examples of a social action approach. Students investigated tracking in their own school and carried out projects to oppose this tracking. In the process, they learned valuable intellectual and organizing skills that well prepared them for university study. Students in the Algebra Project in the South and in Philadelphia have similarly used their studies as a vehicle for organizing and creating school change (Moses & Cobb, 2001). There are a number of curriculum and lesson plan examples of teachers developing social justice projects at *www.rethinkingschools.org*.

Creating Your Own Materials

Teachers and students produce some of the most effective materials themselves. If you analyze your state's standards and you know your subject matter (history, economics, literature, science), you can usually develop quality materials that respect and study the cultural communities and histories of your students. Writing their own curriculum and creating their own media empowers students and their community, whether or not they achieve the graphic quality and professional look of commercial materials. You can download thousands of interesting materials, photos, and lessons from the Internet.

Young students can research and record the history of their classroom. Middle school students (grades 6 to 8) can interview neighborhood residents and research local communities. With the help of computer programs, students can now write their conclusions and leave their studies for next year's class, when students can read and add to the material. In Sacramento, California, for example, immigrant students from Cambodia, Laos, and El Salvador have written textbooks containing their own stories of migration and adjustment to U.S. life. These tales—researched, written, edited, and published by students—provide important writing, editing, and language practice. They also provide far more accurate analyses of the society of young people than most commercial textbooks offer.

Students can write on an event from multiple perspectives and compare their conclusions to those provided in their textbooks. Using the concept of multiple perspectives as a guide, students can question the textbook author's interpretation of events. They become historians and begin to understand the process of content selection and perspective that has excluded many histories, and perhaps their own, from the books. Teachers can use the critical thinking standards and the extensive materials on the internet to extend the curriculum toward multiple perspectives and thus multicultural education.

The Foxfire project and books and the Highlander Folk School in Tennessee both have a long history of validating culture, while supporting young people in recording the history and culture of Appalachian areas. A group called Aspectos Culturales in Santa Fe, New Mexico, records local histories that complement inadequate official texts. Webpage designers have recorded countless quality materials. Particularly interesting are the materials at *www.cradleboard.org* and *www.teachingtolerance.org*. These projective history and cultural recovery efforts offer outstanding guides to the creation of dynamic living history. Students develop cultural knowledge and perspective, reading and writing skills, and self-confidence by producing their own curriculum and by, when possible, writing their own materials and creating their own webpages. Often, the intellectual quality of this material is near to that of commercial textbooks—and it is local and thus relevant to the students' lives. Through this kind of participatory curriculum development, multicultural education can help unite our racially divided nation.

Improving Student Achievement

The single most important thing a teacher can do is to help students succeed with *whatever* materials they use. Revising the curriculum to overcome the current Euro-centric bias is important, but to achieve equality, we need to develop high-achieving democratic schools. For students in underfinanced, poverty-stricken schools, we need to improve academic achievement. Our goal should be to eliminate student failure to the degree possible.

Successful strategies include establishing clear curriculum goals. Then administration, faculty, and staff together must develop comprehensive systems of assessment and accountability. In many areas, this goal setting is connected to establishing standards.

Making the curriculum multicultural will not, by itself, improve these schools. Simply being a student in an urban district with low academic standards, a large administrative bureaucracy, high teacher turnover, crumbling buildings, and a lack of safety often lowers academic achievement. Well-prepared, experienced teaches are needed to improve low-performing schools (Education Trust, 2008). New teachers and experienced teachers must work together to improve academic achievement. This requires goal selection, discipline, and planning and assessment. For example, if the district has a focus on reading, then teachers need assistance with designing reading lessons. Studies of reading involving language-minority students show that reading strategies must move beyond the limited phonics approaches advocated by several current textbook publishers and their sales staffs (see Chapter 11). Improvement of basic reading and writing skills must be part of any multicultural curriculum. Imaginative teachers design their curriculum around the life experiences of their students, using newspapers, magazines, literature, the Internet, video-tapes, and other sources (sometimes at great personal expense) to supplement textbooks.

By working together, teachers can produce their own curriculum materials. Teacher teams can select empowering themes that bridge disciplines. For example, when studying discrimination, students can use reading skills to learn the history of discrimination; writing skills to compose essays and letters; and math skills to calculate and demonstrate tracking, voting patterns, and income inequalities. They can make presentations and video recordings of their work. Teachers can share planning and read samples of student work in other classes. Teachers, not textbooks or curriculum plans, establish high expectation levels.

The Critics of Multicultural Education

In response to the failure of their own reform strategies, conservatives blame the multicultural education movement for declining student performance in public schools. This attack began with Alan Bloom's *The Closing of the American Mind* (1987) and includes works such as *The Disuniting of America* (1992), by Arthur Schlesinger, Jr.; *Slouching*

Toward Gomorrah: Modern Liberalism and American Decline (1996), by Robert Bork; *Left Back: A Century of Failed School Reform* (2000), by Diane Ravitch; and *Where Did Social Studies Go Wrong?* (2003), edited by Leming, Ellington, and Porter.

Because curricula wars over the inclusion of diverse perspectives have continued for more than 100 years, it is reasonable to assume that they will continue. In the media and among textbook authors, conservatives in think tanks and advocacy groups such as the Thomas B. Fordham Institute, the Bradley Foundation, the Olin Foundation, the Heritage Foundation, the American Textbook Council, and the Center for Equal Opportunity (among others) attack and distort efforts at multicultural education in an attempt to regain control of the discussion about race, racism, schools, and democracy (Hirsch, 1996; Ravitch, 2000). Their views dominated the U.S. Education Department under George W. Bush and the No Child Left Behind legislation, which requires a testing and accountability model for school improvement.

In addition to reforming the content of the curriculum, we need to develop a new, coherent assessment system that monitors student progress and assists teachers with their difficult teaching tasks. At the state level, as a consequence of important legal decisions, New York, California, and 14 other states are moving toward measuring the adequacy of school funding, particularly in low-income districts. Early reflections on this effort in New York showed that, as a result of the economic downturn of 2002, New York was actually reducing its funding after being found to have illegally imposed an unequal and inadequate system to finance city schools (Kozol, 2002). Again in the recession of 2008/2009 school budgets were slashed in over 27 states and efforts at school reform were delayed (Johnson, 2008). At present, the available evidence shows that voters and taxpayers, or at least elected officials and the courts, are not willing to provide equal or adequate funding for schools in low-income areas (Kozol, 2002; Oakes & Rogers, 2006; *Williams v. California*, 2000).

Summary

We face a massive challenge: to create a new curriculum based on the full participation of all students. Creating schools that are equitable across race, class, and gender and that provide high-quality education appropriate to a rapidly changing economy requires fundamentally rewriting the curriculum.

There are two distinct curriculum reform movements. The neo-conservative school reform of the 1990s and this decade stresses raising standards, increasing testing, and creating a common culture through textbook selection and publication. Neo-conservative reform also stresses aligning schools and curricula more clearly with business interests and corporate productivity. The multicultural curriculum reform movement developed from a different worldview and holds a different theory of the appropriate role of schooling in society. Multicultural reform seeks to make the curriculum more inclusive and to transform it to empower all students for economic and political participation. Improving students' level of achievement in terms of both content and skills is an important component of multicultural curriculum reform. Multicultural school and curriculum reform can play a role in uniting—in healing—a divided nation.

Questions over the Chapter

1. What do you believe are the differences between the neo-conservative and the multicultural approaches to curriculum?
2. Under what conditions is it appropriate for a group of European American children to study African American history? Under what conditions should African American students study European American history?
3. Explain why there have been major conflicts among scholars over history and literature books but fewer conflicts about multicultural content in math and science texts.
4. Define the *melting pot* thesis. What are the goals of assimilation?
5. Describe your own experiences in reading history and literature. Were your textbooks inclusive and pluralistic?
6. How are textbooks selected or adopted in your school, district, and state?

Activities for Further Study of Curriculum Reform

1. How accurate and complete do you think the textbooks you used in school were? Compare your views with those of a person from another cultural group.
2. Conduct historical research on one of the diversity heroes listed in Figure 12.1. In your opinion, should this person be included in general U.S. history texts? Why do you think the person was left out?
3. List three ways you could use a textbook in your classroom if the book inadequately covered its subject.
4. Design two examples of a transformative approach to curriculum. Share your ideas with your class. What obstacles would prevent you from using a transformative approach?
5. Create a list of social action projects appropriate to the grade level you are working with. Share your list with your class. (Be cautious about the safety level of any project.)

Teaching Strategies for Use with Your Students

1. Find out your district or state standards for your intended teaching level.
2. Plan lessons to teach to the level of the standards. Assess your students' abilities to perform at the level of the standards.
3. Provide supplementary skill development (reading, writing) when necessary.
4. Frequently assess and revise your curriculum. Compare your students' performance to the standards. Change instructional strategies where necessary.

13

Democratic School Reform: How Do We Get from Here to There?

Power concedes nothing without demand. It never did and it never will.
Frederick Douglass

In this chapter, we will briefly review the history of education reform in the United States, describe various school reform efforts, and outline critical issues for teachers to consider when changing and transforming aspects of their classroom and school practices. An underlying assumption in this chapter is that an effective system of public schooling is the bedrock of a vital and healthy democracy. Two important arguments in this chapter are that school reform or school change is a necessity mostly for schools that serve low-income and culturally and linguistically diverse students and that such change or reform, though it will be hard won, is not only worth the effort but also necessary for the future of our democratic society.

A Brief History of Education Reforms

Public education in the United States is a relatively young system, with two competing functions that have been contested territory throughout the development of schooling. In the early years of our nation, children from an elite were educated: boys for professional preparation, women for Dames Schools, and both for reading the Bible. A democratic impulse was also present. Building on the advocacy of Thomas Jefferson and the popular writings of authors such as Thomas Paine, and later the mass migration of Irish and others, schooling become an important and vital element in developing the democracy and in preparing a well-informed citizenry (Carnoy & Levin, 1985). At the turn of the 20th century, approximately 60 percent of school-age children were enrolled in schools (Carnoy & Levin, 1985). The mass migration from 1890 to 1910, along with the rapid development of a capitalist-driven industrializing economy, made mass public schooling an important priority. Schools became active in the processes of "assimilating" newcomers and "training" an industrial workforce, keeping children off the streets and out of the mines, as well as creating, at least in theory, a better life—an American Dream—for the largely immigrant working classes, thus limiting the demand for radical or revolutionary change. By 1920, most states had passed compulsory education laws, and about 80 percent of children were enrolled in schools. By the 1970s, more than 90 percent of school-age children were enrolled in school, and three-quarters of them were graduating from high school (Carnoy & Levin, 1985). As noted in Chapter 4, there were significant class and racial differences in who graduated. Until about World War II, completing a high school education was often not really necessary to earning a livable wage. Today, of course, high school graduation is necessary for even the most menial of jobs, and without advanced schooling, millions of students are being left behind in the postindustrial economy (Mishel & Rothstein, 2007; The New Commission on the Skills of the American Workforce, 2006). In the last 50 years, educational requirements and opportunities have been revolutionized; some students are winning and some students are losing.

There are at least two competing agendas for education policy and school reform that are attempting to influence the control, purpose, and operation of the schools. On the one hand, schools have traditionally trained a workforce and thus reproduced the unequal, hierarchical relations of the workplace; on the other, they have offered an expansion of economic opportunity to subordinate groups and the extension of basic democratic and human rights.

Another major conflict has been the development in the last 50 years of state and federal government interventions in school policy and delivery—recently through testing. Historically, the United States has had a decentralized system of public education—unlike other countries such France or Japan, where a formal national curriculum exists for K–12 programs and even for teacher education. In the United States, the federal government has historically played a minor role in education programming and policy making; for example, less than 11 percent of the funds for education come from the federal government. The restricted federal role is the result of long-held beliefs in the tradition of federalism and the local control of schools. Local control has not always served democratic ends, as when states and communities in the South East used their control of schools to enforce racial segregation prior to the 1970s.

A brief overview of the major education reforms of the 20th century highlights the tensions between the two agendas. During the formative period of our current public education system, roughly between 1900 and 1940, many of the basic practices and organizational models were developed, including local control, testing, and efforts to exclude certain kinds of politicization by "professionalizing" school administration (Dorn, 2007). During this period, a concern of education policy makers was to prepare a small number of students for college and to tailor the education system for other students to meet the needs of the workplace.

After World War II, economic prosperity, New Deal legislation, and the GI Bill greatly expanded high school attendance and college opportunities. State and local governments funded a great expansion of schooling. Enrollment at all levels—including college—exploded.

In 1940, three-quarters of adults either were high school dropouts or never attended high school in the first place. Just 5 percent of the adult population had a four-year college degree or higher. By 1980, less than one-third of adults lacked a high school diploma; by 2007, those without a diploma made up only 14 percent of the population. At the same time, the percentage of adults holding a B.A. rose steadily to reach 29 percent in 2007, with another 25 percent having attended some college but not having graduated with a B.A. This expansion of education produced economic and social class revolutions (Teixeira & Abramowitz, 2008).

In 1957, the launching of the Soviet space probe, Sputnik, in the midst of the Cold War, prompted calls for education reforms in order to improve the United States' economic, scientific, and military competitiveness. Policy makers and politicians demanded that schools pay more attention to accountability and student achievement in math and the sciences. Efforts to train the "best and the brightest" students were encouraged. Federal money was provided for teacher training in math, science, languages, and other fields. The policy debate was shifted away from democratic and economic opportunity to issues of competitiveness, efficiency, and the need to meet workplace demands.

The landmark U.S. Supreme Court civil rights decision *Brown v. Board of Education* (1954), the Civil Rights Act of 1964, and other legislation brought about by the Civil Rights Movement were part of a national effort to make our schools more equal and to open economic opportunity to all students. In the 1960s, turmoil and demonstrations—and, at times, riots—occurred in major cities, including Newark, Detroit, and Los Angeles. Politicians in the established political culture responded with promises of improved educational opportunity. That is, schooling was offered as a response to severe inequality, leaving unquestioned the economic inequality.

In 1965, President Lyndon Johnson signed into law the first Elementary and Secondary Education Act (ESEA) as a component of his "War on Poverty" initiative. The 1965 ESEA established a pattern repeated in subsequent authorizations with separate entitlement programs for low-income students (Title 1), language-minority students (Title 7), gender equity (Title 9), and higher education (Title 2). An important study entitled *Equality of Educational Opportunity* (1966)—commonly known as the Coleman Report, after its author, James Coleman—established much of the basis for the courts and the government to increase enforcement of the earlier *Brown* decision of 1954. The Johnson Administration and later governments sought to use federal funding to lessen discrimination and segregation in schools by funding programs designed to achieve equal opportunity. The ESEA was also a major introduction of federal policy making into education, which in prior years had been an arena of local control. Court desegregation decisions and national legislation were a response to grassroots demands for a more democratic, more equitable education system. By the 1970s, equal opportunity in the form of bilingual education programs, multicultural education, and gender equity efforts were promoted as solutions for education inequity.

This new focus on equity issues led to research into "effective schools" undertaken between 1976 and 2000 (Edmonds, 1979; Levine & Lezotte, 2001; Parish et al., 2006), which identified characteristics of schools where working-class students and students of color performed at national and state averages (see Figure 13.1). This research on effective

Figure 13.1   Summary of Characteristics of Effective Schools

---

A.   A well-functioning total system producing a school social climate that promotes positive student outcomes

B.   Specific characteristics crucial to the development of effectiveness and thus to a positive school social climate

   1.   A safe and orderly school environment

   2.   Positive leadership, usually from the formal leaders

   3.   Common agreement on a strong academic orientation

      a.   Clearly stated academic goals, objectives, and plans

      b.   Well-organized classrooms

   4.   Well-functioning methods to monitor school inputs and student outputs

C.   A positive school social climate

   1.   High staff expectations for children and the instructional program

   2.   Strong demand for academic performance

   3.   High staff morale

      a.   Strong internal support

      b.   Consensus building

      c.   Job satisfaction

      d.   Sense of personal efficacy

      e.   Sense that the system works

      f.   Sense of ownership

      g.   Well-defined roles and responsibilities

      h.   Belief and practice that resources are best expended on people rather than on education software and hardware

---

Source: From "Effective Bilingual Schools: Implications for Policy and Practice" (n.p.), by T. Carter and M. Chatfield, 1986, November, *American Journal of Education,* pp. 200–232. Reprinted with permission.

schools offered hope for equity, in that it demonstrated that some schools (about 1.6 percent) in poverty areas worked well to promote student achievement.

1980s–1990s

The National Commission on Excellence in Education's 1982 report *A Nation at Risk,* designed initially to save the U.S. Department of Education from being eliminated by the new Reagan Administration, initiated a new conservative-dominated reform cycle. The reform slogans of this period convinced the media and then the public to accept a series of "conventional wisdoms" still in use today: Today's graduates do not have the skills needed for a technologically advanced society, academic achievement is stagnant or declining (it is not), and the nation was at risk due to "a rising tide of mediocrity." Central to this agenda was the thesis that none of the problems of schools could be solved by putting more money into schools—or, as conservatives put it, "throwing money at schools." Business groups and conservative political advocates deceptively blamed schools for the nation's economic decline in the 1980s; however, when the economy recovered for a period in the 1990s, the schools were not credited with the recovery (Rothstein, 2008).

The facts, however, contradict the conservative ideological assault. The average U.S. student today does as well as the average student in the 1930s–1950s, but now there are new immigrant populations to serve. Students in the United States do almost as well as their counterparts in Japan or Korea but not as well as students in Finland. Schools in middle-class suburbs are continually getting better (Bracey, 2006; Nichols & Berliner, 2007).

Increased resources were decried as wasteful and leading to a bloated bureaucracy. Conservative advocates viewed school improvement as a management issue and presented school failure as a technical problem, subject to a new science (Chubb & Moe, 1989; Dorn, 2007; Weiss, Cambone, & Wyeth, 1992). Business administration ideas were advocated and applied to schools. Reformers argued that new management and control systems, along with an emphasis on remedial drills for skill development, would improve schools for all students (Carlson, 1992). Common reforms initiated in the 1980s included standards, vouchers, charter schools, and site-based management or decentralization. These efforts suppressed the goals of democracy in education and equal educational opportunity or equity in favor of more competition and business viewpoints.

Conservative ideological advocates, from governors and legislators to business groups, blamed teachers—not poverty—for low scores. They argued that more money was not the answer—a patently false claim. By arguing that all schools were in crisis—even though middle-class schools were doing well—legislators and antitax advocates avoided consideration of basic issues such as class size, per pupil expenditures, and unequal funding of schools serving low-income students.

The 1982–1992 school reform effort had little positive impact on the quality of schooling in urban areas. Seymore Sarason noted that this effort failed to consider schools as an interconnected system of actors. Instead, working from the management–production model, managers, college professors, and "leaders" ignored the perspectives of teachers, students, and parents of disenfranchised students. These business-led reformers advanced their own careers and developed "reform" strategies that scapegoated schools for the problems of inequality and changes in the economy (Sarason, 1990).

Conservatives and their allies in the business community successfully passed legislation in over half of the states, including Texas, California, and Kentucky, that called for standards and accountability-based school reform (Emery, 2007). This reform effort failed to improve achievement in schools, but the themes of conservative reform continued to dominate government discussions. In 1989, the nation's governors, at a meeting cochaired by then Governor Bill Clinton, announced national goals for U.S. education that later became law. Their goals were as follows:

By the year 2000

1. All children in America will start school ready to learn.
2. The high school graduation rate will increase to at least 90 percent.

3. American students will leave grades four, eight, and twelve having demonstrated competence in challenging subject matter including English, mathematics, science, history and geography, and every school in America will ensure that all students will learn to use their minds well, so they may be prepared for responsible citizenship, further learning, and productive employment in a modern economy.

4. U.S. students will be first in the world in science and mathematics achievement.

5. Every adult in America will be literate and will possess the knowledge and skills necessary to compete in a global economy and exercise the rights and responsibilities of citizenship.

6. Every school in America will be free of drugs and violence and will offer a disciplined environment conducive to learning. (p. 3)

After the May 1992 riots in Los Angeles, then President Bush said that these goals for school reform were the cornerstone of the government's response to poverty and a racially divided society. You can judge for yourself if these goals have been met to date. When Bill Clinton was elected President in 1992, he and the Congress continued to focus on Goals 2000, which he had helped to establish as a governor, as the centerpiece for federal school policy. The basic federal legislation, the Elementary and Secondary Education Act, including the Goals 2000 efforts, was reauthorized by Congress in the fall of 1994 (*www.ed.gov/legislation/GOALS2000/TheAct/index.html*).

The No Child Left Behind Act

Over a decade of pressure for conservative education reform efforts culminated in 2001, when the new President Bush, based upon his experience as a Governor in Texas, worked with political leaders in both parties to pass Public Law 107-110; the reauthorization of the Elementary and Secondary Education Act, titled by the Bush Administration—The No Child Left Behind Act (NCLB). NCLB made assessment-based reform (testing) and accountability the central components of a new national policy on school reform. This was a significant shift from state and local control to federal control. The stated purpose of NCLB was positive:

Sec. 1001. Statement of Purpose.

The purpose of this title is to ensure that all children have a fair, equal, and significant opportunity to obtain a high-quality education and reach, at a minimum, proficiency on challenging State academic achievement standards and state academic assessments. This purpose can be accomplished by—

1. ensuring that high-quality academic assessments, accountability systems, teacher preparation and training, curriculum, and instructional materials are aligned with challenging State academic standards so that students, teachers, parents, and administrators can measure progress against common expectations for student academic achievement;

2. meeting the educational needs of low-achieving children in our Nation's highest-poverty schools, limited English proficient children, migratory children, children with disabilities, Indian children, neglected or delinquent children, and young children in need of reading assistance;

3. closing the achievement gap between high- and low-performing children, especially the achievement gaps between minority and nonminority students, and between disadvantaged children and their more advantaged peers. . . . (Public Law 107-110)

Under NCLB, all students in grades 3 through 12 would be tested annually. Schools had to make "adequate yearly progress," and failure to do so would result in a progression of interventions, beginning with additional resources and support and ending with the closure of the school. The act also provides for vouchers for students underserved by a school. Under NCLB, schools can use only programs that are based on "scientifically rigorous research," a code term for the positivist research paradigm (see Chapter 6).

As a future teacher, you should also know that with this new reauthorization of the ESEA, the federal government attempted to define the characteristics of a "highly qualified teacher." Although this definition (bachelor's degree and state certification) is not rigorous, it does represent one of the first times the federal government has asserted its authority over that of the states when determining teacher quality.

Early critiques of the NCLB implementation included the following:

- The amount of federal monies earmarked for education does not begin to cover the costs needed to implement the federal mandates, particularly those around testing.

- The focus on testing as a means of evaluating teachers and schools reinforces the notion that student learning and growth can be accurately expressed by a single test.

- "Adequate yearly progress," as measured by increases in test scores, is flawed on several accounts. (See Nichols & Berliner, 2007.)

- The emphasis on programs founded on "scientifically based research" was an ideological device to promote a specific (behaviorist) view of education and was manipulated by agencies to fund particular reading programs and textbooks selected and implemented in a manner that made some officials rich (see Inspector General, U.S. Office of Education, 2006; Boulay et al., 2008; U.S. Department of Education, 2006).

Competing Paradigms of School Reform

Recall the political context of several of the proposed school reforms. As described in earlier chapters, our public schools have developed with a tension between two competing ideologies and two or more interest groups. The democratic ideology views schools as places where young people prepare for adulthood, careers, and responsible citizenship. This position argues for schools that promote multicultural education, teach critical-thinking skills, and encourage students to create a more democratic society. This viewpoint is associated with Thomas Jefferson, John Dewey, and the very foundations of our public schools. Other advocates of this view have been described throughout this book, including (to varying degrees) Maria Montessori, Paulo Freire, Alfie Kohn, Jean Anyon, James Banks, and the advocates of a critical theory perspective.

Recent politically imposed reform efforts, including NCLB and its state-by-state implementation, argue from a second and competing perspective about schools: The education system should operate primarily in service of the owners of the economic system. Schools should produce workers who can be productive in our economic system—some will be professional workers and others will be prepared for service work and manual labor. Graduates need to have skills in basic literacy and numeracy as well as being technologically competent. Good work habits like being punctual, following instructions, and accepting authority are also valued. This second perspective is the predominant viewpoint framed and advanced by business advocacy groups like the Business Roundtable, is taken for granted in the national media, and has been adopted as law in NCLB. This perspective comes from a political/economic paradigm called *neo-liberalism* (closely associated with the more common terms *capitalism* and *markets*). This paradigm is the dominant ideology of the finance capital economic interests who dominated the U.S. political and economic system until the economic crisis of 2008/2009.

The school reform movement from 1983 to 2008, including NCLB, was largely driven by this corporate goals and corporate thinking. Corporate rule was established through the corporations' influence and contributions to elected officials and their funding of "research" institutes (Emery, 2007). This corporate view of school reform—called neo-liberalism in economics—came to dominate the media and the government. Noncorporate goals such as freedom, the extension of democracy, and equal opportunity were driven from the school curriculum and driven from the reform packages.

The corporate view, or neo-liberalism, is more than an economic policy. It is also a political project that considers people primarily as consumers and negates or limits their role as citizens and as political actors. Glaring examples of this are the development of charter schools and the vast expansion of private, for-profit higher education (e.g., National University, University of Phoenix). As Robert Reich argues in *Supercapitalism: The Transformation of Business, Democracy, and Everyday Life* (2007), democracy (including that in school policies) has been overwhelmed by capitalism and the corporate culture. The United States has experienced a corporate takeover of our politics. Corporate interests presently hold the majority of power in Washington, and they established and protect the No Child Left Behind legislation, with its emphasis on testing and accountability. As corporate domination grows, noncorporate institutions like schools and unions lose their access to the media and to the public conversation about schools, democracy and multiculturalism. Neo-liberalism takes money from public systems, such as public schools, and transfers it to private consumption; thus, public institutions lose resources. Developing democracy requires one form of education; pursuing neo-liberalism requires a very different form of education. And at present, clearly the neo-liberal agenda is winning, particularly as advanced in NCLB, although its reauthorization was stalled in 2008.

A substantial opposition developed to the reauthorization of NCLB. What are the key issues? The current NCLB accountability system provides elected officials with information about which schools and districts are performing well and which are not. Not surprisingly, they found that impoverished schools have impoverished scores. NCLB does not provide teachers with useful information on what to do to improve student learning and instruction. It also does not provide resources to improve the schools, and it ignores the substantial inequality of resources in both schools and neighborhoods. We have yet to learn if a revised NCLB will deal with these issues.

Although market mechanisms may work well for production companies and retailers, they are not an appropriate framework for a public education system in a democratic society. Rather, the neo-liberal viewpoints (often termed neo-conservative in political terms) of the Reagan, Bush, and Bush Administrations pressured schools to abandon a commitment to equity and presented an inaccurate understanding of the role of schools in our society. As numerous scholars (Anyon, 2006; Bracey, 2003; Kozol, 2005; Meier & Wood, ed., 2004; Nichols & Berliner, 2007; Sarason, 1990; West, 2004) have noted, these reforms have failed to improve schools, particularly those schools that serve traditionally low-income and marginalized students.

More on the Problem of the Current Standards

As described in Chapter 12, education standards have been an important component of conservative reform efforts since the 1980s. Industry-related concepts of *performance* and *accountability* support the idea of the standards movement as an essential process for improved levels of student achievement. However, as described in Chapters 1, 3, and 4, when extreme inequities exist within the very structure of the school system, it is unjust and dishonest to insist that all educators and students strive to meet uniform standards unless resources are adjusted to provide a truly level playing field.

By setting goals and standards and refusing to consider the school and community resources needed to achieve these goals and standards and to improve low-performing schools, elected officials and other policy makers create an appearance of responding to the school crisis. In reality, they are refusing to adequately fund the schools and to make real changes in the financing of those schools that systematically fail a substantial portion of our children, particularly poor students and students of color. By passing lists of standards without allocating sufficient resources, elected officials avoid the issues of raising taxes and spending the money that any serious effort to provide equal opportunity would require.

Standards are not necessarily bad. They could be a positive part of a needed school reform program. Following the work of Dewey and Freire, a more democratic approach would move standards away from these elite, professional-dominated committees and insist on broad public participation. Democracy in schooling is the power to participate in making decisions on what enters the curriculum. The standards movement, when combined with testing, is clearly moving us away from democracy and away from local control.

An important reform direction is to advocate for more democracy and more inclusion in the setting of standards (and in testing). It is not an accident that the standards movement has moved away from empowerment and cultural pluralism and toward the exclusion of parents and the domination of the process by a narrow, professional, bureaucratic class (Freire, 1997). For schools serving low-income and culturally and linguistically diverse students in particular, a democratic process around standards needs to be inclusive of the knowledge base, values, and expectations of the community. When standards are imposed from outside, such as from a state department of education committee or other agency, they fail. Schools have not been successfully reformed in this manner. The standards and their related programs and processes must be democratically arrived at and should accelerate student learning, open up education opportunities, and increase student achievement—not simply record the failing of more students.

Testing Issues

Added to the shortcomings of the standards movement is the recent heavy emphasis on high-stakes testing to determine the achievement of the standards. Decades of work have highlighted the effectiveness of authentic assessments (portfolios, student exhibitions, scoring rubrics, etc.) as tools for informing teachers' instructional practices and as methods for communicating to students and parents the knowledge that has been gained. However, the current practice in assessment is the standardized, norm-referenced test, consisting almost wholly of multiple-choice questions. It is problematic that policy makers would mandate the development of elaborate content standards only to couple such policies with low-level and narrow assessments (Dorn, 2007; Nichols & Berliner, 2007).

The long and troubled history of testing and test development in the United States was severely damaged by racism, which the test producers have yet to overcome (Berlak, 2000; Valdés & Figueroa, 1994). Standardized, usually multiple-choice, tests are preferred because they can be mandated by political leaders, be implemented, and deliver clear results. But, as in the case of positivism and reductionism (from which these tests come), they are measuring and evaluating only a small segment of the important learning goals of schools. Low-level tests do not measure human relations, respect, civic courage, and critical thinking, for example. Standardized testing is a political act that often forces teachers to change their teaching strategies (Perlstein, 2007). Teachers need to examine the limits of the testing processes and use classroom-based assessments to inform their teaching. In many states, including Texas, California, and Massachusetts, and in many school districts, including New York, Chicago, and Philadelphia, standards and a test-driven curriculum have been used to reduce teachers' professional choice and decision making.

The most basic failure of the testing/accountability model lies in its refusal to recognize that public education is far more than production; it includes, at a minimum, facts, concepts, generalizations, skills, attitudes, critical thinking, and citizenship. Thus, a business-production model, based on low-level, multiple-choice testing, measures only a small part of the important issues of schools in a democratic society (see Dorn, 2007; Perlstein, 2007; Renzulli, 2002). Meanwhile, governors and legislators committed to the testing movement ignore other parts of the business-production model, such as providing as much support, including tools, training, and technical assistance, as workers need.

Testing systems have grown in part because they are very profitable for the companies that produce and score these low-quality tests—companies that lobby the legislatures to establish testing systems. State funding for testing grew in Texas from $19.5 million in 1995 to $68.6 million in 2001 and at similar rates in other states (Gluckman, 2002; Perlstein, 2007). *Bloomberg News* estimated in 2006 that the testing industry makes over $2.5 billion per year (Gloven & Evans, 2006). Funding increases for testing and test preparation usually are matched by a reduction in funding for other classroom items such as textbooks, dictionaries, libraries, and teacher support. In spite of these large investments, without major improvements in the quality of testing and investments in teacher capacity-building, test-based accountability systems will not produce significant improvement in student achievement in high-risk neighborhoods (Kober, 2001; Nichols & Berliner, 2007; Popham, 2003).

Extensive evidence shows that the current testing emphasis has driven instruction away from the important issues of developing democratic and multicultural content, away from teaching critical-thinking skills, and away from developing citizenship and pro-democratic values (Neil, 2003; Renzulli, 2002). Available testing, particularly multiple-choice testing, is not the only form of assessment. Other assessment devices include teacher observations, rubrics, student presentations, and portfolios (Wood, Darling-Hammond, Neil, & Roschewski, 2007). These forms of assessment can be used to measure progress on goals of critical thinking and democracy and on important multicultural goals such as mutual respect.

Scores on most standardized skill tests actually tell us very little; they measure very imprecisely. Current objective tests measure whether the student can identify letters, words, and rhyming words, but they do not measure the ability to comprehend a paragraph or to write a creative essay. They measure skills and isolated facts rather than significant academic achievement. Tests are usually not actual measures of competencies but measures of isolated skills that can be drilled without improving the student's education (Perlstein, 2007). Rather than investing more money in the current low-quality testing systems, we could develop appropriate and useful assessments, including those using computer technology, that would help the teacher. There are good uses for standardized tests. They should be short tests given frequently that assist the teacher in making decisions about individual students, teaching, and review. But that is not what is happening with testing in K–12 programs today.

When goals and standards are tied to mandated testing systems, as in NCLB, standards and testing gain even more power to shape the school experience. Teacher decision making loses power. A major effect of standards and testing in the last decade has been to take curriculum decisions and teaching decisions away from locally elected officials and teachers who work with children and deliver this power to the national government or the state. Whatever test makers have put on the test has become the curriculum. And multicultural education, self-esteem, value clarity, and democracy itself are not on the tests because test items in these areas are difficult and expensive to measure with current test technology (Berlak, 2000; Perlsein, 2007).

Now, after more than 10 years, NCLB and the standards and testing movement show little real evidence of improving scores and achievement (Fuller, Wright, Gesicki, & Kang, 2007; Lee, 2006). Virtually absent from the discussion of test scores in the mainstream press is the widespread effect of inequality and institutional racism (see Chapter 3) in the schools. We know that children are presented with distinctly unequal schools, teachers, and opportunities, and then we give them all the same test and publish the scores in the newspaper.

Fortunately, a number of civil rights groups and community organizations have now recognized this danger and engaged in a variety of resistances to the high-stakes testing efforts still so popular with elected officials (see FairTest: The National Center for Fair and Open Testing at *www.fairtest.org;* the Forum for Education and Democracy at *www.forumforeducation.org*, and the Institute for Language and Education Policy at *elladvocates.org*).

The No Child Left Behind Law in Practice

While the purposes of NCLB are noble, the act has focused on imposing sanctions and blaming teachers, and as a consequence, it has not produced improved or more equitable student achievement. NCLB allowed politicians and advocacy groups working with corporate leaders to capture the spotlight by doing something for the schools without significantly increasing funding (Emery, 2007). Corporate leaders and elected officials held conferences and made announcements of what would work in schools without talking with teachers. It was a way to establish a business- or neo-liberal–directed view of the national agenda for school reform, which included charters, vouchers, and test-based accountability as central features of the law.

NCLB required that states develop their own standards and tests and that they use test scores to determine if children have achieved grade-level skills in mathematics and reading. These requirements have led to a narrow, test-driven curriculum, as described in Chapter 12, that emphasizes reading and math in the early years. The accountability approach central to the law has limited scientific legitimacy, and there is little evidence that this approach has actually worked for kids (Dorn, 2007). Instead, it represents an ideology of how conservatives think schools should work. Civil rights groups have provided significant evidence that the testing pressure created by NCLB and state accountability systems has actually increased dropouts and push-outs from schools (Oakes & Rogers, 2007).

According to data from the National Assessment of Educational Progress (NAEP), there has been little improvement in student reading scores and only a small improvement in math scores. (See Figure 1.2.) In California, there has been no measured improvement in the scores of its large population of English language learners (of course, those who become proficient in English leave the category). At the same time, the United States has one of the highest high school dropout rates in the industrialized world as well as one of the highest incarceration rates for young people, particularly African American and Latino males.

The Bush Administration used NCLB sanctions, including the shifting of money from public schools to private charters, for failing to raise test scores. One of the unintended consequences of this effort was to actually push schools to encourage poor students to drop out or to transfer to another school. The accountability-driven reforms have not improved schools, but they have produced cheating and fraud (Nichols & Berliner, 2007). The changes on test scores after eight years are marginal (Fuller et al., 2007; Lee, 2006). In 2008, NCLB ran into stiff opposition when it was time to reauthorize the bill. Richard Rothstein (2008b) summarized the arguments well:

Schools and Social Policy

In one respect, NCLB betrays core Democratic principles, denying the importance of all social policy but school reform. Inadequate schools are only one reason disadvantaged children perform poorly. They come to school under stress from high-crime neighborhoods and economically insecure households. Their low-cost day-care tends to park them before televisions, rather than provide opportunities for developmentally appropriate play. They switch schools more often because of inadequate housing and rents rising faster than parents' wages. They have greater health problems, some (like lead poisoning or iron-deficiency anemia) directly depressing cognitive ability, and some causing more absenteeism or inattentiveness. Their households include fewer college-educated adults to provide rich intellectual environments, and their parents are less likely to expect academic success. Nearly 15 percent of the black-white test-score gap can be traced to differences in housing mobility, and 25 percent to differences in child- and maternal-health.

Yet NCLB insists that school improvement alone can raise all children to high proficiency. The law anticipates that with higher expectations, better teachers, improved curriculum, and more testing, all youths will attain full academic competence, poised for college and professional success. . . .

Teachers of children who come to school hungry, scared, abused, or ill, consider this absurd. But NCLB's aura intimidates educators from acknowledging the obvious. Teachers are expected to repeat the mantra "all children can learn," a truth carrying the mendacious implication that the level to which children learn has nothing to do with their starting points. Teachers are warned that any mention of children's socioeconomic disadvantages only "makes excuses" for teachers' own poor performance.

Of course, there are better and worse schools and better and worse teachers. Of course, some disadvantaged children excel more than others. But NCLB has turned these obvious truths into the fantasy that teachers can wipe out socioeconomic differences among children simply by trying harder. (p. 1.)

Neo-Liberal Reforms and the Return to Education Inequality

The school reforms initiated in the 1980s and mostly in vogue currently suppress the ideological issue of equality of opportunity. Conservative school reform advocates portrayed bilingual and multicultural education as divisive and as a "distraction" from important issues (Bloom, 1987; Hirsch, 1987). Not surprisingly, the important equity goals embodied in the reforms of the 1960s and 1970s fell by the wayside, deemed unimportant or promised as trickle-down by-products of current efforts to raise standards. These efforts focused more on school management than on the actual dynamics of teaching and learning in classrooms. Moreover, few conservative reform efforts attended specifically to schools that were failing to meet the needs of poor and cultural minority students. At the same time, liberal responses to conservative initiatives tended toward the piecemeal, suggesting the inclusion of representative heroes and authors or the hiring of minority role models as teachers.

Education Week's editors wrote: "Despite 15 years of earnest efforts to improve public schools and raise student achievement, states haven't made much progress" ("Quality Counts," 1997, p. 3). In fact, these 1980s conservative reform efforts showed pitiful results. In 1996, states earned an average "grade" of "C" for quality of teaching, based on poor preparation and professional support and development opportunities, as judged by *Education Week*. By 2001, California received a D– and Florida a D+, with New York and Texas each receiving a C+ for adequacy of school resources. That is, most states with large minority populations are not investing significantly in improving school conditions.

Schooling for Working-Class and Marginalized Students

Bob Chase (1997), then president of the National Education Association (NEA), noted that "the richest nation in the world has yet to muster the political willpower to provide every child with a decent chance at quality education. At least 15 million children in America attend substandard schools. . . . That's why the states must level up funding for the poorest public schools, especially inner city and rural schools" (p. 2). To date, few states have leveled up their funding, even when ordered to do so by court decisions. In NCLB and in state legislation, governors and legislatures have demanded high standards for all students, and they have mandated testing systems for accountability, but they have not provided the resources needed to achieve these standards. We continue to have separate and unequal education in our nation, a condition that author Jonathan Kozol calls *The Shame of the Nation* (2005).

We spend less per student than 16 other modern industrialized countries (Slavin, 1998). Moreover, of these, we are the only country that does not actively promote equality of educational opportunity. In the Netherlands, for example, schools receive 25 percent more funding for each lower-income child and 90 percent more funding for each minority child than in the United States (Slavin, 1998). Clearly, schools serving working-class students and cultural minorities fail in large part because our nation refuses to invest in its children. Our economy needs well-educated workers. We cannot permit schools to continue to fail. When schools succeed for middle-class students and fail for working-class students and students of color, schools contribute to a crippling division in our society along economic and racial lines. Schools, as public institutions, must find ways to offer all children equal educational opportunity. Yet reformed schools are more exceptions than the common pattern, particularly in our urban areas.

Let us be clear about the reality of schools in our nation. Some middle-class schools could benefit from reform, but most middle-class schools work. Most schools in urban areas, however, are unable to provide the equal educational opportunity called for by our national ideals and by constitutional law. There will be no significant change in the quality of urban education without substantial new funds allocated to these schools. Children in these schools need and deserve the same quality of buildings, teachers, materials, and resources as do students from affluent neighborhoods. Legislation was introduced in the state of Maryland in 2002 to bring all schools up to "adequate" levels of funding. This is a significant step toward equitable funding across districts. In the Maryland case, the budgets of high-performing schools were studied in an effort to understand how much money was available for per-student expenses; these average expenditures were then used to establish an adequate spending formula. The calculated cost was $6,000—$2,500 more than the average state expenditure per pupil at that time (Montgomery, 2002). Campaigns for equal funding of schools and for adequate funding became important in New Jersey, New York, California and other states. In 2008 a federal judge in Texas ruled that the state was failing to provide an equal education to middle and high school students struggling to learn English. He ordered improvements by the 2009–2010 school year (Elliot, Dec. 19, 2008.)

In the economic crisis of 2008/2009, which has been described as the worst economic crisis since the Great Depression, the combination of rising unemployment, declining consumer spending, declining asset values, has led to declining state revenues while the growing number of people in poverty and needing social services has increased.

Most education budgets are state and local funds. As much as 46% of state and local funds go to schools. When state budgets are in crisis, school budgets are in crisis particularly in our large urban areas.

School budgets were cut, class sizes were increased, teacher positions and supplementary programs were eliminated. Although the media savvy school superintendents and politicians continued to make promises, until most state finances recover from the recession, substantive school reform for urban and low income areas has come to a halt.

Neo-liberal reformers, although they claim to be influenced by business management theories, misuse recent developments in management theory. They fail to recognize that teachers' working conditions are students' learning conditions. Most large city schools are highly bureaucratized and control-oriented institutions—based on a high level of control and distrust, as is NCLB. Modern management theory recognizes that in personnel-intensive workplaces, control does not work well. Each year schools place the most inexperienced teachers with the students who most need help. We staff urban schools with large numbers of teachers who failed to find a position in their preferred suburban district, and then we wonder why over 50 percent leave within three years.

Attempts to break the domination of the bureaucracy, such as that occurring in Washington, D.C., under Chancellor Michelle Rhee, often focus on bringing in superintendents with little background in administration and public schools and on firing administrators and some teachers for not reforming failing schools. It is the corporate world of individualism, competition, and consumption, as opposed to the public sphere of civic cooperation and a pluralist democratic ethos. To date, this strategy has produced high teacher and administrator turnover, but it has not significantly improved academic achievement.

There is an approach to rigid school administration made notable by Joel Klein Chancellor in NYC, and Michele Rhee Chancellor in Washington D.C, among others, and applauded, endorsed and supported by a wide variety of news magazines and media outlets.

Rather than incorporate teaches into their planning, these school administrators repeatedly imposed neo-liberal policies including closing schools and attacking teachers unions. They admire what they believe to be corporate culture (not including the revelations of the actual culture of 2008/2009 economic recession) and are arbitrary in management systems with limited input from teachers or parents. Teachers have not been respected nor consulted. Little thought has been given to how these policies, have been destructive to the children and their futures.

Neo-liberal reformers including Rhee, Klein and others blame teachers and particularly the teachers unions for their own failure to improve public schools. In one sense, they are correct. Unions have organized and used political power to limit the expansion of corporate control over schooling. They have defended the traditions of Thomas Jefferson, John Dewey, and others that public schooling should prepare young people for democratic life.

New Goals for Democratic School Reform

As we have documented in this book, the U.S. public education system has consistently failed low-income students; many African American, Latino, and Native American students; and some Asian American students. Many reforms have been initiated, yet few have articulated an agenda that specifically seeks to hold the system accountable for providing equal educational opportunities for all students. A democratic agenda for school reform is long overdue and is imperative for the future health of our society.

Macedo (1993) summarizes some of the results of continuing the present school system:

> It is indeed ironic that in the United States, a country that prides itself on being the first and most advanced within the so-called "first-world," over sixty million people are illiterate or functionally illiterate. . . . To the sixty million illiterates we should add the sizable groups who learn to read but are, by and large, incapable of developing independent and critical thought.
>
> . . . I believe that, instead of the democratic education we claim to have, what we really have in place is a sophisticated colonial model of education designed primarily to train state functionaries and commissars while denying access to millions, a situation which further exacerbates the equity gap already victimizing a great number of so-called "minority" students. Even the education provided to those with class rights and privileges is devoid of the intellectual dimension of true teaching, since the major objective of a colonial education is to further deskill teachers and students so as to reduce them to mere technical agents who are destined to walk unreflectively through a labyrinth of procedures. What we have in the United States is not a system to encourage independent thought and critical thinking. Our colonial literacy model is designed to domesticate so as to enable the "manufacture of consent." (p. 203)

Thus far, we have critiqued the current education system particularly in terms of its performance vis-à-vis low-income and culturally and linguistically diverse students. We have also highlighted the shortcomings of the major education reform initiatives proposed and implemented by federal and state governments and by members of the policy and research communities. If such efforts as standards, charter schools, and vouchers are problematic, particularly because they concede the goals of public education to corporate interests, what kinds of school reforms would be superior and supportive of enriching and strengthening our democracy? It is important to emphasize that establishing education goals, monitoring student progress, maintaining high-quality expectations for teaching and learning, and improving the efficiency and smooth organization and operation of schools do not contradict goals of democracy or pluralism. Far too often, conservative forces have claimed these practices as solely their own, when in fact they also work well with democratic goals. The key questions, however, relate to who determines education standards, who monitors student progress and with what tools, who determines definitions of high-quality teaching, what kinds of resources are available for educationally sound efforts, and how are those resources distributed. This section describes alternative school reforms that have better prospects for creating a public education system that fosters democracy.

School Reform Networks

One pathway to pursuing multicultural and democratic school reform can be found through the efforts of educators and researchers outside of state departments and districts who have developed powerful intervention strategies. Building on the ideas of "effective schools" (see Figure 13.1), such efforts as the Comer School Development Program, the Accelerated Schools Project, the Child Development Project, and the Coalition of Essential Schools offer innovative models for school improvement. For reform efforts like the Comer School Development Program and the Accelerated Schools Project, both rising out of collaboration between school districts and major research universities (Yale University and Stanford University, respectively), changing school governance structures to include a broader group of stakeholders—that is, parents, community members, teachers, and students—is a key component. The Comer program also concentrates on underlying issues of mental and emotional health that often prevent urban students, impacted by poverty, violence, substance abuse, and lack of physical safety, from concentrating on their academics (Mintrop, Wong, Gamson, & Oberman, 1996). The Accelerated Schools Project adds a focus on powerful learning, in which high teacher expectations, peer coaching among teachers, and an enriched curriculum are used to engage students in accelerating their learning. Both of these reform efforts operate large national networks (more than 300 Comer schools and more than 700 Accelerated schools). Their schools are found primarily in low-income urban and rural settings.

The Child Development Project combines a strong commitment to ethical and prosocial curricula with broader changes in school governance and decision making (Mintrop et al., 1996). This program, which is specifically aimed at schools serving poor students and students of color, focuses intensively on helping teachers to transform their instructional attitudes and strategies along with adopting new curricula, structured heavily around literature and language arts. In addition, the project introduces more democratic and participatory forms of school governance. The Coalition of Essential Schools, founded by Theodore Sizer and affiliated with Brown University, uses a limited set of "essential principles" around which school communities transform their schools

(Mintrop et al., 1996). These principles include such ideas as "small is better" and "student knowledge should be demonstrated." This is one of the larger networks and offers participating schools a number of attractive professional development opportunities, including national conferences, regional conferences, and a partner school that acts as a "critical friend." This reform model is considered most appropriate for high schools; early participants tended to be primarily suburban schools, though the network has been expanded recently to include more schools serving diverse populations.

Community-Based Reforms

A central assumption of the market/corporate-based reforms, such as vouchers and charter schools, is that if the qualities of the supply of schools can be changed, then the outcomes of schools will be different. If you are not an economist, this can be a bit difficult to conceptualize. However, using this economic paradigm with a political action twist, community-based organizations have addressed a different part of the market equation: demand. A central premise of this chapter and others in this text is that public schools are generally adequate except for those serving low-income and culturally and linguistically diverse students. One reason why public schools in middle- and upper-middle-class communities work well and send the majority of students on to college or high-status jobs is that parents are able to translate their desires for their children's education into concrete expectations on the system. There is considerable parent demand for a high-quality education. This demand comes in several forms, from large and productive Parent–Teacher Organizations or Associations (PTOs or PTAs); to parents who are unhesitant about communicating their preferences to teachers, principals, and board members; to parents who can marshal resources from business partnerships and the like for school enrichment offerings.

Groups like the Industrial Areas Foundation, a faith-based intercongregational community group, have mounted efforts in low-income communities across the country to help parents make more informed and strategic demands on their local schools. In one case, in Austin, Texas, local organizers engaged in a three-year process of intensive parent education (Murnane & Levy, 1996). The focal points were twofold: involving parents in an extended discussion about a quality education that results in greater understanding of the indicators of a quality education (what do grades mean, what do test scores mean, how does their school compare with the one in a more affluent neighborhood, etc.) and teaching parents about the system and how to intervene strategically in it. As a result of this community-organizing effort, parents became more informed about the poor quality of their children's school and the education that it offered. Through dialogue with teachers, they discovered, though not always easily, that both groups shared similar concerns and goals for the students. Through training by the organizers, both teachers and parents became more adept at advocating for their school through district channels, obtaining external support (from the housing authority for improvements to a local park, from the police department for better patrolling for drug-related activity, from medical organizations for health care services provided at the school), and working as a united group. The end result was high-quality science programs at the school, accelerated math and science programs to better prepare students for junior high school, and a series of culturally based enrichment programs, emanating mostly from the cultural funds of knowledge in the Latino community that predominated in the area.

This approach is particularly appealing because the results promise to endure for the long term. Teaching parents these kinds of advocacy skills and involving them in truly collaborative efforts with teachers will spin off into areas not directly related to the ins and outs of the local school's classrooms. It is also a quintessentially democratic effort that exemplifies all that is possible when people develop the knowledge and access to information that enable their participation in the political process. This kind of community-based organizing is not for every situation and would only work where different kinds of community organizations (with schools being one) come together around a common goal of improving aspects of local public schools (see Figure 13.2).

Figure 13.2   The Industrial Areas Foundation

The Industrial Areas Foundation (IAF) is a cornerstone organization of a national network of broad-based, multiethnic, interfaith organizations that work primarily in poor and low-income communities. This network has been in operation for more than 50 years and works to further the vision of its founder, Saul Alinsky, by building the competence and confidence of ordinary citizens to change the relationships of power and politics in their communities (Cortés, 1996) As the IAF contends: "Any effort to improve the quality of early care and education must be connected to the revitalization of the social and political institutions in our communities. . . . In every community throughout the nation there are literally thousands of people with the potential to participate successfully in public life. Reform strategies won't work unless they recognize and draw upon the resources of these people and their ties to community institutions" (pp. 2–6).

Building from this belief, the IAF has worked in numerous communities to mobilize support for fundamental education reforms. Its efforts have been highly successful, yielding not only substantial improvements in local schools but also compelling insights about the nature of broad-based networks. The IAF observes that the initial forays of parents (particularly immigrant parents or those with their own negative schooling experiences) and community leaders into school reform highlight how unfamiliar they are with basic aspects of school structure and organization. Because they do not yet understand how schools operate or possess skills for effectively working in this arena, they are often ineffective advocates and participants in decision making. IAF organizers use careful and consistent mentoring to help build parents' and community members' skills at such endeavors as identifying and researching issues, organizing action teams, and engaging in public debate and negotiation. As their self-esteem and self-confidence increase, parents become active participants in the reform process who not only respond to but also actually shape the efforts to improve their schools.

The IAF has been most active in school reform in the Southwest. Through the Alliance Schools Initiative, a Texas partnership of districts, cities, and IAF organizations, many schools have seen test scores and attendance rates increase, dropout rates decrease, and parent participation escalate dramatically. In these cases, a compelling cultural shift has occurred: "Principals no longer see themselves as compliance officers of the district, but as leaders of a team. Teachers learn how to negotiate rules and regulations and can contribute their creative ideas to the classroom. Parents learn how to be equal decision-makers at the table with teachers, principals, and officials" (Cortés, 1996, p. 13). During an era when politics and social movements can seem fractured by narrow group interests, the IAF highlights the importance and effectiveness of cross-group coalitions.

Similar organizations are active in other areas, including New York City, New Mexico, and Los Angeles, California (Oakes & Rogers, 2006; Shirley, 1997).

There are some important lessons to be learned from these kinds of efforts. Parents, even when they are low-income, undereducated, and unsure of their English proficiency, care deeply about their children's futures and understand that education is one of the best investments to create brighter opportunities for their children. Many times such parents do not fully understand how the education system works; what is needed to ensure that their voices are heard; what kind of information indicates that it is the system, not their children, that is failing, and how they can make contributions outside the school to their children's learning. Similarly, these parents often confront many other barriers in their professional and personal lives: erratic job opportunities; low wages; limited, if any, health coverage; and so on. Finally, parents need teachers to be allies. The first step in this alliance is realizing the power of a united front around students' learning. For an interesting example of this work see *www.onela-iaf.org*.

Teachers as Reform Partners

Anyone serious about democratic school reform should first address his or her concerns to teachers. Teachers are the major resource available for improving schools. Unfortunately, few legislatures recognize this. Teachers' salaries are the largest part of any school budget. It is teachers—not administrators—who conduct the basic education process. Most teachers want to do better and would welcome an opportunity to help more students succeed. Reformers interested in improving the education opportunities for students should first look to help teachers perform their jobs better.

Various efforts have been made to produce curriculum and instructional strategies that are "teacher-proof"; that is, the authors script and monitor each step a teacher might take in delivering a lesson, hoping that strictly controlling teacher action will guarantee student outcomes (for example, several recent phonics-based reading packages use this approach). But a wealth of research has revealed that good teaching is a highly individual and creative act, based as much on instinct and experience and on theory and philosophy as on a prescribed curriculum. Even the most organized and innovative curriculum can become monotonous in the hands of a mediocre teacher; highly skilled teachers can transform drill and practice into activities that students find engaging and productive.

Some reform efforts have sought to capitalize on teachers' "wisdom of practice" (Shulman, 1987) by empowering them to participate more fully in policy development and other important decisions. School improvement programs such as the Accelerated Schools Project seek to empower teachers, while also expanding their responsibility for the development and implementation of education decisions (Hopfenberg et al., 1993).

Increased involvement of teachers has had many benefits, including more practical and better-implemented policies as well as renewed enthusiasm for and interest in teaching on the part of educators. Thus, recognition and acknowledgment of teacher voice, experience, knowledge, and wisdom can create momentum for school change. At the same time, we must consider several important factors when thinking of teachers as stakeholders in democratic school reform.

Teachers in general, particularly new teachers, are highly committed to their students and care about their education and overall welfare. Education reforms and reform movements should capitalize on this commitment by focusing their efforts on the matters of most importance to teachers: learning and teaching in the classroom. A study at Stanford University (McLaughlin & Talbert, 1993) found that, across the country, reforms that support teacher learning by providing time for study, reflection, and in-service training on concrete classroom issues will have the most chances for improving student learning. Reforms that provide teachers with supportive environments in which to innovate and try new practices will help to unleash the creative ideas that are typically quashed by the more standard teacher-proof curriculum. Reforms that connect teachers to teachers and involve them in a network that can provide a flow of new ideas, new questions, new strategies, and other forms of renewal will solidify in teachers a perspective of continual improvement and high standards.

Teachers need improved organizational and material conditions in order to be active participants in democratic school reform efforts. Most teachers work in conditions that would be deemed unacceptable by other professionals. They have little more than an hour or two per week to plan and develop lessons, they often spend much of their own salaries for basic materials, and in many urban schools they work in classrooms with leaky roofs, broken glass, insufficient lighting, and limited access to telephones. These conditions are demoralizing and devalue the skills and talents that most teachers have developed. It is also essential that democratic school reform grapple with the personnel dimensions of school change. Adding teachers' voices to those already active in democratic school reform will strengthen these movements.

Teachers Unions and School Reform

Teachers' voices are most often expressed through their unions. More than 83 percent of teachers in the United States are represented by unions (National Education Association, 2003). Teachers responded to the growth of educational management and bureaucracy in the 1960s and 1970s by forming unions. In the ensuing decades, unions have become increasingly politically active, using their organization and money to protect their members' interests. Organized teachers unions have often protected school funding in the midst of public fiscal crises. Serious effort at school reform must engage teachers through their unions, and teachers interested in school reform need to enlist their unions' aid. Unions have the organization and political capital that can assist or defeat efforts to democratize public schools.

Teachers work in an environment that is often not professional or free or democratic. Particularly since NCLB and assessment-based reform, teachers' decision making has been restricted. When new teachers begin work in some districts, they leave many of their civil liberties at the door. We can hardly develop democratic behaviors if the teachers spend most of their time in an environment that closely resembles a dictatorship. Unions provide an important limit to the arbitrary power of politicians and administrators.

Teachers in low-performing schools are too often treated as unworthy people—as failures. They are blamed by the media and by politicians for the failure of the schools to educate, ignoring the many economic/social structures that lead to school failure. Teachers are frequently reminded of their low status by conflicts with students, orders from administrators, and stories in the press. Compliance is demanded to a long list of rules: teach this material, give this test, monitor lunch counts, supervise the playground. Unions assist teachers with these matters. Too often the buildings are dismal, rundown, inadequate. The bathrooms are dismal, supplies are lacking, and most of all, time is lacking. Most teachers know how to teach much better than they presently perform, but they need more time to prepare, to plan, and to support students. Many soon succumb to the environment of oppression. The literature may call it burnout, but defeat and oppression are more accurate descriptors.

New teachers seldom are supported in a significant manner. A doctor will spend two years as an intern, learning to help patients. A teacher will typically spend one semester, and usually with too little guidance because the host teacher is busy working with children. Teachers need time to learn and to receive support and coaching from skilled, experienced teachers. Quality teaching makes a difference. Low-performing schools tend to receive too many new teachers who are still learning their craft (Education Trust, 2006). Many administrators have responded during this cycle of "reform" by issuing more commands and setting up accountability systems. This strategy has failed to improve school achievement (Kober, 2001; Valenzuela, 2004). Many administrators are not selected or trained to guide and support new teachers, even though teachers are their most basic resource (Darling-Hammond & Friedlaender, 2008). They are managers. Only a few were skilled teachers themselves. They do not have the time or the skills to help and to coach new teachers.

While unions have long led the efforts to protect school funding and to elect pro-education legislators, more recently they have provided substantial leadership in the struggle to improve the quality of education in our areas of educational crisis. When schools are under attack, unions provide a vital and vigorous defense.

Teacher-activists concerned with producing equal educational opportunity for children from urban districts can work with unions to reconceptualize the roles of their unions. A beginning was made toward union participation in education reform in August 1994 in Portland, Oregon, at a meeting of the National Coalition of Educational Activists. A document produced at this meeting, "Social Justice Unionism" (National Coalition of Educational Activists, 1994), contains the following statement: "Public education is at a crossroads and so, too, are our unions. Our society's children face deepening poverty and social dislocation, challenges and higher expectations with declining resources. . . . As the organized core of the teaching profession, education unions remain central to resolving these crises" (p. 12).

The Portland meeting led to the creation of the Teacher Union Reform Network. This network continues and currently supports a number of local initiatives to improve schools, including modifying seniority provisions, placing highly qualified teachers in low-performing schools, and assisting with professional development (Taylor & Rosario, 2007).

The NEA has been a major and consistent advocate of the position that a quality public education is essential to a successful democratic society and that such an education should be accessible to every child. Its leaders have argued for equity-based reform at conferences, in major media, through paid advertising, and in the Congress and legislatures. The NEA works with state and local affiliates to improve low-performing schools by making fundamental changes—changes that will create a safe, orderly environment and that focus on high standards of teaching and learning for all students.

Both the NEA and the American Federation of Teachers (AFT) teachers' unions urge an increased investment in current federal programs such as NCLB, and particularly Title 1 of that legislation. And both unions have been leaders in the efforts to amend NCLB to make it more supportive of teachers. The NEA and its state affiliates have advocated in support of proposals to provide additional resources and opportunities necessary to improve the quality of poor-performing schools, including

- Class size reduction in the early grades,
- School construction and renovation to help modernize school buildings and alleviate classroom overcrowding, and
- School–community partnerships.

The smaller and more urban-based AFT (affiliated with the AFL–CIO) represents teachers primarily in the East and Midwest, as well as a number of teacher assistants and college faculty, and advocates for school reform positions similar to those of the NEA. The AFT, led by Randi Weingarten, often has been an advocate for a more conservative teaching philosophy, supporting standards and programs in math, phonics, history, and literature as well as National Board certification for teachers. The strongest critics of multicultural education, including Al Shanker, Diane Ravitch, E. D. Hirsch, and Arthur Schlesinger, and the strongest advocates for phonics approaches to reading are frequently featured in the AFT magazine, *American Educator*. On the other hand, the AFT has been a leader in several cities in pursuing education reform. In New York City, the United Federation of Teachers (AFT) has developed two charter schools to demonstrate how one can run a successful school serving high-needs communities with high poverty rates that empowers teachers and parents, while protecting the union rights of faculty. For more examples of school districts working cooperatively with teachers union members to improve schools, see the Center for School Improvement website at *www.aft.org/topics/csi/index.htm*.

There are many teacher and administrator organizations. The largest are the unions, the NEA (*www.nea.org*), the AFT (*www.aft.org*), and their state affiliates. These organizations have professional development goals, staff, and resources. As unions, they advance the interests of their members on issues such as salaries and benefits. In addition, responding to the current era of school reform, a few teachers unions have recognized that the relentless efforts of the White House, school boards, and the business community to "reform" schools usually are designed to reward and punish teachers, as when they link new programs to high-stakes testing systems that fail to recognize the complexity of student learning. As a result, several of the country's large local teachers unions, such as the Montgomery County Education Association (Maryland) and the San Juan Teachers Association (Sacramento) have taken the lead in developing their own programs in social justice and in assisting teachers with professional development (see Taylor & Rosario, 2007). Many unions now argue that the democratization of decision making in schools—that is, promoting teacher professionalism and decision making—is vital to the successful implementation of meaningful school improvement.

Several academic disciplines also have their own organizations, such as the National Council for the Social Studies (*www.ncss.org*) and the National Council of Teachers of English (*www.ncte.org*), each of which impacts the efforts to establish standards. In addition, organizations exist whose purpose is to improve opportunities for marginalized students, such as the National Association for Bilingual Education (*www.nabe.org*), the National Association for Multicultural Education (*www.nameorg.org*), and the Institute for Language and Education Policy (*www.elladvocates.org*).

Clearly, reformers would benefit by drawing on the expertise and resources of the teachers' unions. When reform efforts or antireform efforts reach the state legislators, as with the imposition of a poor testing regime or the elimination of services to language-minority students, the participation of teachers' unions is critical.

Professional Development Schools

Beginning in the mid-1980s, public schools and universities began to work in partnership around issues related to student learning and to teacher preparation and professional development. By the late 1980s, a new model of school reform, the professional development school, was articulated, primarily by universities and by the Holmes Partnership, a national network of school–university partnerships. A professional development school involves the collaboration of two organizations: a local school (or schools, in some cases) and a local university that houses a teacher education program. Both organizations come together to pursue four primary objectives: the improvement of student learning and achievement, enhancement of the field/clinical experiences of student teachers, professional development for all educators (student teachers, cooperating teachers, mentor teachers, and university faculty), and use of inquiry as a tool for understanding and addressing issues in student learning, teaching effectiveness, and teacher education (Hoffman, Reed, & Rosenbluth, 1997; Holmes Group, 1995; Johnston, Brosnan, Cramer, & Dove, 2000).

In a professional development school situation, the teachers and their pupils in the local school benefit because they have additional resources to help them reach their academic goals: Student teachers from the university can tutor students, organize special enrichment days, and assist teachers with particularly labor-intensive activities (like interactive journals). Education faculty members, who usually increase their presence on the school campus, can serve as resources for cooperating teachers and for the school administration; content faculty can also be important resources for teachers, and their knowledge can be tapped to enrich and strengthen the core curriculum. The benefits to the university's teacher preparation program are also significant. Classroom-based teachers can assist university faculty as they shape their methods courses to more realistically address issues that arise in classrooms. Classroom teachers can help redesign the field experience/student-teaching activities to make them developmentally appropriate for beginning teachers. Classroom teachers and administrators can often coteach courses with faculty, lending their expertise particularly in the applications of theoretical and conceptual constructs. The university teacher preparation program is the ultimate beneficiary when university instructors have an opportunity to ground their theoretical knowledge in the practicalities of

Figure 13.3 The Interactive Change Process

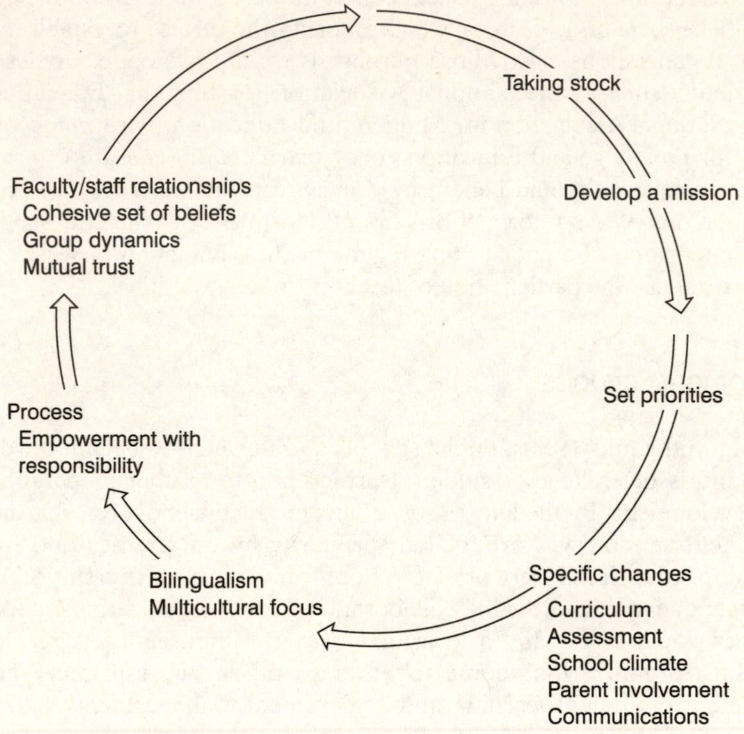

Taking stock

Develop a mission

Faculty/staff relationships
Cohesive set of beliefs
Group dynamics
Mutual trust

Set priorities

Process
Empowerment with
responsibility

Specific changes
Curriculum
Assessment
School climate
Parent involvement
Communications

Bilingualism
Multicultural focus

designing and teaching lessons to diverse groups of students and to wrestle firsthand with the teaching and learning dilemmas faced by classroom teachers daily.

The teacher-centered practices described here contrast with the top-down neo-liberal reforms detailed earlier in terms of their emphasis on education equity, partnerships, and inclusion. These efforts strive to broaden decision making to include teachers (in more significant ways), parents, and community members; emphasize rich learning and meaningful instructional activities; support teacher professional development; and address the unique needs of children from low-income and culturally and linguistically diverse backgrounds. They are based not on the notion that competition will improve schools but on the belief that more community investment, better professional development, and a sharper focus on rich opportunities for learning will.

Figure 13.3 illustrates several necessary elements for teacher-based changes.

Pertinent Reform Questions

As a teacher, you will experience firsthand the forceful winds of change. Calls for school reform are likely to continue as our society experiences more rapid economic and social change. You will likely be asked to consider different reforms and to participate in various reform projects. It will be crucial that you base your decision on serious and probing questioning of these reforms and their objectives. You may consider using the following questions to determine the ability of proposed reforms to meet democratic and multicultural education objectives.

Do the proposed reforms (curricula, materials, strategies, reorganization ideas, etc.) do any or all of the following:

- Build on the cultural and linguistic strengths of students?
- Teach students to develop positive human relations?
- Incorporate meaningful cooperative learning strategies into daily routines?
- Develop students' critical-thinking skills?
- Provide coaching and encouragement for students?
- Structure in opportunities for meaningful dialogue and exchange among participants (teachers, administrators, parents, students, etc.)?
- Address key local issues identified as priorities by participants?
- Create structures of democratic empowerment for all school stakeholders?

There definitely are schools that are dysfunctional. Lack of funds contributes to the problem, but money alone will not fix these schools. These schools need substantial reform. The administration, the faculty, and the students are participating in a culture of failure. In such cases, the schools may need *reconstitution*, as provided for by NCLB and most state laws.

In New Orleans, Philadelphia, Washington, D.C., New York, and elsewhere, reconstitution has been achieved by establishing charter schools and bringing in an outside management company to radically alter the school culture. In other places, school districts have worked with charters such as the KIPP schools or with intervention systems such as WestEd, the Accelerated Schools Project, and the Comer School Development Program.

KIPP, the Knowledge Is Power Program, is one of several school restructuring programs that have emerged in the last two decades. KIPP schools are organized for academic achievement. They insist on a contract between the home and the school. They do not have unions for their teachers. There are currently 57 KIPP public schools in 16 states and the District of Columbia, enrolling more than 14,000 students. Across the KIPP network, 55 of the existing 57 schools are charter schools. The majority of KIPP schools, 48 of 57, are middle schools designed to serve fifth- through eighth-grade students.

KIPP schools are free, open-enrollment, college-preparatory public schools where low-income students develop the knowledge, skills, and character traits needed to succeed in top-quality high schools and colleges. KIPP schools provide a structured, academic-centered learning environment and more time spent in classes. All of the students and the parents sign a contract to complete their work and their homework. If students and parents do not agree to participate in this structured college-prep environment, they are not accepted in a KIPP school. By creating an on-task academic environment for all students, KIPP has been successful in getting a significant number of its students to graduate and to enter college. You can find out more about KIPP schools at www.KIPP.org.

If your school or district is working with an intervention system, you need to carefully read "Don't Face School Reform Alone; Organize" in the following section.

A New Teacher's Survival Guide

You are entering teaching at a time of great controversy about and discussion of school reform. New teachers are central to school improvement. They enter the profession with high expectations and optimism. The following ideas are offered to assist you in maintaining your optimism, while working in a very difficult environment:

1. Have confidence in yourself. Build on your strengths and support that confidence.

2. Maintain a positive attitude by focusing on your students. Many schools have some teachers who say no to all initiatives and new ideas and who will tell you that there are no new ideas, just old failed ideas recycled. Don't let them get you down.

3. Pick a problem to work on, limiting yourself to one (at most, two) of the most important. Select problems that you can actually do something about. For example, you can change name-calling in your classroom, but in your first year of teaching, you probably cannot change the district or state textbook selection. Choose problems that will help you to build a teacher support group.

4. Break problems into pieces. Start small. Pick issues you can win—for example, starting a clothes closet or English-as-a-second-language classes for parents. Your victories will lead to more self-confidence and greater personal power.

5. Take an inquiry approach to classroom challenges. Reflect on root causes rather than superficial behaviors or symptoms. Get the facts. Prepare yourself. Research issues and develop solutions. Ask for assistance and team up with like-minded folks. Often a mentor teacher or a peer teacher can assist you with learning how other teachers have resolved this issue.

6. Learn who has the power to change things. Identify decision makers and persons with influence in your school. What decisions can the principal make? What decisions do experienced teachers make? Does the PTA have influence? Who is your union representative? What decisions are covered by your contract? Keep a list of names, addresses, and telephone numbers.

7. Plan. Sort through your information and decide what you want. What are achievable goals? Who is responsible for providing resources? Be certain to regularly recruit new supporters. Insist that your union join you in the effort. Don't try to change the school by yourself. Who in the community may be willing to assist you and support your teacher network?

8. Develop a range of improvements. Start with recommendations that can be acted on immediately, within existing laws and programs, with little or no money. For those of you teaching in underfunded schools, develop a long-range plan that will require resources to bring your school up to equal financial support for your state. Real reform costs money.

9. Start changing things. Begin with the person closest to the problem. It may be you as the teacher in the classroom. Do not assume that other teachers or administrators are against you until they have actually demonstrated their opposition. Many teachers and administrators are simply used to the way things are. They have each tried their own innovations in their time and may have become discouraged.

Don't Face School Reform Alone; Organize

Let us be clear. A progressive teacher working in a school is good, but it is not school reform. A progressive activist teacher will improve the education of 30 students, or 100 students, and these are significant contributions. But one or two activists are not school reform and neither is a single progressive principal.

The success of some outstanding schools serving low-income neighborhoods, as previously described, indicates that schools can improve and that children in poverty can be provided with high-quality schooling (Chenoweth, 2007). Individual schools that have improved their performance and academic achievement are valuable islands of hope for reform. And hope is a vital ingredient in working for change.

Consistently high-quality education in low-income schools remains a rare exception, not the norm. Few, if any, of the superintendents of major school systems—and their staffs—have reformed their schools to produce equal opportunity. The leaders of most major city school systems—New York, Chicago, Philadelphia, Los Angeles, New Orleans, San Diego, Washington, D.C. and others—have more success at issuing press releases than at working with teachers to improve student achievement. We know from experience in several cities that school reform efforts are not sustained beyond the tenure of a superintendent or a principal. Indeed, there are numerous cases of schools and leaders making important changes, only to be stopped by control-oriented superintendents in the name of reform (Wilms, 2008). And realistically there has been little improvement in reducing the achievement gap in urban systems.

Testing and accountability models are the most common and frequent efforts at administration-driven reform. Inspired by conservative business interests and supported by federal and state legislation, school leaders have imposed testing and control of curriculum decisions. Research on these efforts indicates that when they work, they work at best based on voluntary compliance by teachers—and the effects last for only a few years.

When the reform narrows the curriculum, ignores language-minority populations, and takes the joy and relevance out of schooling and teaching, we should not voluntarily comply. Instead, we should resist. Their repressive system depends on our voluntary compliance—instead, we should organize for justice and educational equity.

Teachers as Organizers: An Introduction to Organizing

Real school reform requires substantive change. Reform will occur when groups of teachers work together to create a new, more democratic school system to better serve all of the students.

We need to develop a new conception of teachers as change agents for those teachers committed to civil rights and the success of their students. This potential role is underdeveloped. We need active and activist teacher leaders to guide and direct the change to a more democratic and a more equal school system. In many schools there are teachers who want to improve student achievement and they do not wish to become administrators. Indeed, it is not clear that most school administrators can improve student achievement.

There currently exist a number of leadership roles for teachers. Teachers fill positions such as lead teachers, grade-level leaders, host teachers, mentor teachers, student advocates, curriculum specialists, teacher organizers, language specialists, union leaders, and change agents. Schools will not change without leaders dedicated to change. You could become one of these leaders. Teacher leaders are needed to provide a teacher voice and advocacy for quality education within the school reform efforts. Teacher organizers are particularly needed when schools are undergoing some form of reconstitution or reorganization to improve achievement.

What does a change agent do? In *Doing Democracy: The MAP Model for Organizing Social Movements* (2001), Moyer lists the roles of change agents as including the following:

- Organizes people power and engaged citizens for the common good;
- Educates and involves the majority of the citizens on the issues;
- Involves preexisting grassroots and parents' organizations, networks, and unions;
- Places issues on the society's agenda; and
- Promotes alternatives.

Each of these roles can be well applied to teachers fostering change in schools. For teacher activists, the first group to organize is other teachers. First, you need to find one ally, then two. We know from organizing that relationships matter. You need to develop positive, ongoing relationships with a number of teachers in your school site. Indeed, this will make your own work life more interesting and bearable.

Parents are a second important component of organizing. With large-scale immigration, there is no reason to limit your organizing to citizens; parents, including immigrant parents, are appropriate partners. An important task is to develop an educational agenda that parents can understand. School talk is often mystifying to parents. And since so much professional talk is used, parents can be misled into pursuing anti-democratic projects. Parents have been recruited and used in the anti-bilingual education campaigns and in the divisive campaigns on reading and vouchers.

Teachers should look for a community-based organization in their area and work with it. Several community-based organizations, such as those affiliated with the Industrial Areas Foundation, PICO, or the Association of Community Organizations for Reform Now, work on school reform and prepare parents to become community leaders (see Anyon, 2005; *www.industrialareasfoudation.org*; Oakes & Rogers, 2006). Parent organizing can provide the power needed for sustained engagement with the power structure of a school district. Teachers, parents, and educational activists need each other. The first step is building relationships of trust among these constituencies.

As soon as you begin to organize for social justice, you will encounter other, already existing groups. Perhaps the most frequent encounter will be with a union activist in your building. It is useful to map out the existing groups and interests and conduct some informal research to see which of these groups may assist you. For example, a union activist may well encourage you to bring your goals within the union effort. This is useful possible approach. Certainly, if you can bring in the union to support your projects, this will assist you. It is important and valuable for teachers to bring their unions along as they pursue progressive change. These are our institutions with staff, money, and resources.

A note of caution is needed. Unions have their institutional agenda, which usually focuses on the salaries and the treatment of employees. These are important issues, particularly for underpaid teachers and teacher assistants. The union agenda is rather well understood. And whenever possible, you want to work in cooperation with the union. However, at times, the invitation to work within the union is actually a recruitment of you to work on the union agenda rather than on your social justice agenda. You can be an activist and will be encouraged to carry out the many valuable service projects of the union. And it is important to have the union with you when you encounter conflict. But consider these significant questions: Does working within the union allow you to pursue your previous goals? Or are you quickly recruited to work on the union goals? This is an area where you need continuous dialogue with your allies. After all, the union may have already developed a valuable strategy that advances your work.

Organizing for school change always involves bringing in new people to the environment. You may need to recruit new teacher allies. Or you may need to recruit new parent allies. In each case, you need to build cooperative working relationships with others. Organizing occurs when relationships are built on trust and solidarity—and a commitment to school reform goals.

It is useful to note some of the differences between activism and organizing.

Activism is getting people together to take on some activity. Activism may set the agenda and move a group onto the offensive. The teachers unions are good at mobilizing activism in most states. Organizing is educating and building a new movement and new relationships. Organizing needs activism, but the two are not the same thing. Organizing involves educational projects and convincing those that are not yet convinced that schools can change. And, importantly, organizing involves building new relationships between people. Organizing must have an achievable agenda and a strategy for how to get the changes you are seeking—or at least the first steps toward change. Usually, organizing involves changing the power relationships in the school, as when you engage and nourish parental participation. For this reason, organizers promptly seek relationships with unions and community-based organizations, particularly those organizations that themselves have an organizing orientation.

To build organizations for the long haul of school reform, we need a balance of both activism and organizing; each is incomplete without the other. Organize strategically. Choose your targets. Not all change strategies are equal. Some build success, some build relationships, some require much more time to implement. A serious analysis of change opportunities will assist in selecting targets for change efforts.

Usually, teachers, parents, and other interested parties will support a change when (1) they recognize a need to change, (2) they understand the change proposed, and

(3) the proposed change will provide greater rewards or less pain than continuing with the present system. Effective organizers do not talk over the heads of their allies. They explain things in school and help other partners such as parents understand the intricacies and interdependent nature of school cultures and structures.

The above three criteria can be useful in selecting change targets. Selecting your early targets is an important decision. You should make a list of priorities for change. In this process, be certain to include the voices of your allies—the parents. What do they see as needing change first? You should also select targets and campaigns that lead to further change. For example, getting the teachers' lounge painted or getting computers for teachers may be a good task, but it does not necessarily develop a culture or process of change. On the other hand, insisting on teacher voice and choice in selecting in-service workshops or initiating teacher support groups will set up conditions for further dialogue and change. You want to select change targets that will generate further dialogue and open future avenues for innovation.

Public Opinion and the Media

A major problem with our campaign for a democratic approach to schooling is that most of the media have been sold on a mind-set or framework of accountability. Corporate-sponsored networks and their access to the media are not likely to change. The domination of the accountability framework within the media and political circles often requires that we craft our preferred reforms within the themes and phrases already popularized by the media—such as testing and accountability. And we should expect to be misunderstood. Education and explaining will be a constant struggle.

Networks of support exist to assist with refining issues so that they are, first, understandable and, second, subject to change. *Rethinking Schools*, at *rethinkingschools.org*, does a good job of this. The Civil Rights Project (currently at UCLA) has conducted both research and media outreach for over a decade on the growing resegregation of U.S. schools. Opponents of democratic schooling have been successful at creating their own networks, funded by conservative foundations, including the Olin Foundation, Bradley Foundation, American Enterprise Institute, Pacific Research Institute, and others. They create advocacy groups and "research" groups, such as the Thomas B. Fordham Institute, to foster a conservative—no new taxes—view of schools. They sponsor conferences and testimony to hold onto the current failing NCLB focus on testing and standards. These organizations use marketing methods, including in particular the "framing of the issue" strategy of focusing on accountability and testing. Both teachers' unions and most professional organizations have public relations staff and offer advice on and tool kits for getting a positive message out about schools.

Conflict and Change

Substantive change usually involves conflict. There is no escape from controversy and conflict when you are trying to change a well-established system like the poor reading scores and high dropout rates in many schools and the current distribution of money, power, and decision making in schools and the legislatures that supports these failures. While you probably cannot avoid conflict, you can avoid unnecessary conflict.

When there are unjust situations such as the achievement gap in schools, the controversy must be faced. As you raise the issues, if you describe the reality, you may be accused of starting trouble, being divisive, or creating conflict. Most administrators would rather ignore or gloss over differences. They prefer a continuation of the present power distribution—since they are in charge. Becoming a change agent includes

1. Early recognition of and preparation for conflict,
2. Avoidance of unnecessary and merely destructive conflict,
3. Willingness to face the pain and tension of a conflict,
4. Willingness to do the research necessary to select and promote changes, and
5. Willingness to make a change in yourself and your views.

By setting some clear goals and recognizing progress, you can usually keep the conflict manageable. An important practice is to select achievable goals and then recognize your progress toward these goals. Engaging in unnecessary conflict—caused, for example, by an overemphasis on the personality traits and behavior of an opponent—may cost you allies and prevent progress toward school improvement. When you encounter opposition—which you will—your first response should not be to run to the barricades and engage the conflict. You should first begin to analyze your opposition.

What are the forces keeping the current practice in place? How do your opponents usually react to ideas from outside the system? How would school administrators react to

1. Criticism at a school board meeting?
2. Picketing at the school or their office?
3. A school walkout, strike, or boycott?

Are there school board members who may be allies? Can your opponents be divided? Opposition research is vital. If you do not analyze your opposition, you may well lose the issue, even if you have good reasons and good analysis.

Not everything will change at once. And you cannot change the entire local school system this year. It is far easier to initiate and to sustain a change at your school site if the proposed change is understood by students, parents, faculty, administrators, and even the media. For example, at present most groups are convinced of the need for standards-based reform. As described in Chapter 12 and earlier in this chapter, there are significant limits to standards-based reforms, but the concept has great acceptance in most arenas.

If you are advocating an alternative effort, such as adoption of the Algebra Project, it will ease your entrance into the change dialogue if you use the vocabulary of standards-based reforms and you include references to standards in your proposals. You do not need to convince the members of your audience of the need to abandon their basic beliefs. If, on the other hand, you propose changes that include few opportunities to measure and demonstrate progress, and few references to standards your proposal will encounter more resistance and might fail.

Remember also that transforming a school requires the unified efforts of many actors. Students themselves can be active in this process by being given opportunities to articulate their ideas about their education and the kinds of opportunities they would like to have. Teachers are key actors in school change and should be given the tools (e.g., resources such as planning time, sufficient instructional materials) to be active players in developing programs for their school. Parents should work in tandem with teachers and be given opportunities to communicate their hopes and desires to school staff as well as to share their cultural funds of knowledge when making curricular and instructional decisions. Administrators provide the needed leadership for a school that is hoping to make significant changes: They must run interference with their district office to ensure that the voices of their teachers are heard; they must learn how to create structures at the school that maximize student, teacher, and parent involvement, while also protecting and bolstering learning time and opportunities. Finally, teachers unions can be important players in the school change process. Though unions have historically been more concerned with "bread and butter" issues like salaries and benefits, many teachers unions, particularly those involved with the Teacher Union Reform Network, are beginning to take a more active role in shaping a professional teaching force that has at its core an ethos of continuous learning and renewal. If unions can be brought in to support school-based reforms that further goals of educational equity, this will also lend strength to these efforts.

A Choice Between Two Futures

The United States and the school systems in most of our cities are currently in crisis. Schools can continue as they are, and one segment of society will be well educated, while another segment will continue to fail. The economic crisis for working people and people of color will continue to grow (Ehrenreich, 2008; Mishel, Bernstein, & Allegretto, 2007; Reich, 2007). Alternatively, schools can be transformed, through some of the strategies described in this book, into places where education is a rich, compelling, and affirming process that prepares all young people to make thoughtful contributions to their community in economic and civic terms. The election of Barack Obama and his own focus on educational reform gives hope for positive, democratic change.

The possibility for change exists. Current proposals promoted by conservative institutes, such as school choice and the use of public monies to fund private education, will not lead to democratic reform. Rather than continuing these privileges, a reform movement must build on the democratic ideals of progress and equality of opportunity. These traditional values can triumph over the hostility and violence produced by racism, sexism, and class bias presently accepted as "normal" and natural in our schools.

The growth of the African American, Asian, and Latino middle class—a direct result of the Civil Rights Movement's use of political power to reduce discrimination based on race—provides powerful evidence that racism can be combated through education and public policy. Frederick Douglass spoke to this issue in 1849 when he wrote the following:

The whole history of the progress of human liberty shows that all concessions yet made to her august claims have been born of earnest struggle. The conflict has been exciting, agitating, all absorbing, and for the time being putting all other tumults to silence. It must do this or it does nothing. If there is no struggle there is no progress. Those who profess to favor freedom, and yet depreciate agitation, are men who want crops without plowing up the ground. They want rain without thunder and lightning. They want the ocean without the awful roar of its many waters. This struggle may be a moral one; or it may be a physically one; or it may be both moral and physical; but it must be a struggle. Power concedes nothing without demand. It never did and it never will. (1849/1991, p. vii)

Summary

This is the time for a change in our society and in our schools. This generation must renew our democratic society. As described in this book, we face marked crises in government, politics, families, and communities—and in the schools. Public schools have a particular responsibility to reverse these crises and to renew our democratic society. The first mission of pubic schooling is to equip all students for the responsibilities and privileges of citizenship—and many of the schools in low-income areas are presently not fulfilling this mission. If we do not solve the problems of low-performing schools, our democracy suffers. For our democracy to prosper, we need to create schools that value all of our children and that encourage the educational achievement of each one.

All children need a good education to participate in our democracy and prepare for life in the rapidly changing economy. Making schooling valuable and useful is vital to prosperity for all. Lack of education is a ticket to economic hardship. The more years of school that students complete, the more money that they are likely to earn as adults and the better their chances are that they will get and keep a good job. Unemployment is highest among school dropouts, as is incarceration for crimes. When we fail to educate all of our children, the high costs of this failure come back to hurt us in the form of unemployment, drugs, crime, incarceration, violence, social conflict and economic stagnation.

We need to invest in urban schools, provide equal educational opportunities in these schools, and recruit a well-prepared teaching force that begins to reflect the student populations in these schools. We must insist on equal opportunity to learn, without compromise. When we do these things, we will begin to protect the freedom to learn for our children and our grandchildren and to build a more just and democratic society.

Teacher advocates for democratic, multicultural education challenge those social forces acting to preserve the present inequalities and injustices in our schools. We consider schools as sites for the struggle for or against more democracy in our society. The struggle for education improvement and education equality will be a long one. The struggle for multicultural education, based in democratic theory, is an important part of the general struggle against race, class, and gender oppression and for democracy.

Schools serving urban and impoverished populations need fundamental change. At present these schools do not open the doors to economic opportunity. They usually do not promote equality. Instead, they recycle inequality. The high school dropout rates alone demonstrate that urban schools prepare less than 50 percent of their students for entrance into the economy and society. A democratic agenda for school reform includes insisting on fair taxation and adequate funding for all children. Political leaders in most states have not yet decided to address the real financial costs of school reform. We cannot build a safe, just, and prosperous society while we leave so many young people behind.

At present, there is not a political agreement to make the necessary investments to bring about substantial school reform. The U.S. government and your state government will not make the necessary investments to improve education or to improve health care or to rebuild the economic infrastructure until we stop investing over $850 billion in the wars in Iraq and Afghanistan and whichever military intervention follows. Funding choices made at the federal, state, and local levels directly affect our children.

The conservative/media emphasis on accountability for schools is a distraction from the real issues. We know which schools need improvement, and we know how to improve them. Teachers can pursue democratic opportunity with instruction in multicultural education, critical thinking, cooperative learning, improved reading and language skills, and empowerment. Teachers and parents together face a political choice: Shall we continue to call for high standards without providing the necessary resources for all schools to have a reasonable chance to attain such standards? Shall we continue to punish schools and their staffs for low test scores, even when we know that the tests are poor instruments for measuring learning and that their construction guarantees the failure of many students? Are increased competition and privatization the answer for schools when they have not been the answer in other sectors of our society, particularly for low-income and marginalized people? Did free market economics work in the housing and banking industry or did they contribute to the economic crisis.

The problem is to provide the resources, including well-prepared teachers with adequate support, needed to make the current schools successful. We face a political choice: We can choose to provide high-quality schools only for the middle and upper classes and underfunded, understaffed schools for the poor. Or we can choose to work together to improve the schools for all of the children.

Question over the Chapter

1. Most school reform reports recognize a need for new skills. What skills are needed for entrance into the emerging economy?

Who are the major advocates of reform in your state? In your district?

Activities for Further Study of School Reform

1. Make contact with your teachers union. What kinds of reform activities is it engaged in?
2. List three reasons why some parents are frustrated with schools. Share your list with your class. Brainstorm ideas for addressing these concerns.
3. What kind of change efforts have you been a part of in a personal or community setting? What kinds of skills and dispositions did these changes require? Do these same skills and dispositions apply to making changes in a classroom or school?

4. Decide on the three most urgent reforms you could initiate as a student teacher (language support, coaching, or conflict resolution, for example). Make a plan for initiating one of these efforts.
5. Decide on three urgent reforms you would initiate as a tenured, experienced teacher. What are the differences between your answer to this question and that for question 4?
6. Contact one of the following organizations or another school intervention effort and request materials. Determine whether the organization's recommendations (if any) are appropriate to your school. Discuss in class how you would present them at a faculty, staff, or other schoolwide meeting.

Accelerated Schools Project. National Center for Accelerated Schools Project, University of Connecticut, 2131 Hillside Road, U-7, Storrs, CT 06269-3007. 860-486-6330. *info@acceleratedschools.net*

Association for Effective Schools. Ben A. Birdsell, President. 8250 Sharpton Road, R.D. Box 143, Stuyvesant, NY 12173. 518-758-9828.

California Tomorrow. Laurie Olsen, Director. Fort Mason Center, Building B, San Francisco, CA 94123. 415-441-7631.

Coalition of Essential Schools. Theodore Sizer, Chairman. Brown University, Box 1969, Providence, RI 02912. 401-863-3384.

Success for All. Robert Slavin, Director. Center on Research on Effective Schools for Disadvantaged Students, Johns Hopkins University, 3505 North Charles Street, Baltimore, MD 21218. 410-516-8809.

References

A Broader, Bolder Approach to Education. Accessed at http://www.boldapproach.org/ (2008).

A man of Flint: How General Motors lost the loyalty of its workers in Flint, Michigan. (1998). *Economist, 347*(8073), 79.

Abu El-Haj, T. (2002). Contesting the politics of culture, rewriting the boundaries of inclusion: Working for social justice with Muslim and Arab communities. *Anthropology & Education Quarterly, 33*(3), 308–316.

Achilles, Chuck M. (1999). STAR: Student-Teacher Achievement Ratio.

Acuña, R. F. (1996). *Anything but Mexican: Chicanos in contemporary Los Angeles.* London: Verso.

Acuña, R. F. (2007). *Occupied America: A history of Chicanos* (6th ed.). New York: Longman.

Adams, J. (1995). Proposition 187: What's to be learned? *RaceFile, 3*(1), 19–29.

Adams, M. J., Foorman, B. R., Lundberg, I., & Beeler, T. (1998). The elusive phoneme. *American Educator, 22*(1–2), 18–29.

Adler, M. (1982). *The Paideia proposal: An educational manifesto.* New York: Macmillan.

AFL–CIO. (2002). *Working women.* Retrieved June 28, 2002, from www.afl-cio.org/women/wwfacts.htm

African American Male Task Force of Milwaukee Public Schools. (1990, May). *Educating African American males: A dream deferred.* Milwaukee, WI: Milwaukee Public Schools.

Albert, M., Hahnel, R., Sklar, H., King, M., Cagan, L., Sargent, L., et al. *Liberating theory.* Boston: South End Press.

Alcoff, L. M. (1999). Latina/o identity politics. In D. Batstone & E. Mendieta (Eds.), *The good citizen* (pp. 93–112). New York: Routledge.

Alington, R. L., & Woodside-Jiron, H. (1999). The politics of literacy teaching: How "research" shaped educational policy. *Educational Researcher, 28*(8), 4–13.

Allport, G. W. (1979). *The nature of prejudice.* Reading, MA: Addison-Wesley.

Almaguer, T. (1994). *Racial fault lines: The historical origins of White supremacy in California.* Berkeley, CA: University of California Press.

Al-Qazzaz, A. (1996). The Arab lobby: Political identity and participation. In W. C. Rich (Ed.), *The politics of minority coalitions: Race, ethnicity and shared uncertainties.* Westport, CT: Praeger.

America on trial: Fire and fury. (1992, May 11). *Newsweek,* 24–29.

American Anthropological Association. (1997, November). *Anthropology Newsletter, 38*(11), 1.

American Association of Physical Anthropologists. (1996). *American Journal of Physical Anthropology, 101,* 569–570.

American Association of University Women. (1992). *How schools shortchange girls.* Washington, DC: Author.

American Association of University Women. (1998). *Gender gaps: Where schools still fail our children.* Washington, DC: Author.

American Psychological Association. (2007). *Report of the APA Task Force on the Sexualization of Girls.* Washington, DC: Author.

Amott, T. L., & Matthaei, J. A. (1991). *Race, gender and work: A multicultural economic history of women in the United States.* Boston: South End Press.

Amrein, A. L., & Berliner, D. C. (2002, December). *The impact of high-stakes tests on student academic performance: An analysis of NAEP results in states with high-stakes tests and ACT, SAT, and AP test results in states with high school graduation exams.* Tempe, AZ: Educational Policy Research Unit, Arizona State University. Retrieved Jan 11, 2009, from http://www.boldapproach.org/

Anderson, J. A. (1988, January–February). Cognitive styles and multicultural populations. *Journal of Teacher Education, 39*(1), 2–9.

Anderson, S., Cavanagh, J., & Lee, W. T. (2000). *Field guide to the global economy.* New York: Institute for Policy Studies, New Press.

Annie E. Case Foundation. (2006). *Kids count data book.* Baltimore, MD: Author.

Ansary, T. (2004). The muddle machine: Confessions of a textbook editor. *Edutopia: The New World of Learning, 1*(2), 30–35.

Anyon, J. (1980). Social class and the hidden curriculum of work. *Journal of Education, 162*(1), 7–92.

Anyon, J. (2005). *Radical possibilities: Public policy, urban education, and a new social movement.* New York: Routledge.

Anzaldúa, G. (1987). *Borderlands/La frontera: The new mestiza.* San Francisco: Spinsters/Aunt Lute.

Appiah, K. A., & Gutmann, A. (1996). *Color conscious: The political morality of race.* Princeton, NJ: Princeton University Press.

Apple, M. (1979). *Ideology and the curriculum.* London: Routledge & Kegan Paul.

Apple, M. (1988). *Teachers and texts: A political economy of class and gender relations in education.* New York: Routledge & Kegan Paul.

Apple, M. (2001). *Official knowledge: Democratic education in a conservative age.* New York: Routledge.

Apple, M., & Bean, J. (1995). *Democratic schools.* Alexandria, VA: Association for Supervision and Curriculum Development.

Apple, M., & Christian-Smith, L. K. (Eds.). (1991). *The politics of the textbook.* New York: Routledge.

Arizona proposal would prohibit race-based student groups. (2008). *Chronicle of Higher Education*/blog: Chronicle of Higher Education. Retrieved from http://chronicle.com/news/article/4338/arizona-proposal-would-prohibit-race-based-student-groups

Arlington, R. L., & Woodside-Jiron, H. (1999). The politics of literacy teaching: How "research" shaped educational policy. *Educational Researcher, 28*(8), 4–13.

Armor, D. J. (1995, August 2). Can desegregation alone close the achievement gap? *Education Week*, p. 68.

Arnstine, D. (1995). *Democracy and the arts of schooling.* Albany, NY: State University of New York Press.

Aronowitz, S. (1973). *False promises: The shaping of American working class consciousness.* New York: McGraw-Hill.

Aronowitz, S., & Giroux, H. (1985). *Education under siege: The conservative, liberal, and radical debate over schooling.* South Hadley, MA: Bergin & Garvey.

Aronson, J., Zimmerman, J., & Carlos, L. (1998). *Improving school achievement by extending school: Is it just a matter of time?* San Francisco: WestEd.

Aronstein, M., & Olsen, E. (1974). *Action learning: Student community services projects.* Washington, DC: Association for Supervision and Curriculum Development.

Asante, M. K. (1991, Spring). Multiculturalism: An exchange. *American Scholar, 60*: 267–272.

Association for Supervision and Curriculum Development. (1988). *Dimensions in thinking.* Alexandria, VA: Author.

Au, K. H. (1993). *Literacy instruction in multicultural settings.* New York: Harcourt Brace Jovanovich.

Au, K. H., & Kawakami, A. (1994). Cultural congruence in instruction. In E. R. Hollins, J. King, & W. Hayman (Eds.), *Teaching diverse populations: Formulating a knowledge base* (pp. 5–23). Albany, NY: State University of New York Press.

Au, W. W. K. (2001). What the tour guide didn't tell me: Tourism, colonialism, and resistance in Hawaii. In B. Bigelow (Ed.), *Rethinking our classrooms: Teaching for equity and justice* (Vol. 2. Pages 76–80). Milwaukee, WI: Rethinking Schools.

August, D. A., & Hakuta, K. (1997). *Improving schooling for language-minority children: A research agenda.* Washington, DC: National Academy Press, National Research Council.

Ayers, W., Hunt, J. A., & Quinn, T. (Eds.). (1998). *Teaching for social justice: A democracy and education reader.* New York: Teachers College Press.

Baird, P. (2001). *Children's song-makers as messengers of hope.* Unpublished doctoral dissertation, University of San Francisco, California. (UMI No. 3012660)

Baker, P. (2007, September 27). An extra S on report card. *Washington Post*, p. A10.

Banks, J. A. (1988). Approaches to multicultural reform. *Multicultural Leader, 1*(2), 1–3.

Banks, J. A. (1989). Multicultural education: Characteristics and goals. In J. A. Banks & C. A. McGee Banks (Eds.), *Multicultural education: Issues and perspectives* (pp. 2–3). Needham Heights, MA: Allyn & Bacon.

Banks, J. A. (1992). African American scholarship and the evolution of multicultural education. *Journal of Negro Education, 61*(3), 273–285.

Banks, J. A. (1995). Multicultural education: Historical development, dimensions, and practice. In J. A. Banks & C. A. McGee Banks (Eds.), *Handbook of research on multicultural education* (2nd ed.). (pp. 1–24). New York: Simon & Schuster/Macmillan.

Banks, J. A. (1997). *Educating citizens in a multicultural society.* New York: Teachers College Press.

Banks 2004, Multicultural Education; Historical Development, Dimensions and Practice, in Banks, J. A., & McGee Banks, C. A. (Eds.). (2001). *Handbook of research on multicultural education* (2nd ed.). pp. 3–29. San Francisco: Jossey-Bass.

Banks, J. A. (2008a). *An introduction to multicultural education* (4th ed.). Boston: Pearson.

Banks, J. A. (2008). *Teaching strategies for ethnic studies* (8th ed.). Needham Heights, MA: Allyn & Bacon.

Banks, J. A., & McGee Banks, C. A. (Eds.). (1989). *Multicultural education: Issues and perspectives*. Needham Heights, MA: Allyn & Bacon.

Banks, J. A., & McGee Banks, C. A. (Eds.). (1995). *Handbook of research on multicultural education*. New York: Simon & Schuster/Macmillan.

Banks, J. A., & McGee Banks, C. A. (Eds.). (2004). *Handbook of research on multicultural education* (2nd ed.). San Francisco: Jossey-Bass.

Barber, B. (2007). "Supercapitalism." *Truthdig*. Retrieved Dec.13,2007 from http://chronicle.com/news/article/4338/arizona-proposal-would-prohibit-race-based-student-groups

Barber, B. R. (2003). *Strong democracy: Participatory politics for a new age*. Berkeley, CA: University of California Press. (Original work published 1984)

Barth, P. (Ed.). (2000, Spring). "You might start by fixing the bathrooms": Actions for communities and states. *Thinking K–16, 4*(1), 26–27.

Barth, P., Haycock, K., Jackson, H., Mora, K., Ruiz, P., Robinson, S., et al. (1999). *Dispelling the myth: High poverty schools exceeding expectations*. Washington, DC: Education Trust.

Bartlett, D. L., & Steele, J. B. (1992). *America: What went wrong?* Kansas City, MO: Andrews & McMeel.

Bastian, A., Fruchter, N., Gittell, M., Greer, C., & Hoskins, K. (1985). *Choosing equality: The case for democratic schooling*. Philadelphia: Temple University Press.

Batiste, D. (1998). *A World Of Difference® Institute anti-bias study guide*. New York: Anti-Defamation League.

Batstone, D., & Mendieta, E. (Eds.). (1999). *The good citizen*. New York: Routledge.

Beane, J. A. (1990). *Affect in the curriculum: Toward democracy, dignity and diversity*. New York: Teachers College Press.

Becker, H. J. (2000, Fall/Winter). Children and computer technology: Who's wired and who's not: Children's access to and use of computer technology. *Future of Children, 10*(2), 44–75.

Becker, J., & Siklos, R. (2007, June 25). Murdoch reaches out for even more. *New York Times*.

Bell, D. (1992). *Faces at the bottom of the well*. New York: HarperCollins.

Bellah, R., Madren, R., Sullivan, W. H., Swidler, A., & Tipton, S. M. (1986). *Habits of the heart: Individualism and commitment in American life*. Berkeley, CA: University of California Press.

Benner, C., Brownstein, B., & Dean, A. B. (1999). *Walking the lifelong tight rope: Negotiating work in the new economy*. Washington, DC: Working Partnerships U.S.A. & Economic Policy Institute.

Bennett, C. (1986). *Comprehensive multicultural education: Theory and practice*. Needham Heights, MA: Allyn & Bacon.

Bensman, D. (1987). *Quality education in the inner city: The story of Central Park East schools*. New York: New York Community Trust.

Berends, M., Kirby, S. N., Naftel, S., & McKelvey, C. (2001). *Implementation and performance in new American schools: Three years into scale-up*. Santa Monica, CA: Rand.

Berlak, A., & Berlak, H. (1981). *Dilemmas of schooling: Teaching and social change*. London: Methuen.

Berlak, H. (2000). Cultural politics, the science of assessment and democratic renewal of public education. In A. Filer (Ed.), *Assessment: Social practice and social product*. London: RoutledgeFalmer. (pp. 189–207).

Berlak, H., Newman, F. M., Adams, E., Archbad, D. A., Burgess, T., Raven, J., et al. (1992). *Toward a new science of educational testing and assessment*. Albany, NY: State University of New York Press.

Berliner, D. (2006a, February). Fixing School Isn't Everything. *NEA Today*. Retrieved from http://www.nea.org/home/12206.htm

Berliner, D. (2006b). Our impoverished view of educational reform. *Teachers College Record, 108*(6), 949–995.

Berliner, D. C., & Biddle, B. J. (1995). *The manufactured crisis: Myths, fraud, and the attack on America's schools*. Reading, MA: Addison-Wesley.

Berliner, D., Glass, G. V., & Nichols, S. L. High-Stakes Testing and Student Achievement: Problems for the No Child Left Behind Act." (2005

Berman, S. (1990). The real ropes course: The development of social consciousness. In J. C. McDermott (Ed.), *Beyond the silence: Listening for democracy* (pp. 117–131). Portsmouth, NH: Heinemann.

Bernstein, B. (1977). *Class, codes, and control*. London: Routledge & Kegan Paul.

Bernstein, J., McNichol, E., & Nicholas, A. (2008). *Pulling apart: A state-by-state analysis of income trends*. Washington, DC: Center on Budget and Policy Priorities & Economic Policy Institute.

Bernstein, R. J. (1983). *Beyond objectivism and relativism: Science, hermeneutics, and praxis*. Philadelphia: University of Pennsylvania Press.

Beyer, B. (1988). *Developing a thinking skills program*. Needham Heights, MA: Allyn & Bacon.

Biddle, B., & Berliner, D. C. (2003). *What research says about unequal funding for schools in America*. San Francisco: WestEd.

Bigelow, B. (2002). Social studies standards for what? *Rethinking Schools, 16*(4), 9.

Bigelow, B. (2006a). *The line between us: Teaching about the border and Mexican immigration.* Milwaukee, WI: Rethinking Schools.

Bigelow, B. (2006b). *Whose wars? Teaching about the Iraq War and the war on terrorism.* Milwaukee, WI: Rethinking Schools.

Bigelow, B., & Peterson, B. (Eds.). (2002). *Rethinking Columbus* (2nd ed.). Milwaukee, WI: Rethinking Schools.

Bilingual writing center. (1993). [Computer program]. The Learning Company.

Black, W. K. (2005). *The best way to rob a bank is to own one: How corporate executives and politicians looted the S & L industry.* Austin, TX: University of Texas Press.

Blakeslee, N. (2002, February 15). Naked emperors and wet rats: As Enron goes under, Texas pols scramble for cover. *Texas Observer.* Retrieved April 20, 2003, from www.texasobserver.org/showArticle.asp?ArticleID=557

Bliatout, B. T., Downing, B. T., Lewis, J., & Yang, D. (1988). *Handbook for teaching Hmong-speaking students.* Folsom, CA: Southeast Asia Community Resource Center, Folsom Cordova Unified School District.

Bloom, A. (1987). *The closing of the American mind: How higher education has failed democracy and impoverished the souls of today's students.* New York: Simon & Schuster.

B'nai B'rith Antidefamation League. (1986). *The wonderful world of difference: A human relations program for grades K–8.* New York: Author.

Bobo, K., Kendall, J., & Max, S. (1991). *Organizing for social change: A manual for activity in the 1990s.* Washington, DC: Seven Locks.

Bohn, A. (2006). A framework for understanding Ruby Payne. *Rethinking Schools, 21*(2). Accessed Jan.11. 2009 from http://www.rethinkingschools.org/archive/21_02/fram212.shtml

Bomer, R., Dworin, J. E., May, L., & Semingson, P. (2008). Miseducating teachers about the poor: A critical analysis of Ruby Payne's claims about poverty. *Teachers College Record, 110*(12), 2497–2531

Bomotti, S. (1998, April 13–17). *School choice: Complexities, cross-currents, and conflicts.* Paper presented at the American Educational Research Association annual meeting.

Bond, J. (2007, Fall). We must persevere. *Teaching Tolerance, P. 32.*

Bork, R. H. (1996). *Slouching toward Gomorrah: Modern liberalism and American decline.* New York: Reagan Books, HarperCollins.

Boulay, B., Bozzi, L., Caswell, L., Horst, M., Smith, W. C., St. Pierre, R. G., et al. (2008). Reading First Impact Study: Interim Report. U.S. Department of Education, National Center for Educational Evaluation and Regional Assisstance. Accessed. Dec. 13, 2008. from http://ies.ed.gov/ncee/pdf/20084016.pdf

Boushey, H., Brocht, C., Gunderson, B., & Bernstein, J. (2001). *Hardships in America: The real story of working families.* Washington, DC: Economic Policy Institute.

Bowers, C. A., & Flanders, D. J. (1990). *Responsive teaching: An ecological approach to classroom patterns of language, culture and thought.* New York: Teachers College Press.

Bowles, S., & Gintis, H. (1976). *Schooling in capitalist America: Educational reform and the contradictions of economic life.* New York: Basic Books.

Boyer, E. (1983). *High school: A report on secondary education in America.* Princeton, NJ: Carnegie Foundation for the Advancement of Teaching.

Boyer, R. O., & Morais, H. M. (1955). *Labor's untold story.* New York: United Electrical Workers.

Boyte, H. C. (2000, July/August). The struggle against positivism. *Academe, 86*(4), 46–51.

Bracey, G. (2000). *Bail me out: Handling difficult data and tough questions about public schools.* Thousand Oaks, CA: Corwin Press.

Bracey, G. (2003). *On the death of childhood and the destruction of public schools: The folly of today's education policies and practices.* Portsmouth, NH: Heinemann.

Bracey, G. (2006). The 16th Bracey report on the condition of public education. *Phi Delta Kappan, 88*(2), 151–166.

Bracey, G. (2007a). The first time "everything changed": The 17th Bracey report on the condition of public education. *Phi Delta Kappan, 89*(2), 119–136.

Bracey, G. (2007b). *The Rotten Apples in Education Award for 2006.* America Tomorrow. Retrieved from http://www.america-tomorrow.com/bracey/EDDRA

Bradley, A. (1994, September 14). Education for equality: The story of Ron Rodriguez. *Education Week,* pp. 28–32.

Branch, C. W. (1994). Ethnic identity as a variable in the learning equation. In E. R. Hollins, J. E. King, & W. G. Hayman (Eds.), *Teaching diverse populations: Formulating a knowledge base* (p. 222). Albany, NY: State University of New York Press.

Brant, R. (1990, February). On knowledge and cognitive skills: A conversation with David Perkins. *Educational Leadership, 47*(2), 50–54.

Bridgeland, J. M., DiIulio, J. J., Jr., & Morison, K. B. (2006). *The silent epidemic: Perspectives of high school dropouts.* Washington, DC: Civic Enterprises, with Peter D. Hart Research Associates for the Bill and Melinda Gates Foundation.

Brittingham, A., & de la Cruz, G. P. (2005). *We the people of Arab ancestry in the United States* (CENSR-21). Washington, DC: U.S. Census Bureau.

Brock, D. (2004). *The Republican noise machine: Right-wing media and how it corrupts democracy.* New York: Crown.

Brooks, A. K., & Kavanaugh, P. C. (1999). Empowering the surrounding community. In P. Reyes, J. D. Scribner, & A. P. Scribner (Eds.), *Lessons from high-performing Hispanic schools: Creating learning communities* (pp. 61–93). New York: Teachers College Press.

Brown v. Board of Education, 344 U.S. 141 (1954).

Brown, D. (1987). *Principles of language learning: Theory and practice* (2nd ed.). Upper Saddle River, NJ: Prentice Hall.

Brown, P. A., & Haycock, K. (1984). *Excellence for whom? A report of the planning committee for the Achievement Council.* Oakland, CA: Achievement Council.

Bruner, J. (1996). *The culture of education.* Cambridge, MA: Harvard University Press.

Bruner, J., & Cole, M. (1973). Cultural differences and inferences about psychological processes. In J. M. Anglin (Ed.), *Jerome S. Bruner: Beyond the information given: Studies in the psychology of knowing* (pp. 452–467). New York: W. W. Norton.

Bugliosi, V. (2001). *The betrayal of America: How the Supreme Court undermined the Constitution and chose our President.* New York: Thunder's Mouth Press.

Burkins, G., & Simpson, G. R. (1996). As Democrats meet, the teachers' unions will show their clout. *Wall Street Journal, 128*(39), A1.

Bushman, J. H., & Bushman, K. P. (1997). *Using young adult literature in the English classroom* (2nd ed.). Upper Saddle River, NJ: Merrill/Prentice Hall.

Buteyn, R. J. (1989). *Gender and academic achievement in education.* Washington, DC: U.S. Department of Education. (ERIC Document Reproduction Service No. ED 313 103)

Butler, J. E. (1989). Transforming the curriculum: Teaching about women of color. In J. A. Banks & C. A. McGee Banks (Eds.), *Multicultural education: Issues and perspectives* (pp. 145–163). Needham Heights, MA: Allyn & Bacon.

Cagan, E. (1978, May). Individualism, collectivism, and radical educational reform. *Harvard Educational Review,* Vol. 48, 227–266.

California Department of Education. (1987). *History–social science framework for California public schools: Kindergarten through grade twelve.* Sacramento, CA: Author.

California Department of Education. (2000). *History–social science content standards for California public schools.* Sacramento, CA: Author. Retrieved Dec 5, 2007 from www.cde.ca.gov/be/st/ss/documents/histsocscistnd.pdf

California Department of Education. (2006). *Language census report for California public schools, 2006.* Sacramento, CA: Educational Demographics Unit, California Department of Education.

California Department of Education, Bilingual Education Office. (1981). *Schooling and language minority students: A theoretical framework.* Los Angeles: Evaluation, Dissemination, and Assessment Center, California State University.

California Department of Education, Bilingual Education Office. (1986). *Beyond language: Social and cultural factors in schooling of language minority students.* Los Angeles: Evaluation, Dissemination, and Assessment Center, California State University.

California Department of Education, Educational Demographics Unit. (2007). Retrieved Language Census. December 10, 2008, from dq.cde.ca.gov/dataquest

California Department of Education, Educational Demographics Unit. (2008). Language Census. Retrieved from December 9, 2008 dq.cde.ca.gov/dataquest

California Tomorrow. (1988). *Immigrant students and the California public schools: Crossing the schoolhouse border.* San Francisco: Author.

California Tomorrow. (1994). *The unfinished journey: Restructuring schools in a diverse society.* San Francisco: Author.

Cameron, S. C., & Wycoff, S. M. (1998, Summer). The destructive nature of the term *race*: Growing beyond a false paradigm. *Journal of Counseling & Development, 76,* 277–285.

Campbell, D. (2006). *Why we vote: How schools and communities shape our civic life.* Princeton, NJ: Princeton University Press.

Campbell, D. E. (1980). *Education for a democratic society: Curriculum ideas for teachers.* Cambridge, MA: Schenkman.

Campbell, D. E. (1987). How the Grinch stole the social sciences: Moving teaching to the right in California. *Journal of the Association of Mexican American Educators,* 43–49.

Carinci, S. T. (2002). *Gender equity training in selected California preservice teacher preparation programs.* San Francisco: University of San Francisco.

Carinci, S. T. (2007). Examining gender and classroom teaching practices. In G. Stahly (Ed.), *Gender, identity, equity, and violence: Multidisciplinary perspectives through service learning* (pp. 63–83). Sterling, VA: Stylus.

Carlson, D. (1992). *Teachers and crisis: Urban school reform and teachers' work culture.* New York: Routledge.

Carlson, D. (2006). Are we making progress? Ideology and curriculum in the age of No Child Left Behind. In L. Weis, C. McCarthy, & G. Dimitriadis (Eds.), *Ideology, curriculum, and the new sociology of education: Revisting the work of Michael Apple* (pp. 91–114). New York: Routledge.

Carnegie Corporation. (2002). *The civic mission of schools: The Civic Mission of Schools report.* New York: Carnegie Corporation & CIRCLE. Retrieved Sept. 16, 2006 from www.civicmissionofschools.org

Carnegie Council on Adolescent Development. (1995). *Great transitions: Preparing adolescents for the 21st century.* New York: Carnegie Corporation.

Carnegie Foundation for the Advancement of Teaching. (1988). *An imperiled generation: Saving urban schools.* Lawrenceville, NJ: Princeton University Press.

Carnes, J. (Ed.). (1999). *Responding to hate at school: A guide for teachers, counselors, and administrators.* Montgomery, AL: Southern Poverty Law Center.

Carnoy, M. (1984). *The state and political theory.* Princeton, NJ: Princeton University Press.

Carnoy, M. (1989). Education, state, and culture. In H. A. Giroux & P. McLarne (Eds.), *Critical pedagogy, the state, and cultural struggle* (pp. 3–23). Albany, NY: State University of New York Press.

Carnoy, M. (1994). *Faded dreams: The politics and economics of race in America.* Cambridge, England: Cambridge University Press.

Carnoy, M. (1998). National voucher plans in Chile and Sweden: Did privatization reforms make for better education? *Comparative Education Review, 42*(3), 309–337.

Carnoy, M., Hannaway, J., Chun, M., Stein, S. and Wong, P. (1995) *Urban and Suburban School Districts: Are They Different Kinds of Educational Producers?* Camden, N.J.: Consortium for Policy Research in Education.

Carnoy, M., & Levin, H. M. (1985). *Schooling and work in the democratic state.* Stanford, CA: Stanford University Press.

Carreon, C. (2008). March 31, 2008. School walkouts seek to hike status of Chavez holiday. *Sacramento Bee,* p. B3.

Carter, C. J. (1997, March). Why reciprocal teaching? *Educational Leadership, 54*(6), 64–68.

Carter, S. C. (2000). *No excuses: Lessons from 21 high-performing, high poverty schools.* Washington, DC: Heritage Foundation.

Carter, T. P. (1990). *Effective schools and the process of change.* Unpublished manuscript, California State University, Sacramento.

Carter, T. P., & Chatfield, M. L. (1986). Effective bilingual schools: Implications for policy and practice. *American Journal of Education, 95*(1), 200–232.

Carter, T. P., & Segura, R. (1979). *Mexican Americans in school: A decade of change.* New York: College Entrance Examination Board.

Case, R., & Bereiter, C. (1984). From behaviorism to cognitive behaviorism to cognitive development: Steps in the evolution of instructional design. *Instructional Science, 13,* 141–158.

Casey, L. (2006). The educational value of democratic voice: A defense of collective bargaining in American education.

Cass, J. (May/June, 2002). The Moses factor. *Mother Jones,* 56–59.

Castañeda v. Pickard, 648 F.2d 989 (5th Cir. 1981).

Center for Civic Education. (1991). *Civitas: A framework for civic education.* Calabasas, CA: Author.

César Chávez Foundation (Ed.). (in press). *Education of the heart: César E. Chávez in his own words.* Keene, CA: Author.

Chandrasekaran, R. (2006). *Imperial life in the emerald city: Inside Iraq's Green Zone.* New York: Random House.

Charles, C. M. (1989). *Building classroom discipline: From models to practice* (3rd ed.). New York: Longman.

Charles, C. M. (2008). *Today's best classroom management strategies: Paths to positive discipline.* Allyn & Bacon, Pearson. Boston.

Chase, R. (1997, April 27). All children are equal: But some children are more equal than others. *NEA Today,* 2.

Chávez, L. (1998). *The color bind: California's battle to end affirmative action.* Berkeley, CA: University of California Press.

Chavez Comeron, S., & Macias Wycoff, S. (1998, Summer). The meaninglessness of race: Growing beyond an artificial paradigm. *Journal of Counseling & Development, 76*(3), 277–285.

Cheney, L. V. (1987). *American memory: A report on the humanities in the nation's public schools.* Washington, DC: National Endowment for the Humanities.

Chenoweth, K. (2007). *It's being done: Academic success in unexpected schools.* Cambridge, MA: Harvard Education Press.

Chick, K. A. (2008). *Teaching women's history through literature: Standards-based lesson plans for grades K–12.* Silver Spring, MD: National Council for the Social Studies.

Childers, K. W., & Brown, J. (1989, Spring). No blank slate: Teen media awareness mirrors upbringing. *Media & Values, 46,* 8–10.

Children's Defense Fund. (2001). *The state of America's children 2001.* Washington, DC: Author.

Children's Defense Fund. (2004). *The state of America's children 2004.* Washington, DC: Author.

Children's Defense Fund. (2005). *The state of America's children 2005.* Washington, DC: Author.

Children's Defense Fund. (2007). *America's cradle to prison pipeline.* Washington, DC: Author.

Chubb, J. E., & Moe, T. M. (1989). *Politics, markets and America's schools.* Washington, DC: Brookings Institution.

Cintrón, J. (1993). A school in change: The empowerment of minority teachers. In H. T. Trueba, C. Rodriguez, Y. Zou, & J. Cintrón (Eds.), *Healing multicultural America: Mexican immigrants rise to power in rural California* (pp. 115–132). Washington, DC: Falmer.

Civil Rights Act of 1964, Pub. L. No. 88-352.

Cloward, R., & Piven, F. F. (2000). *Why Americans still don't vote and why politicians want it that way.* Boston: Beacon Press.

Cobell v. Norton, No. 96CV01285 (D.D.C. 1996).

Cohen, E. (1986). *Designing groupwork: Strategies for the heterogeneous classroom.* New York: Teachers College Press.

Cohen, E., & Lotan, R. A. (1997). *Working for equity in homogeneous classrooms: Sociological theory in practice.* New York: Teachers College Press.

Cohen, E., Lotan, R. A., & Whitcomb, J. A. (1992). Complex instruction in the social studies classroom. In R. J. Stahl & R. L. Van Sickle (Eds.), *Cooperative learning in the social studies* (p. 87). Washington, DC: National Council for the Social Studies.

Coleman, J. (1966). *Equality of educational opportunity.* Washington, DC: Office of Education, U.S. Department of Health, Education, and Welfare.

Coleman, J. (1987). *Public and private high schools: The impact of communities.* New York: Basic Books.

Coleman, J. (1990). *Equality and achievement in education.* Boulder, CO: Westview.

Coley, R. J. (2002, March). *An uneven start: Indicators of inequality in school readiness.* Princeton, NJ: Education Testing Service.

Colin, G. (1975). *The great school legend: A revisionist interpretation of American public education.* New York: Basic Books.

Collier, V. (1995). *Promoting academic success for E.S.L. students: Understanding second language acquisition for school.* Elizabeth, NJ: Teachers of English to Speakers of Other Languages—Bilingual Educators.

Collins, P. H. (1996). *Fighting words: Black women and the search for justice.* Minneapolis, MN: University of Minnesota Press.

Colvin, R. L. (1998, 19 May). Too many teachers are ill prepared. *Los Angeles Times,* pp. R1, R5, R6.

Comer, J. P. (1988). *Is parenting essential to good teaching?* Washington, DC: National Education Association.

Comer, J. P. (1997). *Waiting for a miracle: Why schools can't solve our problems—and how we can.* New York: E. P. Dutton.

Comer, J. P. (2001). Schools that develop children. *American Prospect, 12*(7). Retrieved July 11, 2003, from www.prospect.org/print/V12/7/comer-j.html

Comité de Padres de Familia v. Honig (Comité De Padres De Familia v. Honig (1987) 192CalApp.3d528)

Commission on Chapter 1. (1993, January 13). Making schools work for children in poverty. *Education Week,* pp. 47–51.

Congressional Black Caucus. (1991). *Quality of life budget, FY 1991* (Executive Summary). Washington, DC: Author.

Consortium for Policy Research in Education. (1998, May). *States and districts and comprehensive reform* (CPRE Policy Brief RB–24). Philadelphia: University of Pennsylvania.

Cook, T. D. (2001, April 5). The school development program: A synthesis of findings with musings on evaluation strategy. A paper presented at *Rockefeller Foundation Symposium.* Washington, DC: Rockefeller Foundation.

Coons, J. E., & Sugarman, D. S. (1978). *Education by choice: The case for family control.* Berkeley, CA: University of California Press.

Corbett, C. (2008, Spring/Summer). Where the girls (and boys) are—and where the real crisis is. *AAUW Outlook, 102*(1), 7–10.

Corbett, C., Hill, C., & St. Rose, A. (2008). *Where the girls are: The facts about gender equity in education.* Washington, DC: American Association of University Women.

Cornbleth, C. (1985). Critical thinking and cognitive process. In W. B. Stanley ed., *Review of research in social studies education: 1976–1983* (pp. 11–55). Silver Spring, MD: National Council for the Social Studies.

Cornbleth, C. (1999, Summer). An American curriculum? *Teachers College Record, 99*(4), 622–646.

Cornbleth, C., & Waugh, D. (1995). *The great speckled bird: Multicultural politics and education policymaking.* New York: St. Martin's Press.

Cortés, E. (1996). *The IAF and education reform: Organizing citizens for change* (Mimeograph). Dallas, TX: Industrial Areas Foundation.

Costa, A. (1985). *Teaching for intelligent behavior.* Orangevale, CA: Search Models Unlimited.

Costa, A. (2008). The thought-filled curriculum. *Educational Leadership, 65*(5), 20–24.

Costa, A. L., & Kallick, B. (1996). *Assessment in the learning organization: Shifting the paradigm.* Alexandria, VA: Association for Supervision and Curriculum Development.

Cotton, K. (1989). *Expectations and student outcomes.* Portland, OR: Northwest Regional Laboratory.

Couto, R. A., & Guthrie, C. S. (1999). *Making democracy work better.* Chapel Hill, NC: University of North Carolina Press.

Cradleboard Teaching Project. Retrieved Jan 11, 2009 from www.cradleboard.org/main.html

Crain, W. C. (1985). *Theories of development.* Englewood Cliffs, NJ: Prentice-Hall.

Crawford, J. (1992). *Hold your tongue: Bilingualism and the politics of "English only."* Reading, MA: Addison-Wesley.

Crawford, J. (1999). *Bilingual education: History, politics, theory and practice* (4th ed.). Los Angeles: Bilingual Educational Services.

Crawford, J. (2002). Obituary: The Bilingual Ed Act, 1968–2002. *Rethinking Schools, 16*(4), 5.

Crawford, J. (2004). *Educating English learners: Language diversity in the classroom* (5th ed.). Los Angeles: Bilingual Educational Services.

Crawford, J. (2007). *Selling NCLB: Would you buy a used law from this woman?* http://www.elladvocates.org/nclb/spellings2.html Accessed. Jan. 11, 2009.

Crawford, J. (2008). *Framing the debate over No Child Left Behind.* Retrieved December 14, 2008, from www.elladvocates.org/nclb/politics2.html

Cross City Campaign for Urban School Reform. (2005). *A delicate balance: District policies and classroom practice.* Chicago: Author.

Cuban, L. (2001). *Oversold and underused: Computers in the classroom.* Cambridge, MA: Harvard University Press.

Cuban, L., & Shipps, D. (Eds.). (2000a). *No exit: Public education as an inescapably public good.* Stanford, CA: Stanford University Press.

Cuban, L., & Shipps, D. (Eds.). (2000b). *Why is it so hard to get "good" schools?* Stanford, CA: Stanford University Press.

Cummins, J. (1986). Empowering minority students: A framework for intervention. *Harvard Educational Review, 56*(1), 18–36.

Cummins, J. (1989). *Empowering language minority students.* Ontario, CA: California Association for Bilingual Education.

Cummins, J. (1996). *Negotiating identities: Education for empowerment in a diverse society.* Sacramento, CA: California Association for Bilingual Education.

Cummins, J., & Sayers, D. (1995). *Brave new schools: Challenging cultural illiteracy through global learning networks.* New York: St. Martin's Press.

Dahl, R. (1985). *A preface to economic democracy.* Berkeley, CA: University of California Press.

Darder, A. (1991). *Culture and power in the classroom: A critical foundation for bicultural education.* New York: Bergin & Garvey.

Dare, S. (2001). A continent in crisis: Africa and globalization. *Dollars & Sense, 236,* 12–33.

Darling-Hammond, L. (1990). Instructional policy into practice: The power of the bottom over the top. *Educational Evaluation & Policy Analysis, 12*(3), 339–348.

Darling-Hammond, L. (1995). Inequity and access to knowledge. In J. A. Banks & C. A. McGee Banks (Eds.), *Handbook of research on multicultural education* (pp. 465–470). New York: Simon & Schuster/Macmillan.

Darling-Hammond, L. (1997). *The right to learn: A blueprint for creating schools that work.* San Francisco: Jossey-Bass.

Darling-Hammond, L. (2000). *Solving the dilemmas of teacher supply, demand, and standards: How can we ensure a competent, caring and qualified teacher for every child?* New York: National Commission on Teaching and America's Future.

Darling-Hammond, L. (2001). Inequality and access to knowledge. In J. A. Banks & C. A. McGee Banks (Eds.), *Handbook of research on multicultural education.* New York: Simon & Schuster/Macmillan.

Darling-Hammond, L., & Ancess, J. (1996). Democracy and access to education. In R. Soder (Ed.), *Democracy, education and the schools* (pp. 151–181). San Francisco: Jossey-Bass.

Darling-Hammond, L., & Friedlaender, D. (2008). Creating excellent and equitable schools. *Educational Leadership, 65*(8), 14–21.

Darling-Hammond, L., LaPointe, M., Meyerson, D., & Orr, M. T. (2007). *Preparing school leaders for a changing world: Lessons from exemplary leadership development programs.* Palo Alto, CA: Stanford University.

Darling-Hammond, L., & Wood, G. H. (2008). *Democracy at risk: The need for a new federal policy in education.* Amesville, OH: Forum for Education and Democracy.

Davis, M. (1986). *Prisoners of the American dream: Politics and economy in the U.S. working class.* London: Verso.

Dear, J. (1995). *Creating caring relationships to foster academic excellence: Recommendations for reducing violence in California schools.* Sacramento, CA: Advisory Panel on School Violence, Commission on Teacher Credentialing.

DeAvila, E. (1987). *Finding out: Descubrimiento, teacher's guide.* Northvale, NJ: Santillana.

DeAvila, E. (1990, September 10). *Assessment of language minority students: Political, technical, practical, and moral imperatives.* Paper delivered at the National Symposium on Limited English Proficient Students, Washington, DC.

DeAvila, E. (1997). *Setting expected gains for non and limited English proficient students* (NBCE Resource Collection Series No. 8). Washington, DC: National Clearinghouse for Bilingual Education. Retrieved Feb.15, 2004 from www.ncela.gwu.edu/pubs/resources/setting/index/html

DeMott, B. (2003). *Junk politics: The trashing of the American mind.* New York: Nation Books.

Dewey, J. (1966). *Democracy and education: An introduction to the philosophy of education.* New York: Free Press/Macmillan. (Original work published 1916)

Dinkes, R., Cataldi, E. F., & Lin-Kelly, W. (2007). Kena, G., and Baum, K. *Indicators of school crime and safety.* Washington, DC: National Center for Education Statistics, Institute of Education Sciences, U.S. Department of Education & Bureau of Justice Statistics, U.S. Department of Justice.

Domhoff, G. W. (2002). *Who rules America? Power and politics.* Boston: McGraw Hill.

Dorn, S. (2007). *Accountability Frankenstein: Understanding and taming the monster.* Charlotte, NC: Information Age Publishing.

Douglass, F. (1991). Letter to an abolitionist associate. In K. Bobo, J. Kendall, & S. Max (Eds.), *Organizing for social change: A manual of activity in the 1990s* (cover page). Washington, DC: Seven Locks.

Dray, P. (2002). *At the hands of persons unknown: The lynching of Black America.* New York: Random House.

Dreikurs, R., Grunwald, B. B., & Pepper, F. C. (1971). *Maintaining sanity in the classroom: Classroom management techniques.* New York: Harper & Row.

Dreikurs, R., Grunwald, B. B., & Pepper, F. C. (1998). *Maintaining sanity in the classroom: Classroom management techniques* (2nd ed.). London: Taylor & Francis.

Dreikurs, R., & Stoltz, V. (1964). *Children: The challenge.* New York: Hawthorn.

DuBois, W. E. B. (1975). *Color and democracy: Colonies and peace.* Millwood, NY: Kraus-Thompson. (Original work published 1945)

Dweck, C. (1977). Learned helplessness and negative evaluation. *Educator, 19*(2), 44–49.

Dyson, M. E. (2000). *I may not get there with you: The true Martin Luther King Jr.* New York: Simon & Schuster.

Dyson, M. E. (2006). *Come hell or high water: Hurricane Katrina and the color of disaster.* New York: Basic Civitas Books.

Edmonds, R. (1979). Effective schools for the urban poor. *Educational Leadership, 37*(1), 15–24.

Edmonds, R. (1982). Programs for school improvement: An overview. *Educational Leadership, 40*(3), 4–12.

Education Trust. (2006a). *How poor and minority students are shortchanged on teacher quality.* Washington, DC: Author.

Education Trust. (2006b). *Yes we can: Telling truths and dispelling myths about race and education in America.* Washington, DC: Author.

Education Trust. (2008). *Their fair share: How Texas-sized gaps in teacher quality shortchange low-income and minority students.* Washington, DC: Author.

Ehrenreich, B. (1989). *Fear of falling: The inner life of the middle class.* New York: Pantheon.

Ehrenreich, B. (2001). *Nickel and dimed: On (not) getting by in America.* New York: Henry Holt.

Ehrenreich, B. (2005). *Bait and switch: The (futile) pursuit of the American dream.* New York: Metropolitan Books, Henry Holt.

Ehrenreich, B. (2008). *This land is their land: Reports from a divided nation.* New York: Henry Holt.

Ehrenreich, B., & Ehrenreich, J. (1979). The professional-managerial class. In P. Walker (Ed.), *Between labor and capital* (pp. 5–45). Boston: South End Press.

Eisner, E. (1994). *Education update.* Alexandria, VA: Association for Supervision and Curriculum Development.

Linda Elder and Richard Paul. (2008, November/December). Critical thinking in a world of accelerating change and complexity. *Social Education, 72*(7), 388–392

Eldredge, J. L. (1995). *Teaching decoding in holistic classrooms.* Upper Saddle River, NJ: Merrill/Prentice Hall.

Elkind, D. (1988). *The hurried child: Growing up too fast too soon.* Reading, MA: Addison-Wesley.

Eller-Powell, R. (1994). Teaching for change in Appalachia. In E. R. Hollins, J. E. King, & W. G. Hayman (Eds.), *Teaching diverse populations: Formulating a knowledge base* (pp. 61–75). Albany, NY: State University of New York Press.

Elliot, J. (2008, December 19). Bilingual programs spark a legal battle. *Houston Chronicle.* Retrieved December 20, 2008, from www.chron.com/disp/story.mpl/metropolitan/6174610.html

Emery, K. (2007, Spring). Corporate control of public school goals: High stakes testing in its historical perspective. *Teacher Education Quarterly, 34*(2), 25–44.

Emery, K., & Ohanian, S. (2004). *Why is corporate America bashing our public schools?* Portsmouth, NH: Heineman.

Engle, S. H., & Ochoa, A. S. (1988). *Education for democratic citizenship; Decision making for the social studies.* New York: Teachers College Press.

Equal Educational Opportunities Act of 1974, Pub. L. No. 93-380 (20 U.S.C. § 1701 *et seq.*).

Equity Resource Center Digest. (1997). Newton, MA: WEEA Resource Center at Education Development Center.

Erkut, S., Fields, J. P., Sing, R., & Marx, F. (1996). Diversity in girls' experiences: Feeling good about who you are. In B. J. R. Leadbeater & N. Way (Eds.), *Urban girls: Resisting stereotypes, creating identities* (pp. 53–64). New York: New York University Press.

Esquibel Tywoniak, F., & Garcia, M. T. (2000). *Migrant daughter: Coming of age as a Mexican American woman.* Berkeley, CA: University of California Press.

Etzioni, A. (2008). Moral dimensions of ethical decisions. *School Administrator.* May 2008. Accessed Dec. 13, 2008 from http://www.aasa.org/publications/saarticledetail.cfm?ItemNumber=10332&snItemNumber=950.

Every child reading: An action plan of the Learning First Alliance. (1998). *American Educator, 22*(1–2), 52–63.

Faludi, S. (2006). *Backlash: The undeclared war against American women.* New York: Crown. (Original work published 1991)

Faux, J., Scott, R., Salas, C., & Campbell, B. (2001). *NAFTA at seven: Its impact on workers in all three nations.* Washington, DC: Economic Policy Institute.

Feagin, J. R. (2001). *Racist America: Roots, current realities, and future reparations.* New York: Routledge.

Federal Interagency Forum on Child and Family Statistics. (2008). *America's children in brief: Key national indicators of well being, 2008.* Washington, DC: Author. Retrieved July 16, 2008, from www.childstats.gov

Feinberg, W. (1998). *Common schools/uncommon identities: National unity and cultural differences.* New Haven, CT: Yale University Press.

Fernandez, J., & Underwood, J. (1993). *Tales out of school: Joseph Fernandez's crusade to rescue American education.* Boston: Little, Brown.

Fine, M. (1993). Sexuality, schooling, and adolescent females: The missing discourse of desire. In L. Weis & M. Fine (Eds.), *Beyond silenced voices: Class, race, and gender in United States schools* (pp. 75–99). Albany, NY: State University of New York Press.

Finn, P. J. (1999). *Literacy with an attitude: Educating working class children in their own self-interest.* Albany, NY: State University of New York Press.

Fitzell, S. (1997). *Free the children: Conflict education for strong, peaceful minds.* Gabriola Island, British, Columbia, Canada: New Society Publishers.

Fix, M., & Passel, J. (1994). *Immigration and immigrants: Setting the record straight.* Washington, DC: Urban Institute.

Flood, C. P. (2000, November). Safe boys, safe schools. *WEEA Digest,* 3–6.

Florio, G. (1998, June 8). Bilingual classes are a hit in Texas: There is no plan to cut back. *Philadelphia Inquirer,* p. 1.

Foley, D. A., Levinson, B. A., & Hurtig, J. (2001). Anthropology goes inside: The new educational ethnography of ethnicity and gender. *Review of Research in Education, 25,* 37–98).

Foner, E., & Werner, J. (1991, July 29). Fighting for the West. *Nation,* 163–166.

Foner, P. P. (Ed.). (1970). *W. E. B. Du Bois speaks: Speeches and addresses, 1920–1963.* New York: Pathfinder.

Ford, D. Y., & Harris, J. J., III. (1999). *Multicultural gifted education.* New York: Teachers College Press.

Fordham, S. (1988). Racelessness as a factor in Black students' success: Pragmatic strategy or Pyrrhic victory? *Harvard Education Review, 58*(1), 54–84.

Fordham, S. (1996). *Blacked out: Dilemmas of race, identity, and success at Capital High.* Chicago: University of Chicago Press.

Foster, M. (1994). Effective Black teachers: A literature review. In E. R. Hollins, J. King, & W. Hayman (Eds.), *Teaching diverse populations: Formulating a knowledge base* (pp. 225–241). Albany, NY: State University of New York Press.

Foster, M. (1995). African American teachers and culturally relevant pedagogy. In J. A. Banks & C. A. McGee Banks (Eds.), *Handbook of research on multicultural education* (pp. 570–581). New York: Simon & Schuster/ Macmillan.

Frank, T. (2004). *What's the matter with Kansas? How the conservatives won the heart of America.* New York: Metropolitan Books, Henry Holt.

Freire, P. (n.d.). *Conscienticizing as a way of liberating.* Washington, DC: LADOC, Division for Latin America.

Freire, P. (1972). *A pedagogy of the oppressed.* New York: Continuum.

Freire, P. (1985). *The politics of education: Culture, power, and liberation.* New York: Bergin & Garvey.

Freire, P. (1997). *Pedagogy of hope: Reliving pedagogy of the oppressed.* New York: Continuum.

Freire, P. (1998a). *Pedagogy of freedom: Ethics, democracy, and civic courage.* Lanham, MD: Rowman & Littlefield.

Freire, P. (1998b). *Politics and education.* Los Angeles: Latin American Center, University of California.

Freire, P., & Macedo, D. (1987). *Literacy: Reading the word and the world.* South Hadley, MA: Bergin & Garvey.

Freire, P., & Shore, I. (1987). *A pedagogy for liberation: Dialogues on transforming education.* South Hadley, MA: Bergin & Garvey.

Fremon, C. (1995). *Father Greg and the home boys.* New York: Hyperion.

Friedman, L. J. (1972). *Sex role stereotyping in the media: An annotated bibliography.* New York: Garland.

Friend, R. A. (1993). Choices, not closets: Heterosexism and homophobia in school. In L. Weis & M. Fine (Eds.), *Beyond silenced voices: Class, race and gender in United States schools* (pp. 209–235). Albany, NY: State University of New York Press.

Fry, R. (2006). *The changing landscape of American public education: New students, new schools.* Washington, DC: Pew Hispanic Center.

Fullan, M. (1991). *The new meaning of educational change* (2nd ed.). New York: Teachers College Press.

Fuller, B., Wright, J., Gesicki, K., & Kang, E. (2007). Gauging growth: How to judge No Child Left Behind? *Educational Researcher, 36*(5), 268–278.

Gagnon, P. (1995). What should children learn? *Atlantic Monthly, 276*(6), 65–73.

Gaines, P. (2002). Title IX at 30: Making the grade? *AAUW Outlook, 96*(1)1.

Gamse, B. C., Jacob, R. T., Horst, M., Boulay, B., & Unlu, F. (2008). *Reading First impact study: Final report.* Washington, DC: National Center for Educational Evaluation and Regional Assistance, Institute of Education Sciences, U.S. Department of Education.

Gándara, P. (1995). *Over ivy walls: The educational mobility of low-income Chicanos*. Albany, NY: State University of New York Press.

Gándara, P. (1997). *Review of the research on instruction of limited English proficient students: A report to the California Legislature*. Davis, CA: Education Policy Center, Linguistic Minority Research Institute, University of California at Davis.

Gándara, P. (2007). *NCLB and California's English language learners: The perfect storm*. Chicago: American Education Research Association.

Gándara, P., O'Hara, S., & Gutiérrez, D. (2004). The changing shape of aspirations: Peer influence on achievement behavior. In M. Gibson, P. Gándara, & J. P. Koyama (Eds.), *School connections: U.S. Mexican youth, peers, and school achievement* (pp. 39–62). New York: Teachers College Press.

Gándara, P., Rumberger, R., Maxwell-Jolly, J., & Callahan, R. (2003, October 7). English learners in California schools: Unequal resources, unequal outcomes. *Education Policy Analysis Archives, 11*(36).

Garcia, E. (1994). Attributes of effective schools for language minority students. In E. Hollins, J. King, & W. Hayman (Eds.), *Teaching diverse populations: Formulating a knowledge base* (pp. 93–104). Albany, NY: State University of New York Press.

Garcia, E. (1995). Educating Mexican American students: Past treatment and recent developments in theory, research, policy, and practice. In J. A. Banks & C. A. McGee Banks (Eds.), *Handbook of research on multicultural education* (pp. 372–387). New York: Simon & Schuster/Macmillan.

Garcia, E. (2001). *Hispanic education in the United States: Raices y alas*. Lanham, MD: Rowman & Littlefield.

Garcia, M. T. (1994). *Memories of Chicano history: The life and narrative of Bert Corona*. Berkeley, CA: University of California Press.

Garcia, O., Kleifgen, J., & Falchi, L. (2008). *From English language learners to emergent bilinguals* (Equity Matters: Research Review No. 1). New York: Campaign for Educational Equity, Teachers College, Columbia University.

Gardner, H. (1983). *Frames of mind: The theory of multiple intelligences*. New York: Basic Books.

Gardner, H. (1993). *Multiple intelligences: The theory in practice*. New York: Basic Books/HarperCollins.

Gardner, H. (1999). *The disciplined mind: What all students should understand*. New York: Simon & Schuster.

Gardner, H. (2006). *Five minds for the future*. Boston: Harvard Business School Press.

Gardner, R., & Lambert, W. (1972). *Attitudes and motivation in second language learning*. Rowley, MA: Newbury.

Gauntlett, D. (2002). *Media, gender and identity*. New York: Routledge.

Gay, G. (2000). *Culturally responsive teaching: Theory, research and practice*. New York: Teachers College Press.

Gay, G. (2003). Deracialization in social studies teacher education textbooks. In G. Ladson-Billings (Ed.), *Critical race theory perspectives on the social studies: The profession, policies, and curriculum* (pp. 123–149). Greenwich, CT: Information Age Publishing.

Gee, J. P. (2001). Identity as an analytic lens for research in education. In W. G. Secada (Ed.), *Review of research in education*. Washington, DC: American Educational Research Association. (pp. 99–125).

Genesee, F., Lindholm-Leary, K., Saunders, W., & Christian, D. (2005). English language learners in U.S. schools: An overview of research findings. *Journal of Education for Students Placed at Risk, 10*(4), 363–385.

Gerson, J., & Miller, S. (2006). Exterminating public education. *Slate*.

National Council of Teachers of English. Retrieved from http://www.ncte.org/about/issues/slate/126874.htm.

Gibbs, J. (2001). *Tribes, a new way of learning and being together*. Windsor, CA: Center Source Systems.

Gibbs, J. C. (1977). Kohlberg's stages of moral judgement: A constructive critique. *Harvard Educational Review. 47*(1) 43–61.

Gibson, M. (1976). Approaches to multicultural education in the United States: Some concepts and assumptions. *Anthropology & Education Quarterly, 7*(4), 7–18.

Gibson, M. (1987). The school performance of immigrant students: A comparative view. *Anthropology & Education Quarterly, 18*(4), 262–275.

Gibson, M., & Ogbu, J. O. (1991). *Minority status and schooling: A comparative study of immigrant and involuntary minorities*. New York: Garland.

Gilligan, C. (1982). *In a different voice*. Cambridge, MA: Harvard University Press.

Gimenez, M. (2007). Back to class: Reflections on the dialectics of class and identity. In M. Yates (Ed.), *More unequal: Aspects of class in the United States*. New York: Monthly Review Press. 109–118.

Ginorio, A., & Huston, M. (2001). *¡Si, se puede! Yes, we can: Latinas in schools*. Washington, DC: American Association of University Women.

Gipson, L. M. (2002). Poverty, race and LGBT youth. *Poverty & Race, 11*(2), 1–11.

Giroux, H. A. (1979). Schooling and the culture of positivism: Notes on the death of history. *Educational Theory, 29*(4), 263–284.

Giroux, H. A. (1988). *Teachers as intellectuals: Toward a critical pedagogy of learning*. New York: Bergin & Garvey.

Giroux, H., & Giroux, S. S. (2004). Take back public education: A task for intellectuals. In D. R. Walling (Ed.), *Public education, democracy, and the common good*. Bloomington, IN: Phi Delta Kappa Educational Foundation.

Gitlin, T. (1995). *The twilight of common dreams: Why America is wracked by cultural wars*. New York: Henry Holt.

Glanzer, P. L., & Milson, A. J. (2006). Education laws in the United States: legislating the good: A survey and evaluation of character. *Educational Policy, 20*(3), 525–550.

Glass, R. D. (2001, March). On Paulo Freire's philosophy of praxis and the foundations of liberation education. *Educational Researcher, 30*(2), 17–21.

Glazer, N. (1991, September 2). In defense of multiculturalism. *New Republic,* pp. 18–20.

Glazer, N. (1997). *We are all multiculturalists now.* Cambridge, MA: Harvard University Press.

Glidden, H. (2008). Common ground: Clear, specific content holds teaching, texts and tests together. *American Educator, 32*(1), 13–19.

Gloven, D., & Evans, D. (2006, December). How test companies fail your kids. *Bloomberg News* (Special Supp.).

Gluckman, A. (2002, January–February). Testing . . . testing . . . one, two, three: The commercial side of the standardized-testing boom. *Dollars & Sense, 239,* 32–37.

Goals 2000: Educate America Act, Pub. L. No. 103-227.

Gold, N. (2006). *Successful bilingual schools: Six effective programs in California.* San Diego, CA: San Diego Office of Education.

Goldenberg, C. (2008). Teaching English language learners. *American Educator, 32*(2), 8–22 .

Gonzalez, J. (2000). *Harvest of empire: A history of Latinos in America.* New York: Penguin Books.

Goodlad, J. (1984). *A place called school: Prospects for the future.* New York: McGraw-Hill.

Goodlad, J. (1996). Democracy, education, and community. Chapter 4 in R. Soder (Ed.), *Democracy, education, and the schools.* San Francisco: Jossey-Bass.

Goodlad, J., & Keating, P. (Eds.). (1990). *Access to knowledge: An agenda for our nation's schools.* New York: College Entrance Examination Board.

Gordon, B. M. (1995). Knowledge construction, competing critical theories, and education. In J. A. Banks & C. A. McGee Banks (Eds.), *Handbook of research on multicultural education* (pp. 184–199). New York: Simon & Schuster/Macmillan.

Gordon, K. (1991). *When good kids do bad things: A survival guide for parents.* New York: W. W. Norton.

Gore, A. (2007). *The assault on reason.* New York: Penguin Press.

Gorski, P. (2006). Savage unrealities: Classism and racism abound in Ruby Payne's work. *Rethinking Schools, 21*(2), 1–9.

Gorski, P. (2008). The myth of the culture of poverty. *Educational Leadership, 65*(7), 32–36.

Gray, H. (2002). The Native American struggle: One century into another. *Democratic Left, 29*(4), 8–11.

Green, J. F. (1998, Spring–Summer). Another chance. *American Educator, 22*(2), 74–79.

Greene, M. (1998). Teaching for social justice. In W. Ayers, J. A. Hunt, & T. Quin (Eds.), *Teaching for social justice.* Xxviii–xLv. New York: Teachers College Press.

Greer, C. (1972). *The great school legend: A revisionist interpretation of American public education.* New York: Basic Books.

Greider, W. (1992). *Who will tell the people? The betrayal of American democracy.* New York: Simon & Schuster.

Greider, W. (2002, April 8). ENron Democrats. *Nation,* 11–16.

Greider, W. (2003). *The soul of capitalism: Opening paths to a moral economy.* New York: Simon & Schuster.

Grelle, B., & Metzger, D. (1996). Beyond socialization and multiculturalism: Rethinking the task of citizenship education in a pluralistic society. *Social Education, 60*(3), 147–151.

Grey, P. (1991, July 8). Whose America? *Time, 138,* 12–17.

Grieco, E. M., & Cassidy, R. C. (2001). *Overview of race and Hispanic origin 2000.* Washington, DC: U.S. Census Bureau.

Grisold del Castillo, R. (1979). *The Los Angeles barrio: 1860–1890: A social history.* Berkeley, CA: University of California Press.

Grissmer, D. W., Flanagan, A., Kawata, J., & Williamson, S. (2000). *Improving student achievement: What state NAEP test scores tell us.* Santa Monica, CA: Rand.

Gross, R. E., & Dynneson, T. L. (1991). *Social science perspectives on citizenship education.* New York: Teachers College Press.

Grubb, N., & Oakes, J. (2007). *The rhetoric and practice of higher standards.* Tempe, AZ: Educational Policy Archives, Arizona State University.

Grubb, W. N., & Huerta, L. A. (2001). *Straw into gold, resources into results: Spinning out the implications of the "new" school finance.* Berkeley, CA: Policy Analysis for California Education.

Guinier, L. (2002). Race, testing, and the miner's canary. *Rethinking Schools, 16*(4), 13, 23.

Guinier, L., & Torres, G. (2002). *The miner's canary: Enlisting race, resisting power, transforming democracy.* Cambridge, MA: Harvard University Press.

Gurian, M., & Stevens, K. (2005). *The minds of boys: Saving our sons from falling behind in school and life.* San Francisco: Jossey-Bass.

Guthrie, J., & Brazil, E. (1999, February 16). Tentative deal settles suit before trial. *San Francisco Examiner*, p. 1. Retrieved February 18, 1999, from www.examiner/archive/1999/02/12news

Gutiérrez, K., Baquedano-Lopez, P., & Asato, J. (2000). English for the children: The new literacy of the old world order, language policy and educational reform. *Bilingual Research Journal, 24*(1 & 2), 87–112.

Guttmacher, D. (1999). *Teen sex and pregnancy.* New York: Guttmacher Institute.

Guttmacher. D. (2006). *Facts on American teens' sexual and reproductive health.* New York: Guttmacher Institute.

Habermas, J. (2001, September–October). Why Europe needs a constitution. *New Left Review, 11,* 5–26.

Hacker, A. (1992). *Two nations: Black, White, separate, hostile, unequal.* New York: Scribner's.

Hahn, C. L., & Torney-Purta, J. (1999). The IEA civic education project: National and international perspectives. *Social Education, 65*(7), 425–431.

Hahn, J. (2007, Fall). Schoolgirl dreams. *Ms.* Vol. VII, #4, 46–47.

Hakuta, K. (2001, April 5). *Key policy milestones and directions in the education of English language learners.* Washington, DC: Rockefeller Foundation.

Hall, M. (1981). Teaching reading as a language experience. In J. L. Eldredge (Ed), *Teaching decoding in holistic classrooms* (p. 9). Upper Saddle River, NJ: Merrill/Prentice Hall.

Handlin, O. (1957). *Race and nationality in American life.* Garden City, NY: Doubleday.

Hannah, L. S., & Michaelis, J. U. (1977). *A comprehensive framework for instructional objectives: A guide to systematic planning and evaluation.* Reading, MA: Addison-Wesley.

Hannaway, J., & Carnoy, M. (Eds.). (1993). *Decentralization and school improvement: Can we fulfill the promise?* San Francisco: Jossey-Bass.

Hansen, C. H., & Hansen, R. D. (1988). How rock music videos can change what is seen when boy meets girl: Priming stereotypical appraisals of social interactions. *Sex Roles, 7*(3). 287–316.

Hansen, J. F. (1979). *Sociocultural perspectives on human learning: Foundations of educational anthropology.* Upper Saddle River, NJ: Prentice Hall.

Harrington, M. (1962). *The other America: Poverty in the United States.* New York: Macmillan.

Harrington, M. (1989, May). *The new American poverty.* Lecture delivered at Haverford College, Haverford, PA.

Hart, P. K. (2006, October). Why Juan Can't Read. *Texas Monthly.*

Hartocollis, A. (2002, March 26). Racial gap in test scores found across New York. *New York Times.*

Hartoonian, H. M. (1991). The role of philosophy in the education of democratic citizens. In R. E. Gross & T. L. Dynneson (Eds.), *Social science perspectives on citizenship education* (pp. 195–219). New York: Teachers College Press.

Harvard Project on American Indian Economic Development. (2007). *The state of the native nations: Conditions under U.S. policies of self-determination.* Oxford, England: Oxford University Press.

Haycock, K. (1998, Summer). Good teaching matters: A lot. *Thinking K–16, 3*(2), 3–14.

Haycock, K. (2000). No more settling for less. *Thinking K–16, 4*(1), 3–5.

Haycock, K. (2001, Spring). New frontiers for a new century. *Thinking K–16, 5*(2), 1–2.

Haycock, K., & Crawford, C. (2008). Closing the teacher quality gap. *Educational Leadership, 65*(7), 14–19.

Haycock, K., Jerald, C., & Huang, S. (2001, Spring). Closing the gap: Done in a decade. *Thinking K–16, 5*(2), 3–22.

Heath, S. B. (1986). Sociocultural contexts of language development. In California Department of Education, Bilingual Education Office, *Beyond language: Social and cultural factors in schooling of language minority students* (pp. 143–186). Los Angeles: Evaluation, Dissemination, and Assessment Center, California State University.

Heath, S. B. (1995). Ethnography in communities: Learning the everyday life of America's subordinated youth. In J. A. Banks & C. A. McGee Banks (Eds.), *Handbook of research on multicultural education* (pp. 114–128). New York: Simon & Schuster/Macmillan.

Hechinger, F. M. (1992). *Fateful choices: Healthy youth for the 21st century.* New York: Carnegie Council on Adolescent Development.

Heintz, J., Folbre, N., & The Center for Popular Economics. (2000). *The ultimate field guide to the U.S. economy.* New York: New Press.

Helping youth navigate the media age: A new approach to drug prevention. (2001). Washington, DC: The White House.

Henry, S. (2000). What is school violence? An integrated definition. *School Violence, 567*(1), 16–29.

Heredia-Arriaga, S., & Campbell, D. (1991). *How to integrate cooperative learning for the elementary teacher: Video and training program.* Carson City, NV: Superior Learning Programs.

Hernandez Sheets, R. (2000, December). Advancing the field or taking center stage: The White movement in multicultural education. *Educational Researcher, 29*(9), 29–35.

Herrnstein, R. J., & Murray, C. (1994). *The bell curve: Intelligence and class structure in American life.* New York: Free Press.

Heubert, J. P. (1998). High stakes testing and civil rights: Standards of appropriate test use and a strategy for enforcing them. In *Conference report: The Civil Rights Project.* Cambridge, MA: Harvard University. Retrieved June 13, 2004 from www.law.harvard.edu/civilrights/conference/testing98/drafts

High Performance Learning Communities Project. (1999). *Examining data with your school community.* Berkeley, CA: Author.

Hill, D. (1997, August–September). Sisters in arms. *Education Week,* p. 1.

Hirsch, E. D., Jr. (1987). *Cultural literacy.* New York: Houghton Mifflin.

Hirsch, E. D., Jr. (1996). *The schools we need, and why we don't have them.* New York: Doubleday.

Hoffman, D. M. (1996). Culture and self in multicultural education: Reflections on discourse, text, and practice. *American Educational Research Journal, 33*(3), 545–569.

Hoffman, D. M. (1998, September). A therapeutic moment? Identity, self, and culture in the anthropology of education. *Anthropology & Education Quarterly, 29*(3), 324–346.

Hoffman, L., & Sable, J. (2006). *Public elementary and secondary students, staff, schools, and school districts: School year 2003–04.* Washington, DC: National Center for Education Statistics, Institute of Education Sciences, U.S. Department of Education.

Hoffman, N. E., Reed, W. M., & Rosenbluth, G. S. (Eds.). (1997). *Lessons from restructuring experiences: Stories of change in professional development schools.* Albany, NY: State University of New York Press.

Hollins, E. R., King, J. E., & Hayman, W. C. (Eds.). (1994a). *Ethnic identity as a variable in the learning equation.* Albany, NY: State University of New York Press.

Hollins, E. R., King, J. E., & Hayman, W. C. (Eds.). (1994b). *Teaching diverse populations: Formulating a knowledge base.* Albany, NY: State University of New York Press.

Holmes Group. (1995). *Tomorrow's schools of education.* East Lansing, MI: Author.

Holyroyd, H. J. (1985). Children, adolescents, and television. *American Journal of Disordered Children, 139,* 549–550.

Hooks, B. (1994). *Teaching to transgress: Education as the practice of freedom.* New York: Routledge.

Hooks, B. (2000). *Where we stand: Class matters.* New York: Routledge.

Hoose, P. (1993). *It's our world, too! Stories of young people who are making a difference.* Boston: Little, Brown.

Hoover, R. L., & Kindsvatter, R. (1997). *Democratic discipline: Foundations and practice.* Upper Saddle River, NJ: Merrill/Prentice Hall.

Hopfenberg, W. S., Levin, H. M., Chase, C., Christensen, G., Moore, M., Soler, P., et al. (1993). *The accelerated schools resource guide.* San Francisco: Jossey-Bass.

Horwitz, E., Horwitz, M., & Cope, J. (1991). Foreign language classroom anxiety. In E. Horwitz & D. Young (Eds.), *Language anxiety: From theory and research to classroom implications* (pp. 27–36). Upper Saddle River, NJ: Prentice Hall.

House, T. W. (2000). *The President's new markets trip: From digital divide to digital opportunity. Highlighting technology's economic opportunity in Shiprock.* Washington, DC: The White House. Retrieved April 20, 2000, from www.whitehouse.gov

Howell, J. C. (1998). *Youth gangs: An overview.* Washington, DC: Office of Juvenile Justice and Delinquency Prevention, Office of Justice Programs, U.S. Department of Justice.

Hu, W. (2007, May 12). Middle school manages distractions of adolescents. *New York Times.* Accessed from http://www.nytimes.com/2007/05/12/education/12middle.html?_r=1&scp=2&sq=Hu%20+%20Middle%20School%20&st=cse

Huff, C. R. (1989). Youth gangs and public policy. *Crime & Delinquency, 35*(4), 524–537.

Humes, K., & McKinnon, J. (2000). *The Asian and Pacific Islander population in the United States, March 1999* (P20-529). Washington, DC: U.S. Census Bureau.

Hunter, M. (1982). *Mastery teaching.* El Segundo, CA: TIP.

Hursh, D. W., & Ross, E. W. (Eds.). (2000). *Democratic social education: Social studies for social change.* New York: Falmer Press.

Ignatiev, N. (1995). *How the Irish became White.* New York: Routledge.

Institute for Puerto Rican Policy. (1991). *The Puerto Rican exception: Persistent poverty and the conservative social policy of Linda Chavez.* New York: Author.

Irvine, J. J. (2003). *Educating teachers for diversity: Seeing with a cultural eye.* New York: Teachers College Press.

Isaacs, J. (2007). *Economic mobility of families across generations.* Philadelphia: Pew Charitable Trusts.

Ivins, M., & Dubose, L. (2003). *Bushwhacked: Life in George W. Bush's America.* New York: Random House.

Jackson, T. (1993–1994). Everyday school violence: How disorder fuels it. *American Educator, 17*(4), 4–9.

Jargowsky, P. A., & Bane, M. J. (1991). Ghetto poverty in the U.S., 1970–1980. In C. Jenks & P. E. Peterson (Eds.), *The urban underclass* (pp. 235–273). Washington, DC: Brookings Institution.

Jencks, C. (2001, December 20). *Who should get in: Part II* [Review of books on immigration]. *New York Review of Books, 48*(20). Accesed from http://www.nybooks.com/articles/article-preview?article_id=14942

Jenkins, H. (with Clinton, K., Purushotma, R., Robison, A. J., & Weigel, M.). (2006). *Confronting the challenges of participatory culture: Media education for the 21st century.* Chicago: MacArthur Foundation.

Jensen, A. S. (1969). How much can we boost IQ and scholastic achievement? *Harvard Educational Review, 39*(1), 1–123.

Jimerson, L. (1998, April 13–17). *The students "left behind": School choice and social stratification in non-urban districts.* Paper presented at the annual meeting of the American Educational Research Association, San Diego, CA.

Johnson, A. G. (2006). *Privilege, power and difference* (2nd ed.). Boston: McGraw Hill, 2006.

Johnson, C. S. (2008). A culturally consonant tone: African American teacher theorizing on character education policy. *Theory & Research in Social Education, 36*(1), 66–87.

Johnson, D. W., & Johnson, R. T. (1992, September). Teaching students to be peer mediators. *Educational Leadership, 50*(1), 10–18.

Johnson, D. W., & Johnson, R. T. (1999). *Learning together and alone: Cooperative, competitive and individualistic learning* (5th ed.). Boston: Allyn & Bacon.

Johnson, D. W., Johnson, R. T., Holubec, E. J., & Roy, P. (1984). *Circles of learning.* Alexandria, VA: Association for Supervision and Curriculum Development.

Johnson, D. W., Johnson, R. T., & Stanne, M. B. (2000). *Cooperative learning methods: A meta-analysis.* Minneapolis, MN: University of Minnesota.

Johnson, N., Hudgins, E., & Koulish, J. (2008). *Most states are cutting education.* Washington, DC: Center on Budget and Policy Priorities. Retrieved December 17, 2008, from www.cbpp.org/12-17-08sfp.pdf

Johnston, D. C. (2003). *Perfectly legal: The covert campaign to rig our tax system to benefit the super rich—and cheat everybody else.* New York: Penguin.

Johnston, D. C. (2005, June 5). Richest are leaving even the rich far behind. *New York Times*, Accessed from http://www.nytimes .com/2005/06/05/national/class/HYPER-

Johnston, D. C. (2007). *Free lunch: How the wealthiest Americans enrich themselves at government expense (and stick you with the bill).* New York: Penguin.

Johnston, M., Brosnan, P., Cramer, D., & Dove, T. (2000). *Collaborative reform and other improbable dreams. The challenges of professional development schools.* Albany, NY: State University of New York Press.

Johnston, R. C. (1998, April 8). Minority admissions drop sharply at California universities. *Education Week*, p. 1.

Jones, V., & Jones, L. (2007). *Comprehensive classroom management: Creating communities of support and solving problems.* Boston: Pearson/Allyn & Bacon.

Kagan, S. (1985). *Cooperative learning.* San Juan Capistrano, CA: Author.

Kagan, S. (1986). Cooperative learning and sociocultural factors in schooling. In California Department of Education, Bilingual Education Office, *Beyond language: Social and cultural factors in schooling of language minority students* (pp. 231–298). Los Angeles: Evaluation, Dissemination, and Assessment Center, California State University.

Kagan, S. (1989). *Cooperative learning: Resources for teachers.* San Juan Capistrano, CA: Resources for Teachers.

Kahne, J., & Westheimer, J. (2004). What kind of citizen? The politics of educating for a democracy. *American Educational Research Journal, 41*(2), 237–269.

Karp, S. (1992). Trouble over the rainbow. *Rethinking Schools 7(3),* 8–11.

Karp, S. (2007). Money, schools, and justice. *Rethinking Schools, 21*(4), 27–30.

Keyes v. School District #1, 576 F. Supp. 1503 (D. Colo. 1983).

Kilbourne, J. (1999). *Can't buy my love: How advertising changes the way we think and feel.* New York: Simon & Schuster, Touchstone.

Kilbourne, J. (2000). *Killing us softly III* [Video]. Northampton, MA: Media Education Foundation.

Kilsen, M. (2007, December 20). Reflections on Black group will and identity in the 21st century. *Black Commentator, 258.* Accessed from http://www.blackcommentator.com/258/258_black_group_will_kilson_ed_bd.html

Kincheloe, J. E. (2000). Cultural studies and democratically aware teacher education: Post-Fordism, civics, and the worker-citizen. In D. W. Hursh & E. W. Ross (Eds.), *Democratic social education: Social studies for social change.* pp. 97–120. New York: Falmer.

King, J. E. (1992). Diaspora literacy and consciousness in the struggle against miseducation in the Black community. *Journal of Negro Education, 61*(3), 317–335.

King, J. E. (1995). Culture-centered knowledge: Black studies, curriculum transformation, and social action. In J. A. Banks & C. A. McGee Banks (Eds.), *Handbook of research on multicultural education* (pp. 349–380). New York: Simon & Schuster/Macmillan.

King, K., & Gurian, M. (2006, September). With boys in mind/Teaching to the minds of boys. *Educational Leadership, 64*(1), 56–61.

King, M. L., Jr. (1986). *Testament of hope: The essential writings and speeches of Martin Luther King, Jr.* (J. Washington, Ed.). San Francisco: Harper.

Kinzer, S. (2006). *Overthrow: America's century of regime change from Hawaii to Iraq.* New York: Henry Holt.

Kirsch, I., Braun, H., Yamamoto, K., & Sum, A. (2007). *America's perfect storm: Three forces changing our nation's future.* Princeton, NJ: Educational Testing Service.

Kirschenbaum, H. (1992). A comprehensive model for values education and moral education. *Phi Delta Kappan, 73*(10), 77–176.

Klein, S. P., Hamilton, L. S., McCaffrey, D. F., & Stecher, B. M. (2000). *What do test scores in Texas tell us?* Santa Monica, CA: Rand. Retrieved May 14, 2003, from www.rand.org/publications/IP/IP202

Knapp, M., & Woolverton, S. (2001). Social class and schooling. In J. A. Banks & C. A. McGee Banks (Eds.), *Handbook of research on multicultural education.* New York: Simon & Schuster/Macmillan. (pp. 636–681).

Kober, N. (2001). *It takes more than testing: Closing the achievement gap.* Washington, DC: Center on Education Policy. Retrieved January 15, 2002, from www.ctredpol.org

Kober, N., Chudowsky, N., & Chudowsky, V. (2008). *Has student achievement increased since 2002? State test score trends through 2006–07.* Washington, DC: Center on Education Policy.

Kohn, A. (1993). *Punished by rewards: The trouble with gold stars, incentive plans, A's, praise and other bribes.* New York: Houghton Mifflin.

Kohn, A. (1999). Offering challenges: Creating cognitive dissonance. In C. McDermott (Ed.), *Beyond the silence: Listening for democracy* (pp. 6–15). Portsmouth, NH: Heinemann.

Kohn, A. (2005, September). Unconditional teaching. *Educational Leadership, 63*(1), 20–24.

Kozol, J. (1991). *Savage inequalities: Children in America's schools.* New York: Crown.

Kozol, J. (2002, June 10). Malign neglect: Children in New York City public schools are being shortchanged: Again. *Nation.*

Kozol, J. (2005). *The shame of the nation: The restoration of apartheid schooling in America.* New York: Crown.

Krashen, S. (1996). *Under attack: The case against bilingual education.* Culver City, CA: Language Education Associates.

Krashen, S. (2002a). Don't Trust Ed Trust. Accessed July 13, 2008 from http://www.sdkrashen.com/articles/dont_trust/dont_trust.pdf;

Krashen, S. (2002b). Why bilingual education? *Eric Digest.* (ERIC Document Reproduction Service No. ED403101)

Krashen, S. (2003). *Explorations in language acquisition and use.* Portsmouth, NH: Heinemann.

Krashen, S., & McField, G. (2005). What works? Reviewing the latest evidence on bilingual education. *Language Learner, 1*(2), 7–10, 34. Retrieved July 13, 2008 from Users.Rcn.Com/Crawj/Langpol/Krashen-Mcfield.Pdf

Krashen, S., & Terrell, T. D. (1983). *The natural approach: Language acquisition in the classroom.* Hayward, CA: Alemany.

Kroft, S. (2007, April 1). Under the influence. *60 minutes* [Television broadcast]. New York: Columbia Broadcasting System.

Kronowitz, E. (2008). *The teacher's guide to success.* Boston: Allyn & Bacon.

Krugman, P. (2007). *The conscience of a liberal.* New York: W. W. Norton.

Kuhn, T. S. (1970). *The structure of scientific revolutions* (2nd ed.). Chicago: University of Chicago Press.

Kurusa. (1995). *The streets are free.* New York: Annick Press.

Labaree, D. F. (1997). Public goods, private goals: The American struggle over educational goals. *American Educational Research Journal, 34*(1), 39–81.

Labaree, D. F. (2000). No exit: Public education as an inescapably public good. In L. Cuban & D. Shipps (Eds.), *Reconstructing the common good in education: Coping with intractable American dilemmas* (pp. 110–129). Stanford, CA: Stanford University Press.56

Labov, W. (1970). *The study of nonstandard English.* Champaign, IL: National Council of Teachers of English.

Ladson-Billings, G. (1992, September). The multicultural mission: Unity and diversity. *Social Education, 56,* 308–311.

Ladson-Billings, G. (1994a). *The dreamkeepers: Successful teachers of African American children.* San Francisco: Jossey-Bass.

Ladson-Billings, G. (1994b). Who will teach our children? Preparing teachers to successfully teach African American students. In E. Hollins, J. King, & W. Hayman (Eds.), *Teaching diverse populations: Formulating a knowledge base* (pp. 129–135). Albany, NY: State University of New York Press.

Ladson-Billings, G. (Ed.). (2003). *Critical race theory perspectives on the social studies: The profession, policies and curriculum.* Charlotte, NC: Information Age Publishing.

Laitsch, D. (2006). *Assessment, high stakes, and alternative visions: Appropriate use of the right tools to leverage improvement.* Tempe, AZ: Educational Policy Research Unit, Arizona State University. Retrieved Sept. 10, 2007 from epsl.asu.edu/epru/documents/EPSL-0611-222-EPRU.pdf

Lareau, A. (2003). *Unequal childhoods: Class, race and family life.* Berkeley, CA: University of California.

Latigua, J. (2001, April 20). How the GOP gamed the system in Florida. *Nation.* Retrieved April 30, 2001, from www.thenation.com/doc.mhtml?i20010430&s=Latigu

Lau v. Nichols, 414 U.S. 563 (1974).

Lawrence-Lightfoot, S. (1994). *I've known rivers: Lives of loss and liberation.* Reading, MA: Addison-Wesley.

Leadbeater, B. J. R., & Way, N. (Eds.). (1996). *Urban girls: Resisting stereotypes, creating identities.* New York: New York University Press.

Lee, J. (2006). *Tracking achievement gaps and assessing the impact of NCLB on the gaps: An in-depth look into national and state reading and math outcome trends.* Cambridge, MA: Civil Rights Project, Harvard University.

Lee, J. (2007). *The testing gap: Scientific trials of test-driven school accountability systems for excellence and equity*. Charlotte, NC: Information Age Publishing.

Lee, J., Grigg, W., & Dion, G. (2007). *The nation's report card: Mathematics 2007*. Washington, DC: National Center for Education Statistics, Institute of Education Sciences, U.S. Department of Education.

Lee, J., Grigg, W., & Donahue, P. (2007). *The nation's report card: Reading 2007*. Washington, DC: National Center for Education Statistics, Institute of Education Sciences, U.S. Department of Education.

Leming, J. (1985). Research on social studies curriculum instruction: Interventions and outcomes in the socio-moral domain. In W. B. Stanley (Ed.), *Review of research in social studies education, 1976–1983* (pp. 123–194). Washington, DC: National Council for the Social Studies.

Leming, J., Ellington, L., & Porter, K. (Eds.). (2003). *Where did social studies go wrong?* Dayton, OH: Thomas Fordham Institute.

Lever-Duffy, J., & McDonald, J. B. (2008). *Teaching and learning with technology*. Boston: Allyn & Bacon.

Levin, H. (1994, Spring). Powerful learning in accelerated schools. *Accelerated Schools Project Newsletter,* 14–18.

Levin, H. M. (1999, July). *High stakes testing and economic productivity* (Rev. ed.). Retrieved July 3, 2001 from www.law.harvard.edu/civilrights/conferences/testing/98/drafts/levin

Levine, D. U., & Lezotte, L. W. (1995). Effective schools research. In J. A. Banks & C. A. McGee Banks (Eds.), *Handbook of research on multicultural education* (pp. 525–547). New York: Simon & Schuster/Macmillan.

Levine, D. U., & Lezotte, L. W. (2001). Effective schools research. In J. A. Banks & C. A. McGee Banks (Eds.), *Handbook of research on multicultural education* (pp. 525–547). New York: Simon & Schuster/Macmillan.

Levy, A. (2005). *Female chauvinist pigs: Women and the rise of raunch culture*. New York: Free Press.

Lewis, O. (1968). Culture of poverty. *Scientific American, 215*(4), 19–24.

Lieberman, A. (Ed.). (1995). *The work of restructuring schools: Building from the ground up*. New York: Teachers College Press.

Limerick, P. N. (1988). *The legacy of conquest: The unbroken past of the American West*. New York: W. W. Norton.

Lipsitz, G. (2001). *The possessive investment in whiteness: How White people profit from identity politics*. Philadelphia: Temple University Press.

Llanes, J. (1982). *Cuban Americans: Masters of survival*. Cambridge, MA: Abbott.

Loeb, S., Byrk, A., & Hanushek, E. (2007). *Getting down to facts: School finance and governance in California*. Palo Alto, CA: Stanford University.

Loewen, J. W. (1995). *Lies my teacher told me: Everything your American history textbook got wrong*. New York: New Press.

Lortie, D. (1975). *Schoolteacher*. Chicago: University of Chicago Press.

Loveless, T. (2001a). *The 2001 Brown Center report on public education: How well are American students learning?* (Vol. 1, No. 2). Washington, DC: Brookings Institution.

Loveless, T. (2001b). *The great curriculum debate: How should we teach reading and math?* Washington, DC: Brookings Institution.

Lowe, R., & Miner, B. (Eds.). (1996). *Selling out our schools: Vouchers, markets, and the future of public education*. Milwaukee, WI: Rethinking Schools.

Luhman, R. (1996). *The sociological outlook* (5th ed.). San Diego, CA: Collegiate.

Lynn, M. (2002). Critical race theory and the perspectives of Black men teachers in Los Angeles public schools. *Equity & Excellence in Education, 35*(2), 119–130.

MacDonald, G. J. (2005, June 6). Conservatives see liberal bias in class—and mobilize. *Christian Science Monitor*, http://www.csmonitor.com/2005/0606/p01s03-legn.html

Macedo, D. P. (1993, Summer). Literacy for stupification: The pedagogy of big lies. *Harvard Educational Review, 6.* 183–204.

Macedo, S. (2000). *Diversity and distrust: Civic education in a multicultural democracy*. Cambridge, MA: Harvard University Press.

MacLeod, J. (1987). *Ain't no making it: Leveled aspirations in a low-income neighborhood*. Boulder, CO: Westview.

Mansilla, V. B., & Gardner, H. (2008). Disciplining the mind. *Educational Leadership, 65*(5), 14–19.

Manzo, K. (2006, October 4). Scathing report casts cloud over "Reading First." *Education Week*, p. 1.

Marable, M. (1985). *Black American politics: From the Washington march to Jesse Jackson*. London: Verso.

Marable, M. (1992). Multicultural democracy: The emerging majority for justice and peace. In M. Marable, *The crisis of color and democracy: Essays on race, class and power* (pp. 249–251). Monroe, ME: Common Courage.

Marable, M. (2007). Race, *reform and rebellion: The second Reconstruction and beyond in Black America, 1945–2006* (3rd ed.). Jackson, MS: University Press of Mississippi.

Marable, M., & Mullings, L. (Eds.). (2000). *Let nobody turn us around: Voices of resistance, reform, and renewal: An African American anthology*. Lanham, MD: Rowman & Littlefield.

Marks, H. M., & Louis, K. S. (1997). Does teacher empowerment affect the classroom? The implication of teacher empowerment for instructional practice and student academic performance. *Educational Evaluation & Policy Analysis, 19*(3), 245–275.

Marri, A. R. (2005). Building a framework for classroom-based multicultural democratic education: Learning from three skilled teachers. *Teachers College Record, 107*(5), 1036–1059.

Marshall, R., & Tucker, M. (1992). *Thinking for a living: Education and the wealth of nations.* New York: Basic Books.

Martinez, M. (1978). *Self concept and behavioral change through counseling, consulting interventions.* Unpublished doctoral dissertation, Texas Tech University, Lubbock.

Matute-Bianchi, Maria E. (1991). Situational ethnicity and patterns of school performance among immigrants and nonimmigrant Mexican-descended students. In M. Gibson & J. O. Ogbu (Eds.), *Minority status and schooling: A comparative study of immigrant and involuntary minorities.* 205–245. New York: Garland.

McCaleb, S. P. (1994). *Building communities of learners.* New York: St. Martin's Press.

McCarthey, K. F., & Vernez, G. (1997). *New immigrants, new needs: The California experience* (Publication No. RB-8015). Santa Monica, CA: Rand Institute on Education and Training.

McCarthy, C., & Dimitriadis, G. (2000). *All-consuming identities: Race and the pedagogy of resentment in the age of difference.* In P. P. Trifonas (Ed.), *Revolutionary pedagogies: Cultural politics, instituting education, and the discourse of theory* (pp. 47–60). New York: Routledge.

McCarthy, J. D., & Yencey, W. L. (1971). Uncle Tom and Mr. Charlie: Metaphysical pathos in the study of racism and personal disorganization. *American Institute of Sociology, 76*, 648–672.

McClaren, P. (2000). Unthinking whiteness: Rearticulating diasporic practice. In P. P. Trifonas (Ed.), *Revolutionary pedagogies: Cultural politics, instituting education, and the discourse of theory* (pp. 140–173). New York: Routledge.

McClaren, P. (with Giroux, H.). (1995). Radical pedagogy as cultural politics: Beyond the discourse of critique and anti-utopianism. In P. McClaren, *Critical pedagogy and predatory culture: Oppositional politics in a postmodern era* (pp. 1–29). London: Routledge, 1995.

McDermott, R. (1974). Achieving school failure: An anthropological approach to illiteracy and school stratification. In G. Spindler (Ed.), *Education and cultural process* (pp. 173–209). New York: Holt.

McDermott, R., & Varenne, H. (1995). Culture as disability. *Anthropology & Education Quarterly, 26*(3), 324–328.

McDowell, L. (1999). *Gender, identity and place: Understanding feminist geographies.* Minneapolis, MN: University of Minnesota Press.

McFadden, J. (1975). *Consciousness and social change: The pedagogy of Paulo Freire.* Unpublished doctoral dissertation, University of California at Santa Cruz.

McGarrell, E. (2001). Restorative justice conferences as an early response to young offenders. *Juvenile Justice Bulletin.* Washington, DC: Office of Juvenile Justice and Delinquency Prevention, Office of Justice Programs, U.S. Department of Justice.

McGee Banks, C. A. (1997, Spring). The challenge of national standards in a multicultural society. *Education Horizons*, Vol. 75. (3), 126–132.

McGhee, P. E., & Freuh, T. (1980). Television viewing and the learning of sex-role stereotypes. *Sex Roles, 2*, 179–188.

McIntyre, A. (1997). *Making meaning of whiteness: Exploring racial identity with White teachers.* Albany, NY: State University of New York Press.

McKenna, G. (1992, March 27). Heartware, not hardware. *Los Angeles Times*, p. A11.

McKeon, D. (1994, May). When meeting "common" standards is uncommonly difficult. *Educational Leadership*, Vol. 51 (8), 45–49.

McKinnon, J. (2001, August). *The Black population: 2000* (C2KBR/01-5). Washington, DC: U.S. Census Bureau.

McKinnon, J. (2003). *The Black population of the United States: March 2002* (P20-541). Washington, D.C.: U.S. Census Bureau.

McLaren, P. (1989). *Life in schools: An introduction to critical pedagogy in the foundations of education.* New York: Longman.

McLaren, P. (1997). Decentering whiteness: In search of a revolutionary multiculturalism. *Multicultural Education, 5*(1), 4–11.

McLaren, P. (2000). *Che Guevara, Paulo Freire, and the pedagogy of revolution.* Lanham, MD: Rowman & Littlefield.

McLaughlin, M. W. (1991). The Rand change agent study: Ten years later. In A. Odden (Ed.), *Educational policy implementation* (pp. 143–156). Albany, NY: State University of New York Press.

McLaughlin, M. W., & Oberman, I. (Eds.). (1996). *Teacher learning: New policies, new practices.* New York: Teachers College Press.

McLaughlin, M. W., & Talbert, J. (1993). *Contexts that matter for teaching and learning: Strategic opportunities for meeting the nation's educational goals.* Stanford, CA: Center for Research on the Context of Secondary School Teaching.

McLeod, B. (1996). *School reform and student diversity: Exemplary schooling for language minority students.* Washington, DC: Institute for the Study of Language and Education, National Clearinghouse for Bilingual Education, George Washington University.

McNamara, O., & Rogers, B. (2000). The roots of personal worth and the wings of self-responsibility: A research-based enquiry into a business-education mentoring programme. *Mentoring & Tutoring: Partnership in Learning, 8*(2), 85–97.

McNeil, L. (2000). *Contradictions of school reform: Educational costs of standardized testing.* New York: Routledge.

McNeil, L., Coppola, E., Radigan, J., & Vasquez Heilig, J. (2008). Avoidable losses: High-stakes accountability and the dropout crisis. *Education Policy Analysis Archives, 16*(3). Retrieved May 5, 2008, from epaa.asu.edu/epaa/v16n3

McNeil, L., & Valenzuela, A. (2000). *The harmful impact of the TAAS system in Texas: Beneath the accountability rhetoric.* Cambridge, MA: Civil Rights Project, Harvard University. Retrieved May 1, 2000, from www.harvard.edu/civilrights/conferences/testing98/drafts/mcneil_valenzuela.html

McNeil, L., & Valenzuela, A. (2001). The harmful impact of the TAAS system of testing in Texas. In G. Orfield & M. L. Kornhaber (Eds.), *Raising standards or raising barriers: Inequality and high-stakes testing in public education.* (pp. 127–150). New York: Century Foundation Press.

McPartland, J. M., & Slavin, R. E. (1990). *Increasing achievement of at-risk students at each grade level.* Washington, DC: U.S. Department of Education.

McTighe, J., Seif, E., & Wiggins, G. (2004, September). You can teach for meaning. *Educational Leadership, 62*(1), 26–30.

Media Literacy Summit. (2001). *Helping youth navigate the media age: Findings of the National Youth Anti Drug Campaign, Media Literacy Summit.* (2001). Washington, DC: The White House.

Medina, J. (2008, January 21). New York measuring teachers by test scores. *New York Times*, p. A1.

Medina, M., & Escamilla, K. (1992). Evaluation of transitional and maintenance bilingual programs. *Urban Education, 27*(3), 263–290.

Mehan, H. (1992). Understanding inequality in schools: The contributions of interpretive studies. *Sociology of Education, 65*(1), 1–20.

Mehan, H., Lintz, A., Okamotoa, D., & Wills, J. S. (1995). Ethnographic studies of multicultural education in classrooms and schools. In J. A. Banks & C. A. McGee Banks (Eds.), *Handbook of research on multicultural education* (pp. 163–183) 2nd edition. New York: Simon & Schuster/Macmillan.

Meier, D. (1995). *The power of their ideas: Lessons for America from a small school in Harlem.* Boston: Beacon Press.

Meier, D., & Wood, G. (Eds.). (2004). *Many children left behind: How the No Child Left Behind Act is damaging our children and our schools.* Boston: Beacon Press.

Mendez v. Westminster School District, 64 F. Supp. 544 (C.D. Cal. 1946), aff'd, 161 F.2d 774 (9th Cir. 1947)

Mihesuah, D. A. (2003). *Indigenous American women: Decolonization, empowerment, activism.* Lincoln, NE: University of Nebraska Press.

Mill, J. S. (1985). *On liberty.* Indianapolis, IN: Hackett. (Original work published 1859)

Miller, J. (1992, July/August). Silent depression. *Dollars & Sense, 242,* 6.

Miller, R. (Ed.). (1995a). *Culture, imperialism, and Goals 2000.* Brandon, VT: Resource Center for Redesigning Education.

Miller, R. (1995b). *Educational freedom for a democratic society: A critique of national goals, standards, and curriculum.* Brandon, VT: Resource Center for Redesigning Education.

Miller-Jones, D. (1991). Informal reasoning in inner-city children. In J. F. Voss, D. N. Perkins, & J. S. Segal (Eds.), *Informal reasoning and education* (pp. 107–130). Hillsdale, NJ: Lawrence Erlbaum.

Miner, B. (1996). Splits on the right: What do they mean for education? *Rethinking Schools, 10*(3), 11–18.

Mintrop, H., Wong, P., Gamson, D., & Oberman, I. (1996). *Evaluation of the San Francisco Foundation school reform portfolio.* San Francisco: San Francisco Foundation.

Mishel, L., Bernstein, J., & Allegretto, S. (2007). *The state of working America, 2006/2007.* Ithaca, NY: Cornell University Press.

Mishel, L., & Rothstein, R. (2007). *Response to Marc Tucker.* Washington, DC: Economic Policy Institute.

Moll, L. C., Vélez-Ibañez, C., & Greenberg, J. (1992). *Community knowledge and classroom practice: Combining resources for literacy instruction: A handbook for teachers and planners.* Arlington, VA: Development Associates.

Momaday, N. S. (2002, July/August). And we have only begun to define our destiny. *Native peoples: Arts & lifeways, 15*(5).

Montgomery, L. (2002, April 22). Maryland seeks "adequacy," recasting school debate. *Washington Post*, p. A1.

Moore, J. (1988, April). *An assessment of Hispanic poverty: Is there an Hispanic underclass?* San Antonio, TX: Tomás Rivera Center.

Mora, C. (2007). *Latinos in the West: The student movement and academic labor in Los Angeles.* Lanham, MD: Rowman & Littlefield.

Moraga, C., & Anzaldúa, G. (Eds.). (1981). *This bridge called my back.* New York: Kitchen Table, Women of Color Press.

Mosak, H., & Dreikurs, R. (1973). Adlerian psychology. In R. Corsini (Ed.), *Current psychotherapies* (pp. 35–84). Itasca, IL: Peacock. Quoted in Martinez, M. (1978). *Self concept and behavioral change through counseling, consulting interventions.* Unpublished doctoral dissertation, Texas Tech University, Lubbock.

Moses, R. P., & Cobb, C. E. (2001). *Radical equations: Civil rights from Mississippi to the Algebra Project.* Boston: Beacon Press.

Moyer, B. (with McAllister, J. A., Finley, M. L., & Soifer, S.). (2001). *Doing democracy: The MAP model for organizing social movements.* Gabriola Island, British Columbia, Canada: New Society Publishers.

Moynihan, D. P. (1993–1994, Winter). Defining deviancy down. *American Educator,* Vol. 18. 10–18.

Münch, R., & Smelser, N. J. (Eds.). (1992). *Theory of culture.* Berkeley, CA: University of California Press.

Murnane, R., & Levy, F. (1996). *Teaching the new basic skills: Principles for educating children in a changing economy.* New York: Free Press.

Musil, C. M. (2007, Fall). Scaling the ivory towers. *Ms.* pp. 43–45.

Nai-Lin Chang, H., Nguyen Louie-Murdock, B., Pell, E., & Femenella, T. S. (2000). *Walking the walk: Principles for building community capacity for equity and diversity.* Oakland, CA: California Tomorrow.

Nathan, J. (1996–1997, Winter). Progressives should support charter public schools. *Rethinking Schools, 11*(2), 20–21.

National Center for Children in Poverty. (1991). *News and issues.* New York: Columbia University School of Public Health.

National Center for Immigrants' Rights. (1979). *Immigration defense manual.* Los Angeles: Author.

National Center on Education and the Economy. (2007). *Tough choices or tough times: The report of the New Commission on the Skills of the American Workforce.* Washington, DC: Author.

National Coalition for Women and Girls in Education. (2002). *Title IX at 30: Report card on gender equity.* Washington, DC: Author.

National Coalition for Women and Girls in Education. (2008). *Title IX at 35: Beyond the Headlines.* Washington, DC: Author.

National Coalition of Advocates for Students. (1991). *The good common school: Making the vision work for all children: A comprehensive guide to elementary school restructuring.* Boston: Author.

National Coalition of Educational Activists. (1994, Autumn). Social justice unionism. *Rethinking Schools, 9*(1), 8, 12–13.

National Commission on Excellence in Education. (1983). *A nation at risk.* Washington, DC: U.S. Government Printing Office.

National Council for Excellence in Critical Thinking. (2003). *Critical thinking.* Accessed Web, 2008. May 5, 2008. http://www.criticalthinking.org/page.cfm?PageID=411&CategoryID=51

National Council on Education Standards and Testing. (1992). *Raising standards for American education: A report to Congress, the Secretary of Education, the National Goals Panel, and the American people.* Washington, DC: U.S. Department of Education.

National Economic and Social Rights Initiative. (2007). *Deprived of dignity: Degrading treatment and abusive discipline in New York City and Los Angeles public schools.* New York: Author.

National Education Association. (1990). *Tracking: Report of the NEA Executive Committee on academic tracking.* Washington, DC: Author.

National Education Association. (1998). *American education statistics at a glance: NEA research, March 1998.* Washington, DC: Author. Retrieved February 5, 1999, from www.nea.org/society/edstat98.pdf

National Education Association. (2003). *Status of the American public school teacher 2001.* Washington, DC: Author.

National Geographic Society. (1993). *The world of the American Indian.* Washington, DC: Author.

National Research Council. (1997). *Schooling for language minority children.* Washington, DC: Author.

Neil, M. (2003, February). The dangers of testing. *Educational Leadership, 60*(5), 43–46.

Nelson, B., Berman, P., Ericson, J., Kamprath, N., Perry, R., & Silverman, D. S. D. (2000). *The state of charter schools, 2000.* Washington, DC: Office of Educational Research and Improvement, U.S. Department of Education.

Nelson, J., Lott, L., & Glenn, H. S. (2000). *Positive discipline in the classroom.* New York: Ballantine Books.

New York State Education Department. (1989, July). *A curriculum of inclusion: Commissioner's Task Force on Minorities: Equity and excellence.* Albany, NY: Author.

New York State Education Department. (1995). *Curriculum, instruction and assessment: Preliminary draft framework for social studies.* Albany, NY: Author. Retrieved March 15, 2007 from www.emsc.nysed.gov/ciai/socst/pub/ssframe.pdf

New York State Social Studies Review and Development Committee. (1991). *One nation, many peoples: A declaration of cultural interdependence.* Albany, NY: New York State Education Department.

Newcomer, S., & Brown, J. D. (August,1984). *Influences of television and peers on adolescents' sexual behavior.* Paper presented at a meeting of the American Psychological Association, Toronto, Canada.

Ngo, B. (2002). Contesting "culture": The perspectives of Hmong American female students on early marriage. *Anthropology & Education Quarterly, 33*(2), 163–188.

Nichols, S., & Berliner, D. (2007). *Collateral damage: How high-stakes testing corrupts America's schools.* Cambridge, MA: Harvard University Press.

Nichols, S. L., Glass, G. V., & Berliner, D. (2005). *High-stakes testing and student achievement: Problems for the No Child Left Behind Act.* Tempe, AZ: Arizona State University.

Nieto, S. (2004). *Affirming diversity: The sociopolitical context of multicultural education* (5th ed.). Boston: Allyn & Bacon, Pearson.

Njeri, I. (1991, January 13). Beyond the melting pot. *Los Angeles Times,* pp. E1, E8, E9.

No Child Left Behind Act of 1991, Pub. L. No. 107-110 (20 U.S.C. § 6301 *et seq.*).

Nord, M., Andrews, M., & Steven Carlson, Household Food Security in the United States, 2007. See the full report Economic Research Report No. (ERR-66), November 2008 U.S. Dept. of Agriculture.Retrieved from http://www.ers.usda.gov/Publications/ERR66/ERR66_ReportSummary.html

Noel, J. (2001). Examining the connection between identity construction and the understanding of multicultural education. *Multicultural Perspectives, 3*(2), 3–7.

Noguera, P. (1999). Transforming urban schools through investments in social capital. *In Motion*. Retrieved June 14, 2008 from www.inmotion.com

Norton, J. (1998, Spring). High standards for all—experienced teachers for some. *Changing Schools in Long Beach, 2*(2), 1–2.

Oakes, J. (1985). *Keeping track: How schools structure inequality*. New Haven, CT: Yale University Press.

Oakes, J. (1988). Tracking in mathematics and science education: A structural contribution to unequal schooling. In L. Weis (Ed.), *Class, race and gender in American education* (pp. 106–125). Albany, NY: State University of New York Press.

Oakes, J. (2005). *Keeping track: How schools structure inequality* (2nd ed.). New Haven, CT: Yale University Press.

Oakes, J., & Lipton, M. (1990). Tracking and ability grouping: A structural barrier to access and achievement. In J. Goodlad & P. Keating (Eds.), *Access to knowledge: An agenda for our nation's schools.* New York: College Entrance Examination Board.

Oakes, J., & Rogers, J. (with Lipton, M.). (2006). *Learning power: Organizing for education and justice.* New York: Teachers College Press.

Oakes, J., & Rogers, J. (2007). *Latino educational opportunity report: 2007.* Los Angeles: Institute for Democracy, Education, and Access, UCLA.

Oakes, J., & Saunders, M. (2007). *Multiple pathways: High school reform that promises to prepare all students for college, career, and civic responsibility.* Los Angeles: Institute for Democracy, Education, and Access, UCLA.

Obama, B. (2004). *Dreams from my father: A story of race and inheritance*. New York: Crown.

Obama, B. (2007). *The audacity of hope: Thoughts on reclaiming the American dream*. New York: Crown.

O'Cadez, M. D. P., Wong, P. L., & Torres, C. (1998). *Education and democracy: Paulo Freire, social movements, and educational reform in San Paulo.* Boulder, CO: Westview.

O'Callaghan, S. (2000). *To hell or Barbados.* Dublin, Ireland: Brandon.

O'Connor, T. (1998). The rhythms and routines of democratic classrooms. In C. McDermott (Ed.), *Beyond the silence: Listening for democracy.* pp. 44–51. Portsmouth, NH: Heinemann.

O'Day, J., & Smith, M. S. (1993). Systemic reform and educational opportunity. In S. Fuhrman (Ed.), *Designing coherent educational policy: Improving the system.* pp. 233–267. San Francisco: Jossey-Bass.

Odden, A. (Ed.). (1991). *Educational policy implementation.* Albany, NY: State University of New York Press.

Odden, A. (1992). School finance and educational reform. In A. Odden (Ed.), *Rethinking school finance: An agenda for the 1990s* (pp. 1–40). San Francisco: Jossey-Bass.

Ogbu, J. U. (1978). *Minority education and caste: The American system in cross cultural perspective.* New York: Academic Press.

Ogbu, J. U. (1995). Understanding cultural diversity and learning. In J. A. Banks & C. A. McGee Banks (Eds.), *Handbook of research on multicultural education* (pp. 582–596). New York: Simon & Schuster/Macmillan.

Ogunwole, S. U. (2006). *We the people: American Indians and Alaska Natives in the United States* (CENSR-28). Washington, DC: U.S. Census Bureau.

Olsen, L. (1988). *Crossing the schoolhouse border: Immigrant students and the California public schools.* San Francisco: California Tomorrow.

Olsen, L. (1992, Fall). Whose curriculum is this? Whose curriculum will it be? *California Perspectives, 2,* 3B.

Olsen, L. (1997). *Made in America: Immigrant students in our public schools.* New York: New Press.

Olsen, L. (2001, April 5). *Looking to the future: Immigrant students in our schools.* Washington, DC: Rockefeller Foundation.

Olsen, L., Chang, H., De La Rosa Salazar, D., Dowell, C., Leong, C., McCall Perez, Z., McClain, G., Raffe. L. (1994). *The unfinished journey: Restructuring schools in a diverse society.* San Francisco: California Tomorrow.

Olsen, L., & Dowell, C. (1997). *The schools we need now: How parents, families and communities can change schools* (published simultaneously in Spanish as *Las escuelas que necesitamos hoy: De cómo los padres, las familias y las comunidades pueden participar in el cambio escolar*). San Francisco: California Tomorrow.

Olsen, L., & Mullen, N. (1990). *Embracing diversity: Teachers' voices from California.* San Francisco: California Tomorrow.

Olson, L. (1986, January). Effective schools. *Education Week*, pp. 11–21.

Olson, L. (1997, January 22). Keeping tabs on quality. *Education Week*, pp. 7–17.

Olson, L., & Hendrie, C. (1998, January 8). Pathways to progress. *Education Week*, pp. 32–34.

Omi, M., & Winant, H. (1986). *Racial formation in the United States: From the 1960s to the 1980s.* New York: Routledge & Kegan Paul.

O'Neil, J. (1997). Building schools as communities: A conversation with James Comer. *Educational Leadership, 54*(8), 6–10.

Orfield, G., & Ashkinage, C. (1991). *The closing door: Conservative policy and Black opportunity.* Chicago: University of Chicago Press.

Orfield, G., Bachmeier, M., James, D. R., & Eitle, T. (1997). *Deepening segregation in American public schools.* Cambridge, MA: Harvard Project on School Desegregation, Harvard University.

Orfield, G., Eaton, S. E., & Harvard Project on School Desegregation. (1996). *Dismantling desegregation: The quiet reversal of Brown v. Board of Education.* New York: New Press.

Orfield, G., & Gordon, W. N. (2001). *Schools more separate: Consequences of a decade of resegregation.* Retrieved July 2, 2002, from www.civilrightsproject.harvard.edu/research/deseg/call_separateschools.php?Page=1

Orfield, G., & Lee, C. (2006). *Racial transformation and the changing nature of segregation.* Cambridge, MA: Civil Rights Project, Harvard University.

Orfield, G., & Lee, C. (2007). *Historic reversals, accelerating resegregation, and the need for new integration strategies.* Los Angeles: Civil Rights Project, UCLA.

Organization for Economic Cooperation and Development. (2006). *Society at a glance.* Author. Paris, France.

Osborne, A. B. (1996). Practice into theory into practice: Culturally relevant pedagogy for students we have marginalized and normalized. *Anthropology & Education Quarterly, 27*(3), 285–314.

Ovando, C. J., Collier, V. P., & Combs, M. (2006). *Bilingual and ESL classrooms: Teaching in multicultural contexts* (4th ed.). Boston: McGraw Hill.

Owen, D. (2006, September 24–29). *What research tells us about the implementation of education for democracy materials in classrooms: A review of stated goals and achieved results.* Paper presented at the Conference on Democracy-Promotion and International Cooperation, cosponsored by the Center for Civic Education and the Bundeszentrale fur politische Bildung, Denver, CO.

Padilla, A. M., & Lindholm, K. J. (1995). Quantitative educational research with ethnic minorities. In J. A. Banks & C. A. McGee Banks (Eds.), *Handbook of research on multicultural education* (pp. 97–113). New York: Simon & Schuster/Macmillan.

Palast, G. (2002). Ex-con game: How Florida "felon" voter purge was itself felonious. *Harper's, 304*(1822), 48–49.

Palast, G. (2006). *Armed madhouse: Who's afraid of Osama Wolf? China floats, Bush sinks, the scheme to steal '08, no child's behind left, and other dispatches from the front lines of the class war.* New York: Penguin.

Scribner, A. P. (1999). High Performing Hispanic Schools. In P. Reyes, J. D. Scribner, & A. P. Scribner (Eds.), *Lessons from high-performing Hispanic schools: Creating learning communities.* (pp. 1–18). New York: Teachers College Press.

Parish, T. B., Pérez Merickel, M., Linquanti, R., (2006). *Effects of the implementation of Proposition 227 on the education of English learners, K–12: Findings from a five-year evaluation.* Palo Alto, CA: American Institutes for Research and WestEd.

Parker, R. (1972). *The myth of the middle class.* New York: Harper & Row.

Parker, W. C. (2003). *Teaching democracy: Unity and diversity in public life.* New York: Teachers College Press.

Parker, W. C. (2009). *Social studies in elementary education* (13th ed.). Boston: Allyn & Bacon.

Partnership for 21st Century Skills. (2008). *21st century skills, education and competitiveness: A resource and policy guide.* Tucson, AZ: Author.

Passel, J. S., & Cohn, D. (2008). *U.S. population projections: 2005–2050.* Washington, DC: Pew Research Center.

Pastor, J., McCormick, J., & Fine, M. (1996). Making homes: An urban girl thing. In B. J. R. Leadbeater & N. Way (Eds.), *Urban girls: Resisting stereotypes, creating identities* (pp. 15–34). New York: New York University Press.

Pastor, M. (1993). *Latinos and the Los Angeles uprising: The economic context.* Claremont, CA: Thomas Rivera Center.

Paul, R. (1988). Program for the Fourth International Conference on Critical Thinking and Educational Reform, Sonoma State University, Rohnert Park, CA. In R. J. Marzano, R. Brandt, C. S. Hughes, B. F. Jones, B. Z. Presseisen, S. C. Rankin, et al. (Eds.), *Dimensions of thinking: A framework for curriculum and instruction* (pp. 18–22). Alexandria, VA: Association for Supervision and Curriculum Development.

Payne, R. (1996). *A framework for understanding poverty.* Highlands, TX: aha! Process.

Payne, R. (2008, April). Nine powerful practices. *Educational Leadership, 65*(7), 48–52

Pelo, A., & Pelojoaquin, K. (2006/2007). Why we banned Legos. *Rethinking Schools, 21*(2), 8–12.

Peregoy, S. F., & Boyle, O. F. (2005). *Reading, writing, and learning in ESL: A resource book for K–12 teachers* (4th ed.). Boston. Allyn & Bacon.

Pérez, B. (1998). *Sociocultural contexts of language and literacy.* Mahwah, NJ: Lawrence Erlbaum.

Perie, M., Grigg, W., & Dion, G. (2005). *The nation's report card: Mathematics 2005.* Washington, DC: National Center for Education Statistics, U.S. Department of Education.

Perie, M., Grigg, W., & Donahue, P. (2005). *The nation's report card: Reading 2005.* Washington, DC: National Center for Education Statistics, U.S. Department of Education.

Perkins, D. (1986). *Knowledge as design.* Hillsdale, NJ: Lawrence Erlbaum.

Perkins, D. (1999, November). The many faces of constructivism. *Educational Leadership, 57*(3), 6–11.

Perkovich, G. (2005, July/August). Giving justice its due: The missing principle. *Foreign Affairs, 84*(4), 6–10.

Perlstein, L. (2007). *Tested: One American school struggles to make the grade.* New York: Henry Holt.

Perry, T., & Delpit, L. (Eds.). (1997). The real Ebonics debate: Power, language, and education of African American children. *Rethinking Schools, 12*(1), 1–34.

Perry, T., & Delpit, L. (Eds.). (2002). *The real Ebonics debate: Power, language, and the education of African-American children.* Milwaukee, WI: Rethinking Schools.

Pfaelzer, J. (2007). *Driven out: The forgotten war against Chinese Americans.* New York: Random House.

Phillips, K. (2002). *Wealth and democracy: A political history of the American rich.* New York: Broadway Books.

Pickney, A. (1986). *The myth of Black progress.* Cambridge, England: Cambridge University Press.

Pipher, M. (1994). *Reviving Ophelia: Saving the selves of adolescent girls.* New York: Ballantine Books.

Poggioli, S. (2008). Jan.22.2008. Muslim activist critical of "multicultural mistake." *Morning edition* [Radio broadcast]. Washington, D.C.: National Public Radio.

Pogrow, S. (1996, June). Reforming the wannabe reformers: Why education reforms almost always end up making things worse. *Phi Delta Kappan*, Vol. 77. p. 656–663.

Pool, C. R. (1997, March). Maximizing learning: A conversation with Renate Nummela Caine. *Educational Leadership, 54*(6), 11–16.

Popham, W. J. (1999, March). Why standardized tests don't measure educational quality. *Educational Leadership, 56*(6), 8–15.

Popham, W. J. (2003, February). The seductive allure of data. *Educational Leadership, 60*(5), 48–51.

Popham, W. J. (2004). *America's "failing" schools: How parents and teachers can cope with No Child Left Behind.* New York: RoutledgeFalmer.

Popkewitz, T. S. (1987). Knowledge and interest in curriculum. In T. Popkewitz (Ed.), *Critical studies in teacher education: Its folklore, theory, and practice* (pp. 338–339). London: Falmer.

Popkewitz, T. S. (1998). Restructuring of social and political theory: Foucault, the linguistic turn, and education. In C. A. Torres & T. R. Mitchell (Eds.), *Sociology of education: Emerging perspectives* (pp. 47–89). Albany, NY: State University of New York Press.

Popkewitz, T. S., Tabachnick, B. R., & Wehlage, G. (1982). *The myth of educational reform.* Madison, WI: University of Wisconsin Press.

Porter, G. (1995). The White man's burden, revisited. In R. Miller (Ed.), *Educational freedom for a democratic society. A critique of national goals, standards and curriculum.* Resource Center for Redesigning Education. Brandon, VT.

Porter, R. P. (1998, May). The case against bilingual education. *Atlantic Monthly, 281*(5), 28–29, 38–39.

Posner, R. A. (2003). *Law, pragmatism, and democracy.* Cambridge, MA: Harvard University Press.

Powell, J., Blackorby, J., Marsh, J., Finnegan, K., & Anderson, L. (1997*). Evaluation of charter school effectiveness.* Palo Alto, CA: SRI International.

President's Initiative on Race. (1998, September 18). *One America in the 21st century: Forging a new future.* Washington, DC: The White House.

Putnam, R. D. (1995, January). Bowling alone: America's declining social capital. *Journal of Democracy, 6*(1), 65–78.

Putnam, R. D. (2000). *Bowling alone: The collapse and revival of American community.* New York: Simon & Schuster.

Putnam, R. D. (2007). E pluribus unum: Diversity and community in the twenty-first century. *Scandinavian Political Studies, 30*(2), 137–174.

Quality counts: A report card on the condition of public education in the 50 states. (1997, January 22). *Education Week* (Supp. to Vol. 16).

Quality counts: The urban challenge: Public education in the 50 states. (1998, January 8). *Education Week* (Supp. to Vol. 17).

Quality counts: A better balance: Standards, tests, and the tools to succeed. (2001, January 11). *Education Week, 20*(17).

Quality Counts at 10: Two Decades of Standards Based Education. (2006, January 5). *Education Week, 25*(17).

Quality counts 2008: Tapping into teaching. (2008, January 11). *Education Week.*

Technology Counts Archive: 2008. Education Week.

Quality Education for Minorities Project. (1990). *Education that works: An action plan for the education of minorities.* Cambridge, MA: MIT Press.

Ramirez, J. D. (2000). *Bilingualism and literacy: Problem or opportunity? A synthesis of reading research on bilingual students.* Washington, DC: U.S. Department of Education.

Ramirez, J. D., Yuen, S. D., & Ramey, D. R. (1991). *Final report: Longitudinal study of structured English immersion strategy, early-exit and late-exit transitional bilingual education programs for language-minority children.* Washington, DC: U.S. Department of Education.

Ramirez, M., III, & Castañeda, A. (1974). *Cultural democracy: Bicognitive development and education.* New York: Academic Press.

Ramirez, R., & de la Cruz, G. P. (2003). *The Hispanic population in the United States: March 2002* (P20-545). Washington, D.C.: U.S. Census Bureau.

Rasell, M. E., & Mishel, L. (1990). *Shortchanging education: How U.S. spending on grades K–12 lags behind other industrialized nations.* Armonk, NY: Economic Policy Institute.

Raths, L. E., Harmin, M., & Simon, S. B. (1966). *Values and teaching: Working with values in the classroom.* Columbus, OH: Charles E. Merrill.

Ravitch, D. (1974). *The great school wars*. New York: Basic Books.

Ravitch, D. (1990, Spring). Diversity and democracy: Multicultural education in America. *American Educator, 15*(1), 16–48.

Ravitch, D. (1991, Spring). Multiculturalism: E. pluribus plures. *American Scholar, 37*(3), 337–354.

Ravitch, D. (1997). *Student performance today* (Brookings Policy Brief No. 23). Washington, DC: Brookings Institution.

Ravitch, D. (2000). *Left back: A century of failed school reform*. New York: Simon & Schuster.

Ravitch, D. (2003). *Language police*. New York: Alfred A. Knopf.

Ravitch, D., & Viteritti, J. P. (1997). *New schools for a new century: The redesign of urban education*. New Haven, CT: Yale University Press.

Ravitch, D., & Viteritti, J. (Eds.). (2000). *Lessons from New York City schools*. Baltimore, MD: Johns Hopkins University Press.

Raymond, C. (1991, October 30). Results from a Chicago project lead social scientists to a rethinking of the urban underclass. *Chronicle of Higher Education*, p. A9.

Redovich, Denis. (2001). *The phony intellectualism of Diane Ravitch*. Retrieved June 6, 2005 from www.mediatransparency.org

Reich, R. B. (1991a, January 20). Secession of the successful. *New York Times Magazine*, p. 44.

Reich, R. B. (1991b). *The work of nations: Preparing ourselves for 21st century capitalism*. New York: Alfred A. Knopf.

Reich, R. B. (1997, May–June). Up from bipartisanship. *American Prospect, 8*(32), 27–35.

Reich, R. B. (2007). *Supercapitalism: The transformation of business, democracy, and everyday life*. New York: Alfred A. Knopf, 2007.

Reidford, R. (1972). Educational research. In C. Weinberg (Ed.), *Humanistic foundations of education* (pp. 257–280). Upper Saddle River, NJ: Prentice Hall.

Renzulli, J. S. (2002). *The definition of high end learning*. Retrieved June 10, 2002, from http://www.gifted.uconn.edu/sem/semart10.html

Reveles, F. (2000). *Encuentros: Hombre a hombre*. Sacramento, CA: California Department of Education.

Reyes, P., Scribner, J. D., & Scribner, A. P. (Eds.). (1999). *Lessons from high-performing Hispanic schools: Creating learning communities*. New York: Teachers College Press.

Richart, R., & Perkins, D. (2008). Making thinking visible. *Educational Leadership, 65*(5), 57–61.

Rist, R. C. (1970, August). Student social class and teacher expectations: The self-fulfilling prophecy in ghetto education. *Harvard Educational Review, 40*(3), 411–451.

Rizvi, F. (1993). Children and the grammar of popular racism. In C. McCarthey & W. Crichlow (Eds.), *Race, identity, and representation in education*. 126–138. New York: Routledge.

Rogers, J., Kahne, J., & Middaugh, E. (2007). *Multiple pathways, vocational education, and the "future of democracy."* Los Angeles: Institute for Democracy, Education, and Access, UCLA.

Rose, P. (1974). *They and we: Racial and ethnic relations in the United States* (2nd ed.). New York: Random House.

Rose, S. (1992). *Social stratification in the United States: The American profile poster* (Rev. ed.). New York: New Press.

Rosen, R. (2000). *The world split open: How the modern women's movement changed America*. New York: Viking/Penguin Books.

Rosen, Y., & Salomon, G. (2007). The differential learning achievements of constructivist technology-intensive learning environments as compared with traditional ones: A meta-analysis. *Journal of Educational Computing Research, 36*(1), 1–14.

Rossinow, D. (1998). *The politics of authenticity: Liberalism, Christianity, and the new left in America*. New York: Columbia University Press.

Rotheram-Borus, M. J., Dopkins, S., Sabate, N., & Lightfoot, N. (1996). Personal and ethnic identity, values, and self esteem among Black and Latino adolescent girls. In B. J. R. Leadbeater & N. Way, *Urban girls: Resisting stereotypes, creating identities* (pp. 35–52). New York: New York University Press.

Rothstein, R. (1993, Spring). The myth of public school failure. *American Prospect, 4*(13), 20–34.

Rothstein, R. (1998, May). Bilingual education: The controversy. *Phi Delta Kappan, 79*(9), 672–678. Retrieved March 31, 2000, from www.pdkintl.org/kappan/krot9805.htm

Rothstein, R. (2004). *Class and schools: Using social, economic and educational reform to close the Black-White achievement gap*. Washington, DC: Economic Policy Institute; New York: Teachers College Press.

Rothstein, R. (2008a, Jan/Feb). Leaving "No Child Left Behind" behind. *American Prospect. 19*(2), pp. 50–54.

Rothstein, R. (2008b, April). "A nation at risk" twenty-five years later. *Cato Unbound*. Retrieved from http://www.cato-unbound.org/archives/april-2008/

Rothstein, R. (2008c). Whose problem is poverty? *Educational Leadership, 65*(7), 8–13.

Rothstein, R., Jacobsen, R., & Wilder, T. (2006, November 13–14). *"Proficiency for all"—an oxymoron*. Paper presented at the symposium *Examining America's commitment to closing achievement gaps: NCLB and its alternatives*, sponsored by the Campaign for Educational Equity, New York.

Rothstein, R., Wilder, T., & Jacobsen, R. (2007). Balance in the balance. *Educational Leadership, 64*(8), 8–14.

Ruiz, N., Garcia, E., & Figueroa, R. (1996). *The OLÉ curriculum guide: Creating optimal learning environments for students from diverse backgrounds in special and general education.* Sacramento, CA: California Department of Education.

Ryan, J., & Sackrey, C. (1984). *Strangers in paradise: Academics from the working class.* Boston: South End Press.

Hoffman, L., & Sable, J. (2006). *Public elementary and secondary students, staff, schools, and school districts: School year 2003–04.* Washington, DC: National Center for Education Statistics, U.S. Department of Education. Retrieved from http://nces.ed.gov/pubsearch/pubsinfo.asp?pubid=2006307

Sadker, M., Sadker, D., & Long, L. (1989). Gender and educational equality. In J. Banks & C. A. McGee Banks (Eds.), *Multicultural education: Issues and perspectives* (pp. 106–123). Needham Heights, MA: Allyn & Bacon.

Said, E. (2000). *The Edward Said reader* (M. Bayoumi & A. Ruben, Eds.). New York: Random House.

Saks, J. (1997). *The basics of charter schools: A school board primer.* Alexandria, VA: National School Boards Association.

Sampson, R. J., Sharkey, P., & Raudenbush, S. W. (2008). Durable effects of concentrated disadvantage on verbal ability among African-American children. *Proceedings of the National Academy of Sciences, 105*(3), 845–852.

San Juan, E., Jr. (2002). *Racism and cultural studies.* Durham, NC: Duke University Press.

Sanbonmatsu, J. (2004). *The postmodern prince: Critical theory, left strategy, and the making of a new political subject.* New York: Monthly Review Press.

Sanchez, R. (1997, October 13). Mixed results on gifts to education. *Washington Post*, p. A1.

Sapon-Shevin, M. (1999). *Because we can change the world: A practical guide to building cooperative, inclusive classroom communities.* Boston: Allyn & Bacon.

Sarason, S. B. (1990). *The predictable failure of educational reform: Can we change course before it is too late?* San Francisco: Jossey-Bass.

Sawicky, M. B. (1991). *The roots of the public sector fiscal crisis.* Washington, DC: Economic Policy Institute.

Scales, P. C., & Leffert, N. (1999). *Developmental assets: A synthesis of the scientific research on adolescent development.* Minneapolis, MN: Search Institute Press.

Scherer, M., & Gardner, H. (1999, November). The understanding pathway: A conversation with Howard Gardner. *Educational Leadership, 57*(3), 12–16.

Schlesinger, A. M., Jr. (1991a). A dissenting opinion. *One nation, many peoples: A declaration of cultural interdependenc*e (Appendix to Report of the New York State Social Studies Review and Development Committee). Albany, NY: New York State Education Department.

Schlesinger, A. M., Jr. (1991b, Winter). The disuniting of America. *American Educator, 16*, 57–61.

Schlesinger, A. M., Jr. (1992). *The disuniting of America.* New York: W. W. Norton.

Schmalleger, F., & Bartollas, C. (2008). *Juvenile delinquency.* Boston: Pearson, Allyn & Bacon.

Schmidt, P. (1994, September 28). Idea of "gender gap" in schools under attack. *Education Week*, pp. 1, 16.

Schmitz, B., Rosenfelt, D., Butler, J., & Guy-Sheftall, B. (2001). Women's studies and curriculum transformation. In J. A. Banks & C. A. McGee Banks (Eds.), *Handbook of research on multicultural education* (pp. 708–727). New York: Simon & Schuster.

Schnaiberg, L. (1997, March 5). The politics of language. *Education Week*, pp. 25–27.

Schniedewind, N., & Davidson, E. (1998). *Open minds to equality: A sourcebook of learning activities to affirm diversity and promote equity.* Boston: Allyn & Bacon.

Schofield, J. W. (2001). Improving intergroup relations among students. In J. A. Banks & C. A. McGee Banks (Eds.), *Handbook of research on multicultural education* (pp. 635–646). New York: Simon & Schuster.

Schultz, J. (2002). *The democracy owners' manual: A practical guide to changing the world.* New Brunswick, NJ: Rutgers University Press.

Schultz, K., Buck, P., & Niesz, T. (1999, January). Democratizing conversations: Racialized talk in a post-desegregated middle school. *American Education Research Journal, 37*, 33–65.

Schwartz, J. (2008). *The future of democratic equality: Rebuilding social solidarity in a fragmented United States.* New York: Routledge.

Schwartz, W. (1996). *How well are charter schools serving urban and minority students?* (ERIC/CUE Digest No. 119). New York: ERIC Clearinghouse on Urban Education, Institute for Urban and Minority Education. (ERIC Document Reproduction Service No. ED410332)

Schwickart, D. (2002). *After capitalism.* Lanham, MD: Rowman & Littlefield.

Scribner, J. D., & Reyes, P. (1999). Creating learning communities for high-performing Hispanic students: A conceptual framework. In P. Reyes, J. D. Scribner, & A. P. Scribner (Eds.), *Lessons from high-performing Hispanic schools: Creating learning communities* (pp. 188–210). New York: Teachers College Press.

Scribner, J. D., Young, M. D., & Pedroza, A. (1999). Building collaborative relationships with parents. In P. Reyes, J. D. Scribner, & A. P. Scribner (Eds.), *Lessons from high-performing Hispanic schools: Creating learning communities* (pp. 36–60). New York: Teachers College Press.

Scriven, M., & Paul, R. (1994). *Defining critical thinking* (Draft Statement for the National Council for Excellence in Critical Thinking Instruction). Rohnert Park, CA: Sonoma State University.

Secada, W. G. (Ed.). (2001). *"Othering" education: Sexualities, silences, and schooling.* Washington, DC: American Educational Research Association.

Sewell, G. T. (1991). *Social studies review.* New York: American Textbook Council.

Shapiro, S. (1990). *Between capitalism and democracy: Educational policy and the crisis of the welfare state.* New York: Bergin & Garvey.

Shaps, E. (2002). *Community in school: Central to character formation and more.* Washington, DC: White House Conference on Character and Community.

Shaver, J. (Ed.). (1977). *Building rationales for citizenship education* (Bulletin No. 52). Arlington, VA: National Council for the Social Studies.

Shemo, D. J. (2007, March 9). The war over the teaching of reading. *New York Times.* Retrieved from http://www.nytimes.com/2007/03/09/education/09reading.html

Shin, H. B., & Bruno, R. (2003). *Language use and English-speaking ability: 2000* (C2KBR-29). Washington, DC: U.S. Census Bureau.

Shirley, D. (1997). *Community organizing for urban school reform.* Austin, TX: University of Texas Press.

Shorris, E. (1992). Latinos: The complexity of identity. *NACLA Report on the Americas, 26*(2),19–27.

Shulman, L. (1987). Knowledge and teaching: Foundations of the new reform. *Harvard Educational Review, 57*(1), 1–22.

Simon, S. B., Howe, L. W., & Kirschenbaum, H. (1972). *Values clarification.* New York: Hart.

Sklar, H., Mykyta, L., & Wefald, S. (2001). *Raise the floor: Wages and policies that work for all of us.* New York: Ms. Foundation for Women.

Slavin, R. E. (1995). Cooperative learning and intergroup relations. In J. A. Banks & C. A. McGee Banks (Eds.), *Handbook of research on multicultural education* (pp. 628–634). New York: Simon & Schuster/Macmillan.

Slavin, R. E. (1997–1998, December–January). Can education reduce social inequity? *Educational Leadership, 55*(4), 6–10.

Slavin, R. E., Chamberlain, A., & Daniels, C. (2007). Preventing reading failure. *Educational Leadership, 65*(2), 22–27.

Slavin, R. E., Chamberlain, A., & Hurley, E. A. (2003). Cooperative learning and achievement: Theory and research. In W. M. Miller & G. E. Reynolds (Eds.), *Handbook of psychology* (Vol. 7, pp. 177–198). Hoboken, NJ: Wiley.

Sleeter, C. E., & Bernal, D. D. (2004). Critical pedagogy, critical race theory, and antiracist education: Implications for multicultural education. In J. A. Banks & C. A. McGee Banks (Eds.), *Handbook of research on multicultural education* (2nd ed., pp. 250–258). San Francisco: Jossey-Bass.

Sleeter, C. E., & Grant, C. (2007). *Making choices for multicultural education: Five approaches to race, class and gender* (5th ed.). Hoboken, NJ: Wiley.

Smith, H. (1998). To teachers and their students: The question is "How can we learn?," not "What are we going to do today?" In C. McDermott (Ed.), *Beyond the silence: Listening for democracy* (pp. 24–32). Portsmouth, NH: Heinemann.

Sommers, C. H. (2000, May). The war against boys. *Atlantic Monthly, 285*(5).

Sommers, C. H. (2000). *The war against boys: How misguided feminism is harming our young men.* New York: Simon & Schuster.

Southern Poverty Law Center. (2007). *Close to slavery: Guestworker programs in the United States.* Montgomery, AL: Author.

Sowell, T. (1991, May–June). Cultural diversity: A world view. *American Enterprise,* 45–54.

Spindler, G., & Spindler, L. (with Trueba, H., & Williams, M. D.). (1990). *The American cultural dialogue and its transmission.* London: Falmer.

Spindler, G., & Spindler, L. (1991, October). *The process of culture and person: Multicultural classrooms and cultural therapy.* Paper presented at the Cultural Diversity Working Conference, Stanford University School of Education, Stanford, CA.

Spindler, L., & Spindler, G. (1992, April). *The enduring and the situated self.* Paper presented at California State University, Sacramento, CA.

Sping, J. (1988). *Conflict of interests: The politics of American education.* New York: Longman.

Spradley, J. P., & McCurdy, D. W. (1994). *Conformity and conflict: Readings in cultural anthropology* (8th ed.). Boston: Little, Brown.

Squires, D. A., Huitt, W. G., & Segars, J. K. (1983). *Effective schools and classrooms: A research-based perspective.* Alexandria, VA: Association for Supervision and Curriculum Development.

Steen, D. R., Roddy, M. R., Sheffield, D., & Stout, M. (1995). *Teaching with the Internet: Putting teachers before technology.* New York: Resolution Business Press.

Steinberg, S. (1995). *Turning back: The retreat from racial justice in American thought and policy.* Boston: Beacon Press.

Stiggins, R. J. (1997). *Student-centered classroom assessment* (2nd ed.). Upper Saddle River, NJ: Merrill/Prentice Hall.

Stiglitz, J. E. (2002a, May 23). A fair deal for the world [Review of the book *On globalization*]. *New York Review of Books, 49*(9). Retrieved from http://www.nybooks.com/articles/15403

Stiglitz, J. E. (2002b). *Globalization and its discontents.* New York: W. W. Norton.

Stille, A. (1998, June 11). The betrayal of history [Review of history textbooks]. *New York Review of Books, 45*(10), 15–20.

Stutz, T. (2008b, March 28). State board ditches suggested reading lists. *Dallas Morning News*, Retrieved from http://www.texastextbooks.org/pdfs/3.28-DMN-State%20board%20ditches%20suggested%20reading%20lists.pdf

Stutz, T. (2008c, April 14). TAKS may lose its sting: Texas lawmakers consider school ratings that reward student progress. *Dallas Morning News*, http://www.dallasnews.com/sharedcontent/dws/dn/latestnews/stories/041408dntexachievement.3da4bc3.html

Sullivan, M., & Miller, D. (1990, February). Cincinnati's Urban Appalachian Council and Appalachian identity. *Harvard Educational Review, 60*, 105–124.

Sunderman, G. (Ed.). (2008). *Holding NCLB accountable: Achieving accountability, equity, and school reform.* Thousand Oaks, CA: Corwin Press.

Swanson, C. B. (2006). *Making the connection: A decade of standards-based reform and achievement.* Washington, DC: Editorial Projects in Education Research Center.

Takaki, R. (1989). *Strangers from a different shore: A history of Asian Americans.* Boston: Little, Brown.

Tannen, D. (1990). *You just don't understand: Women and men in conversation.* New York: Ballantine.

Task Force on the Education of Maryland's African-American Males (Report). (2006). Annapolis, MD: Maryland State Department of Education.

Tate, K. (1992). Invisible woman. *American Prospect, 8*(1), 74–81.

Tatum, B. D. (1992, Spring). Talking about race, learning about racism: The application of racial identity development theory. *Harvard Educational Review, 62*(1), 1–24.

Tavris, C. (1992). *The mismeasure of woman: Why women are not the better sex, the inferior sex, or the opposite sex.* New York: Simon & Schuster.

Taylor, D. (1993). *From the child's point of view.* Portsmouth, NH: Heinemann.

Taylor, D. (1998). *Beginning to read and the spin doctors of science: The political campaign to change America's mind about how children learn to read.* Urbana, IL: National Council of Teachers of English.

Taylor, W. L., & Rosario, C. (2007). *Fresh ideas in collective bargaining: How new agreements help kids.* Washington, DC: Citizens' Commission on Civil Rights.

Teachers of English to Speakers of Other Languages. (1998). *ESL standards for pre-K–12 students.* Washington, DC: Author.

Teixeira, R., & Abramowitz, A. (2008, April). *The decline of the White working class and the rise of a mass upper middle class.* Washington, DC: Brookings Institution.

Teller-Elsberg, J., Heintz, J., & Folbre, N. (2006). *Field guide to the U.S. economy.* New York: New Press.

Tennessee Education Association & Appalachian Educational Laboratory. (1993). *Reducing school violence: Schools teaching peace.* Charleston, WV: Appalachian Educational Laboratory.

Tetreault, M. K. T. (1989). Integrating content about women and gender into the curriculum. In J. A. Banks & C. A. McGee Banks, (Eds.), *Multicultural education: Issues and perspectives* (pp. 124–144). Needham Heights, MA: Allyn & Bacon.

Tharp, R. G., & Gallimore, R. (1988). *Rousing minds to life: Teaching learning and schooling in social context.* Cambridge, England: Cambridge University Press.

The other gap: Poor students receive fewer dollars. (2001, March 16). Washington, DC: Education Trust.

Thomas, W. P., & Collier, V. P. (2002). *A national study of school effectiveness for language minority students' long term academic achievement.* Santa Cruz, CA: Center for Research on Education, Diversity, and Excellence, University of California.

Thornburg, D. (2000). *The new basics: Education and the future of work in the telematic age.* Alexandria, VA: Association for Supervision and Curriculum Development.

Thurow, L. C. (1996). *The future of capitalism: How today's economic forces shape tomorrow's world.* New York: William Morrow.

Tienda, M., & Stier, H. (1991). Joblessness and shiftlessness: Labor force activity in Chicago's inner city. In C. Jenks & P. E. Peterson (Eds.), *The urban underclass* (pp. 135–154). Washington, DC: Brookings Institution.

Thomas Rivera Center. (1993). *Resolving a crisis in education: Latino teachers for tomorrow's classrooms.* Claremont, CA: Author.

Torres, C. A. (2006). Schooling, power, and the exile of the soul. In L. Weis, C. McCarthy, & G. Dimitriadis (Eds.), *Ideology, curriculum, and the new sociology of education: Revisiting the work of Michael Apple.* pp. 47–61. New York: Routledge.

Torres, C. A., & Mitchell, T. R. (Eds.). (1998). *Sociology of education: Emerging perspectives.* Albany, NY: State University of New York Press.

Trueba, E. T. (1999). *Latinos unidos: From cultural diversity to the politics of solidarity.* Lanham, MD: Rowman & Littlefield.

Trueba, H. T. (1989). *Raising silent voices: Educating linguistic minorities for the 21st century.* Boston: Heine & Heine.

Trueba, H. T., Rodriguez, C., Zou, Y., & Cintrón, J. (1993). *Healing multicultural America: Mexican immigrants rise to power in rural California.* Washington, DC: Falmer.

Tyack, D. (2003). *Seeking common ground: Public schools in a diverse society.* Cambridge, MA: Harvard University Press.

Tyack, D., & Cuban, L. (1995). *Tinkering toward utopia: A century of public school reform.* Cambridge, MA: Harvard University Press.

Tyler, R. W. (1949). *Basic principles of curriculum and instruction.* Chicago: University of Chicago Press.

Tyson-Bernstein, H. (1988). *A conspiracy of good intentions.* Washington, DC: Council on Basic Education.

Unger, R., & Crawford, M. (1992). *Women and gender: A feminist psychology.* Philadelphia: Temple University Press.

United Nations Children's Fund. (2000). *The progress of nations.* New York: Author.

United Nations Children's Fund. (2008). *The state of the world's children.* New York: Author.

U.S. Census Bureau. (1997). *Poverty in the United States: 1996* (P60-198). Washington, DC: U.S. Government Printing Office.

U.S. Census Bureau. (2001). *Poverty in the United States: 2000* (P60-214). Washington, DC: Author.

U.S. Census Bureau. (2005). *Areas with concentrated poverty: 1999* (CENSR-16). Washington, DC: Author.

U.S. Census Bureau. (2006). *Current population survey, 2006 annual social and economic supplement.* Washington, DC: Author. Retrieved July _16__, 2008, from www.Census.Gov/Population/Socdemo/Hh-Fam/Cps2006/Tabc8-All.Xls

U.S. Census Bureau. (2007). *Income, poverty, and health insurance coverage in the United States: 2006* (P60-233). Washington, DC: Author.

U.S. Census Bureau (2008). *Public education finances, 2006.* Washington, DC: Author.

U.S. Commission on Civil Rights. (1975). *A better chance to learn: Bilingual-bicultural education* (Publication 51). Washington, DC: Author.

U.S. Commission on Civil Rights. (2001). *Voting irregularities in Florida during the 2000 presidential election:* Retrieved June 11, 2009, from http://www.usccr.gov/pubs/vote2000/report/exesum.htm

U.S. Department of Education. (1987). *Schools that work: Educating disadvantaged children.* Washington, DC: Author.

U.S. Department of Education. (1991). *America 2000: An education strategy.* Washington, DC: Author.

U.S. Department of Education, Office of Educational Research and Improvement, National Center for Education Statistics. (1995). *The educational progress of Hispanic students.* Washington, DC: Author.

U.S. Department of Education, National Assessment of Educational Progress, National Assessment Governing Board. (2001a). *National Assessment of Educational Progress achievement levels 1992–1998 for reading.* Washington, DC: Author.

U.S. Department of Education, Office of Educational Research and Improvement, National Center for Education Statistics. (2001b). *The nation's report card: Fourth-grade reading highlights 2000.* Washington, DC: Author.

U.S. Department of Education, Institute of Education Sciences, National Center for Education Statistics. (2004). *The condition of education 2004.* Washington, DC: Author.

U.S. Department of Education, Institute of Education Sciences, National Center for Education Statistics. (2005). *NAEP 2004 trends in academic progress: Three decades of student performance in reading and mathematics.* Washington, DC: Author.

U.S. Department of Education, Office of the Inspector General. (2006). *The Reading First Program's grant application process: Final inspection report.* Washington, DC: Author.

U.S. Department of Education, Institute of Education Statistics, National Center for Education Statistics. (2007). *State education reforms.* Retrieved December 14, 2008, from nces.ed.gov/programs/statereform/saa_tab11.asp

U.S. Department of Health and Human Services, National Reading Panel. (2000). *Teaching children to read: An evidence-based assessment of the scientific research literature on reading and its implications for reading instruction.* Retrieved April 16, 2007 from www.nichd.nih.gov/publications/nrp/next.htm

U.S. General Accounting Office, Health, Education, and Human Services Division. (1997, February). *School finance: State efforts to reduce funding gaps between poor and wealthy districts* (GAO/HEHS 97–31). Washington, DC: Author.

U.S. Immigration and Naturalization Service. (1997). *Statistical yearbook, 1996.* Washington, DC: U.S. Government Printing Office.

University of California All Campus Consortium on Research for Diversity & UCLA Institute for Democracy, Education, and Access. (2007). *California educational opportunity report 2007.* Los Angeles: Authors. Retrieved April 5, 2008 from www.edopp.org

Valdés, G. (1996). *Con respeto: Bridging the distances between culturally diverse families and schools: An ethnographic portrait.* New York: Teachers College Press.

Valdés, G., & Figueroa, R. (1994). *Bilingualism and testing: A special case of bias.* Norwood, NJ: Ablex.

Valentine, C. A. (1968). *Culture and poverty: Critique and counter-proposals.* Chicago: University of Chicago Press.

Valenzuela, A. (1999). *Subtractive schooling: U.S.-Mexican youth and the politics of caring.* Albany, NY: State University of New York Press.

Valenzuela, A. (2004). *Leaving children behind: How "Texas style" accountability fails Latino youth.* Albany, NY: State University of New York Press.

Van Allen, R., & Allen, C. (1976). *Language experience activities.* Boston: Houghton Mifflin.

Vaughan, P. (1997). *Web trek: Social studies Internet directory*. Vallejo, CA: Web Trek.

Viadero, D. (2001). Whole-school projects show mixed results. *Education Week*. Retrieved November 7, 2001, from www.Edweek .org/ew/newstory.cfm?slug=10memphis.h21

Vicini, J. (2008, February 28). *U.S. incarcerates more than any other nation: Report*. Retrieved March 3, 2008 from www.reuters .com/article/domesticNews/idUSN2862169320080228

Vise, D., & Malseed, M. (2006). *The Google story: Inside the hottest business, media, and technology success of our time*. New York: Delta.

Vossekuil, B., Fein, R. A., Reddy, M., Borum, R., & Modseleski, W. (2002, May). *The final report and findings of the Safe School Initiative: Implications of school attacks in the United States*. Washington, DC: U.S. Department of Education.

Vygotsky, L. S. (1978). *Mind in society: The development of higher psychological processes* (M. Cole, J. Teiner, S. Scribner, & E. Sauberman, Eds.). Cambridge, MA: Harvard University Press.

Wade, R. (2000). *Building bridges: Connecting classroom and community through service learning in social studies*. Silver Spring, MD: National Council for the Social Studies.

Walker, P. (Ed.). (1979). *Between labor and capital*. Boston: South End Press.

Walsh, J. (1999). A new racial era for San Francisco schools. *Salon Magazine*. Retrieved February 18, 1999, from salonmagazine.com/news/1999/02/18news.html

Warner, W. L. (1949). *Democracy in Jonesville: A study in quality and inequality*. New York: Harper.

Washington, J. M. (Ed.). (1986). *Testament of hope: The essential writings and speeches of Martin Luther King, Jr.* San Francisco: Harper.

Waters, M. C. (1990). *Ethnic options: Choosing identities in America*. Berkeley, CA: University of California Press.

Waters, M. C., & Ueda, R. (with Marrow, H. B.) (Eds.). (2007). *The new Americans: A guide to immigration since 1965*. Cambridge, MA: Harvard University Press.

Watkins, K. (2005). *Human development report*. New York: United Nations.

Weatherford, J. (1988). *Indian givers: How the Indians of the Americas transformed the world*. New York: Crown.

Webb, J. (2004). *Born fighting: How the Scots-Irish shaped America*. New York: Random House.

Weber, D. J. (1973). *Foreigners in their native lands: The historical roots of the Mexican Americans*. Albuquerque, NM: University of New Mexico Press.

Weiler, K. (1988). *Women teaching for change: Gender, class and power*. South Hadley, MA: Bergin & Garvey.

Weinberg, C., & Reidford, R. (1972). Humanistic educational psychology. In C. Weinberg & R. Reidford (Eds.), *Humanistic foundations of education* (pp. 104–132). Upper Saddle River, NJ: Prentice Hall.

Weiner, R., & Pristoop, E. (2006). *The funding gap 2006: Low income and minority children shortchanged by most states*. Washington, DC: Education Trust.

Weis, L. (1988). High school girls in a de-industrializing economy. In L. Weis (Ed.), *Class, race and gender in American education* (pp. 183–208). Albany, NY: State University of New York Press.

Weis, L. (1990). *Working class without work: High school students in a deindustrializing economy*. New York: Routledge.

Weis, L. (2004). *Class reunion: The remaking of the American White working class*. New York: Routledge.

Weis, L., & Fine, M. (Eds.). (1993). *Beyond silenced voices: Class, race and gender in United States schools*. Albany, NY: State University of New York Press.

Weis, L., & Fine, M. (Eds.). (2000a). *Free spaces unbound: Families, community, and Vietnamese high school students' identities*. New York: Teachers College Press.

Weis, L., & Fine, M. (Eds.). (2000b). *Re-writing/-righting lives: Voices of pregnant and parenting teenagers in an alternative high school*. New York: Teachers College Press.

Weis, L., & Fine, M. (Eds.). (2000c). *Sheltered "children": The self-creation of a safe space by gay, lesbian and bisexual students*. New York: Teachers College Press.

Weis, L., McCarthy, C., & Dimitriadis, G. (Eds.). (2006). *Ideology, curriculum, and the new sociology of education: Revisiting the work of Michael Apple*. New York: Routledge.

Weiss, C. H., Cambone, J., & Wyeth, A. (1992). Trouble in paradise: Teacher conflicts in shared decision-making. *Educational Administration Quarterly, 28*(3), 350–367.

West, C. (1993a). *Prophetic thought in postmodern times: Beyond Eurocentrism and multiculturalism* (Vol. 1). Monroe, ME: Common Courage.

West, C. (1993b). *Race matters*. Boston: Beacon Press.

West, C. (2004). *Democracy matters: Winning the fight against imperialism*. New York: Penguin Press.

Westheimer, J., & Kahne, J. (2003). Teaching democracy: What do schools need to do? *Phi Delta Kappan, 85*(1), 34–40, 57–66.

Westheimer, J., & Kahne, J. (2004). What kind of citizen? The politics of educating for a democracy. *American Educational Research Journal, 41*(2), 237–269.

Westminster School District of Orange County v. Mindez, 161 F.2d 744 (9th Cir. 1947).

Wexler, P. (1989). Curriculum in the closed society. In H. Giroux & P. McClaren (Eds.), *Critical pedagogy, the state, and cultural struggle* (pp. 92–104). Albany, NY: State University of New York Press.

Whitmore, K., & Crowell, C. (1994). *Inventing a classroom: Life in a bilingual, whole language learning community*. York, ME: Stenhouse.

Wilbur, G. (1991). Gender-fair curriculum. Research report prepared for Wellesley College Research on Women. Cited in American Association of University Women, *How schools shortchange girls* Washington, DC: American Association of University Women. p. 112.

Wilkins, A. (2006). *Yes we can: Telling truths and dispelling myths about race and education in America*. Washington, DC: Education Trust.

Williams v. California, No. 312 236 (San Francisco County Super. Ct., filed May 17, 2000).

Williams, B. (1995). *The Internet for teachers* (2nd ed.). Foster City, CA: IDG Books Worldwide.

Williamson, B. (1988). *A first-year teacher's guidebook for success: A step-by-step educational recipe book from September to June*. Sacramento, CA: Dynamic Teaching.

Willingham, D. T. (2007, Summer). Critical thinking: Why is it so hard? *American Educator 31*(2), pp. 8–19.

Wilms, W. (2008). *Liberating the schoolhouse*. Retrieved May 28, 2008 from www.truthdig.com/report/item/20080430_liberating_the_schoolhouse

Wilson, W. J. (1978). *The declining significance of race*. Chicago: University of Chicago Press.

Wilson, W. J. (1987). *The truly disadvantaged: The inner city, the underclass and public policy*. Chicago: University of Chicago Press.

Wilson, W. J. (1988, May–June). The ghetto underclass and the social transformation of the inner city. *Black Scholar 19*(3), 10–17.

Wilson, W. J. (1996). *When work disappears: The world of the new urban poor*. New York: Alfred A. Knopf.

Wilson, W. J. (1999). *The bridge over the racial divide: Rising inequality and coalition politics*. Berkeley, CA: University of California Press.

Wink, J. (1997). *Critical pedagogy: Notes from the real world*. New York: Longman.

Wolf, N. (1991). *The beauty myth: How images of beauty are used against women*. New York: William Morrow.

Wong-Filmore, L. (1991). When learning a second language means losing the first. *Early Childhood Research Quarterly, 6*(3), 323–346.

Wood, G. H., Darling-Hammond, L., Neil, M., & Roschewski, P. (2007). *Refocusing accountability: Using local performance assessments to enhance teaching and learning for higher order skills*. Washington, DC: Forum for Education and Democracy.

Wu, F. (2003). *Yellow: Race in America: Beyond Black and White*. New York: Basic Books.

Wynn, M. (1994). *The eagles who thought they were chickens*. Marietta, GA: Rising Star.

Yates, M. (2007). *More unequal: Aspects of class in the United States*. New York: Monthly Review Press.

Yoon Louie, M. C. (2001). *Sweatshop warriors: Immigrant women workers take on the global factory*. Cambridge, MA: South End Press.

Zinn, H. (1990). *Declarations of independence: Cross-examining American ideology*. New York: Harper.

Zinn, H., & Macedo, D. (2005). *Howard Zinn on democratic education*. Boulder, CO: Paradigm.

Zou, Y., & Trueba, E. T. (Eds.). (1998). *Leadership, education, and political action: The emergence of new Latino ethnic identities*. Albany, NY: State University of New York Press.

Author Index

Subject Index

European American working class
benefited from education, 127
financial pressure to keep jobs, 127–128
Finnish immigrants, 126
formation, 125–128
German immigrants, 126
international economic restructuring, 127–128
Irish Americans, 125–126
Italian immigrants, 126
lack of class consciousness, 128
melting pot worldview, 127
mixed, cultural heritage, 127
Polish immigrants, 126
urban immigrant communities, 126
European Americans, 49
anti-affirmative action movement, 86
ideological bias, 106
immigrants, 54
majority of people, 74
public schools, 126
redefining, 63
schools, 51
teaching profession, 162–163
working poor, 124
worldview, 53
Evaluation, 266
Evans, Charlie, life story of, **90–91**
Experts, 269–270
Expressive language, 317
Extended participant observation, 185
Extreme materialism, 161

Faces at the Bottom of the Well (Bell), 92
Facts, constructing meaning from, 48
Facts About Working Women (AFL-CIO), **163**
Failing public school districts, 314
Failing schools, 39, 386
Fair Test Web site, 383
Fairness, 239
curriculum, 241
primary grades, 220
Families
cross-gender and cross-racial respect, 148
dramatic changes in structure, 162
income growth, **114**
prejudice, 299
working with schools, 190
Farming and Japanese workers, 100
Federal Emergency Management Agency, 36
Federal home loans, 127
Federal tax rates, 19–20
Feedback, 249
Female-centered community, 164
Female-centered home, 164
Female heads of households, 120
Female students
See also girls
European American, 148–152
growing up fast, 157
intellectually rigorous classes, 152
journals, 166
lure of beauty myth, 152–153

media literacy, 156–157
minority cultures, 149
models, 155
non-college-bound, 159–161
personal conflicts, 192
rapport with, 192
self-esteem, 147–148
sexual issues, 152
sexual orientation, 158–159
sexualization of girlhood, 153–156
silenced voices, 152
support from teachers, 150
tracking, 146–159, 165
women teachers and, 157–158
Feminist movement (1970s and 1980s), 158, 186
Feminist scholars, 216
Feuerstein, Rueven, 139
Field Guide to the Global Economy, The (Anderson, Cavanagh and Lee), 128
Filipino students, 135
Filipinos, hostility and discrimination, 100
Financial markets crisis, 18
Finding Out/Descubrimiento Project, 295, 300
Finn, Chester, 16, 108, 213
Finnish immigrants, 126
"Fire Next Time, The," 25
First grade and social skills, 194
Florés-Magon, Enriqué, 96
Florés-Magon, Ricardo, 96
Florida
2000 presidential election, 36–37
temporary bilingual schools, 310
Fluency, 318
Fluent-English-proficient (FEP) students, 307
Food and Drug Administration, 169–170
For-profit higher education and neo-liberalism, 379
Forced assimilation, 54
Ford, Henry, 310
Formal curriculum, 227
Forum For Education Web site, 383
Foxfire curriculum development projects for Appalachian students, 367–368
Framework for Understanding Poverty, A (Bomer et al), 139–140
Francis, Joe, 155
Franklin, John Hope, 27
Free Lunch: How the Wealthiest Americans Enrich Themselves at Government Expense (and Stick You with the Bill) (Johnston), 20
Free trade, 102
Freedom marches, 223
Freire, Paulo, 185–186, 216, 218, 379
From the Child's Point of View (Taylor), 184
Fuerze Unida, 97
Funding Gaps 2006, 141
Funding public schools, 385

Gagnon, Paul, 213, 354
Gang-associated youth, 263–264
Gang identity, 66
Gang interventions, 197, 261–263
Gang members, 66

Gangs, 262264
problem for schools, 238
role relationships and communication styles, 194
Garcia, Eugene, 70
Gardner, Howard, 268
Gay, lesbian, bisexual, and transgender (GLBT) issues, 159
Gender
equal treatment, 165–166
importance of issues, 161
interrelationships, **107**
open discussion of, 226
racism, 83
social and biological category, 145
society stratified by, 105
Gender, Diversities and Technology Institute website, 158
Gender bias, 183
Gender equity
attacks on, 169–170
efforts, 374
entitlement programs, 374
Gender-fair curriculum, 167–168
Gender groups, disempowering, 230
Gender identities, 66
Gender-neutral terms, 166
Gender roles
schools and, 145–146
stereotyping, 149
General Motors Corporation, 137
German immigrants, 126
German language rights, 310
Germans immigrants, 95
GI Bill, 127
Girls
See also female students
achieving better than boys, 146
Advanced Placement and higher track classes, 153
anger, 153
career choices, 152
communication styles, 150
conformity, 153
coping styles, 153–154
depression, 153
drugs, alcohol, and questionable sexual behavior, 154
early pregnancy, 157
Hollywood and, 154
identities and roles, 191–192
interacting with peers, 147
journals, 168–169
learning and relating to others, 150
low track, 291
male-imposed expectation, 154
math, **151**
middle school, 151
oversexualization, 154
peer group expectations and norms, 154
peer pressure, 152, 156–157
personal image, 152
pregnancy, 152
primary grades, 149
reality shows, 154–155
school, 146
school behavior, 161